D1029791

QUICHEAN
CIVILIZATION

QUICHEAN
CIVILIZATION

The Ethnohistoric, Ethnographic, and Archaeological Sources

by Robert M. Carmack

UNIVERSITY OF CALIFORNIA PRESS
Berkeley, Los Angeles, London

University of California Press
Berkeley and Los Angeles, California

University of California Press, Ltd.
London, England

Contents

Plates

Maps

QUICHEAN
CIVILIZATION

Nijaib royal coat-of-arms. The symbol of the Austro-Spanish empire was granted to the Nijaib Quiche as recognition of their aristocratic standing. From the Buenabaj Pictorials.

CHAPTER I

Introduction

My main concern is with the written document, a source of information not always associated with the anthropologist. This study, therefore, is not typical of anthropological work. It is neither an ethnography, nor an ethnohistorical reconstruction; nor is it addressed to general problems in anthropology. Extensive use of documents is not new. In fact, Maine, Tylor, Durkheim, and Morgan relied heavily on their use. As anthropologists specialized on the "primitives," peoples without a written language, it was necessary to develop methods to obtain data through direct observation. Ethnography became the methodological stronghold of anthropology, Evans-Pritchard (1962) has argued, and with it a strong antidocumentarian attitude became entrenched. Anthropologists frequently ignored data in documents where their use would have seemed obvious. This methodological trend was related to the turn away from evolutionary themes—which necessarily require cultures of the past and, hence, documents—toward a concentration on synchronic problems of structure and function. It even went beyond that. The so-called "historical school" of American anthropology relied primarily upon trait distributions rather than on documents to reconstruct culture historical processes.

During the last quarter century, anthropology has renewed its interest in the use of documents for sociocultural studies, mainly because we realized we are running out of nonliterate peoples. It forced the conclusion on us that literate civilizations and Western influenced societies are equally apt subjects of anthropological investigation. We can no longer ignore the rich documentation available on these societies and, consequently, more anthropologists engage in cultural analysis of such diverse documentary materials as Sumerian cuneiform tablets, medieval English texts, American Indian land claims, Aztec codices, and colonial administrative records.

The practical considerations to turn to documentary sources are accompanied by similar theoretical arguments. The structure-functional approach was adopted by cultural anthropologists, who argued that it should be combined with the culture historical orientation of ethnologists. Eggan (1956), the most lucid spokesman of this position, called for "controlled comparison" of structure-functional systems with similar geographical and historical milieus. It became clear that structure and function of past social forms could not be reconstructed from a study of the geographic distribution of the traits of remnant groups (Herskovitz 1965; Leacock 1961). Thus, the flowering of ethnohistoric interests in anthropology, in recent years, is the result of a new theoretical orientation.

Despite continuing criticism that the work of British social anthropologists is too synchronic (Sturtevant 1968; Harris 1968), there is growing acceptance among anthropologists that the most fruitful social field is the structure-functional unit over time. Indeed, Evans-Pritchard (1962) has convincingly argued that the concepts of structure and function can be shown to have validity only if they are placed in historical context. The importance of documents is taken seriously by the younger generation of social anthropologists, and I have suggested (1970) that they have made outstanding progress in controlled comparison.

During the past twenty years, the use of documentary materials was fostered by the vigorous return to evolutionary studies. An evolutionary explanation consists of a demonstration of the necessary development of one structure-functional system out of another, and hence has the same high data requirement as the more restricted comparisons of the social anthropologists. It is not accidental that the writings of the evolutionists Sahlins (1958), Wolf (1962), Harris (1964), and Steward (1963) show heavy reliance on documentary sources. In fact, the evolutionists' approach is a case in point where theoretical demands so dominate methodological considerations that not enough care is taken in handling the sources.

Anthropologists who attempt to give historical or genetic explanations make limited use of documents. Though history has meant different things to different anthropologists (Swartz 1958), it usually refers to specific antecedent persons, purposes, places, and times which clarify certain social conditions under investigation (Brown 1963). However, it is evident that sequences of events are not sufficient explanation, but in themselves must be explained by generalization and other external factors (Nagel 1952; Swartz 1958). Perhaps this is why genetic explanations are not often used in anthropology, and why the approach has not led to an extensive use of documentary sources. Nevertheless, the use of historical materials to provide data for functional, evolutionary, and other general law explanation has become pervasive.

Middle America (Mexico and northern Central America) seems to be ideally suited to apply the method of controlled comparison. It is not a uniform geographical region, but its broad highland-lowland pattern can be exploited for comparison and contrast. In prehispanic times, most of the area was inhabited by peoples sharing a Mesoamerican sociocultural tradition (Kirchhoff 1952). After the conquest, for about three centuries, the Spanish imposed a common colonial sociocultural system. Since independence, the republican era has brought about parallel social conditions, though in northern Central America social change has notably lagged behind that of Mexico.

The source materials are ideal. For the prehispanic phase we have better documentary sources and archaeological remains than for any other part of the world, except the ancient Near East. The Spanish were obsessed with the need to keep extensive administrative records and, consequently, documentation for colonial Middle American society is excellent. The record-keeping proclivity continued into the newly independent Middle American administrations. This fact, and the favorable conditions for ethnographic study of the cultural descendants of the prehispanic cultures, provide a continuity of source materials in Middle America that is probably better than for any other area in the world.

I believe the potential for diachronic (time-depth) structure-functional studies of Middle American society has not been sufficiently exploited, though there are a few notable studies. One might point to the important contribution to the concept of acculturation made by Middle Americanists (Redfield, Linton, Herskovitz 1936; Beals 1951; Tax 1952); the masterful analysis of sociocultural change in the formation of nation states by Wolf (1962); the insights into internal peasant community dynamics by Middle American ethnographers (Lewis 1963; Wolf 1955b; Foster 1967); and the pioneering work on the evolution of urbanization and civilization by a host of Middle Americanists (Steward 1963; Adams 1966; Sanders 1968; Caso 1966). These studies have theoretical importance for anthropology, and in part resulted from advantageous use of the special historical materials available.

Ethnohistoric methods have been widely applied to prehispanic cultures of Middle America (Nicholson 1960), but the approach has been more descriptive than theoretical. Likewise, ethnographic studies are numerous for modern peasant communities, but structure-functional analysis and a temporal perspective are generally lacking (Carmack 1970; Nash 1967b). Anthropological inquiries into colonial society are even more limited, but some have been of high quality and related to theoretical problems (e.g., Harris 1964; Wolf 1953; 1955a; Gibson 1964; Carrasco 1961a). By calling attention to the deficient theoretical sophistication in the writings on Middle America, I do not wish to imply blanket criticism, but only wish to assess the general state of our science.

We are at a preparatory stage for more sophisticated, theoretically oriented work in Middle American studies; sharpening our tools, as it were, for the work at hand. Considerable effort has gone into preparing the documentary sources for analysis through translation, textual evaluation, classification and publication. Two entire volumes of the forthcoming *Handbook of Middle American Indians* will consist of a guide to ethnohistoric manuscripts. This is the sort of laborious ground spading necessary before the theoretically interesting problems can be effectively dealt with (a conclusion which would seem to be supported by the case of the Near East, where years were spent in making available a usable form of the source materials).

4

The study of the Quichean sources should be viewed in a similar preparatory context. It was motivated by the forces which stimulated the production of the ethnohistory volumes of the *Handbook*. I hope it will serve, in a more complete way, the same purpose for the cultures of highland Guatemala as the *Handbook* will for all Middle America. I have paid special attention to problems of methodology as related to the preparation and use of documents with the idea that my work may serve as a case study in ethnohistoric methodology.

In his overview to Middle American ethnohistory that will appear in the *Handbook*, Nicholson notes that documentary source materials on the prehispanic cultures of Mesoamerica tend to cluster in certain regions, the densest clusters being in the Basin of Mexico, Western Oaxaca, Highland Guatemala, and Northern Yucatán. The distribution of documentary sources corresponds to the distribution of the most highly evolved prehispanic Mesoamerican societies, who had complex social forms and elaborate modes of communication, including written books and codices. These regions offer the best opportunities for work within the theoretical strictures we discussed.

Nicholson goes on to state that "bibliographic organization" and "reconstructive syntheses" are needed for all Mesoamerica, though some regions are in greater need than others. He notes that we still lack adequate synthesis for central Mexico, the best documented region. Even more in need of synthesis are the Quichean cultures of highland Guatemala. More than twenty years ago Kidder (Kidder, Jennings, and Shook 1946) argued that what was needed most in the study of native culture in highland Guatemala was a reconstruction (through documentary sources) of contact-time cultures. Without deprecating in the least the important preliminary studies of Quichean culture made by Villacorta, Recinos, and Wauchope, I believe it will be clear to the reader that highland Guatemala is a region particularly rich in documentary source materials, and abjectly poor in bibliographic organization and reconstructive synthesis. I hope my study will lay the foundation for the solution of the problem of bibliographical organization and provide some necessary tools for reconstructive synthesis.

In prehispanic times the Quichean peoples were located in the central Guatemalan highlands and in the lowlands immediately to the south. The word « Quichean » is generally used for the group of languages which includes Quiche, Rabinal, Cakchiquel, Tzutujil, and Uspantec (McQuown 1956). I have expanded the scope of the term to include the whole sociocultural tradition characteristic of these linguistic units. This seems justified because approximately one hundred years before the conquest these peoples were either part of or closely allied with the largest and most important political system of highland Guatemala known to us. I have referred to this political system as the "Quiche state" (Carmack 1968), arguing that possibly it was the largest political unit ever to develop in highland Guatemala. At the time of the conquest, the Quiche state had fragmented, the Cakchiquel and Tzutujil maintained independent and competitive political systems, while the Rabinal Quiche were more a confederate partner than a subordinate province.

The political and social integration of these linguistic groups, along with their common highland cultural background produced close cultural similarity among them. In spite of their political separation, the cultural homogeneity of the Quiche, Cakchiquel, and Tzutujil peoples is proven by similarities in form and content of their documentary sources (see Native Documents). This fact is important, for it allows us to use information from the writings of one linguistic group in reconstructing the culture of another. This should be done with caution, for we must not forget that they were politically separate.

Other linguistic groups were less intensely influenced by the Quiche state, and for shorter periods. The *Pokomán*, *Mam*, *Kekchí*, *Pipil*, *Aguacatec*, and *Ixil*, were not culturally transformed to the same degree as the Cakchiquel and Tzutujil. Consequently, they did not produce similar documentary sources after the conquest, and we are not directly concerned with them, except when their documents provide information on the Quichean cultures, or a useful contrast to them.

I have divided the Quichean sources into five sections: Primary Native Documents, Primary Spanish Documents, Secondary Documents, Modern Anthropological Sources, and A Case Study: *Título C'oyoi*. The arrangement reflects the relative importance of each category of documents for reconstructing Quichean culture; but the analysis of the *Titulo C'oyoi* is placed last because it illustrates the significance and use of all other sources discussed. The Primary Native Documents form the most important corpus of documents for the study of Quichean culture, closely followed by the Primary Spanish Documents. Most Secondary Documents date from the mature colonial period, and generally offer a vaguer, more ambiguous view of native culture than the primary documents (see Introduction to Secondary Documents). The Modern Anthropological Sources, a special category, consist of ethnographic and archaeological descriptions of high reliability but problematic authenticity (due to their cultural and temporal removal from prehispanic Quichean culture).

The Appendices contain documents or parts of documents of important information on Quichean culture. I have included only unpublished documents with a few exceptions (which I explain in the sections that refer to particular appendices). Where necessary, I have transcribed or translated the appendices into Spanish rather than English, because it is more appropriate to use the language of the area from which they come, and because this facilitates their use by Latin American scholars.

In analyzing, evaluating, and classifying, I was especially concerned to identify primary sources, to summarize their history (how, when, and where they were written, transcribed, translated, and finally located and published), and the purposes for which they were intended. Nicholson (1968) notes that such textual criticism, though commonplace to the trained historian, is often ignored by anthropologists. I have attempted rigorous textual criticism of the Primary Native and Spanish Documents, and applied it more generally to the Secondary and Modern Anthropological sources (some of which are of minor importance). But the analysis of the *Titulo C'oyoi* is designed as a model of the evaluatory techniques which were used in more abbreviated fashion throughout the study.

The introduction to each section outlines the history of anthropological thought and epistemology as related to studies of the Indians in highland Guatemala. In a limited way I show how the history has paralleled, or diverged from, the development of worldwide anthropological studies (systematic ethnographic description of native peoples). Where available information warrants it, I have explained the history in terms of the social contexts from which it emerges. In a limited way, therefore, I also give a historiographic analysis of anthropological writings on the Quichean Indians of Guatemala.

The Quichean Sources evolved from my doctoral dissertation, *The Documentary Sources, Ecology, and Culture History of the Prehispanic Quiche-Maya of Highland Guatemala,* which was based on published sources and a short visit to Guatemalan archives. But I was dissatisfied with the dissertation because I had been unable to control many sources which I knew existed, and because methodological problems connected with the use of the sources prevented me to do much sociopolitical reconstruction. I therefore continued to search for Quichean sources in order to reconstruct Quichean society and culture with the result that I can now discuss them with more confidence and completeness. I had also hoped to present social reconstruction but gathering, transcribing, translating, and evaluating the sources proved to be so formidable an undertaking that social reconstruction must be deferred.

I am indebted to several persons, universities, and granting agencies. Professor H. B. Nicholson of the University of California, Los Angeles, first pointed out to me the need for a synthesis of the sociocultural data contained in important documentary sources from highland Guatemala. Professor M. G. Smith, now in Great Britain, influenced me to direct my research toward a reconstruction of the prehispanic and contemporaneous sociopolitical system of the Quiche. Professors Pedro Carrasco of the State University of New York, Stony Brook, and Munro Edmonson of Tulane University offered suggestions and encouragement. Arizona State University and the University of California, San Diego, provided research grants and various technical services. Grants from the Ford Foundation and the Social Science Research Council enabled me to visit many libraries with Quichean holdings in the United States (Newberry, University of Pennsylvania Museum, American Philosophical Society, Peabody Museum, Tulane University, Pius XII Memorial, University of Texas, Brigham Young University, and Bancroft Library), several archives in Spain, the National Archives of Mexico, and the Archivo General de Centroamérica in Guatemala.

Plates 1 to 6 were drawn by Karen Lockwood, Del Mar, California.

Inasmuch as gathering and evaluating the sources was a necessary methodological procedure, I hope other students of Mesoamerican culture will benefit from my description of the methods.

R. M. C.

CHAPTER II

Native
Documents

INTRODUCTION

Before we examine the native documents on which any study of the prehispanic Quichean society and culture must be based, it is necessary to understand the origin and function of the documents. Wherever possible, it is important that we establish the tie, if any, between a document and its aboriginal antecedents; and where this is not possible, that we at least ascertain the reasons for its composition, and take them into consideration in interpreting the document for ethnohistoric reconstruction.

Therefore, in this section on the native sources, we will analyze each document in order to establish its relationship to aboriginal tradition. We will attempt to clarify for each document details about authorship, available texts and translations, and basic content. This, then, is a form of textual evaluation for authenticity and reliability; an essential step in any ethnohistorical study, but one too often neglected (Nicholson 1968:7).

Before we turn to the individual documents, it will be useful to understand generally the nature of the prehispanic and early posthispanic native documents, and to clarify the orthographic symbols used.

Prehispanic Codices

There can be little doubt that the Quiche and related groups had written books or codices before the arrival of the Spaniards. According to the sources (Recinos 1953:222; 1950:56), the Quiche and other highland peoples brought books (*u tz'ibal*) and cal-

Buenabaj Pictorials. Photograph of two sixteenth century pictorials in possession of the Indians of aldea San Vicente Buenabaj, Santiago Momostenango.

endars (*chol k'ij, may k'ij*) with them when they came to the highlands after visiting Tulan. In fact, the *Popol Vuh* now in our possession was written, we are told, because the original "book of the council, *Popul Vuh,* as it is called, cannot be seen any more" (Villacorta 1962a:16).[1]

Unfortunately, no prehispanic books have survived into modern times, though Las Casas had seen some of them around 1540, while he was in Guatemala. He describes them (1958:346) as consisting of "figures and characters by which they could signify everything they desired; and that these great books are of such acuteness and subtle technique that we could say our writing does not offer much of an advantage" (my translation). He explained they were partly phonetic and partly based on the rebus principle (similar to Aztec writing).

Fuentes y Guzmán describes two native codexlike documents which apparently were aboriginal. One, a map showing the territory of the Quiche state, was drawn prior to the conquest (though a few characters were added after that event). He describes the document as almost exclusively pictographic (1932-33:7:108), though lines in the form of spokes of a wheel connecting various *caciques* were used ideographically to represent the concept of political pact or agreement. He included a copy of the other document in his chronicle (1932-33:7:112; see Appendix I) without stating its source. His interpretation of its characters suggests a basically Mexican writing system. It is primarily pictographic, though there are ideographic symbols for numbers and rebus symbols for the names of conquered settlements. He claims it was the writing system used by the Cakchiquel at the time of the conquest, but unfortunately he does not elaborate on the source of these "pictorials."

Two other "paintings" or "cloths" are mentioned in a sixteenth century record of a dispute over leadership at Santiago Atitlán (Carrasco 1967b). They were purportedly painted by Tzutujil lords from Atitlán, probably before the conquest. Apparently, the contents were exclusively pictorial—representations of fifteen Tzutujil rulers and their royal residences.

---

[1] Part of the account which follows has been taken from my article in *Revista Mexicana de Estudios Antropológicos.* I have included phrases from that and other articles I published in various journals to give continuity, and because they were primarily written in preparation for this study.

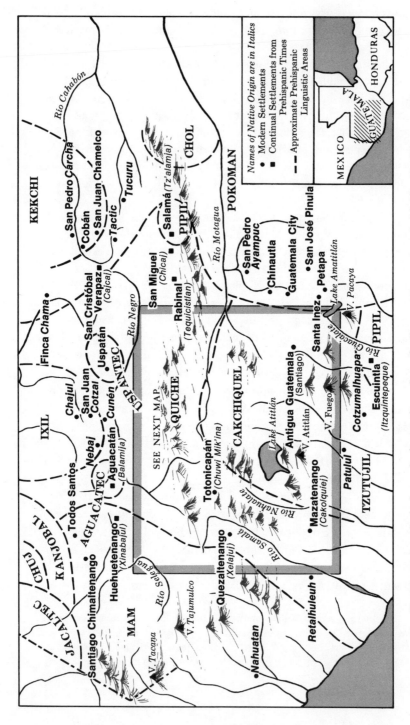

1. Prehispanic ethnic boundaries and modern Indian settlements of highland Guatemala.

The map on the following pages presents
a detail of map 1 on the left.

1. Prehispanic ethnic boundaries and modern Indian settlements of Guatemala.

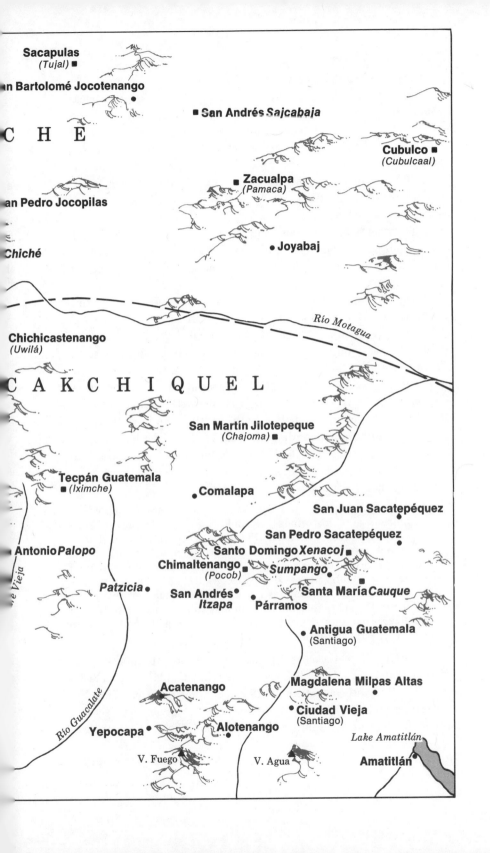

Other sixteenth century pictorials which have come to us manifest strong Spanish influence, though an indigenous background also shows through. Perhaps the most aboriginal is an undated "map" from the Sacapulas area (AGC Al:337-7091). It consists of three concentric circles; the outermost is divided into twenty-eight sections, which contain the names of locations circumscribing Sacapulas (see Appendix V). If the idea of a circular map is aboriginal, it may have derived from representations of the native calendar.

The other two pictorials, one from Momostenango (Carmack n.d.b) and one from Quezaltenango, are perhaps too hispanicized to provide much accurate information about prehispanic cultural forms.

Possibly our best clue to the nature of prehispanic writing in the codices comes from the archaeological record. At the site of Iximché, Guillemin (1965:16-17) discovered several murals with human figures painted in a variant of the Mixteca-Puebla style. At the site of Chuitinamit, Lothrop (1933:80-85) found pictographs carved in stone strongly reminiscent of the same style. The implication is that Quichean codices were similar to those of central Mexico, presumably both in style and content.

Our information regarding the use of the codices is limited, though Las Casas (1958:346) has left us an important statement. He describes the native codex as a "book of the state," containing precedence for public ritual and policy:

> Among other offices and officials were those who served as chroniclers and historians . . . and they (i.e., trainee historians) came to him (the chief historian) when they were doubtful about any articles or steps of history; and not only those new historians, but also the kings, lords, and priests (came) about any doubts they had with respect to the ceremonies and precepts of religion, festivals, the gods, and in any other thing related to ancient government and profane things of quality; each one consulted in that area which pertained to him (My translation).

Assuming Las Casas' statement is accurate, it appears that writing and interpreting history was in the hands of specialists, and that their office and knowledge was transferred patrilineally. Unfortunately, the titles of the offices are not given, nor is there any indication of the number of patrilineal offices. Nevertheless, we may surmise that the term, *aj tz'ib* ("scribe, painter") (Vico n,d.a; Sáenz 1940), was their general title, while *aj may wuj* ("he of the 400-day calendar book") and *aj chol k'in* ("he who counts the days," i.e., of the 260-day calendar), (Recinos 1958:168) may have referred to priests with special knowledge of the calendric system.

The number of patrilineal lines with books and guardian officials to maintain them may be indicated by the number of major native *títulos* written in the initial years after the conquest.[2] Following this line of reasoning, we may conclude that only the major political-descent groups of the Quichean peoples had such officials—perhaps some twenty to thirty in all (the Cawek, Tamub, Nijaib, Canil, Tzutujil, Quejnay, Xajil, Xpantzay).

One reason why we know so little about Quichean "historians" (*aj tz'ibab*) is that shortly after the conquest they ceased to function in the way they had before the conquest. In almost every case, the sixteenth century native documents were written by heads of aboriginal political divisions, not by the trained priest-historians. This is probably the result of social overspecialization, that is, the aj tz'ibab had been trained to read and interpret the books and calendars which were closely connected with native religion, and they were left without a role to play when, as Las Casas states (1958:346), "these books were seen by the friars, who had them burned because it seemed to them that they dealt with religious matters" (my translation).

The codices, guarded and interpreted by a special class of officials, must have been used in connection with important affairs of the state. The books themselves served as symbols of the power and esoteric knowledge of Quichean rulers. There is some indication that the prehispanic *Popol Vuh* was periodically viewed (probably at a distance) by subject lords during their visits to the Quiche capital as a form of homage and tribute to

---

[2] As I note elsewhere (Carmack n.d.c), the assumption here is that areas without historians and codices in prehispanic times would have been unable to initiate títulos after the conquest. This is not true in every case (see *Título Mam*,) but I believe it generally holds. Politically underdeveloped peoples would be lacking a historical tradition, and the idea of composing a título would be absent. Even if that idea somehow came into existence, the problem of meaningful content of the documents would still arise.

the rulers (Recinos 1953:238-239). The very fact of having produced, or at least possessed, such documents must have been inspiring, and probably intensified by the pomp and ceremony which apparently surrounded their guardianship.

Probably, certain historical and legendary accounts in the codices functioned to legitimatize and sanctify the political supremacy of the Quichean rulers. Undoubtedly, political aspects of Quichean history were recounted to the various subjects of the state during periodic public ceremonies (Las Casas 1958; Carrasco 1967a), but, unfortunately, we lack substantiating details.

A divinatory use of the codices is emphasized in the statement from Las Casas about the *Popol Vuh* quoted above; that is, the book, somehow, was used to divine answers to questions about public policy. Abundant evidence from many sources (Berendt n.d.; Ximénez 1929-1931:1) indicates that most Quiché divination was based on the 260-day calendar and its permutations with other calendars, and apparently this was an important use of the calendars contained in prehispanic Quichean codices.

Mythological and possibly legendary portions of the codices were repositories for the ideas and tales behind the great rituals of Quichean society. Probably, the *Popol Vuh* accounts of the demigods derive from representations in the codices, and served as a kind of text for ceremonial drama. This may also be true for the well-known drama, *Rabinal Achí* (Edmonson 1964:263: 272). Apparently, the priests consulted these accounts in order to clarify detail, to assure correct recitation and chanting, and to interpret the associated ritual (Las Casas 1958:346).

I believe the codices contained elements which might be termed, "charters of the existing social order." Apparently, well-known social conditions were explained and represented in standardized ways in these prehispanic documents. An example of a social situation possibly represented in this manner would be the hostile relations between the Quiche and their earliest Vuk Amak' neighbors, symbolized in the *Popol Vuh* by the episodes about begging for fire, and seduction by the enemy maidens (Recinos 1953:186ff:206ff).

It is not possible to generalize further on the prehispanic Quichean codices, for even the above reconstructions are based on sparse evidence. Surely, the find of just one aboriginal codex would modify the few suggestions on posthispanic sources that I have made. Indeed, the difficulty with the study of Quichean sources is the puzzling absence of samples of the prehispanic codices, though they were known to have existed shortly after the conquest. Even more puzzling is the paucity of posthispanic native books based on prehispanic models, a form of colonial Indian expression widespread in the Mexican area. One can only conclude that the tradition of writing (whether in Mexican or Mayan characters) was more limited and less developed in highland Guatemala than in central Mexico or Yucatán.

Posthispanic Native Documents

To evaluate the native documents written shortly after the conquest, we must understand the purposes for which they were written, especially how these purposes might have affected forms which were once a part of prehispanic culture. Obviously, these documents were not mere transcriptions into Spanish or Quichean languages of the native codices, and it is important that we determine the origin of their different components. Generally, an understanding of the purposes for which they were written will help clarify apparent distortions from native patterns. Fortunately, in many cases these specific purposes are stated by the authors.

The early posthispanic native documents appear to have been written primarily for legal and political purposes. Edmonson (1964:257-263) has summarized the way the native documents functioned as land titles, though it is clear that some were not designed primarily as land titles, and in a few cases land was not an issue at all (e.g., *Título Tzutujil*; Recinos 1953: 249-251). I think a good case can be made that at an early time some of the documents were *not* written primarily as land titles, but later came to function as such, as contests over land became more critical (Carmack 1967). Nevertheless, a claim to land was an important part of most documents, and was almost the sole purpose of some minor documents.

As noted by Edmonson (1964:259), rights to land were divided and complex, and different rights could be claimed by different social segments. Most documents refer to either local rights of administration, or to rights of tribute. Administration rights, usually, were based on mytholegendary associations between the land and the local groups, or on mere occupancy, in which case land boundaries and markers were given. Tribute rights were based on narration of the conquest of the territory and subsequent instances of tribute payment by the subjected peoples.

Besides land claims, some documents contain claims to special cacique privileges given by the Crown to *señores naturales* (members of the aboriginal ruling stratum, though not priests). Most claims were made in the decade of 1550-1560, possibly in response to the Crown's attempt to limit the tribute rights and other privileges of Indian caciques (Gibson 1964:197). Evidently, under increasing pressure for acceptable verification of ties with prehispanic nobility, the Spanish courts began to demand of the caciques special native documents on their genealogy and history.[3]

The documents make it clear that the most direct path to cacique standing was through the ruling line of the Quiche at Utatlán. That connection could be established in several ways: by showing genealogical or political relationship with the ruling line, by demonstrating the possession of the same titles and insignia, and by acquiring the testimonial signatures of their living descendants. An important component of almost all documents is the genealogy of the rulers of the local area. Their linkage with the Quiche ruling line is often the focal point of the genealogy, thereby drawing attention to their claim to quiche nobility, and *ipso facto* to cacique privileges.

The titles of the highest Quiche office (*ajpop, k'alel*) were widely granted throughout the territory of the Quiche state, and possession of a title was important evidence for the claim to caciqueship after the conquest. The approving testimony and signature of Quiche lords with such titles was important. In a few

---

[3] I have argued (Carmack n.d.c) that this was a logical policy for the Spaniards to pursue, once they discovered that only the ruling lines of aboriginal society had access to the traditions of significant complexity, for the missionaries, at first, had taught reading and writing skills only to the nobility (Anonymous 1935b:191). In a sense, therefore, a selection of "señores naturales" had already been made, for only the nobles would have been capable of transcribing native tradition with Latin script.

cases lords from several areas were brought together, as if to assure the claim by weight of numbers (Recinos 1957; Carmack n.d.c). Often, too, lesser-titled local officials and elders signed the documents, apparently to testify to their acceptance of the caciqueship to be placed over them (Recinos 1957:115).

In varying degrees, all native documents show evidence of Christian influence (Contreras R. 1963). This points to acculturation, but also suggests another important purpose of the documents—they are pleas to the Spaniards to relax colonial demands, in exchange for the natives' acceptance of and faithfulness to Christianity. In many cases the missionaries taught the natives to merge their migration stories with the Biblical story of the dispersion of the Irsaelites from Babylon. Presumably, they believed that a demonstration of their relationship with Old Testament peoples made them worthy to be treated as free men rather than as servants, the status imputed to them by many of the *encomenderos*. No doubt, this explains why the native accounts of the conquest so often portray the native rulers as giving ready acceptance to Christianity (Recinos 1957:91-93), or granting special favors to the *conquistadores* (Recinos 1957:89; Gall 1962).

The above uses of the documents—as land titles, as testimonies for cacique standing, and as pleas for relaxation of Spanish demands—show direct Spanish influence on the natives. Simultaneously, the documents continued to function like the prehispanic codices; and like the codices, they became important symbols of power, and were guarded with ceremonial care. In addition to their providing support for cacique claims, they continued to legitimatize the authority of local rulers in the traditional political system (some accounts appear to refer *only* to local or lineage positions) (Recinos 1957:165-169; 1950:195-207), and they provided explanatory statements about the social order of the 16th century. However, with the atomization of the Quichean states by the Spaniards, intercommunity relations greatly diminished, and some of the social "charters" in the documents were narrowed down to lineage referents within individual communities (Recinos 1957:24-67; 1950:211-242).

Because the Spaniards suppressed native religious activities, the sixteenth century documents did not retain important divinitory functions, nor did they serve as repositories for myth and ritual. For a short time, the latter function may have been served by the *Popol Vuh* but native ritual was mostly lost or continued in modified form through ceremonial drama. Divination continued to be practiced, secretly, but the only written form of it comes from copies made long after the conquest (Berendt n.d.), for after the conquest the knowledge and procedures of divination appear to have been transmitted orally.

Orthography

Several orthographic systems are currently in use for transcribing Quichean texts and speech. The early missionaries generally adapted Latin characters to represent Quichean sounds, though five special symbols were invented for the glottalized consonants not found in Spanish (Vázquez 1937-44:14:125-127; Sáenz 1940: 10). In the eighteenth century, Ximénez followed the same Latinized system of orthography, though his representation of glottalized consonants had been simplified.[4] Some modern writers have followed the orthography of Ximénez (Recinos 1950; 1953), though there has been a trend toward further hispanicizing the system (Villacorta 1934).

In 1949, under the auspices of the Instituto Indigenista Nacional, an official alphabet was established for the Mayan languages of Guatemala, including the Quichean (Quiche, Cakchiquel, Tzutujil). The alphabet adopted was a compromise between the requirements of a Spanish-speaking and reading country, and the more standardized phonetic symbols of linguistics.[5] This com-

[4] The five symbols invented by Father Francisco de la Parra in the 16th century were as follows: the cuatrillo, or "4" (phonetic c'); the tresillo, or backward "3" (k'); the 4 with comma, "4," (tz'); the letter "k" (phonetic k, a glottal uvular stop); and the "4h" (ch') (Vázquez 1937-1944:14:126-127; Sáenz 1940:10).

There were other adaptations, too, such as the use of "x" for the "sh" sound of English; "h" for the Spanish "j" sound, and "v" for the English "w" sound. Ximénez transcribes "c" and "k" both as "c"; "c'" and "k" both become "g"; "ch'" is given as "gh"; and the other glottal consonants (tz', t') are not distinguished from their nonglottal froms (Villacorta 1962a:14).

[5] It would belabor the point to list the standard phonetic equivalents for the official alphabet of Guatemalan Indian languages. Edmonson in his Quiche

promise system has proven to be practical, and a great deal of literature since published has used it (Fox 1965). It is the system I used during my field studies in modern Quiche communities and in this book.

The following symbols represent Quichean sounds roughly equivalent to those used in Latin American Spanish: *c* or *qu* (when followed by e, i), *ch*, *j*, *l*, *m*, *n*, *p*, *r*, *s*, *t*, *y*, *a*, *e*, *i*, *o*, *u*. In addition, the following symbols represent sounds not found in Spanish: *b*, glottal bilabial stop; *c'* or *q'u* (before e or i), glottal palatal stop; *ch'*, glottal alveopalatal affricate; ', glottal stop (before and after vowels); *k*, uvular stop; *k'*, glottal uvular stop; *r*, alveopalatal, retroflex semivowel (with affrication); *t'*, glottal alveolar stop; *tz*, alveolar affricative; *tz'*, glottal alveolar affricative; *w*, bilabial, median resonant (as in English "w"); *x*, grooved, alveopalatal fricative (as in English "sh"); *a*, median vowel (as the vowel in English "run;" not differentiated in the early documents) (Anonymous 1950:13-20; Gleason 1961:252).[6]

There have been phonological changes in the Quiche language since the time of the conquest, though we do not know all the changes. Because the symbols listed were worked out for modern Quiche, they only approximate the language spoken by the Quichean peoples when the Spaniards arrived. Some early texts do not distinguish between all the meaningful sounds, especially not between *c*, *c'* (or *qu*, *q'u*) and *k*, *k'*. For these texts, the reconstructed orthography must ultimately be based on modern Quichean phonology, and is therefore subject to error in a few cases.[7]

---

dictionary (1965) retains some of the orthography used by Ximénez, but applies standard phonetic symbols for Quiche velar and uvular glottalized stops (k', and q', respectively). Wick, in his recent study of spoken Quiche (1966), and Edmonson's reconstruction of classical Quiche (1967) employ standardized phonological symbols.

[6] I have given a phonemic alphabet. For example, I have ignored the fact that the symbol, "r", not only stands for the retroflex semivowel, but also for the resonant alveolar flap in medial position. The official alphabet given by the Instituto Indigenista de Guatemala is basically also phonemic, though some of their symbols (and their description of the sounds) appear to refer to allophones rather than phonemes (Anonymous 1950:14-15).

[7] The problem is especially obvious in the translation of proper names: Are we to transcribe the name of the most famous Quiche ruler as *Qui cab*,

MAJOR QUICHE DOCUMENTS

There are four categories of native documents: major Quiche documents, major documents of peoples related to the Quiche, minor documents of the Quichean peoples, and native documents cited by later writers.

The documents of the first two categories are the richest in substantive content and the most important. In part, they appear to have been based upon prehispanic historical and cultural traditions, which in several cases must have been transcribed in native codices. They were written by descendants of the most important ruling lines in prehispanic highland Guatemala, and thus express the "official" versions of native history.

Popol Vuh

This summary of the *Popol Vuh*, hereafter abbreviated *P.V.*, the most important source on the Quiche, will be brief because an extensive discussion can be found in the introduction to Recinos' translation of the book (Recinos 1953).

The author or, more likely, authors of the *P.V.* are not known. A suggestion that it might have been written by Diego Reynoso, a Quiche Indian who in 1539 was taken to Guatemala City in order to be taught how to read and write Spanish, has been refuted by Recinos on rather complex historical grounds (1953:31-37). What is clear about the authorship, as revealed by the dynastic lists at the end of the document, is that those who wrote the account were descendants of the "royal" Cawek, Nijaib, and Ajaw Quiche lines at Utatlán (the Quiche capital) (Recinos 1953:242-248).

The Quiche manuscript was found in Chichicastenango by Father Ximénez. Presumably, it had been written by Quiche lords originally from Utatlán (who may have moved there short-

---

Qui k'ab, Q'ui cab, or *Q'ui k'ab*? Depending on the orthography used, the name would be variously translated as, "the honey," "the arms," "much honey," "many arms." The only published ancient Quiche manuscript for which there has been a thorough attempt to reconstruct the orthography so as to correspond to phonological transcriptions of modern Quiche is the translation of the *Popol Vuh* by Burgess and Xec (1955).

ly after the conquest), between 1554 and 1558. After being hidden some 150 years, Ximénez was permitted to see it around 1701 (Recinos 1953). From my experience in modern Quiche Indian communities, I would suggest that the original manuscript is still in the possession of the *principales* of Chichicastenango, though this is denied by officials of the *municipio*.

Ximénez, who knew the Quiche language well, translated the text into Spanish, in a literal and a paraphrastic version. His literal translation was first published in 1857 in Vienna (Scherzer 1857), and a reprint of that version was later published in San Salvador (Larde 1926). The paraphrastic version, along with a commentary by Ximénez, was published in Guatemala in 1929 (Ximénez 1929-1931:1).

In 1861, Abbé Brasseur de Bourbourg (hereafter Brasseur) published a French translation of Ximénez's transcription of the original Quiche text (Brasseur 1861). Although there are many errors and omissions in the translation, it contains Brasseur's commentaries, which are valuable for historical interpretation.

There are many other translations, only four of which are of special importance to us. These are by Schultze-Jena (1944), Recinos (1953), Burgess and Xec (1955), and Villacorta (1962a). Each is based on a copy of the complete Ximénez manuscript, now in the Ayer Collection of the Newberry Library.

Schultze-Jena conveniently places the Quiche text alongside his German translation. His insight into Quiche culture cannot be found in other translations because they lack his sound understanding of modern Quiche language and culture. However, he was confused on certain grammatical features of the Quiche language.[8]

Recinos' Spanish edition is probably the most accurate translation, a result of his exceptional knowledge of the classic Quichean

[8] Schultze-Jena's confusion about aspects of the Quiche language shows when his grammar (1933:282-329) is compared with those of present-day linguists (Fox 1965; Wick 1966). Nevertheless, he understood well the Quiche language spoken at Chichicastenango and Momostenango, contrary to the insinuations by Tax (1947b:10). With the aid of native informants, I have gone through the texts and German translations recorded by Schultze-Jena at these communities (1933); for the most part they are linguistically and culturally sound.

languages. His elegant style more than any other translation captures the literary quality of the original Quiche account. Recinos relied heavily on Ximénez translation, but he also used the early dictionaries extensively. I have followed Recinos' version for my studies more than any other translation.

Burgess and Xec have prepared a Spanish translation which they place opposite the Quiche text. The text was transcribed into the "official" alphabet for the Quiche language.[9] Their success is evidence for the continuity of Quiché language and culture to this day, and it makes feasible a limited use of modern dictionaries in interpreting the *P.V.* With the aid of Quiche-speaking students from different communities of Guatemala, the translators were able to find instances of modern usage for almost all the words in the text, and to ascertain their meaning. This makes their translation a kind of ethnographic approach to the *P.V.* It would have been more valuable had they included notes elaborating on the meaning of terms now obscure.

Recently, Villacorta produced an entirely new Spanish translation, which he placed, word for word, under the Ximénez Quiche text. Becàuse his earlier translation from the Brasseur transcription (Villacorta y Rodas N. 1927) had been criticized, he undertook the task of forming a vocabulary list of all the words from the Quiche text. Based on the meanings of nouns and modifying particles from this vocabulary, he translated the document (Villacorta 1962a:10). The translation appears to contain many errors, but, because it is placed next to the text, I have found it a convenient edition for consulting the Quiche text when detailed analysis is required.

---

[9] The Burgess and Xec translation of the *Popol Vuh* (1955) is the most complete transcription of all the meaningful Quiche phonemes available (though Schultze-Jena had transcribed most of the sounds into somewhat different orthographic symbols). Their purpose was to transcribe the text so that it could be read and understood by modern Quiche speakers. With my informants from Momostenango, I have verified that this is the case, though there are a few words of the text which they do not understand. Had Burgess and Xec coupled their knowledge of presentday Quiche with the old dictionaries, I am convinced, their translation would be the most correct and insightful of all attempts.

In 1950, an English version of the Recinos' Spanish translation was made by Delia Goetz and Sylvanus G. Morely. It is an excellent rendering of the Spanish. Occasionally, I have made use of this edition for citations of a general nature. I am also informed by Edmonson that he has retranslated the entire Quiche text into English, and that this edition will soon be published by the Middle American Research Institute of Tulane University.

The *P.V.* represents, in part, a claim to supremacy by the Cawek, Nijaib, and Ajaw branches of the Quiche. It describes the immigration of their founding ancestors from the East; their dynastic lines from the time of the ancestors until the conquest; and the growth, conquests, and tribute rights of the Quiche state. Unlike the other títulos, it also contains an elaborate recounting of Quiche myths (in the first section of the book). Edmonson has suggested that these are calendar myths, but that only six of the original twenty are recounted (1964:263). An analysis beyond the scope of the present study would be necessary to evaluate his suggestion.

The ultimate source of the contents in the *P.V.* is difficult to determine, though I am inclined to believe that most of the account had some representation in aboriginal codices which the authors once possessed. As the authors state in the preface (Goetz, Morley 1950:79-80):

> This we shall write now under the law of God and Christianity; we shall bring to light because now the *Popol Vuh*, as it is called, cannot be seen any more . . . The original book, written long ago, existed, but its sight is hidden to the searcher and to the thinker.

Because the authors were well educated in Quiche culture, and were directly descended from the ruling lines at Utatlán, it is reasonable to assume that they had seen and listened to recitations from the great book of the council, which was frequently consulted in aboriginal times by the lords of state.

Perhaps equally as important as their recollections of the characters in the codices were various oral devices of transmission. The mythological accounts (Recinos 1953:85-173) could have been remembered through association with the chants and rituals which must have accompanied their periodic presentation. The middle section has a legendary ring (Recinos 1953:174-224), and appears to have been put together by transcribing a series of songs and sagalike tales. In the final and most detailed section (Recinos 1953:224-248), recent events of Quiche history are treated in such detail as to suggest that they had been remembered by persons trained in these matters. The use of oral devices does not detract from the book's authenticity, nor does it deny that much of its contents were at one time recorded in some "official book of the state."

Though the authors admit to being under the influence of the Spaniards, almost all who have studied the *P.V.* have concluded that it is almost wholly indigenous. This conclusion is supported by the elegant Quiche in which it was written (almost completely free of Spanish words), as well as by the native imagery and concepts. Especially intriguing are the Christian ideas so subtly woven into its fabric that they are virtually imperceptible. For example, the Quiche version of the creation is harmoniously combined with some of the spirit of Genesis (Recinos 1953: 85ff). The Xquic myth is ever so slightly twisted so as to parallel parts of the Adam and Eve tale (Recinos 1953:125ff). Even the narration of the coming from the East is smoothly modified to conform to the Tower of Babel tale in the Old Testament (Recinos 1953:200-201).

There is some distortion in the historical parts of the book, where the group occupying the Quiche capital, especially the Cawek ruling line, is given special attention. Because this group exercised a controlling influence throughout the highlands, the view presented is more catholic than that of the other native documents. As the "official" historical tradition of the Quiche state (Ximénez 1929-1931: 1:54), and our most extensive account, the *P.V.* profitably may be used as a standard of comparison in establishing the authenticity and reliability of other native documents.

Título Totonicapán

The authors of this document are not known, except for the part which recounts a "second" journey to the East, written by Diego Reynoso (Recinos 1953:31). The document is basically a title of territorial possession held by the Quiche princes ruling at Totonicapán.[10] The original Quiche manuscript was probably presented as a claim to the Spanish Crown for cacique privileges.

In 1834, upon appeal by the Indians of Totonicapán, the provincial governor commissioned Dionisio José Chonay, the priest at Sacapulas, to translate the Quiche text into Spanish. It took three weeks, "because of the difficulty of understanding a thing so full of words or terms that are no longer used and of things we do not know" (Goetz 1953:166). He states that he did not translate the initial pages of the manuscript, because their contents were very similar to those of Genesis and the Old Testament. He may have referred to a mythological section similar to the one in the first part of the P. V., though we may never know because the Quiche manuscript has disappeared.

It is possible that the original título is still in possession of the principales of Totonicapán. I am told that they have preserved among their many ancient documents the "mother título of the town," which may be the document under discussion here. I have tried on several occasions to obtain permission to study their títulos (which include other important documents as well), (García Elgueta 1962:189-190), but they have always refused because of the sacred qualities they now attach to them.

Brasseur made a copy of Chonay's translation in 1860, calling it *Título de los Señores de Totonicapán*, and from this Charencey published French and Spanish versions in 1885. Recinos' edition of Chonay's Spanish translation was also taken from Brasseur's copy (now in the Bibliothèque Nationale of Paris; see Recino's discussion, 1950:211-213). Recinos claims that Chonay's translation "is clearly and elegantly written and seems to be a faithful rendering of the history of the Quiche people." As pointed out, the student has no access to the original Quiche, though fortunately Chonay left the spelling of names as they were in the original text. I have generally used Recinos' Spanish edition, though Delia Goetz' (1953) excellent English rendering of Recino's version is suitable for citations not involving precise analysis.

[10] In the *Título Totonicapán* (Recinos 1950:195) the Quiche ruler at Totonicapán is called Quik'ab Nima Yax. Quik'ab is the name of the most famous Quiche ruler, but here is used as a title of authority. Nima Yax means "great, wise, or mature man," that is, "chief" (Edmonson 1965; interview with the late Jesus Carranza Juárez).

As a land claim by the leading descent lines of the Quiche, the Totonicapán document begins with the legendary migration of the Quiche ancestors from Tulan. There is a description of the conquests and glories of their descendants down to the reign of Quik'ab, after which the account abruptly breaks off, ending with the signatures of the señores.

Like one section of the *P.V.*, the Totonicapán document appears to be a series of dramatic tales (there is frequent use of dialogue), roughly tied together into a chain of events. Each episode appears to be built around one or more central figures (the founding ancestors, C'otuja, Quik'ab). As founders of different descent groups, tales about each ancestor might have been told by elders from various groups (who would be expected to remember more about their own ancestors than those of other groups). This may explain why Diego Reynoso is specifically mentioned in connection with the journey to the East.[11] Possibly, a genealogical pictorial of the important persons of the narration, or some other written document, was used as a mnemonic device for recording the events. This seems especially plausible for the last section of the document (Recinos 1950:236-240), where the boundaries of a territory are recounted in a way that suggests a map was being used.

Except for an abvious attempt to connect the coming of the founding fathers from the East with the scattering of the Israelites in Babylon (Recinos 1953:215-216, 241), the document is free of direct Spanish influence. Like the *P.V.*, its political bias is in favor of the Cawek ruling dynasty from Utatlán, though the Nijaib line was dominant at Totonicapán according to local tradition (García Elgueta 1962:117). In its focus on the boundaries of a specific territory around the modern town of Totonicapán indirect Spanish influence is strongest (i.e., in the face of the dis-

---

[11] Diego Reynoso claims to be telling of a second journey to the East, but it is clear that he merely gives a slightly abbreviated version of the same journey already given in the *Título Totonicapán* (Recinos 1950:223-224) and also found in the *Popol Vuh* (Recinos 1953:219-220). In transcribing this episode of the Totonicapán narration, there may have been a difference of interpretation, which was resolved by recording both views. It should be noted that Diego Reynoso, who was from Utatlán rather than Totonicapán, gives a version very similar to that of the *Popol Vuh*.

ruption brought by the conquest, traditional claims had to be reasserted).

Título Tamub

The date and author of the document are given as follows: "On the twelfth of the month of October of the year 1580. . . Don Juan de Torres, the old Lord Ahpop Atzih Vinak Ekoamak united with my younger brother, Don Diego Ramires, Rahop Achih Eskah" (Recinos 1957:63). The account was written by members of the Ekoamak' line of the Tamub Quiche. Unfortunately, we are not sure where it was written, though it refers to places which suggest that the Tamub people were located somewhere between Totonicapán and Utatlán (there are boundaries given which mention places northeast of Totonicapán) (Recinos 1957:65).[12]

William Gates obtained a copy of the Quiche manuscript while in Guatemala and it is now part of the Robert Garrett collection of the Princeton University Library. In 1957, Recinos published the Quiche text and a Spanish translation entitled, *Historia Quiché de Don Juan de Torres* (Recinos 1957:24-67). I have used Recinos' Spanish translation and the Quiche text.

The *Título Tamub* is a claim to land and tribute by the Tamub, a major division of the Quiche state. To back the claim, the Tamub describe migrations by their ancestors from the East, elaborate their genealogy, and summarize the organization of Tamub "colonies." The título is of inestimable value in reconstructing Quiche social institutions, for the data on the Tamub ruling line and other lineages are complementary to those for the Cawek, Nijaib, and Ajaw Quiche contained in the *P.V.* It also provides clarification of Quiche "colonial" organization.

The detailed sagalike narrations of the *P.V.* are lacking in the Tamub account, though many identical events are mentioned. The author states, he is passing on what was told him of old by

---

[12] I learned from a título in the possession of *municipio* Patzité (Department of Quiché) that the northeastern part of their jurisdiction was formerly called, *parcialidad Tamú*. These lands passed into the hands of the Spanish Crown, and were later incorporated within the boundaries of Patzité when it was established as a municipio. It would seem that at least some of the Tamub Quiche were located in a region to the south and west of Utatlán.

the forefathers, though I think it also possible that his memory on some matters had been aided perhaps by a largely genealogical codex he had seen. Most of the account, however, consists of complex Tamub genealogical relations, which were probably still viable and well-known to the author and the other lords who no doubt aided him. Much of the document (Recinos 1957:49-67) appears to be a record of Tamub social and cultural forms which would have been part of the knowledge common to important members of the ruling Quiche stratum during the sixteenth century.

The document shows almost no direct Spanish influence. The only Spanish words in it refer to Christian dates, though there is also a feeble attempt to connect the departure point of the forefathers with Babylon (Recinos 1957:25, 63). However, the presentation of specific land boundaries, and the emphasis on Tamub political equality with the Quiche of Utalán probably are the result of indirect Spanish pressures—the document is both a land claim and a plea for cacique privileges. Though the text is far more extensive than would be required simply to back cacique claims before the Crown, obviously it was also intended as a memorial.

Though lacking the details which accompany the *P.V.* narrations, the *Título Tamub* agrees well with the *P.V.* about the flow of historical events, and their spatial specification. The major point of divergence is in genealogy, where, as may be expected, data on the Utatlán ruling line is fragmentary and in error, while Tamub genealogy is given in all its complexity.

Títulos Nijaib

Four documents have come to us which contain claims to prehispanic territorial holdings by the Nijaib branch of the Quiche. (I follow the *P.V.* spelling of this group, though it is often given as Nejaib in other sources). I have classified them *Nijaib I, II, III, IV*.

Nijaib I. — The authors of this document are not known, though we may safely assume that they were representatives of the Nijaib branch of the Quiche. They state that their account was left to them by their forefathers as "title and proof" of their rights. The document was written at Quezaltenango, but the date of its composition is not given. It purports to have been written in the presence of Don Pedro de Alvarado and the four priests who allegedly had come with the conquistadores, though this is a spurious claim. There is no evidence of authorizations of Indian claims by Alvarado, and these four priests did not accompany Alvarado during the conquest (Remesal 1932:4:19; Gall 1963). Inasmuch as most Quiche títulos were written between 1550 and 1560, that decade may be the approximate period of of its composition. Other títulos written during that decade were signed by the same Quiche lords listed at the end of this document (Recinos 1953:31-37).

The original Quiche manuscript was presented before the Spanish court as part of a land claim in the middle of the seventeenth century by one of the illustrious families of Totonicapán. The court ordered a translation made of it, a copy of which was later deposited in the museum of the Sociedad Económica de Guatemala. From that Spanish copy, the *Título Nijaib I* was first published in 1876 in *La Sociedad Económica*, and again in 1941 in the *Anales de la Sociedad de Geografía e Historia*. In 1957, Recinos published it again, based on the 1876 edition, correcting it through comparison with an earlier copy made by Brasseur which had come to rest in the Institute for Advanced Study, Princeton University; he entitled it, *Título de la Casa Ixquin-Nehaib, Señora del Territorio de Otzoya* (1957:13-16).

I discovered another version of *Título Nijaib I* in the canton book of San Vicente Buenabaj, municipio Santiago Momostenango. Unfortunately, the Quiche text is missing, though it is obviously a translation from the same source upon which the document published by Recinos was based. Most of my references are from the Recinos edition, with a few exceptions where the Buenabaj version adds useful information.

As a Nijaib land claim the document contains a description of the conquest of Mam speakers in the western highlands, occupying a territory known as Otzoya. The conquests occurred during the reign of Quik'ab, though one important military expedition to the coast apparently postdates the life of the great ruler. The account ends with a fascinating description of the Spanish conquest of Quezaltenango.

Nijaib II. — The authors of the document are said to be "the lords of Quiche, Santa Cruz Utatlán." Inasmuch as many geographic places are listed in the same order as in the *Título Nijaib I*, it is probable that some of the same authors participated in the composition of both documents. It was written at Chwa Tz'ak (Momostenango) in 1558, a date which, incidentally, helps date the *Título Nijaib I* (Recinos 1957:97:115).

The original Quiche manuscript was obtained by Brasseur in the 19th century and later, through Gates, passed on to the Institute for Advanced Studies, Princeton University (Glass n.d.). Brasseur made a French translation of the document which he sent to Guatemala, but its present location is unknown. Recinos translated it from the original Quiche to Spanish and published it along with the Quiche text as, *Título Real de Don Francisco Izquin Nehaib* (Recinos 1957:96-113).[13]

There is a Spanish translation of *Título Nijaib II* in the same canton book of San Vicente Buenabaj I mentioned. In comparing this translation with that of Recinos and both with the Quiche text, it becomes clear that the Recinos translation is inadequate in some key passages (see Appendix II where I have retranslated some of the passages with the aid of the Buenabaj version).[14]

The *Nijaib II* account is basically a description of the post-conquest entitlement of Don Francisco Izquin and his brother Don Juan (at Momostenango), and a justification of this delegation of office. To this end there is a description of the conquests of "Captain" Izquin, including a detailed list of many settle-

---

[13] A fragment of a copy of the Quiche text made by Brasseur is located in the Archivo Nacional de Guatemala. Recinos used the original at Princeton University.

[14] The few passages which are poorly translated by Recinos are not the result of any lack of ability to translate Quiche. Rather, they contain references to places and events specific to Momostenango, which only would be fully understood by persons familiar with that area. Whoever translated the version of the *Título Nijaib II* found at Buenabaj presumably was from that area, and present-day principales there still recognize most of the place names.

Problems of this kind point to the inevitable inadequacies in translating the native documents. Such problems could be corrected only by a thorough knowledge of each area mentioned in the various sources (Carmack 1967), a requirement impossible to fulfill.

ments and geographical features of the territory to the north and west of Utatlán. The document is signed by the lords of the Cawek, Ajaw Quiche, Ilocab, and Tamub divisions of the Quiche.

Nijaib III. — The small document was written in 1542 on behalf of the principales from Momostenango, and if the date is accurate, is one of the earliest documents. In 1964, during an anthropological survey in Momostenango, I found a Spanish copy of it and restudied it during fieldwork there in 1966-1967 (Carmack 1967). The original Quiche text has disappeared, but a copy of it is located in the Archivo General de Centroamérica, apparently in the handwriting of Brasseur (AGC, A1:6074-54879), (see Appendix III).

The document contains a land claim based on the description of a series of conquests carried out by Don Francisco Izquin Nijaib and Don Juan Gómez Ilocab in the territory around present-day Momostenango. Since the principle figure is from the Nijaib branch of the Quiche, I have included it here with the other Nijaib títulos.[15] In 1775, it was presented to the courts by the *alcaldes* of Momostenango in a land dispute with Santa María Chiquimula.

In spite of its brevity, the document provides important information on the political geography of the Momostenango area, and on political relations between the Nijaib and Ilocab divisions of the Quiche.

Nijaib IV. — The document was originally composed both in Quiche and Spanish at Santa Cruz del Quiché, on behalf of Cawek and Nijaib lords residing in Quezaltenango. The date of composition is given as 1505, which is probably an erroneous

---

[15] In another article (Carmack 1966b) I referred to the document as an "Ilocab" título. Even though Juan Gómez Ilocab is a prominent figure in the document, there can be no question that Francisco Izquin Nijaib is the principal personage. We have so little information about the Ilocab that one might want this to be an Ilocab document; however, it is not. I recently visited San Antonio Ilotenango, where descendants of the Ilocab now reside, but unhappily learned that no early título was made for that group. Perhaps, then, we shall never know much about the Ilocab, the third major division of the Quiche (the other two divisions were the Nima Quiche and Tamub).

rendering of 1555. Its many similarities to the *Título Nijaib II*, written in 1558, points to the 1550-1560 decade.

No version of the Quiche text has come to us, although two Spanish copies are in the Archivo General de Centroamérica (AGC, Al:6074-54883, 54884). Crespo (n.d.), who does not distinguish it from the *Título Nijaib I*, states that his version was taken from a copy made by Brasseur. I have transcribed an identical but later copy of it, taken from the same packet of documents in the Archivo General de Centroamérica, as Appendix IV. Recinos, no doubt, was aware of this document, but probably considered it too small to include in his *Crónicas Indígenas* (1957).

The document is a título for the Otzoya territory, written on behalf of Don Quebek and Don Nejaib, by most of the same Quiche lords mentioned at the end of the other Nijaib documents. It clearly delineates the political boundaries of that important territory. It also sheds important light on political relations between provincial rulers of the Quiche state.

Many persons, places, and events mentioned in the four Nijaib títulos are the same and point to at least partial common authorship. However, the *Nijaib I* account is much the fullest, and probably represents the official (state) version of the role played by the Nijaib in Quiche history. Possibly, it was based in part on an early codex, perhaps largely genealogical in form (the narration is closely tied to Cawek and Nijaib dynastic successions). The other three documents (and especially *Título Nijaib III*) are more limited in scope, and though possibly in part derived from an official source, appear to be largely elaborations of matters known to provincial lords. Most certainly, the many landmarks listed in the *Títulos Nijaib III* and *IV* were primarily provincial matters recorded especially for these documents.

Direct Spanish influence is evident in all four accounts, as seen by the use of several Spanish terms (especially in *Nijaib II*). In addition, *Nijaib I* contains an account of the conquest and early Christianization of the Quezaltenango area, and all but *Nijaib III* have erroneous Christian dates referring to the prehispanic period (Recinos 1957:76:109). In *Nijaib I*, there is also an attempt to portray the Quiche lords as cooperating with the Spaniards, both in aiding them in subsequent conquests and in accepting Christianity (see their claim that Alvarado and the first

Spanish missionaries were witnesses to their documents), (Recinos 1957:85-94). However, there is no attempt to alter native history to make it conform with Biblical accounts. In general, the four documents must be considered authentic.[16]

Título Sacapulas

As part of an eighteenth century land dispute between the *parcialidades* of Santo Domingo Sacapulas, one of the factions presented an ancient título and a crude circular map of the town boundaries. Both a Quiche text and a Spanish translation of the título apparently existed at the time, but only the Spanish version was transcribed into the court record (AGC, A1:6025-53126).[17] A note at the bottom of one *folio* of another document in that archive indicates that Brasseur made a copy of the título in 1859 (AGC, A1:6074-54887).[18] In addition, there are two small documents, one written in Quiche, and one in Spanish, the first of which appears to be a postscript to the *Título Sacapulas* (AGC, A1: 337-7091; Acuña 1968). A map with Quiche inscriptions located in the same section of the archives differs from the Spanish version found with the litigation papers, and may be the original. It would seem to date the original composition of the map and the

---

[16] This is perhaps best illustrated by the *Nijaib II*. In spite of many Spanish terms in the Quiche text (*gobernador, probanza, rey, capitán*), it contains one of the best accounts we have of the symbols, ritual, and ideas associated with Quiche authority (Recinos 1957:99:103).

[17] The Sacapulas título is quite lengthy, and contains valuable information about prehispanic Quiche institutions. The whole complex of problems connected with its texts, translation, and analysis have been discussed by Acuña in a recent publication (1968) of the Spanish text.

I have gathered various related documentary and ethnographic data from Sacapulas, though I have been unable to locate the original Quiche text. It may still be among the ancient documents jealously guarded by the *cofrades* at Sacapulas, but they would not permit me to see any.

[18] The Brasseur fragment of the Sacapulas título is a slightly different translation from the one with the litigation papers. Presumably it was taken from the Quiche text, for some names are retained in their Quiche forms. These Quiche names make it a useful supplement to the complete version. For a good discussion of the several versions of the título, see Acuña (1968).

título at 1551.[19] I include the texts of the Quiche postcript and map as Appendix A.

The document was written by lords of the Canil and Toltecat ruling lines at Sacapulas, primarily as a claim to the mineral springs located there. It was probably written at the same time the map was composed, possibly in 1551, and accordingly grand-children of the contact-time rulers are mentioned in the account.

The clearest part of the document is a description of the migration by the ancestors of the people of Sacapulas from the "seven caves and hills." Other parts tell of the founding of many sites around modern Sacapulas, and of wars and their subjugation by political rivals. Near the middle of the document a short succession line of guardian rights to the main *nawal* of the group is given, and at the end of the document there is a similar line of rights to political office within the community.

The Spanish translation is not good. In some places it is too literal to be understandable, and in other places it is badly garbled. To make matters worse, the translator attempted to render names and titles in Spanish, so that comparisons and correlations with other native documents are difficult to make. Because of this, the reliability of this source must be constantly questioned, though its authenticity cannot be doubted.

It is clear that most of the Sacapulas account hinges on references to places represented in the map. The map conceivably derives from a prehispanic model, whose form in turn might have been suggested originally by circular representations of the calendar. Whether or not the map has prehispanic antededents, in connection with the título it must have served as an important mnemonic device. Many places represented in it appear to have been associated with traditional stories or tales which are re-

[19] The Spanish inscription in the center circle of the map records the date of 1151, which is probably a transpositioning of 1551. The boundary names in the map correspond well with persons and places mentioned in the título and the postscript. This is not true of the Spanish version of the map in the litigation papers, which appears to be a new and later composition rather than a translation from the early Quiche map (cf. Acuña 1968). This explains why the Quiche map has only 28 boundary names, while the Spanish version has 30. The map and small postscript in Spanish were probably composed in 1758, at the time of the litigation. (See Secondary Sources, Records).

counted in the document. Oral tradition in this case was apparently not extensive, for the accounts are sketchy. The chronological sequence is vague, perhaps because of the heavy emphasis on spatial representation. Apparently, the last part of the account is based on the memory of the authors, and primarily consists of genealogical information dating to the conquest and early postconquest periods.

The authors expressly state that they are writing after Christianity had been introduced, and they refer to the aboriginal period as one of "darkness and night." Nevertheless, the events and ideas recorded in the document are almost wholly native, and unabashed religious worship of native idols and patron deities is described. The major Spanish influence is to be seen in the purposes for which the document was written—the claim to land and certain mineral springs had to be made because of the social and political shifts occurring at Sacapulas as a result of the conquest. Tlaxcallan auxiliaries had apparently settled there, and were a threat to the autochthonous owners of the mineral springs.

Título C'oyoi

The important document was written at Utatlán by the C'oyoi Sakcorowach, a lineage of the Quejnay branch of the Quiche.[20] The principal author was Juan de Penonias de Putanza, who claims to have been a close kinsman to one of the C'oyoi military lords killed in the conquest. Unfortunately, in each place where a Christian date is given the document is defective. Nevertheless, the appearance of several names found in other early documents (especially *Títulos Nijaib I* and *II*) point to a date of compositon sometime during the 1550-1570 period.

The original Quiche text, with two pictorials, is located in the Princeton University Library, as part of the Robert Garrett Collection of Middle American Manuscripts. The manuscript is badly fragmented in many places and the pages (some 56 now exist) were badly out of order. What remains, however, is clearly

---

[20] The C'oyoi Sakcorowach lineage controlled a territory just east of Quezaltenango, which is variously called Baca, Xeoj, Xequi. It is mentioned in other sources (Recinos 1957:72:105), including the *Annals of the Cakchiquels* (Recinos 1950:71).

written, and full use is made in the script of the special characters for sounds with glottal stops. I have prepared a translation and notes for those parts of the text which are sufficiently intact, as a case study for the final section of this study.

The account parrallels in many places the *P.V.* and other Quiche documents. There is a narration of the coming of the forefathers from the East, the dawning, a series of migrations, with the eventual founding of Utatlán, the conquests of Quik'ab, particularly those in the Quezaltenango area, and a view of the Spanish conquest. Of particular interest is a description of Quiche preparations for the conquest, especially as they relate to their hero, Tecum Umam.

The C'oyoi Quejnay were aided in the composition of this document by other officials of the Quiche state, so that at least some parts of the account appear to be taken from an "official" version of Quiche history. We are told in several places that the "words of the forefathers" were being recorded, and there are a few instances where the narration includes dialogue. This is similar to the use of poetic sagas in the *P.V.*, which, we noted, may ultimately derive from song and chant accompaniments to codices. The two pictorials show considerable Spanish influence, and were probably composed after the conquest (without prehispanic referents). Nor should we expect the topographic description of the Quezaltenango area or the account of the conquest to be based on prehispanic sources, but rather, they must have been reconstructed as they were remembered by Quiche lords still living in the 16th century.

The document is relatively free of direct Spanish influence, though there are a few words given in Spanish (e.g., *cimientos, título, poder*). The only attempt to "Christianize" the account I can find is in a reference to the coming from the East, "on the other side of the sea." The few references to religious matters seem entirely indigenous.

To some extent the document was written, "to paint the glory of the Quiche." Primarily, though, it is a claim to land and caciqueship by members of the *C'oyoi* lineage. Repetitiously, descent from the prehispanic Quiche ruling line is asserted, and association with each of the famous rulers is established (Balam Quitze, Quik'ab, Tecum Umam). Midway into the document we are told that it is their "title, proof, and power," and later the boundaries of the *C'oyoi* lordship are enumerated.

Título Huitzitzil Tzunun

The título was written at Quezaltenango in 1567 by Quiche lords from Santa Cruz del Quiché, Quazaltenango, and probably other nearby towns.

The original Quiche text has disappeared, and the Spanish translation which remains was made upon the request of a great grandson of the principal figure of the título, sometime in the 18th century. The document became part of the Ayer Collection in the Newberry Library, where photocopies of it were obtained by a Guatemalan commission studying the historical facts surrounding the life and death of the national hero, Tecum Umam (Anonymous 1963). In 1963, the Sociedad de Geografía e Historia de Guatemala published it under the title, *Título del Ajpop Huitzitzil Tzunun*, with paleography and notes by Francis Gall.

The título contains a testimonial in support of Martín Ajpop Huitzitzil Tzunun and his descendants, confirming his position as *"principal y cabeza de su calpul"* and his claim to lands. It contains a brief narration of the Quiche conquests of the Mam in the Culajá area (Quezaltenango), and of events connected with the Spanish conquest there. The territorial boundaries of the "province" of Culajá, and the *encomienda* rights of Juan de León Cardona are given.

The lords of Utatlán, who went to Quezaltenango to aid in producing the document, clearly were acquainted with the official verson of Quiche history. Very little of that history is given, however, and then only as it related to events occuring in the Quezaltenango area. Because most of the description is of the conquest and subsequent colonization of Quezaltenango, it may be considered a new tradition in the process of formation through the testimony of eyewitnesses. Even though it does not shed much new light on Quiche cultural patterns, it is authentic, and provides an insight into the special knowledge and view held by Quiche rulers during the mid16th century (Gall 1963:8-9).

The purposes and motives of the authors had been influenced by the Spaniards, and there was a conscious attempt to portray

Huitzitzil Tzunun as a Christian leader among his people (he is analogized with Moses). This, along with a description of how he gave aid to the Spaniards during the conquest of Utatlán, were designed to procure special privileges for him and his descendants. In general, the distortion of historical and cultural patterns resulting from this "bias" are more a simplification (to focus attention on the role of Huitzitzil Tzunun) than a willful alteration of the facts.

Título Zapotitlán

The names of the authors of the document are not known, though they were members of the Quejnay branch of the Quiche. We do not know the precise date and place of composition; but because it was attached to the *Relación Zapotitlán* (1579), we can assign it generally to the province of Zapotitlán with a *terminus ante quem* of 1579. The document, apparently a Spanish translation of an original Quiche text, was composed in answer to a question in the *Relación* about "who the Indians were in their gentile times" (Estrada 1955). The original Spanish version is now in the Latin American Library, University of Texas.

It was first published by Recinos, along with the *P.V.* under the title, *Papel del Origen de los Señores* (1953:249-250). It has since been translated into English by Goetz and Moley (1950).

The Zapotitlán account is basically a claim to legitimation by rulers of the Zapotitlán area, and contains an outline of their connection with the dynastic line of Utatlán. The same matters are further portrayed in a pictorial, showing what appears to be a network of ropes or strings. The knots stand for different rulers and branches which lead off the central ruling line. Unexpectedly, the historical part of the account refers to the early period, when the Quiche were in the general area of Rabinal. For this reason, the *Título Zapotitlán* is a valuable supplement to certain sections of the *P.V.* and *Título Totonicapán* which describe the same period.

Because we lack details about the authors of this account, it is difficult to determine the sources from which it was composed. It does not appear that Quiche lords from Utatlán were present to aid in its composition, with the result that we have a view of history somewhat different from the official version maintained at the capital. Their knowledge of Quiche history was specialized, being primarily restricted to events associated with those Quiche rulers who gave rise to the Quejnay ruling line. In that specialized knowledge, however, they surpass in detail even the *P. V.*

This raises the possibility of their having possessed a codex at one time, with representation of such matters. The pictorial of the genealogical line further suggests this, and may have come directly from such a prehispanic document. It is similar to the description given by Fuentes y Guzmán (1932-7:33:108) of a codex from Utatlán, which he claims also contained a drawing of a string with knots to represent the Quiche ruling line.

The account appears to be essentially free of Spanish influence, presumably because it was written in answer to a question about native life (it would be similar to an informant's reply to the ethnographer's inquiries). In view of this, it is significant that it is in close agreement with other Quiche documents, especially the *P. V.*, and *Título Totonicapán.*

Título Santa Clara

The authors of the document claim to be descendants of the Cawek ruling line of the Quiche. It was written in 1583 at Santa Cruz del Quiché, and was presented before the Spanish court in 1640 by elders of Santa Clara as evidence to support their litigation with the Indians of San Juan Atitlán (Recinos 1957:173).[21]

The original Quiche text, preserved in the Archivo General de Centroamérica, was published by Recinos along with a Spanish translation under the title, *Título de los Indios de Santa Clara la Laguna* (1957:171-181). Generally, I have followed Recinos' Spanish translation, though I have also consulted the original

---

[21] From other documents among these litigation papers we learn that the Indians of Santa Clara were originally from Santa Catarina Ixtahuacán. The town was established about 1580 in order to block the encroachment of the Tzutujil into their lands. San Juan Atitlán was established somewhat later (ca. 1600), under the direction of the Tzutujil at Santiago Atitlán (AGC, Al: 5942-51997; see Secondary Sources, Records).

Quiche text and the partial Spanish translation included in the litigation papers.

The Santa Clara account is basically a Cawek Quiche claim to territory along the borders of Lake Atitlán and in the lowlands to the south. The claim is based on conquest of the area, described as part of a military expedition led by Quik'ab, beginning at Utatlán, continuing on to Tzololá, passing alongside Lake Atitlán (where the Indians of Santa Clara and San Juan were subjected), and dropping down to the coast. Many rulers of the Cawek line are recorded in the document, and it is signed by representatives of the four major Nima Quiche descent groups at the time of the conquest—i.e., the Cawek, Nijaib, Ajaw Quiche, and Zaq'uic.

Though the document was written almost 50 years after the conquest, it is important. There is little likelihood that any part of it was based on prehispanic codices, but the authors were direct descendants of the ruling line at Utatlán. They had learned first-hand from their fathers the official version of Quiche history, as is evident from the similarity between the dynastic list presented here and the one in the *P.V.* For the part of history which interested them (in connection with the litigation against the Tzutujil), many details of name and place are presented. Just how these details were retained for such use I do not know, though they were probably linked in some way to a standardized account of a major military thrust into the area. This would account for the close similarity between this document and a part of *Título Nijaib I* (Recinos 1957:79-84).

There is little direct Spanish influence evident in the document, though some communities are listed by their Spanish names. Of course, its focus on the Santa Clara area is the result of posthispanic litigation at the Spanish court, but this area was already a source of conflict between the Quiche and the Tzutujil before the conquest.

Rabinal Achí

Unlike the other documents mentioned, the *Rabinal Achí* is a native drama, which, under the name, "Dance of the Tun," continued to be performed by the natives of Rabinal during the centuries following the conquest. Its transcription seems to have been as follows: In the year 1850, Bartolo Sis of San Pablo Rabinal transcribed the dialogue into Quiche, "to leave a remembrance to my descendants." Six years later, Brasseur, then priest of Rabinal, had the drama performed for him. He was so impressed that, with the aid of his Quiche-speaking servants, he copied Sis's version, and translated the Quiche into French (Brasseur 1945-49:21:163; Mace 1967). It was published in 1862 with the title *Rabinal Achí*, along with a grammar of the Quiche language (Brasseur 1862).

Apparently, the original Quiche transcription by Sis has disappeared, and various subsequent versions have followed the Brasseur publication (Mace 1967). Of special importance among these later editions is the Monterde translation into Spanish of the Brasseur Quiche text accompanied by an extensive commentary (1955).

In spite of the long time which had elapsed between the conquest and the transcription of the *Rabinal Achí* (over 300 years), it appears to be almost wholly aboriginal. As Edmonson states (1964:272): "The monotonous, heroic and totally nonromantic style and the obscure and archaic language rule out the possibility of European authorship that has sometimes been hinted." And Mace, in a recent study of the text, concluded that it "descended from an authentic preconquest dance drama" (1967:17).

The drama tells the story of a Cawek military leader who attacks the Rabinal province. He is captured and taken prisoner to the provincial fortress, where his guilt is determined, and he is sacrificed. The account is much less important for the legendary events which it narrates, than for the cultural values and patterns which it so extensively and dramatically expresses. From that point of view, apart from the *P.V.* it may be unsurpassed in value among the sources relating to the prehispanic Quiche.

The sources from which the *Rabinal Achí* was composed have long puzzled students of Quiche culture. The suggestion that it derives from Spanish influence has been generally abandoned, because of the totally aboriginal nature of the theme, language, and cultural setting (Armas Lara 1964:43-44; Mace 1967:16-19; Edmonson 1964:273). Not a single Spanish word appears in the Quiche text. Mace believes that it suffered some changes through oral transmission during the colonial period (1967:17-18), but it is also possible that the original had been transcribed some three centuries before its alleged date of composition (by Sis) in 1850. That is, when Sis stated that he had "made the original of this dance of the Tun," possibly, he meant that he was copying a transcription of a Quiche text which had been in the town since the 16th century.[22]

The text of the *Rabinal Achi* could have been written shortly after the conquest, for the Rabinal Quiche came into close contact with the Dominican missionaries as early as 1541 (as part of the famous Las Casas' pacification of Verapaz). The Rabinal Indians must have been impressed with the missionaries' ability to write the native language (Remesal 1932:4:185), and probably importuned the missionaries into teaching them this writing system before it came into use by other Quiche caciques. Because the ritual of human sacrifice is so clearly expressed in the drama, and would have been offensive to the Spaniards, the transcript must have been kept from the eyes of the Spaniards during the period of Spanish domination. Other dances were altered so as to be less offensive to the Spaniards, while still others were derived wholly from the missionaries (Mace 1967:9; see the discussion of ceremonial drama in Secondary Sources).

If the above reconstruction is correct, the *Rabinal Achi* should be placed along side the *Popol Vuh* in terms of its authentic expression of native culture. Presumably, it is a fairly accurate transcription of some of the dialogue and scenario accompanying one of the important ceremonial dramas presented in prehispanic times by the Rabinal Quiche.

---

[22] The Quiche words used by Sis were, "*mixchiwelesaj wi original rech wae xajoj tun.*" *-elesaj* is the active form of the verb, "to take from, remove, deliver" (Edmonson 1965; Sáenz 1940). Most translators have accepted the meaning of the verb as, "to deliver" (i.e., "to deliver the original"), but it is possible that he used the term in the sense of, "to take from" (i.e., "to take it from the original"). I would not force the latter interpretation, however, as the former seems more natural, and, closer to the meaning of the Spanish word *sacar*.

It might be noted that in the short paragraph written by Sis in Quiche he used several Spanish words. This is what one would expect of a Quiche speaker of the 19th century, and it stands in sharp relief with the Quiche text itself.

MAJOR DOCUMENTS OF GROUPS RELATED TO THE QUICHE

I have somewhat arbitrarily separated documents written in Quiche (or by Quiche speakers in Spanish) from those composed by other Quiche, and highland Maya speakers (Cakchiquel, Tzutujil, Pokomán, Kekchi). This seems useful because of the Quiche's special importance in highland Guatemala, and because documents written by non-Quiche speakers, even other Quichean peoples, are "outsider" accounts, potentially hostile toward the Quiche. Nevertheless, cultural forms were widely held in the highlands at the time of the conquest, and much can be learned about Quiche culture in particular and Quichean culture and society in general from documents of the neighboring cultures. The different Quichean peoples became separated only late in their history, so that a document like the *Annals of the Cakchiquels* contains valuable historical information about the Quiche as well as the Cakchiquel.

Annals of the Cakchiquels (Memorial de Sololá)

The original document was written at Sololá in the Cakchiquel language, mostly by two members of the Xajil lineage of the Cakchiquel. The author of the first part was Hernández Arana, grandson of the Cakchiquel ruler, Jun Ik', and a witness to the conquest in 1524. At least by 1573 (Recinos 1950:124), he had begun to transcribe the traditions of his lineage, continuing the record until his death (probably in 1582). After 1583 Francisco Díaz, also of the Xajil lineage, continued the account by recording the important events of the town (i.e., births, deaths, the purchase of church equipment) (Recinos 1950:17-21). A copy was made of the original Cakchiquel text, presumably in the 17th century, and most available translations have come from that copy. The omnipresent Brasseur was shown the manuscript in 1855, and he translated it into French. Leaving a copy of the translation behind, he returned to France with the early Cakchiquel text. This manuscript was eventually purchased by Brinton, who published an English translation of most of it under the title, *The Annals of the Cakchiquels* (1885). From the same manuscript, in 1934, Villacorta published the complete Cakchiquel text, along with a Spanish translation of most of it.

I have used Villacorta's version for direct study of the Cakchiquel text. In some places his translation appears to be more accurate than Recinos' recent Spanish version (1950), though generally I have followed the Recinos edition. Also useful is the fine English translation of the Recinos edition by Goetz (1953).

The *Annals* are more a chronicle of history and tradition than a título, though a claim to territory is implicit in the account. The narration begins with a brief description of the creation, followed by a version of the legendary migration of the Cakchiquel ancestors from Tulan to the Lake Atitlán region. In the middle section, numerous details of social and cultural patterns form a matrix within which Cakchiquel legendary history is recorded. Towards the end of the preconquest period, in chronicle fashion, dates are given in the native calendar system for the events which transpire. These dated events begin during the equivalent Christian year A.D. 1493, and continue into the 17th century.

Though I cannot agree with Edmonson (1964:266) that the *Annals* are "incomparably better history than any of the other sources," they do provide the most complete account available of prehispanic history in the highlands. Up to the separation of the Cakchiquel from the Quiche (Recinos 1950:101), the document is in every way similar to large sections of the *P.V.* and other Quiche documents. However, from that point on the account becomes a chronicle with all events dated according to a native long-count system. In terms of the sources from which the *Annals* were compiled, how is this to be explained? Was it the result of a "happy idea," hit upon by one of the Xajil to record the traditions which for generations bad been orally passed on, as suggested by Recinos (1950:17)?

Unfortunately, the authors are silent on this point. Arana, who wrote the section which refers to the prehispanic period, only states that these things were told to them (i.e., the Xajil) by the forefathers. He also indicates that he saw the coming of the Spaniards, so that we may assume that all posthispanic descriptions are based on personal observation. The large number of details in the first part of the *Annals*, including extensive dialogue, would seem to argue against an exclusively oral transmission. In view of the fact that, along with the Quiche, the Cakchiquel leaders brought "paintings" and calendars with them from the East (Recinos 1950:52), it seems likely that some book or codex served as primary source for much of the early part of the account. Surely, Arana, as a descendant of the second most highly ranked Cakchiquel ruling line, would have had access to codices not immediately destroyed after the conquest. Some Indians of Sololá were taught to read and write in Cakchiquel by the missionaries in 1542, and, presumably, sometime after that Arana began to write (and, perhaps, in part transcribe) his work. If, in fact, much of the first part of the account was based on a prehispanic codex, this would explain why the document is not just a land title (at least, in any direct sense of the word).[23]

As to why the account in the *Annals* becomes chronological after the Cakchiquel separated from the Quiche, we may assume that their own history became more important and more precise once they had gained autonomy. There is no reason to believe that they did not record calendar dates in their codices to date the events which transpired after their separation from the Quiche. And, later, when they chose a beginning for their long count, they selected the most significant event affecting their internal structure, that is, the revolt of the Tukuchée.

Presumably, then, Arana took his account for the prehispanic part of Cakchiquel history from a native chronicle, one resembling the chronicles of central Mexico for the same period. Unfortunately, however, this reconstruction must remain speculative until additional evidence is uncovered. We are still left with the question why only in this case a long count was used by the Quichean peoples of highland Guatemala in recording their prehispanic history.

[23] In the absence of an explanation by Arana, we cannot know for sure why he decided to write (and, in part, transcribe) the *Annals*. Perhaps, the presumed codex was badly torn, and unreadable for the natives. This transcription would have provided a permanent, readable record.

But other explanations are possible. For example, we know the Xajil, along with other Cakchiquel Indians, had some of their privileges removed in 1557 (Recinos 1950:145), and the *Annals* might have been written in order to seek their restoration. Or it might have been prepared as evidence in land-claim cases, which were common during the period (e.g., Recinos 1950:147ff). It is even possible that the account was made (whether with the help of a codex or not) to satisfy requests by the missionaries for information about aboriginal life.

The section of the *Annals* that refers to the prehispanic period appears to be devoid of direct Spanish influence. This is seen by the fact that, prior to the mention of the conquest by "Tunatiuh" (Pedro de Alvarado), (Villacorta 1934:263), not a single Spanish word is used in the Cakchiquel text. There are many references to native beliefs and institutions which would have been offensive to the Spaniards (such as the worship of stone idols). Nevertheless, the predominance of political matters in the account must be, in part, the indirect result of Spanish influence. There is an attempt to document the connection between the Xajil and the other important ruling lines in the highlands, and this includes ties between the Cakchiquel and the most famous Quiche rulers.[24] Though, in part, this emphasis on political matters may reflect the nature of their presumed prehispanic codices; probably it also is the result of Spanish policy which rewarded with cacique privileges only those natives who could demonstrate direct descent from the prehispanic rulers.

Títulos Xpantzay

The Títulos Xpantzay are three documents written in the 1550s by Cakchiquel lords from Tecpán Guatemala, near the old Cakchiquel capital of Iximché.[25] Two documents, *Historia de los Xpant-*

---

[24] The attempt in the *Annals* to show a connection between the Cakchiquel rulers and those of the Quiche is a fortunate circumstance. It crossties the ruling dynasties of the two groups, and greatly facilitates their historical reconstruction (Wauchope 1949; Carmack 1966a).

[25] The first of the three Xpantzay documents published by Recinos bears the fictitious date of 1524, the year the conquest began. Obviously, this was a device designed to add prestige and legitimacy to the document.

In another place in the same document, Franciscan friars are mentioned, and, because they taught the Cakchiquel as early as 1542, that year becomes a *terminus post quem* for the beginning of this Xpantzay título (Recinos 1957: 125, footnotes 3, 4; Recinos 1950: 139-140). It also means that the quotation ascribed in this document to Four Imox, the Ajpotzotzil, is fictitious, for he was hanged by Alvarado in 1540 (Recinos 1950:136-137).

A *terminus ante quem* for the document is provided perhaps by the death date of Juan Pérez in 1552, one of the witnesses to the document (Recinos 1950:141). Alonso Pérez, who witnessed the document as the Ajaw Xpantzay, apparently did not receive that position until sometime shortly before 1554 zay de Tecpán Guatemala, and *Guerras Comunes de Quiche y Cak-chiquel,* hereafter *Títulos Xpantzay I* and *II,* apparently were written by the Tzotzil, Tukuchée, and Xpantzay divisions of the Cakchiquel (Recinos 1957:120-149). The other document, *Testamento de los Xpantzay,* or *Título Xpantzay III,* was written by Alonso Pérez, a direct descendant of the ruling line Xpantzay (Recinos 1957:152-169).

Originally composed in Cakchiquel, the Spanish authorities ordered the three documents translated into Spanish in 1659 as evidence in a dispute over land between Francisco de Argueta and the Indians of Tecpán Guatemala (Berlin 1950:40-41). In 1950, Berlin published the Spanish translations of the three títulos, along with other smaller native documents. In 1957, Recinos corrected the Spanish translations and published them along with their Cakchiquel texts.

The *Título Xpantzay I* is the least significant of the three, though it does contain a useful list of lineage and place names which can be correlated with other Cakchiquel documents. The *Título Xpantzay II* contains an extremely important account of how the Cakchiquel participated in Quiche military activities during the reigns of K'ucumatz and Quik'ab. We can correlate events described there with those given in the *P.V.* and other Quiche documents, and thereby clarify certain details in the Quiche sources.

The *Título Xpantzay III* is basically an attempt to trace the history of the ruling line of the Xpantzay, and in the process gives many details about Cakchiquel migrations into the area northeast of Lake Atitlán. The document provides one of our clearest insights into the internecine struggles which were fought between rival houses for the highest political offices.

The documents show no direct evidence that they were based on a prehispanic codex. However, in the first part of the *Título Xpantzay II* (Recinos 1957:132-143), the extensive use of dialogue is similar to sections of the *P.V.,* and might have been taken from native codices. When we recall that matters associated with

---

(Recinos 1957:165-169). The *Título Xpantzay III* bears Alonso Pérez' signature for the year 1554.

Therefore, the account was prepared sometime between 1542 and 1552, probably early in the 1550-1560 decade.

the Quiche hero rulers are narrated in this document and that it was written in collaboration with the most important Cakchiquel officials, the possibility of some connection with a prehispanic codex becomes credible. This does not apply to the *Títulos Xpantzay I* and *III*, however, for in these two sources we are specifically told that they are based on "ancient sayings" passed from father to son (Recinos 1957:152-153). Nor have these accounts the epic or poetic characteristics of the *Título Xpantzay II*, a fact which is perhaps further related to the secondary ranking of the author in the case of *Xpantzay III*.[26]

Títulos Xpantzay II and *III* are relatively free of direct Spanish influence, which is more evident in the *Título Xpantzay I*. Except for one date, the *Título Xpantzay II* does not contain a single Spanish word in the Cakchiquel text. The narrow focus of the account, however (restricted to relations with famous Quiche rulers), suggests that its purpose was to establish cacique standing for the Cakchiquel ruling lines by demonstrating affiliation with the Quiche ruling line (the line accepted by the Spaniards as the dominant political power in the highlands at the time of the conquest). The Cakchiquel were proud of recounting (or transcribing) their past glories. We find this statement in the documents: "May the glory of our city and clan never decline!" (Recinos 1957:148, translation mine). In the *Título Xpantzay III*, Spanish words appear in the text only in connection with events occurring after the conquest (Recinos 1957:162ff). The primary purpose of the document is quite clear, and it significantly affects the nature of its contents. The Bishop had interceded on behalf of Alonso Pérez in the power struggle between the ruling lineages of Tecpán, and Don Alonso writes to demonstrate that his lineage can legitimately claim descent from the Xpantzay ruling line, and thence from the Tzotzil rulers.

---

[26] Again we note that oral mnemonic devices were probably used in the production of these documents, whether there was a prehispanic codex or not. This suggestion is reinforced by the continual use of such phrases as "it is said," "the ancient saying," and "true words." This seems to be the only reasonable explanation of how the extensive tales about K'ucumatz and Quik'ab (*Título Xpantzay I*), or the detailed migration tales, with associated names and places (*Título Xpantzay II*) could have been composed so many years after their occurrence.

The *Xpantzay I* case is somewhat different. The document is explicitly a title to land, and the territorial boundaries are listed. As backing for the claim, prior acceptance of and affiliation with Spanish institutions by the rulers of the lineage are cited, along with statements about prehispanic possession of the land. Their traditions of Tula are linked with Old Testament tales of Babylon, and testimony of their baptism and indoctrination under the hands of the early missionaries found its way into the account.

Título Chajoma

The document was originally composed in 1555 in the Cakchiquel language by the leaders of the Chajoma branch of the Cakchiquel living at San Martín Xilotepeque (Jilotepeque). In 1689, a Spanish translation of it was used as evidence in a land dispute between San Martín and Santo Domingo Sinacao (Xenacoj). Crespo published this Spanish version under the title, *Trasunto de un Título de los del Pueblo de San Martín Xilotepeque* (1956:13-15). I have used this published version and the Spanish copy in the Archivo General de Centroamérica (Al:5981-52131).

The document is primarily a land title, and contains a valuable list of prehispanic toponyms and names of social groups residing in the eastern part of the Cakchiquel hegemony. It gives brief references to Cakchiquel history, including a description of an early period in the Joyabaj area. The list of rulers from that early period is incomplete and confused, but some names correspond to those given in important Quiche sources (Recinos 1950: 218:245-247).

The Cakchiquel-speaking authors of the document state that they are writing the things they "remember" and "recognize" as being true and, indeed, the account is probably based on oral tradition. A substantial number of details on names and events are given for the early period of their history. Possibly, at least part of their account was based (remembetred?) on some prehispanic document. The extensive list of boundary markers is derived from information well known to the lords of that area during the 16th century.

The document was used by the inhabitants of San Martín Jilotepeque legally to defend themselves against the claims of other nearby communities. The supreme rulers of the Quiche and Cakchiquel lines are mentioned, but no attempt is made to gain special cacique privileges by demonstrating close affiliation with them.

Relación Tzutujil

Though the document is not a título, I have included it because it is a native composition and contains valuable information on the prehispanic aboriginal condition. It was sent to the Spanish Crown in 1571 by the "caciques y principales" of Santiago de Atitlán. They petition for privileges which they believed to be appropriate to their position as sons and kinsmen of native rulers. If there was a Tzutujil original, we have no record of it; only the 1571 Spanish version has come to us.

A French translation of *Relación Tzutujil* was published by Ternaux Compans in 1838; and the Sociedad de Geografía e Historia de Guatemala published it from the original Spanish version in the Real Academia de la Historia, Madrid, under the title, *Relación de los caciques y principales del pueblo de Atitlán* (Anonymous 1952).

The document contains a brief, clear description of the political organization of the Tzutujil at Atitlán (and in that respect is in close agreement with the Quiche and Cakchiquel documents), and an interesting account of the conquest and subsequent imposition of tribute on the Tzutujil by the Spaniards.

The opening section of the *Relación*, which refers to the prehispanic period, is good evidence that it was, in part, based on prehispanic sources. The names of three of the signers are found in another document from 1563, which records a dispute between two factions of the Tzutujil at Atitlán (Carrasco 1967b317-331). In that dispute two "paintings," *lienzos*, which pictorially represented the houses and rulers of the Tzutujil in prehispanic times, were used as evidence. The six lords mentioned in the *Relación Tzutujil* are also listed in the 1563 document. We may therefore conclude that such largely pictorial codices served as mnemonic devices for transcribing lists of subject towns, kinds of tribute paid, and the titles of offices and special groups—like those given in the *Relación Tzutujil*. Presumably, the narration of posthispanic events in the document was based on the personal observation and memory of the authors.

In the absence of any Tzutujil text, it is difficult to judge the extent to which the prehispanic account was influenced by contact with the Spaniards (e.g., the Spanish names given for the towns subject to the Tzutujil might have been listed by their aboriginal names in the presumed native text). It quite clearly describes native, and not Spanish patterns, though the purpose for the description reflects Spanish influence. The document was written as a plea for special privileges—the right to collect small "rents" and to bear arms. They deviced evidence that their fathers had held special privileges of service and tribute in aboriginal times, and recounted the many services, both ecclesiastical and secular, which they had rendered to the Crown since the conquest. Possibly, therefore their claims to prehispanic authority and privilege are somewhat exaggerated.

Título Cajcoj

It is a historical título written by the elders of San Cristóbal Verapaz (the settlement was called Cajcoj or Kajcoj in aboriginal times). We do not know the precise date of composition, but it can be assigned to the second half of the sixteenth century on the basis of events described which took place there after the pacification of Verapaz.[27] The original document was apparently written in Pocomchi, but only a Spanish version, copied in 1785, has come to us (AGC, Al:6074-54885). Crespo (n.d.) recently transcribed that version for his study of Guatemalan native documents, and I have used his transcription as well as the copy in the Archivo General de Centroamérica.

[27] Though we cannot give the precise year in which the document was written, probably it was sometime between 1550 and 1580. Pacification of the region began in earnest in 1542 (Sáenz 1964:53-54). Juan de Torres was the first missionary to work at Cajcoj, according to this título. Two other missionaries mentioned toward the end of the document, Fray Gallego and Fray de Viana are known to have written a relación from Verapaz in 1574 (a date which may roughly serve as a *terminus ante quem*). There were two successions to the ruling line at Cajcoj after the Spanish contact. This fact suggests a period of composition some twenty to forty years after the pacification of Verapaz (i.e., 1560-1580).

Título Cajcoj contains a mythological account of the creation of the first Cajcoj people, and legends about their conflicts with neighbors from Tucurub and Taltique (Santa María Tactic). There are brief references to other surrounding peoples, the Chinautec and Rabinaleb. The account centers on the pacification of the area by the Dominicans, especially Fray Juan de Torres. At the end is a list of some twenty-three successions of rulers, twenty of which purportedly took place before Spanish contact.

Though the document contains minimal ethnographic data (and only a few words about the Quiche), it is important as the most substantive *título* of the Pokomán speakers. It provides a basis for comparison with the Quichean *títulos*, especially on ideas about the founding of their respective political systems. It is unfortunate that the Pocomchi original is not available, for some words which have been translated into Spanish (e.g., tribes, jefe) would be of comparative interest.

It is difficult to reconstruct the sources for the composition of the document because we lack the presumed Pocomchi text, and it is not possible to state whether the references to the pre-hispanic period were based on written codices or oral tradition. Both modes of transmission were known in the Verapaz region (Las Casas 1958:346), but according to one statement in the document, it is a "memorial by the forefathers giving account to their sons and grandsons about the creation and birth of the first men." It is perhaps noteworthy that the section referring to the pre-hispanic period is brief, compared to the sections describing post-hispanic events and boundary markers. The long dynastic line given at the end of the document lists twenty-one prehispanic successions. Such a list of names could have been memorized for there is almost no narration connected with any of the rulers. It seems likely, however, that they were transcribed from one of the native "paintings."

A direct and important Christian influence can be detected throughout the account, and the description of the pacification of Verapaz was primarily written to prove that the people of Cajcoj had cooperated with the missionaries. However, underlying it all was the idea of defending the territorial rights of San Cristóbal against surrounding communities. Because of this overriding purpose, one must read with caution statements about Cajocj political superiority before the conquest, and the cooperative reaction of the people there to the "peaceful" conquest by the friars.

MINOR QUICHEAN DOCUMENTS

This category of native documents consists of small accounts with little or no information about prehispanic history and limited substantive data on cultural patterns. They are generally provincial accounts, which do not appear to have been based upon well developed prehispanic historical traditions (with a few possible exceptions). Nevertheless, they are important for the view they give us of conditions in the Quichean provinces and surrounding territories.

Título Paxtoca

Under the title, *Memorial de la conquista y títulos de mojones, Paxtoca*, this document was used during the colonial period as evidence in a prolonged land dispute between San Miguel and San Cristóbal Totonicapán. The original was written in 1558 by members of the Excamparitz parcialidad from Paxtoca, probably in Quiche, though only a Spanish translation of it has come to us (Crespo n.d.; AGC, Al:6074-53386). Important extracts from this document are in Appendix VI.

There are a few references to indigneous political organization, and the boundaries of the *parcialidad del calpul de San Sebastián Paxtoca* are listed. Paxtoca is now an *aldea* within the municipal territory of San Miguel Totonicapán.

The account is definitely provincial, and there is no evidence that the authors had access to any major portion of the official Quiche state historical tradition. The purpose of the document was to maintain the territorial rights of the Excamparitz by obtaining favorable testimony from native rulers of surrounding communities.

Título Retalulew

The document is very similar to the Título Paxtoca. It was used as evidence in 1797 as part of a land dispute between the elders of San Antonio Retaluhleuh and a Spaniard named Mariano de la Torre. It is now reposited in the Sección de Tierras, Archivo de la Escribanía de Guatemala. It was originally written in 1557 (though it bears the erroneous date of 1537),[28] by Quiché lords from Santa Cruz del Quiché, on behalf of Don Francisco Tatzuy from Retaluhleuh. Though it was probably written in Quiche, only a Spanish translation is attached to the litigation papers now available. I have transcribed the document as Appendix VII.

With the exception of a brief reference to the conquest of the Retaluhleuh area by the Quiche lord, Tatzuy, there is no historical information about the prehispanic period. It sheds some light on the political geography of that part of the Quiche state, and it contains the names and titles of a number of important Quiche lords.

This document was written by sons of the contact-time rulers at Utatlán, persons who were well acquainted with official Quiche historical tradition (and who may have had some of the prehispanic codices). However, they confine themselves to an affirmation of Tatzuy's high rank, and his lordship over the Retaluhleuh area.

Título Chuachituj

The brief but important document was written in 1592 at Santa Cruz del Quiché. Though possibly written in Quiche, originally, only a Spanish translation of it used as evidence in an 1824 land dispute between San Antonio Ilotenango and Santa María Chiquimula has survived (Archivo de la Escribanía, Sección de Tierras, Department of Totonicapán). I have included a copy of the document as Appendix VIII.

The author was Martín Pérez Quik'ab, a Quiche lord who apparently witnessed the conquest and who, many years later,

---

[28] Two places in the document give the date of March, 1537, but this surely is an error in translation or transcription. There is no evidence whatsoever that native títulos were being produced at that early date, and if they were, the first ones certainly would have been made at Utatlán. Many names of Quiche lords mentioned in the document can be identified with those listed in other documents from the decade of 1550-1560. It is highly probable, therefore, that the second "5" in 1557 was transposed to "3" by a scribe who did not realize the incredibly low probability of such an early date of composition.

as an old man, was brought especially from Quezaltenango to serve as a witness for the land title.[29] The document was also witnessed and signed by other principales from Santa Cruz, including the cacique, Juan de Rojas.[30]

The account is mainly important for its brief references to the prehispanic vassalage condition of the Soc at Utatlán, and for the toponyms which are listed for the territory of Chuachituj.

Apparently, the author of this document based his account on information known to him from full participation in the political life of the prehispanic Quiche. His purpose was to legitimatize holdings given to former vassals of the Quiche state. He attempted to do this by testifying that these rights had been granted by the Quiche ruler himself, and by pointing out the controlling powers of Quiche rulers to the royal land title granted to the community of Santa Cruz del Quiché.

Título Chacatz-Tojin

The document contains a small land claim made by the Chacatz and Tojin calpules at Santa Cruz. It was originally written in Quiché in 1607, and subsequently translated into Spanish at the request of the same calpules. Later, in 1783, the Spanish translation became part of the *protocolos* from Santa Cruz, which are

---

[29] The identification of Martín Pérez Quik'ab is made difficult by references to him as "Montesuma," "the Quiche King," and "representative of Montesuma." He states that he was the "younger brother of Montesuma;" that he lived at Utatlán before the conquest; and that his residence was expropriated by the conquistadores. It would appear that he uses the title "Montesuma" as a synonym for ruler or king, so that such references were to the Quiche supreme ruler (Ajpop) and not to the Aztec emperor.

Possibly Don Martín of Quiche, who signed some other native documents, is the same person as the one discussed here (Recinos 1957:115).

[30] The date of composition given in the document is 1592, though Juan de Rojas is said to have attached his signature in 1594. Therefore, either Juan de Rojas lived well beyond the 1558 date by which time Recinos suggests that he had died (1953:30), or the name was a title taken by his descendants. The latter possibility is supported by other papers from the archives in Guatemala (Contreras R. 1965; Carrasco 1967a), in which the name continues to appear for several generations.

The statement that the document was signed by Pedro de Alvarado, Hernán Cortés, and the early missionaries is fictitious.

now preserved in the Archivo General de Centroamérica (erroneously under the Department of Totonicapán) (Al:1497-9974). A copy of the document is included as Appendix IX.

The document contains only the briefest reference to the prehispanic period. Its primary, though limited value, lies in the list of lineage and place names given, for some can be correlated with their equivalents in other native documents. This kind of information is of special importance because of the political dominance of the area to which it refers—the prehispanic Quiche capital, Utatlán.

The authors of the account were not acquainted with the historical tradition of the Quiche state, presumably because of the late date at which it was composed, and perhaps because the Chacatz and Tojin people came from descent groups peripheral to the ruling line at Utatlán. When listing territorial boundaries and the calpules located within them, the authors clearly write from firsthand knowledge. Their purpose is made explicit: They want to prepare a land title which can be taken to the *alcalde mayor* in cases of dispute over lands at Santa Cruz.

Título Lamaquib

The brief document was written in 1595 by the elders of the Lamaquib, later called parcialidad Santo Tomás, of Santa Domingo Sacapulas. There is no indication that it might have been originally composed in Quiche, though the account contains many toponyms in that language. The local scribe who wrote it in Spanish probably translated from Quiche as it was recited to him by the elders. This would have required no great effort, for the account is extremely brief.

We do not know the specific purpose for which the document was originally composed, though obviously it had to do with clarifying Sacapulas' western boundaries siding with the Indians from Aguacatán. It was used in 1739 as evidence in support of claims made by Sacapulas in a dispute with Aguacatán over territorial rights. I obtained a copy of it from the Archivo General de Centroamérica in Guatemala (Al:5978-52518), which I include as Appendix X.

There is no prehispanic history in the account, but the location of several ethnic and political units from the aboriginal period are specified. The document should be useful for reconstructing the prehispanic political geography of the area (an area of primary importance for the rise of the Quiche state).

The information contained in this document must have been common knowledge to the leaders of the Lamaquib in 1595. Possibly, one or two of the older people alive could remember the prehispanic period; but, more than that, the aboriginal names of places and peoples had persisted without much change during the first generations after the conquest. The account involves no tie-in with any historical tradition, but rather is a simple recitation of a few social and geographic facts pertinent to that specific area. We should expect these facts to be accurate, though the territorial claims of the Lamaquib are probably somewhat exaggerated.

Título Uchabaja

The small document, written in Quiche in 1600, was attached to litigation papers from Sacapulas, now preserved in the Archivo General de Centroamérica (A1:5936-51914). The 1601 dispute for which it was used as evidence was over land claimed by both San Andrés (Sajcabaja) and parcialidades Tolteca and Canil from Sacapulas. Apparently the territory described in the small título was part of the land disputed by the two communities.

The Quiche text was written legibly, though the Parra characters were only partially applied by the scribe, Francisco Aceituno (who also transcribed in 1613 a small land title discussed in Secondary Sources, Native Language Documents). I have copied the Quiche text (minus some insignificant testimonial at the end) and have given a translation of it as Appendix XI.

The primary importance of the document is in the prehispanic lineage names which it records, and its brief reference to prehispanic history. The Quiche military invasion of the Sacapulas area is mentioned, and that on that occasion the Tolteca faction gained control over the disputed lands. Apparently, this territory had been the sole possession of the Uchabaja lineage prior to the Quiche conquest.

In view of the late date of composition, the document's contents must be viewed with caution. The source of the tradition from which the historical account was taken was probably the same as the one given in the *Título Sacapulas*. That document also mentions the Tolteca, Canil (but not the Uchabaja), and the coming of the warring Quiche. One would suppose that the heads of all the major lineages at Sacapulas had seen the pictorial map used in connection with the *Título Canil*, and heard many times the traditional account associated with it.

Buenabaj Pictorials

Among ancient papers in a leather-bound look possessed by the elders of aldea San Vicente Buenabaj, municipality of Santiago Momostenango, are three pictorials or paintings, and a Quiche inscription below one of them. The elders kindly allowed me to photograph them, and I include them along with a translation of the inscription as Appendix XII.

The drawings are not dated, nor is there an indication to which documents they might have been attached originally. Subject matter and style clearly indicate that they are posthispanic, though there is evidence that indigenous patterns also went into their composition.[31] The collection of papers included a version of *Título Nijaib I*, which contains a claim that the Quiche paid tribute to Motecuzoma. Inasmuch as the inscription states the same thing, it may be inferred that the pictorials accompanied that document. This would suggest a tentative date sometime during the decade of 1550 to 1560 (See *Título Nijaib I* above). The authors are given in the inscription as, "we, the lords in the city of Quiche, Utatlán."

---

[31] The pictorials are an interesting syncretism of native and Spanish cultural patterns and symbols. Some significant native motifs are: the representation of a horse below the tail of the twin-headed eagle symbolizing the Spanish Crown; the highly stylized mountains, river, and lake, as part of the "map" (this part of the pictorial is similar to the map which accompanies the *Relación Geográfica Santiago Atitlán*); the loin cloths of the Quiche and Mexican rulers, which undergird their Spanish style robes; the bow and arrow and large drum placed beside a Spanish *escopeta*. These features show the mixture of native and Spanish cultural patterns.

The primary significance of the pictorials is the additional evidence they provide that the Quiche had established strong ties with the Aztecs. The inscription contains a startling statement to the effect that Motecuzoma had married two of his daughters to the Quiche ruler. Unfortunately, no clarification of this statement is made.

Presumably, the two-headed eagle emblem represents the royal title granted by the Crown to the lords of Momostenango. The "map" was undoubtedly based upon common knowledge of the authors, and some of the individual features of the cathedrals portrayed were probably taken directly from those structures at Momostenango, Ilotenango, and Santa Cruz del Quiché. The form in which the mountains and river were portrayed may have their basis in prehispanic models. The "marriage" scene was apparently based on events occurring shortly before the conquest, and which were still remembered in the 1550s. However, the many Spanish elements incorporated in this scene suggest that it did not derive from prehispanic models.

The purpose of the paintings seems clear. The authors wanted to establish the legitimacy of cacique privileges held by the rulers of Momostenango (Chwa Tz'ak), by showing their affiliation with the ruling line of Utatlán. The map shows Momostenango to be one link in a chain extending west from Utatlán. The Spanish coat of arms demonstrated the acceptance of the Utatlán rulers by the Crown, while the linkage with the house of Motecuzoma shows an acceptance of their prehispanic nobility and rulership by the Aztecs.

Testament Catalina Nijay

The small document is the last will and testament of Catalina Nijay of San Antonio Suchitepéquez. It was written in 1569 in Nahuatl (the language in which the will was presumably expressed, though the scribe might have translated from Quiche to Nahuatl as he wrote), and rendered into Spanish in 1586. Both the Nahuatl and the Spanish versions are now in the Archivo General de Centroamérica (A1:5930-51849), where I obtained the Spanish copy included as Appendix XIII.

The document contains no direct reference to prehispanic cultural patterns, but sheds light on inheritance rules, and lineage and political titles which existed in that region shortly after the conquest. The use of the Nahuatl language, either by the scribe or by Catalina (or both), is significant.

Obviously, this document was of local importance only, and appears to have no relationship to prehispanic historical tradition. It is somewhat surprising to find a native using the testamentary privilege at such an early date, though the fact that Catalina was of noble status may explain it. She was apparently worried that the property of her first husband would be taken by her second husband (or his children), and hence, not passed on to her sons (from her first husband).

Relación Pacal

Among the papers at the end of the *Annals of the Cakchiquels*, are five small documents written by Diego López, a representative of the Pacal Cakchiquel lineage. As grandfather of Francisco Díaz, the second of the great Xajil chroniclers, his accounts were logically included in the *Annals*. The documents are not dated; though they are inserted next to other native records written in the last decade of the 16th century, I would suggest a somewhat earlier date of composition (sometime between 1550 and 1590).[32]

Recinos includes a Spanish translation of the Pacal documents at the end of the *Annals* (1950:197-205), and the Cakchiquel texts were published by Villacorta (1934:323-325:328-330:331-332).

There are numerous references in these documents to prehispanic events, though few details are given. Their primary importance derives from the detailed information they provide on the Pacal, a sublineage of the Xajil descent group. Besides an elaborate genealogy for the lineage, there are details on land rights, political offices, and rights of succession. I have oversimplified things by grouping together these documents and calling them

---

[32] A careful reading of the Pacal accounts suggests that their author was one generation removed from the conquest. The author's grandson, Francisco Díaz, was an adult by 1583 (when he entered into his first marriage), and probably died around 1604 (the point at which his chronicle ends). Therefore, Diego López was probably an important member of the Pacal lineage as early as 1540-1550, and might have written these documents anytime after that.

Relación Pacal, but they are similar to many other documents for which this designation seems entirely appropriate.

Diego López does not specify the source of his information, but merely states that he is leaving his memorial, *memoria*, and his sign, *retal*. The account is perhaps simple enough for one man to have remembered (most likely aided by other elders), and, significantly, most references are to events and persons after the conquest. But as an important contemporary to the author of the prehispanic section of the *Annals*, he might have seen some of the presumed prehispanic Cakchiquel codices, or heard of their contents from older men who had seen them. This suggestion is particularly relevant to his description of early Cakchiquel history (Recinos 1950:201), and his list of genealogical ties between the Pacal and prehispanic Xajil rulers (Recinos 1950:198).

The *Relación Pacal* documents show little direct Spanish influence, and the few Spanish words are names (even so; there is extensive use of the native method of appelation) (Carrasco 1964).[33] Stronger Spanish influence can be detected in the testamentary and memorium for the dead ancestors found in two of the documents.

Títulos Felipe Vásquez

The two small documents were written in 1581 and 1602 by Felipe Vásquez, a descendant of the Xpantzay ruling line at Tecpán Guatemala. The history of their origin is similar to that of the *Títulos Xpantzay* discussed—they were translated from Cakchiquel to Spanish in 1659, were used in a land dispute between Tecpán Guatemala and Francisco de Argueta, and Spanish translations were published by Berlin (Documents B and E, 1950), along with *Títulos Xpantzay I, II, III*, and one unimportant document. I obtained a copy of the original Cakchiquel texts from the Archivo General de Centroamérica (A1:6062-53957).

---

[33] The *Relación Pacal* also contains dates in Spanish, giving the day of the week and the month, but not the year. Apparently Diego López was not acquainted with the long-count used by his grandson, Francisco Díaz (who might have learned of it from reading the section of the *Annals* written by his predecessor).

Both documents contain brief references to prehispanic events, and in these matters they are generally consistent with other Cakchiquel sources. Their primary importance, however, lies in the list of names of places and lineages from the Iximché area. In some cases, aboriginal activities associated with these places are briefly indicated.

Felipe Vásquez was acquainted with the *Títulos Xpantzay* written by his father and grandfather 30 to 50 years earlier, and some of his account derives from those sources (see his statement that the Xpantzay came from Tulan Zuyva). Other things, such as the list of place names and their prehispanic associations, probably came from local tradition.

Vásquez, who was alcalde when he wrote the first of the two documents, obviously had been greatly influenced by Spanish culture, though mostly he wrote about Cakchiquel affairs. The first document is expressly a land title. The second document contains a claim to noble ancestry and was to be used in court in the continuing struggles for political office between competing Xpantzay lineages.

Testament Ajpopolajay

The small document was written in 1569 as a testament and land title of Gerónimo Mendosa, head of the Ajpopolajay political descent group. It may have been recorded originally in Tzutujil, but only a Spanish copy has been preserved. In 1641, the document was used as evidence by the Tzutujil Indians of San Juan Atitlán in their dispute over lands with the Quiche of Santa Clara la Laguna. Along with the *Título Santa Clara*, a copy of it was transcribed as part of the litigation papers of that case (AGC, A1:5942-51997; Appendix XIV).

The main part of the document contains a description of the disposition by Mendosa of several houses and plots of lands to his family and kinsmen. Of particular importance are the boundary markers which are listed by their Tzutujil names for this native group located west of Lake Atitlán. The document also suggests the mode of political succession, for it provides for Don Gerónimo to be succeeded by one of his sons.

Carrasco (1967b:325-326) has suggested that the Ajpopolajay may have been one of several calpules in which the Tzutujil were divided, according to the early sources. If this is true, it must have been a minor group, for it is not mentioned in the Tzutujil calpul lists given in the *Relación Tzutujil, Título Totonicapán*, or a judicial record to be discussed in the next section (Primary Spanish Sources, Records). This may also explain why the document lacks historical information of the kind found in the títulos described above. Presumably, the head of the Ajpopolajay lineage was too far down in the Tzutujil political hierarchy to have competency in matters relating to the codices and history.

Título San Bartolomé

The small document was written in "lengua Sotoxil" (Tzutujil) by Juan López from San Bartolomé[34] (to be identified with a barrio of that name in the present-day municipality of Chicacao). Though the account is not dated, the author and his witnesses claim to have been taught Christianity by the first missionaries that came to the area, and to have personally contacted both Pedro de Alvarado and Hernán Cortés.[35] The Tzutujil text is surely from the 16th century, but it is not possible to date it more precisely than that. The text was translated into Spanish in 1712, and a copy of the translation was published by Crespo (1956:12-13). I have a copy of the Tzutujil original from the Archivo General de Centroamérica (Al:5963-52303).

---

[34] San Bartolomé may be tentatively identified in modern times with a barrio of that name in the piedmont town of Chicacao (Anonymous 1961-1962). According to a *Relación Geográfica* from there which was attached to the *Relación Santiago Atitlán* (Bretancor and Arboleda 1964), the aboriginal name of the settlement was *Xeoj*. The Nahuatl translation of Xeoj is *Aguacatepec*, the name by which San Bartolomé was known during most of the colonial period.

[35] I am not well enough acquainted with the technicalities of early postconquest history to determine whether or not these Tzutujil from San Bartolomé actually met with Alvarado and Cortés. Nor do I know whether the two missionaries mentioned in the document were indeed the first friars to perform labors in that zone. I suspect that part or all the claims are spurious, although their credibility is enhanced, perhaps, by the fact that the name of the nephew of Pedro de Alvarado (who allegedly was sent to support them in their land claim under dispute) is given in the document.

The account contains no direct references to prehispanic events and conditions, but does list a few names of places in the general area of San Bartolomé. Its chief importance, perhaps, derives from the fact that it is the only example of 16th century Tzutujil language which has come to us.

Apparently, the information contained in the account was based on the postconquest observations and experiences of the author and other elders from San Bartolomé. Spanish influence is evident in the attempt to appeal to the *audiencia* in their land dispute with San Juan Nahualapa. Several Spanish words were used in the four-page Tzutujil text.

Título Mam

The brief document was written in 1583 by elders from San Juan Ostuncalco and Concepción Chiquirichiapa, Department of Quezaltenango. They claim to have witnessed the conquest, and to have gone to the audiencia in about 1561 over a land dispute with the Quiche from Quezaltenango. The document was written, possibly in the Mam language, to be presented as evidence in litigation against the Quezaltecos. The Spanish version which has come to us was paleographized and published by Crespo (1956).

There is a brief reference in the document to prehispanic events, and a valuable description of political boundaries between the Quiche and Man in the area is given. Its importance is magnified by the fact that it is the only early Mam document extant.

There is no evidence that the account was based on prehispanic writings, though the sketchy reference to war with the Quiche suggests a historical tradition passed on from their forefathers (probably through oral devices). Most references are to postconquest affairs, which, apparently, were personally observed by the authors. Spanish influence is evident throughout the account, most obviously in the attempt to obtain legal support from Spanish officials in their land struggles with the Quiche of Quezaltenango.

Título Chama

The original of this small document was written in 1565 in the Pokomchí language (sometimes grouped with Pokomán) (Miles

1957) by elders from Santa Ana Chama, Verapaz. They were directly aided in this by the early missionaries, who signed the document (including Fray Juan de Torres). The town was later attached as a barrio to San Cristóbal de Verapaz (Cajcoj), to where the elders took their badly mutilated título and recopied or at least summarized it.[36] Toward the close of the 19th century, the copy was found in San Cristóbal by a local school teacher, Vicente Narciso. Under the direction of Karl Sapper, the native text and a Spanish translation by Narciso were published, along with a German translation and linguistic notes by Otto Stoll (Sapper 1904b; Stoll 1904).

There are few references to the prehispanic period, though the document contains a valuable list of boundary names persisting from early times. As pointed out by Sapper (1904b:403), it is primarily important for the information on the territorial boundary line between the Pokomchí speakers to the south and the alcalá Chol and Lacandón to the north.

The direct involvement of the missionaries in the original composition of the título probably precludes the possibility that it was taken from a prehispanic codex. This is also suggested by the brief references to the prehispanic period, and its focus on posthispanic events. As noted by Stoll (1904), the account is narrowly provincial, and clearly does not derive from any great historical tradition. Written under heavy Spanish influence, the intent of the authors was to provide evidence in support of the land claims of barrio Santa Ana in disputes with surrounding communities.

Título Chamelco

The small document apparently was written in 1611 by the elders of San Juan Chamelco. Presumably, it was originally composed in Kekchí, the native language of the region, though only a Spanish version has been preserved. Sapper found a copy of it in the local archives of Cobán in the late 19th century, and published a German

---

[36] The later transcription apparently was carried out after 1589, because that date is mentioned in the document. Apparently, like the original, it was written exclusively in Pokomchí.

translation of it (1897). He did not publish the Spanish text and does not refer to any Kekchí original. He also found two pictorials among the papers, one of which may have been taken from an earlier original (1897a:97; Miles 1957:770). Dieseldorff found another copy of the same document in possession of a *cofradía* at Carchá, and published both the Spanish text and a German translation of it (1904).[37]

Though brief, the document provides a direct view of political events in the Kekchí area just prior to Spanish penetration. Especially important is a description of the "treading of the bone" institution, which regulated hostile relations between feudalistic lords. The map provides a brief list of place names continuing from prehispanic times, and a few hints as to possible prehispanic pictorial writing style.

Apparently, the account is based on an early posthispanic tradition held by certain caciques in the area, for there is nothing in the description itself which would suggest derivation from a prehispanic codex. The map, however, may be derived from an indigenous original (see the comments by Sapper, 1904b:97), and might have served as a mnemonic device for the written account. The narration is clearly indigenous, even though it was produced for purposes resulting from Spanish influence—i.e., to counteract in the Spanish courts the land claims being made by the people of San Pedro Carchá.

Testament Magdalena Hernández

The document consists of a small will and testament written entirely in Kekchí. The text was recorded by a native scribe from the proceedings of the testamentary session held in 1583 at either San Pedro Carchá or San Juan Chamelco. Around 1900 an unidentified German found the document at Carchá, and sent it to the Berlin Museum. From there Karl Sapper sent it along to

[37] Dieseldorff gives no particulars of his finding the document, except for the statement that it was an "extract from the ancient book preserved by the Carchá *cofradia*" (1904:399), nor does he give the 1611 date. He erroneously assumes that the prehispanic events described in the document occurred in 1471 (70 years before 1541), rather than 1541 (70 years before 1611) (1904:402).

Burkitt, who transcribed and analyzed it in a letter published by the *American Anthropologist* (1905).

The will records a transfer of possessions by Magdalena Hernández (who leaves several household objects, foodstuff, and land to the Church), to Luis Caal and Juan Yat. The proceedings were witnessed by Indian church and town officials, and signed by resident Spaniards.

The document shows considerable Spanish influence—36 of the 148 readable words are Spanish. Its only value for studying aboriginal culture is that it places many Kekchí words in contexts which may help clarify their meanings. In this regard, it is probably less useful than an early catechism from Cajabón, commented on by Burkitt (1902), but unfortunately never published.

NATIVE DOCUMENTS CITED BY LATER WRITERS

This is a special category, consisting of documents cited and summarized by later writers, especially the 17th century Guatemalan chronicler, Fuentes y Guzmán. Several documents are important for any study of Quichean culture, but they must be interpreted with great caution. It is always risky to study potential primary sources secondhand. This is especially true in the case of Fuentes y Guzmán and Brasseur. Both men tended to exaggerate and distort native history because they themselves were confused by their sources.

In this section I discuss separately each document in terms of its date of composition, author(s), and important contents. This is not an easy task in the case of Fuentes y Guzmán, for he does not always clearly cite his sources. He tried to synthesize their content and in some cases the original manuscripts from which his account was composed cannot be disentangled. The following reconstruction, therefore, may contain errors of interpretation in the case of Fuentes y Guzmán, though I believe it is generally correct (cf. Villacorta 1934:133-154).[38]

---

[38] I have omitted from this discussion native documents cited by Fuentes y Guzmán which do not provide significant substantive historical or cultural data. Specifically, documents not discussed here but cited by Fuentes y Guzmán are *Ms. Kachiquel, Título Aruchilaba, Ms. Pokoman, Título del Cacique Gatu Pocom Moxim, Escrito Calel Cacoh Atzihuinac, Ms. Purom Chitabal.*

After I have discussed the documents separately, I will evaluate them as a whole. I will attempt generally to determine the distortions introduced by the writers who cite them, and the relationship of these sources to the other native documents from highland Guatemala. Unless otherwise specified, references to Fuentes y Guzmán will be cited by volume (6, 7, 8) and page numbers from the *Biblioteca "Goathemala"* (1932-1933).

Título Ixtahuacán Tzumpam (Fuentes y Guzmán)

The document was written in 1561 by the leading cacique from Santa Catarina Ixtahuacán, Francisco García Calel Tzumpam, at the command of the first Bishop of Guatemala, Francisco Marroquín (7:391). It consisted of some 28 folios, the first five of which contained a description of the early history of the Tamub branch of the Quiche, including a narration of the migrations by which the founding fathers came from the East (7:391-398). The first two folios apparently also contained a description of the events preceding the conquest (including preparations by the Quiche for war) (7:395-398:402), while folios 3 to 11 recorded the Spanish conquest of the Quiche, Ixil, and Mam (8:58-64, 110-129, 468-475).

The important account of the "bride capture" of a Quiche princess by the Tzutujil, and subsequent wars between these two groups was based, in part, on this source (folios 17 to 23) (7:37-39). Villacorta argues (1934) that this narration was intercalated in the first portion of Fuentes y Guzmán's book, because he had found the *Título Ixtahuacán Tzumpam* later. Though this may be true, it must be recoginzed that much information on the events came from the Torres Macario document.

Título Ixtahuacán Torres Macario (Fuentes y Guzmán)

Apparenty, the document was written in 1568 by Juan de Torres from Santa Catarina Ixtahuacán, son of Chignahuivcelut (Chiconavi Ocelotl, probably the Mexican equivalent of the Quiche ruler, Belejeb Tz'i') (8:48).[39] A painting was attached to it which was

---

[39] Fuentes y Guzmán identifies Juan de Torres as the author of the Ixtahuacán document (7:388), and states that his son's name was Juan Macario.

still in the hands of the elders of Ixtahuacán at the time of Fuentes y Guzmán (8:158). This source should not be confused with its companion, the *Título Ixtahuacán Tzumpam,* or the *Historia Quiché de Don Juan de Torres* (*Título Tamub*), published by Recinos (1957). The latter account was not written until 1580, and the author appears to have lived near present-day Patzité.

The document contained the usual description of the migrations from the East by the ancestors of the leading Quiche groups (8:157-158), and the founding of the Quiche state by Acxopil and his sons (6:6-10; 7:34-37, 387-388).[40] Largely from this source, Fuentes y Guzmán reconstructed, unsuccessfully, the Quiche ruling dynasty (7:389-390).

The specific contents of this source are not clearly cited by Fuentes y Guzmán, though it appears, at least it contained accounts of the early political history of the Quiche (folios 1-5) (6:8-10; 7:387-388), and the later Quiche-Tzutujil wars (folios 7-13) (7:37 *passim*). Fuentes y Guzmán apparently considered this source less important and reliable than the *Títulos Ixtahuacán Tzumpam* and *Torres Macario* (7:38); a careful reading of the text, where it is cited, suggests that he used it as a supplement.

Título Xecul Ajpop Quejam (Fuentes y Guzmán)

This account was written by Don Juan Macario, the prehispanic ruler of Xecul, and a participant in the battle between the Quiche and the conquistadores over Quezaltenango (8:159). The date of its composition is not given. It must have been written sometime near the middle of the 16th century. I searched through the town records of modern San Andrés Xecul, but could find no trace of the document.

The manuscript contained an account of some events immediately preceding the conquest in Guatemala, including the military preparations made by the Quiche in anticipation of their

When citing the document, Fuentes y Guzmán apparently used the names of both father and son—i.e., *Torres Macario,* both of whom might have been involved in its composition.

[40] A slightly different version of the Acxopil account as given in Fuentes y Guzmán is contained in a small document written by an anonymous Franciscan (see Appendix XV).

battle against the Spaniards on the plains of Quezaltenango (folios 10-11, 15-16) (8:161-164). It formed the basis for Fuentes y Guzmán's description of prehispanic wars between the Quiche and Mam (folios 11-12) (8:200-203), and it supplemented the writings of Gonzalo de Alvarado in providing information for his account of the Spanish conquest of the Mam (folos 15-17v) (8:110-129).

Título Pipil (Fuentes y Guzmán)

Fuentes y Guzmán gives no information where or when this document was produced, though it is possible he obtained it while acting as Alcalde mayor of Escuintla or Sonsonate, two well-known Pipil centers. It must be distinguished from the two Pipil scrolls, which he saw at Sonsonate, that served as the basis for his discussion of Pipil writing (7:109).

I favor Thompson's (1948:13) suggestion that the *Título Pipil* contained the account of Mexican incursions into Guatemala during the time of the Aztec ruler, Ahuitzotl (6:47-48; 7:90), as well as the description of Pipil political organization (7:90-92). It seems likely that Fuentes y Guzmán's discussion of Pipil law and custom partly came from the same source (7:125-128, 145-147), though much of it must have come from personal observation made while serving as Alcalde Mayor in the Pipil area. The manuscript apparently also contained a few details on the conquest of the eastern part of Guatemala, at Jumay, Azacualpa, and Mitla (folios 6, 13, 15) (7:144, 172, 204).

Fragment of the Crónica Franciscana (Anonymous Franciscan)

In a small collection of documents on colonial Guatemala in the Peabody Museum Library, Harvard, there is a fragment of a manuscript written by an anonymous Franciscan historian who apparently had access to a native document. Though the authorship of the fragment is unknown, it seems probable that it was part of a late 17th or early 18th century chronicle known as the *Crónica Franciscana*. The native source used is not cited, nor is there any indication when it might have been written. However, it contains an account which in some places is almost word for word the same as passages in Fuentes y Guzmán which he claims to have been taken from the *Título Ixtahuacán Torres Macario* (1932-1933:6:6-10), so we may assume that it is that document. This is not at all surprising, for Fuentes y Guzmán received much material from the Franciscans, and the anonymous author of this document was apparently his contemporary (see Secondary Sources, Historians). Inasmuch as the fragment from the Peabody Library has never been published to my knowledge, I include it as Appendix XV.

The fragment contains information already cited in Fuentes y Guzmán, though in describing the early establishment of the Quiche state at Utatlán, the Nahua names of the supreme ruler and his sons are given more accurately than in Fuentes y Guzmán. The account seems exaggerated and flowery like the writings of Fuentes y Guzmán. From this source and from the *Título Ixtahuacán Tzumpam*, he produced his account of the Tzutujil "bride capture" and Quiche-Tzutujil wars (he drew his information from folios 11-17), (7:37-59).

Título Xawila Tzumpam (Fuentes y Guzmán)

It is easy to confound this document with the *Título Ixtahuacán Tzumpam*, as was done by Villacorta (1934:135). Nevertheless, there appear to have been two different documents written by persons having the name Francisco García Tzumpam. The Tzumpam lord who wrote the Xawila document was apparently the son of the ruler of Xequiquel (Olintepeque), and was a witness of the conquest at the tender age of 11. He reportedly composed his account in 1544; it was later included in a book of ordinances put together by *Licenciado* Francisco de Briceño, Governor of Guatemala.[41] About a century later it came into the hands of Fuentes y Guzmán (8:47:157).

[41] The identification of "Don Francisco García Calel Tzumpam Xawila" (8:157) with the son of the ruler of Olintepeque (8:47) is a somewhat tenuous reconstruction. I have put together two negatively correlated conditions: one, the son of the ruler of Olintepeque could not be the Tzumpam from Ixtahuacán, for the latter was the son of the Quiche ruler, Belejeb Tzi'; two, if Tzumpam Xawila wrote his account in 1544, he could not be the same Tzumpam from Ixtahuacán, who prepared his account in 1561.

Xequiquel is the usual Quiche name given for Olintepeque, but that des-

Only once in all his writings does Fuentes y Guzmán definitely cite this document, and in so doing so he does not list folio numbers (8:157-158). This suggests that the document was brief, or that other citations which I have interpreted as referring to the *Título Ixtahuacán Tzumpam* actually refer to this source. At any rate, we can say with some certainty that it contained an account of the Toltec origin of the Tamub Quiche, however brief the reference might have been.

Título Gómez Ajtz'ib (Fuentes y Guzmán)

Fuentes y Guzmán claims to have received this document from Fray Francisco Vázquez, who apparently had obtained it from the Cardona family (7:386). It was written by "Don Francisco Gómez, Primer Ahzip Quiché," probably in the vicinity of the Quezaltenango valley (the area in which Juan de León Cardona held his encomienda) (Gall 1963). The date of composition, unfortunately, is not given.

Título Tzutujil (Brasseur)

In the second volume of Brasseur's, *Histoire des Nations Civilisées du Mexique et de l'Amérique Centrale* (1857), he summarizes the contents of a Tzutujil document similar to some títulos discussed above. He claims that the document, which he calls "Ms. Zutujil," was part of the *Crónica de San Francisco de Guatemala* (*Crónica Franciscana*, now lost). In view of the fact that Tzutujil native sources are so scarce, I have translated it into English and included it as Appendix XVI.

Not much can be said about the document because of the brevity of Brasseur's summary. Nevertheless, it is noteworthy that the Tzutujil tradition is similar to the Quiche sources in ascribing a Toltec origin to their founding fathers. The peregri-

---

ignation apparently was made after the conquest (in memory of the sanguinary battles in the plains below the settlement) (Recinos 1957:91). Xawila may have been the prehispanic name for Olintepeque, for it is etymologically close to the aboriginal name of a river and an aldea of that municipio, called Siwila. A further corruption of its name to Xepau was apparently made by the Cakchiquel (who so referred to Olintepeque) (Recinos 1950:130).

nation described is similar to accounts in the Quiche and Cakchiquel sources, too, though I do not recall seeing the place name, Xenimain, in those documents.

It is obvious that this título existed and that Brasseur has accurately summarized part of its contents. We do not know if the entire document was recorded in the *Crónica Franciscana*, or if it contained only a synopsis of the original.

The native sources used by the anonymous Franciscan (except the document about *Acxopil*, where he apparently cited the *Annals of the Cakchiquels*) and by Brasseur are insignificant. They provide little to no information about their sources, though I do not doubt the authenticity of the documents.

More important and equally authentic are the documents used by Fuentes y Guzmán. Fortunately, he usually gives enough information about their origins to demonstrate that they were composed by well-informed native rulers, and during the same general period as the other native títulos discussed. Though none of them seems to be identifiable with documents known to exist today (with the exception of the *Manucrito Cakchiquel*, which might be the *Annals*), there are enough parallels to show, indisputably, their intimate relationship to one another. Seen against the background of the modern corpus of Quiche documents, many distortions of the Fuentes y Guzmán sources can be detected and the valuable information about native history and culture is brought to light. Someday, we hope some of the documents he describes will be found and compared with his writings, and so provide further guidelines for their proper interpretation.

Fuentes y Guzmán was convinced of the authenticity of his sources; he claimed they were based on prehispanic paintings which were transcribed into the Spanish system of writing after the native ruling class had been taught to read and write by the friars (7:125-126). He had seen fragments of the codices, but argued that most of them had disappeared because of the early attempt of the priests to destroy them. With the possible exceptions of the *Título Xawila Tzumpam* and *Título Xecul Ajpopquejam*, Fuentes y Guzmán was probably correct in ascribing an aboriginal codical basis to them. However, he apparently did not sufficiently appreciate the special motives resulting from Spanish domination that influenced the native rulers who wrote the documents.

He recognized that some documentary accounts were closer to the official version of Quiche history than others, and he favored those written by lords closest to the ruling line of Utatlán (7:38, 389, 391). This bias caused some of his distortions. He was interested in describing the grandeur of native culture and political history, so that the feats of the conquistadores might thereby be magnified. This would account for his outlandishly high figures for the size of native armies (7:37-59; 8:160-161), his characterizing the Quiche miltary and administrative organization in terms reminiscent of the political systems of Europe (7:387, 393-394), and the over long dynastic lines he ascribes to the Quiche (7:388-390).

Fuentes y Guzmán's distortions of his sources because of linguistic problems is difficult to assess. He specifically states that some documents had originally been written in Quiche and then translated into Spanish (7:386; 8:157). This is born out by his use of many Quiche names, and by certain expressions which appear to be literal translations from the Quiche language (e.g., 7:39-40).[42] Yet, there are obvious cases of mistranslations and misunderstanding of Quiche terms (7:53, 387): The expression, "by the lords" (*rumal ajaw*), is rendered as a name, and the names of four maidens sent to tempt the Quiche rulers are said to be four Quiche chiefs.

As far as I can determine, Fuentes y Guzmán did not claim to read or speak any of the Maya languages. His denigrating attitude toward them probably precludes that possibility (8:407). He was aware of the diversity of native languages spoken in Guatemala, and of the subtle differences between them (8:406-407). I donot think he would have attempted to translate any text

---

[42] In a speech by a Quiche ruler which, Fuentes y Guzmán claims, was taken from the *Título Ixtahuacán Torres Macario* (7:39-40), are several expressions which appear to be derived from forms in the Quiche language. Thus, *vasallos y capitanes* could derive from the Quiche expression, *al, c'ajol, k'alel* (or *rajop, utzam) achij*; *los reinos de los cantones* from the Quiche, *tinamit, wuk amak'*; *no se desiguala en la sangre* suggests the Quiche form, *xa junam c'oyewal*; and *dentro de veinte días* probably comes from the Quiche, *pa winak k'ij* (Recinos 1957:96 *passim*).

written in Quiche or any other Quichean language, though he could etymologize the more familiar and important Quiche substantives. He apparently used Spanish translations (7:386), some of which he might have had produced specifically for his studies (he was familiar with the use of interpreters) (8:406). As for the mistranslations, they usually appear as isolated errors amid reconstructions which seem to be generally accurate. I suspect most errors of this kind resulted from misinterpreting the Spanish translations with which he worked, for they were probably literal and abstruse.

Fuentes y Guzmán has been criticized for his distortions and obvious biases, but in his use of native documents criticism must be tempered with gratitude and admiration. It is to his credit that he saw the value of the documents for the reconstruction of prehispanic native history and culture, and that he used them in his important narration of the events of the conquest (8:157). There will always be problems of interpretation in using native sources as they appear in the writings of Fuentes y Guzám, but by comparing them with the extensive corpus of documents now available, much valuable information can be obtained.

CHAPTER III

Primary
Spanish
Documents

INTRODUCTION

The rich corpus of native documents written during the 16th century was in part stimulated by Spanish influence, though a highly specialized native literary tradition had already existed. More important for the study of Quichean culture, however, is the fact that the Spaniards themselves were literate. From the arrival of the first conquistadores to the retreat of the last Spanish official at the time of independence, the Spaniards recorded their impressions of the native peoples. Indeed, the propensity of the Spaniards to keep detailed records of affairs in their colonies has been commented upon many times by students of Spanish America (Gibson 1966:110-111). The Spanish documents written in Guatemala during the 16th century are a body of information about native life which is complementary, and almost equal, in ethnohistoric value to the native sources. These documents are classified, described, evaluated, and in some cases, transcribed in this section.

Illustration: Bartolomé de Las Casas. From a painting of the famous Dominican friar, in Remesal (1932:4:143).

Primary Sources

We will designate the Spanish documents written during the 16th century as primary, and those composed thereafter as secondary sources, even though it is somewhat arbitrary (see introduction to Secondary Sources). Throughout the sixteenth century, many patterns of native culture were relatively unchanged. As a total configuration, Quichean culture was in its early stages of transformation and in some areas was close to its aboriginal condition. In dealing with cultural changes over time, it is not possible to establish precise dates when one culture form becomes another; in highland Guatemala culture changed differentially, and in some areas patterns of native culture have persisted to the present (Nash 1967b; Madsen 1967).

It is convenient, then, to indicate a *terminus post quem* for the discontinuation of native culture and the crystalization of the syncretic culture which predominated in Indian communities during the colonial period. In working with the documentary materials from Guatemala I have found that after 1600 the sources are less interesting to the student of native cultures, while seventeenth and eighteenth century documents are interesting because they refer to earlier, sixteenth century, accounts. I agree with LaFarge (1962) and others who argue that by 1600 the violent disruption of native culture had abated, and that a new phase of culture history had begun.

Spanish Ethnomethodology

In evaluating the sources to be described in this section, we will emphasize to what extent ethnographic techniques were used to obtain information on native culture. We will say little about the literary qualities of the written sources, or their potential for reconstructing Guatemalan history, or colonial society. Instead, we will examine the way the authors obtained their data, especially the kinds of observations they made, their attitudes toward the Indians, and the purposes of the gathered information. This should help us to understand potential bias in the Spanish sources, and, in some cases to clarify the conceptual framework, or theory, in which they placed their data. This part of the analysis, therefore, may be considered a minor contribution to the early history of anthropological theory.

I have subclassified the primary Spanish documents as conquistador writings, quasi ethnographies, dictionaries, relaciones, and records. The conquistador writings may be ethnomethodologically characterized by their direct observations of nearly untouched native culture, their generally unsympathetic attitude toward the Indians, and their authors' underlying desire to gain privilege as a result of their accounts. The criteria for classifying the documents by type are presented at the beginning of each discussion.

A comparison between all types suggests certain generalizations about the ethnomethodology used by sixteenth century Spanish writers. As for mode of observation, we will note that, with few exceptions, the friars were the only persons to observe Quichean culture in detail. Zorita, an early *oidor*, might have been such an observer, but he was transferred to Mexico at a critical time in his studies, and consequently he left us limited information. Likewise, other Spanish judges were in a position to investigate native culture in connection with legal proceedings involving aboriginal participants. However, with the exceptions of Briceño and Palacio, they showed limited interest in native cultural patterns, and ethnographic data are treated as secondary to the issues being disputed.

In contrast, several priests carefully observed native culture, and some have left important ethnographic accounts. There was no Sahagún or Motolinía, but the detailed description of native culture left by Las Casas, the elaborate dictionaries by Vico and others, and the ethnographically rich *Relación Geográfica* prepared by Arboleda attest to the careful attention the 16th century friars gave to native culture.

The attitude of the earliest Spanish officials toward the Indians generally ranged from harsh to indifferent. There were few priests in Guatemala at that time, and the few apparently were not strong in their defense of the Indians. Even the humanitarian Bishop Marroquín appears to have been ambivalent in his defense of the Indians against the ruthless Spanish *encomenderos* (cf. Sáenz 1963). With the exception of the few harsh statements about the Indians by Alvarado, and a brief description of their pitiful condition left us by Marroquín (Sáenz 1963), little was written during the first 20 years after the conquest, either in their defense, or as description of their culture.

Around 1540, Las Casas came to the defense of the Indians of Guatemala and initiated his program of peaceful pacification in Verapaz. The sympathetic, ethnographic tradition of the Dominicans of Guatemala that he started, persisted for over two centuries. Men like Vico, de Viana, Remesal, and Ximénez, successively, turned their attention to the Indians and their problems. The Franciscans, who first came to Guatemala between 1540 and 1542 (CDI, 1925:155), never developed an ethnographic tradition equal to that of the Dominicans. Nevertheless, their excellent Quiche and Cakchiquel dictionaries attest to an early interest in the native cultures; and if we ever rediscover the famous *Crónica Franciscana*, we may find that they had a stronger ethnographic interest than present evidence indicates.

It was not until Cerrato became president of the audiencia in Guatemala in 1549 that secular leadership displayed genuine concern for the Indians and their cultural heritage. Cerrato was apparently too occupied in administering the affairs of the audiencia to write much about the Indians, but he was sympathetic to their cause. His two judges, Zorita and Tomás López Medel, were interested in native culture and have left us important descriptions. The ethnographic spirit subsided after the Cerrato regime, but reappeared in the period of the Relaciones Geográficas (ca. 1575-1585). During that decade several important reports were prepared by such varied Crown officials as Valverde, president of the audiencia, Palacio, judge of the audiencia, and Estrada, a corregidor.

Overwhelmingly, the documents were written for administrative purposes: to report to higher officials on the general condition of the Indians, or to gather specific information about native culture for some immediately practical use. In either case, they were political instruments. Only rarely were data gathered for theoretical reasons (cf. Las Casas, López Medel), and even then that purpose was probably subordinated to more instrumental ones. This meant that most categories within which the officials placed native culture were Spanish in origin. Fortunately, though, some instrumental tasks required recording of native categories (especially in the case of the dictionaries and the *Relaciones Geográficas*).

Within each subclass of documents, occasionally, some officials went beyond the call of duty and provided more information than would have been necessary for strictly official purposes. Often this was done because the officials had become interested in native culture, though the Crown's repeated call for information on the Indians in order to facilitate their governance and Christianization makes it difficult to distinguish what was required and what was reported anyway. Examples of pure ethnographic works would be Zorita's first report to the king, Vico's Quichean dictionary, Palacio's account, and Briceño's prosecution of the claim to privileges by the Cawek caciques of Utatlán.

In addition to the general ethnographic tendencies in sixteenth century Spanish writings, other generalizations can be made by comparing them. I am perplexed by the large number of important sixteenth century documents from Guatemala that are known to be lost. Ethnographic treasures mentioned in later sources are missing: a report to the Crown on the condition of Guatemala prepared by Alvarado, Marroquín's census, two descriptions of native religion prepared by Vico and Cipriano, several *Relaciones Geográficas*, some of the earliest Cakchiquel dictionaries, and a seventeenth century chronicle (*Crónica Franciscana*) which referred to sixteenth century documents. This is a complaint of all historians, but it seems an especially serious one in the Guatemalan case.

The sixteenth century Spanish corpus on the Guatemala Indians is biased in favor of data on Quichean culture. There are records covering the administration of all Indian groups in Guatemala, but only those for the Quiche, Cakchiquel, Tzutujil and, to a less extent, the Pokoman and Kekchi of Verapaz, contain much ethnographic data. The Mam, Kanjobal, Ixil, Pipil, Chorti, and Lenca are slighted in these early documents. Among the Quichean cultures, the Quiche and Cakchiquel received about equal attention, and the Tzutujil were not far behind (except that Tzutujil dictionaries are lacking).

As for the Quichean ethnographic material, it is seriously deficient in data on native religion. This is partially compensated for by the *Popul Vuh*, and by Las Casas' description of religion in Verapaz; but compared to sources on the Aztecs, the Guatemalan material is seriously deficient. This is due to the loss of the studies by Vico, Cipriano, and the Franciscans.

Two characteristics of the sixteenth century documents are in no way unique to Guatemala: The strong tendency of one author to copy the work of another, even during the same century. This is especially obvious in the dictionaries, but is also in the conquistador writings (e.g., Díaz del Castillo copied another source for his account of the conquest of Guatemala), and the judicial records (where citations of previous judicial records must constantly be sorted out). And, from the viewpoint of ethnohistoric evaluation, the judicial records emerge as an unusually important source of ethnographic information. If used with caution, the testimony of witnesses in the records becomes similar to data gathered from informants by ethnographers. Though we would want to ask different questions of them, at least the witnesses often had first hand knowledge of aboriginal culture. The Archivo de las Indias has many judicial records in the form of *residencias* and *visitas* which go beyond the small but ethnographically rewarding documents I was able to review.

Explaining the Spanish Sources

Some general characteristics of the 16th century Spanish sources we have summarized can be explained in terms of historical factors and the sociocultural conditions of Spain and Guatemala. For example, the superiority of the accounts of the friars over those of civil officials in providing us early ethnographic observations on native life is a reflection of the strong humanistic tradition that the clergy brought to the New World. The humanistic component of the Renaissance (Ubieto et al. 1967:301-307; Wolf 1962:165-167) came to Spain primarily through the Church, and from there to the New World. Rowe (1965) has pointed to another facet of the Renaissance tradition imbibed by the Spanish clergy—the study and comparison of different cultures (begun with the comparison of European with classic culture). The friars translated their anthropological and humanistic interests in Guatemala into action; they produced important studies of native culture (e.g., Las Casas in Verapaz).

At first, civil rulers tended to follow an aristocratic warrior tradition (Wolf 1962:157). Later, as Renaissance humanism was infused into the political system, the tradition turned into a form of political absolutism rather than a concern for the native peoples. This is painfully obvious in Guatemala. Not until Las Casas sponsored the selection of a president (Cerrato) did civil officials begin to prepare substantive ethnographic descriptions. Significantly, Cerrato and his most ethnographically oriented judge were also ecclesiastics (Sáenz 1963:122). Only later, after the Crown had become more absolutist, and economic crisis at home and demographic catastrophe in America had caused the government to study more carefully the Indians and their culture, did civil authorities in Guatemala make a more substantial ethnographic contribution (e.g., Palacio, Pineda).

The dearth of ethnographic contribution by civil officials generally, and during the early part of the sixteenth century in particular, is related to historical and sociocultural factors: Guatemala was less economically or culturally advanced than other areas of the New World, and, consequently, was not assigned the most capable Spanish officials. A good example is Alvarado. He helped to create an atmosphere of exploitation and indifference toward the Indians which was difficult for later officials to overcome. In collaboration with other conquistadores, he established one of the harshest encomienda systems of the colonies (Zavala 1967), and long after his death the conquistadores or their descendants fought to perpetuate the condition. Even the humanitarian Bishop Francisco Marroquín was influenced by him for, though he repudiated many excesses committed against the Indians, as Alvarado's friend and participant in the original exploitation he was never able to escape its influence. Though he defended the Indians and worked among them to some extent, he failed to leave any significant writings on their culture (his doctrinal in Cakchiquel and a presumed Quiche grammar constitute his sole contributions) (Sáenz 1963:124-125).

The dominating personality among the early friars in Guatemala was the Dominican, Bartolomé de Las Casas. Whatever opinion one may have with respect to the black *vs.* the white legend (Sáenz 1963; Durán 1963), the fact remains that Las Casas rather than his opponents left us an important account of native cultures (cf. the *Apologética Historia* with any writings of his opponents, Marroquín and Maldonado). That the ethnographic tradition of the Dominicans was stronger than that of the Franciscans was due to him, though the Franciscans were superior in this regard in Mexico (Motolinía and Sahagún were Franciscans). In Guatemala Las Casas' influence was important in the development of an ethnographic interest among the friars. He was attracted to the area because of its state of neglect (hence, the opportunity for his pacification experiment) and, significantly, he left soon after his purpose was accomplished.

The loss of many early documents from Guatemala requires explanation. Chroniclers mention some documents were lost in a fire in the archives of Guatemala City during the early colonial period, and that others were lost during the destruction of Ciudad Vieja in 1541. These natural disasters perhaps explain the disappearance of Alvarado's relación and Marroquín's census, though we would expect that copies had been sent to Spain. Other now lost documents were seen by Remesal in the first half of the seventeenth century, and the *Crónica Franciscana* was used as late as the second half of the nineteenth century. Probably, many documents still exist in various archives, but have not yet been located because of inadequate research. Interest in Guatemalan history and ethnohistory have not been sufficient to uncover the valuable documents, mainly because interested Guatemalan scholars lack a strong global archival tradition and the funds to expand their research to all archives of Guatemala, México, and Europe. I will continue to search for these documents, and hope this study will inspire other students to do so.

The prominence of ethnographic data about the Quichean vis-à-vis other native Guatemalan cultures is easy to understand. Quichean Indians had reached the highest sociocultural level of Indian groups, and at the time of the conquest they politically dominated most other highland peoples (Carmack 1968). They had complex administrative systems into which the Spaniards could tie, in order to extract tribute and labor from the Indians. In the case of the less developed native groups this was more difficult to do (Service 1955); as a result the most important encomiendas were established among the Quichean peoples. Because most ethnographic studies were primarily designed to facilitate administration of the native peoples, it follows that the bulk of these studies were made on the Quichean Indians.

The deficiency of information on the religious practices of the Indians is partly to be explained by the decisive influence of Bishop Marroquín during his thirty-three years in Guatemala. Apparently, he was more concerned with conversion of the Indians than with understanding their culture. No doubt, this spirit affected the attitude of other priests working there in the early years. Another explanation was suggested by other priests: Eradication of native religion proved to be difficult, and ethnographic descriptions seemed only to exacerbate the problem. Whereas Las Casas was anxious to clarify the nature of native religion, Remesal, though an admirer of the friar showed little interest to do so. To elaborate on a religious stysem so embarrassingly strong many years after the conquest, would have been too negative an admission. Apparently, information about the persistence of native religious practices was partially suppressed, though the reality of the situation was specifically exposed from time to time (e.g., by Ximénez and Cortés y Larraz in the eighteenth century). The few descriptions of native religion which were made are now missing (e.g., the accounts by Vico and Cipriano); their loss may be due to the friars' tendency to suppress reports about the persisting native religion.

CONQUISTADOR WRITINGS

Introduction

The accounts of the conquest of Guatemala left us by the conquistadores are disappointing. They are not comparable to the rich and useful accounts written by Cortés or Díaz del Castillo on the conquest of Mexico. For Guatemala we have only one major original account; the two letters sent to Córtes by Alvarado in 1524. All other references are either brief notations or secondary summaries of original accounts.

Conquistador writings provide peculiar advantages and disadvantages to the student of native culture. To start with the disadvantages: We can cite the oft repeated caveat about the conquistadores' tendency to exaggerate in order to dramatize their exploits. Though we must be aware of this bias, by the general consensus of modern scholars who evaluated conquistador writings, the problem is said to have been exaggerated. We have found that conquistador statements about demography (Borah and Cook 1963) and social stratification (Caso 1963) are generally consistent with information obtained from other sources.

But the superficiality of their accounts is critical. Often they give only the obvious features of native cultures. The accounts are all too brief even on the cultural items they emphasize and they fail to mention many cultural features of primary concern to the anthropologists. We have good, but tantalizingly limited, information on native military institutions, demographic levels, language distributions, community names and locations, and technology—especially metallurgy. Usually, we are told little or nothing about kinship and family, religion (especially the less spectacular aspects), property relations, economic patterns in the rural areas, and world view.

The special advantages to be gained from using conquistador writings, is that the descriptions are based on first hand observation when native culture was in a pristine state. The political alliances and confederations the conquest catalyzed, had occurred in an aboriginal culture milieu. Our most important data on political relations in highland Guatemala, therefore, derive from events of the conquest as described by the conquistadores.

Then, too, there is something special about the conquistadores' style. Their accounts, often transcribed in the field of action, have immediacy and freshness in their descriptions. Their accounts are dominated by personal impression and concrete detail of special value to the ethnohistorian, and this orientation is useful for modern theoretical purposes. The conquistador tendency to evaluate each cultural thing they observed in terms of relative size and likeness to their own civilization caused them to make discriminations that are useful for our theoretcial schemes (e.g., placement in evolutionary stages).

In spite of the brevity of their accounts on the conquest of Guatemala, and the necessary caution against possible exaggeration, the conquistador writings are an important and unique source for the study of Quichean culture.

Pedro de Alvarado

The most important account of the conquest was written by Pedro de Alvarado. His record of the events is primarily contained in two reports he sent to Cortés. The first was composed just outside the Quiche capital of Utatlán in April, and the second from the Cakchiquel center of Iximché in July, 1524. The two letters have been widely circulated and published since the first half of the sixteenth century, and were used by the Spanish chronicler López de Gómara. My study is based on a modern Spanish edition of the letters published in Madrid (1946).

From other documents written shortly after the conquest, we know Alvarado later prepared and sent to the Crown a complete description of the province of Guatemala, detailing its geography and peoples. Unfortunately, we do not know what happened to it. Alvarado's letters and testimonial statements contain fragments of information useful in reconstructing the history and culture of the natives (see Spanish records; also AGI, Patronato 180, No. 64). The letters are cited in Recinos' seminal biography of the *adelantado* (1952). A few comments on the conquest by Alvarado are in a *proceso de residencia*, placed against him in Mexico in 1529.[1] The record of the trial was first published in Mexico in 1847 and has been reproduced by the Sociedad de Geográfia e Historia de Guatemala (Anonymous 1934; Ramírez 1930-1931).

Alvarado's account of the events of the conquest is sketchy and only covers the period of first contact. His description of native life is even briefer, though he mentions native techniques of warfare, settlement pattern, population size, and agricultural production.

---

[1] Testimony of other witnesses to the conquest is also there; it aids in the interpretation of Alvarado's account. Recinos, effectively, used this source in his reconstruction of the life of Pedro de Alvarado (1952).

Because Alvarado observed the natives in their aboriginal state, his writings are of special importance. However, he apparently was not as careful an observer as Cortés (or Díaz del Castillo). Historians of the conquest generally agree that Alvarado was cruel and ruthless toward the Indians (Recinos 1952:205ff), that he represents the archetypal conquistador who viewed the natives as source for exploitation. There is indication that he practiced his philosophy during and after the conquest, and this, presumably, prevented him to give serious attention to their culture; though his bias adds a touch of realism to his account.

The purpose of his two letters to Cortés was to report on the military progress in Guatemala. One detects some optimism and perhaps exaggeration in his accounts, though not much, as prospective ruler of the area he could not afford to deceive. In the *proceso*, where his position and prestige were on the line, his testimony is more liable to distortion. Any fact it contains must be sifted from less reliable information.

Alvarado's letter sent from Soconusco to Cortés (1946:457), which Cortés acknowledges as having received (1961:230) presents a special problem. The letter has been lost, though there is evidence that two early chroniclers had access to it and that they extracted certain parts from it for their narration of the conquest (Recinos 1952:63).

One, Pedro Mártir, in his eighth and last decade (1912:2:358-364) tells of events involving Alvarado which took place "towards the end of the year 1523" (a time when he was at the frontier of a "powerful kingdom" he had been sent to find). Alvarado departed for the conquest of Guatemala from Soconusco in late 1523 or early 1524, so Pedro Mártir's description must have been from Alvarado's first letter to Cortés.[2] This is an important consideration, for Pedro Mártir's account contains valuable information on social and political affairs in Guatemala at the time.

The same event, in slightly different form, is related by López de Gómara in his history of the conquest of the Indies (1946).

[2] Pedro Mártir is apparently mistaken when he states that Alvarado returned to Cortés in order to receive instructions before marching into the territory of the "powerful kingdom" (1912:2:363). His report to Cortés was by letter, not in person, though an envoy bearing the letter and the spoils of conquest apparently was sent to Cortés.

Though he ascribes the account to Alvarado, and dates it 1523, he erroneously interprets it as having occurred while Alvarado was at Tututepec, before Cortés sent him to conquer Guatemala (1946:284-285).[3] Gómara's version clarifies the fact that the powerful kingdom was Cuauhtemallan (Guatemala).

Recinos could not decide whether the López de Gómara and Pedro Mártir accounts were spurious or genuine (1952:54-56). Once we recognize the accounts are based on Alvarado's letter to Cortés from Soconusco (the most plausible explanation), then both can be seen to be based in fact, and can be checked against each other.

Díaz del Castillo

In two chapters of his *Historia Verdadera de la Conquista de la Nueva España*, Díaz del Castillo describes events related to the conquest of Guatemala. The most detailed chapter (No. 164), however, is not based on personal observation, for Díaz del Castillo did not accompany Alvarado during that conquest. This part of the account was taken from a manuscript written by Gonzalo de Alvarado, who accompanied his brother Pedro de Alvarado. Apparently, Gonzalo took his information from the letters Pedro de Alvarado sent to Cortés.

In another chapter (No. 214), Díaz del Castillo describes the situation in Guatemala as he found it in 1526. That year, he accompanied Alvarado from Honduras to Guatemala and saw the province for the first time. They stayed only a few days in the Quezaltenango area and then returned to Mexico.

The two chapters probably were written between 1564 and 1568, some forty years after the events (Cerwin 1963:221-222).[4]

---

[3] Alvarado conquered Tututepec in 1522, almost two years before his expedition to Guatemala when the events under discussion took place (Cortés 1961; Recinos 1952:52-56). It would appear that López de Gómara also erroneously interpreted the visit of the Cakchiquel with Cortés as occuring after these events (1946:285).

[4] In his biography of Díaz del Castillo, Cerwin presents evidence (1963) that the conquistador wrote the first sixteen chapters of his book as early as 1552-1557. He put the manuscript away for several years, but returned to it in 1564. A first draft was completed in 1568, and seven years later a finished version was sent to Spain. Díaz del Castillo continued to revise it

The Gonzalo de Alvarado manuscript he used was written many years before 1564. Publication of Díaz' book was delayed until 1632, almost half a century after his death. I have used a 1933 Madrid edition of the original seventeenth century publication.

The chapter describing the conquest of Guatemala parallels in fact and order of events Alvarado's account in his letters to Cortés, with a few added details, such as the role played by the Quezaltec Indians in discovering the alleged Quiche plot to trap and burn the Spaniards. The other chapter provides a sketchy view of the rebellious condition of the Indians two years after the conquest.

An analysis of the purpose of Díaz de Castillo's account is unimportant here. His account of the conquest is largely second-hand, and must be considered supplementary to Alvarado's.

Hernán Cortés

Cortés briefly mentions the Indians of Guatemala in two letters to the Crown. The first reference is in his fourth letter written toward the end of 1524. He tells (1961:218-219) of receiving emissaries from the rulers of Utatlán and Guatemala, as he returned from the province of Pánuco. In the fifth letter, written from Tenochtitlan during the latter part of 1526, he mentions (1961:310) the rebellious condition of the natives of Utatlán and Guatemala.

Brief as Cortés' Guatemalan references are, they contain important information about political relations between the aboriginal groups in Mexico and Guatemala at the time of the conquest.

There would seem to be no reason for Cortés to distort his brief description of the natives in Guatemala, and his remarks are perfunctory. In describing the visit of the Cakchiquel emissaries, Cortés merely recites his personal experience. The source of information for his brief statement on the rebellious conditions in Guatemala in 1526 is uncertain. The information could have been brought by messengers or by Alvarado during his visit to Mexico in the latter part of 1526.

---

until his death in 1584, and that revision of the manuscript is probably the one now in the Archivo General de Centroamérica (Cerwin 1963:199ff).

Mexican Auxiliaries

From the Mexican warriors who accompanied Alvarado, we have two limited accounts of the conquest. The less important account is in the writings of the Texcocan prince, Ixtlilxochitl (1952:391-396). Written some time before 1608, his account appears to be based on the two letters by Alvarado. In telling of the conquest, Ixtlilxochitl refers primarily to the Mexicans' role in it. The few additions to the Alvarado letters were probably based on general information known to Ixtlilxochitl, and not on any primary source.[5]

A more important Mexican source is a pictorial codex portraying the Spanish conquest of Guatemala as seen through the eyes of the Tlaxcalan auxiliaries. Known as the *Lienzo de Tlaxcala* (Chavero 1892), it was painted about 1550 by important Tlaxcalan lords who had participated in the conquest. It was probably prepared by the same men who provided information for the famous Niza history of the conquest (now lost), to which it may be regarded as a pictorial counterpart (Gibson 1952:146). Both documents were meant to provide the Crown with information on the events of the conquest.

The *Lienzo* pictorials show five Guatemalan settlements taken in the conquest.[6] The pictorials show such cultural forms as native dress, weaponry, and name glyphs. In the absence of prehispanic pictorials from Guatemala, the Tlaxcalan paintings take on added significance.

The *Lienzo* tends to magnify the role of Tlaxcalan warriors in the various conquests, and this is probably true of the five

---

[5] The following additions to the Alvarado account of the conquest of Guatemala are made by Ixtlilxochitl (1952): he corrects the Nahua forms of the names of Guatemala settlements (e.g., Otlatlan, Cuauhtemalan); he designates the province of modern west El Salvador which was conquered as Toltec; he indicates that some Mexican warriors remained at Iximché during the conquest of Salvador; and that upon return to Iximché some Mexican soldiers carried Alvarado's letter back to Mexico, and there reported to Cortés and to the rulers of Texcoco and Tenochtitlan.

[6] The conquered places listed in the *Lienzo de Tlaxcala* were Tzapotitlán, Quetzaltenanco, Tecpán Atitlán, Quauhtemallan, and Itzcuintepec (Anonymous 1963: Laminas 34-38). Interestingly, the conquest of Utatlán is not shown, whereas that of Tecpán Atitlán (Tzololá) is, though it is not mentioned in Alvarado's report to Cortés.

pictorials. However, there is little reason to believe that this distorted their portrayal of the Indians of Guatemala, though it is possible that the adornment of Quichean warriors might have been toned down to provide a sharper contrast with that of the Tlaxcalans.

There are a number of small 16th century documents in the Archivo de Indias with petitions to the Crown by Mexican auxiliaries; some refer to their participation in the conquest of Guatemala. Generally, however, the references are so brief that little information is given (AGI, Guatemala 52). There are similar documents, though of later date, in the national archives in Guatemala (AGC, A3:241-4797).

Conquistador Writings in Fuentes y Guzmán

Fuentes y Guzmán cites several sources on the conquest of Guatemala which, unfortunately, are no longer available. His account of them provides important information, even though it is secondhand. The two most important sources were a history of the conquest of the Mam by Gonzalo de Alvarado, and notes on the conquest of eastern Guatemala by Hernando de Chávez. Fuentes y Guzmán used various other papers left behind by the conquistadores, and supplemented these sources with the first Book of the *Cabildo* (Santiago, Guatemala).

Fuentes y Guzmán claims (1932-1933:8:465) that shortly after 1526 Gonzalo de Alvarado, brother of Pedro, began writing a history of the conquest. His motive was to clear his name of accusations of cruelty against the Indians during the time he was in charge of the province (while his brother was absent in 1526). Gonzalo's history has been alluded to by Díaz del Castillo, and in the 17th century Fuentes y Guzmán obtained a manuscript copy of it from Father Vides y Alvarado, a descendant of the famed Alvarados (1932-1933:8:106).[7] We do not know what happened

---

[7] Fuentes y Guzmán believed that the manuscript in his possession was only a "notebook" (*cuaderno*) belonging to Gonzalo, and that the *History* had been lost (1932-1933:8:465). In view of the rather extensive nature of the contents of the notebook, I think it likely that he had obtained Gonzalo's full account. Perhaps Fuentes y Guzmán expected too much because he had seen the impressive manuscript by Díaz del Castillo.

to the Gonzalo manuscript after it was used by Fuentes y Guzmán.

From Fuentes y Guzmán's citations of the "notebook," it would seem that it contained an extensive account of the conquest, especially as it related to the fall of the Mam speakers in the Huehuetenango area (1932-1933:8:109-129). Other battles described, which took place in the years following the initial contact between Spaniards and Indians, were at Mixco (6:295-305), Sacatepéquez (6:313-329), Chimaltenango (6:367-372), and Olintepeque (8:468-475).[8] All references to the conquest are rich in detail on native life and political relations.

Because Gonzalo witnessed the conquest, his account is of considerable importance, even though we receive it secondhand through Fuentes y Guzmán. Of the probable distortions in the book, most appear to be in relation to the deeds of the conquistadores, who Gonzalo and then Fuentes y Guzmán attempted to vindicate and glorify.

Fuentes y Guzmán also had in his possession certain papers left to him by his forefather, the conquistador Hernando de Chávez, referring to these papers as the *Probanza Original de Hernando de Chávez* (7:194). He claims to have received them from his elder kinsmen (7:175). Apparently, the contents were somewhat confusing, and he was forced to use the *Libro de Cabildo* and "simple tradition" in order to interpret them (7:175, 177). Presumably, the papers included an original account written by Chávez.

Based upon this source, Fuentes y Guzmán has left us an interesting description of the conquest of the Esquipulas area of eastern Guatemala, including an account of battles fought around the famous classic Maya archaeological site of Copán (7:169-183, 203-209).

Again, we must use the source cautiously. Besides the problems of egocentric distortion and changes suffered in Fuentes y

---

[8] Fuentes y Guzmán was not always explicit about his sources in describing this phase of the conquest, but the Gonzalo manuscript appears to have been his main source. At the same time, he also used other documents, including some written by the natives. In the case of the conquest of Sacatepéquez, we are specifically told that Fuentes y Guzmán had once possessed papers containing "notations on the conquest of Sacattepéques," but that he no longer had them, and so was forced to rely more on the Gonzalo notebook (6:315-316).

Guzmán's hands, the original source appears to have been not as carefully prepared as the documents described earlier. Nevertheless, it is our only source of information on the conquest of eastern Guatemala, and bears evidence that it was originally composed by someone who witnessed the events.

Fuentes y Guzmán had access to other records on the conquest that are no longer available, but these are of minor importance. His description of the conquest of Uspantán appears to have been based on a lost Spanish source (along with a native document), though he does not cite it (8:58-64).[9] He also obtained a few scraps of information from notes on the conquest of Sacatepéquez (the sources are three conquistadores named Vásquez, Guelamo, and Carrillo) (6:315), and from a *probanza* by Don Laureano Guerra Veintemilla and Don Alonso Enríquez de Larios on the conquest of the Mam (8:118).

Others

The writings of the conquistadores of Guatemala described above clearly represent the most important sources available. Undoubtedly, there are additional references to the events of the conquest to be found in the personal probanzas, claims, reports, and testimonies of the conquistadores and their descendants, deposited in the archives of Spain and Guatemala. I have not attempted to exhaust such sources, and it is important to recognize their potential additional contribution.

I am aware of the following documents: the *"Información de méritos y servicios de Diego de Usagre"* (1564), which mentions an expedition by Pedro de Alvarado into the Lacandón area (Recinos 1952:112-114); a claim by Ortega Gómez in which he indicates that he had participated in the conquest of Cuzcatlán (1537) (AGI, Justicia 1031, No. 1); and various claims about the conquest made by children of the conquistadores (AGI, Guatemala 53).

---

[9] An official report of this conquest was registered in the *Libro de Cabildo*, and Fuentes y Guzmán acknowledges it as the source for some of his information (8:59). Herrera briefly described the conquest of Uspantán (1934-1957:9:ch. 29-30), and Fuentes y Guzmán was aware of that account (7:170).

These sources are of minor importance to the anthropologist, for they generally lack information about native cultural patterns. They would be essential, however, for any definitive historical study of the conquest of Guatemala.

QUASI-ETHNOGRAPHIES

Introduction

In modern times, we consider a study to be ethnographic if it, provides a description of the way of life—the culture—of a society based on direct observation. It is assumed that the study is made with an attitude of sympathy or admiration for the native culture, or, as it is often expressed, with objectivity toward it. The ethnographer is expected to learn the native's point of view on things while, at the same time, placing that viewpoint in some theoretical or comparative perspective.

If we describe ethnography in this way, we may properly classify some Spanish writings with descriptions of native culture in Guatemala as quasi ethnographies. Men like Las Casas and Zorita were interested in native culture *per se*, whatever their other purposes for studying the Indians might have been. Characteristically, they aimed for objectivity in reporting their observations, though they also felt a kind of missionary calling to promote respect and sympathy for the native cultures which, they believed, were misunderstood.

Perhaps what distinguished them from modern ethnographers is the comparative framework in which their own cultural tradition required them to place their descriptions. They were concerned with Greek deductions about the nature of man, the superiority of Christianity, and efficiency in the control and subordination of the Indians. Both Las Casas and Zorita attempted to compare native culture with the civilizations of antiquity, and López Medel's comparison reached a state of refinement analogous, in significant ways, to modern theories of cultural evolution. The mixed framework of scientific comparison and classic scholasticism in their writings should not surprise us. It reflects the state of epistemology in Spain during their time.

In classifying some Spanish writings on native culture as ethnographic, we do not suggest that Guatemala was blessed in this regard. There was no Sahagún—no one attempted thoroughly to capture Quichean culture through extensive use of informants and the native language. But, then, the Quiche or Cakchiquel were not the Aztecs; as highly developed as their culture was, it did not attract the same attention as the Aztecs' spectacular way of life. I classify only the work of three sixteenth century Spaniards as quasi ethnographies: Las Casas, Zorita, López Medel. (One might also add the sixteenth century dictionaries, though they will be discussed separately).

Probably, other equally important ethnographic studies were made in the sixteenth century which have not come to light in modern times. Notable among the lost works is a study of native religion by Domingo de Vico entitled, *De la Historia, Fábulas, y Errores de los Indios*. Referring to this work, Remesal states (1932:4:429), it was a large book about native religion and history, written in the Cakchiquel and Verapaz (Pokoman or Kekchi) languages. I have been unable to find this unpublished manuscript during my search of the various archives and libraries of Spain, France, and the Americas, though I hope it may yet be found.

Remesal also mentions (1932:4:429) a book written in Quiche about "the idols and the province of Sacapulas," by Friar Salvador de San Cipriano (early 17th century). The present location of this undoubtedly important ethnographic document is unknown. There were others about which we know even less. Some information upon which the *Crónica Franciscana* was based (see Secondary Sources) apparently came from early ethnographic documents now unknown, written by the first priests in Guatemala.

To learn about documents of obvious ethnographic value cited in later publications, and yet not to have access to them is frustrating to the ethnohistorian. It requires patience to wait for their gradual though not inevitable appearance. Meantime, we will evaluate the sources which have survived the destruction of time.

Las Casas

The most important Spanish source on prehispanic Quichean culture are the writings of the Dominican Friar Bartolomé de Las Casas. In his *Apologética Historia*, he devotes some thirteen chapters to the Indians of Guatemala, and there are scattered references to them in his other writings. The thirteen chapters form a body of ethnographic information which is the closest thing we have for the Guatemalan area to the writings of Sahagún for central Mexico, or the *Relación* of de Landa for Yucatán.

According to Hanke (1949:75), Las Casas began his account of native life in the Indies as early as 1527, several years before he had seen Guatemala. He continued working on it through the years, originally intending it to be part of his *Historia de las Indias* (1951), (a book written largely during the last years of his life). About 1550, he finished the *Apologética Historia* as a separate manuscript, shortly after he had returned to Spain. The manuscript remained in the library of the Academy of History, Madrid, for many years, and was finally published in 1909 under the title, *Apologética Historia de las Indias*. I have used a more recent edition, published as part of the *Biblioteca de Autores Españoles* (1958).

The information in the *Apologética Historia* on the Guatemalan Indians was apparently obtained by Las Casas during his residence in Guatemala between 1536 and 1544 (Hanke 1949:37). Much of that time, no doubt, was spent in Santiago Guatemala, where he probably learned about Quichean culture from interested Spaniards (like Bishop Marroquín, who spoke Quiche), Indian lords, who came to the capital on official business, and from other Indian peoples in the many native villages surrounding the city. He visited the important Quiche centers of Utatlán, Sacapulas, and Rabinal. He must have directly questioned important Quichean lords about their aboriginal way of life, for in various places in the *Apologética Historia* he cites his source of information as "some of the old men," or simply, "they say" (1958:342ff). Remesal certifies that he knew the language spoken in the province of Utatlán and Guatemala (i.e., Quiche and Cakchiquel, which were probably still mutually intelligible), though apparently he was not very proficient in it (Remesal 1932:4:204:213).[10]

[10] Las Casas has been criticized for writing about the Indians without a knowledge of their languages. Sáenz has argued (1966:345) that Remesal was in error in crediting Las Casas with knowing any Guatemalan languages, especially those used at places distant from the capital. There is no reason to believe, however, that he did not learn at least the rudimets of Quichen during his months in the capital, and that he did not expand on it during his

Nevertheless, Las Casas appears to have been more an armchair ethnographer than a fieldworker. He relied on the tremendous quantity of accounts and reports which he gathered wherever he went (his traveling library was apparently an object of considerable commentary), (Hanke 1949:ch. 7). In his description of the Indians, he freely recognized his reliance on information obtained by the priests, who "with more diligence, alone have conversed and studied in depth the language and customs of the peoples" (1958:345). That was especially true of his account of Tezulutlán or Verapaz, which, he explains, was based on written information supplied him by Dominican priests who lived there and spoke the native languages (1958: 354:360).

Most references to the Indians of Guatemala are in the second volume of his *Apologética Historia*, though the first volume also contains important comments on native religion and settlement patterns (1958:105:157-158:427-428). A more complete account of native religion is in the second volume, where almost five chapters are devoted to the topic (1958:147-157:346-348:361-363). Las Casas also paid special attention to political organization (1958:341-343:348-352), laws and customs (1958:343-345: 356-360), and kinship organization (354-356).

The problem with Las Casas' writings is how to differentiate the groups to which he refers in the various parts of his account. He was aware of the prehispanic existence of several provinces, and specifically mentions those of Utatlán, Guatemala, Tequicistlán (Rabinal), Atitlán, and Verapaz. However, his descriptions refer primarily to either Utatlán or Verapaz. In the major section of his writings on the Guatemalan Indians he appears to refer first to the natives of Utatlán (i.e., the Quiche) (1958: 341-351), and then to those of Verapaz (1958:351-363).[11]

---

visits to the outlying communities of Sacapulas and Rabinal. It is my impression from statements by Las Casas in the *Apologética Historia* (1958:345), that he admitted ignorance of the languages of Verapaz (probably the Kekchi and Pokoman of the Cobán area), but not of those of the provinces of "Guatemala and Utatlán."

[11] In the part which apparently refers to the Quiche of Utatlán (1958:341-351), there are references to Verapaz, though these are always so specified (1958:344:347:348) He seemed to feel that his Verapaz information was of greater depth than that for Guatemala proper (1958:345-346).

It is unclear to what area he refers in his chapter on kinship (1958;354-356). Miles (1957:760), following Torquemada, assigns it to the Indians of Verapaz, while Ximénez (who knew Quiche culture firsthand), (1929-1931:1:96), and Fuentes y Guzmán (1932-1933:6:13) associate it with the Quiche. Las Casas repeatedly warns of the similarity between culture in the various provinces of Guatemala (and with that of Mexico as well), and probably intended this chapter to refer to both areas.[12] I do not believe, however, that Las Casas intended to include the Quiche-speaking peoples of the Rabinal area within the province of Verapaz (in spite of my earlier statement, Carmack 1966b:43). He refers to Verapaz as being inhabited by natives with a different language from that of Utatlán and Guatemala, and appears to rely exclusively on written sources for that part of his account (1958: 354:360).[13] At any rate, matters of kinship must have been similar throughout the highlands of Guatemala before the conquest, especially for the common classes.

Another section whose referent is unclear treats of "the religion that the Indians of Guatemala had" (1958:147-157). Las Casas claims, it refers to the "people of the kingdoms of Guatemala" (1958:148), and there is internal evidence that some material is specifically about the Quiche.[14] He apparently felt that his description applied to central Mexico as well, and, accordingly,

[12] The chapter in question is ascribed by Las Casas to the "Indians of Guatemala" (1958:354). Elsewhere the designation refers primarily to the Quiche of Utatlán, and perhaps secondarily to the Cakchiquel. In this chapter, he refers to a statement in an earlier chapter, which clearly seems to deal with the Quiche (1958:345:355).

[13] Remesal is not clear on this point but his account seems to suggests that the dividing line between Verapaz (Tezulutlán) and the province of Guatemala was just east of present-day Rabinal. He specifically associates Cobán with Verapaz (1932:1:205), and that seems to agree with statements by Las Casas (1958:347). In the early relaciones, Rabinal is placed in the province of Guatemala, rather than Verapaz (López de Velasco 1952:38; Viana, Gallego, Cadena 1955).

[14] Las Casas' statement that the ball game was frequently played "in high places" (1958:149) suggests the Quiche in the central highlands of Guatemala (Recinos 1953: passim; Smith 1955) But he also specifically mentions Guatemala within the chapter (1958:153:154), and even uses a few Quiche words (1958:153:156).

the account is similar to some Mexican sources (e.g., Sahagún). His description would seem to correspond to a social environment more urban than that existing in most parts of prehispanic Guatemala (1958:150-152).

It is clear that Las Cases believed many religious practices in Guatemala to be similar to those of Mexico, and he defined a "culture area" of 800 leagues in circumference, which included Guatemala and Nicaragua (1958:157). He may have used a Mexican source for part of the section under discussion, though it was written primarily as an account of religion in Guatemala. Apparently, after he had completed his description of religion in central Mexico, and had gone on to state that it was similar to that found in Guatemala, he decided to add the Guatemalan section.[15] Presumably, he would not have done this, nor ascribed it to Guatemala, had he not been using some non-Mexican sources.

The anthropological strengths and weaknesses of Las Casas' *Apologética Historia* have been ably summarized by Hanke (1949: 69-101), and need not be repeated in detail here. Las Casas wrote with a definite bias—to prove that the Indians had a civilization of their own, not different from those of the ancient Mediterranean world. He followed Aristotelian guidelines, and thus restricted his attention to standardized topics such as agriculture, crafts, warfare, priesthood, politics, and law. He tended to gloss over native customs which he considered to be bad, though such matters are not entirely absent from his writings. He recognized the importance of knowing the native language to understand fully and record their culture. He had a respect and appreciation for the Indian cultures he attempted to describe, the characteristic which, Hanke believes, qualifies him as an anthropologist (1949:100).

These characteristics appropriately describe the anthropological value of the Guatemalan sections taken alone. In them, Las Casas focuses upon those aspects of culture which he believed would prove that the Indians were creators of a worthy civili-

[15] The evidence that the section on Guatemala was inserted later is in a footnote by the editor about the original manuscript (1958:157, footnote 1). We learn that chapter 180 was originally a continuation of chapter 176, and that Las Casas crossed out the last part of chapter 176, apparently in order to insert the additional three chapters on Guatemalan religion. Chapter 180, then, followed the three new chapters.

zation (e.g., he notes that their writing system was nearly as functional as the Spaniards') (1958:346). He does not completely neglect the less spectacular aspects of culture, as shown by his description of commoner affairs related to kinship and the life crises. His forceful statements on the importance of language for properly understanding native cuture are impressive. In fact, his own knowledge of Quiche (and Cakchiquel), as limited as it might have been, makes his Guatemalan section of special significance. Because of this, along with his familiarity with the area and its people (both native and Spanish), of the Indian cultures discussed in the *Apologética Historia*, perhaps only his section on native life in the Caribbean Islands is of comparable ethnographic value.

Though he biases his account by trying to prove the civilized condition of the Guatemalan Indians, I must agree with Hanke that he rises above it. "He felt . . . the true uneasiness of the anthropologist who consecrates himself to rescue all possible information about the language and customs of peoples disappearing from the face of the land" (1949:100). The general accuracy of his account is demonstrated by numerous correlations which exist between it and the native sources described earlier.

The most serious criticism to be made about his Guatemalan section is its lack of adequate citations. Because of that, it is not always clear to which native group Las Casas refers, though I hope most problems have been solved by my analysis.

Zorita

It is sometimes overlooked that the important writings of Alonso de Zorita (Zurita) on native customs in New Spain contain references to the Indians of Guatemala. The Guatemalan references are contained in two books written after his return to Spain in 1566: *Breve y sumaria relación de los señores de la Nueva España*, and *Relación de cosas notables de Nueva España*. The *Breve y Sumaria Relación* remained unknown for over a century, and an adequate published edition of it did not appear until 1891 (García Icazbalceta 1886-1892). Since then, two additional Spanish editions have appeared (Zorita 1941; 1963a), and an English translation (1963b). Only the first part of the *Relación de Cosas*

Notables has been published to date (1909), though the complete manuscript is preserved in the Biblioteca del Palacio Real in Madrid.

In the *Breve y Sumaria Relación* Zorita states explicitly, he is writing in answer to a request made by the Crown in 1553 that Spanish officials report on the pre- and early posthispanic political organization of the Indians, especially with respect to their system of tribute payment. He explains that he left Guatemala before he could make his report there, and that he arrived in Mexico too late to be able to report from that province. He never forgot the Crown's request, and after returning to Spain determined to make "a clean copy of that which I have had for many years in my memorials and notebooks" (Zorita 1941:72). The chapters are organized according to the questions of the 1553 royal *cédula*, though he does not strictly adhere to the topics prescribed by them.

Apparently, Zorita considered the *Relación de Cosas Notables* to be his magnum opus. From the sources used in the work, information specifically relevant to the proper administration of Indian tributes was extracted for his *Breve y Sumaria Relación*. In the larger work, Zorita attempts to give a complete view of native life, and to narrate a history of events from the time of the arrival of the Spaniards in the New World. The first part, consisting of 27 chapters, deals with the full range of customary native practices in New Spain and surrounding provinces. In the second part, consisting of sixteen chapters, he describes the aboriginal political system of New Spain. The third part, with 37 chapters, refers to the conquest of New Spain and Central America. The fourth part contains 23 chapters of description of the missionization and proselytization of the Indians of New Spain, concluding with extracts from the writing of Fray Toribio de Benavente (Motolinía), (Zorita 1941:XXIX-XXIV).

Throughout the four parts of *Cosas Notables*, Zorita evaluates, moralizes, compares, and contrasts the Indians and their treatment by the Spaniards with the customs and morals of the ancients (as contained in the scriptures and the writings of the Greeks). As a consequence, even though the smaller *Breve y Sumaria Relación* appears to be confined by the questionnaire around which it is organized, it is in fact closer to an ethnography than the larger *Cosas Notables*.

In describing the customs of the natives of Guatemala, Zorita is careful to cite the sources of his information[16] In most cases his account is based on personal observation and questioning, and he is careful to state who gave the information and to which settlement or province it pertained (Zorita 1941:69 passim). During the three years Zorita was oidor in Guatemala he visited almost all regions of the province, including the centers Salamá, Sacapulas, Utatlán, and Tecpán Guatemala.[17] He claims that he had been careful to converse with "the principal and elder Indians, whom one could believe they would say the truth" (1941: 72). He must have talked to them through interpreters in most cases, for he apparently did not speak the native tongues. According to his own testimony, he made notes of the things he had learned, and this is borne out by his specific references to persons and places some 20 to 30 years later. At Utatlán, with the aid of a Dominican priest there (probably Pedro de Angulo, first Bishop of Verapaz), he was shown a native codex and given an explanation of its contents. Unfortunately, he has little to say about its style or contents (1941:204).

Most of Zorita's ethnographic notes on the Indians of Guatemala refer to their mode of government, and economic organization (including the tribute system). Throughout, he shows special competence, and these parts of his *Breve y Summaria Relación* are outstanding ethnography in every respect. This is due to

---

[16] Zorita begins the *Relación de Cosas Notables* with a list of important sources known to him on the history and native cultures of the New World (Zorita 1909:8-24). He candidly informs the reader which of the works he had read and the extent of their use in preparing his account. For Guatemala, he lists Las Casas (probably the *Apologética Historia*, and his polemical account of the conquest), Román y Zamora (whose references to Guatemala came from Las Casas' *Apologética Historia*), López de Gómara, Pedro Mártir (who used the letters of Alvarado), and Díaz del Castillo (Zorita saw the first part of his *Historia Verdadera*).

[17] According to a letter copied by Muños (n.d.: Vol. 69), in 1555, Zorita spent six months visiting different parts of the province, mostly on foot. He attempted to congregate the Indians into towns, and to eradicate their idolatries. Perhaps his most important activity was his attempt to eliminate the unjust treatment which the encomenderos imposed upon the Indians. For his role in this, he incurred the wrath of the encomenderos, who complained to the Crown.

his genuine interest in political administration, and to the fact that as an official of the audiencia he dealt constantly with related problems. He was also conscientious about the request made by the Crown for information on native government and tribute collection, and he specifically made inquiries about that aspect of native culture.

The four chapters devoted to Central America in the third part of his *Relación de Cosas Notables* are disappointing from an ethnographic point of view. His discussion of Guatemala is confined to the etymology of the name *Quahutimalam,* and the events surrounding the destruction of Ciudad Vieja in 1541 (most of this information came from Motolinía). He also gives a history of the origin of the Nahua speakers in Nicaragua, based on one of Motolinía's missing manuscripts.[18]

As a judge who spent most of his time in the urban Spanish centers of America, Zorita was a good ethnographer. He was careful to obtain reliable, firsthand information, and properly to cite the sources. He was interested in the history and customs of the Indians, and, like most good ethnographers, he defended them and their way of life. He did not think it unjust to collect tribute from the Indians, but he vigorously opposed the excesses of the encomenderos. He felt the Indians had been unfairly categorized as a people without abilities and achievements worthy of respect. He explained their submissive attitude toward the Spaniards as the result of fear instilled in them by the cruelties to which they had been subjected (1941:84). In many places he calls attention to their praiseworthy customs and beliefs (especially their good government and firm social order), and favorably compares them with the peoples of the Old World. Unlike many of his contemporaries, his works do not pivot around any grand theme or thesis, which would have unduly biased his account.

I value highly Zorita's ethnographic contribution for material on New Spain and Guatemala. His focus on native political administration is especially valuable, for on this topic we gener-

---

[18] I am indebted to the director of the Biblioteca del Palacio Real, Madrid, for providing me with photocopies of chapters 34-38 of the *Relación de Cosas Breves y Notables.* The Motolinía document used by Zorita, apparently was also used by Torquemada for his description of the Pipil migrations to Central American (1943:1:331; Nicholson n.d.a:73).

ally lack detailed writings by the other sixteenth century Spanish "ethnographers." We can only wish that the had dealt as extensively with the native culture of Guatemala as he had with that of Mexico.

López Medel

Licenciado Tomás López Medel's geographically oriented quasi-ethnographic study contains many references to the prehispanic native culture of Guatemala. It is entitled, *Tradato cuyo título es de los tres elementos, aire, agua y tierra . . . acerca de los occidentales Indios*, and was composed in Spain sometime around 1560.[19] Most of it was copied by Muñós, and now forms part of volume 42 of his collected manuscripts in the Real Academia de la Historia, Madrid. The important section for this study is the third part, which contains 21 chapters dealing mostly with Indian cultural patterns (Muñós n.d.:42:168-248).[20] Chapter 20 was translated and published by Tozzer as an appendix to the de Landa *Relación* (1941:221-229).

Presumably, López gathered the material for his book while serving as audiencia judge (oidor) in Mexico, Guatemala, and Colombia (New Granada). For three years, he resided as judge at Santiago Guatemala (from the establishment of the audiencia in 1549 to his reassignment to New Granada in 1552). Apparently, much of his time was taken up in adjusting and regulating Indian tributes, a task at which he became proficient. He was sent to Yucatán in 1552 specifically to put in order the tributary system of the province (Tozzer 1941:70-73). From the ordinances on tribute payment which he issued while in Yucatán, we learn

---

[19] The manuscript is undated, though usually bibliographies date it 1612— perhaps the year a copy of it was made. It is evident from remarks in the document that it was written after López had returned to Spain (sometime around 1558-1560). The approximate date of composition is suggested by a leaf inserted into the account by López' nephew, written in the year 1561 (Muñós n.d.:42:248).

[20] I am indebted to Carl Sauer of the Department of Geography, University of California, Berkeley, for providing me with a copy of this and other sections from the Muñós collection. The department had obtained its photocopy from the Real Academia de la Historia, Madrid.

that he had studied native social patterns closely—e.g., he had to determine the tributes traditionally paid to native caciques, in order to be able to adjust them. He gained additional knowledge about native life from litigation involving the Indians, though most cases coming before the audiencia probably pertained to political rather than everyday affairs.

Unfortunately, López does not cite sources in his account. Throughout, the language used suggests that his primary source was personal observation, and this is substantiated by his emphasis on patterns from areas where he had served as judge. He may have made personal notes, though he does not say so; and in one place he states that he was using his memory ("now that it comes to me") (Muñós n.d. 42:239v). His description is long, though not detailed, and might have been written largely from memory.

A major problem in the interpretation of this source is to determine the native group to which López refers for any given matter. In most references to Guatemala, he lumps all native groups together, even though he was aware of differences. He is more specific in some instances, however, as in his references to "the valley of Guatemala," the "city of Guatemala," "Guatemaltecas y Utlatecas," the "southern coast of Guatemala." Apparently, López considered the cultures of Mexico and Guatemala to be very similar, though he recognized that native culture in Guatemala was less developed than in Mexico. At any rate, in most places he discusses the two regions together.

López designates group referents only in his discussion of religious practices. In chapter 20, he specifically refers to the "Utlatecas" (Quiche). Possibly, his information on this aspect of native culture was fuller, perhaps based on notes. He was also more interested in religion because he was an ecclesiastic.

In turning to the ethnographic information on Guatemalan native culture, we immediately note the importance of the chapter on religion, because it details and specifies native groupings. Other chapters contain useful general descriptions of native kinship and marriage, inheritance, political organization, use of natural resources, and plant domestication. Unfortunately, López fails to mention Guatemala in his somewhat understated account of native arts and crafts (weaving, writing, architecture), (chapter 18), presumably because he felt his remarks about Mexican Indians were generally true for Guatemalan Indians as well. While he lived in Guatemala, it is unlikely that he could not have noticed the natives' ability in these areas of technology.

The anthropological value of López' writings is difficult to assess because his purposes and motives were complex. His attitude toward the Indians and their culture was patronizing. He considered them barbarians, without the light of Christianity and its attendent civilization. Yet, he thought, they were not to be blamed for this, and in a sense, they represented a "natural" way of life of which the Spaniards had lost sight as a consequence of the artificiality and ceremonialism into which their civilization had fallen. Furthermore, the barbarism in the Indies was not unlike that in ancient Greece and Rome, or Spain, even though the former nations had the great philosophers, and the latter Christianity. Therefore, López wrote primarily to enlighten the Spaniards on their own "idiocies," and exhorted them to the task of saving the Indians from "their abominations and errors" (Muñós n.d. 42:221v-222v, 242v).[21]

His ambivalent attitude toward the Indians (at least as compared to Las Casas) resulted in an account in which he defends the Indians in a few places, but denigrates the uncivilized condition of their culture in most. He generally underestimated the level of native cultural development in the New World. Fortunately, however, his description is often more accurate than his doctrine, so that the highly developed nature of native culture emerges, nevertheless.[22]

López also wrote as scholar, and responded to questions posed by the learned men of his day and the sages of the past (especial-

[21] This attitude can be seen in his actions as oidor. He sided with the friars in Yucatán, and gained the hate of the encomenderos there. Yet, he did not act as a friend of the Indians, who resented his strenuous attempts to eradicate their traditional way of life (through congregation and forced education) (Tozzer 1941:70-72, notes 316-319). In Guatemala he had the friendship of the encomenderos, but was in conflict with Cerrato, the friend of the Indians (Muñós n.d.).

[22] In his chapter on arts and crafts, López states that "no nation in the world is to be found with lower artifices and curiosities than the occidental Indians" (Muñós n.d.:42:219v). He contradicts this, then, by describing the complex technical achievements in metallurgy, weaving, writing "like the Egyptians," carpentry, elaborate architecture, and the like.

ly Aristotle). Through logic and fact he attempted to dispose of such theories as the transformation of stone into gold by active volcanoes, or the origin of the Indians from various Old World peoples (whether the ten tribes, Carthaginians, or Romans). He was also interested in classification, as his extensive lists of plant and animal types show. He presented an interesting classification of native societies in which he placed them on three levels or "estates." At the top were the Indians of Guatemala, along with the natives of Mexico and Peru.[23]

López's scholarly side somewhat counterbalances his ethnocentric bias, and adds importance to his work. Unfortunately, his "scientific" approach was rather haphazard, especially in classifying culture patterns by place and social grouping. His failure to specify in most instances the groups in Guatemala is the major ethnographic weakness of his account.

DICTIONARIES

Introduction

The dictionaries prepared by the early priests in Guatemala contain rich ethnographic data. Ostensibly, they were written to facilitate the Christianization of the Indians, but the priests who wrote them invariably show an interest in native culture above and beyond the practical reasons for which they were produced.[24] Languages themselves are important aspects of native culture, though they are perhaps best studied through early grammars and the native texts already described. We have two important

[23] López' classification of native societies is remarkably similar to some recent anthropological schemes (Service 1964; Sanders 1968). At the lowest level he lists the hunters and gatherers, who were without chiefs. Next came the small chiefdoms, the unions of 1 to 3 communities under a single head. Finally came the empires, the three most important of which were the Haitian, the Mexican, and the Peruvian. The Maya empires were at this level, though somewhat less developed (Muñós n.d.: 42:226v-227v).

[24] The genuine interest of many friars in native customs was not inconsistent with Crown policy. From the beginning of missionization in the area, the friars were ordered to prepare descriptions of native life in order to be able to better eradicate such ideas, and "because of their curious nature" (Remesal 1932:4:428-429).

16th century grammars (Vico n.d.b; Martinez n.d.) and several later ones (Edmonson 1967).

To the ethnohistorian, more important than language grammars are the lexicons contained in the early dictionaries. These lexicons provide a blueprint to much of the content of the cultures of which they are a part and point to the native way of classifying the world. For this reason the early dictionaries are of fundamental ethnographic importance.

In analyzing the primary dictionary materials from Guatemala, we will emphasize those written in the 16th century. Most dictionaries prepared in the following two centuries borrowed extensively from the early sources. The later sources will be included here only where they contain ethnographic material of special value from earlier dictionaries. We will attempt to trace their entries to the original sources.

The dictionaries we will discuss, do not represent the entire extant corpus of 16th century Guatemalan dictionaries. To sort out all original dictionary sources available by comparing the holdings of several important archives would require time and funds much beyond those available to me. I hope I have included the most important dictionaries (see also Recinos 1950; Sáenz 1959). Certainly, the sources I mention contain a treasure of ethnographic information waiting to be tapped. Compared with the dictionary sources used by Carrasco (1950) or Roys (1943) to reconstruct Otomí and Yucatecan Maya culture, the Quichean lexical materials are relatively abundant.

Vico's Cakchiquel-Quiché Dictionary

Perhaps the most important dictionary source for the study of Quichean culture, is the Cakchiquel-Quiché dictionary written by the "Saint Thomas of Guatemala," Domingo de Vico.[25] It was written before 1555 (the year of Vico's martyrdom), probably while he was prior of the Dominican convent in Santiago Guatemala (ca. 1548-1550). Copies of the original dictionary were made

---

[25] Remesal noted approvingly (1932:5:380) that another priest had compared Vico's writings on the Indian languages with those of Saint Thomas in Latin.

to be used by the Dominicans (Gates n.d.) and eventually two copies found their way into the *Bibliothèque Nationale* of France, presumably as part of the Brasseur manuscript collection. Gates obtained photographic copies of them, and these later became part of the holdings of the Peabody Museum and the Newberry Library.

The photocopy from the Newberry Library I have used[26] is entitled, "Vocabulario de la lengua Cakchiquel y Kiche" (Vico n.d.a). It is undated and unsigned, but a reference in it to Maldonado's, *Ramillete manual* . . ., suggests it was written sometime in the seventeenth century. The copy is in a clear hand, but in a personal communication to me, René Acuña pointed out that it contains many entries by an anonymous seventeenth century Franciscan priest (presumably additions to a Vico original).

Vico was famous for his linguistic ability more than any other priest of the sixteenth century in Guatemala. Remesal claims (1932:5:370-380) that he was dedicated to learning the languages of the native groups wherever he went (including dialectical differences between towns), and that he knew seven Indian languages. Most of his ten years in Guatemala were spent in the Verapaz region, so he undoubtedly knew the Pokoman and Kekchi languages, as well as Chol (the language probably spoken in Acalá) (Thompson 1938:586).

He must have learned Quiche and Cakchiquel before his priorship in Guatemala, for his understanding of these languages was prodigious. Besides the dictionary, he wrote a Quiche grammar (Vico n.d.b), and a huge volume of doctrinal treatises transcribed into the Quiche language (called *Theologia Indorum*).[27]

---

[26] These U.S. institutions kindly permitted me use of their materials and provided me with facilities to obtain copies of selected important documents: Bancroft Library, University of California, Berkeley; the Newberry Library in Chicago; the American Philosophical Society of Philadelphia; the University Museum Library, University of Pennsylvania; the Princeton University Library; the Latin American Library, Tulane University; the Graduate Research Library, University of California, Los Angeles; the University of Texas Library; Peabody Museum Library, Harvard University; Pius XII Memorial Library, St. Louis University; Brigham Young University Library; Hispanic Foundation, Library of Congress.

[27] Gates (n.d.) has commented on the linguistic worth of these religious writings, noting that Vico probably transcribed them in Cakchiquel and Tzu-

The Cakchiquel-Quiche dictionary reveals Vico's profound knowledge of the two languages. He gives numerous grammatical clarifications, carefully distinguishes between Quiche and Cakchiquel forms, and meticulously applies the Parra phonemic symbols. Though the setting for much of the vocabulary appears to be the region surrounding the Guatemalan capital (he mentions such places as Pank'an—Santiago—Santa María Cauque, Alotenango, Itzapa, Comalapa), he also draws material from Quezaltenango, Samayac, Utatlán, and Chiquimula. We cannot help admire and appreciate the breadth of linguistic data in this work.

Following is a brief, representative summary of the ethnographic contents of the Vico dictionary: the months and days of the year, numerals of all kinds, political titles and their insignia, some mythology and ritual, complete kinship terminology, crafts and craftsmen, agricultural products and techniques, settlement patterns and forms.

Vico was the ideal ethnographer in almost every way. He was well organized (Las Casas had lured him away from the Dominican college at Salamanca), and he was vitally interested in the Indians and their culture (note the legends grown up around him, as recited by Remesal) (1932:5:373ff). He spent much time with the Indians, quickly learning their languages in order to communicate with them, and he compared and analyzed different native cultures (especially the languages). His work is unexcelled among Spanish writings in terms of accuracy and familiarity with native culture.

Yet ethnographic information for many important cultural categories is scanty (which, of course, is to be expected; otherwise this long dictionary would have become unwieldy). Also, we detect in the dictionary the influence of Vico's desire to bring Christianity to the natives. He gives special attention to the terms which were important for translating Christian concepts, and many word examples are in a biblical context. But even here Vico demonstrates an ethnographic fidelity by carefully employing native terms which seemed most closely to approximate

---

tujil as well as Quiche. Several copies of Vico's *Theologia Indorum* are in the *Bibliothèque Nationale*, Paris. Gates obtained photographic copies of them, some of which are in the Newberry Library of Chicago.

Christian meanings. His putting Christian concepts into native molds later led to religious squabble (Vásquez 1937-44:14:120), but helped preserve native categories of meanings.

Varela Cakchiquel Dictionary

Unfortunately, the earliest Cakchiquel grammars and dictionaries on which the Varela Cakchiquel dictionary is based have disappeared. One, *Arte de la lengua de Guatemala*, was written ca. 1545 by the Franciscan friar, Pedro de Betanzos. He is reputed to have been a great linguist who spoke some fourteen languages (including Nahuatl and several Maya tongues) (Vázquez 1937-44:17:127). Also lost is the early dictionary composed by Francisco de la Parra sometime between 1544 and 1560 entitled, *Vocabulario trilingüe guatemalteco*. Parra was famous in his day for having adapted five special characters to represent the glottal stops of the Guatemalan native languages (ca. 1545) (Vázquez 1937-44:14:126). Pedro de Betanzos and Francisco de la Parra were the best "linguists" among the early Franciscan missionaries; it is unfortunate that both their vocabularies have disappeared without surviving copies.

Varela's dictionary probably incorporates much of the lexicons contained in the Parra and Betanzos works, though this is not certain.[28] Apparently, Varela did not write his dictionary until around 1600; he arrived in Guatemala in 1596 and lived there until 1630 (Vázquez 1937-44:16:299). The late date of composition seems inconsistent with the archaic and aboriginal form of the lexical contents of the dictionary, and the contrast provides our strongest evidence that it is based on earlier sources.

---

[28] In the copies of Varela's dictionary that have survived, there is no reference to the earlier works, and, of course, comparison with them is not possible. A statement by Vázquez, however, is somewhat suggestive in this regard (1937-44:16:299): "Varela. . .succeeded in producing an excellent work, that for many years had been desired, and which, because of its difficulty had not been reached in the perfected form as it was done by Friar Francisco. He has made a dictionary of the type made by Ambrosio Calepino, as copious as that, for the principle languages of this province." It sounds as though Varela was building on the foundation of his Franciscan predecessors.

At least two copies of the Varela dictionary have come to us. Another dictionary by Francisco Barela, in the Museo Nacional de México, titled, *Vocabulario Kakchiquel*, was reputed by Recinos to be another copy of that dictionary (1950:253). However, in a personal communication, Acuña has suggested that it may be an entirely different dictionary.

The copy in the American Philosophical Society bears the title, *Calepino en lengua Cakchiquel*, and the author is given as Francisco Varea (the copyist was Fray Francisco Zerón, 1699). It is written in a clear hand, using the Parra characters, and is the version I have used for this study. Apparently, another copy of the Vare(l)a dictionary was obtained from the Maya Society (Gates 1937:24) by Father Rossbach of Chichicastenango shortly before 1940, for he provided Sáenz de Santa María with photocopies of it,[29] and most of its contents can be conveniently found in Sáenz's published version (though some valuable ethnographic information has been left out), (1940).

It is not known precisely where Varela learned Cakchiquel, but it most surely was in the vicinity of Lake Atitlán. The few geographical references in the dictionary are to places near the lake—*viz.*, Pank'an (Santiago Guatemala), Patulul, Atitlán. The meanings of words appear to be taken exclusively from Cakchiquel culture, and there are no Quiché references. For example, the descent groups referred to are the same as those mentioned in the *Annals of the Cakchiquels—Tukuchee, Bac'ajol, Xajil, Ajpop*, etc. Thus, it is narrower in scope than the Vico dictionary, and must be considered independent of that source.

Though more limited in the number of words listed, the Varela dictionary is comparable in ethnographic content to that of Vico. There is information on kinship terms, social and political organization, the native calendar, method of counting, and many other customs and beliefs. Practically every page contains some information which would be useful for reconstructing the prehispanic Cakchiquel culture.

[29] Sáenz states that the copy of the Varea dictionary he used had 400 folios, which is the exact number of pages ascribed to the original Varela manuscript by Vázquez (1937-44:16:299). In contrast, the Barela *Vocabulario* in Mexico has 267 pages, and the Varea *Calepino* in Philadelphia 453 (see Note 30).

It is difficult to evaluate adequately this dictionary because we know so little about the author and the sources that went into its composition. Nevertheless, on the basis of internal evidence I would rate if of high ethnographic quality. Many entries make it clear that much of the aboriginal way of life was still viable at the time they were first recorded. Christian elements are not absent in the dictionary, but they are certainly attenuated. It is my impression that the author(s) was even more inclined than Vico to transcribe the native language as he found it, and less inclined to seek correlations between native concepts and Christian beliefs.

Calepino Cakchiquel

The history of this presumed 16th century dictionary is complex and only some of the obscurities connected with its writing and subsequent copies can be clarified here. To begin, there appear to be several anonymous versions of it available. One of these versions, *Calepino Grande, Castellano y Quiche* (in the Newberry Library), (Butler 1937:196), is probably a 17th or 18th century copy of an earlier document. Identical to the *Calepino Grande* are two copies of a dictionary from the Gates collection, now in the Library of Brigham Young University entitled, *Vocabulario en lengua castellana y guatemalteca que se llama Cakchiquelchi* (Cline n.d.a). They appear to be later copies (perhaps 18th century) of the same vocabulary. The format and most entries in the Tirado dictionary (copied in 1787 at Sacapulas), (Edmonson 1965) were taken directly from either the original or a copy of the *Calepino Cakchiquel*—as I shall call this dictionary.[30]

Because all copies we have of the *Calepino Cakchiquel* were made by Franciscans, we can be certain that the author of the original Spanish-to-Cakchiquel document was a Franciscan. Gates

---

[30] The Spanish-to-Quiche dictionary copied by Fermín Joseph Tirado in 1787, leaves out many terms which are defined in the *Calepino Grande*. As a result, the usefulness ascribed to the *Calepino Grande* does not entirely hold true for the Tirado dictionary. Tirado's technique for shortening his copy was to transcribe only the first word or two of each entry, and to delete many terms no longer of significance in the second half of the 18th century (cf. Edmonson 1965).

believed (n.d.) the author to be Fray Félix Solano, because his name was given as author on the fly leaf of a copy. This is probably not so because Fray Solano is not mentioned by Vázquez (1937-1944), Coto (n.d.), or other Franciscans who wrote about early Guatemalan missionaries. Surely the author of this important dictionary would have been worthy of mention by the early colonial chroniclers.

Possibly, the author was Fray Juan de Alonso, known as the foremost Franciscan student of native languages of Guatemala during the second half of the 16th century (Vázquez 1937-44: 14:249). Significantly, Alonso knew both Cakchiquel and Quiche (he labored at Totonicapán),[31] and his vocabulary is reputed to have been written in a Spanish-to-Cakchiquel format. An entry in Coto's dictionary ascribed to Alonso is identical with the corresponding entry in the *Calepino Cakchiquel* (see the gloss for *sacrificarse* in both sources). In view of these facts, and the fame of Alonso as a Franciscan linguist, it seems more realistic to ascribe to him the authorship of this dictionary than to Solano.

From references in the *Calepino Cakchiquel* to the Xajil and Tzotzil lineages and to several named places near Santiago Guatemala, its composition may be located in the Cakchiquel area east of Lake Atitlán. The suggested Alonso authorship, and its many references to native categories and activities point to an early date of composition, though it is not possible to specify this more than to say it probably was the second half of the 16th century.

The Spanish entries in the *Calepino* tend to be somewhat repetitious, and the Cakchiquel glosses are brief. Nevertheless, the total number of words and concepts given is impressive. Especially important are the native terms referring to social positions and rank, divination and ritual, and domestic activities. This fact, plus its presumed early date of original composition make this dictionary an important source for studying Quichean culture.

---

[31] A comparison between the *Calepino Cakchiquel* and the dictionary written by Vico reveals that they are independent of each other. However, many entries in the Coto dictionary are identical to corresponding entries in the *Calepino*. Surprisingly, the version of this dictionary at Newberry is said to have Spanish glosses, even though they are identical to the equivalent Cakchiquel glosses in the Gates and Coto dictionaries. The original appears to have had exclusively Cakchiquel glosses.

Coto Dictionary

Though not written until the close of the seventeenth century, the *Vocabulario de la Lengua Cakchiquel y Guatemalteca*, written by the Franciscan friar, Tomás Coto, is one of the most ethnographically complete dictionaries. Coto labored at least fifty years in the Cakchiquel-speaking region around Santiago Guatemala (Vázquez 1937-1944:15:229), and finally compiled his dictionary shortly before his death (ca. 1690).[32]

The numerous Spanish-to-Cakchiquel entries in the dictionary are rich in ethnographic detail. Some were taken from the Varela dictionary, others came from the works of Maldonado and Saz (seventeenth century). Coto also took data from a sixteenth century vocabulary prepared by Fray Juan de Alonso. The *Calepino Cakchiquel* appears to have been the basic source to which Coto added words from his own knowledge and from the vocabularies listed above. The result was a comprehensive dictionary which contains the most important entries of all Franciscan vocabularies at the end of the seventeenth century.

Pokoman Dictionaries

An important ethnographic source for the Pokoman speakers who lived east of the Quiche are the Zúñiga and Morán dictionaries. Both are based on a sixteenth century dictionary written by the Dominican friar, Francisco de Viana. Viana first went to Verapaz in 1556, where he became well known for his knowledge of the native languages and customs in the Cobán area (apparently he resided for many years in San Crisóbal Cajcoj), (Remesal 1932: 5:381-382). The exact date when he wrote the dictionary is not known. It was probably before he collaborated with two other priests in writing the *"Relación de la Provincia de la Verapaz"* (1574), (Viana, Callego, Cadena 1955).

Viana's dictionary survived only through the works of his two successors. One, Dionysius Zúñiga, arrived in Verapaz in 1597, and became Viana's pupil (Miles 1957:736). In 1608, after

---

[32] An entry into the dictionary records an earthquake at Almolonga for March 29, 1691. Therefore, Coto was in the process of writing his vocabulary in the first part of the last decade of the seventeenth century.

Viana's death, Zúñiga recopied many of the well-worn manuscripts of his teacher, including the dictionary. The resulting Zúñiga dictionary, *Diccionario Pocomchí—Castellano y Pocomchí de San Cristóbal Cahcoh*, was based primarily on Viana's work, but also contains additions from Zúñiga's studies and another early dictionary witten at Cobán. In 1875, Berendt obtained a fragment of the Zúñiga dictionary (400 of some 1000 original leaves) from the parish priest of San Cristóbal. This fragment is now in the University of Pennsylvania Museum Library.

In 1720, the Dominican priest Pedro Morán copied the Zúñiga dictionary verbatim, noting only a few dialectical differences between the northern and southern Pokoman speakers (Miles 1957:739). He entitled his work, *Arte breve y compendioso de la lengua Pocomchí de la Provincia de la Verapaz*, and gave full credit to Zúñiga (though not to Viana). Fragments of Morán's dictionary have survived, and photocopies of them are part of the Gates collection (Miles consulted them at the Peabody Museum Library). Fortunately, Miles noted, (1957:736), Zúñiga's manuscript is partially complementary to that of Morán, one filling in the gaps of the other.

Even though we do not have Viana's original work, it seems clear that Zúñiga's transcription is accurate, and his own additions are also valuable. Viana and Zúñiga were good ethnographers. Many entries in their dictionaries show a profound interest in native culture, and suggest that they attempted to investigate native language and custom in detail (Miles 1957:738, note 4). They showed comparative interest in dictionaries, so that we find specific comments about different communities within Verapaz and about separate linguistic groups outside that area. Viana never knew Vico, but he and Zúñiga carried on the ethnographic and linguistic tradition started by Vico among the Indians of Verapaz.

The ethnographic information in these dictionaries has been summarized by Miles in her study of the sixteenth century Pokoman (1957). She uses the Zúñiga and Morán dictionaries to reconstruct native political organization, religion, kinship, marriage, and family. Her study is a brilliant demonstration of the tremendous ethnographic potential of the early dictionary sources.

RELACIONES

Introduction

From the time of the first conquests in the New World until the end of the colonial period, the Spanish Crown demanded that its officials send reports describing conditions in the possessions. Many reports contain valuable accounts of native life which can be used for the reconstruction of native culture. A general caveat is called for, however, in using the sources. The Crown requested information in order to formulate policy for the newly subjected peoples, and to evaluate the performance of its officials. The officials who wrote these reports were aware of their uses, and often biased their accounts to further their own interests. Therefore, in evaluating the relaciones, it is important that we determine the degree of disinterestedness of the reporting officials.

In this section, I am grouping a rather diverse collection of reports. All were based on personal observations made in Guatemala, and all contain substantive information on native customs in the sixteenth century. They differ from the quasi-ethnographic sources mentioned mainly in terms of size and purpose. The relaciones were clearly originated by directive, their information is more controlled, and hence, briefer than the quasi ethnographies. In general, these reports show little interest in native cultures *per se*—the authors are not studying native culture, but are reporting on administrative subjects. Nevertheless, many reports are of high quality, and in some cases native informants were used to supply basic ethnographic information.

The best known relaciones are the *relaciones geográficas*, written between 1578 and 1586 (Cline n.d.b). The reports were prepared by various Spanish officials (usually corregidores or alcaldes mayores) in repsonse to questionnaires sent to them from the Crown's chronicler cosmographer. Of the fifty questions asked, numbers 13 to 15 are of special interest because they required that the officials describe native institutions "in heathen times." Unfortunately, of the ten to twenty relaciones geográficas which were probably prepared in Guatemala, only two are now known (*Relación Zapotitlán*, and *Relación Santiago* Atitlán).[33] During

---

[33] The loss of potential ethnographic information that this represents can be appreciated when one considers the importance of the relaciones geográficas

the rather tumultuous history of the relaciones geográficas, many may have been lost; though it is possible some may turn up, perhaps as a fairly large collection now hidden in some archive.

I have arranged the relaciones in chronological order. They span the period from 1552 to 1594. It is unfortunate that we have no relaciones written before 1550 (e.g., we are missing a report on the condition of the province prepared by Alvarado shortly after the conquest), though some records refer to that period.[34]

Relación Cerrato

Among the many reports to the Crown by Alonso López Cerrato, president of the *audiencia de los confines*, is a small relación on the political organization of the Guatemalan Indians before the conquest. It was written from Guatemala in 1552, almost thirty years after the conquest. Juan Bautista Muñós, the royal cosmographer, copied it in the 18th century, and it is now part of the Muñós collection of the Real Academia de la Historia, Madrid (Volume 68).[35] It has been published (CDI,1875:561-563); I include a copy as Appendix XVII.

At the beginning, Cerrato states that he was writing in fulfillment of a royal mandate to find out about the prehispanic political condition of the Indians of Guatemala. From the tenor of his report, it is clear that the mandate referred especially to tribute collection and judicial process. Unfortunately, Cerrato does not cite the source of his information. In his position of high authority, he could have easily called the leading caciques among

---

written in Texcoco (Pomar 1941) and Cholula (Rojas 1927). It is not inconceivable that comparable reports existed for Utatlán and Tecpán Guatemala, and perhaps also for Quezaltenango and Totonicapán. The loss may also be appreciated by comparing Guatemala's paltry two relaciones geográficas with the fifty-four we have for Yucatán (Cline n.d.b).

[34] I am indebted to the directors of the Archivo General de Indias, Sevilla, Spain, who allowed me to make photocopies of several relaciones and many other documents and supplied me photographic services.

[35] I am indebted to the directors of the Real Academia de la Historia, Madrid, who provided me with microfilm copies of parts of the Muñós collection. I cite from this collection by volume number, according to the numeration in the catalogue of Gómez Canedo, Volume I (1961).

the Indians into court to query them on such matters. Possibly, he merely relied on reports already available in the city of Santiago, though if this were true, it is likely he would have cited his source. At any rate, the fact that three Cakchiquel political groups are mentioned in the account along with the Quiche of Utatlán suggests that the information came from a Cakchiquel source.

His report is brief. The ethnographic information relates to the way tribute was paid to the prehispanic ruling class, and to the severity of judicial sanctioning imparted by the rulers.

Cerrato tried to treat the Indians fairly, and his presidency of the audiencia in Guatemala (1549-1555) was a period when they received much needed social justice (Recinos 1950:141, note 271). The Cakchiquel testified to this (Goetz 1953:136-151): "he condemned the Spaniards, he liberated the slaves and vassals of the Spaniards, he cut the taxes in two, he suspended forced labor and made the Spaniards pay all men, great and small. The lord Cerrato truly alleviated the sufferings of the people." As president of the audiencia he probably had direct but limited contact with the Indian caciques, and this is borne out by his *residencia*, which contains no major references to Indian affairs.

Cerrato was opposed to the tribute excesses exacted from the Indians by the encomenderos, and this possibly led him to minimize the severity of the native tribute system. Other sources make it clear that in spite of a statement by Cerrato to the contrary, the Quiche and Cakchiquel rulers collected taxes or tributes in addition to the services they received. For this reason and because of its brevity this relación must be classed as a minor document, to be used cautiously in conjunction with more reliable sources.

Relación Betanzos

This small report was included in a letter sent from Guatemala in 1559 to the King by Pedro de Betanzos. Probably prepared at the request of the audiencia in Guatemala, it was designed to provide expert testimony in connection with cacique Juan Cortés' appearance before the royal court to plead for special privileges. Though the other papers used at this important hearing have disappeared, Betanzos' report was preserved, and is now in the Archivo General de Indias (México 280; an incomplete version is in the Archivo Histórico Nacional, Madrid). Carrasco has published it in a study on the descendants of the prehispanic Quiche ruling lineage (1967a:255-259).

Betanzos does not indicate the source of his information, though he was renown for his knowledge of native language and custom (Vázquez 1937-1944:14:122-128). Apparently, he took a rigid stand against non-Christian practices,[36] and in the letter his testimony strongly condemned Juan Cortés' attempt to regain some of the privileges he had held as head of the leading lineage at Utatlán.

The ethnographic information is limited, but important. Because of the nature of the report his focus, necessarily, was on the kinds of relations which existed between the ruling lines of Utatlán and adjacent settlements and provinces. It also contains a few references to events in Quiche history.

No doubt, Betanzos was well acquainted with Quichean culture (by 1559 he had been in Guatemala fifteen years), and he provided insightful ethnographic material in his report. However, he underestimated the power and scope of the Quiche state centered at Utatlán apparently for two reasons: First, he derived his information mainly from the enemies of the Quiche—especially the Cakchiquel. Second, his own working philosophy favored rigid control by the Spaniards over the Indians for, as he clearly states, only by these means could the Indians be effectively proselytized. Therefore, it was logical for him to oppose any statement which would have imputed substantial influence by the native rulers over their people.

Once Betanzos' bias is taken into account, his report can be a useful supplement to other sources on the Quiche and their neighbors.

---

[36] In the debate between the Franciscans and the Dominicans over what term should be used for "God" in the doctrinals, the latter argued in favor of the Quichean term, *c'abawil*, while the former opted for the Spanish form, "*Dios*." Betanzos strongly opposed the use of the native term, its usage, he claimed, was a form of irreverence toward God. At his insistence, the term was prohibited to be used by all the religious orders by the presiding ecclesiastical authority (Vázquez 1937-1944:14:127).

Relación Garcés

This relación was sent by Diego Garcés, alcalde mayor of the province of Zapotitlán, to the audiencia in Guatemala (de los confines). The document is not dated, though from a reference to it in a later letter to the King, it can be placed in the year 1570. It was filed away with many other papers coming to the Spanish Council from the Indies, and is now located in the Archivo General de Indias (Guatemala 968). I have included a copy as Appendix XVIII.

Garcés was reporting to the audiencia on the tribute capacity of native settlements along the Pacific piedmont of Guatemala. He recognized that diverse reports from that zone had been given, and that as an official of the Crown it was his duty to set the record straight. He claimed to know his large province well, asserting that he had visited every part of it. Indeed, according to his statement in another letter he had served the Crown as an official in Guatemala for eighteen years (perhaps much of it in the Zapotitlán area).

The ethnographic information in this relación is limited. He describes in brief terms the distribution and quality of cacao production along the coast, and the general political geography there— especially the location of settlements and political ties between them.

Later, in a letter sent by Garcés to the King (1572), he provides a few observations about native customs of marriage and political control (AGI, Guatemala 55), (see Appendix XVIII). In that letter, Garcés again states his desire to fulfill the obligation of all officials of the Crown to report on conditions in their jurisdictions. His main objective in writing, however, was to obtain an encomienda grant for himself and his family. He mentions problems the Indians had in connection with paying tribute in cacao, and points to difficulties with the Indians because of their customs of early marriage, marriage outside the community, and collusion between elders and priests.

Garcés' description of cacao production is probably accurate, and provides us with the most useful information of the two letters. In the second letter, he wrote for his "bread," and his report is more biased; it should be used cautiously, and only in conjunction with more reliable sources.

Relación García de Palacio

This report was made in 1574 by Licenciado Diego García de Palacio, oidor of the audiencia of Guatemala.[37] It was sent to King Philip II as a response to one of the questionnaires about native life which had been sent to colonial officials by Ovando Godoy, and López de Velasco.[38] Palacio combined his special obligation to answer the questionnaire with his standing duty periodically to report on the condition of the peoples in his jurisdiction. As he visited the eastern provinces adjacent to the audiencia, he gathered information to aid in answering the questionnaire.

Herrera used data from Palacio's report in his early 17th century history, but the first full publication of it did not appear until the 19th century. I have used an 1866 edition appearing in the *Colección de Documentos Ineditados del Archivo de Indias,*

Much of Palacio's report was based on his personal observations—especially the geographical descriptions. He also queried the elders of each place he visited, presumably through interpreters, about their aboriginal history and customs. Apparently, from the area around Copán, he obtained a native "book," which he claims contained an account of the origin of the inhabitants of that area.[39] His report demonstrates that he was able to gather

---

[37] According to a note appended to the Miranda relación (1954:358), the original Palacio manuscript bears the date 1574. The published editions of the report all give the date of composition as 1576.

[38] These were precursors to the questionnaire of the *Relaciones Geográficas.* Palacio was probably responding to the 135-question form, for this questionnaire was sent out in 1573, the year after Palacio first entered service in the audiencia (Cline n.d.b). Apparently, Palacio did not attempt to answer all questions individually. It is unfortunate for us that he did not do so.

[39] Palacio does not give enough information about the "book" to enable us to determine whether it had a hieroglyphic text like those from Yucatán, a Mexican-style script like the ones used in the Quiche area, or a transcription into Spanish of a native language using Latin characters. He says of the book: "I have not found any books with their antiquities, nor do I believe that there is more than the one which I have in all this district. They say that anciently a great lord from the province of Yucatán had gone there and made these edifices, and that after a few years he returned alive to his land, and left it vacant (unpopulated). Of the fables they recount this appears to be the most correct one, because from the said memorial it appears that anciently the people of Yucatán conquered and subjected the provinces of

considerable ethnographic information during his circuit of the eastern provinces, for he claims that he had much additional material which he was not including in the report.[40]

The Palacio relación contains an important summary of linguistic boundaries in Guatemala at the time, and provides a list of various traits characteristic of native culture along the coast of El Salvador and eastern Guatemala. The most important part of the account is a detailed description of Pipil culture centered at Asunción Mita. Along with a few references in Fuentes y Guzmán, it makes up nearly our entire corpus of material on early Pipil culture in Guatemala.

Though we do not know much about the methods Palacio used, he appears to have been a good ethnographer. He obviously sought out persons who knew native customs well, but he does not usually cite them (e.g., where did he obtain his Pipil data?). The Miranda relación from Verapaz suggests that Palacio received some data on native custom from Spanish priests living in different areas of Guatemala. It is possible that his description of the Pipil from Mita came from such a report. If we were forced to rely on Palacio for any study of the Pipil, it could be done with some degree of confidence, for he is a fairly reliable source.

Relación Verapaz

This relación was written from Cobán toward the close of the year 1574 by Prior Francisco de Viana and two Dominican priests, Lucas Gallego and Guillermo Cadena. It was addressed to the king, most likely in response to the same questionnaire which prompted the relación prepared by Palacio earlier that year. This seems plausible because Verapaz was a province separate from Guatemala, though under the jurisdiction of the same audiencia. Appropriately, ecclesiastical authorities were the ones to respond, for Verapaz had been under Dominican rule in both secular and religious matters since its "pacification." Like several other re-

---

Acajal, Lacandón, Verapaz, the land of Chiquimula, and this one of Copán" (García de Palacio 1866:91-92).

[40] This is borne out by a later account prepared by Palacio (Paso y Troncoso 1939-1942:15:104-125). It shows that he possessed considerable knowledge of native social institutions.

laciones from Guatemala, the original manuscript is part of the Latin American collection of the University of Texas Library,[41] where a copy was obtained and published in 1955 by the Sociedad de Geografía e Historia de Guatemala.

The contents of the report show that it was composed by persons well acquainted with the geography, history, and native customs of Verapaz. Viana had come to Verapaz in 1556, and was famed for his knowledge of native language and culture there. Though nothing is known about Cadena, we know that Gallego had been in Verapaz at least since 1565, and that he had a good knowledge of native language and culture.[42] Much of their ethnographic data was based on personal observation and on studies carried out during the previous 15 to 20 years. Working at the provincial capital of Coban, they had access to the official records which were kept there in conjunction with the ecclesiastical and secular administration of the Indians. They cite tribute figures obtained from there different censuses, including the first tribute census for Verapaz in 1561 (Viana, Gallego, and Cadena 1955:29).

The ethnographic information of principal value for this study are the tribute (and hence population) figures, an outline of the distribution of native languages in the province, and a description of native production techniques (e.g., maize horticulture, quetzal feather "harvesting," cacao production). Each major community is described separately, but except for data on tribute payment, most information relates to the condition of Church property.

This relación appears to be highly reliable due to the authors' firsthand knowledge of native culture. One possible bias in the report (though a legitimate one), lies in the responsibility these and the other priests had for the material well-being of the Indians

[41] For a discussion of the history of the *Relaciones Geográficas* and similar documents as they were moved from one archive to another, see the article by Cline for the *Handbook of Middle American Indians* (n.d.b). All Guatemala *Relaciones* now in the University of Texas Library are part of a collection of documents purchased by that Library in 1934 from the heirs of Joaquín García Icazbalceta. Icazbalceta had obtained them in the 19th century from an unnamed source in Spain.

[42] Both Viana and Gallego signed the *Titulo del Barrio de Santa Ana* in 1565. Inasmuch as that document was written in Pokomchí, there can be little doubt that both knew the language.

in Verapaz. The report, in part, was a plea to the Crown for material aid to the province, and this may have caused them to con-
centrate on negative social conditions to the exclusion of information on aboriginal customs. Of course, they were biased on
those aspects of native culture directly related to their evangelical
work. One must be skeptical about statements like: "They (the
Indians) manifest enthusiasm for the things of our sacred religion,
without any trace of their ancient beliefs (*antigüedades*)" (Viana,
Gallega and Cadena 1955:29).

Relación Miranda

Fray Francisco Montero de Miranda sent his relación about Verapaz
to the oidor of the audiencia of Guatemala, Licenciado Palacio,
sometime between 1574 and 1579.[43] He claims that at the Audiencia
he overheard Palacio express an interest and curiosity in the "new
and notable" things of the province. He remembered this, and
upon being sent to labor in Verapaz he was careful to take note
of the "memorable things" there. His subsequent report was a
"work of love," sent to Palacio or "anyone to whom he might want
to give it." What happened to the manuscript after that is not
known, except that it went from Guatemala to Spain, then to
Mexico, and eventually into the Latin American Library of the
University of Texas. It was published by the Sociedad de Geográfia e Historia de Guatemala in 1954.

The information contained in the report was based on personal observation. Miranda queried some Indians, but it is doubt-
ful that he spoke any of their languages—he complained of the
large number of languages spoken there, and of the fact that hardly anyone spoke Mexican, probably the only native language with
which he was familiar. Apparantly, he did not consult the resident
friars about native customs.

---

[43] Miranda must have gone to Verapaz shortly after 1572; in that year he
served as a scribe for the royal audiencia in Guatemala (Vázquez 1937-44:
14:217). His report probably did not reach Palacio until after 1574, for in
Palacio's relación, written in 1574, there is no description of Verapaz. A *terminus ante quem* is provided by the year Palacio left the audiencia of Guatemala, 1579 (Warren n.d.).

The ethnographic information in his relación concerns matters of technology, such as craft manufacturing, cultivation of copal, extracting quetzal feathers. His best and most extensive data are on the natural and domesticated flora and fauna of Verapaz.

Miranda was an acute observer of the things that interested him, and he left us some high-quality descriptions. However, he did not penetrate deeply into the character of native culture. He was shocked by their condition of poverty, and this was a barrier which prevented him from taking their culture seriously.

Relación Geográfica Zapotitlán and Suchitepéquez

This is a standard composite relación geográfica (Cline n.d.b), prepared under the direction of the alcalde mayor of the province, *Capitán* Juan de Estrada. Estrada received the questionnaire from the audiencia in 1579, and with the aid of a scribe set out immediately to answer the questions. He sent copies of the questionnaire to several priests working in the area, asking for their help. When his correspondents did not respond quickly, he prepared the report himself, including a map of the province, completing it in the same year, 1579. The original is now part of the University of Texas, Latin American Library collection. The Sociedad de Geografia e Historia de Guatemala obtained a photocopy of the document, and published it in 1955 under the title, *Descripción de la Provincia de Zapotitlán y Suchitepéquez*. The map was published later by the same institution (Estrada 1966).

Estrada admitted that he did not know as much about his jurisdiction as he should, explaining that he had been there only a short time, and that he had been sick part of the time (1955:69). To make matters worse, none of his "expert" witnesses returned their responses to the questionnaire in time to include them in the report. Nevertheless, he communicated orally "with them and with others" (1955:81), and his contacts were either important Indian leaders or had ties with such persons, as shown by the important native título which he attached to his report (Recinos 1953:249; see Native Documents). Though information in his report about native customs came to him secondhand (he probably spoke no Indian language), the data about geographic matters are based on his own observations.[44] In addition, of course, he had access to official records kept in the *alcaldía mayor*, and from them he obtained the figures on tribute payment which were included in his map.

His ethnographic statements on native culture are brief, but specific. He gives important information concerning the languages spoken in the area, local flora and fauna (both natural and domesticated), native dress, weapons of war, saltmaking, and a few other cultural items. However, there is no extensive discussion of these cultural elements.

Estrada was not particularly sympathetic toward the Indians, and held little respect for their culture. He tends to play down or simplify their cultural accomplishments. It is to his credit, that he obtained information from people who understood aboriginal culture much better than he, and included it in his report. For this reason, his relación is a valuable addition to the corpus of documents on the Indians living along the Pacific coastal lowlands.

Relación Ponce

In 1584, Alonso Ponce was commissioned to visit the Franciscan convents scattered throughout New Spain to help put their affairs in order, and to report on conditions he found there. He was accompanied in his travels by a secretary and a Mexican-speaking interpreter. His relación, based on notes taken by his secretaries, was given the title, *Relación breve y verdadera de algunas cosas de las muchas que sucedieron al Padre Fray Alonso Ponce*. It was published in Madrid in 1873.

Ponce visited many Indian communities, especially those in the Pacific coastal lowlands. The notes describing each settle-

---

[44] Estrada's map demonstrates that he knew the Pacific coastal part of his jurisdiction well. Apparently his sickness (at least this is the reason he gives) prevented him from visiting its extension into the highlands of Western Guatemala. When one considers the size of this alcaldía mayor, and the difficult terrain it included within its boundaries, one can understand why the Spanish officials there did not make regular visits to all towns. Some seven years earlier Garcés deemed the fact that he had visited the northern part of the same alcaldía mayor worthy of mentioning in a letter to the king.

ment and province were apparently made on location. Much information came from local priests, some was obtained by the interpreter, who found Mexican speaking Indians all along the coast from Soconusco to Nicaragua. Other data consist of observations made by the scribes and Ponce.

The report contains only sketchy ethnographic descriptions on cacao production and methods of fishing. Its primary significance consists in the outline it provides of the linguistic, economic, and physical geography of the Indians of the Pacific lowlands (for an effective use of Ponce's report, see Thompson 1948).

The Ponce report is like a diary; straightforward narration and description seem to dominate over any special purposes for which it might have been composed. The Indians are treated as a natural part of the land, and as subjects (more or less faithful) of the Church. A usual notation about the Indians states how well they had received Ponce during his visit. Each description typically consists of only a phrase or two, and not even the affairs of the friars are given in detail. We get the impression that the trip and its accompanying rigors were the important matters, somewhat in the manner of a modern travelogue. Though the report is of some value in studying the Indians of Guatemala, it is primarily a history of one important visita.

Relación Geográfica Atitlán and Aguacatepec

This is a complex relación geográfica (Cline n.d.b) written in 1585 in response to the second edition of the questionnaire sent by the Crown's cosmographer. It was prepared under the direction of the corregidor and guardián of Atitlán, with collaboration from Tzutujil-speaking elders. Two separate reports were made, one for Santiago Atitlán, the other for San Bartolomé Aguacatepec. They are closely connected with each other; much of the second report repeats information contained in the first.

A map of the Lake Atitlán area was attached to the report. We are not told who prepared the map, though judging from statements by the scribes, it would appear that the native elders played an important role in its composition. The report was sent to the audiencia and from there to Spain. Like the other relaciones geográficas from Guatemala, it became part of the University of Texas collection. Based on photocopies from Texas, the report from Santiago Atitlán was published by the Sociedad de Geográfia e Historia de Guatemala in 1964, and the following year the same organization published the map and report from Aguacatepec (Betancor and Arboleda 1965).

The geographical observations and general statistical information in the report were supplied by Fray Pedro de Arboleda and the corregidor, Alonso Páez Betancor. They had access to official ecclesiastical and civil records, and Arboleda had lived among the Tzutujil speakers for at least eight years by 1585 (Vázquez 1937-44:14:219, note 1). He knew the Tzutujil language well, having worked in both Aguacatepec and Atitlán, and having visited the other Tzutujil towns of the district. Betancor's participation appears to have been minor.

Both at Atitlán and Aguacatepec the oldest and most important native leaders, including the governor of each town, were used as informants on all matters specifically relating to prehispanic native history and culture. The relevant questions were asked of them either in Tzutujil by Arboleda, or in Mexican by the scribe,[45] and an unusually large number of native terms were transcribed in their Nahua forms. Because many responses of the Aguacatepec report are identical in phraseology to those for Santiago Atitlán, it would appear that where the officials found no great variation in the responses given, they merely rewrote what had been recorded at Atitlán.

This relación is a rich source of information on prehispanic Quichean culture and the geography of the area. Especially detailed are the descriptions of native political organization, dress, military arms, ritual sacrifice, and the medicinal use of natural herbs and plants. The Aguacatepec report adds details on the use of divination by the prehispanic rulers and the kinds and uses of tobacco.

This is the most useful relación available. Almost all the ideal ingredients of a sound ethnographic study went into its

---

[45] It is not clear why Mexican was used to obtain information from the elders, for we are told that in Atitlán and Aguacatepec only a few men spoke that language. Because the scribe, apparently, could speak Mexican but not Tzutujil, it is possible that it was used so that he could obtain data independent of Arboleda, or in order to facilitate the transcription of data obtained by Arboleda.

production. Arboleda was a good observer, and had long exposure to native languages and culture. Informants who had lived during aboriginal times were questioned in their native language. Key native terms were not only translated, but transcribed in the report. A broad range of cultural topics was described. The best statistics available for the inhabitants under study were included.

The ethnographic characteristics of the report are the direct result of the questionnaire which produced the other relaciones geográficas. The relación shows the enormous ethnographic potential of this type of report. Perhaps its only weak point is that it was written by the scribe rather than by Arboleda, and therefore has a slight Nahua bias.

Relación Pineda

This report was made by Juan de Pineda in fulfillment of a commission to discover the reasons why native tributes paid to the Crown were less than those paid to the encomenderos. He was ordered to visit the settlements and provinces under the jurisdiction of the audiencia, to take a tribute count, and to inform the president and judges on the kind of adjustments which were needed. The investigatory trip was apparently made at the beginning of the last decade of the 16th century and the report was written in 1594. It was first published in 1925 by the Sociedad de Geografía e Historia de Guatemala under the title, *Descripción de la Provincia de Guatemala.*

It is apparent from the document that Pineda had been concerned with Indian tribute payment long before his commission toward the end of the 16th century. As an official of the audiencia in 1557, Pineda had been commissioned to count prospective tributaries among Indians living around Santiago Guatemala (those who had until then been free from tribute payment). Thereafter, he apparently continued to serve at the audiencia, for in his report he notes the inaction on the part of its high officials with respect to what he felt were abuses against the Crown's rightful tributes (1925:357). It must be assumed, therefore, that his information on the Indians was derived from long experience in dealing with them as an official, as well as from his later visit to most of the major communities of the province. Surprisingly, he never learned any of the native languages and had to rely on interpreters when conversing with the Indians.

The ethnographic data in the report are related to economic matters of tribute payment, though there are a few more general descriptions (e.g., on the way kinship ties facilitated trade between lowland and highland natives). His report does not include specific figures for tribute and population sizes.

Pineda was not sympathetic towards the Indians, and felt they were cheating the Spanish government. As a zealous supporter and apologist for the Crown, he was biased, and probably overestimated the economic capacity of the Indians. His report was made late, though this is perhaps compensated for by the knowledge he had gained during his forty years of prior residence. For these reasons, the Pineda report, though it contains useful information on the Indians, must be used with caution.

RECORDS

Introduction

In varying degrees the relaciones we discussed are official records, i.e., reports prepared for an official organization so that its business might be effectively conducted. The records grouped together here differ from the relaciones in several ways. In the records, information specifically about the Indians and their way of life is generally more abbreviated than in the relaciones. In many cases the Spanish officials who compiled the records attempted to gather data in a form so condensed that they could be quantified. Here I have included various statistical reports, covering such aspects of native society as population size, eligible tributaries, production potentials, number of settlements, and the like. Obviously, the data represent abstractions of native culture, and the abstracting was done in Spanish, not in native categories. This meant that the Spaniards could more readily convert the data into programs of action. For the student of native culture, however, reconversion to aboriginal forms is problematic and difficult.

Another characteristic of the records is their tangential or incidental references to native culture. The information is strongly biased by the specific goals the officials had in mind as they gathered and reported their data. This must be taken into consideration. Because the categories are tightly controlled, other information on native culture often was allowed to vary randomly. This is especially true of the judicial records, where ethnographic facts about the Indians that were incidental to the case appear in relatively neutral or unbiased form. The advantage to the ethnographer is somewhat counterbalanced, however, by the brevity and scarcity of data.

The large number of records, and the differences in their size and quality, make it inappropriate to discuss each document separately. I have grouped them into three categories, somewhat arbitrarly, though I think they have heuristic value. They roughly correspond to the *hacienda*, *patronato*, and *judicial* categories of Spanish political organization. I shall refer to them as statistical, administrative, and judicial records.

The collection of Spanish records is especially incomplete. The number of records of this type for 16th century Guatemala must be tremendous.[46] I have included only those records with information on the Indians of 16th century Guatemala which have been published, or which I have been able to locate (mostly in the Archivo General de Indias, and Archivo General de Centroamérica).[47] My emphasis, in each category, is on the significant records for this study, though I realize that for other purposes records absent or barely mentioned may be of considerable importance.

Statistical Records

I have been unable to find tribute records on the Guatemalan Indians for the 25 years following the conquest, though there

---

[46] I understand that Dr. Reina of the University of Pennsylvania in cooperation with faculty members from the Universidad de Sevilla is attempting to obtain photocopies of all important records for 16th century Guatemala from the Archivo General de Indias. This monumental undertaking is important for the future of ethnohistoric research and I hope a listing of the films will be made available to interested scholars.

[47] I am indebted to the directors and staff of the Archivo General de Centroamérica, Guatemala, for the excellent service they rendered during my visits in 1964, 1966, 1968, and 1969, and for allowing me to obtain Xerox copies of several documents.

are scattered figures in the Spanish and native documents we have discussed.

Both Marroquín and Maldonado took tribute censuses before 1540, but unfortunately the records are no longer available (Sáenz 1963:95-96; CDI, 1925:155). Marroquín claims that by 1537 he had visited all towns of Guatemala, and that he had "made a census of the whole *gobernación*" (Sáenz 1963:95). Probably, Marroquín is the source of the few population figures given by Las Casas (Las Casas 1958:105:157; Sáenz 1963:96). The earliest and most important tribute record available is the famous 1549-1551 census (Roys 1957:10), which is now in the Archivo General de Indias (Guatemala 128). It gives the number of tributaries, names of encomenderos, and amount of tribute payment for most towns of Guatemala (but not Verapáz), Yucatán, and the other provinces of Central America. The list for Guatemala was prepared between 1548 and 1551 by President Cerrato, assisted by his oidores (especially Ramírez).

From other references to the census, we have a few details on how it was carried out (especially in Muñós n.d.: Vols. 66-69). Cerrato visited many towns in order to take the census, and used local caciques and elders to assure an accurate count. Apparently, part of the census was made through reports from some towns instead of visits. Marroquín severely criticized Cerrato for the practice (Sáenz 1963:96). The figures obtained were not popular with the Spaniards who argued that the new census was unnecessary because earlier counts existed. Apparently the number of eligible tributaries was significantly lowered by Cerrato, presumably in recognition of native losses through death, and by granting additional tribute immunities to caciques. In addition, the amount of tribute payment required of each tributary was curtailed, which, along with the freeing of Indian slaves, brought down on Cerrato the everlasting wrath of the Spanish residents of Guatemala.[48]

---

[48] The courageous action Cerrato took on behalf of the Indians is impressive. He incurred the anger of Spanish officials, secular and ecclesiastic, high and low, and of the encomenderos, whose attitude toward the Indians can be gauged by their evaluation of Cerrato. This mid-16th century humanitarian is worthy of a serious biography, especially because there is considerable docu-

Inasmuch as I do not wish to analyze the census data, I will mention briefly some problems connected with their use. We should recognize that Cerrato attempted to make an accurate and complete assessment of eligible native tributaries, though he probably was only partially successful. There must have been distortions by the natives, for it was to their advantage to report a smaller number of inhabitants than actually lived in any town (the Indians paid tribute by town not by individual). There were many Indians who had not come under the jurisdiction of any town, and who did not figure in the tribute lists. Evidence of this is scattered in the writings of Spanish officials of the period; even today large numbers of Indians escape modern census counts. Caciques, the sick, the old, and children exempt from tribute payment are not listed, and will have to be estimated through other sources.

There are more direct problems connected with the use of the census for reconstructing native population. Tributaries are not recorded for all towns listed in the report, whereas some towns have two or even three counts recorded for them (probably because of the division of the population of some towns between two or more encomenderos). Nor is it possible to identify all town names with prehispanic settlements or modern communities. The names of almost all towns are given in Mexican form, a usage not nearly so widespread today as it was for Spanish officials in the 16th century.

In spite of these problems, the Cerrato census is an important record for the study of early native demography and economy. We are aided in its use by the fact that Juan López de Velasco, the first cosmographer-chronicler of the Crown, used it in compiling his section on Central America for the *Geografía y Descripción Universal de las Indias y Demarcación de los Reyes de Castilla* (1952). His account is mainly a tributary record, and even though it was prepared in 1571-1574, it is mainly based on the 1549-1551 census.[49] Evidently, Velasco had access to other

---

mentary material available (including his unfinished residencia) in the Archivo General de Indias.

[49] This can be determined by comparing his tribute figures with those of the Cerrato census. His use of that record provides a lead to the meaning

kinds of data which he included in his report, such as tributary figures for Verapaz (apparently from a census made in 1561).

Muñós summarized the tributary data of this census in the 18th century, and provided a few interpretive remarks on their meaning (n.d.: Vol. 85). More recently, Paso y Troncoso published that part of the record which refers to Yucatán; it includes data on a few Guatemalan towns (1939:5:208-217).

For the twenty years following the Cerrato census, we lack detailed tributary and population statistics. However, two documents from this period are of extreme importance for early Gautemalan demography. One is a detailed tributary census taken in 1562 by the audiencia (the task was assigned to a *regidor* from Santiago Guatemala). We have data for Chimaltenango, Zumpango, San Juan and San Pedro Sacatepéquez, Comalapa (Cakchiquel); Petapa, Santa Inéz, and Amatitlán (Pokomán) (AGI, Gautemala 45).[50] The quantitative data in these records are less important than the other kinds of information they contain. For example, the process of taking a census is clearly illustrated—much of the responsibility for accuracy and completeness was laid upon the shoulders of the local officials and elders. The percentage and specific components of native population exempted from tribute payment are clearly defined. Some basic social divisions of the communities are identified—that is, tributaries are given by *parcialidades*, usually by their aboriginal names. This is a valuable list of sixteenth century surnames and economic activities for each town because the tributaries are listed by names and often by profession. The other document, a census taken in Vera-

---

of some of the information it contains. The Velasco case should serve as a warning to the ethnohistorian reconstructing early demographic patterns, for often tribute figures cited for one year are based on data gathered many years earlier.

[50] Apparently, the census record for Amatitlán mentioned is the same 1559-1562 "account book" to which Miles refers in her study of the Pokoman (1957: 742:779). She used a Bureau of American Ethnology copy of the original, which is probably the document from the Archivo General de Indias, Audiencia de Guatemala, Legajo 45. Unfortunately, I do not have a photocopy of that document to compare with Miles' notes.

There is a list of Indian inhabitants from Amatitlán in the 1570 residencia of Licenciado Briceño (AGI, Justicia 317), which I suspect is a more formal version of the 1562 census.

paz sometime between 1561 and 1567[51] is now in the Real Academia de la Historia, Madrid. We do not know who prepared it, nor does it contain information about the process of census taking. In one half of the document the tributaries are numerically accounted for, in the other, numbers of tributaries and their specific requirements are given in narrative form. Unlike the first document, the social components of each town are not indicated, though in one instance the existence of Alcalá Indians at Cobán is mentioned. An important feature of the record is that it contains a list of the number of caciques, of old and sick people, and of deserters not paying tribute in each town. Along with similar data from other documents, we can use this kind of information to interpret other census records (including the Cerrato census of 1549-1551).

We have noted that some relaciones contain Guatemalan tributary numbers for the 1570-1585 period (especially the *Relación Geográfica Zapotitlán*). In addition, I have located four other census records prepared by ecclestical officials between 1570 and 1585. The first census was written in 1570 by the *fiscal* of the province of Guatemala, who purportedly gives the number of *vecinos* within the jurisdiction of the bishopric (AGI, Guatemala 394). When we compare the figures with those from other sources, it becomes apparent that tributaries instead of individual persons have been recorded. The author warns that his data are based on "common knowledge," and that there were actually many more persons in the province than had been recorded. A second census record, similar to the first, though more limited in scope, was prepared in 1575 by the head of the Franciscan Order. He purportedly lists all persons in Guatemala administered by the Franciscan priests (AGI, Guatemala 169). Here again, the figures appear to refer to tributaries rather than to individuals. The census is incomplete, for other Indians were under Dominican and Mercedarian control, and some were administered by the

[51] The document is not dated, but contains a statement to the effect that the year 1567 had not yet arrived. Because it cannot be the first census, which was taken in Verapaz in 1561 (Viana, et al. 1955:29), the date of composition must be somewhere between 1561 and 1567.

seculares.[52] The two records should be used with utmost caution, only in conjunction with other sources for which we have better information on the meaning of their contents.

The third census from this period formed part of the official 1570 registry on Guatemala in the Council of the Indies (CDI, 1925:178-180). It consists of a simple list of towns in the "district of Guatemala" which had priests, grouped according to religious order. For each town the number of vecinos is given, along with the rent (in pesos) paid to the resident priests. No details are given how the data were collected, though we may assume that the work was done under ecclesiastical direction. The figures apparently refer to tributaries rather than to individual members of the population.

The fourth document is perhaps the most useful one. It is a census record for the Indians of Guatemala made by the *deán* and *cabildo de catedral* of Guatemala, at the command of Juan de Ovando, *visitador* in 1572 (the original document is in the University of Texas Library). The Indian towns of the province of Guatemala are listed according to the religious orders amdinistering them, beginning with the secular priests, followed by the Franciscans, Mercedarians, and Dominicans. Except for Indian towns under Dominican jurisdiction, for larger towns the *cabecera* name, subject towns, encomenderos, tributary number, and names of caciques are given. The value of the document is greatly enhanced by statements (in most cases) on the sources of information for each entry. For example, in the case of Samayaque, we are told that the data were taken from a census made by the *cura* and *vicario* living there. The data for all Dominican towns came from a memorial sent by that order. Throughout the report population figures are given as representing individual persons, though actually they represent tributary units. This is recognized, for the authors at the end of the document state that "many sons, daughters, women, widows, and orphans" are not given in the report. The

---

[52] The Franciscan priest who prepared this record sent a similar document to the Crown in 1582 (AGI, Guatemala 171), in response to a request that the religious orders justify their need for additional priests. The good friar appears to have performed the task conscientiously, for the population figures, though close to those oi 1575, show a slight decrease in numbers.

independent and local sources from which the various data were obtained mean that the record is somewhat unbalanced, but also make it one of the most important population censuses we have for the 16th century.

About 1580, Licenciado García de Valverde, president of the audiencia of Guatemala, carried out the second major 16th century tributary census. He specifically mentions Cerrato 's earlier census (AGI, Guatemala 10), arguing that many years had passed since that count had been made, and that the Indians and the encomenderos had requested the new count. Assisted by his oidores, he personally directed the census work between 1578 and 1582. The record of the census, prepared by the audiencia scribe, was sent to the Crown toward the end of 1582, and is now in the Archivo General de Indias (Guatemala 966).

The census contains numerous references to a prior tributary count for each town, apparently a modified version of the original Cerrato figures. In studying the new count and tribute assignment, it becomes clear that the population had declined, and that Valverde lowered both the total tribute assignment for each town, and the amount of each individual payment.

Like Cerrato, it appears that Valverde attempted to treat the Indians more fairly than his predecessors.[53] Because of this we might expect his census record to be more accurate than those made by less enlightened officials.[54] His record has special value because of the double set of tributary figures it contains. Its value is impaired, however, by the fact that data for many towns are lacking.

---

[53] That year, Valverde, in a report to the Crown, (1582) (AGI, Guatemala 10), deplored the situation which had developed in Guatemala, where living tributaries were forced to pay for the dead. He began to require that the priests keep records of deceased tributaries, so that the total tribute assessment of a town might be lowered accordingly. The new census of the Indian population, in part, revealed the decline in eligible tributaries which had occurred over the previous twenty to thirty years.

[54] With the possible exception of Las Casas there appears to be little likelihood that any Spanish official would have been so zealous in his defense of the Indians as to bias Indian tributary figures downward. The most that can be expected in the cases of Valverde and Cerrato is that, probably, they did not bias the figures upward.

Administrative Records

To reconstruct prehispanic Indian culture, the administrative records are less important than the statistical and the judicial records. However, they are useful for studying early colonial history, and the Spaniards', administration of their colony. For this reason I include only a brief description of a small portion of the extant documents.

The earliest documents are letters and reports written by Spanish officials at Santiago Guatemala. One such source is the first cabildo record of Santiago Guatemala, which was initiated in 1524 (the year of the conquest) and terminated in 1530. Already by 1590 the first few pages of this record were in bad state of repair, and an official of the cabildo put the pages in order and prepared a new cover for the volume. With this new protection, the entire book, except the first entry (on the founding of the city of Santiago), was preserved. It was published in 1934 as *Libro Viejo de la Fundación de Guatemala*, by the Sociedad de Geografía e Historia de Guatemala. As might be expected, its references to the Indians are limited. There is a brief description of early ecological differences between the plains of Chimaltenango and the valley of Almolonga (now Antigua); the continuing conquest of the Indians is cursorily noted.

Brief notices on the Indians are also contained in a number of scattered official reports and letters sent during the 1530s from the gobernación. The originals can be found in the Archivo de Indias (especially, Guatemala 45, 156), and most have been published in four important collections: *Cartas de Indias* (CDI, 1875), *Colección de Documentos Antiguos del Ayuntamiento de Guatemala* (Anonymous 1935a), *Papeles del Consejo de Indias* (CDI, 1925) and *Los Escritos de don Francisco Marroquín* (Sáenz 1963:193-312).

The *Papeles del Consejo de Indias* contains an especially valuable synopsis of early colonial history, based on reports from the 16th and the 17th centuries. This and the other documents contain scraps of ethnographic information on the Indians. For example, a 1530 report made by the treasurer at Guatemala, refers to the conquest proceeding at the time, mentioning by name the rebellious Quiche and Cakchiquel rulers (AGI, Guatemala 45).

Another early record is a 1535 visita report made by Maldonado (oidor from the audiencia of México) to the province of Guatemala (AGI, Patronato 180, no. 64). Mainly matters of Spanish government are recorded, though there are also a few references to continuing phases of the conquest of the Indians. The testimony of both Alvarado and Maldonado are recorded, so that their accounts can be compared with each other in order to derive a fairly accurate picture of the condition of the Indians at the time (1535).

Some data on the names of specific native rulers and the events of the conquest are contained in a series of formal title and privilege grants made by the Crown to the Indian caciques who aided the Spaniards in the conquest. Undoubtedly, as noted by Remesal (1932:4:227), some of these *cédulas reales* have been lost. We have a record for: A certificate issued in 1541, in which Don Juan of Atitlán, Don Jorge of Tecpán Atitlán, and Don Miguel of Chichicastenango are granted permission to aid the Dominicans in the pacification of Verapaz (Remesal 1932:4:228); a 1542 grant of privilege and coat of arms to Don Juan of Atitlán for his aid in the pacification of Verapaz and Lacandón;[55] a similar grant (without coat of arms) issued in 1543 to the Mam cacique of Sacatepéquez (AGC, A3:226-4086); and a 1544 grant of privilege to Don Jorge of Tecpán Atitlán, for service rendered in the peaceful conquest of Verapaz (Remesal 1932:I:227). A related document is a cédula issued by the Crown in 1555, praising the mode of government existing among the Indians of Verapaz under the rule of cacique Apobatz (Konetzke 1953:1962:I:330-332).

For the period of 1545 to 1555, many letters and brief reports were sent to the Crown from the audiencia (they are now in the Archivo General de Indias). Most contain only the briefest references to the Indians and their culture, and perhaps their primary importance is in the view they provide of the Indian's continual struggles against Spanish domination. One such example is a report by Cerrato to the Crown in 1550, in which he describes the encomiendas of Guatemala, in a few instances outlining the way

---

[55] This cédula contains a pictorial representation and written description of the coat of arms granted to Don Juan. It has been erroneously classified with the audiencia of Charcas (#56) in the Archivo General de Indias.

they were established through conquest (AGI, Guatemala 968A). Muños has conveniently summarized and extracted pertinent parts of a series of these varied reports from Guatemala for the years 1542 to 1555 (Muños n.d.: Vols. 65-69). His extracts refer to the pacification of Verapaz, Zorita's congregation activities in Sacapulas, and other bits of information on Spanish-Indian relations.

Finally, two later records are worthy of mention. One is a set of instructions and ethnographic orientations prepared by Licenciado Palacio, oidor of the audiencia, for officials assigned to take tribute counts for the Crown. The document is not dated, but was probably written shortly after his relación of 1574 (certainly long after the 1549-1551 tribute list with which it is filed in the Archivo General de Indias). Paso y Troncoso published it in 1939 (Vol. 15). It contains references to a few native customs, but does not specify the source of information, or social group to which they pertain. It is clear that in at least one instance his account was taken from the Pipil source he used in his relación (1939:4:123), though he felt that the practices he described were general to the whole province (and even to all of New Spain).

The other report was prepared in 1582 by García de Valverde, as part of his duties as president of the audiencia (AGI, Guatemala 10). He describes problems associated with Indian tribute payment in the province, and refers to a few native customs from the Salvadorean community of Izalcos.

Judicial Records

The documents summarized in this category are records of land disputes between Indian communities during the first decades after the conquest. In many instances they are incorporated in legal papers which postdate the conquest by two or more centuries, and thus served as evidence of prior possession of the disputed territory. For this reason, these valuable primary documents tend to be hidden within large land title *expedientes* of the 17th and 18th centuries, and no doubt many important sources await discovery.

They are the kind of judicial records which in other cases yielded the native títulos. In fact, the classification of a document as título instead of judicial record is in some cases arbitrary. In any case, we are dealing with 16th century native testimony on the prehispanic condition of land relationships. Generally, where the native rulers prepared a detailed document with specific references to the preconquest period, I have classified it as a native document. Where the testimony of native witnesses was recorded by Spanish officials, or a small petition prepared by native litigants was brief or briefly summarized by the Spanish scribe, I have classified the document as judicial record.

Several judicial records refer to the Quiché Indians of the central highlands. Perhaps the most important are records of attempts by descendants of the Quiché rulers to retain control of servile groups they had held before the conquest. They did this successfully during some 275 years of Spanish rule, and in the process were required, many times, to present documentary substantiation of their claims. Contreras (1965) has commented on one collection of such records of 1788, which contains references to documents written in 1569, 1730, 1774, and 1788 (AGC, Al: 202-4090). He notes that the "feudal right" was finally ended by royal decree in 1801.

Carrasco (1967a:252-260) has commented upon this same expediente, and describes another one from the same archive which contains citations to documents from 1574, 1592, and 1596 (AGI, Al:205-4985). He also clarifies (1967a:252-260) the fact that one of the descendants had taken the case to Spain, and quotes an important document written there in 1557 (AGI, Guatemala 386). In addition, Carrasco cites (1967a) a letter sent in 1595 from the audiencia on this same subject (AGI, Guatemala 10).

I have located two other collections of documents related to this case in the Archivo General de Centroamérica (AI:1587-10231; 205-4985). These records contain citations to documents from 1569, 1574, 1589, 1592, 1593, 1692, 1730, 1788. I have extracted from these sources the most relevant material for reconstructing prehispanic Quiché relations, and, with pertinent parts from the published extracts of the documents cited by Carrasco, include them as Appendix XIX.

These records provide an important view of 16th century social structure at the Quiché capital. In addition, principles of succession within the ruling line, and family organization of the servile group are clarified. We can be reasonably sure of the accuracy of the information because of the care and even hostility with which the officials of the audiencia processed this grant of special cacique privileges.[56]

We have other judicial papers which record an attempt by the descendants of a secondary ruling line at Utatlán to claim special privileges (AGC, Al:4678-40252). Cacique Juan de Rosales made the claim in 1603 to the audiencia, presenting a petition which his father (Diego Pérez) had used in 1564. A few names of social groupings and persons from the prehispanic period are mentioned, including the name of the descent group to which Rosales belonged, Ajtzic Winak.[57] There is also a brief description of the principle of succession under which Quiche rule operated. The data rest rather firmly on the testimony of several important elders from Utatlán, called as expert witnesses by the audiencia.

Another judicial record with information on 16th century native political relations contains a 1588 claim to *rezago* (residue) tributes made by the Crown against the communities of Tecpán Guatemala (Sololá) and Quezaltenango (AGC, A3:2800-40485). Through the treasurer of the audiencia, the Crown charged that local tribute collectors in the two communities had not turned in the full tribute amount during previous years. In the process of investigating this case, through witnesses and written records of various kinds, many features of social organization in these communities are clarified. I have extracted the most significant ethnographic parts from the documents and included them as Appendix XX.

Carrasco has called attention (1964) to the importance of this document for reconstructing 16th century Indian social pat-

---

[56] The Spanish officials, some of them creoles, argued it was not just that the Indians should continue to receive special services which had been discontinued for the encomenderos. The royal grant continued, nevertheless, though some rights of service were restricted in ensuing years.

[57] On this record, it is difficult to make out the name of the parcialidad which Rosales and his father headed. In one place it appears to be given as Awich huinah abac, and in another as Xazih huinah avah. My identification of this with the Quiche descent group, the Ajtzic Winak (Abaj?) (Recinos 1953:231) is probably correct, though the Spanish scribe so badly garbled the terms that I am not certain of this transcription.

terns, and I have warned (Carmack 1966b) of the possibility that significant modification in these patterns already had taken place by 1588. This is not to say that there is any reason seriously to question the accuracy of statements in these documents about social organization in the Indian towns at the time. Both the description of how tribute was collected, and of the organization of the calpules, were made by persons who had firsthand acquaintance with the facts.

I have located a few additional land-dispute documents from Quiche-speaking communities of the highlands in the Archivo General de Centroamérica. One document is a 1596 dispute over land situated between Joyabaj and Sacualpa (AGC, A1:5933-51884). In the testimony given by the elders of each community, we learn that the Indians of Sacualpa (at least some) had been resettled with those of Joyabaj, at a time when they were called the chajoma. Various toponyms for the area are listed in the document, and the economic uses made of the land in aboriginal times are described. Because witnesses from the disputant communities agreed about the kind of social relations which existed between the two groups before the conquest, the accuracy of the document on that point seems assured.

There are two documents from Sacapulas similar to the one from Sacualpa. In one, (AGC, A1:6025-53132), a record from 1572 is cited, which contained a description of a dispute between two parcialidades from Sacapulas over land, political office, and rights to graze sheep. We learn that three Indian towns (Sacualpa, Coatán, Iztapaneca) were grouped together into one parcialidad (Citalá). This same packet of documents contains a small land title from Sacapulas written in Quiche (1613), (see Appendix XXV), and a record of tributaries from the two disputant parcialidades (AGC, A1:5942-51995). The tribute list, apparently made around 1572, has been summarized and included as Appendix XXI. The other document from Sacapulas (AGC, A1:5936-51914), records a dispute over territory situated between Sacapulas and San Andrés Sajcabajá. Among the papers are three small testimonials written by Indian caciques from Sacapulas (dated 1600-1601), two in Spanish and one in Quiche. These documents, along with the *Título Sacapulas* refer to the names of several aboriginal social groupings and geographical boundaries in the area. The small Quiche document written in 1600 has already been described as *Título Uchabaja* (see Native Documents).

Three small judicial records from the highlands which contain minimum information about 16th century Quiche patterns may be mentioned. The first, written in 1537, is the record of a dispute between Pedro de Alvarado and another conquistador, Ortega Gómez, over encomienda rights to the Indians of Chichicastenango (AGI, Justicia 1031, No. 1). The aboriginal name of the leading cacique and parcialidad of the town is revealed— Izquin. The second document contains a request made to the audiencia in 1570 by a Spaniard, Gómez de Escalante, for vacant lands located to the east of Quezaltenango. The Quiche names of several important topographical features near the site are recorded. The third document records a dispute in 1600, over land within the territory of Rabinal (Tequicistlán) (AGC, Al:5935-51899). A few native toponyms in the vicinity are the only ethnographic data of significance.

Another cluster of 16th century judicial records referring to Quiche-speaking Indians is available from the Zapotitlán province in the Pacific lowlands. The two most important records were transcribed in the residencia against Licenciado Briceño in 1570, at the completion of his service as governor of the Audiencia de los Confines (AGI, Justicia 316, 317). The first is a report of a tribute count taken at Samayaque in 1570. Upon completion of the census the official sent by Briceño (Pablo de Escobar) demanded that the Indians of the town provide him with fresh fish to take back to Guatemala (so several witnesses testified). The description of how the fishing expedition was organized and the techniques used to catch the fish provides a useful view of native economic patterns in that area. Descriptions of this kind are highly reliable, because they are incidental to the main issue of the judicial proceedings, and are repeated by several witnesses, both caciques and commoners.

Another case in the Briceño residencia concerns a 1561 dispute over lands situated between San Francisco Zapotitlán and Zambo. Testimony gathered by the defender of the Indians, sent to the disputant towns to resolve the dispute, includes useful information on the names of important aboriginal rulers in that area, and the names of boundaries which existed between Zambo and Zapotitlán before and after the conquest. The testimony of several witnesses living before the Spaniards had arrived are of special value.

The record of another land dispute in which Zambo figured prominently has been located in the Archivo General de Centroamérica (A1:5928-51825; see also A1:5929-51833). In 1578-1579 an attempt by the natives of Zambo to obtain lands along the coast for agricultural use was stringently resisted by the caciques of Mazatenango, Zapotitlán, and other towns, who claimed that they had occupied the lands "since time immemorial." Testimony given during the litigation reveals much about the geography of the area and the kind of agricultural production practiced there. There is a brief, illuminating account of the changes taking place in the settlement pattern of Zambo in the first years after the conquest. The ethnographic information in this document was meant to be secondary to the facts of the dispute, and, therefore, is less susceptible to distortion; it was also repeated by several witnesses.

In connection with the Zapotitlán coastal lowlands, there are two additional small records in the Princeton University Library (Robert Garrett Collection, Quiché 103). They contain the record of disputes over land between Samayaque, Suchitepéquez, and San Luís (1587-1589). There is little information of ethnographic interest, except native names. In the case of the San Luís document, a brief account of the rules of succession to cacao plantations is given.

For the Cakchiquel, Kekchi, and Pokoman Indians to the east of the Quiche, we have a few litigation papers worthy of mention, though none as important as those discussed.[58] For the Cakchiquel, I have located three important packets containing documents on 16th century land dispute litigation. One, written in 1565, is the record of a dispute over land between San Jaun and San Pedro Sacatepéquez, and Sumpango (AGC, A1:5928-51820). In another 17th century dispute from Chimaltenango, a 1577 do-

[58] Obviously, I have not searched as diligently for records from this area, but instead have concentrated on the Quiche area. It is my impression that 16th century litigation papers are not as common for that area, though additional research might turn up more. Especially worthy of research is the Verapaz region, where German ethnologists found several such documents at the close of the 19th century.

cument is cited which records a conflict over land between Indians from that town, and Párramos and Itzapa (AGC, Al:6064-53973). In another case, the Indians of San Juan Sacatepéquez presented a 1590 título to support them in their 18th century litigation with surrounding towns over lands on their borders (AGC, Al: 5984-59612). The useful ethnographic data contained in these documents are a few aboriginal names of groups and places still in use after two or three centuries of Spanish domination.

For the Pokomán of the Amatitlán area we have extracts of judicial records made at the audiencia in 1561 and 1572 (Latin American Collection, University of Texas, G19-29). In recording the process by which legal rights to the use of the lake were transferred first from the Indians to the Dominicans, and later to the Crown, a few data of ethnographic interest are given. Of special note are the aboriginal toponyms listed for the area, references on the Indians' use of the lake, and a brief description of events associated with the conquest.

From the Verapaz region we have the record of a 1596 dispute over land between Cajabón and San Agustín (AGC, Al:5933-51888). Among other things, it contains testimonials given by persons who had lived before the conquest. Also included is a 1569 "declaration" by Fray Gallego on the rights of the Indians of Cajabón to the lands, and two 16th century reports on the agricultural products grown in the disputed lands. Of special ethnographic value are references to the names of the ruling parcialidad at San Agustín, as well as a brief description of changes taking place in Verapaz after the coming of the Spaniards.

One of the most important judicial records we have was prepared in connection with a struggle between the two leading parcialidades of the Tzutujil-speaking Indians centered at Santiago Atitlán. Carrasco (1967b) has discussed it fully, and has provided us with extracts of the pertinent parts (the originals are now in the Archivo General de Centroamérica, Al:5946-52042). From testimony given by caciques from Sololá, Nagualapa, and other important towns in the region, we have detailed information on the internal organization of the Tzutujil political system. Carrasco has shown that during aboriginal rule succession was assured by a standby lineage which provided a ruler in the event that a mature successor was not available from the ruling lineage.

Two "cloths" or codices are also mentioned, and from their use, the function of prehispanic writing in highland Guatemala is illuminated (see Native Sources). This document is the ideal judicial record: it contains numerous references to aboriginal cultural and social patterns, and its accuracy seems assured by the direct and independent testimony of several witnesses.

The last category of judicial records concerns a number of documents containing litigation over territories extending between different ethnic and political groupings. The most important is an audiencia record from 1667, in which testimony taken in 1565 is cited. The dispute involved the Pipil Indians of Esquintepeque (Escuintla) and the Cakchiquel of Alotenango.[59] Witnesses from surrounding towns, some of whom had seen the conquest, testify to the respective rights of the two communities to the disputed land. They describe the nature of prehispanic political ties between the Cakchiquel and Escuintla Indians at this zone where the two groups had come into physical contact. They describe some aboriginal institutions by which Quichean peoples interacted with potential enemies in frontier zones. In addition, the names of important rulers in this part of the eastern coastal lowlands are revealed, along with various toponyms (See Appendix XXII).

Ximénez cited certain legal papers in his possession which contained the record of a 16th century boundary dispute between the Pokomán of Yampuc and the Cakchiquel of Sacatepéquez (1929-1931:1:69:77). He also had learned from "some ancient papers" of a dispute over land between the Indians of Rabinal and Cobán (1929-1931:1:74:195-196). Miles has commented on the ethnographic significance of the information of these citations by Ximénez in her study of the 16th century Pokoman (1957:742-743: 775). I have searched in the national archives of Guatemala for the records cited by Ximénez, but apparently they have disappeared. Naturally, their interpretation is made more difficult by our secondary access to them, but they remain important, nevertheless.

---

[59] The document belongs to a private party in Guatemala City, and cannot be properly cited. There can be no question as to its authenticity. It is like hundreds of similar documents housed in the Archivo General de Centroamérica, where it also belongs.

A dispute over land, somewhat similar to the one between Alotenango and Esquintepeque, is recorded in a document from Patulul, written in 1587 (AGC, Al:2811-24781). The disputed land (Tzacbalcat) was claimed by both the Cakchiquel of Patulul and the Tzutujil of Atitlán, and testimony from various witnesses brings out the fact that the site was probably a hostile frontier zone before the conquest (probably it had come under Tzutujil control a few years before the Spaniards arrived). The account contains useful data on place names, the kinds of relations holding between the Cakchiquel and Tzutujil at this point of physical contact, and many of the titles held by native rulers in that region.

From a large expediente in the Archivo General de Centroamérica (Al:5942-51977), we learn of certain lands west of Lake Atitlán which had been contested since prehispanic times by the Tzutujil Indians of San Juan la Laguna and the Quiche of Santa Clara. In 1640, several documents were brought forth as evidence, including the *Títulos Santa Clara* and *Ajpopolajay*, discussed in Native Sources. In addition, the testimony of some older witnesses reviewed events taking place almost sixty years before—i.e., in the 1580's. From this testimony we learn of the boundaries which existed between the Quiche and Tzutujil at the time and before, and of the original posthispanic formation of the towns of Santa Clara and San Juan. And because Santa Clara was formed by Indians from Santa Catalina Ixtahuacán, we also learn something of the 16th century internal organization of that town.

This completes the discussion of judicial records, and the primary Spanish records in general. I must emphasize the incompleteness of the collection of documents. It represents only the limited search of a few scholars, and in the future we will surely see the appearance of many more important documents.

CHAPTER IV

Secondary Sources

INTRODUCTION

Secondary vs. Primary Sources

What is or is not a primary or secondary source is always somewhat arbitrary judgement. Technically, primary source classification should be assigned only to those works whose authors had direct contact with aboriginal culture. However, I prefer to be less restrictive and include within the primary classification the many important documents written in the sixteenth century, when native culture was known at least in its early stages of change, if not in its aboriginal condition. I designate all works with information about Quichean groups written after the sixteenth century and before the development of modern anthropology as secondary sources.

Certainly, by the turn of the century many changes had taken place in the native cultures of highland Guatemala. Mesoamericanists generally are agreed that by then the violent disruption of native culture had largely taken place (LaFarge 1962; Beals 1952; Cámara Barbachano 1964). It is unlikely that by 1600 persons were still living who could remember the precontact period. Therefore we can set apart with sound justification works written after 1600 from those written before.

Illustration: Shield of Santiago de los Caballeros, Guatemala. Colonial symbol of Guatemala. From the frontispiece of the *Anales de la Sociedad de Geografía e Historia de Guatemala*.

Because a work is classified as a secondary source, it does not mean it is less important than a primary document. The later writers based their writings on sixteenth century sources (Fuentes y Guzmán is the most striking example), and others describe obviously aboriginal cultural patterns not clarified in the sixteenth century sources (e.g., Ximénez' description of Quiche settlement patterns). A secondary classification of a source signifies that special care should be taken in its interpretation. We should carefully differentiate between aboriginal patterns and those resulting from Spanish influence, or other distortions that normally accompany the transmission of culture over time.

The secondary source material, which I have been able to find, is subdivided into three categories: native language documents, colonial histories, and colonial records. I briefly outline the conditions under which they were produced, and give simple explanations why they were originally written.

History of the Secondary Documents

After the close of the sixteenth century, the natives generally ceased to transcribe their history and culture in either their own languages or Spanish. Because the Spaniards did not extensively marry into the aristocratic Indian families of Guatemala, mestizo accounts of aboriginal culture were not written (cf. the writings of Pomar, Camargo, and Garcilaso for Mexico and Peru).

A new sociocultural reality had come into existence as a result of the jokeying for power between descendants of the native ruling lines and the dominating policies of the Spaniards. The new reality was more provincial, involving local caciques and principales, resident priests, cofrades, alcaldes, corregidores. In a sense, a new legal base had been established for settling problems involving the Indians. It was a system of relations laid down by the conquest and the subsequent process of political and ecclesiastical subjugation. Colonial period disputes were mainly settled through reference to this system, rather than to aboriginal arrangements.

Obviously, the culture of the higher levels of aboriginal political structure faded into nonexistence with the onset of colonial society, and the relatively few references made to it by Spanish writers were based, for the most part, on native titulos written during the century of conquest. Nevertheless, aboriginal language and culture in slightly modified form continued into the colonial period, especially within the framework of rural social organization and the extended family. To a limited extent these cultural continuities were observed and recorded by the Spaniards and creoles, especially the priests. Their observations were incorporated into chronicles and histories of Guatemala, while others were transcribed into texts using the native languages. Some native language documents have come to us, and form a valuable supplement to the native titulos.

The pace of events in colonial Guatemala slowed considerably after the close of the 16th century, and a rather drab, provincial period replaced the heroic age of conquest. As Indian culture was inalterably changed and by a slow process of adaptive modification was transformed into a syncretic peasant culture (Wolf 1955b), Spanish writings on the Indians changed too. The Indians in their new condition of isolation and peasantism were less impressive, and hence less interesting, to the Spaniards. It was no longer possible simply to report native customs with a fair assurance that aboriginal forms were being described. The task of separating native from Spanish cultural patterns required more intellectual investment than many were willing to give. Most colonial writings about the Indians are historical. The Indians were primarily studied through native and Spanish writings produced during the previous century, and the quasi ethnographies and relaciones were generally replaced by chronicles and other historical works.

Spanish writing became more provincial, too, because Iberian historians were joined by creole writers from Guatemala. The void in action, brought about by the end of the conquest era and the subjugation of the Indians, led to the production of long, detailed histories of the religious orders and provincial political systems. They were usually accompanied by pompous classical commentaries written in a baroque literary style. These works are largely irrelevant to a study of native culture, and massive volumes of pages and folios must be reviewed in order to cull the limited information which they contain on native cultural forms.

Caution must be used in studying native culture through secondary sources, especially in the case of the colonial histories. Nevertheless, they contain critical information on the Quichean cultures.

The number of official records produced by the Spaniards during the post 16th century colonial period in order to administer their colony is prodigious. I discovered the impact of this fact when, in 1966, I attempted to study all documents in the Archivo General de Centroamérica for one Indian community, and found it an impossible task. Though these records represent a marvelous treasure for reconstructing colonial society and culture, their value for studying aboriginal cultural patterns is limited. This is related to the Spaniards' loss of interest once the native populations were subjugated and semi-Christianized. The Indians of the 17th and 18th centuries had become mere subjects to be administered and controlled, and the records of colonial administration show signs of "ethnographic" indifference. Then, too, native culture had changed significantly, especially in the outward manifestations, the stuff of which official records are made.

Strong evidence of the drop in ethnographic quality in the colonial records is provided by the Momostenango case I describe. An exhaustive investigation of almost the entire corpus of documents from that community sheds pitifully little light on any traditional Indian patterns which might have been perpetuated in the community during the colonial period. There is a tremendous contrast between the impression given by the colonial records and the all pervasive traditional Indian patterns which the ethnographer observes around him in Momostenango today.

Even with the ethnographer's knowledge of what to look for in the colonial records, they provide a disappointingly meager yield of information on native cultural forms. Indeed, I discuss the colonial records more for their importance for reconstructing colonial than aboriginal culture.

Social Explanation of the Secondary Documents

Almost all commentators on the social condition of the Middle American Indian during the colonial period have argued that fundamental socioeconomic changes occurred during the transition from the 17th to the 18th century. This was the period when the haciendas replaced the encomiendas as the dominant Spanish social institution for controlling the Indians. As a result, the Indian was able to retrench and reintegrate aboriginal cultural patterns with Spanish ones (LaFarge 1962; Beals 1952; Cámara Barbachano 1964). Gibson has noted that creole writing was influenced by these changes, and that it became "complex, stylized, lavish, involuted," preoccupied with insignificant detail, and generally unaffected by early 18th century enlightenment (1966:132-143).

The Guatemalan documents described in this section certainly fall under Gibson's indictment for Spanish American documents in general. Nowhere is this literary decadence more telling than in the diminished interest in the Indians which is characteristic of the writings. As best as I can determine, they provide little evidence for the thesis that Indian culture underwent significant change or reintegration during that period. Life in the Indian villages remained much the same during the 17th and 18th centuries, the haciendas simply serving as exploiting agencies functionally equivalent to the encomiendas.

Apparently, there was a minor flowering of writing about the Indians close to the turn of the 18th century. The representative works were produced by the friars: e.g., the histories of Ximénez, Vázquez, anonymous priests (*Isogoge Historia, Crónica Franciscana*); and the dictionaries by Guzmán, Basseta, Ximénez, Coto, and others. One might connect this flowering with the enlightenment of Europe, though it would seem to be more directly related to events occuring in Guatemala. In particular, it should be noted that one of the reasons why the creole *hacendados* were able to increase their power in the colonies during the 17th and 18th centuries is that the regular orders of friars were being phased out. There must have been tremendous pressure to remove the remaining friars, the persons who produced the writings, and the two events must be interconnected. Apparently, the friars turned their attention to the Indians in hopes of recapturing some of the spirit and power of the earlier friars, and thereby justify their existence in colonial society.

The large number of land dispute documents which were prepared during the second half of the 18th century also appears to have its basis in internal social conditions. It was a period of hacienda growth, concurrent with the growth of native Indian population. Faced with creole *congregaciones, denuncias,* and *composicioues* (Gibson 1966:154-159), the land-deprived, expanding Indian population began to fight for its lands through the courts. They were not usually successful in their struggle, but the records of their attempts are an invaluable source of information for the modern ethnohistorian.

NATIVE LANGUAGE DOCUMENTS

Documents of this type are described and analyzed in five subgroups: dictionaries, native calendars, ceremonial drama, religious manuals, and official records. These documents contain information on native cultural patterns; all were written by Spaniards or Creoles, and at least in part in the native language.

The purpose of their composition was to aid in the education of the Indians—teaching the doctrines of the church, inculcating Spanish customs, presenting evidence for the need to eradicate "superstitions." Indeed, strictly theological writings copied and composed in the native languages during the colonial period are exceedingly numerous (see Butler 1937; Gates n.d.).

Though these works were meant to educate, almost without exception they also show their authors' genuine interest in native culture. This was especially true for the twenty years preceding and following the turn of the eighteenth century, when the study of native language and culture underwent a minor resurgence.

Dictionaries

The preparation of dictionaries of the Indian languages to aid in the work of the priests and missionaries continued into the seventeenth and eighteenth centuries. Some colonial dictionaries were based on earlier vocabularies (e.g., the Coto dictionary, discussed in Primary Spanish Sources), but others were produced *de novo* by new generations of priests facing different problems. Generally, the later dictionaries suggest that the priests were less interested in native culture, and the long, ethnographically valuable glosses tend to be replaced by brief pragmatic ones, lower in cultural content. Presumably, this reflects the fact that the period of dramatic cultural change had ended, and that the priests now required only enough of the language to function adequately within the now standardized Spanish-Indian relationships that had evolved. Yet some of the dictionaries are impressive and valuable to the student of Guatemalan Indian culture.

In the various archives and libraries of the world many of these dictionaries have been preserved. It would be tedious to discuss them all. The interested student may consult the bibliographic summaries in Recinos (1950), Butler (1937), and Sáenz (1959). In this section I describe what I hope is a representative sample of the corpus, and focus on those dictionaries which would be most useful in reconstructing native cultural patterns.

Pantaleón de Guzmán. — This dictionary has entries arranged according to topical subjects, reminiscent of the ethnographically oriented dictionaries of the 16th century. It was prepared around the turn of the 17th century by a creole, Fray Pantaleón de Guzmán. A copy of the manuscript entitled, *Compendio de nombres en lengua Cakchiquel,* is in the Newberry Library, Chicago. The Cakchiquel-to-Spanish entries are numerous, in perfect Parra characters, and are conveniently arranged under the following headings: birds, insects, metals, social positions, plants, astral bodies.

Guzmán's glosses are extremely brief, but define the meanings of more words on the relatively few topics covered than perhaps any other dictionary source. Some material may have come from earlier sources (e.g., some entries parallel those in Varela), but it appears that many came from his own studies of the Cakchiquel language at Santa María de Jesus Pache (and perhaps other communities).

Basseta. — In 1690, the Dominican friar, Domingo de Basseta, prepared perhaps the most complete Quiché dictionary. It consists of two large sections, one Spanish-to-Quiche, the other Quiche-to-Spanish. Brasseur apparently obtained the manuscript from a fiscal of one of the Dominican convents in Guatemala, and later proudly refers to it as a "magnificent vocabulary"

(1857:LXXXVIII). The manuscript has since become part of the American collection of the Bibliothèque Nationale in Paris, from where various photocopies have been obtained by American libraries.[1]

I have been unable to find biographical information on the life of Fray Basseta, except for a notice of his death in 1699 (Ximénez 1929-1931:3:409). His knowledge of Quiche was apparently gained in the Baja Verapaz region, for he mentions Rabinal and Cubulco in his dictionary. His entries do not seem to be based to any great extent on the early dictionaries, though he probably made some use of them. After a few definitions, he explains that the particular words were no longer in use. In a few cases he gives the meaning of words which are not found in most other dictionaries (e.g., this and the Ximénez dictionary are the only ones to define *chajal pokob*, "an ancient dance" (see *Título C'oyoi*).

Though the glosses in the Basseta dictionary are brief and his use of Parra characters is imperfect, it remains a solid contribution to the study of Quiché culture. It is in the tradition of the work of Ximénez and Guzmán, and shows that an interest in the Indians of Guatemala continued well into the colonial period.

Ximénez. — Around the turn of the 18th century, Fray Francisco Ximénez produced one of the most important studies of the Quiche language.[2] The work, entitled *Tesoro de las lenguas K'ak'chiquel, Quiche, y Tz'utuhil*, contained among other things a magnificent Quiche grammar and a large Quiché, Cakchiquel, and Tzutujil-to-Spanish dictionary.[3] Brasseur copied the Quiche grammar when it was part of the library of the University of Guate-

---

[1] I obtained a copy of the Quiche-to-Spanish part from the Middle American Research Institute Library, Tulane University. An incomplete later copy is in the Pius XII Memorial Library, St. Louis University (cf. Landar 1967).

[2] I imagine Ximénez produced this work while serving in the Franciscan convent of Santo Tomás Chichicastenango from 1701 to 1703, the period when he found the *Popol Vuh*, and probably began its translation. We know that he had already completed the dictionary when he began writing his chronicle in 1715 (Ximenez 1929-1931:1:65; see Colonial Historians).

[3] The dictionary contains only a few Cakchiquel and Tzutujil terms, though Ximénez meant it to be a dictionary for the three Quichean languages. Almost all entries are in Quiche, the language he knew best.

mala, and later published it under his name along with a few brief grammatical notes in French (1862). A new edition of this has recently been published in Guatemala, unfortunately retaining Brasseur's name as author (1961). The dictionary, however, has never been published. Around the middle of the 19th century it also came into the hands of Brasseur, and after his death became part of the collection of American Indian manuscripts of the Bancroft Library of Berkeley.[4]

The grammar is quite complete, more so than Vico's grammar (n.d.b), and is useful in translating the 16th century native sources. In addition, it contains an abbreviated vocabulary of Quiche roots and the best collection of Quiche numerical terms available.

Ximénez states, he had access to earlier vocabularies when he prepared his dictionary (and because of this, he says, the word *tesoro*, treasure, in his title is not a boast). Nevertheless, most entries appear to be based on his own knowledge of Quiche, some of it he learned while working on the *Popol Vuh*.

Like the Basseta dictionary, Ximénez gives meanings for an extensive number of words with brief glosses. In some cases, however, he goes beyond Basseta and other postsixteenth century dictionaries in providing ethnographic content. He includes valuable toponymic identifications, explanations of the counting system, correlations of words with Quiche mythology (as contained in the *Popol Vuh*), and brief descriptions of native customs and beliefs.

Ximénez' ethnographic interests are seen clearly in the two works, especially in the dictionary. He makes a remarkable statement in the dictionary: "These are the things that made it seem like they are committing idolatry, because they are (things) of their forefathers; but it is nothing more than a reminder of what their fathers were, and it is not superstition for all of us do the same, and it is a praiseworthy custom" (part of the entry for the word *cwal*).

---

[4] This important document should be published in order to make it readily available to scholars. I was permitted to study the original at the Bancroft Library, and the library kindly loaned me a microfilm copy of it.

Ximénez was deeply interested in native history and culture, especially after he had discovered the manuscript of the *Popol Vuh*. I think it likely that his reason for preparing the two works was to use them as tools in his studies of the great book (the Quiche text and his Spanish translation of the *P.V.* were attached to the volume that included the grammar). They were also useful in the work of the ministry, and indeed Ximénez says it was his primary reason for preparing the dictionary.

The preparation of dictionaries of the native languages continued until the close of the 18th century, though most works appear to be copies of earlier vocabularies. Many can be found among the manuscripts or photocopies of the Newberry Library (Butler 1937). After Ximénez, no outstanding student of the native languages emerges, though the Franciscan Friar Ildefonso Joseph Flores enjoyed considerable fame for his grammar, published with special characters in 1753. Not until the middle of the 19th century do ethnographically significant vocabularies appear again; by then the purpose for which they were being written had changed (see Modern Anthropological Sources).

The Tirado Spanish-to-Quiche dictionary deserves to be mentioned here (see Primary Spanish Sources, Dictionaries). Though many Quiché glosses were taken directly from an earlier Spanish-to-Cakchiquel dictionary (the *Calepino Cakchiquel*), some Quiché forms appear to be independent contributions by an anonymous Franciscan friar (probably from Sacapulas). The same author added a small vocabulary at the end of the Tirado dictionary, arranged according to subject categories (lists of birds, foods, dress, kinship terms). This appended vocabulary is identical with a small anonymous Spanish-to-Quiche dictionary now in the Bibliothèque Nationale (Anonymous 1924-25:93), a copy of which is at the Newberry Library. The Tirado dictionary also served as the primary source for Edmonson's recent Quiche-to-English dictionary (1965).

Native Calendars

Clandestinely, many aspects of the aboriginal calendar system continued to be used in Guatemala during the colonial period, and even in modern times. Its use is mentioned in the early native sources (especially in the *Annals of the Cakchiquels*). The historians of the 17th and 18th centuries testify to its ubiquitous use among the Indians (e.g., Ximénez 1929-1931:1:101-102), Cortéz y Larraz claims that it was in use "in all parishes of the Quiche and Cakchiquel" (1958:11:57); García Elgueta (1962) describes its use among the Quiche during the 19th century; and many 20th century anthropologists (including myself) have discovered its importance in modern Indian communities (Miles 1952). Following are the three most important references to the native calendar recorded before the beginning of modern anthropological studies.

The first is a 1685 Cakchiquel calendar recorded by the anonymous Franciscan priest who wrote the *Crónica Franciscana* (see Colonial Historians). In 1887, Berendt made a copy of chapter 7 in the manuscript which contained the calendar (his handwritten copy is in the University of Pennsylvania Library). From a photocopy of the Berendt manuscript, Rodríguez and Crespo published the calendar in *Antropología e Historia de Guatemala* (1956).

Unfortunately, we do not know exactly where this particular calendar came from, probably from an important Cakchiquel center near Santiago Guatemala. From the text given by Berendt, it is clear that the Franciscan priest who transcribed it used a knowledgeable Cakchiquel Indian as his informant and asked him specific questions about how it worked. It certainly seems closer to the aboriginal version of the Quichean calendar than the two later versions we will discuss.

The 1685 calendar is an example of the 365-day solar cycle, correlated with the Christian calendar for the year 1685. The eighteen 20-day periods (months) are named and their meanings for the agricultural cycle are given (but not their etymologies). The thirteen number and twenty day name permutations are given according to month, and the "good days" are noted (but not the "bad days"). The last five "closing days" are listed, after which the new year was said to begin on the last day of January.

The second calendar, written in Quiche in 1722, actually consists of three calendars grouped together. It was copied by Berendt in 1877 from a manuscript in the Museo Nacional de Guatemala. His copy is in the University of Pennsylvania Museum

Library, but has never been published as far as I know.[5] I have summarized its contents in Appendix XXIII.

Berendt believed that the calendar had come from the Quezaltenango area, and that it was the one given to Cortés y Larraz by the resident priest there (1958:II:157). This is probably true, for it is similar in form and content to calendars recorded at nearby Totonicapán and Ixtahuacán (García Elgueta 1962:163-182; Hernández Spina 1932).[6]

The first of the three calendars is the solar cycle, called the *chol powal k'ij, macewal k'ij* (the count of the round of days, the common days). It contains a list of the eighteen "months," the five closing days, the twenty day names, the yearly permutations of the thirteen number and twenty day names, and the four year-bearer day names. These cycles are correlated with the Christian calendar for the years 1722-1727.

The other two calendars called *ajilabal k'ij* (the count of the days), are 260-day divinatory calendars, written by two different persons. The days are organized in sets of five days, the days of each set sharing the same number (e.g., one *canil*, one *hunajpu*, one *ee*, one *c'at*, one *ajmak*). Each cycle of thirteen numbers totals 65 days, and four units of 65 days make up the 260-day sacred calendar. Good, bad, and mixed fates are given in Quiche glosses for most sets of five days. Edmonson (n.d.) has suggested that these divinatory entries might have been taken from hieroglyphic codices still available in the 18th century. Though this is a possibility, it seems unlikely to me. Esoteric, rhetorical phrases of this type could have been memorized fairly easily and perpetuated on a strictly oral basis.[7] The fates given in the two

[5] A photographic copy of the calendar is in the Newberry Library of Chicago, where I obtained a copy of it. I hope someone will prepare a copy of it for publication.

[6] Unfortunately, we do not have a complete record of the month names from the heart of the Quiche area, though we know they were similar to those given in the 1685 Cakchiquel calendar (Ximénez n.d.). In comparing Ximénez' list of day names with those of the 1722 calendar, we find a difference at the 6th day (1929-1931:1:101-102). Whereas Ximénez records it as *balam*, it is given as *ik'* in the 1722 calendar; the latter form agrees with the Totonicapán calendar recorded by García Elgueta (1962:164).

[7] I find Edmonson's hypothesis stimulating and pregnant with leads for research problems. However, in the Quiché text there are no allusions to the

calendars are similar but not identical in phraseology and content, proof of their separate but nearly contemporaneous composition.

Unfortunately, we do not know the purpose for which these calendars were transcribed. Possibly it was done at the request of some interested priest around 1722, and the manuscript was then kept in the convent until it was turned over to Cortés y Larraz in 1770.[8] The transcriptions must have been made by educated members of the cacique class at Quezaltenango, Christians still steeped in Quiche tradition.

Another Quiche calendar was recorded in 1845 by the resident priest of Santa Catarina Ixtahuacán, the Presbiter Vicente Hernández Spina. Brasseur obtained this manuscript from the chief archivist in Guatemala City shortly thereafter (Brasseur 1857: LXXXVI), and toward the close of the nineteenth century it became part of the Brinton Collection of the University of Pennsylvania Museum Library. A copy of it was later translated into English and published by Gates in volumes 1 and 2 of the *Maya Society Quarterly* (1932).[9]

The Hernández account lists the twenty day names with their associated good and bad fates. The month names are not given, but in a somewhat confused explanation of the operation of the calendar, Hernández indicates that there were eighteen twenty-day units. He also gives the starting point of the Quiche solar year in relation to the Christian calendar (on the first of May), and indicates the year-bearer pattern (*noj*, and, therefore, also

---

glyphs Edmonson argues for. For example, *ka tzij* should not be translated as "it says" (that would be *catzij*), rather it is a familiar phrase of affirmation (in truth). This form of affirmation is used in the native títulos in such a wide context as to preclude the specialized meaning for it suggested by Edmonson. In further opposition to Edmonson's interpretations, I would argue that though antiphonical couplets are an aspect to Quiche syntax, they do not appear as universally as he claims, nor are they necessarily always purposefully given.

[8] Cortés y Larraz arrived in Quezaltenango in the early part of 1770, and the entry date in one of the calendars was March 18, 1770. Probably, the same priest who gave him the calendar manuscript ascertained the current date in the native calendar and recorded this for him (cf. Edmonson n.d.).

[9] The Tulane Middle American Research Institute Library has a typewritten copy of the original Spanish and Quiche manuscript from Pennsylvania. They were kind enough to provide me with a Xerox copy of that document, which I have consulted along with the Gates publication.

ik', quej, ee). In addition, Hernández recorded in Quiche a long magical prayer given by one of the priest-shaman (*ajk'ij*) of Santa Catarina, and translated it into Spanish. He also included a brief summary of native beliefs and customs, and a list of sacred toponyms and the names of renowned priest-shamans in the area.

It is clear that Hernández interrogated several important priest-shamans of the community in order to learn about their calendar. One must have trusted him so that he permitted Hernández to record the prayer in its entirety, and then revealed the list of important priests residing in the area. It is unfortunate that the month names were not recorded also, because apparently they were still remembered at the time.

Ceremonial Drama

Ceremonial dance, drama, song, and chant were important modes of artistic expression and oral communication of culture in aboriginal highland Guatemala. This is conclusively established by the native documents (especially the *Popol Vuh* and *Título C'oyoi*) for the aboriginal period, and ethnographic studies have shown that folk dance and drama play a similar role in modern times (Armas Lara 1964; Kurath and Marti 1964).

I have suggested elsewhere (Carmack n.d.c) that there were at least two basic kinds of aboriginal ceremonial drama: those representing great cyclic themes about nature and society, and those representing famous legendary events. Examples of the former type from the native sources would be the "Song of the Camucu," the "Dance of the Monkey Jun Ajpu," the "War Dance," and the "Dance of the Drum" (Recinos 1953:136:217; *Título C'oyoi*). The *Rabinal Achi* is the most important example of a native drama with a legendary theme (see Native Sources), and the "Dance of Tolk'om" is an illustration of the same type among the Cakchiquel (Recinos 1950:78).

After the conquest, the Spanish missionaries introduced several dance dramas to the Indians in order to facilitate their conversion to Spanish culture and Christianity (Kurath 1967). One had the conquest as a theme, and became extremely popular among the Indians of highland Guatemala. Known as "The Dance of the Conquest," many local versions were elaborated, and apparently presented continuously during the colonial and independence periods to the present day (Bode 1961). If it was composed in Quiche, the texts have disappeared, and we are left with several Spanish versions from the 19th and 20th centuries (Bode 1961: Appendix I). The earliest text is from 1872 (Bode 1961:Appendix II). A very important version from Santa Cruz del Quiche (Silva n.d.) is not listed by Bode in her useful study of the dance (1961).

Though the story is obviously placed in a Spanish mold, there are enough references to 16th century Quiche institutions to suggest the aid of native informants (e.g., prehispanic wars with the Tzutujil, and Mam, the counting system by 400s, calpul organization are mentioned). There is reason to believe that originally it was written in Quiche as well as Spanish (to aid in the conversion of the Indians), an accomplishment probably also requiring the help of native speakers.

Local variation in the text of the drama is especially well illustrated by comparing the Silva text (n.d.), written at Santa Cruz del Quiche with that published by Bode (1961:Appendix II) presumably from Quezaltenango. The latter document contains detailed references to the specific Quiche lords from Xelajú taking part in the conquest, and to places around that settlement where the events of the conquest occurred. The Silva account has more to say about the lords of Utatlán, including Tojil and Quik'ab, and of places situated nearby (e.g., Paizmachi).

Armas Lara has uncovered evidence that the original of the drama was written in 1542 by a Dominican priest at Santiago Guatemala, and that it was performed for Bishop Marroquín somewhat later at San Juan del Obispo (1964:75). This is a plausible explanation for the origin of the famous dance, to which I would add the suggestion that it was used in the pacification of Rabinal and Verapaz by the Dominicans—in the year 1542 and thereafter (Sáenz 1966).

On internal evidence alone, we may conclude it was written by Spanish missionaries, with the aid of native informants, during the first half-century after the conquest, and that significant changes in it were made in each area where it was performed.[10] The ver-

---

[10] The text suggests that the author(s) was strongly biased against the conquistadores and their method of conquest and conversion (Bode 1961; Silva

sions which have come to us, contain the accretions of time, and it is impossible to say precisely what the original text was like.[11] Of the surviving Spanish versions, I believe the Silva text comes closest to a native viewpoint in comparison to other versions— the conquistadores are dealt with harshly, and the Quiché do not accept Christianity.

The discovery of three native títulos from the Quezaltenango valley (Recinos 1957:71-94; Gall 1963; *Título C'oyoi*) permit us to see that the Dance of the Conquest is consistent in many ways with early native traditions on the events of the conquest (cf. Edmonson 1964:273). Nevertheless, it is too general and too hispanicized to be of much use in reconstructing native historiography. It is much more important as a folk expression of resistence and pride (Bode 1961:231-234). By studying its regional variations, the ethnologist is in a position to understand the way the drama was changed in accordance with local geographical and sociopolitical conditions.

A second dance drama about the conquest called, "Zaki C'oxol," or "Dance of Cortés" has come to us from the colonial period. It has been confused with the Dance of the Conquest (Gates n.d.; Edmonson 1964:272-273), but clearly is an entirely different production. It was probably written somewhere near the Verapaz region, from where our texts appear to come and where the dance is still performed today (Bode 1961:211; Brinton 1900:14).

Edmonson (1964:273) suggests, it was written by a Spanish missionary, possibly in the 18th century. In view of the fact that the several extant texts are all in an archaic Quiche, it seems more likely that the dance was composed during the 16th century, like the Dance of the Conquest. All copies of the Dance of Cortés now available are from the 19th century, ranging in dates from 1800 to 1875 (Gates n.d.; Brinton 1900:14). I have used an 1875 Berendt copy from the University of Pennsylvania Museum Library,

---

n.d.). It seems favorable toward Indian culture, except for matters related to religion. These characteristics are what one would expect from Las Casas influenced Dominicans of the time.

[11] Bode, in her able study of the Dance of the Conquest concludes it was not written until the 19th century. However, she presents enough evidence to convince any skeptic that it must derive from 16th century traditions of the conquest (1961:216-219).

one of six versions of the drama from the Gates collection at that library.

One of the principle characters of the drama is zaki c'oxol, "white demon," a term used by the Quiche to refer to certain dwarflike creatures who inhabited volcanoes, mountains, and forests (Edmonson 1965:159; Recinos 1950:65). In the story he symbolizes the magical power of the Quiche, and accordingly, his name is sometimes substituted for the witch aj itz in the Dance of the Conquest (Bode 1961:213).

The general theme of the dance is the conquest of Mexico by Cortés and the Spaniards, though its focus is on the communication which passed between the Aztecs and the Quiche preparatory to the arrival of the Spaniards. That such contact between these important independent powers existed is verified by many native sources (e.g., *Titulo Nijaib I*; Pictorial Momostenango), a fact which suggests an early original composition of the dance.

From modern ethnographic studies we know that many other native dance dramas were transmitted from the conquest to modern times: e.g., "Dance of the Deer," "Dance of Corn," "Dance of the Serpent," "The Flying Pole," "The Patzca" (Dance of the Jesters), and others (Termer 1957; Armas Lara 1964; Edmonson 1964; Mace 1961). These dances have retained considerable native cultural forms, and a thorough, comparative study of them is badly needed.

Other dances no longer performed, but briefly described by colonial writers are the "Quiche Winak," "Dance of the Volcano," and the "Three Drum" (Ox Tun) (Ximénez 1929:78; Fuentes y Guzmán 1932-33:6:7:367-368:388; Chinchilla 1963:9-19). Unfortunately, none of these men recorded the dialogue of the dance ceremonies they witnessed, so we are left without native texts. The tremendous ethnographic loss that this represents can be appreciated by considering the importance of the one native dance drama which was recorded, the *Rabinal Achí*.

Religious Manuals

We have a few catechisms and doctrinal treatises prepared by the priests during the colonial period. Four manuals written in Cakchiquel during the 17th century are of special interest, for they contain useful information on native customs persisting to that time.

Three manuscripts are in the American Philosophical Society, where they were sent in 1836 along with several other important documents as gifts from President Gálvez. The first, *Ramillete manual para los indios sobre la doctrina cristiana*, is a copy of an original manuscript written by Fray Francisco Maldonado. The date of composition is not known, but it must have been several years after 1605, the year Maldonado entered the Franciscan Order in Guatemala (Vázquez 1937-44:16:318).[12] One small part of the Cakchiquel text (folio 37) has been translated into Spanish by Carrasco (1963), who notes its importance for reconstructing the form of Cakchiquel prehispanic clans and lineages. In the untranslated pages which follow that section, additional information on kinship patterns, including a useful list of kinship terms, is given.

The other two manuscripts given by Gálvez contain a collection of religious writings, some in Cakchiquel and some in Spanish. We do not know who is the author of the first, and it is not dated, though a probable date of 1692 is assigned to it by Freeman (1962). It contains a list of kinship terms similar to the ones given by Maldonado. The other document is a *confesionario*, prepared sometime before 1664 by the Franciscan Friar Antonio del Saz. Saz was well-versed in the Cakchiquel language, and wrote several other doctrinal works in that language (Chinchilla 1963:25-26). His confesionario was included in a religious manual of twenty -pláticas, *Manual de pláticas de todos los sacramentos para la administración de estos naturales* (1664). It contains a large questionnaire dealing with misconduct in the areas of public administration, marriage and family life, and religious practices. As noted by Chinchilla (1963:22), "life in the Indian towns is projected and objectified in the seventy-six questions which a vast experience in the daily practice of confession has put in the lips of Fray Antonio del Saz."

---

[12] The manuscript copy in the American Philosophical Society was made in 1748. Besides the "dialogues" composed by Maldonado, it contains a treatise on Christian doctrine, composed by an unknown priest in 1556 (Freeman 1962).

Another example of this kind of document is a Quiché-to-Spanish catechism written by an anonymous priest in 1680. Daniel Contreras R. found the document in the Museo Nacional de Guatemala while serving as director of that institution in 1950, and later Chinchilla Aguilar published the chapter from it on worship (1957). The text is mainly important for the Quiché titles of religious practitioners which are listed there, and for the sketchy but penetrating view it gives of native religious beliefs still extant at the time.

Because all three works were catechismal in purpose, we can be sure that the authors viewed persisting aboriginal practices as anachronisms to be corrected (and this is so stated in each document). Nevertheless, each was a rather careful student of the culture he was trying to change. One cannot resist suggesting that they had discovered in their investigations of native "superstitions" an ethnographic interest that went beyond the purely pragmatic purpose of establishing doctrinal orthodoxy. At any rate, their works contain useful ethnographic data which the student of native cultures should not ignore.

Official Records

Name Lists. — After the conquest the Quichean Indians began to take Spanish names (Carrasco 1964). Almost everyone received at least a Spanish given name, and generally members of the cacique class also began to use Spanish surnames and the title "Don" (Carrasco 1967b). Some ruling class members and most commoners continued to use native lineage and family names into colonial times, and this has persisted to the present day.

Documents containing lists of lineage names are important to the student of native culture for several reasons. Most obvious is the fact that the names are an aspect of native culture. Knowledge of them adds a concreteness to cultural reconstruction; a study of their etymologies can reveal aboriginal semantic patterns. The lists also provide evidence of the distribution of important lineages among the various settlements of the Quichean area. In important prehispanic communities, lineage names which figured prominently in the history contained in native títulos can usually be recognized. The lists help us to determine how representative the lineages mentioned in the native sources were within the total aboriginal society (e.g., they force the student to realize that native history contained in the títulos is primarily the history of a ruling class, not of the common man). Often patterns of native kinship, marriage, stratification, political position, and segmentation are suggested by name lists.

One source of native name lists are Church baptismal, birth, death, and marriage records. In 1964, I made a search of such records in the convents of several Quichean communities of the central highlands. Unfortunately, none of the parishes there have records earlier than the 17th century, and for some the earliest dated records were prepared during the 18th century. A further disappointment was the discovery that hamlet or barrio origin of the persons listed is not given, so that patterns of internal endogamy or exogamy could not be worked out (though community exogamy-endogamy can be determined).

The communities for which I have name lists from the earliest available church records are as follows (Carmack n.d.a:Appendix V): Quezaltenango (1739-1746), Mazatenango (1645-1695), San Francisco Zapotitlán (1680-1690), Santa Catarina Ixtahuacán (1600ff), Santiago Atitlán (1683ff), Santa Clara la Laguna (1681-1709), Sololá (1778ff), Santa Cruz del Quiché (1757-1790), San Miguel Totonicapán (1682-1702), and Santiago Momostenango (1745-1756).

Another type of document often containing native name lists is the tributary record. The practice of recording the names of all tributaries for the 16th century continued into the colonial period. I have not fully exploited this source of information, but it is clear that many tributary records have been preserved in the Archivo General de Centroamérica (in an unpublished manuscript, Lawrence Feldman has compiled a long though not exhaustive list of such documents in the AGC). In contrast with the kinship patterns suggested by the name lists in the church records, tributary lists usually point more to patterns of stratification and political standing.

As an example of such documents (see colonial records from Momostenango), a 1751 tributary list from Chichicastenango might be cited (AGC, A3:2831-41163). In listing all tributaries from the community, some eight lineage names which are mentioned in the *Popol Vuh* and other native títulos are given. The use of calendric names is clearly revealed. Marriages with persons from other communities suggest the closeness of social relations between Chichicastenango and these communities. Persons of the cacique class, free of tribute obligations, are listed separately by name, and so provide information on the probable prehispanic ruling lineages of the area. Even where only Spanish names are given, the information is valuable, for the ethnographer can contact the descendants of these people living today, and in some cases discover their aboriginal names (Carmack 1967).

In this context I recall that most modern ethnographers include local native names scattered or listed in their reports or notes. Even some superficial, quasi-ethnographic accounts of Guatemalan communities contain such lists. A good example is Teletor's "monograph" on Rabinal, which contains an excellent list of the native family surnames in the community (1955:195-198).

Transactions. — A few official civil records continued to be written in the native language during the colonial period. The most important of these were records of transactions, especially the testamentary, and bills of sales (especially of land). A few administrative accounts were also transcribed in the Quichean languages. These sources contain far less information on native culture than their equivalent documents from the 16th century but they should not be ignored.

The Archivo General de Centroamérica in Guatemala City has six small testaments written in Cakchiquel around the turn of the 17th century (AGC, A1:6071-54705; 6074-54901). Two include Spanish translations of the native texts, in which it is erroneously stated that they were written in Popoloca. The file card indicates that one of the documents was used in connection with a land measurement made in the territory of Chichicastenango, though all appear originally to have been prepared at Sololá.[13]

---

[13] The fact that they were written in Cakchiquel suggests that Sololá rather than Chichicastenango was the place of composition. More important, Francisco Hernández, one of the persons mentioned in these documents was the head of a calpul at Sololá. In addition, one of the testators had the surname Can, a name which is found in the Francisco Hernández (Arana) calpul list at Sololá (see Appendix XX).

The testators were Diego Can (1596), Antón Quej (1600), Pedro Méndez (1601), Gáspar Yaqui (1607), Pedro Wuch (1607), and Gáspar Wuch (1608). The records are important for the Indian clan and lineage names they contain, the political titles of some of the officials, and the several named topographical features in the territory around Sololá (some of which bordered on the land of Iximché).

In the same *legajo* of the Archivo General de Centroamérica, there is an interesting "memorial" from Escuintla, written in 1600 (Al:6074-54891). It was composed entirely in Nahuatl by the cabildo scribe, Andrés García, and there is no translation of it. It is a record of the activities of the cofradía and civil officials of that community during the celebration of Holy Week that year. It is mainly important for the aboriginal names of titles, persons, and places that are inscribed in it.

From the records of the cabildo at San Cristóbal Totonicapán, several land-purchase documents have come to us (AGC, Al:6047-53386). These were written in Quiche between the years 1713-1750. I have transcribed the texts and prepared a translation of the most important of the documents, and include them as Appendix XXIV. The documents contain the names of important native leaders and topographical features around Paxtoca, and this information can be correlated with the 16th century títulos (especially the *Títulos Paxtoca* and *C'oyoi*).

Gates obtained some fifty testaments written between the years 1762 and 1777 in the Quiche language, and copies of them can now be found at various libraries, including the Newberry Library and Middle American Research Institute Library, Tulane University. Their origin is not given, but a comparison between the Indian surnames in the wills and those listed by Teletor for Rabinal (1955:196-198) reveals so many identical cases as to make it highly likely that they came from that community.[14] Except for the Indian surnames and a few Quiche titles which these testaments contain, there is little in them to suggest aboriginal cultural patterns. They are mainly important as a documentation

[14] A quick comparison resulted in the following list of surnames found in both the wills and Teletor's book: Pank'an, Ajanel, K'ojom, Iboy, Coloch, Cajbon, Konalej, Chun, Toj, Tum, Sis, Raxcaco, Chen, Xpatac, Tzakol.

of the changes occurring in legal relations between the Indians during the colonial period.

Similar to the above in content and significance are documents from other parts of the highlands (Gates 1937:11). For example, I have a copy of a document written in Quiche from the Archivo General de Centroamérica which is the record of a 1783 land sale at Totonicapán (Al:3058-29330). Juan Zapeta Uxcabutiuj sells a house and plot of land to three men by the name of Solís, in the presence of the "King, common justice, and officials of the royal cabildo." Among the few aboriginal clan or lineage names mentioned in the document is Extayul, a name which appears in the *Popol Vuh*.

An almost identical land document was recorded in the Quiché language at Sacapulas in the year 1734. The handwriting of the scribe is poor, but it is legible, and he left a crude Spanish translation of it (AGC, Al:6025-53126). The document contains a description of a parcel of land owned by Domingo Ulwan and later inherited by his sons, who apparently had this small title drawn up in preparation for selling the land. I include a copy of both the Quiche and Spanish texts as Appendix XXV, along with an earlier (1613) small land document from Sacapulas, also written in Quiche (AGC, Al:5942-51995). The latter document contains the testimony of local officials who walked around the boundaries of a parcel of land inherited by members of the Lamak'ib clan at Sacapulas. It is important for the native names and titles recorded in it, and it provides an interesting basis for comparison with the Ulwan document written more than a hundred years later.

Besides containing a few native names, the documents of transactions are useful for showing the way native patterns were adapted to the requirements of a Spanish controlled colony. That also is the significance of a collected summary of documents entitled, *Petición ruc ahau President*, from the Bibliothèque Nationale, Paris. This synthetic document contains various requests made by leaders of Indian communities to higher colonial officials, and vice versa (Butler 1937:197). The original documents were written around 1790 (one of them contains a 1794 date), at the Quiche-speaking communities of Samayaque, Sambo, Quezaltenango, San Miguel Totonicapán, San Cristóbal Totonicapán, Momostenango, Sacapulas, and others.

COLONIAL HISTORIES

I have arranged the colonial histories according to the chronological order in which they were written, rather than in the order in which they were published. The works included form a fairly coherent collection, with the exception of Gage's book. He was not writing as a historian, except in the sense of narrating his own life and the events occurring during his travels in New Spain and Guatemala. He did not use documentary materials, and his descriptions of native culture were not commentaries on earlier accounts. His ethnographic observations are similar in many ways to those by Fuentes y Guzmán, Ximénez, and Tovilla; therefore I have included his work here.

I have evaluated the historial works for their ethnographic content. For a consideration of their historical value, one should consult the important study of Esteve Barba (1964), or the informative introductory essays which accompany the publication of most of the books.

Remesal

The first Guatemalan chronicle entitled, *Historia General de las Indias Occidentales y Particular de la Gobernación de Chiapa y Guatemala*, was written between 1615 and 1617 by the Dominican Friar Antonio de Remesal. As a history of the Spaniards in that province, it proved to be polemical, and its distribution was suppressed for several years after its publication in 1620 (Esteve Barba 1964:276-277). Since then it has been widely acclaimed as an important source on the early history of Central America. It was published by the Sociedad de Geografía e Historia de Guatemala in 1932 (two volumes), and more recently as a part of the famous *Biblioteca de Autores Españoles* (Remesal 1964).

Remesal had been in Guatemala only two years at the time he began his book, and had experienced little contact with the Indians. Understandably, then, his study is not important as an ethnography of the Indians. Nevertheless, he used many documentary sources which contained references to the Indians, and he alone preserved some information of great importance on them.

He summarized an important account of the pacification of Verapaz, and included a few ethnographic details about the Indians of Rabinal (1932:4:200-217). The source for this account was a manuscript prepared by a friar at Sacapulas, Francisco Salvador de San Cipriano, written in Quiche around the turn of the century. Besides containing a history of the pacification of Verapaz, the original source had a description of the "idols of the province of Sacapula" (Remesal 1932:4:429). The part on the pacification of Verapaz was translated for Remesal by another priest.

Scattered throughout Remesal's two volumes are brief comments on the activities of the Indians around the time of the conquest, apparently based in part on the lost letter sent by Alvarado to Cortés. He did not have access to the two letters, and so describes only the events preceding the conquest, passing over the conquest in silence (except for a comment he took from the grandson of the ruler of Sacapulas at the time of the conquest) (1932: 4:19-20).

Remesal briefly commented on the conquest of the Lacandón, and the missionization of Manche Chol (1932:5:374ff: 571-589). According to Sáenz (1964:42), the source of his Lacandón account was a document from the audiencia in Guatemala.[15] The Manche information came from the Cipriano document mentioned above.

Remesal gives a few brief reports on the congregation of Indian towns through the efforts of the early missionaries (1932: 5:242-247:331-337). These were taken from official civil and ecclesiastical documents.

Sáenz (1964; 1966) has pointed out a number of errors and inconsistencies in the history of Remesal, especially in connection with his account of the pacification of Verapaz. Though I cannot agree with him on all his arguments,[16] he is correct in stating that

[15] The same account is given about a century later by Villagutierre (1933: 60ff), and has been discussed by other students (Thompson 1938; Villa Rojas 1967). The Lacandón mentioned were Chol speakers, occupying Lacam tun (hence, Lacandón), an island fortress in the lake of presentday Laguna de Miramar, eastern Chiapas (Villa Rojas 1967:29).

[16] Sáenz is undoubtedly correct in stating that Sacapulas was afforded a prominent place in the pacification story because the story was written there, though it is also possible that the rulers there assisted the priests in their missionary labors in Verapaz. Much confusion is removed, however, if it is assumed that cacique Juan was from Rabinal, not Sacapulas. The context in which he is described suggests this correlation and it is an error which easily could have been made.

Cipriano is a late source, and that the major thrust of the pacification of Verapaz was not until 1542 (CDI, 1925:156-157; Viana et al. 1955). Fortunately, the ethnographic information contained in the account is not affected by the errors in historical detail.

Remesal was not a good ethnographer, nor was he sympathetic toward Indian culture. As he expressed it, "they were idolators, this is all that can be said (of them)" (1932:4:429). He claims to have had considerable data on the religion and customs of Chiapas, but as in the case of the Cipriano material on the religion of the Quiche at Sacapulas, he did not think it worthy to be included in his book. The only useful purpose he could see in studying the beliefs and customs of the Indians was to facilitate their eradication, or to show their inferiority to Christianity. He decided that it was no longer necessary to study the ancient religion, and that to do so might stir the Indians to a return to their pagan ways. He included a few lines on the customs of the Indians in Chiapas, but they are prejudicial and distorted (1932:4:430-432).

More than anything else, Remesal's book is what he claimed of it, a history "whose truth consists in knowing true events (taken) from reports, relations, and authentic writings" (1932:4:14). The documents he found in Guatemala were the primary stimulus for his writing, and their preservation will always make his book an important source on the early history and cultures of Guatemala.

Thomas Gage

This fascinating book about life in early 17th century Guatemala was written by an unusual Dominican priest, Thomas Gage. He

---

It must also be realized that Verapaz did not include Rabinal, though the rulers of the two provinces were linked through marriage (cacique Juan's brother married a princess from Cobán). This interpretation is substantiated by the *Rabinal Achi* (Brasseur 1862), which records a similar marriage arrangement.

I disagree with Sáenz on two other minor points. I see no reason to doubt at least an initial congregation of Rabinal before the more widespread activity there after 1542. In fact, the whole congregation process should be considered as ongoing, and never fully completed. Sáenz notwithstanding, it seems clear that Las Casas in fact visited both Rabinal and Verapaz (Muñoz n.d.: Vols. 65-67). He, along with the other Dominicans, was exempt from the ban on the entrance of Spaniards into the area.

spent twelve years in Chiapas and Guatemala (1625-1637) laboring as the only English priest in the province, and upon returning to England (where he renounced his catholic affiliation) he wrote an account of his travels and life in the New World.[17] Though his book is propagandistically anti-Catholic, it nevertheless contains a useful description of the colonial life of Spaniards and Indians.

Gage shows no interest in historical matters, and does not cite a single document relating to the Indians. His book includes many ethnographic observations, the most important of which may be summarized as follows: He identifies several Pokoman towns in terms of the etymology of their names, agricultural production, and other special cultural features found there; he provides an insightful summary of the language, customs, social organization, and beliefs of the Pokoman Indians of eastern Guatemala (1958:214-247); he describes several incidences involving Indians which occurred while he was serving as village priest. These accounts reveal important facets of native character and world view at the time (1958:268-277).

Gage's description of native life was based on personal observation made during the seven years he lived at Mixco, Pinula, Petapa, and Amatitlán. He was fluent in the Pokoman language, and unquestionably came to understand well native culture. As noted by Thompson (Gage 1958:xlvi), he kept a journal during his stay in Guatemala, and much of his book is based on that source.

Gage was favorably impressed with the Indians and their way of life, though to a certain extent this was because he was anxious to prove they were superior to the Spaniards. He found their culture interesting, and his description of their customs is both sympathetic and insightful.[18]

---

[17] There have been several editions of Gage's book since the first edition, *The English-American by Sea and Land: or, A New Survey of the West-Indies,* published in 1648. I have found it convenient to use Thompson's edited version (1958), since nothing is gained by retaining the old English forms, nor the tirades against the Catholic church. No ethnographic information on the cultures of Guatemala is omitted in the Thompson edition (as I have verified by comparing it with an unedited version).

[18] Gage was not sympathetic to the native practices of idolatry and witchcraft. He appears to have been a genuine zealot in opposing these practices,

It is clear from his account that many prehispanic patterns had persisted in almost unchanged form. His references to the Indians, however, were focused on their relationship with the Spaniards. In fact, I know of no other book which more clearly portrays (though with some exaggeration) the exploitation of the Indians during the colonial period than Gage's, though the information is of little value in reconstructing aboriginal cultural patterns.

In spite of Gage's biases—his anti-Catholicism, and his focus on Spanish-Indian relations—his book remains an important source for the study of Pokoman cultural patterns (see Miles' use of Gage, 1957). He was a keen observer of social life and, fortunately, quite "truthful and reliable" (Gage 1958:xlvl; cf. Esteve Barba 1964:289).

Tovilla

In 1635, Martín Alonso Tovilla, the alcalde mayor of Verapaz, wrote a description and history of that region entitled, *Relación Histórica Descriptiva de las Provincias de la Verapaz y de la del Manche*. He apparently took his manuscript to Guatemala where it was later found by Fuentes y Guzmán, who used it as a source for his description of the conquest of the Manche Chol. Finally, it came to the public library of Toledo, Spain, from where photocopies were obtained by Scholes for his recent publication of it (Tovilla 1960).

Primarily, the book is important for its description of the conquest, pacification, and Christianization of the Chol and Lacandón area. In addition, it provides limited information on the Quichean Indians. The data may be summarized as follows: Besides a description of Verapaz which Tovilla extracted from Remesal, there are brief ethnographic notes for the region (e.g., on the methods used to "harvest" quetzal feathers) (1960:55-59: 141-149). These notes were based on Tovilla's observation during the five years he spent in the province. He comments on the geography and customs of a few Quiché-speaking towns which he visited—Rabinal,

---

and his description of them is disappointingly moralistic; perhaps because he wrote for a protestant England where idolatry was associated with the Catholics.

Salamá, Sacapulas, Cunen, Jocopilas, Ilotenango, Santa Cruz del Quiché, Chichicastenango, Sacualpa (1960:207-224). He gives a detailed description of the saltmaking industry at Sacapulas (1960; 217-219), and the mode of prehispanic government in Utatlán (1960:221-223). Apparently, he talked to Indian caciques at Sacapulas, and while at Utatlán obtained his information from Joseph Cortés, grandson of the "natural king," as they walked through the ruins of the old Quiche capital.

Tovilla has a noncommittal attitude toward the Indians. He reports on them in a factual way, without moral judgements (though he notes their extreme misery and poverty in some cases). He appears to have been genuinely interested in obtaining what information he could on native customs during his visits to their towns. He concludes some ethnographic notes with the comment that such "curious things are worthy of being known" (1960:219).

Tovilla's account is fundamentally a report to the audiencia on what he was able to find out about the provinces over which he had been put in charge. It was especially useful for him to know about the unconquered Indians in the northern part of his jurisdiction, and he made a special effort to obtain data—e.g., he had the account of the Chajul Indian translated and then recorded for him (1960:203-211). He was personally interested in the Indians, and was probably aware of his special capacity to dispassionately describe their customs. He was careful to cite his sources. Even though he was unacquainted with the literature already available on the Indians of Guatemala his account is generally authentic and pertinent.[19]

Fuentes y Guzmán

Francisco Antonio de Fuentes y Guzmán was born in Santiago de los Caballeros de Guatemala in 1643. As a descendant of the conquistadores, including Bernal Díaz del Castillo, he came from one of the most respected Spanish families of his time. He twice

---

[19] Tovilla's description of political rule in prehispanic Sacapulas and Utatlán testifies that aboriginal traditions were still strong in the heart of the Quiche area during the early part of the 17th century. The information Tovilla obtained from Joseph Cortés in 1631 is not very different from what Zorita recorded there almost a century earlier (1941:204).

served as alcalde of Santiago, and later became alcalde mayor of Totonicapán (ca. 1661) and Sonsonate (ca. 1699) (Gavarrette 1932). In these positions of prestige he gained access to many important documents referring to the history of Guatemala, written by religious and secular authorities, and Indian caciques. These sources, along with other documents in the possession of his family, formed the basis for his massive history of Guatemala.

The initial impetus to undertake the study came in 1675 from reading the first edition of the history of the conquest, written by his great-great-grandfather, Díaz del Castillo (see Primary Sources, Conquistadores). When he compared that edition with the manuscript in the possession of his family, he found many "errors" in it,[20] and thenceforth began searching for materials to prepare his own history. The first part was completed by 1690, and sent to Spain as part of an appeal for the title of *cronista real* of Guatemala (which apparently was never officially granted, nor was the manuscript published until 1882) (Aguilar 1933:4-5). A second part of his history was completed in 1699, but the contemplated third part was apparently cut short by his death in 1700. The first two parts were published together in the *Biblioteca "Goathemala"* (1932-1933) under the title, *Recordación Florida: Discurso Historial y Demostración Natural, Material, Militar y Política del Reyno de Guatemala*. The original manuscript is preserved in the Archivo General de Centroamérica.

The *Recordación Florida* has always been recognized as an important source for the study of the history and culture of early Guatemala, though Fuentes y Guzmán has been severely criticized for his exaggerations, disorganization, confusion and errors of fact, rambling, flowery style, and his obvious bias in favor of the conquistadores (Gavarrette 1932:xx; cf. Aguilar 1933:3-40). Granting the general validity of these criticisms, it is my considered opinion that Fuentes y Guzmán was a better student of Indian culture than is usually recognized, and that his work is of inestimable importance for any study of prehispanic Quichean cultural patterns.

---

[20] The discrepancy between the accounts is probably due to the fact that the family manuscript contained the additions and revisions made by Díaz del Castillo during the sixteen years which elapsed after his first draft was sent to Spain (Cerwin 1963).

In a general statement by Fuentes y Guzmán on the sources which he used to reconstruct the history and customs of the Indians, he tells of certain "papers which some principal Indians and ecclesiastical ministers have communicated to me, and others, which coming into the hands of lawyers from the audiencia for Indian disputes and litigation have come into my hands" (1932-1933: 6:5).

We find scattered throughout his work references to the sources of his writings. The quality and quantity of these sources are impressive. To give but a partial listing, he made use of native informants, native manuscripts or títulos, personal observation, special reports from priestly and secular officials, tradition, unpublished Spanish manuscripts, native pictorials and maps, official statistics of the Crown, litigation papers, old pictures in churches and private houses, personal and reported surveys of archaeological sites,[21] cabildo records, and published works (Remesal, Torquemada). Any modern ethnographer would be proud to claim a similar list of sources.

Though Fuentes y Guzmán did not speak the native languages, he had access to translations. It is now possible to correct many errors and exaggerations he made because of new perspectives resulting from advances in knowledge and passing time. When these corrections are made, his work remains as an important contribution to the study of native culture.

The most important ethnohistoric materials in the work by Fuentes y Guzmán are on native history and culture, taken from early documents no longer available (see Native Documents). Other materials of importance are: Various accounts of the conquest of Guatemala, based mostly upon documents written by the

---

[21] Fuentes y Guzmán showed a strong interest in the study of archaeological remains. He visited several sites, and transcribed pictorial and written descriptions of them.

His descriptions of Iximché and Zaculew have proven to be reasonably accurate (Guillemin 1965; Woodbury and Trik 1953), whereas the one for Utatlán is grossly distorted (Maudslay 1899). In addition to personal inspection of various sites, he solicited descriptions of some from priests who were living in the communities where they were located (8:109:197). His drawing of the ruins of Uspantán (8:197) was obtained from Friar Amaro Fernández, "after the solicitation of many letters and untiring pleas."

conquistadores (see Primary Spanish Documents, Conquistador Writings). Scattered descriptions of native customs and laws, which appear to have been taken from priestly documents not generally cited by Fuentes y Guzmán (e.g., 6:11-14; 6:156-158; 7:125-128; 8:396-401). Geographical data on population figures, domesticated plants and animals, natural flora and fauna, for the various provinces of Guatemala. He apparently derived this information from personal observation, official reports and statistics of the audiencia, and special reports from priests, prepared at his request (see his comment in 7:412).

Fuentes y Guzmán's attitude toward the Indians was ambivalent. He saw much in their culture and their persons to admire: they had a developed aristocracy, with associated luxurious accoutrements (including impressive military and religious buildings); they were physically well-proportioned and attractive; they were hardworking and resolute; they had a well-ordered political system, and kept impressive histories. However, he considered most of their religious practices abominable, and many of their customs barbarian. They could not be compared favorably with the Spaniards, and their old way of life should be replaced by Spanish culture—he argued that they should learn Spanish in place of their native languages, and that their licentious rituals should be replaced with Christian orthodox ones (6:210ff;8:406-407). He did not deny the impressive steps toward civilization they had made before the conquest, for the Indians were a kind of propaganda resource to Guatemala, whose worth should not be underestimated. I think, too, that he was surprised at the degree of development of native culture before the conquest, and as he consulted the early sources, he increasingly became aware of and interested in it.

His purposes in writing are clear. He wrote first as a creole patriot, desirous of lauding the Kingdom of Guatemala and its inhabitants (Esteve Barba 1964:281), which meant that not only the acts of the Spanish population would be exaggerated, but those of the Indians too. He was willing to accept a Mexican origin for the native kingdoms in Guatemala, but he would not concede that they represented a lower level of development than the political systems of the Indians of Mexico and Peru (6:5). This is why he focuses on the political accomplishments of the

Quichean and other native groups, exaggerating the size of their armies, cities, and jurisdictions. It explains why he was more interested in the documentary accounts of the Indians than in personal observation of them. Many comments on the contemporaneous Indians around him are in the form of a lamentation for the miserable state into which they had fallen (especially he regretted the loss of prestige and position suffered by the descendants of the prehispanic aristocracy) (8:422). One detects a special bias in reporting those instances where his own forefathers played an important role—Díaz del Castillo, Hernando de Chávez.

He was influended, too, by the nature of the documentary information which he found in the archives at Santiago, and later obtained from the priests (including Vázquez). He claims to have searched for over fourteen months in the archives of the city and, finding many important documents there, he made an index of them, and resolved to write a history. In part, he wrote as a historian who had discovered sources with "things very worthy of being remembered," not known to those who had written before him (6:2). Curiously, he was probably less successful at writing history than describing native culture and history. Fortunately for students of the Guatemalan Indian, Fuentes y Guzmán was a better ethnologist than historian.

Vázquez

An important book for the study of Guatemalan Indians is a chronicle written by the Franciscan creole, Francisco de Asís Vázquez de Herrera. Twenty-one years after entering the order, Vázquez became chronicler of the Province of Guatemala (1683), and from that time until near the year of his death (in 1713-1714) he continued to work on his mammoth history (Lamadrid 1937: x-xiv). It was published two years later in Guatemala under the title, *Crónica de la Provincia del Santísimo Nombre de Jesus de Guatemala*, and more recently (1937-1944) as four volumes of the *Biblioteca "Goathemala."* For the latter edition, Fray Lamadrid has prepared a useful introductory biography on Vázquez, footnotes to the text, and a complete index of proper names.

Inserted at the beginning of the fourth volume of the work is a document written in 1689 under the direction of Vázquez, and entitled, *Descripción de los conventos de la Santa Provincia del Nombre de Jesus de Guatemala*. Though not part of the original chronicle, it is of importance to us (the original is in the Latin American Collection of the University of Texas Library).

In addition to strictly historical matters concerning the Franciscan Order and government of Guatemala,[22] Vázquez' writings contain significant information on Quichean culture.

He provides a few details on events surrounding the conquest of the Indians (14:16-27;15:157-159). He appears not to have had the two letters sent by Alvarado to Cortés, though he may have had Cortés' fourth letter to the king, which mentions the visit of the Cakchiquel emissaries to Mexico. His account of the circumstances surrounding the conquest was apparently based on native títulos, possibly the *Título Huitzitzil Tzunun* and the *Título Nijaib I* (Gall 1963; Recinos 1957:91-93).

Scattered throughout his book, especially in the first volume, are vrief references to native customs, based on observation either made by Vázquez in the 17th century, or other Franciscans during the 16th century.[23]

In a survey of the convents of the Franciscan Order, Vázquez recorded for each settlement data on population size (i.e., numbers of parishioners), native languages spoken there, local geographical features, and, in a few cases, local native customs (17:33-67). Except for a few of the population figures (14:170, 249), these data are contained in the *Descripción* inserted in the fourth volume of the chronicle.

Vázquez claims to have had several Indian títulos in his possession (15:26), probably many of those used by his friend, Fuentes y Guzmán. Yet he makes almost no use of them. Vázquez saw the Indians as a recalcitrant people, rebellious against the

[22] Vázquez was inaccurate on many historical points, and has been criticized for this. Ximénez pointed out some errors (1929-1931), and modern historians have found others (Gall 1963:7-19). Esteve Barba says that he was "credulous and thin in certain affirmations of a historical type" (1964:275).

[23] E.g., reciting events from the life of Fray Francisco del Colmenar (who labored in Guatemala from 1544-1581), Vázquez tells (1937-1944:15:82-83) of his converting an Indian cacique from Sololá. Kakawitz, as the old man was called, had several wives, and did not want to leave them, though, according to the report, he finally gave them up.

true religion, and deceived by the devil. Native society and culture were impediments to Spanish subjugation and Christian conversion, which apparently he accepted unquestioningly as the right order of things. He sides with both the conquistadores and the missionaries in their contests of power with native resisters.

Vázquez wrote primarily as historian of the Franciscan Order, and as creole patriot. The Indians were somewhat incidental to his purposes, and information about them, for the most part, is contained in sources cited by him. Nevertheless, he included material of interest on the religious history of Guatemala (with a Franciscan bias). I agree with Esteve Barba's evaluation of his chronicle: "it is a repository of interesting notices, lost among inopportune facts . . . one must review it with attention in order to discover among his copious, disorganized and massive text, notices about the teachings of the Indians, indigenous clergy, or customs from the time of the viceroyalty" (1964:276).

Ximénez

Francisco Ximénez, a Dominican friar, came to Guatemala in 1688 at the age of twenty-one. For the next third of a century, until his death in 1729-1730, he lived among the Quiche and Cakchiquel-speaking Indians. He claims to have spoken Quiché for twenty years and to have acquired a "perfect mastery" of it (1929-1931:1:65), as a result of his three years in Chichicastenango, ten years in Rabinal, and four years in Sacapulas. I think it fair to say that Ximénez qualifies as the foremost linguist and ethnographer of Quichean culture during the colonial period.

Apart from his transcription and translation of the *Popol Vuh* (see Native Sources) and his work on the Quiche language, his most important contributions to the study of Quiche cultural patterns are the first volume of his *Historia de la Provincia de San Vicente de Chiapa y Guatemala* (1929-1931), and his *Historia Natural del Reino de Guatemala* (1967). An account of his other works, and the circumstances surrounding the production of the above works is given by Recinos in his introduction to the *Popol Vuh* (1953:37-55). It is in reference to the *Historia de la Provincia*, and the *Historia Natural* that the following evaluation of Ximénez is made.

Ximénez began the *Historia de la Provincia* in 1715, at a time when he had already spent some fourteen years in Quiche-speaking communities. He was intimately familiar with Quiche culture by then, as may be learned by studying the following items relevant to the Quiche found in that work.

During his many years among the Quiche, Ximénez became familiar with their clan and lineage organization, which in several places he clarifies and relates to prehispanic patterns (1929:71-74: 101-105).

During his residence in Xenacoj, Rabinal, and Chichicastenango, he gained access to important documentary materials which contained references to prehispanic patterns. Specifically, he describes the movement of the Pokoman to Yampuc (1929:69:76:149), the political boundaries of the Rabinal before the conquest (1929:75:195-196), the genealogy of the ruling line at Utatlán (1929:119-210), and the function of Quichean temples in aboriginal culture (1929:74).

His discussion of Quiche religion provides original ethnographic materials (1929:78: 101-102), as well as important additions to the writings of Las Casas (1929:81-100).[24]

Ximénez' account of the conquest and pacification of Guatemala (1929:113 *passim*) provides a few corrections to the writings of Fuentes y Guzmán, Vázquez, and in some cases Remesal, as well as giving limited ethnographic and geographic details.

Ximénez' *Historia Natural*, recently published by the Sociedad de Geografía e Historia de Guatemala (1967), was written in 1722 at Sacapulas. It was probably our most important geographical study on Guatemala until McBryde's monograph was published in 1945. He confines his account to geographical factors of im-

[24] Ximénez fully acknowledged that he was taking several chapters directly from Román, and he was also aware that Román's writings were based on Las Casas (1929:96). These are the relevant chapters in Ximénez which can be correlated with chapters in Las Casas' *Apologética Historia* (1958): the description of sacrifice (X. 1929:81-83) comes from Chapter 177 (L.C. 1958: 147-149); the so-called *Cuaresma* ceremony (X. 1929:83-86) from chapter 178 (L.C. 1958:150-153): the places of sacrifice (X. 1929:87-90) from chapter 179 (L.C. 1958:153-157); the description of government and laws (X.1929: 90-96) from chapters 234 and 326 (L.C. 1958:341-345, 351-354); the chapters on marriage (X. 1929:96-98) and burial (X. 1929:360-362) from Las Casas, chapters 238 and 240 (1958:354-356: 360-362).

portance to the Indians, and includes much ethnographic material learned from his long residence in the Indian communities. Unfortunately, his treatment of geographical features is uneven with perhaps the most complete description being on the domestication of bees. His discussion of plant domestication is rather skimpy for a subject of such economic importance.

Ximénez is best known for his discovery and translation of the *Popol Vuh*, but it should be remembered that he was an ethnographer of considerable ability, and his observations about Quichean language and culture are still important. He appears to have been the first Spanish writer effectively to combine documentary data on the Indians with observations of their contemporaneous culture. He was led to do this because of his intimate knowledge of Quichean language and customs, and the chance discovery and subsequent translation of the *Popol Vuh.*

Ximénez' attitude toward the Indians is perhaps more favorable than that of any other Spanish writer during the colonial period. Without reservation he claimed that Quiche culture was advanced, and that the Spaniards had much to learn from it (1929: 1). Their mode of government and manner of writing came in for special praise, but even more impressive to him was their language. He stated, "I have become persuaded that this language is about the principal one of the world" (1929:65). He had some doubts about the Indian's natural capabilities (1929:59), but accepted the thesis that they were descendants of the Israelites, and that they had been visited by Saint Thomas (1929:53-64). He felt they had later fallen into error under the influence of Satan, but were not nearly so "bestial" as the conquistadores had portrayed them. Hence, he argued, the Indians were apt subjects for conversion to Christianity—they tenaciously held to their ancient traditions, but were capable of changing their beliefs if the message could be brought to them in their own tongue, according to their manner of understanding (1929:59).

In part, then, Ximénez wrote his history to present the materials he had gathered on the Quiche, and thereby express his viewpoint as to who they were and where they came from. Beyond that, he was a chronicler of the Dominican Order, continuing a tradition of history begun by Fray Juan de Torres, and continued by Remesal and Molina. He updated those chronicles to about 1720, and made corrections and additions to them and other works preceding his own study (including rather severe criticism of Fuentes y Guzmán and Vázquez). As noted by Esteve Barba (1964:280), his chronicle becomes rather monastic and provincial after the founding of the Dominican convent in 1541, though later sections contain important accounts of the conquest of the Chol and Lacandón, and the rebellions of the Tzendales in Chiapas.

Minor Historians

A few other histories from the colonial period are, for various reasons, not sufficiently significant for the study of Quichean culture to warrant a detailed analysis here. I shall briefly discuss them in the chronological order in which they were written. Emphasis will be placed on the ethnographic information in them.

Vázquez de Espinosa. — Between 1612 and 1621, Vázquez de Espinosa, an erudite Carmelite friar traversed almost the whole extent of Spanish America, studying its geography, society, and economic conditions. Upon his return to Spain he prepared a comprehensive account of his observations and information received from other people in the Indies, a mammoth work not quite completed at the time of his death in 1630. The manuscript was lost to the scholarly world until, in 1929, it was found in the Vatican library by Mr. Charles Upson Clark of the Smithsonian Institution. Clark translated the entire manuscript into English, entitled it, *Description of the Indies*, then supplemented his translation with an extremely useful index to its contents (1968).

The account is not historically oriented, by Vázquez' own admission, but contains numerous historical facts, and in general is like the other works described above. Some eleven chapters are devoted to Guatemalan matters, and there are a few scattered references to Guatemala in other chapters of the book. Most descriptions are of Spanish affairs, though considerable information on the geography of Guatemala is included. Information on the Indians is confined to a few population figures, and brief mention of their languages, the customary use of the sweat bath, and general social conditions.

Molina. — In 1677-1678 the Dominican friar, Antonio de Molina initiated a chronicle of the events occurring after 1628 which involved his order. It was continued to 1721 by Friars Agustín Cano and Francisco Ximénez, and the latter took information from it for his own history of Guatemala and Chiapas. The entire chronicle was published in Guatemala in 1943 under the title, *Antigua Guatemala.*

. This source is not important for the study of the Indians of Guatemala. It is a useful account of the culture history of the Dominicans in Guatemala, and especially of the role the order played in the founding of the Universidad de San Carlos (see Esteve Barba 1964:281).

Crónica Franciscana. — A manuscript history was written around 1685 by an anonymous friar of the Franciscan Order entitled, *Crónica de la Santa Provincia del Santíssimo Nombre de Jesus de Guatemala.* It was found in the archives of the Archbishopric of Guatemala by Juan Gavarrete in 1829, who later placed it in the library of the Sociedad Económica. Berendt saw it there toward the close of the 19th century, and made a copy of its seventh chapter (n.d.). Brasseur also obtained a copy of it, about 1855 (1857:LXXXIV), and took it back to France. At the dissolution of the Sociedad the manuscript apparently disappeared, and its present location is unknown.[25] Sadly, the Brasseur copy also seems to have disappeared; at least I have been unable to find any trace of it in the repositories to which the other Brasseur documents were sent after his death.

Berendt states that the manuscript contained 283 folios, 141 of which covered the period of Guatemalan history from 1524

[25] The original *Crónica Franciscana* is probably somewhere in Guatemala, and an all-out attempt should be made to locate it. I carefully looked for it in the Archivo General de Centroamérica, and made inquiries about it with Guatemalan historians, but I found no trace of it. Nor did I find it in the archives of the Archbishopric, though many documents preserved there are not available to scholars. It is my guess that the *Crónica Franciscana* is in the Archbishopric archives, which, hopefully, will someday be completely opened to inspection by serious scholars.

The library of the Sociedad Económica was taken to the Sociedad de Geografía e Historia de Guatemala, but the president of that association told me that the *Crónica Franciscana* was not part of the transfer.

to 1541 (48 chapters), and 140 the period from 1541 to 1600 (42 chapters). His extract of chapter seven on the Cakchiquel calendar (Berendt n.d.), shows the tremendous potential value of this source for the study of Quichean cultural patterns. This is also evident from Brasseur's use of it in his study of Quiche history (1857; Appendix XXIII).

A small fragment of a document from the Peabody Museum Library of Harvard University appears to be part of chapter four of the *Crónica Franciscana*. The fragment is introduced with the simple explanation that it was written by an anonymous Franciscan historian, and that the original manuscript was in the Franciscan convent in Guatemala. The heading is given as chapter four, apparently three chapters in front of the calendar mentioned above.[26] The text contains citations from Torquemada (so must be dated after 1615), and a statement that almost 200 years had passed since the conquest. The author had access to the *Annals of the Cakchiquels*, and, most importantly, to a native título which Fuentes y Guzmán used for his account of Acxopil (see Native Sources; Appendix XV).

Isogoge Histórica Apologética. — Sometime between 1700 and 1711 an anonymous Dominican priest wrote a long, religiously oriented history of the province of Guatemala. The manuscript was found in modern times in the Dominican convent of Guatemala, and published as a volume of the *Biblioteca "Goathemala"* (Anonymous 1935b). It contains little information on the Indians, and of the little there is, some was taken from Fuentes y Guzmán (e.g., Anonymous 1935:183:205). The only native terms included are in a sentence taken from testimony given by Diego Reynoso, a Quiche lord from Utatlán: *chupan quaresma xul donadi, capitan ajlabal, waral paquiche, la poroj tinamit; ta xkaj ajawarem, ta xtane patan, rumal ronojel amak' xpatawij chiquiwach kamama, kakajaw, paquiche* ("Tonatiuh, the military captain, came here in Quiche at the time of 'Quaresma,' when the fortified center

---

[26] The existence of this manuscript with its apparently elaborate account of native culture may explain why Vázquez was so sketchy in his references to Indian history and customs. The *Crónica Franciscana* may have been considered the standard work on the Indians at the time, a possibility which makes it even more important that it be located.

was burned, and the lordship fell; then the tribute which all the settlements payed to our grandfathers and fathers in Quiche ceased") (Anonymous 1935b:191).

Rivera. — In the Archivo General de Centroamérica (Al:4501-38360) there is a brief history of the pacification and Christianization of the province of Verapaz, written in 1750 by the Dominican Friar Juan de Rivera. The full title of the document is, *Visión de Paz . . . Nueva Jerusalén, construida y figurada en los primitivos héroes de la fundación de esta provincia, antes Tierra de Guerra, hoy Verapaz.* It contains an account of the activities of the earliest Dominican priests to labor in Verapaz, including Las Casas, Angulo, Torres, Vico, Viana, Zúñiga, and others. The account is based largely on sources already available (mostly Remesal, and Ximénez), and adds no significant new information.

Juarros. — Domingo Juarros' famous history of Guatemala, *Compendio de la Historia de la Ciudad de Guatemala,* was written at the close of the colonial period (between 1805 and 1818). It is perhaps the best known of the Guatemalan chronicles, mainly because it is the only one to have been translated into English (1823). The most recent Spanish edition of it was published in Guatemala in 1937.

It is of little importance in studying the Indians, for almost all references to them were taken directly from Fuentes y Guzmán. Somewhat more useful is its geographical information, though the time period is so late that every fact must be checked against data in earlier accounts in order to establish its authenticity. The population figures he cites from the 1778 census can be compared with those of Cortés y Larraz, and used to reconstruct a growth curve which might eventually be helpful in extrapolating prehispanic population figures.

COLONIAL RECORDS

I have divided the documents in this section into administrative records, judicial records, and records from Momostenango. Under administrative records, I group together the documents which were separately discussed in Primary Spanish Documents as statistical and administrative records, and relaciones. This is not because there is a decrease in the quantity of records. On the contrary, the corpus is substantially larger for the 17th and 18th centuries than it is for the 16th century. The records correspond to a new social reality, and shed less and less light on aboriginal cultural patterns as they were written later in time. For example, tributary records were continued throughout the colonial period, though with the passing of time they become less useful to the ethnohistorian as prehispanic demographic trends radically changed. Instead, we have more convenient summaries of such demographic patterns in the writings of the colonial chroniclers. However, we must sift through large numbers of colonial records in order to cull a relatively few kernels of aboriginal material. It seems, therefore, best to lump them together and abbreviate their description.

The administrative records to be described consist of reports made by civil and ecclesiastical officials of the Crown. Data on Indian culture is scarce in the documents, but the report made by Cortés y Larraz proves that important observations on native culture could still be made as late as the last quarter of the 18th century.

The land dispute judicial records again prove to be of considerable importance for identifying the aboriginal names of places and social groupings mentioned in the native títulos. Sacapulas is a Quiche-speaking community for which we have an especially rich corpus of land dispute documents. A detailed description of their contents shows their potential value for studying native patterns. In the last part of this section, the entire post16th century corpus of documents from Momostenango is described in order to provide a check on the completeness and representativeness of the documents discussed in the precedings parts of the section.

Administrative Records

We will note that the first documents to be described correspond to the relaciones of the 16th century, though they are also similar to the administrative records classified above as one kind of primary Spanish source. The documents described toward the end of this section are more characteristically "official" records, generally containing a simple record of legal acts and a quantification of facts for administrative use. Documents of this kind are truly abundant in both the Archivo General de Indias and Archivo General de Centroamérica, and I have selected for discussion only the more promising examples. The following account will illustrate the corpus of such documents in the latter archive, but scarcely suggests their richness in the famous Indian archive of Spain.

Official Reports. — I include in this category several reports sent by Spanish officials to the Crown. One of the earliest documents is a report sent in 1603 by the Bishop of Guatemala, telling of the abuses received by the Indians at the hands of Spanish officials (AGI, Guatemala 156). The good bishop definitely sides with the Indians on this issue, enumerating Spanish abuses in lurid detail. He even sees the sacking of Puerto de Caballos by the English as a punishment sent from God. The document contains a useful description of relations between the Spaniards and Indians around the turn of the century, and in this sense is a companion to the account left us by Gage. But there is little information on surviving native cultural forms.

In a 1628 mandate sent by the Crown to the audiencia, the contents of a report made three years earlier by an oidor of that court are summarized (Konetzke 1953-1962:2:319-322). Some of "the ancient rites which the Indians had in their gentile condition" are briefly recited in order that they might be eradicated. The description is prejudiced, but aboriginal patterns of marriage, family organization, ceremonial drama, and cacao production are recognizable. The same topics are more clearly presented in the primary sources, but their persistence into colonial times sheds light on their functional dependence or independence of the upper levels of prehispanic political organization.

From an anonymous Spanish official, whose jurisdiction included the Mam-speaking peoples east of Quezaltenango, we have another report, apparently written in 1688 (Casteñeda and Dabbs 1939:Gll-43). For each community the number of tributaries is given, and unusual geographical features are noted. Except for a few Indian names of topographical features, no other information on aboriginal culture is given.

In 1740, the Crown sent a small questionnaire to the audiencia, requesting information on "the number of cities, villages, towns in each of the provinces of the kingdom and, respectively, their inhabitants, fruits, crops, mines, manufacturing, distances from the capital, and the location and climate of each town." The relaciones geográficas of 1740 are answers which were sent to the Crown by various officials. The reports from the Valley of Guatemala (Antigua), Escuintla, Huehuetenango, Totonicapán (1743), Atitlán, and Tecpán Atitlán were published in the *Boletín del Archivo General del Gobierno*, Guatemala (Anonymous 1935c). Those from Quezaltenango and Chiquimula are also in the Archivo General de Centroamérica (Al:210-5009), and similar but subsequent relaciones geográficas exist for Suchitepéquez (1755), and Verapaz (1816) (AGC, Al:206-4141; Al: 29-845).

All relaciones are brief and contain virtually no information on aboriginal cultural patterns.[27] They are variable in the amount of information which they contain (those for Escuintla and Huehuetenango are the most extensive), but in every case they are brief compared to the 16th century relaciones geográficas. Nevertheless, they contain useful statistical data on demographic and economic patterns.

In 1763, Narciso Barquín Monte Cuesta, the ex-alcalde mayor of Suchitepéquez, sent a report to the Crown on the problem created for cacao producers of that province because of having to pay tribute in money rather than cacao beans (AGC, Al:206-4149). Three years later on further inquiry into the matter by the Crown, an additional report was filed by the fiscal of the audiencia. Monte Cuesta claims in his report that he had waited until after his retirement to inform on this matter, so that he would not be accused of personal interest. Indeed, it appears that he was able objectively to report the abuses and exploitation of the Indians perpetrat-

---

[27] Possibly the most ethnohistorically useful of the 18th century relaciones geográficas is the one from Escuintla. It was written in 1740 by Alonso Crespo, the justicia mayor of the provinces of Escuintla and Guazacapan. In it we are given a good picture of the Escuintla area at the time, the towns located there (some of which have since disappeared), languages spoken, the agricultural products of the different communities, and something about the natural flora and fauna. The document is also helpful in establishing boundary lines between the Pipil and Cakchiquel peoples, and the Xinca, and Popoloca.

ed by the Spaniards in that province. Unfortunately, there are no significant data in his report on aboriginal culture, though along with the report of the fiscal, it is an important source of information on the kind of exploitation suffered by the Indians during the colonial period. Both documents indicate that the Indians were suffering from a heavy loss of lands, and fraudulent and excessive tribute payments.

Another interesting report was written in 1778 by an anonymous official of the hacienda section of the audiencia in Guatemala.[28] The report contains a brief description (mostly statistical in nature) of the provinces of Chiquimula, Verapaz, Sacatepéquez, Escuintla, Suchitepéquez, Chimaltenango, Atitlán and Sololá, Totonicapán, Quezaltenango, and New Guatemala. There is little information on native cultural patterns, though we are given a revealing view of socioeconomic conditions in Guatemala at the time.

Another report, also filed toward the end of the 18th century (1779-1783), was prepared by an anonymous official commissioned by President Gálvez to survey the coastal areas of Guatemala in search of possible saltmaking sites. His itinerary took him to the coastal plains below Escuintla, then to El Salvador and the Suchitepéquez area. Later, he traversed the Totonicapán and Huehuetenango region on his way to Chiapas, Mexico. We are given a sketchy view of the haciendas, towns, and topography of the areas visited, but essentially no information on native life.

Cortés y Larraz. — Probably the most useful report made during the colonial period is the *Descripción Geográfico-Moral de la Diócesis de Goathemala*, by Archbishop Pedro Cortés y Larraz (1958). It is based on observations which he made during a visit to the curates under his jurisdiction in the years 1768 to 1770,

---

[28] This document and the one to be described next were copied in Spain by Carl Sauer, and are part of the Sauer collection of microfilms in the Department of Geography, at the University of California, Berkeley.

The first report entitled, *Noticias del Reyno de Guatemala, frutos que produce, pueblos, habitantes, y tributarios que tiene, y quanto pagan al Rey*, came from the Real Academia de la Historia, Mata Linares Collection, Vol. 1, ff. 220-246v.

The second report, *Varias noticias del Reyno de Goatemala y Monterrey, y la distancia de unos pueblos a otros*, came from the Museo Naval, Madrid #570, Virreinato de Mexico, Vol. IV, Exp. #7.

and on the written answers to a questionnaire which he sent to the priests of these convents.[29] Cortés y Larraz' use of the replies by the priests varies from brief summaries of their contents (e.g., the report from Uspantán), to extensive extracts (e.g., the report from San Cristóbal Totonicapán). However, he always uses them for his own purposes, and his final report clearly shows an emphasis on the impressions which he gained from his visit to each community in his jurisdiction. For this reason, both his final report and the individual replies by the priests must be studied.

The reports, from almost every community in Guatemala, contain some ethnographic information about aboriginal cultural patterns. One finds useful data on the native languages spoken in each community, local production and trade, family organization (1958:II:30-31), and settlement patterns (1958:II:299-300). Of special importance are the descriptions by several priests of native "superstitions and idolatries," a topic on which they were specifically queried by the Archbishop. Solano Pérez Lila culled most of the data on native religious practices (1963), and demonstrated how they are related to prehispanic religious patterns.

The population figures given by Cortés y Larraz must be taken as approximations (1958:XII), and they are too recent to be of value in reconstructing prehispanic demographic patterns. It might also be noted that Cortés y Larraz presents information which clarifies the extent of native rebellion during the colonial period—both in terms of physical opposition to the Spaniards, and ideological resistance to Christianity.

Cortés y Larraz was not sympathetic to native culture, but saw it as a weapon of the enemy which had to be removed. In this regard, some priests were more lenient than he, and were

---

[29] The replies to Cortés y Larraz' questionnaire were recopied and placed with the manuscript text of his *Descripción Geográfico-Moral*, and are now located in the Archivo General de Indias (Guatemala 948). I have a microfilm copy of those replies which refer to curates within the boundaries of present-day Guatemala. Francisco Solano Pérez Lila has recently completed a doctoral dissertation at the Universidad de Madrid on the Indians of Guatemala during the 18th century, based almost wholly on the summary by Cortés y Larraz and the replies from the resident priests. Besides extracting demographic and ethnographic materials from these sources, he transcribed the replies and placed them in appendices. We hope the dissertation will be published soon, so that his reconstruction might be carefully studied.

severely criticized by him. Paradoxically, Cortés y Larraz' attitude was nevertheless more conducive to the eliciting of aboriginal cultural data than was that of the priests. Whereas they were afraid to admit the substantial strength of native tradition still extant in the villages, he was driven to expose it on every side, that he might thereby try to extirpate it (1958:II:43-44). Cortés y Larraz' approach would lead to an accelerated disappearance of aboriginal patterns, but it also provided a record which is a boon to the ethnohistorian.

Church Records. — As noted above in the discussion of the name lists, Church baptismal, birth, death, and marriage records are valuable sources for the reconstruction of native kinship and marriage patterns (Carrasco 1961b;1964). I have already listed the communities from which I obtained seventeenth and eighteenth century Church statistics. Clearly, the list of names obtained from these records are secondary to the lists contained in some of the statistical records cited in Primary Spanish Documents, but for some communities they represent the only source of information we have about matters of kinship and marriage during the colonial period.

Other church documents which have come to us are the official record books of Indian cofradías. Gates obtained copies of two such books written in Quiche—one from Cofradía San Nicolás (at Sacapulas), written between the years 1664 and 1852, and the other by Cofradía Rosario, written in 1689 (Gates n.d.; Butler 1937:197). There are other surviving examples, but they appear to contain little useful information on aboriginal cultural patterns, and even the two documents mentioned, aside from the Quiché language in which they were written, reveal little about aboriginal culture. But they are useful for studying the changes in religious patterns which occurred after the conquest period.

A related document is a record of a *quinto* (one-fifth) tax assessment on church ornaments made in 1801 against the cathedral and cofradías of Totonicapán (AGC, A3:5305-21). In listing the names of cofradía and town officials, a few aboriginal clan and lineage names are given.

I should also mention two documents prepared by ecclesiastical authorities around 1690 (Casteñeda and Dabbs 1939: G19 37).

One contains a list of Indian towns under Franciscan jurisdiction and was discussed with the writings of Fray Vázquez. The other document has a list of the Franciscan priests working in Guatemala in 1690. In noting the languages spoken by the priests in the different Indian communities, we are given an indication of the languages indigenous to each place. The document is far more important, however, for the view it affords of the Franciscan Order at the time—it shows that there was already a large number of creole priests in Guatemala.

Judicial Records

The 17th and 18th centuries were a time of considerable unrest with respect to controlling rights to Indian lands. Populations expanded beyond the capacity of the land to support them, and ravenous hacendados usurped Indian lands through purchase, legal fraud, or outright seizure (Gibson 1966). This condition spawned the many transactional documents (testamentaries, bills of sale) discussed in Native Language Documents. It also fostered inter- and intracommunity land disputes, the legal records of which have been preserved in large numbers in the Archivo General de Centroamérica, and to a less extent in the Archivo de la Escribanía, Sección de Tierras, Guatemala.

In some land disputes the natives brought forth 16th century títulos as supporting evidence for their claims, and these documents constitute an important primary source for the study of native cultural patterns (see Primary Spanish Sources). In other cases, early documents used as evidence are alluded to but not attached to the legal papers. These references, along with contemporaneous 17th and 18th century testimony are the main data of interest. Generally, the references are to the names of places and social groups which had continued from prehispanic times into the colonial period.

Again the student is faced with the challenge of many potentially valuable documents. The catalogue descriptions in the Archivo General de Centroamérica are helpful in this regard, for they usually give a brief but clear indication of the contents of each bundle of documents. From this it is often possible to determine whether or not the document contains references to matters likely to be related to aboriginal cultural forms. As an additional limiting device I have generally concentrated on documents from the central highlands, especially the areas around Santa Cruz del Quiché and Totonicapán. It becomes obvious when studying the catalogue references that there is a particularly rich corpus of land dispute documents for Sacapulas, and I have attempted to exploit this source more thoroughly.

In a summary such as this, only a sample of the relevant documents can be described. I hope it is a representative sample of these documents, but necessarily leaves out many available sources which also contain substantive information about aboriginal cultural patterns. With this limitation in mind, I shall discuss the colonial judicial records in the following order: land dispute papers from Quiche and Cakchiquel-speaking communities, similar documents from San Miguel Totonicapán and Santo Domingo Sacapulas, and judicial records which relate to the granting of privileges to Indian caciques.

Quiché and Cakchiquel Communities. — There is a disappointing scarcity of land dispute documents from the Santa Cruz del Quiché region, though the Archivo General de la Escribanía, Guatemala, Sección de Tierras contains a fairly large number of less important documents from there, written in the 19th century. An interesting available record is of a dispute in 1628 between Santa Cruz and San Pedro Jocopilas over lands called Chichuchu, Chicul, and Mocwel (AGC, Al:5939-5162). Besides containing references to a few toponyms of importance, the town of San Pedro Jocopilas is called Uquin, which is the name given an important Ilocab settlement in the *Popol Vuh* (Recinos 1953:195). Another brief document from Jocopilas is the record of a dispute in 1703 over lands within that community, and contains the Quiche names of a few principales (AGC, Al:5958-52210).

Later documents from Santa Cruz (1752-1779) provide a general list of the boundary-marker names of the town (AGC, Al:5996-52754; Al:6021-53078), and a 19th century document (1831) which I studied in the municipality during a visit there in 1967 contains additional boundary names, along with a brief description of the economic condition of the town. During that same visit, I was permitted to study early land títulos from Lemoa, Patzité, and

Ilotenango. The elders of aldea San Sebastían Lemoa have an 1836 título, kept in a metal tube, which contains a map showing the limits of the aldea's territory, and a list of names of important boundary markers shared with Santa Cruz, Chiché, and Patzité. The título from Patzité[30] contains an explanation that Indians from Chiquimula and parcialidad Tamu(b) had been combined in the formation of this town and a crude map of the boundaries which were established at the time.

San Antonio Ilotenango also lacks an ancient título, their main land title having resulted from an 1894 dispute over lands with Santa Cruz. In spite of its late date of composition, it contains a good list of toponyms, and has a map showing the territory and location of the most important boundary markers.

During the 18th century the Indians of Ilotenango became involved in a dispute with Santa María Chiquimula and Santa Cruz over Chuachituj, a section of land which had been granted to the former servants of the Quiche rulers at Utatlán (see *Título Chuachituj* in Native Sources). In two other documents which refer to this conflict in 1774 and 1779 (AGC, Al:6021-53078; Al: 1801-24615), we are given more information on the location of the lands and the social condition of the beneficiaries of the grant. Apart from their value in reconstructing prehispanic social relations, these documents provide a revealing view of the process by which native institutions underwent change during the colonial period.

Other Quiche-speaking communities that generated useful land dispute documents are:

Joyabaj. — two documents from the seventeenth century record a struggle between this town and Sacualpa (AGC, Al:5940-5196; Al:5940-51970). In the first document, we are told that the aboriginal name of Sacualpa was Pamaca, and in the second, we are given a good list of toponyms, including the name of the hill dividing Joyabaj from Rabinal (Raxaj).

---

[30] I failed to record the date the Patzité título was written, though I recall that it was during the 19th century. Legally, Patzité became a *municipio* in 1872 (Anonymous 1962:II).

Rabinal. — litigation papers contain an account of a dispute in 1771 with San Pablo Cobán (AGC, Al:6017-53025). A few toponyms are given, as well as the location of the Raxcaco Indians and a cacique named Silvestre Sánchez.

San Cristóbal Totonicapán. — a document contains an account of a 1722 struggle over lands with San Francisco el Alto (AGC, Al:5968-52387). The aboriginal name of San Cristóbal is given as Pujila, and some principales from there are listed by their native names.

Zunil. — a 1770 measurement of the territory of that town is recorded (AGC, Al:5967-52374). The names of many important places and persons in the vicinity are given.

Santa Catarina Ixtahuacán. — an 1810 dispute within the territory of the town over a hamlet called San Miguel is described (AGC, Al:204-4115). It contains a good list of the surnames of the leading elders of the community.

San Bartolomé Mazatenango—a document from there refers to coastal land granted in 1644 to the town of San Lorenzo (AGC, Al:2173-15692). It contains a list of the aboriginal names of the elders, and in some cases gives their native titles of authority.

More useful land dispute documents from Cakchiquel-speaking communities in the highlands come from the following places:

Tecpán Guatemala. — a record of the 1663 litigation over lands between the Cakchiquel Indians and the Argueta family which called forth the *Títulos Xpantzay* (AGC, Al:6062-53957). The documents contain a map of the area surrounding Iximché and list important land marks there.

Patzicía. — a 1682 dispute over lands within the community is described (AGC, Al:2355-17798). The name of one of the disputant factions is given (the Xico people of the Yamole parcialidad), and the native names and titles of a few elders are recorded.

San Juan Comalapa. — a document from there contains the record of a 1692 dispute with Santa Cruz Balanyá over lands called Juchixat, Pixcaya (AGC, Al:5951-52132).

Santo Domingo Xenacof. — a 1740 dispute over lands within the territory of the town resulted in a document which contains several native names and titles of the original inhabitants (Ajuchan, Iboy, Tepew, Ismachí), (AGC, Al:5981-52580).

The Cakchiquel-speaking piedmont community of San Pedro Yepocapa was, in 1656, in a complicated land dispute with Ichanhuehue (AGC, Al:2347-17671). The litigation papers from this case contain a map showing the boundaries of Yepocapa, and a list of local names of persons, places, and Indian settlements (some now extinct). Also from the Cakchiquel-speaking part of the piedmont we have the record of an early dispute (1604) over lands between San Juan Alotenango and Santiago Cotzumalhuapa (AGC, Al:5937-51927). Several Indian communities now extinct are named for the region adjacent to the disputed land (Chiahuitl).

From the region just below the Cakchiquel piedmont zone comes a 1678 land document (AGC, Al:5949-52101) which contains an account of the disappearance of the Pipil-speaking settlement of Tehuantepeque, and the subsequent assignment of the vacant lands to the Indians of Santa Lucía de la Costilla. Many similar documents exist for Pacific coastal communities in the Archivo General de Escribanía, Seccion de Tierras, Guatemala, but I have not sufficiently studied them to be able to review their contents.

Totonicapán and Sacapulas. — Perhaps the utility and scope of land documents from Indian communities in highland Guatemala can be clarified by examining in depth the corpus available in two specific cases—San Miguel Totonicapán and Santo Domingo Sacapulas. In the case of Totonicapán, there are enough documents to allow the student to trace prehispanic sociocultural patterns through the colonial period to the present time. I have demonstrated this in an earlier study (Carmack 1966b), and will not repeat the results here.

Sacapulas is another case for examination in depth. Shortly after the conquest the town was established at its present location by bringing together several different native settlements of that region, in some cases by requiring the Indians to abandon their traditional lands and take up new ones near the town center. Eventually (especially during the 18th century) the various ethnic groups congregated in the town came into conflict over land boundaries and the relative sizes of their holdings. Several litigation papers which record the disputes have come to us and are now in the Archivo General de Centroamérica, Guatemala. These documents are an important source for the study of changing social conditions during the colonial period, but more importantly they contain references to aboriginal social and cultural patterns.

One of the earliest documents is the record of a 1640 dispute over a section of land called Ixpapal between the community of Sacapulas and a parcialidad known as Citala (AGC, A1:5942-51995). In addition to the valuable primary documents which were inserted into the record (see Appendices XXI, XXII), there is a description of the entire judicial process. The derivation of the Citala faction from three aboriginal settlements (Coatan, Sacualpa, Iztapaneca) is clarified, and several indigenous boundary markers are named and can be correlated with names in the *Título Sacapulas*.

Two documents written in 1739 contain a record of a dispute between Sacapulas and Aguacatán over territory called Pechiquil (AGC, A1:5979-52536; A1:5978-52518). Testimony recorded in these documents states that the disputed lands were once part of the settlement of Xolchun, and belonged to the Lamaquib political group.[31] The names of several prehispanic political units adjacent to these lands are given (Ak'aab, Balamija, Matomal, Baijon). One document also contained the *Título Lamaquib* (see Appendix X).

In 1793, there was a dispute, similar to the one with Aguacatán, with San Bartolomé Jocotenango according to another document from Sacapulas (AGC, A1:6044-53348). It does not contain much information on aboriginal social groupings, but many important boundary markers are listed (including Mumux, a mountain mentioned in títulos cited by Fuentes y Guzmán). There is also a map of the territory of Jocotenango, which designates the precise location of many toponyms cited in the text of the legal document.

In the last quarter of the 18th century, land rights conflict was endemic between the several ethnic components (parcialidades) of Sacapulas. One document from 1776 is a record of a

[31] The Lamaquib are mentioned in the *Popol Vuh* (Recinos 1953:180) as one of the groups coming from the East with the Quiché forefathers. From this document we learn they were located at Xolchun, a fact which enables us to identify them with the archaeological site by that same name (Smith 1955).

dispute over lands between the Santo Tomás and San Francisco factions residing at Sacapulas (AGC, Al:6021-53084). The territory of the Santo Tomás faction is precisely demarcated, using native toponyms, and the whole process of land control by the factions is clearly outlined by the local priest. A second document from 1786 has a description of how descendants of Indians brought to Sacapulas from Magdalena attempted to repossess lands they had left vacant in their home territory (AGC, Al:6037-53258). The account has little on aboriginal cultural patterns but provides a good view into the internal social dynamics of the community at the time.

During this stormy period the most valuable of the land dispute documents from Sacapulas was prepared. Written in 1778, it records litigation between the San Sebastián-Santiago and San Pedro factions over a small plot of land located just north of the Tujal river (AGC, Al:6025-53126). This bundle of papers contained the Spanish translation of the *Título Sacapulas* and its accompanying map (see Native Sources). In the other papers, many important identifications are made between places and social groupings mentioned in the título and geographical points in the territory of 18th century Sacapulas.[32] The territorial organization of the community at the time is beautifully shown in a large map painted with different colors. Among the several small documents attached to the litigation bundle is a small title to the disputed land. I discussed its contents in Native Language Documents (see Appendix XXV).

A collection of litigation records of a complicated 1795 land dispute between the Santo Tomás and San Francisco factions of Sacapulas is also valuable (AGC, Al:6042-53327). It contains the names of the tributaries of the two factions, as well as the amount of land possessed by each family. In addition, named boundary markers for the whole community are given, and the territories of each faction are designated by different colors on a large map.

---

[32] Testimony clarifies that calpul Santiago traced its ancestry back to Lord Canil, who came from Tula according to the título. We also learn that members of calpul Santiago, along with calpul San Sebastián, lived in the section of land where the salt springs were located.

This brief summary suggests the richness of the data on aboriginal forms which can be derived from the land dispute documents. Even more important, they provide documentation of changes in Indian social institutions over time. A complete analysis of such changes for Sacapulas easily could be produced by combining these with primary native documents and modern ethnographic investigation.

Cacique Records. — Information on native sociocultural forms is scarce in judicial records other than land disputes. Apparently, land was the permanent object and symbol to which aboriginal ways could be most easily anchored, and disputes over land easily brought them to light. To a less extent, rights to leadership also continued to be associated with aboriginal forms. I have found three cases dealing with problems of cacique standing which have limited data on native cultural patterns.

The most interesting of these is a complaint registered in 1672 against the Toltec caciques from Sacapulas by several Indians from that town (AGC, A1:1564-10208). The document describes the way the descendants of the prehispanic ruling class of that community attempted to dominate most of the affairs of the cofradías, civil administration, local adjudication, and control of the economically important salt springs.

Another brief document of this type, written in 1642, refers to the cacique of calpul Aj Cucumatz from Santa Cruz del Quiché (AGC, A1:1559-10203). Though the document contains little additional information about native forms (it is mainly a confirmation of cacique privileges), the persistence of the prehispanic descent group is significant.

The other cacique document involves a complaint made in 1820 to the Spanish officials by the caciques of San Cristóbal Totonicapán, who argued that they were being forced to perform labors from which they had been exempted because of their special status (AGC, A1:1082-55024). The data of interest consist of the names of the three descent lines which were said to extend back to the prehispanic rulers of that settlement (the Mejía, Tucur, and Wonon). It is surprising to find sociopolitical relations originally established before the conquest still viable after 300 years of Spanish domination.

Records from Momostenango

In order to better appreciate the potential and limitations of the records which have been described generally, I will summarize the full corpus of such documents found after exhaustive search in the relevant archives of the Indian town Santiago Momostenango, a Quiché-speaking community a few miles north of Quezaltenango. The objective for which the documents were originally sought was to provide a diachronic dimension to an ethnographic investigation which I carried out in the community in 1966-1967. Since the conclusion of that field work, I have continued to gather documentary materials on Momostenango from various archives which I have visited.

Most documents were found in the Archivo General de Centroamérica, Guatemala, during my five months there in 1966, and another month's search in the summer of 1968. Additional documents were found in the Archivo de la Escribanía del Gobierno, Sección de Tierras, Guatemala, and in the Juzgado de Primera Instancia, Departmento de Totonicapán. A few documents of importance were found in the community itself, either in the municipal archives, or in the care of trusted guardians living in the rural hamlets. A few references to Momostenango were found in documents from the Archivo General de Indias, Seville, and one document in the Gates Collection at Brigham Young University.

Instead of the substantive data in these documents, I will emphasize information bearing on the problem central to this study; nor will I give complete citations to the documents, as this would unnecessarily detract from the purpose of the discussion. I am in the process of preparing a monograph on the sociopolitical history of Momostenango, where the interested student will be able to find full citation to the documents briefly mentioned here.

The Momostenango documentation may be taken as representative of the materials to be expected by the ethnohistorian for most Indian communities of Guatemala. We will see that the corpus is extensive, though it contains less information on aboriginal patterns than the above description of judicial records might lead one to expect. We must remember, too, that this discussion excludes the primary sources (we have two native títulos from Momostenango), and does not include documents from Momostenango after 1875.[33]

Histories. — Momostenango is mentioned in the chronicles of Fuentes y Guzmán, Vázquez, and Juarros, though they provide no information on native cultural patterns. Their accounts give us an important look into the changing social conditions of the community during the colonial period, describing the community population size, production specialization, and ecclesiastical organization.

Administrative Records. — In the description of Momostenango given by Cortés y Larraz and in the report sent to him by the resident priest, there is no reference to native customs or superstitions. From the vantage point of one who has lived in the town and observed in action the elaborate traditional native way of life which still exists there, this seems an incredible oversight. As charged by Cortés y Larraz, the priest at Momostenango must have hidden the native religious practices of the Indians. The Cortés y Larraz account is valuable for its data on the population size and social organization of the town, and for its description of a strong rebellious Indian faction active there.

The 1740 relación geográfica for Huehuetenango and Totonicapán is too brief to record any indigenous practices at Momostenango. However, it reveals Momostecos had already become specialized in the manufacturing of woolen blankets, a craft for which they are famous today.

If the Momostenango case is at all representative, we can be certain that the Guatemalan archives contain extensive holdings on numbers of tributaries living in the Indian towns during the colonial period. At the request of the Indians of Momostenango, Crown officials took a complete census there in 1714. The resulting record, over 100 pages long, lists the names of all tributaries, their wives and children, their ages, the wards from which they came, and their property holdings. Obviously, this is a rich source for the study of demographic patterns, and of Indian clan and lineage names, marriage arrangements, family organization, and

---

[33] I have summarized in another publication the documentation available for Momostenango, including records written in modern times (Carmack 1970).

economic conditions. There is a similar but less complete census from 1825, though the Indians are not listed as tributaries. In addition, we have an eighteenth century tributary census for the adjacent town of San Bartolomé Aguacaliente, which among other things would permit us to determine the degree to which the people of that town had become interrelated through marriage with Momostecos.

Church records from Momostenango are fairly abundant and cover such topics as the establishment of *capillanías* (1647-1692), the construction of a hermitage (1686), conflicts between local inhabitants and resident priests (1773-1785), taxing of cathedral adornments (1799), and the operational affairs of cofradías (1802-1805). The document which contains a description of the hermitage construction provides a valuable view into the internal social organization and dynamics of the community, but neither it nor the other sources have much to contribute on native cultural forms.

Judicial Records. — I found few civil records, wills, deeds, bills of sale, from Momostenango for the colonial period, though there are several protocols (inheritance registries) instigated by creole residents in the area. The one bill of sale (1780) and testamentary (1804) I found are more interesting for the indication of social change they provide than of native cultural patterns.

I found some 15 to 20 documents recording major land disputes in and around Momostenango during the colonial period. They provided considerable data on the aboriginal names and locations of many important topographical features and aboriginal political descent groups in the area. With these documents I was able to connect the genealogy of prehispanic rulers of the area with one of the prominent families of the town, and to match the boundary markers of a 16th century native título with presently known places in the area (Carmack 1967).[34]

Several documents have come to us which contain charges and countercharges over abuses of cacique privileges at Momostenango. From these it is possible to reconstruct some aspects

---

[34] The turn of the 18th century appears to have been a time of considerable adjustment and change in Momostenango with respect to relations of land control. The reason for this appears to have been the growth and expansion of creole haciendas located along the borders of the community.

of the prehispanic political organization of the Momostenango area, and to identify the ruling lines which were given special status at the time of the formation of the town. However, though one cacique line can be traced back to prehispanic rulers mentioned in the native títulos (the Nijaib), the available documents do not provide enough information to make a similar identification for the other cacique line (the Guzmán-Herrera family).

A category of judicial documents which represents a fairly large corpus in the case of Momostenango are the records of criminal wrongs committed. For the colonial period I have found only a few criminal records from Momostenango, and these were cases primarily involving important people of the community (such as Diego Vicente, the Indian cacique, or Spaniard residents of the town). Since 1825, however, the Archivo General de Centroamérica has kept all criminial records from the courts of first instance throughout the country, including those from Totonicapán, the relevant court for Momostenango. The number of extant documents increases tremendously through time. Whereas there are only 26 cases between the years 1825-1830 for the Totonicapán court, they increase to 760 for the years 1895-1900. I examined all criminal records from Momostenango to independence, and thereafter those written between 1820-1835, 1860-1865, and 1895-1900.

Criminal records are useful in studying judicial process and social structure at Momostenango, but they contain little information on native cultural patterns. One exception is a postindependence homicide case from 1864, which reveals patterns of internal conflict over land between members of Indian clans, and the practice of witchcraft as a technique of political counteraction. Other than this, the cases concern the few creoles living in the town, or do not probe into the lifeways of the Indian participants.

Spanish Records. — Though not relevant to the study of aboriginal culture at Momostenango, we nevertheless noted that there is an important corpus of documents from Momostenango which illuminates the nature of relations between the Spaniards and Indians living there. A document from the Archivo de la Escribanía provides us with a record of the foundation in 1601 of the Spanish town of San Carlos Sija on the northern outskirts of Momostenango. Several capillanías from the 17th century and protocols from the early 18th century document the growth of haciendas near Sija, and their conflicts with Momostecan Indians over land, labor exploitation, and damages to crops by cattle. An 1810 census of non-Indians in Momostenango points to the increasing dominance of the creoles of the town, a tendency also suggested in the administrative and criminal records.

Near the time of independence, there were wide-spread rebellions by the Indians of Momostenango against Spanish rule. Clearly the reinstitution of tribute payments shortly after they had been abolished in 1811 served as a *causus belli* at Momostenango. The documents show that the Indians of the town actively participated in the Indian rebellion of 1820, led by Atanasio Tzul from Totonicapán (Contreras R.1951). According to other documents in the Archivo General de Centroamérica, they rebelled even more in 1824 and again in 1828 against the newly organized Federation of Central America. Obviously, much can be learned about sociopolitical movements in the history of Guatemala from documents available on Indian towns like Momostenango.

CHAPTER V

Modern Anthropological Sources

INTRODUCTION

Ethnography and Ethnohistory

I should like to explain why I include a discussion of ethnographic sources in a basically ethnohistoric study. Briefly, I will give some reasons why it is to the advantage of the ethnohistorian to combine ethnographic work with his study of documents (see Carmack 1970; Sturtevant 1968).

Ethnographic research among the descendants of the culture bearers described in the documents adds a strong element of realism to ethnohistoric reconstruction. It enables us to place the peoples of the past more concretely in their geographical, racial, technological, and cultural setting. Historical documents, in part, are written to enhance and enlarge cultural symbols, and the reader and ethnohistorian are sometimes fooled by this. A few weeks or months of living among the people will make him view the documentary accounts more realistically. The excessive statements about prehispanic Quichean cultures one finds in the writings of Fuentes y Guzmán or Brasseur do not appear in the works of the German ethnologists who spent time studying the living Indians in Guatemala.

The substantive data that are not in the documents but were obtained through ethnographic research are of great importance. As Steward noted (1963:60-61), societies have different sociocultural levels of integration, and lower levels may persist long

Ixtahuacán Indian man and woman. From a drawing made by a nineteenth century visitor to Santa Catarina Ixtahuacán (Tempsky 1858).

after the upper levels have been completely altered. In Spanish America, including Guatemala, at the household level where such activities as family education, sex life, milpa agriculture, food and dress, and family ritual took place, aboriginal patterns have persisted, and can still be studied by the modern ethnographer. These cultural matters are not described in the documents; they were screened out of the writings, for the Spaniards were not particularly interested in them. If they had been, they would probably have suppressed them and we could not study them today.

There are practical reasons why the ethnohistorian should utilize ethnographic studies. Foremost is the knowledge of native languages which ethnographers obtain. This skill facilitates translating and analyzing native documents. This is well illustrated by the ease with which Stoll (1958:157-180) and Schultze-Jena (1944) moved from ethnographic investigation to the translation of the *Popol Vuh*. The ethnographer is in a strategic position to obtain valuable documents which were inaccessible to other scholars, often kept secret by trusted village elders. There are many discoveries by ethnologists in Guatemala, such as the Kekchí will found by Burkitt and the *Título Chamelco* located by Sapper in the Verapaz region.

For these reasons I have chosen to include in this study a discussion of ethnographic materials. After all, we wish to reconstruct Quichean culture, and the thoughtful student will employ all resources and methods available.

History of Anthropological Studies in Guatemala

The Guatemalan Indians were virtually unknown to the Western world at the time of independence in 1821. Several years of political instability followed in Central America, creating a climate unconducive to contact with the outside world. However, with the coming to power of the conservatives in 1839 (led by Rafael Carrera), Guatemala entered into a long period of stability (more properly, stagnation), (Rodriguez 1965; Contreras R. n.d.: 109ff). Foreigners, other than Spaniards, visited Guatemala in significant numbers for the first time, and their accounts placed the tiny country and its people before the eyes of a curious non-Spanish world.

The foreign travelers' writings on Guatemala prepared during this early period (roughly 1840-1900) are not easily defined, even if we limit ourselves to an examination of those on the Indians. With few exceptions the authors were not specifically interested in the Indians *per se*, but rather in all of nature—the flora and fauna, topography, natives of the land, antiquities, history, social and political conditions. They were adventurers, and their travelogues were written to interest and excite the readers.

We will call them protoethnologists, for they prepared the way for the ethnological investigations conducted toward the end of the nineteenth century. They called attention to the Indians of Guatemala, published native documents, posed questions which could only be answered by specific research, and generally represented the natives as subjects worthy of serious study.

Toward the end of the nineteenth century, the Indians of Guatemala were seriously and directly investigated by ethnologists who used modern methods. Practical considerations were subordinated to the goal of understanding culture in its many manifestations and of working out the general laws of cultural change, growth, and relationships. The pragmatically oriented geographical and historical reports and the adventurous travelogues gave way to the newly emerging science of culture. The transition was gradual and the writings of the forerunners Scherzer and Brasseur already show a strong ethnological theme.

The ethnology practiced between 1875 and 1925 seems superficial from the viewpoint of modern studies. Cultural elements were seen as atomistic traits, with little regard for their functional relationships to each other. Exasperatingly little attention was paid to cultural boundaries, except for vague references to linguistic groups (tribes), or to the Indians of Guatemala as a whole.

The deficiencies resulted from the questions that were being asked at the time. These early ethnologists were not interested in discovering how cultural traits fit together in an ongoing social system; instead, they asked how these traits had come to be present in particular times and places. They were interested in traits of aboriginal origin, which they wanted to record before they disappeared, and tried to show how they had been perpetuated from cultures of the past. They were also interested in the influence of geographical factors on culture, and the way languages and antiquities (archaeological remains) could be used to reconstruct the history of particular cultures.

In spite of their limitations, these early studies remain important for the student of native culture. Because of their historical interest, these ethnologists often included extensive descriptions of aboriginal patterns that would not have been recorded had they been equally interested in the dominant Ladino culture of the time. They investigated more regions than they would have, had they believed it important to conduct extensive investigation of individual communities. Consequently, we have a broad sample of cultural data on the Indians back to the nineteenth century. In a few crucial cases, the cultural groups they described have since become extinct.

By 1930-1940 some anthropologists studied the Guatemalan Indian cultures with newly specialized methods and theories. Ethnological studies gave way to a spectrum of new subdisciplines within the general field of anthropology. Material cultural remains were examined by the special excavational techniques of archaeology; native customs were observed within the functional context of community studies; native languages were analyzed and compared by linguists; the environment and its technological exploitation were studied as geography.

The initiation of community studies toward the end of the 1930s was a reflection of the general trend in anthropology away from culture history toward functionalism. In order to understand cultural traits as interrelated elements of functional systems, it became necessary to confine the unit of investigation. The community or municipality rather than the "tribe" became the standard sociocultural unit (Redfield and Villa Rojas 1934; Redfield 1939; Tax 1937). This narrowed scope made it possible to view cultures holistically, as ongoing, functioning systems.

As a result of this approach, ethnological interest shifted from Indian culture and its history, to a study of the cultural interaction between Ladinos and Indians, communities and the nation state. Guided by functional instead of historical problems, communities were selected for study which were not necessarily important (or even existent) in prehispanic Guatemala. This detracted from the culture historical value of the community studies, as did the tendency to pay less attention to aboriginal patterns of low functional significance. A further consequence was that the native languages were slighted in favor of Spanish, the language spoken by the politicially dominant Ladinos. However, this approach provides one main culture historical dividend: In cases where the functionally oriented ethnographer did obtain information on native cultural patterns, it was far more detailed and integrated than similar data recorded by earlier ethnologists. In spite of some limitations, the community studies appear to be as useful as the earlier ethnological studies (which, to some extent, have continued concurrently with them). I have argued (Carmack 1966b; 1970), that more useful data for culture historical and functional analysis could be obtained by combining the ethnological and community approaches.

Modern archaeological work must be seen as a direct continuation of the culture historical research of the ethnologists. Most ethnologists included descriptions of artifacts and of social customs of living peoples in their writings. This was especially true of the 19th century ethnologists. In the early part of the 20th century one notes a tendency of some ethnologists, like Lothrop and Villacorta, to show more interest in archaeology than in ethnography.

By the 1940s, highly specialized archaeological research was being conducted in Guatemala. The turning point came with the excavations by Kidder and his colleagues (1946) at Kaminaljuyu, a work which overshadowed all previous archaeological research. This suggests that the beginning of modern archaeology, like the first community studies, was a reflection of more general developments in anthropology. The specific techniques applied by Kidder at Kaminaljuyu were first developed in the U.S. Southwest, and their application in Guatemala changed the direction of all subsequent archaeological work there.

Explanation of Modern Anthropological Studies

The social condition of the Indians in Guatemala changed in cyclic fashion after independence had been achieved. The so-called liberal governments, pressured the Indians to abandon their traditional way of life and assimilate into the developing Ladino national culture. These were periods of disruption for the Indians, and devaluation of native culture from the viewpoint of the Ladinos. The liberal periods were between 1824 and 1839 (the time of the Union of Central America), 1870 to 1885 (the reign of Justo Rufino Barrios), and 1944 to 1954 (the Revolutionary period) (Rodriguez 1965; Adams 1968).

The policy of the conservative governments generally was to protect the Indians, and preserve their traditional social and cultural patterns, which, of course, to a large extent were castelike in form. The Indians must have viewed these periods of diminished social pressure with relief, and the national prestige of the Indian *qua* Indian undoubtedly increased. The conservative periods, after the failure of Union, were between 1839 and 1870 (especially the time of Carrera), the post-Barrios governments, 1885 to 1930 (typified by the dictatorship of Cabrera), and the recent period since the fall of Arbenz, 1954 to 1964 (Adams 1968; Rodriguez 1965).

There is a rough correlation between cycles of policy toward the Indians and differences in writings on them by Guatemalan scholars. A broader, historical and national interest seems to be characteristic of writings during liberal periods, of which the histories of García Peláez (ca. 1835), Milla (ca. 1879), and Contreras (1951; n.d.) are examples. The Indian is certainly not ignored in their writings, but he is viewed as one element in a much larger and more important social unit, the nation (actually, most liberal authors strongly favored Central American union over nationalism).

It seems to me, most Guatemalan writings about native culture *per se* have been produced during conservative periods. As typical examples, one might cite the 1866 study of Gavarrette, the turn-of-the-century works of García Elgueta, Recinos, and Villacorta, the Indianism begun by Goubaud Carrera in the late 1930s, and the interest in classic Quichean language and culture persued by several Guatemalans after the revolutionary period (typified by Recinos, Villacorta, and Gall). In these works there is a tendency to acclaim Indian culture and generally treat it as a unit worthy of investigation.

However, the most evident correlation is not between the Guatemalan sources on the Indian and internal political events but between anthropological studies and external influences. Guatemala's postindependence history is not its own, for the tiny nation has been profoundly affected by foreign powers. To an important degree, the study of Guatemala and its Indians has been in the hands of foreigners for the past 150 years.

This is evident if we look at the national origins of those who studied Guatemala and its cultures during the past two centuries. The strong British commercial and political influence on Guatemala from independence until 1851 (Rodriguez 1965:88) is reflected in the early nineteenth century studies of Thompson, Dunn, Baily, and Dunlop. Then came the Germans, who were perhaps the dominant commercial influence on Guatemala during the second half of the nineteenth century, primarily through their interest in coffee production. The influence is clearly reflected in the consequent monopoly of the German ethnologists. Anthropology in Germany during the nineteenth century was apparently well developed (this was not unconnected with the country's bustling commercial activities), (Lowie 1937), and the German ethnologists we will discuss reflect that development. The German interest in geographic and historical determinants of culture is evident in the writings of their ethnologists. This fact explains the absence of evolutionary schemes in the nineteenth century ethnologies on the Guatemalan Indians.

Since 1909, (Rodriguez 1965:116ff), U.S. influence in Guatemala has been continuous and considerable. Originally, it was based on political and economic considerations—the desire to control the Canal Zone, and the development of American plantations in Guatemala during the last quarter of the nineteenth century. Anthropological work by American scholars corresponds in time and intensity to U.S. political and economic interests. American anthropological studies in the first quarter of the twentieth century are sporadic, and reflect the culture historical particularism of the American school of anthropology. American anthropology becomes continuous and pervasive in Guatemala by the 1930s and 1940s, reflecting newly discovered functional approaches.

Recent anthropological trends suggest that American interest continues unabated, though it appears that other nations have now joined in the endeavor. These include a handful of well-trained Guatemalans, French archaeologists and sociologists, Mexicans, and again the Germans. Even a Russian scholar is seriously working on the history and culture of Quichean Indians (Kinzhalov n.d.).

Obviously, linguistic developments changed the direction of Guatemalan language studies. By the 1950s, after an intermediate period of partly ethnographic, partly linguistic studies, linguistic research was written with little or no accompanying ethnographic description (Mayers 1966 is a partial exception). Even the so-called pedagogical grammars which appeared, required technical knowledge of linguistic theory for their effective use (Wick 1966). Some Quichean language studies continued to show a concern for culture historical problems; others have been useful to the ethnographer who must learn a native language; and still others contain lexical and grammatical information useful for studying native cognitive categories.

The specialization of geographical studies has had a somewhat different direction since the 1940s. Instead of narrowing and refining method and theory, the tendency has been to specialize on subject matter. It is my impression that most geographical work is now guided by current national socioeconomic problems. Some interest in historical geography has continued, especially with Guatemalan historians and officials of the statistical and geographical agencies.

Anthropological Subdivisions

The sources uncovered by the application of modern anthropological techniques are divided into four categories: ethnology, archaeology, community studies, linguistics and geography. For each subdivision I cite the works with a focus on the Quichean peoples —the Quiche, Cakchiquel, and Tzutujil—though cultural information from adjacent peoples considered to be of special significance is also mentioned.

Important anthropological research has been published in Guatemala which is not reviewed here because it contains little information on aboriginal Quichean cultural forms; for example, the studies with a specific focus on Ladino culture by Adams (1964) and Méndez (1967). No one seems to doubt the value of such studies; while research more specifically oriented toward aboriginal cultural forms finds minimal support at present.

I have included certain studies of native culture in Guatemala which are perhaps best classified as linguistic or geographical, two fields closely tied to anthropology. They are briefly discussed so as to add to our understanding of how the study of native culture in Guatemala has developed.

ETHNOLOGY

Introduction

I will trace the development of ethnological studies from the first steps taken by a heterogeneous group of visitors to Guatemala, whom I call the protoethnologists, to the accomplishments of a group of theoretically oriented social scientists, the ethnologists. Protoethnologists is not a satisfactory term, but ambiguous research roles were characteristic of the social and biological sciences in the nineteenth century. Ethnologist is a more satisfactory term because it points to the fact that anthropology had become established as a separate field of social science (albeit incipiently), and to the culture historical (*vs.* evolutionary) orientation of the early anthropologists.

The broad ethnological tradition of the nineteenth century, which combined ethnographic, linguistic, geographic, and archaeologic interests, has generally been continued into modern times by Guatemalan scholars. This tradition has roots in the colonial past and can be traced through the works of Remesal, Fuentes y Guzmán, Ximénez, Juarros, Peláez, and Jáuregui. In recent times, Guatemalan scholars within this tradition have produced some of our most important syntheses of prehispanic Quichean history and culture: Villacorta (1934; 1938; 1962b), Vela (1935; 1944), Recinos (1953; 1959), Gall (1962;1963), Contreras R. (1963; 1965), Crespo (n.d.), Acuña (1966; 1968), and Chinchilla (1963).

Protoethnologists

In the first half of the nineteenth century, visitors with various interests traveled throughout Guatemala and Central America. The published descriptive accounts of what they had observed represent the beginning of modern anthropological studies. The visitors whose descriptions of Guatemala only secondarily touched upon Indian culture I shall call travelers.

Two mid-century visitors are of special importance because of their unusually intense and sophisticated interest in the Indian cultures: Brasseur and Scherzer. They are the precursors of the ethnologists, and their writings will be discussed in detail.

While outsiders were taking new approaches to the study of Guatemala and its Indians, traditional historic, geographical studies and reports were made by Guatemalan officials and an increasing number of foreigners. The latter continued the tradition which is seen today in the works of the above group of Guatemalan scholars.

Travelers. — The two earliest noteworthy visitors to the newly independent Federal Republic of Central America were British, Henry Dunn, and the British commisioner to Mexico, G. A. Thompson, Esquire. Both traveled through Guatemala during the late 1820s, Dunn for business reasons, Thompson at the request of his government. Dunn's memoranda were published under the title, *Guatimala, or the United Provinces of Central America* (1828), whereas Thompson's report was called *Narrative of An Official Visit to Guatemala from Mexico* (1829). Both accounts contain valuable geographic surveys (population, agricultural products, trade, ethnic composition), and their descriptions of Ladino social life in Guatemala City are especially insightful. Unfortunately, both authors were prejudiced. Thompson's interest in the Indians was in terms of national politics and economics, and as they knew little of the capital or its policies, he viewed them as "stupid, ill-informed, and very diminutive." Dunn viewed them more kindly, largely because of his blatant anti-Catholicism. He left us a useful description of social life on the plantations.

The most important early visitor to Guatemala was John Lloyd Stephens, whose 1839-1840 journey through Central America is well known. His book, *Incidents of Travel in Central America, Chiapas, and Yucatán* (1853), contains numerous references to the condition of the Indians in Guatemala, and is a valuable source of reconstructing posthispanic social life. It contains little information about surviving aboriginal customs, though his reference to a sacred stone in the cathedral at Tecpán Guatemala is of interest. Stephens' most important contribution is archaeological rather than ethnological. This is especially true of his account of the Indians of highland Guatemala, where his useful descriptions accompany the beautiful Catherwood drawings of the archeological remains of Utatlán. Because the site has badly deteriorated since, and in the absence of major excavations, Stephens' description remains important to this day.

Several French-speaking travelers visited Guatemala during the mid-nineteenth century, and some have left us written accounts of their observations of the republic. Besides the famous Brasseur de Bourbourg, they included Philippe de La Renaudiere (1843), Alfred Valois (1861), and a pair of geologists named Dollfus and Mont-Serrat (1868). The most ethnologically inclined of the early French travelers was Arthur Morelet, an adventurer who wrote a stirring account of an 1847 journey through northern Guatemala. It was translated into English by E. G. Squier under

the title, *Travels in Central America* (1871), and is the source
I have consulted.

The narrative refers to his travels in the Yucatecan and Peten
lowlands, but it includes a description of a visit to Verapaz and
a subsequent journey to Guatemala City.

Besides being an entertaining writer (his story is replete with
adventure, character sketches, and even a love affair with a girl
at Cobán), Morelet astutely observed flora, fauna, and Indian
life. His account of the Indian-dominated area of Verapaz contains valuable information on native agricultural practices, the
natural resources, and traditional Indian methods of using the
blowgun and hunting quetzal birds. Yet he was not sympathetic
toward the Indians, and his references to their traditional ways
are secondary to the information he provides on general Ladino
sociocultural conditions.

Less important for the study of Guatemalan Indians are the
accounts by two mid-century British travelers, John Baily and
Robert Dunlop. Both men were historically and geographically
oriented, and their books mainly refer to Ladinos.

Dunlop's work entitled, *Travels in Central America* (1847),
gives no details on native life, but contains an excellent description of social conditions in Guatemala City, along with an account
of the techniques involved in cochineal production. He includes
a useful history of Guatemala from independence to the time of
his writing.

Baily's book, *Central America* (1850), ostensibly was written
to attract immigrants to Guatemala, and the theme runs throughout
his book. He was interested in the geography of Guatemala and
the other Central American states; his description of the Indians
is even more general than that of Dunlop.

A somewhat more useful account of life in Guatemala around
the mid-century was given by Gustav Ferdinand von Tempsky,
the famous European traveler. In 1854, as part of a journey through
Mexico and Central America, Tempsky spent eight months in
Guatemala (seven months of it in the capital), and later described
his experiences there in a book entitled, *Narrative of Incidents
and Personal Adventures on a Journey in Mexico, Guatemala, and
Modes of Life in Those Countries* (1858). He claims that his goal
was to give a life-like portrayal of what he observed, free of pre-

judice. Compared to his contemporaries he succeeds quite well in doing this.

His account has much useful information on Ladino life at Guatemala City, especially as it related to activities of the genteel class. He did not neglect the Indians either, for he was quite favorably disposed toward them. Especially important from an ethnological standpoint is his description of the native customs which he observed at Santa Catarina Ixtahuacán (1858:359-413). In vivid language he describes native use of the sweat bath, their suicidal tendencies, mode of self-government, religious beliefs, traditional dress, and conditions of rebellion. Of special importance to the student of native culture are two beautiful line drawings which portray the dress of the Ixtahuacanos at the time.

Serious travel narratives continued to be written into the 1880s, long after ethnological studies had been initiated in Guatemala. Most noteworthy of these are Brigham's, *Guatemala, the Land of the Quetzal* (1887), and Maudslay's, *Glimpses at Guatemala and Some Notes on the Ancient Monuments of Central America* (1899).

Brigham's book is a narration of his experiences during three trips to Guatemala and Honduras and includes some careful observations on the fauna of highland Guatemala. His attitude toward the Indians, however, was demeaning and he pays little attention to them except to comment on their "stupidity" and "wretchedness."

One is surprised to find in Brigham's book a fairly good outline of prehispanic Quiche history, based on a few primary sources and a 19th century work on Indian culture (Brasseur and Stoll).[1]

Maudslay's account is very similar to Stephens'—his main contribution lies in the description of archaeological rather than ethnographic matters. Of special significance are his notations on the sites of Utatlán, Uspantán, and an unidentified settlement between Rabinal and Cubulco.

---

[1] Brigham's book has an impressive bibliography which helps us to reconstruct the sources on the Guatemalan Indians available during the 19th century. Apparently, Brigham was afflicted with a nearsightedness to which man has always been susceptible—he appreciated the Indians' past accomplishments but denigrated their present way of life.

Maudslay also briefly refers to a few traditional native customs which he had observed—e.g., the use of a hollow shuttle with seeds by female weavers living near Lake Atitlán. Mostly, however, his ethnographic observations are important for the light they shed on social conditions as they existed just before the close of the 19th century.

Early Ethnologists. — The distinguished German physician, Karl Scherzer, visited Guatemala in 1854, and conducted ethnological studies of a quality not known since Ximénez. Scherzer explains in his *Natur- und Völkerleben im tropischen Amerika* (1864) that he had come to Guatemala in order to study tropical life, the potential of the country for German business, and to "observe native culture (Völkerleben)." While in Guatemala he obtained a copy of Ximénez' translation of the *Popol Vuh*, and published it later in Vienna (1857).

Stimulated by the past grandeur of the Quiche, he decided to visit Santa Catarina Ixtahuacán, whose inhabitants, because of their isolation, he hoped had preserved much of the aboriginal culture. His hopes were fulfilled, and some of our most valuable information on Quiche religion resulted from that visit.

Fray Hernández Spina, the resident priest at Ixtahuacán, in preparation for Scherzer's visit prepared an informative document on Quiche religion and language. It included a general account of the religious ideas of the Ixtahuacanos, their calendar day names, an explanation of how the calendar worked, a recorded prayer offered by a Quiche priest-shaman (written in Quiche *and* Spanish), a list of important sacred centers and names of priest-shamans in the vicinity, and a small Quiché grammar. Scherzer published the grammar the following year (1855), and the next year (1856) published the Quiche prayer along with his own commentaries on religion at Ixtahuacán. This material is repeated in Scherzer's *Natur- und Völkerleben*, which also contains a description of native dress and appearance at Ixtahuacán and adjacent communities.[2]

___

[2] More recently, the *Instituto Nacional de Antropología e Historia*, Guatemala, published a convenient Spanish translation of Scherzer's 1856 article on Ixtahuacán religion. Brasseur obtained a copy of the Hernández Spina document from the chief archivist in Guatemala City, and took it to France

Scherzer was stimulated by the 18th century description of American Indians by Alexander von Humboldt, and he in turn initiated a long-term German interest in Guatemalan Indians. In his writings he shows an unusually enlightened attitude toward them; and this influenced the later German ethnologists. The data obtained by Scherzer was limited, but of greater depth than the corresponding information gathered by his contemporaries. He placed the information in a comparative framework, comparing the Guatemalan Indians with those of North America, using them as a test case for solving the fundamental theoretical issue of the day (i.e., the origin of the American Indians).

The writings of the French priest and scholar, Charles Etienne Brasseur de Bourbourg, are of fundamental importance to the student of Guatemalan Indian culture. He has been justifiably criticized for the unscrupulous way in which he obtained several important native manuscripts, and for his fabulous theories about the origin and development of civilization in Middle America (Mace n.d.),[3] though in my opinion his contributions to the study of Guatemalan Indians far outweigh the distortions he introduced.

His theories appear to have had little effect on his generally straightforward reconstruction of late Guatemalan (and Mexican) prehispanic history (1857), or on his monumental undertaking of transcribing and interpreting the *Popol Vuh* (1861) and *Rabinal Achi* (1862). The importance of his gathering many important aboriginal documents is universally recognized. Brasseur should be evaluated in the context of the times in which he wrote, and if we do this, we will realize that he was ahead of his contemporaries. He recognized the scientific importance of Indian culture and

---

with him. It is now in the Bibliothèque Nationale, and from there a photocopy was obtained by Gates (now in the Newberry Library), (Butler 1937). A copy of it is also in the Latin American collection of the Tulane University Library.

[3] In his *Histoire des Nations Civilisées du Mexique et de L'Amérique-Centrale*, Brasseur argues that the Quiché ancestors originally came from Scandanavia (1857:15), though his reconstruction of later Quiche chronology is quite reasonable. His suggestion that K'ucumatz and Quik'ab ruled between 1225 and 1420 A.D. is close to the reconstruction of modern scholars (Wauchope 1949; Carmack 1966a). Later on, Brasseur's theories became fantastic, as he sought to link the myths of the *Popol Vuh* and other native documents with the legendary continent of Atlantis.

history; he placed importance on the study of native documents; he dedicated himself to learning native languages in order to study native culture; he recognized the utility of living in the Indian villages in order to learn of their culture firsthand in order to be able to interpret the documents; and he attempted to link Quiché and Mexican history and culture.

Fortunately, most Guatemalan documents which Brasseur collected have been preserved (mostly in the Bibliothèque Nationale). An exception to this is the *Crónica Franciscana* (see Colonial Historians), which Brasseur cites from time to time. In another place, he summarizes the contents of a Tzutujil título, which formed part of the *Crónica Franciscana* (Brasseur 1957:II:83-84; see Native Documents). Other citations indicate that Brasseur had access to the Nijaib títulos, the *Título Sacapulas*, the *Annals of the Cakchiquels*, as well as the *Popol Vuh* and many important Spanish writings.

The numerous ethnographic notes scattered throughout Brasseur's work are important—especially the footnotes to the *Popol Vuh*, *Rabinal Achí*, *Histoire des Nations Civilisées*, and several letters describing his travels in Guatemala (1945-1949). The many toponymic correlations in these notes are almost indispensable for interpreting the native títulos, though in a few cases Brasseur is in error. He apparently made the most of his short stay in Rabinal, San Juan Sacatepéquez, and other Guatemalan town by interrogating many natives about the place names and customs mentioned in the ancient títulos.

Historical Geographers. — After independence, the Indians of Guatemala continued to receive official attention, now from the republic instead of the Spanish administration. These officials generally either reported on geographical matters related to the Indians, or attempted to perpetuate the historical tradition begun by Remesal during the colonial period. Their accounts are of limited value, for they are based on descriptons of the Indians at a distance and they generally fail to provide details about surviving aboriginal patterns.

The historical work which chronologically succeeds Juarros' study was written by a Guatemalan priest, Francisco de Paula García Peláez, and entitled, *Memorias para la Historia del Antiguo*

Reino de Guatemala (1943). García Peláez was commissioned in 1834 by the chief of state to write the history of Guatemala, a task which he completed in 1841. His book contains many references to the Indians, but they are based on sources available in primary documents. He gives a detailed account of native Indian agricultural production, which is mainly based on Ximénez' *Historia Natural* (García Peláez 1943:I:16-36).

Almost forty years later (1879) another Guatemalan, José Milla, was commissioned by the government to write a history of Guatemala and Central America. The resulting work, *Historia de la América Central* (1963), is excellent scholarship. It contains the history of events and culture of the peoples of Guatemala from before the conquest until independence. The first volume is about the Indians, and has an accurate though sketchy reconstruction of their prehispanic history and culture. It is based entirely on primary sources available to us and contains no personal ethnographic observations.

The same material is summarized for the English-speaking world by Bancroft in his *Native Races*, Volume II, (1883), and *History of Central America* (1886). Although he perpetuates some of Brasseur's erroneous theories, Bancroft's account of the history and culture of Guatemalan Indians is an accurate summary of the content of the *Popol Vuh*, *Annals of the Cakchiquels*, the writings of Fuentes y Guzmán, Ximénez, and other known colonial authors. No new ethnographic data or primary documentary sources appear in his account.

Also in this historical tradition is an interesting book on the Indians of Guatemala, written in 1894 by a professor from the University of San Carlos, Antonio Batres Jáuregui. Entitled, *Los Indios, su Historia y su Civilización*, the book was written in order to better inform educated Guatemalans of the Indian and his history. Batres wanted to see the Indian integrated into society: "It is very dangerous to allow the Indian to remain a *status in statu*, perpetuating his separation, rustic customs, misery, and all the hate motives against the other castes" (1894:xii). His description of the history and culture of the Indians of Guatemala was based on the same sources Milla used and those before him, and adds no additional information of value about native culture. Of greater significance is the last section of his book, where he describes the various attempts which had been made since independence to bring about change in the Indian segment of Guatemalan society.

The 19th century histories mentioned so far have a strong geographical theme, as it was the case with the colonial histories. However, a number of more strictly geographical reports were also written. The first was a description of the geography of the Verapaz region, written by Fray Alonso de Escobar (1841; also published in Morelet 1871:418-427). It is a good description of the economic conditions of the region at the time and contains a list of aboriginal names of the surrounding mountains, and a brief account of the various indigenous settlements which were joined together at the time of the conquest.

A serious contribution to the geographical study of Guatemala in mid-19th century is E. G. Squier's, *The States of Central America* (1858). Squier became interested in Central America while serving there as U. S. diplomat and discovered the dearth of accurate geographical information available on these states. His geographical observations were mostly motivated by practical goals, such as finding a suitable route for railroad communication between the Atlantic and Pacific oceans.

In his chapter on Guatemala, Squier describes the Indians only in a general way, and adds no new ethnographic information. However, he makes a good survey of the economic, demographic, and political condition of the Indians. His brief history of the Lacandones and the Petén area, based entirely on sources known to us, and his comprehensive bibliography of documentary sources written in the first half of the 19th century are valuable.

An excellent geographical study which focuses particularly on the Indians of Guatemala was made by the German geographer, Gustav Bernouilli. In three articles published in Dr. Pettermann's *Geographische Mitteilungen* (1868-1870), he describes the flora and fauna of Guatemala, the production techniques of the Indians, and in an especially perceptive account, he analyzes the political and economic exploitation suffered by them. Bernouilli's objective was to inform a German audience of the commercial potential of Guatemala.

Juan Gavarrette, the official in charge of Guatemala's most important archives, in 1866, wrote an important paper on the geography of the region around Cotzumalhuapa (1929). Using documents he found in the archives, he reconstructed the prehispanic history of the area, and noted the changes which occurred there in settlement pattern and demogarphy during the 16th century.[4]

Apparently, the Francisco Gavarrete who produced a geographic study of Guatemala around the same time (1868) was a different person. His account is too generalized to be of value to the student of Indian culture.

Ethnologists

Specific studies of native cultures in Guatemala were firmly established by the latter part of the 19th, and continued into the early part of the 20th century. The most influential and productive ethnologists of the period were the Germans. We will discuss them together with particular attention to the writings of Stoll, Sapper, Termer, and Schultze-Jena. A few Guatemalan and American ethnologists were also active at the time. Though their contribution was significantly less than that of the Germans, it is important nonetheless. Even after new approaches to the study of culture became dominant, culture historical studies similar to the Germans' continued to this day. I shall list the more useful of these recent ethnologically oriented works.

German Ethnologists. — Berendt, Lehmann, and Seler contributed in a limited way to the study of Guatemalan Indians. They conducted important linguistic studies, investigated archaeological remains, and to a less extent made observations on surviving Indian cultures, but none wrote exclusively on native culture.

Karl Hermann Berendt, one of the earliest German ethnologists, made several expeditions into Guatemala, where he gathered documents (the Quiche and Cakchiquel calendars), archaeological artifacts, and linguistic terms (for a list of his collected materials,

---

[4] Juan Gavarrete assisted Brasseur in obtaining several Guatemalan manuscripts, and his own research was probably inspired by the French priest-scholar. He was also influenced by the writings of Fuentes y Guzmán which he found in the archives (Fuentes y Guzmán 1932-33:6:xix-xx).

see Brinton 1900). His few published articles (see especially 1872; 1877; 1878) show his scientific approach to the study of culture.[5] His study of relations between the Maya languages of Guatemala is his most solid contribution.

Walter Lehmann's contribution to Guatemalan ethnology is confined to his excellent discussion of the distribution and history of the Pipil languages (1920:1059-1075). His study of the Quiche calendar (1911) is taken from Ximénez (1929); he made an interesting comparison of it and the Pipil calendar.

Edward Seler's contribution to Guatemalan studies is in the interpretation of native documents. He commented on the chronology of the *Annals of the Cakchiquels*, the place of origin of the Quiche founding fathers, and the meaning of mythology in the *Popol Vuh* and *Annals* (1960), (for English translations see Bowditch 1939:1:159-162; 3:4:118-121; 2:1:11-22). His archaeological studies (1960:3:4:578-640; 1901) are of little value for reconstructing contact-time culture, though he describes a few artifacts which might be of Quichean origin (Bowditch 1939:IV:122-128).

The Swiss physician, Otto Stoll, brought ethnological study in Guatemala into its mature phase. His articles and books on native language, geography, and customs are the foundation upon which all subsequent ethnologists have built. His work has been summarized by Goubaud Carrera (Stoll 1958:XV-XLVI; Goubaud Carrera 1964:111-112).

Stoll first described the major native languages of Guatemala (1884; 1958), and later studied the Ixil (1887; 1960), Pokomán (1888; 1896), Tzutujil (1901), and Aguacatec languages (1928). His work contains useful information for the ethnologist who is concerned with the origin and distribution of the Pipil speakers, and the space-time relationship of the Maya languages. The climax of his linguistic work (1912) is a comparative grammatical analysis, which is of the quality of a modern ethnosemantic study.

In terms of ethnographic information, Stoll's account of his travels in Guatemala during the years 1878-1883 is most important

[5] In a lecture before the American Geographial Society of New York, in 1878, Berendt called attention to the importance of the Indian cultures for the study of civilization and pointed out that they had developed independent of Old World civilization, and that linguistic and archaeological data should be used to interpret the native títulos.

(1886). He lived one year in Retalhuleuh, another in Antigua, and he visited Verapaz, Sacapulas, Santa Cruz del Quiché, and other Indian communities of the central highlands. He interspersed his comments on geographical and political matters with descriptions of native beliefs and practices—the ritual of Quiche priest-shamans (160ff), beliefs about an earth and tree god (224), beliefs about volcanoes (282), the deer dance (372), and native marriage customs (378ff). He gives an excellent description of the social conditions of the Indians, including the peons living on Pacific coast plantations (87ff).

Stoll made careful observations and tried to obtain the native viewpoint on matters of custom. He made intercultural comparisons in order to establish historical relationships—to the extent of seeking to establish similarities between shamanistic practices of Guatemala Indians and ethnic Germans. The culmination of his studies is an excellent synthesis of Guatemalan Indian culture, published in 1889. It is based on documentary sources and is an excellent example of using ethnographic materials to supplement and clarify documents.

Karl Sapper lived for more than ten years in the Verapaz region and made geographical and ethnographic studies. Of special note are his articles on native ethnography: dietary customs, dance and drama, and religious beliefs of the Kekchí Indians (1897b; 1904a), and customs practiced by the Pokomán (1904b) and Chol speakers (1906). In 1936, he reconstructed the geography of Verapaz for the sixteenth and seventeenth centuries, and so provided us with an excellent view of the early natural geography, native demographic and economic patterns, and ethnic and linguistic distribution of the area. In addition to his study of aboriginal cultural forms, he inquired into the depressed condition of Guatemalan Indian society at the turn of the century (1890; 1897b; 1902).

Sapper also visited the central highlands of Guatemala where he gathered some ethnological data and described the Quiche ruins of Utatlán (1897b:354ff) and the Pokomán site of Mixco Viejo (1898). During a visit to Quezaltenango in 1923-1924, he gathered information on native calendric and shamanistic beliefs from his German friends living in Quezaltenango, Momostenango, and the Mam area. He combined the information he received from them with Stoll's documentary sources and notes and published an account of ritual practices by Quiche priest-shamans (1925).

Sapper's studies were more oriented toward economic geography than were those of the other ethnologists. But his work was excellent and his description of native culture in Verapaz remains an important contribution in view of the scarcity of material for the region.

Franz Termer continued the German interest in Guatemalan geography and ethnology into the second quarter of the twentieth century. Based on data gathered while traveling in Guatemala between the years 1925-1929, he published numerous articles covering a wide range of ethnological topics (see Termer in Bernal 1962). The articles have been combined in a important monograph (1930b), which has been translated into Spanish (1957).

In his monograph, Termer describes many aboriginal cultural elements of Quiche-speaking and related groups which, in mixed form, had persisted from prehispanic times. Of special importance are his identifications of places and events mentioned in the sixteenth century sources, and his account of native calendrics, dances, witchcraft practices, and ritual.

Termer has continued to contribute to Guatemalan ethnology since his 1930 study, but his articles since then deal more with interpretation than with the presentation of new ethnographic data. The most important of these later works is a study of the interrelation between the Pipil and the Quiche of the highlands (1936a), a summary of the historical geography of the Pacific coast (1939-1940), and a review of ethnological studies on the Indians of northwestern Guatemala (1946-1949), including the Ixil (1958).

Termer trained under Seler and Sapper and was inspired by Stoll. He approaches his work in the typical German ethnological manner. He shows a marked interest in aboriginal culture, especially in terms of the patterns of contact and migration by which it was molded into its modern condition. Like his predecessors he left us important geographical and archaeological descriptions.

Leonhard Schultze-Jena, a student of Walter Lehmann, in 1930-1931, conducted ethnological research among the Indians of Chichicastenango and Momostenango. He recorded prayers, folklore, and other traditional orations in the Quiche language, by using informants to translate language and concept. Later, he extracted cultural content from the texts, and published them with his analysis as *Leben, Glaube und Sprache der Quiche von Guatemala* (1933; 1947 partial translation into Spanish).

Schultze-Jena's book is perhaps the most important modern source for studying aboriginal Quiche culture, because he published the Quiche texts alongside his translations so that the student can directly examine the language of the informants on the more conservative aspects of modern Quiche culture. His description of Quiche religion, derived from an analysis of the texts, is the most insightful and complete study of its kind available for the Quichean peoples.

Schultze-Jena studied native culture from a historical perspective, for he was primarily interested in reconstructing aboriginal Quiche culture and in translating the *Popol Vuh*. The Quiche grammar included in his monograph was prepared with the translation in mind. Though it contains some errors, it is nevertheless an important contribution to the study of the Quiche language. His synthesis of Quiche history and culture was published along with his translation of the *Popol Vuh* (1944:170-198).

Schultze-Jena, like the ethnologists before him, was not precise about cultural boundaries. He has been severely criticized for not always specifying the source of the data he recorded—whether it was from Chichicastenango or Momostenango (Tax 1937:423; 1947a). However, in terms of the ethnological tradition from which he came, his study represents a major advance in method and theory. Unlike his predecessors, he limited his cultural unit to two communities (vis-à-vis whole linguistic groups). His description of religion in the two communities is more functionally integrated than studies before his time.[6] Aside from problems about method and theory in athropology, Shultze-Jena's work will remain a solid contribution to Quichean ethnology.

[6] I have found, in working with Schultze-Jena's materials, that almost all ethnographic details can be assigned to one or the other of the two communities on the basis of statements in the book. The theory that the municipio in Guatemala is the most useful cultural unit for anthropological study has not been proved. I found, in working with a Momostecan native informant on Schultze-Jena texts from Chichicastenango, that in both language and culture the differences between the two communities were insignificantly small.

Guatemalan Ethnologists. — Manuel García Elgueta, a resident and official in Totonicapán, was one of Guatemala's first ethnologists. Toward the close of the nineteenth century, besides several articles of minor significance (1932; 1939), he wrote a long essay on the history and culture of the Quiche Indians of Totonicapán. (It was included as part of a larger study of that community in Carranza 1897 and republished in *Guatemala Indígena*, No. 8, 1962).

Though the source of his ethnographic information is not always clear, much of the account was based on firsthand observations at Totonicapán. Of special interest is his description of native "rites of passage," and calendrics. He also cites a native título from Totonicapán which would otherwise be unknown to scholars (1962:189) and describes a few artifacts from sites within the boundaries of that municipio (1962:180-187).

García Elgueta accepted some of Brasseur's outmoded theories on the origin of the Quiche. But in his respect for native culture (he had a somewhat exaggerated respect for their past grandeur) and in his attempt to describe it based on personal observations, he was modern.

Carranza, the coauthor of the larger monograph on Totonicapán, apparently shared this zeal for Indian culture; his part of the monograph contains a few ethnographic facts of interest (on communal land relations between clans) (1897:227-229). Carranza imbued his son, the late Jesús Carranza, with the same ethnological spirit, as I discovered during an enlightening interview with him in 1964.

In 1913, Adrián Recinos, the well-known Guatemalan statesman, published a valuable ethnological monograph on the Mam-speaking communities of the Department of Huehuetenango. The account consists of geographical and historical information on the various Indian communities in the department and includes a brief culture history of Mam Indians from prehispanic to modern times. Recinos also provided a summary of available information on archaeological sites of the area.

Later, Recinos became Guatemala's most renowned ethnohistorian through his translations of the *Popol Vuh, Annals of the Cakchiquels*, and various *Crónicas Indígenas*. In the process of translating and publishing these documents he made a significant ethnological contribution through the many notes to his translations, and syntheses of Quiché (1953:65-78; also 1959) and Cakchiquel culture history (1950:26-44).

Recinos was not an ethnologist like the Germans or even García Elgueta, for he never carried out fieldwork (even his Huehuetenango monograph was based almost entirely on written sources). Nevertheless, he expressed an interest in the living Indians, and asked questions about the history of their culture in a way similar to that of the ethnologists who flourished at the close of the 19th century.

American Ethnologists. — Daniel Brinton, an American linguist and ethnologist of the late 19th century, approached the study of Guatemalan Indian cultures in the manner of Recinos, though he did not contribute to the same degree. He conducted no ethnographic investigations, but worked on translating the native documents (the *Annals of the Cakchiquels*), and included useful ethnological notes with his translation (1885). In addition, his serious though conservative interpretations of Quichean calendrics (1893) and myth (1881, 1896) served as a useful check against the excesses of some of his predecessors (especially Brasseur).

Samuel Lothrop and Robert Burkitt were the other major American ethnologists of the period. They are best known for their archaeological studies, but they also gathered ethnographic data during their investigations in Guatemala. Lothrop's ethnographic reports are more sketchy and less reliable than those of the German ethnologists, though they provide valuable information on such native cultural patterns as the use of the sacred altar (at Chichicastenango), (1926), canoe construction and other practices around Lake Atitlán (1928; 1929; 1952), native dances (1929), and the Quiche calendar (1930). His archaeological observations are also sketchy, though less so than his ethnographic notes. They are generally similar to the superficial archaeological studies of the German ethnologists.

Burkitt's ethnographic contribution is more substantial than Lothrop's. He was well acquainted with the Kekchi language, and gathered valuable texts and documents written in Kekchi. Among his contributions to Guatemalan ethnology are transcriptions into Kekchi and analyses of a prayer to the earth god, a curse, the speech of a medicine man, a description of tobacco planting, a treatise on Catholic theology, and a list of surnames (1902); a 16th century will (see Primary Spanish Documents, Records), (1905); a folk tale (1920); and a calendar from Salomá (1930-1931).

Burkitt's work is sophisticated, and though linguistically oriented it contains considerable ethnographic data. He also described the remains of a few archaeological sites in the Guatemalan highlands and piedmont (1930), but these reports are even sketchier than Lothrop's.

Oliver LaFarge's research among the Indians of the Jacaltec area of northwest Guatemala holds a similar place among American ethnological studies as Schultze-Jena's does for German ethnology. He was primarily concerned with historical questions, such as the relationship between native culture at Jacaltenango and the Classic Maya civilization (LaFarge and Byers 1931). In the Chuj area, his interest was directly archaeological (LaFarge and Byers 1931:200-243; see also Blom and LaFarge, 1926-27).

Like Schultze-Jena, LaFarge went beyond traditional methods and theories. He and his associates lived in Jacaltenango for a prolonged period of time, and their report on the town presents a picture of the total culture, the components of which are described partially in terms of functional relationships; and, like Schultze-Jena, he recorded native texts, especially about religious matters, and prepared a description of the Jacaltec language.

LaFarge noted that the Jacaltec remained outside the dominating influence of the Quiché in prehispanic times and the Spanish during the colonial period. As a consequence, they retained cultural patterns which were probably similar in form to what they had been like in the central highlands before the coming of Quiche influence. For this reason, one may use LaFarge's study as a control for reconstructing the contact-time Quichean cultures of the central highlands.

Continuing Ethnological Studies. — The ethnological tradition of focusing on surviving aboriginal cultural traits, of attempting to trace the distribution and historical connection of the traits, and of paying attention to archaeological and geographical features has continued to the present time. The tradition has been perpetuated through the publications of the Sociedad de Geografía e Historia de Guatemala, and the Instituto Nacional de Antropología e Historia, though many articles and books have been published on this subject in Guatemalan and the U. S. independent of the two institutions. I will not attempt to list these studies, but will mention the most important of them that contain ethnographic information potentially useful for reconstructing aboriginal highland Guatemalan culture.

Several studies of surviving native calendars have been published, notably by Lincoln (1942), Girard (1948), Miles (1952), and Nash (1957). Surviving native religious belief and ritual are the focus of studies by D. Sapper (1925) and Dieseldorff (1925-1926; 1928-1929) for the Verapaz area, Siegel for San Miguel Acatán (1941; 1943), Girard for the Chorti (1949; 1966), Goubaud Carrera on the Eight Batz ceremony at Momostenango (1935), Mendelson on the Mam and "sacred bundle" traditions at Atitlán (1958a; 1959), and Saler on nagualism at El Palmar (1964).

Surviving elements of native social organization like a bachelor's house at Magdalena Milpas Altas have been described by Adams (1956); and Ordonez Ch. (1957) and I have described the ancient clan systems of Sololá and Totonicapán (1966b).

Surviving elements of native dress have been studied by Osborne J. (1931-1932; 1935), O'Naele (1945), Rodas N. and Rodas Corzo (1938). Native dance has been treated by Correa (1958), Bode (1961), Armas Lara (1964), and Mace (1961; 1967). The persistence of aboriginal settlement patterns into modern times has been explored by Borhegyi (1956a; 1956b), and Tax (1937).

Several Guatemalan scholars have published monographs on various regions of the nation, in a form modeled after Recinos' ethnological study of Huehuetenango. The authors of these works tend to treat the Indians from a culture historical point of view, and provide a general geographical sketch of the region. The most important studies from an ethnological standpoint are by Teletor on Rabinal (1955), Chinchilla Aguilar on Amatitlán (1961), César de la Roca on Quezaltenango (1966), and Bremme de Santos on the Cakchiquel east of Lake Atitlán (1963). Though ostensibly written for a traveler's audience, and covering the entire territory of Guatemala, Osborne's book (1960) is similar to these works.

ARCHAEOLOGY

Introduction

Before introducing the modern archaeological research, I will remark briefly on the interrelationship of ethnohistory and archaeology, and the reasons for including archaeological work in a study of ethnohistoric sources.

Most archaeological reports included here were made on sites believed to have been occupied at the time of the conquest. They contain information on a cultural phase for which we have overlapping documentary information. We can therefore treat archaeological data from these sites similarly to ethnographic traits, and so use the data as a guide and supplement to the documentary accounts. The documents, however, remain the source for reconstructing aboriginal cultural forms. This approach, I believe, has advantages for cultural reconstruction neither ethnohistoric or archaeological methods alone can give.

The artifacts archaeologists study provide information that is lacking in the documents. They are concrete and direct in a way the documentary accounts cannot be. There is no better way to understand an art form than to see it. The direct approach obviates many inevitable distortions and errors made by the authors of the documents.

Archaeological remains also provide information not contained in documents. From the spatial arrangement of residential structures at a site we can infer settlement patterns. Archaeological studies always provide much information about technological and economic matters—the manufacturing of pottery—which are so mundane that they usually are not mentioned in documents.

Of special importance to the ethnohistorian is the fact that the archaeological remains are often susceptible to quantification in a way the data in documents are not. This characteristic of archaeological materials facilitates the determination of the degree of outside cultural influence on a settlement (e.g., by calculating the percentage of newly occurring ceramic types); the relative political ranking and development of different settlements (by studying the number of large structures, the amount of luxury goods buried with the dead); and the approximate dates of construction of buildings and other artifacts (through Carbon 14 dating,

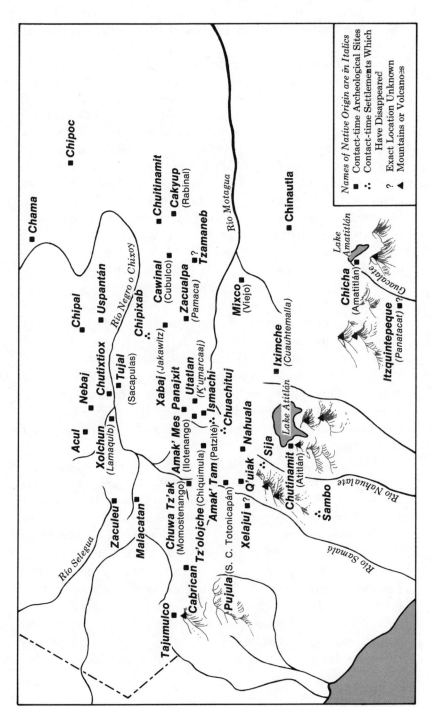

2. Quichean archaeological sites.

obsidian hydration, and ceramic correlations with materials of known date).

Of course, the benefits are reciprocal; the documents provide an important control and add information on aspects of cultural life not evident in the archaeological materials. The standard method of archaeological interpretation is to study individual artifacts in order to determine patterns of style and relationships with other aspects of culture; to compare them with artifacts from other sites in order to establish the history of diffusion and ecological influences; and to date them by absolute and relative methods. Where we have documentary information on the peoples who built and resided at these sites, interpretation can obviously go far beyond what is possible by using archaeological methods alone (Acosta 1956-1957; Wauchope 1948a; Pollock et al. 1962; Guillemin 1965; Carmack 1968). In favorable instances, the documents clarify the purposes and goals for which the material remains were originally constructed, their ideological significance for the practitioners of the culture, and the activities in which they were utilized and manipulated.

The correlation of documentary with archaeological materials is a problem-oriented approach, and has been called the "direct historic method" (Nicholson 1955). There are difficulties connected with it, but it has tremendous potential for improved cultural interpretation. Nowhere is this truer than in the central highlands of Guatemala.

I will first review the 19th century part ethnological, part archaeological reports. I shall call the research protoarchaeology. I will then discuss modern archaeological work in the Quichean zone, followed by work carried out in adjacent areas. I will confine myself to reports on sites which were occupied by peoples living during the postclassic era (ca. 1000-1524 A.D.), who came under the influence of the Quiche state. The restriction seems advisable because we have several excellent summaries of archaeological, findings for all cultural phases of the Guatemalan highlands (Thompson 1943a; Coe 1963; Wauchope 1964; Borhegyi 1965; Rands and Smith 1965; A. L. Smith 1965; Woodbury 1965). I hope this summary will stimulate more archaeological work based on the direct historic method.

Protoarchaeology

The earliest descriptions of archaeological sites in the central high-lands were made by forerunners like Morelet, Stephens, Scherzer (excluding the brief references to the ruins made by the colonial historians). An interesting exception are the drawings of Utatlán and other Guatemalan sites, made in 1834 by order of President Gálvez. A copy of the drawings, catalogued under the title, *Atlas Guatemalteco*, is in the Bibliothèque Nationale, Paris (they are also reproduced in Villacorta 1938).

Most nineteenth century travelers in Guatemala included in their writings a few references to the archaeological sites which they visited, usually associating them with Maya history as known from the *Popol Vuh* or the Yucatecan sources. The more impressive classic Maya sites, such as Copán or Quiriguá, commanded their first attention, though Stephens and Brasseur described the remains of a few contact-time sites.

With the development of ethnology as a field of scientific investigation, archaeological remains came under more systematic and extensive scrutiny. The reports of Maudslay, Sapper, Lothrop, and Termer usually contain scaled diagrams of the sites and their structures, reflecting an advancement over the pictorial representations in Stephen's book or in the *Atlas Guatemalteco*. The ethnologists made an attempt to describe all structural remains at a site, rather than just the spectacular artifacts, and they attempted to place them in space (and to a lesser extent in time) on the basis of the artifacts themselves rather than on documentary information alone.

Admittedly, these early attempts at archaeological investigation had the same deficiencies characteristic of the ethnographic studies of the time (usually made by the same person). The descriptions were based on brief examination of several sites, and little care was taken to distinguish the cultural patterns of one site from those of another. Little effort was devoted to date the artifacts differentially, because external observation, instead of restricted, controlled excavation was the method of obtaining data. Not until the 1940s were modern techniques of archaeology applied in the highlands (e.g., in the work of Wauchope, Kidder, Butler), though a transition can be seen in the research of the

1920-1930s by scholars like Lothrop, Gamio, Termer, Burkitt, and Villacorta.

Quichean Zone

The only complete excavation of a site in the Quichean zone proper was conducted by Wauchope at Zacualpa. This was excellent research; in the present context it is important for its description of culture found in the central highlands before the crystallization of the cultural forms found there at contact time. Unfortunately, the site appears to have been occupied only as a burial place during the last phase of prehispanic culture history.

Guillemin's work at Iximché (1959; 1961; 1965; 1967; 1969) is probably the single, most important excavation so far conducted in the Quichean area, in terms of applying the direct historic method. Iximché was the capital of Cakchiquel speakers who had been an integral part of the Quiche state before 1470 A. D. Guillemin has given us an informative description of their patterns of architecture, artistic decoration, settlement, and burial practices.

Guillemin also provides many useful correlations between the archaeological remains at Iximché and the documentary records. His article (1961) on a "royal" burial found there clearly demonstrates that we can learn about many cultural forms not described in the documents from the archaeological record; it also shows how the documents can aid in the interpretation of that record. By using the documents he is able to hypothesize the name and approximate place and date of death of the individual whose skeleton was found buried at Iximché.

Mixco Viejo, a Pokomán site which came under Cakchiquel influence shortly before the conquest, has been excavated and reconstructed by a French expedition headed most recently by Henri Lehmann. His publications (Lehmann 1968a; 1968b), along with articles by Guillemin (1958), and Navarrete (1962), present considerable data on settlement pattern, architectural style, and ceramics.

Lothrop's excavation at Chuitinamit near Santiago Atitlán (1933) is our only archaeological study of the Tzutujil. The excavations by Lothrop were minor and his report is somewhat disorganized; though his description and illustration of ceramics, pictographs, and sculptured stone pieces are important, for these finds are highly expressive of cultural style and pattern. Lothrop's attempt to relate his archaeological data to the documentary sources was, however, not very successful.

Zaculeu, a site occupied by Mam speakers under Quiche control at the time of the conquest, has been extensively excavated and then restored by Woodbury and Trik (1953). There was a long occupation of this site, extending back into the early classic cultural phase. The report of the sequence of occupation affords a view of highland Guatemala culture before the rise of Quichean influence. Changes in cultural patterns during the last phase (*Xinabajul*) are apparently the result of Quiche cultural influence. Unfortunately, little information was obtained on this last phase, though the report does contain a brief description of its characteristic architectural features, burial practices, and ceramic forms.

Utatlán, the archaeological site of the prehispanic Quiche capital, has never been thoroughly excavated. Therefore, the student of Quiche culture must rely on the sketchy reports of various visitors such as Stephens, Maudslay, and Sapper, and the limited observations and test excavating done there by the archaeologists Villacorta (1938), Lothrop (1933; 1936), Shook (n.d.), Wauchope (1949; 1965), Guillemin (1958) and Michels in a personal communication. The need for controlled excavation at Utatlán is dramatically shown by the fact that the most useful archaeological report available is that of Wauchope. He did little more than sink a few test pits and briefly describe the ceramics and a residential complex.[7] Utatlán should be thoroughly excavated and compared with Iximché and other late postclassic sites.

For other archaeological sites in the highlands where Quichean influence was felt, the lack of excavations is as bad or worse as that of Utatlán. Archaeological reports, where they exist, contain surveys only, based on superficial observation, surface pottery collection, and in a few cases some test-pit sampling. Easily, the most important study of this type is A. L. Smith's reconnais-

---

[7] Brief descriptions of what Wauchope uncovered at Utatlán may be found in his publications of 1949, 1965, and a monograph on protohistoric pottery from highland Guatemala which I have not yet seen. He has elaborated on his work in personal correspondence with me in July, 1968.

sance in the central highlands (1955). His maps, photographs, artifact descriptions, and interpretations are invaluable to the student of contact-time cultures. A similar study, though more limited, was carried out by Shook in the region around Guatemala City (1952).

Other surveys for the Quichean zone are by Wauchope, for the region surrounding Utatlán (1948b; 1949; 1965); Lothrop, at sites around Lake Atitlán, and the zone just northeast of there (1933); Borhegyi, for the region around Antigua (1950); Termer, in the northern Quiche area (1930b; 1931); Shook, throughout the highlands and coastal piedmont, including contact-time sites near Nahualá, Cabricán, Amatitlán, and Escuintla (n.d.); Coe (1959; 1961) and Shook (1965), along the Pacific coastal plains; and Gamio, for the western highlands at the frontier of the Mam speakers (1926-1927).

Additional survey information is available in the Museo Nacional de Antropología e Historia, Guatemala, where apparent contact-time sites are listed for San Andrés Xecul, San Cristóbal Totonicapán, San Miguel Totonicapán, and Chichicastenango. Also, the museum has numerous artifacts from contact-time sites in the highlands which have not been fully described. I spent several days in the museum studying Quichean artifacts for their specific decorative motifs and styles.

Adjacent Areas to the Quichean Zone

The best known archaeological report from areas adjacent to the central highlands is for Kaminaljuyu (Kidder, Jennings, and Shook 1946; also Shook and Kidder 1952; Miles 1965). Apparently, the site was not occupied at the time Quichean culture flourished, though a few hilltop centers in the basin of Guatemala were in use (Shook 1952).[8] Our understanding of highland culture before

[8] Archaeologists from Pennsylvania State University have been conducting large-scale excavations at Kaminaljuyu for the past two years. They have discovered many new occupational sites in the valley, and excavated structures not previously studied by Kidder and his associates. So far as I have been able to learn, there is still no evidence of any important contact-time occupation at Kaminaljuyu.

the development of the Quichean cultures continues to be based mostly on data from Kaminaljuyu.

Another area where extensive archaeological remains have been found is the Motagua valley, northeast of the basin of Guatemala. Smith and Kidder long ago (1943) found several structures and a long cultural sequence at Acasaguastlán in the heart of the valley. Much of their attention was directed to the classic cultural phase manifest at the site, but in a brief note they refer to nearby hilltop ruins, which they suggest are of postclassic and possibly contact-time date.

For the Pacific piedmont region we have reports by Thompson (1948), and a group of archaeologists from the Milwaukee Public Museum (Parsons, Borhegyi, Jenson, Ritzethaler 1963; Parsons and Jenson 1965). It now seems likely that most remains from the region around Cotzumalhuapa are from the preclassic and classic cultural phases, and should not be associated with the Pipil people of the documentary sources.

Away from the piedmont region into the coastal plains the archaeological evidence for contact-time occupation is slight. In Coe's studies of the Ocós region (1959, 1961b), he found abundant preclassic materials, but little from the postclassic Period. Similarly, Shook found almost no postclassic remains along the central and eastern coastal plains (1949). It must be remembered, however, that the whole pacific coastal area is archaeologically virtually unknown for the contact-time period and merits much more attention than it has hitherto received.

For the far western highlands, we have two somewhat out-dated reports—one for the southern site of Tajumulco (Dutton and Hobbs 1943), and the other for the northern site of Chaculá (Seler 1901). The Tajumulco report, though incomplete, contains a useful description of an early postclassic phase there and is supplemented by useful drawings of artifacts (the drawings are by Tejeda) (1947).

Seler's work at Chaculá and adjacent sites was done before the development of modern archaeological techniques, but is nevertheless important because of the abundance of artifacts he encountered. His description of them suggests that preclassic, classic and early postclassic phases once existed in that area.

Excavations by Smith and Kidder at Nebaj (1951) provide us with information on classic and early postclassic cultural phases in that part of the highlands. Apparently, because of the limited nature of their excavations, no contact-time remains were encountered. However, recent excavations in this same Ixil area at Acul, carried out by Becquelin (1966), have turned up evidence of early and late postclassic cultural phases. Becquelin labels these phases, "Tziauin" and "Umul," and gives a useful description of their architectural, burial, and ceramic features.

For the Verapaz region, apart from rather indiscriminate artifact descriptions by Dieseldorff (1928-1929), we have site reports only from Chamá-Chipal (Butler 1940), and Chipoc (R. E. Smith 1952; 1955). The long cultural sequences outlined in these reports include some useful description of postclassic cultural phases, though their importance is limited by the fact that they are almost exclusively based on ceramic evidence. In an especially important article for the ethnohistorian, Butler gives additional information on the Verapaz site of Chipal by focusing on the ceramic transition from aboriginal to Spanish times (1959).

COMMUNITY STUDIES

Introduction

At first glance, community studies of Quichean culture appear to be abundant. Tax and Hinshaw claim (1969:69) that some forty communities in the central zone alone have been studied by ethnographers, and good modern summaries and bibliographies of the ethnographic data are available (Tax 1952; Ewald 1956; Arriola 1956; Goubaud Carrera 1964:109-139; Nash 1967b, 1969; Tax and Hinshaw 1969).

Closer inspection reveals that most studies are superficial surveys. Thorough ethnographies are extremely scarce for Quichean culture. The community studies were conducted in town centers rather than in rural zones and lack strong historical orientation; their data is of limited value for the reconstruction of aboriginal Quichean culture. The situation for communities just outside the central area is somewhat better because of the greater cultural conservatism there (Wagley 1969; Reina 1969).

I will first discuss the studies for the Quichean zone proper, especially the community of Chichicastenango, followed by studies of Cakchiquel and Tzutujil towns; next, survey-type community studies for the Quichean area; and, finally, the more useful community studies outside the central zone.

Chichicastenango

Ethnographically, the best known Quiché community is Santo Tomás Chichicastenango. Schultze-Jena's account of religion there I have already cited for its ethnological importance; it is accompanied by a description of family, community, and cofradía life and their associated elements of aboriginal origin (1947:21-44). The Rodas study of Chichicastenango, ethnologically important for its description of native dress, also contains a good description of an internal social organization based partly on aboriginal patterns (Rodas N. and Rodas Corzo 1938:5-28; also Rodas N. 1925-1926).

The most complete studies of Chichicastenango culture were made by Bunzel (1952) and Tax (1947a) in the 1930s. Though Bunzel's description largely represents the viewpoint of the ladinoized Indians of the town center, nevertheless, it contains cultural data of probable aboriginal origin. She describes beliefs about land, conflicts within extended family households, organization of local native political units, food preparation and consumption practices, ideas about religious powers and supernaturals, and life cycle and communal ceremony all of which have roots in the prehispanic past. The culture historical value of her book is enhanced by the inclusion of several native texts (on the training of priest-shamans, prayers). The texts would be more valuable had she included the Quiche along with her English translations.

Tax's unpublished field notes on Chichicastenango (1947a) are strategically complementary to Bunzel's study because, to a considerable degree, his focus is on the rural Indian of the municipality (Bunzel suggested that the studies by Tax and Schultze-Jena would make up for some of the sampling deficiencies in her book), (1952:forward). Tax describes the kinship-oriented activities involved in canton social life, and we can detect a number of surviving aboriginal patterns of family organization, kinship terminology, marriage, and agricultural practices. He was also able to obtain considerable information on native religious beliefs about the native calendar, magic, nagualism, and deities.

As with Bunzel, the culture historical value of Tax's study is limited by his failure to learn the Quiche language, a disadvantage he fully appreciated (and perhaps the reason why he never published anything but his field notes). In defense of Bunzel and Tax, however, it should be noted that they had planned to return to Chichicastenango in order to continue their studies.

Momostenango

I initiated a community study of Santiago Momostenango in 1966,[9] because earlier ethnographic reports from there indicated that many aboriginal cultural patterns had persisted into modern times (Lothrop 1930; Termer 1930c; Tax 1947b). I found that in the rural zones of the municipality, even close to the town center, a basically aboriginal way of life, centered upon lineage organization, is still extant. After having obtained a working knowledge of the Quiché language, I gathered extensive data on such aboriginally derived institutions as land inheritance judicial process, ritual, marriage, and economic exchange. Soon I hope to make these data available to scholars in a forthcoming monograph on social and political institutions in Momostenango from preconquest time to present-day.

A related study is Saler's research at El Palmar, a piedmont community established by Momostecan immigrants during the 19th century (1962; 1964; n.d.). The culture historical value of his

[9] I am indebted to the Foreign Area Fellowship Program for the grant which enabled me to live with my family in Guatemala City and Momostenango for thirteen months in 1966-1967. Five months were spent at the national archives gathering documentary materials on Momostenango and the Quiche in general. During that time I made several short visits to Momostenango, and then spent the last eight months in residence there. Because of my interest in the aboriginal culture of the Quiche, much time was spent in the more conservative rural areas of the municipio. I never became completely fluent in the Quiche language, though I understand it quite well (I almost always kept an informant with me), and often transcribed in Quiche. I returned to Momostenango for four months beginning in April of 1970, in order to complete the study.

study is somewhat limited by the shallowness of the cultural tradition there, and by Saler's failure sufficiently to understand the community's social organization (e.g., ho mentions but fails to clarify the nature of the "patronymic kin groups") (1964:318). Nonetheless, his report contains a useful description of native personality types, and beliefs and practices associated with nagualism, transforming witches, and calendrics.

Lake Communities

The earliest and most sophisticated community studies in Guatemala were conducted in the Cakchiquel and Tzutujil towns around Lake Atitlán. The anthropologists who worked there were members of the Carnegie Institution of Washingtom and strongly influenced by Redfield and his synchronic, holistic approach to the study of culture. That approach and the fact that the lake communities have lost more of ther aboriginal patterns than other highland communities, has somewhat diminished the culture historical value of these ethnographic reports.

The best known study is Tax's monograph on economic culture at the Cakchiquel town of Panajachel (1953; 1964). Tax emphasizes present-day functional relations between socioeconomic units in the community; his references to an aboriginal background are minimal. Nevertheless, the ecological setting portrayed provides useful data for interpreting prehispanic ecological patterns for the lake area. Presumably, his forthcoming study of Panajachel "world view" will contain more data on native cultural forms.

Probably the culture historically most useful study of the lake communities is Mendelson's description of native world view at the Tzutujil town of Santiago Atitlán (1958a, b; 1962; 1965; 1967). Throughout his monograph, Mendelson focuses on ritual and belief associated with cofradía; and in untangling the symbolic themes used in these rituals he sheds considerable light on aboriginal ethics and mythology. We can only imagine the culture historical possibilities had he paid more attention to native language and social organization in the process of obtaining data for his ingenious analyses.

For the lake communities, we have the unpublished fieldnotes by Redfield on the Cakchiquel town of San Antonio Palapó

(1946), and by Paul (1959; Paul and Paul 1962) and Rosales (1949) on the Tzutujil town of San Pedro La Laguna. Their respective notes have information on ecological conditions along the shores of the lake and contain an extraordinary amount of data on folk belief and practice, some of which derives from aboriginal sources. Much of the data in their notes was transcribed in text form, in both Cakchiquel and Tzutujil, so the ethnologist has direct access to native expressions. Of special value, perhaps, is the detailed account of native beliefs about animals and plants provided by Redfield.

There are a few additional ethnographic studies of Quichean communities so acculturated that aboriginal culture patterns are virtually absent; for example the reports by Adams (1956) and Noval (1964) on the Cakchiquel town of Magdalena Milpas Altas, and the monograph by Nash (1967a) for the Quiche town of Cantel.

Survey Community Studies

We have much "exploratory ethnography," (cultural descriptions based on brief visits to Indian communities) for the central highland zone of Guatemala. By their broad scope and the fragmentary nature of the data recovered, these studies are similar to those of the ethnologists. Though they usually lack a strong historical perspective, in most reports a few cultural patterns are described that appear to be of aboriginal origin. A large number of mostly unpublished reports are in the archives of the Instituto Indigenista Nacional. They were initiated in the 1940s by an ethnographic questionnaire prepared under the direction of Antonio Goubaud Carrera, the director of the Institute at the time. The reports have continued into the 1960s, using basically the same questionnaire. For the Quichean area I have found that the reports for San Andrés Xecul (Búcaro n.d.a), Santa Catarina Ixtahuacán (Saquic n.d.), Santiago Momostenango (Bucaro n.d.b), and Rabinal (Goubaud Carrera n.d.) contain rich data on native institutions (especially kinship, marriage, ritual, and agricultural production). Undoubtedly, there are other equally valuable reports, though some were prepared in statistical form and contain little ethnographic detail.

Another collection of survey ethnographies was prepared by anthropologists working for the Carnegie Institution of Washington under the direction of Sol Tax (the reports are on microfilm in the University of Chicago Library). Among these is a report by Tax (1947b) of his brief visits to Momostenango, Nahualá, Zunil, San Miguel Totnicapán, and Huehuetenango. It contains useful ethnographic data on native kinship terminology, calendar practices, and pottery making. In another study, Tax describes (1946) several communities located along the borders of Lake Atitlán which he visited during an eight-months expedition in 1936. The data of greatest culture historical interest are on the geography of the area, native technology for exploiting lake resources, and domestic material culture.

Another reconnaissance study for Indian communities extending from Chiapas to Verapaz was made by Goubaud Carrera, Rosales, and Tax (1944). Besides visits to several communities in northwestern Guatemala and in Verapaz, they stopped at the Quichean towns of Sacapulas, Cunén, Uspantán, Rabinal, Salamá, Chicaj, and San Juan and San Pedro Sacatepéquez. Their notes are sketchy but contain numerous references to cultural forms of obvious aboriginal origin—e.g., witchcraft, clan organization, native dances, religious ritual on mountain tops.

Rosales later returned to Aguacatán for a two-months study, and his report (1949) is a rich source on native beliefs and practices about agriculture, the life cycle (especially marriage), and ritual. Goubaud Carrera returned to San Juan Chamelco, Verapaz, for a four-month study. His report (1949) contains some data of interest, though it is more general and focuses more on Ladinos than does the report by Rosales.

In the years 1964, 1966-1967, and 1968 I conducted ethnographic surveys at several highland communities in the Quiche area. I was interested in surviving aboriginal cultural patterns and modern social conditions. The communities I visited—for periods of time ranging from three weeks (Totonicapán) to half a day (Patzité)—were San Bartolo Aguascalientes, Santa María Chiquimula, San Francisco el Alto, San Miguel Totonicapán, San Andrés Xecul, Santo Domingo Sacapulas, San Pedro Jocopilas, San Andrés Sajcabaja, Santa Cruz del Quiché, Patzité, San Antonio Ilotenango, and Chiché. I obtained culture historical data on the relationship between political descent groups and archaeological sites (at Sacapulas and Santa Cruz del Quiché), clan and lineage territorial distribution (at Santa Cruz and Totonicapán), the location of important sacred mountains and prehispanic settlements (e.g., Jakawitz mentioned in the *Popol Vuh*, was located near present-day Sajcabaja), ecological patterns, and the meanings of names and other terms used in the native documentary sources.

An important survey was conducted by Lincoln in 1940-1941 at the Ixil communities of Nebaj, Chajul, and Cotzal (1946).[10] His posthumous published notes provide evidence of contact between the Ixil and Quichean peoples; they are a rich source of aboriginal cutural patterns (especially as these relate to calendar and religious belief). Lincoln combined a culture historical interest with the community approach, the resulting study is of particular value to the student of aboriginal cultures of the central highlands.

Community Studies for Adjacent Areas

Areas to the west and east of the central highlands which never came under Quichean influence presumably have retained cultural forms roughly similar to those which prevailed in the central area prior to the coming of the Quiche. Special light has been shed on native religion through a number of community studies made in northwest Guatemala, an area which is conservative from a cultural standpoint. The two most important studies were made by LaFarge at the Kanjobal town of Santa Eulalia (1947), and Oakes at the Mam town of Todos Santos (1951). They focus primarily on religion, and attempt to discriminate aboriginal from Spanish cultural patterns. Another important work from this area is Wagley's study of the Mam town of Santiago Chimaltenango (1941; 1949; 1957). Of particular interest is his description of clan and lineage organization. He also provides good information on native agricultural technology, land ownership, and calendric ritual.

---

[10] Lincoln's promising career was cut short when he fell ill while living among the Ixil; he died in Guatemala City in 1941. Recently, Colby initiated ethnographic work once again among the Ixil speakers, and his first published report (coauthored by Van den Berghe) was published in 1969.

The far eastern part of Guatemala is another culturally conservative area, which was generally beyond Quichean influence (it appears to have had closer cultural ties with the northern lowlands than with the highlands). The most important study there, from a culture historical point of view, is Wisdom's monograph on the Chortí (1940; 1961). He describes patterns of land tenure, agriculture, kinship organization, and religious belief which appear to have their origins in prehispanic culture.

An important supplement to Wisdom's work may be found in the several volumes on the Chortí published by Girard (1949; but see the critique by Starr 1951). Much of his writing consists of speculative attempts to interpret the difficult symbolism of various Maya cultures; but his first two volumes on Chortí culture contain useful descriptive material on native religious and social patterns.

Reina's studies of the Pokomán at Chinautla (1959; 1960; 1966) are largely concerned with functional relations of modern cultural forms, though some aboriginal patterns show through the background of modern beliefs and practices (especially domestic and religious activities). This holds true for Gillin's (1951) and Tumin's (1952) earlier studies in the Pokomán community of San Luís Jilotepeque.

LINGUISTICS AND GEOGRAPHY

Linguistics

Research on Quichean languages during the 19th century may be briefly summarized as follows: Brasseur noted that Quiche, Cakchiquel, and Tzutujil were dialects of the same language (1857) and he went on to learn a great deal about classic Quiche grammar and vocabulary (1961). Scherzer published a brief list of Quiche words from Ixtahuacán (1855) and the Quiche text of the *Popol Vuh* (1857). Berendt gathered Quichean vocabularies, and classified the Maya languages into related groups (e.g., he placed the Quiche, Cakchiquel, and Tzutujil languages together, and put Ixil close to Quiche) (1872; 1878). Brinton worked on classic Cakchiquel grammar (1884), and published the Cakchiquel text and an English translation of the *Annals of the Cakchiquels* (1885). Charencey, who, like Brinton confined his Guatemalan studies to interpretation and language analysis, published a French version of the *Título Totonicapán* (1885), and analyzed Quiche prefixes (1891) and verb forms (1896).

All German ethnologists worked on the Quichean languages, primarily gathering vocabularies and determining historical connections between them. Stoll was foremost among these, gathering vocabularies on all the Quichean languages, analyzing briefly their grammatical systems (1958:181-227; 1901), and reconstructing their historical relationships (1958:251-255). He made similar studies of Ixil, Pokomán, Kekchí, and Aguacatec, languages related to Quiché.

Later, the most important linguistic studies were made by Schultze-Jena, who analyzed the grammar of the Quiché spoken at Chichicastenango (1933), and Burkitt (1902), who left us a brief vocabulary and phonological description of Kekchí.

During the 1930-1940s, more attention was devoted to the study of the phonological and grammatical structure of Quichean languages, though historical problems continued to be investigated. Antonio Villacorta in 1927 translated the *Popol Vuh* with aid from Rodas, and later initiated studies on classic Quichean grammar and historical relationships between Quiche and Cakchiquel. He also produced a Spanish translation and useful vocabulary of the *Annals of the Cakchiquels* (1934). He has continued his linguistic work on classic Quiche with a grammatical analysis of the language used in the *Popol Vuh* (1962b), as part of a new translation of the Quiche text (1962a).

Two ecclesiastical scholars who made contributions to the study of Quichean languages during the 1930-1940s were Carmelo Sáenz de Santa María and Celso Narciso Teletor. Sáenz prepared a useful dictionary and grammar of classic Cakchiquel (based mostly on Varela), (1940) and an interesting though somewhat value-tainted comparison between the Quiche and Yucatec languages (1940). Teletor translated part of the *Annals of the Cakchiquels* into Spanish (1946), and later prepared a brief Quiche grammar (1951) and Quiche-to-Spanish dictionary (1959).

Probably the most sophisticated linguist to work in Guatemala during the same period was Manuel Andrade, then associated with the Carnegie Institution of Washington. His notes on the

Quiche, Cakchiquel, and Tzutujil languages (1946a) contain many texts (some with cultural content), a comparison between the three languages and other languages of Guatemala, preliminary phonemic analyses and dialectological information. He gathered similar materials on Kekchí, Pokomán, and other Guatemalan languages (1946b, c).

Goubaud Carrera continued the historical approach to the Quichean languages that was begun by the Germans. Following leads from Stoll, he published an interesting article and map on the distribution and interrelationships of native languages in Guatemala (1946). Later, he led a group of scholars in devising a standard set of alphabetic symbols to represent the Quiche, Cakchiquel, Mam, and Kekchí languages (Anonymous 1950).

Other studies with a historical orientation were made by Whorf (1943) and Thompson (1943b); both analyzed Quiche vocabularies for Nahua loan words and evidence of prehispanic contact between central Mexico and highland Guatemala. Thompson also discussed the distribution of native languages in the highlands, and offered a culture historical interpretation of their internal relationships (1950).

Recent linguistic work on the Quichean languages has been fairly equally oriented toward structural and historical studies. The structural studies have been carried out under the impetus of the Summer Institute of Linguistics in Guatemala and are at least partially pedagogically oriented. Of special interest are the studies of the Quiche language made by Fox (1965; 1966; 1968), for he has given us perhaps our best understanding of that language since the work of Ximénez. Shaw and Neuenswander (1966) also have made an excellent grammar of the Quiche spoken in Baja Verapaz (where it is called Achí).

Townsend's Cakchiquel grammar (1960), the Maynard and Xec Quiche dictionary (n.d.), and Wick's study of the Quiche spoken at San Cristóbal Totonicapán (1966), though primarily pedagogical in intent, are important contributions to the structural and lexical study of these two languages. Herbruger and Díaz' Cakchiquel grammar (1956) is a similar kind of study, though less sophisticated than the above works (especially Wick's).

Based mostly on work by the Summer Institute, an official alphabet for the Indian languages of Guatemala (including Quiche,

Achí, Cakchiquel, and Tzutujil) has been prepared (Anonymous 1962). It contains useful preliminary phonemic analyses of these and other languages.

An interest in the historical aspects of Quichean languages has continued in recent times. Perhaps the most important study is McQuown's work on the internal relationships and classification of the Maya language family (1955; 1956; 1964). Other broadly based studies of proto-Maya include the Quichean group in their formulations, as in the work of Halpern (1942), Diebold (1960), and Kaufman (1964). Swadesh initiated glottochronological study of the languages of highland Guatemala; with a list of 250 words he compares Quiche, Cakchiquel, and Achí with nine other Guatemalan languages (1960).

Edmonson has renewed interest in classical Quiche with his dictionary of classic Quiche words (taken mostly from the early dictionaries, especially the Tirado vocabulary), (1965), his study of classic Quiche grammar (1967), and a new English translation of the *Popol Vuh* (in press). Fox (1968) has recently taken exception to some of Edmonson's comments about dialectical variation of Quiche words in his dictionary, and in the process has helped clarify the present-day Quiché dialect situation.

Dialectology and internal relationships between languages of the Quichean group also have been the subjects of intensive investigation by Grimes (n.d.), who has attempted to reconstruct the phonology of proto-Quiche (1969). He argues that there is only a dialectical relationship between Cakchiquel and Tzutujil (1968), a point denied by Campbell (n.d.) in his general summary of recent historical studies of the Quichean languages.

Geography

In a broad sense the above ethnologists were all geographers. Even in the narrow sense of geography being the study of the physical environment and its use by man, the forerunners such as Morelet, Squier, and Scherzer were strongly geographically oriented. The Germans especially had geographic interests because of their commercial designs toward Guatemala (Bernoulli 1868-1870) and after 1840, when Berghaus made the first cartographic map of Guatemala, the Germans dominated geographical studies in

Guatemala for the next century. Besides the Germans, perhaps the best early geographers were Garcia Peláez, in his history of the kingdom of Guatemala (1943), Squier, in his wide-ranging book on Central America (1858), and Francisco Gavarrete, in his general account of Guatemalan geography (1868).

The German ethnologists incuded large amounts of geographical data in their accounts, though Sapper and Termer stand out in this regard (they are, perhaps, best classified as "cultural geographers"). Both made important contributions in physical (Sapper 1894; 1899; 1905; Termer 1936b) and historical geography (Sapper 1924; Termer 1957; passim; 1936a; 1939-1940). In their many publications, they treated such topics as prehispanic demography (Sapper 1924), markets (Sapper 1897b), native foods and drink (Sapper 1901), Indian routes of travel (Termer 1957), salt, pottery, and limemaking (Termer 1957), coastal agriculture (Termer 1939-1940), and many others.

After Sapper and Termer, the most important name in Guatemalan geography is Felix McBryde, who carried out geographic fieldwork in Guatemala during the 1930s and 1940s. He wrote articles on several different topics—climate (1942), marketing (1933), and demography (1955). Fortunately for students of anthropology, he was interested in native culture, and his most important study is a historically oriented cultural geography of southwestern Guatemala (1947). His focus was on the Quichean area and peoples, especially those living around Lake Atitlán. In describing numerous economic enterprises with undeniable roots in prehispanic culture, he concentrated on agriculture and craft production, marketing, settlement pattern, and population patterns.

Other geographic studies of culture historical interest are Stadleman's intensive investigation of maize cultivation in northwestern Guatemala (1940), Foshag's analysis of jade and other mineral deposits in highland Guatemala (1957), Borhegyi's (1956a; 1956b) and Tax's (1937) description of settlement patterns in highland communities; Ibarra's (1959) and Luna's (1958-1959) notes on native Guatemalan fauna, and Higbee's (1947) classification of agricultural regions.

The historical geography tradition in Guatemala has been carried on recently in part by the Instituto Geográfico Nacional through two of its publications: the *Diccionario Geográfico de*

Guatemala (Anonymous 1961-1962), and the topographic maps (scales 1:250,000, and 1:50,000). The *Diccionario Geográfico*, prepared mostly by Francis Gall, is an invaluable source of information on the names and locations of Indian rural settlements. Gall also included in this work a weatlh of historical notes which accompany the geographical data listed for each department and municipality.

The excellent topographic maps were prepared with the assistance of the U. S. Air Force, and are based on air photographs. They contain topographic and settlement features in fine detail, giving the names of mountains, hills, rivers, hamlets, farms, and archaeological sites. They are a tremendous aid to the ethnohistorians in identifying places mentioned in the early native and Spanish sources. Their importance for studying the aboriginal cultures of Guatemala is illustrated in the last section of this study, where they facilitated the interpretation of the *Título C'oyoi*.[11]

Considerable geographical information has been published by the Dirección General de Estadística, in connection with the five censuses which have been conducted in Guatemala in modern times (Anonymous 1966:5, 6). The general deficiencies and strengths of the various censuses have been discussed elsewhere (Monteforte Toledo 1965:61ff; Whetten 1965:19ff), and the following comments refer only to census data considered to be most useful for studying the Indians.[12]

The 1892 census tabulates population by municipality, and provides a good indication of such things as degree of ladinoization, craft specialization, endogamous marriages, and cultural conservatism (as indicated by literacy and the practice of Spanish crafts). The 1921 census breaks the population down into muni-

---

[11] I am especially indebted to the directors of the Instituto Geográfico Nacional, Guatemala, for the many maps I received free of charge. Similarly, I received free census materials from the Dirección General de Estadística, Guatemala. Throughout my work in Guatemala, I was never treated more generously or kindly than by the administrative personnel of these two institutions. I am indeed grateful.

[12] The 1778 and 1825 censuses can hardly be called censuses in the modern sense of the term. For that matter, subsequent censuses up to 1950 were also defective in many ways, though an attempt was made to standardize and assure accuracy beginning with the census of 1880 (Anonymous 1966).

cipalities, and lists the names of submunicipal settlements (*aldeas, caseríos, parajes*).

Only the 1940 census provides information on the native languages. The languages included were Quiche, Cakchiquel, Mam, Pokomán, Kekchí, and "Others" (see *Boletín del Instituto Indigenista Nacional*, 1946). These data must be used with extreme caution, because we are not told how language determination was made, and because President Ubico deliberately added almost a million persons to the total population count by increasing the population numbers for towns whose citizens had been politically favorable to him (Whetten 1965:20).

The 1950 and 1964 censuses, including the published *agropecuario* (economic) volumes, are as reliable as one can expect for present-day social conditions in Guatemala. The information in them is primarily important for the light it sheds on modern socioeconomic conditions in Guatemala, but data on such topics as population density, land use, agricultural production, ladionoization, and rural settlement patterns can be used as a control in interpreting geographical information contained in some of the primary sources.

A Case Study: *Título C'oyoi*

INTRODUCTION

A Case Study

To provide a specific and detailed description of the nature of source materials for the study of prehispanic Quichean cultures, I am presenting as a case study the *Título C'oyoi*, which is classified as a major Quiche document. (See Native Documents). This título is appropriate for a case study for several reasons : It serves to emphasize the primary importance of the native títulos in studying Quichean cultures in highland Guatemala. Important as the descriptions of the early Spanish writers, or the archaeological and modern ethnographic findings are, the accounts written by the natives still afford us our most direct and profound insights into their culture. This is true for the largest and best known títulos like the *Popol Vuh* and the *Annals of the Cakchiquels* and for the lesser native documents as well. Only when we have comparative texts can we eliminate the most serious historical and cultural distortions (though they are of interest themselves) of the better known sources. The *Título C'oyoi*, one of the smaller títulos, can be used in that way (it is about one third the size of the *P.V.* and the *Annals*, and approximates the size of the *Título Totonicapán*).

The *Título C'oyoi* affords us an opportunity to describe several ethnohistoric techniques usually applied to the study of native documents. It has never been properly identified, transcribed,

Illustration: Pictorial from *Título C'oyoi*. From one of two pictorials in the *Título*. It is supposed to represent the "castle" of the C'oyoi lineage.

or translated from the Quiche, nor has it been compared with the other sources in order to illuminate them and in turn be illuminated by them. It is a privilege to be able to translate an original document and it is the duty of the ethnohistorian to make the material available to scholars, so that they may use it in their investigations. I am happy to present the *Título C'oyoi* in, I hope, accurate and useful form, so that it may belong to mankind.

Unlike the other small documents published for the first time in this book, I have translated the *Título C'oyoi* into English instead of Spanish. I would have preferred a Spanish version but, because it is part of the main text, I felt it should be in English. I hope it will eventually be translated into Spanish so that Latin American scholars will have easier access to it.

Because of the "virginity" of the título and its substantial contents, its analysis requires the use of the major sources described in this book. I believe it illustrates especially well the ethnohistoric importance of the dictionaries, without which the secret of documents like this título would be forever sealed. As I worked on it, I became aware how important my ethnographic experience in modern Quichean communities was for the interpretation of many of its concepts, though it was not practical to cite all aids in the notes.

The study also emphasizes the usefulness of the modern topographic maps on which my map is based. I was pleased to find places mentioned in the sixteenth century document that are still called by approximately the same name 400 years later.

Archaeological sources are little used in this analysis because of the paucity of excavations in the Quezaltenango valley. It would certainly be a worthwhile effort to survey some of the sites of which their location is specified in the document, and so provide yet another situation for the application of direct historic method.

History of the Document

In the summary of the *Título C'oyoi* in the section on Native Documents, I have noted that it was probably written at Utatlán by the C'oyoi rulers from Quezaltenango, aided by Quiché rulers from Utátlan. It is similar to other títulos (e.g., *Título Santa Clara*), apparently written to obtain both land and cacique privileges for the C'oyoi line. Unfortunately, we have no knowledge of any petition or land dispute papers to which it might have been attached originally.

We do not know what happened to the document after the 16th century. Sometime before 1920 it became part of William Gates' collection of manuscripts on Middle American Indian languages. We are not told exactly how it came into his lands, but presumably it was among the manuscripts found during one of three collecting expeditions in Guatemala. Gates sent a man into Guatemala for a 15 months' manuscript search in 1914-1915; he himself went there in 1917-1918; and he obtained manuscripts found by an American woman, who had searched for two to three years "in out of the way places in Guatemala" (Gates 1937:15).

In 1930, the document became part of the holdings of the Maya society, when it was organized as a repository for the Gates collection. It was listed in a 1937 catalogue of the society under the title, *Probanza Ejecutoria del la Casa de Quiché*. Gates noted that it was "wholly unknown, and not mentioned by any writer," and he considered it of "highest importance," to be used along with the *Popol Vuh*, *Annals*, and *Título Totonicapán* in reconstructing ancient Quichean history.

It was later transferred to the Institute for Advanced Studies, Princeton, along with the *Titulos Tamub* and *Nijaib I* and *II*, and was cited as being there by Recinos in 1950. It is now part of the Robert Garett Collection of Middle American Manuscripts of the Princeton University Library. I have consulted the original manuscript at Princeton University, but mainly I have worked from a microfilm copy of the document graciously given to me by Dr. Pedro Carrasco, who obtained it from the library. Dr. Carrasco encouraged me in my translation and analysis of it, and the Princeton University Library willingly gave me permission to publish it.

Preparing the Transcription, Translation, and Analysis

An immediate problem in preparing the Quiche text for transcription was the page order. Only five pages were numbered (2-6), and these later turned out to be improperly so. Much of the ordering was done on the basis of matching configurations of the fragmented edges and perforations in the center of the pages. Later adjustments were made on the basis of continuities in narration, though these could not always be established because in many cases the lower sections of the pages were missing. Comparative knowledge of the format of other native títulos was helpful in establishing the proper order. I now feel confident that the page sequence is mainly correct, though possibly one or two transpositions may have been made, and, as will be seen, the order of the last few completely tattered pages could not be established.

The Quiche text was written in a very legible hand, with almost perfect use of the Parra characters. There is virtually no punctuation and many words are not separated from one another. I have not added punctuation, though I have attempted to establish the proper separation of words. In transcribing the text, I have attempted to convert it to the official orthography established under the direction of the Instituto Indigenista Nacional, Guatemala. Exceptions to this are the suspected Nahua words, which I have left as they appear in the text. Where part of a word is missing, I have indicated this with two dots (..); a word or more with four dots (....); and a phrase or several phrases with eight dots (........).

In translating the text into English, most Quiche words were found listed in the early dictionaries, and the grammatical forms were not difficult (many phrases are similar to phrases in the *P.V.* and other native títulos). Yet, the translation is obviously imperfect. This is due to the many gaps in the Quiche text, some of which seriously disrupt the flow of the narration and eliminate the aid to translation usually provided by context. Then, too, there are a few expressions not clarified by the dictionaries or other títulos. Moreover, my knowledge of classical Quiche is imperfect, and some errors, no doubt, are due to that. In general, however, the translation is probably accurate, an evaluation which I make based on the meaningful association which can be shown to exist between most parts of the narrative, and the vast number of similarities between this document's contents and those of the other títulos.

I have attempted to make the translation as literal as possible without completely disrupting the flow of the narration. I have added only a minimum of punctuation, mostly in the form of commas and semicolons. I did this in order to be consistent throughout the text, for there are some pages which are so fragmented that a more precise punctuation would not be possible. I have retained the Quiche forms for all titles, places, and social groupings of importance. I have often added missing parts where these could be safely assumed from repetitions in the text itself, or from cognate portions in other títulos. Where these insertions seemed problematic, I have explained them in the notes.

The notes explain some of the translation problems and provide a preliminary analysis of the document by comparing its contents with other sources. The notes do not exhaust the information which might have been taken from those sources, but I hope they are representative enough to clarify the document and illustrate the method of study. Another guideline in preparing the notes was to indicate those parts of the document which are of special cultural and historical significance, such as the Nahua derived words, or the exploits of the Guatemalan national hero, Tecum Umam. Finally, as I suggested in the first section of this study, I have used the *Popol Vuh* as the standard of comparison in constructing historical, cultural, and linguistic forms.

Significance of the Document

Before looking at the document itself, it might be useful briefly to summarize some of its more significant contents. The judgments as to what is or is not significant are made on the basis of a comparison with information already available in other native sources.

Perhaps the information which will receive first attention, especially by Guatemalan scholars, is that which relates to Tecum Umam, the officially proclaimed national hero of Guatemala. The document probably contains our most detailed account of that famous Quiché lord, and combined with the Nijaib and Huitzitzil Tzunun títulos should provide the basis for a more accurate reconstruction of the details of his life than has hitherto been possible. In fact, the entire account of the Spanish conquest is of special interest. It provides a unique view of the destruction wrought by the Spaniards on the residences of the native rulers. Unfortunately, much of this information is lost or unintelligible because of the extensive fragmentation of the last pages.

I mention the detailed description in the document of the political organization of the Quiche residing in the Quezaltenango area. This was the second most important Quiche center (after Utatlán), and yet, we have only sparse information about it in the Nijaib and Huitzitzil Tzunun títulos. The C'oyoi document describes how and by whom the area was conquered; whom the Quiche rulers sent to colonize and guard it, and their relationship to the ruling line at Utatlán; the names and titles of the most important rulers in the area, and the location of their political religious centers of stone and mortar. And there is an extensive list of the topographic features of the whole region.

The document helps to clarify certain institutionalized practices of the Quiche which are quite obscure in the other sources. An example of this kind of information has to do with Quiche numerical systems. Their method of counting is well illustrated in the document, and a unit of measurement is employed in one place. There are several references to the native calendar, including the use of calendar names, and a 360-day unit for expressing elapsed time.

Next to the *Popol Vuh* and the *Rabinal Achi*, the C'oyoi document is probably our most important source of information on the native dance drama. The names of several dances, and sketchy descriptions of how they were performed are in the account. The document also reveals a surprisingly strong Nahua influence. Not only are many Nahua words employed, but in one ritual context an entire archaic Nahuat esoteric phrase was used. The *Titulo C'oyoi* provides a good description of the uses of late postclassic town centers: for habitation, dance and other ceremony, legal punishment, astronomical observation, and defense. Two pictorials included in the document, though drawn under Christian influence, perhaps provide clues to prehispanic architecture (e.g., the roof constructions shown represent our only information on such features for prehispanic highland Guatemala).

Many of the cultural features mentioned in the título can be correlated with their counterparts in the other sources. Examples of cultural features with considerable overlap in the other documents are the numerous toponyms (these correlations are pointed out in the notes to my translation), political titles, facts of Quiche history (much of the narration of early Quiche history has been lost in this document), political succession (the same rulers are mentioned as are found in the other sources), and social organization (the título is rather weak in this regard).

The document lacks the extensive information on myth contained in the *Popol Vuh*, or the elaborate chronology of the *Annals of the Cakchiquels*. It definitely is a provincial account of Quiche history, seen through the eyes of the rulers of Quezaltenango. Within that limitation, however, it is authentic, and provides a penetrating view of the history, culture, and geopolitics of that important territory. With the section containing the native viewpoint of the Spanish conquest, it becomes clear that the document is an invaluable source to the student of native culture and society in Guatemala.

QUICHE TEXT OF THE TÍTULO C'OYOI

Page 1. *Wacamic chupam.... so ruc' junab[1].... tiquiba wi nabe tzij[2] uc'oje.... xic kamamaxic oj q'ui.... cha uxeabaj oj puch .... corowach[3] cuchix kak'a.... chun sajcab[4] ....ju..b.... tuy quejnay[5] belej lajuj .... jawar wi kamam kakajaw chup.... tak'aj[6] oj umam uc'ajol .... ak'ab maj[7] ... mam........*

Page 2. *....xal sakcorwach ....wi wacamic mix ....ri c'ute ix- numam ix ....ronojel tzij c'ajolaxi ....jawarem kech ri ajawa .... uy quejnay xeulic ....jawa....am ajawa ....chin qui- tunisaj[8] usuc'uli ....eic nimal rajawarem[9] ka .... kajaw juwinak caib chi aja ....rono..l tzij uni ....etic puch........*

Page 3. *....pam q'uiche juyub tak'aj ta xpe rele[10] .... ka ch'o ch'aka polo ciwan tulan.... kub pec wukub siwan....cha e.... jaw nabe winak balam q'uitze.... ak'ab/ majucotaj/ iqui.... xic kamam kakajaw quim.... c'ut cawek[11] nijaib ajaw q'uich.... oj umam uc'ajol ajaw iqu.... queje ucab q'uiche chi tamub.... chojlan majquinalo ajk'ana il.... ilocab junam quipetic ta.... winak yal chitun....chiyatziquin .... junam quix....*

Page 4. *....xepe relebal k'ij chiri c'ute xepixaba ....juwi juyub xcha c'ut quitzij chila ....be ubi chi pixab[12] e oxlajuj chi ....e quibi quiwach chi conojel ....q'uiche/ tambu/ ilocab ....akchi- queleb/[13] tzutujileb .... nak/ mayuc ajtzunu ....b/ ajch'umilaja/ la ....umatz/ cakajib/ iqu .... ch chi conojel oxlaju ch'ob ....amak' tecpan[14] ta xqui ....c'ut kamam ka ....balam q'uitze chu ....ojel amak' ....ix pu ka........*

Page 5. *tamub[15] a bi chuxic xawi queje aw.... cab are a bi ri chuxic xawi queje awe.... rabinaleb are abi ri chuxic/ xawi awe at cakchiquelab are abi ri.... xawi queje awe at tzutujil.... tuchaxic/ xachi wi queje.... ja tujal winak catuxic/.... awe at cubalcaal catuxic/.... awe at zakajib cakaj.... xawi queje awe at ak'aab.... xic/xawi queje awe balimaja are bi ri chuxic/ xachi wi queje awe.... ch'umilaja are abi ri chuxic/ xachi wi je awe at lamak'ib....at are abi .... xic/ xcha kamam kakajaw ch....*

273

nojel amak' ta xeuk'obisaj ta xeupic.... baj chuwi juyub ubi chi........mak'........cuc'........

Page 6. *....c'ut chiri amak'tan ubi juyub cakibal amak'tan[16] cuchax wacamic are ta xsakiric e c'u xucuxuj quetaji.... tisanic ta xel ula nima ch'u.... ti sakiribal xecha chire caqui.... mixtam pon[17] quecha chire ta.... oxib chi nimak' k'ij[18] chiri a ....juyub xsakir wi ix kama.... ta xquitiquiba c'ut binic.... canok sakiribal.... xpaj tzij ta xepetic xeul chiri chiwaij quetajin tamub ilocab e tac'abai quicabal ta xec'ulunic kamam kakajaw oj..be q'uiche queje c'ut naj chiwi xquiba..i xquita c'abata ucok quicabal chwa tak ....naj xquiban chiri coxichal cach bi....ta xepe chi c'u chiri xeopo........*

Page 7. *xquiban chiri xa wal wonon xa wal sitan[19] .... loo xa ratz'iak che[20] caquik'uuj xeel chi c'ut xeopon chic'u chila ticaj ch'alib[21] xak'an c'ut chiri xawi quekam ri abatz ri xpe relebal.... ruc' ri pisom c'ac'al[22] ma pu que....jik'aj jumul quewaic chi tic'oj naji.... nojel k'ij kitzij elok'olaj winak e.... jaw ri balam q'uitze balam a.... taj iqui balam e nabe winak .... jaw xcok'otaj chic'u canari.... xeul chi chiri jow balam k'ana ulew.... chi c'u chiri xeopon chi c'u chila chi waam .... k'uk' quijaj chi wi xquiban chiri xemay[23] .... chi wi chiri xeel chi c'u chiri xeopon chi c'u ch.... xch'ayab xinbaxuc' xawi kique ka.... abaj xpe relebal k'ij ruc' ri pisom c'ac'al.... tal ajawarem xeok'otaj chi c'u canari xe.... c'u chirij pa tzutuja c'a chiri c'ute........ wi jun....tuja cak.... rowach........*

Page 8. *....quiwach xeel chi c'u chiri xeopon chi.... pa tzekeb chiyaqui ubi juyub aretak....c'owibal ri xquiq'uiz quic'ux pa tak ciwan.... bea pa juyub pa q'uechelaj e kamam e ka ..jaw.... balam q'uitze don balam ak'ab.... aj don iqui balam ta xeel.... culum chi c'ut chiri k'alena....abaj[24] xawi xak'an chi cochoch.... re ral wonon ral sital caqui.... xo.. quiyab xek'anaric xebuwijic xe.... aliric e kaman e kakajaw chi ta usu..uliquil quic'axc'ol[25] ta xquitzucuj ta ....canayisaj kajuyubal katak'ajal ri....quimam quic'ajol xcok'otaj chi c'u cana.... ta xeul chi c'u chila pache e chik'ojom ubi juyub naj chiwi xquiban chiri e kamam.... kakajaw ajq'uix ajcab[26] xcok'otaj chi c'u.... nari xeul chi ..chiri chiq'uix[27] chic'........yub c'a ji....xqui........*

Page 9. *jawab e katit quixoki....xur/xpuch/ xtax[28] quibij ta xtica ....cumal kamam kakajaw xawi....cak sutz'[29] c'ut xok'ojol k'e..al*

ja....k'ol sutz' mayul cakulja[30] *....wonon sital xoc chiquech....*
uxiquin amak' ta xesachic .... queje c'u ri ix kamam ix....
chiq'uix chich'at rumal kam.... kilzij uzuc'uliquil aroka[31] *pu....*
bi binaam wi tibil xc'alakam k'uy[32] *uxiq... chuchaxic queje qui-*
sachic quicamic ri ch.... q'uix chich'at ta xepe chi c'u chira ta
xel.... c'u chiri jumetaja culba cawinal[33] *.... naj chiwi xqui-*
ban chiwi xajumet cocho.... xquiban chiri chiri c'ut xquic'ulwi
rajawa.... ak'aab cawinal[34] *..uchaxic xa c'u xquib.... quitzij*
camel nabej chiquic'ux xac'.... ya utzij cawinal xax xre.... na
pwakin boj[35] *k'ana puakim cu.... quecha chire xqui..t.nij*[36] *ch....*
ta xepe chi c'u jumetaba.... xe .... machi c'a chiri....wa..
am ta xa k'a.... chun sajcab[37] *.... cumal aja....*

Page 10. *Castillo*[38] *del segundo rey q'uiche utlatlecat*[39]*.*

Page 11. *Castillo*[40] *del calpul Ju° penonias de putanza*[41] *tercero*[42]*.*

Page 12. *....robanza executorio....culic nabe winak e kamam*
e ka..ol chiri chupam ismachi[43] *ta xban c'ut.... eje wae uchi-*
wach quitz'ak qui....e chupam titulo c'o camic xax....wi chi
chupam q'uiche jun rech ca....rech nijaib jun rech ajaw ....ruc'
chituy quejnay ta xban c'ut ch'u k'ak'al xic'owisax c'ut pokob
chanal[44] *ta x..oj c'ut junajpu coy wukub cakix*[45] *jo....tumum*
liquinza[46] *chuchaxic cakix....xic'owisakex pokob ruc' quel cuyuch*[47]
....bex c'ut rismal ta xban ta xtijto[48] *....ch'uti k'ak'al chiri*
ta xek'abaric ta xe....chupam nima quicotem chupam.... ja-
nal ta xquisipaj quimial....jubabal[49] *tzijbal sic*[50] *xecha chire*
sub....ak' tibaac'[51] *rajawiche xecha chire....quimial xajun k'ebal*[52]
chisaka....natal oj rapujutic'ab chi..tza....jer. Are....ta xe
....m q'uitze

Page 13. *balam ak'ab ma*[53] *....quikajaw ajawa.... che chituy*
quejnay xawi.... chojlan majq'uinalo ajma.... ruc' ilocab yal-
chitun chira.... chiyatziquin rajawal wukm.... nija rokche[54] *ca-*
jib Aj ta.... quib chiri chiismachi oxib ....nima q'uiche ucab
q'uiche ro.... jachow quib ta x....j nima q'uiche .... chij queje
uca.... c kamam ka.... ri paismachi queje c'u ri xoc ubic....
panq'uib panpacay[55] *chuchaxic ri xet .... mam kakajaw are c'u*
ri ilocab xeo.... chiri mukuis[56] *ilocab chuchaxic........*

Page 14. *....xmuk chex na....unojixic quech....ruc' nim q'uiche*
ruc' malcatz[51] *....c'ojeic ruc' quilok' quib*[58] *....xel chak'ixel*
c'a chupam ucaj....ta xticar c'ut nimal ajawa....na ronojel
umam ajaw....tz chak' ta xticar c'ut uchu....tinamit aban c'ut

nimak....catak wikab oxtak wikab[59] *xo....jaa tanata.... mej*
ulok mej[60] *.... nim rab rax....chixibin chic chisach.... nakil*
upam[61] *ta xticar chapic etaxic....queak'anic coxichal cakan aja-*
wa[62] *....rech nima q'uiche xawi cak'an rech ta.... ilocab role*
wakle[63] *ta xticar c'ut cho....zinteut*[64] *tz'akil........*

Page 15. *tzatz nabe xban paq'uiche ix kamam kac'a.. uq'uial nabek*
chi oyowal achijilal[65] *xquiban e nawal winak*[66] *ekamam kakajaw*
que.. relebal k'ij[67] *quetaam ukajibal k'ij quetaam puch unic'ajal*
caj unic'ajal ulew queje xban ri ojer xcha utzijoxic xubij..anajok
e kamam e kajaw xkatao x..bij oj ajaw mixkilo rulic utzij dios
ru.... c'ut don pᵒ Albarado[68] *nim.... itan Adelantado conquistar*
petina .... astilla ruc' kanim.... wal dios rey[69] *.... c'ut xchika-*
tiquiba.... ucholic wae nimal labal xquiban chuw.... wuk amak'[70]
tecpan xquimino ronoj.... mak' tinamit xkaj utinamit rabinal....
chiquel/[71] *tzutujil tujaleb cubul..al/ cunen cakquilaj/ booj/ choxa*
.... naj xjil winak/ balimaja/ yoc....chebex/ chele/ chun sitzol
ri c'u te....kaj utinamit cuma........

Page 16. *chiquic'ojeic ruc' ronojel ajawab nima rajop achij ch'uti*
rajop achij[72] *pa xicaja pa balimaja*[73] *xel wi banal labal ta xebec*
are c'ut xchikabij quibi ajawab wae xeajawar paq'uiche oj jun
chi q'uiche chi chituy q..jnay wae nabe ajaw nabe culel[74] *....*
nimal ajpop sakimox ruc'ajaw k'ali camja........ ajaw uk'ale
ch....yoi 9 Aj[75] *....ajaw rajpop achij c'oyoi ucabal....wi ruc'*
ajaw utzam achij sitai sitalan[76] *....ey c'u ajawab ri e wil tzij*
e pu ujolom tzij c'o nabe c'ut quiq'uial quicab cox catzqui chak'
xawi la xchikalemo xchikatajo qui....quiwach chi conojel e bele-
jeb caja....ol chituy quejnay xa wiil tzij ri caib cubulel nabe
cubulel xax uc'o....icwi...cak ma c'o ta la tzij........

Page 17. *jawarem are nabe cubulel ri don min mejia 9 Aj*[77] *cu-*
chaxic xawi c'o chi wi usuc'uliquil ri quech cawekil ri ajcot ajbalam[78]
nabe cubulel ri ajpop raxaj[79] *xa chi wi queje rech ajaw q'uiche*
are nabe cubulel ri runum c'abawil[80] *k'alel ajaw xawi c'o quicab..*
e uwil tzijo.. pu ujolom tzij tzatz qui..oxic naj nakaj xawi c'u
queje ucab q'uiche tamub are....cubulel are ri k'ale cakoj[81] *atzij*
wi....cakoj/ k'ale tam/ ajpop tam....c'u ajawab ri e uwiil tzij
e nabe culel queje xawi c'u queje quech ajawab i..cab are nabe
cubulel ri/ cortes k'alel ro..che ruc' atzij winak rokche ruc' ....
cajib aj.. utzam pop rokch[82] *....xic e rajawal q'uiche xeul........*
are.... junam........

Page 18. *nima rajop achij chita usuc'uliquil are ri cortes k'alel rokche caknoy e worom e c'a..m*[83] *c'o chi wi usuc'uliquil xchinbij Are c'u wae ajawab xeworic xcc'akic chi tatil chi k'ana abaj*[84] *lotzqui*[85] *..ak che ri xtz'akcot*[86] *balambak tatil k'ana abaj....ocob pich quij tzic wil coj tzic wil ba....toc matacuz....yom aztapulul ..be relebal k'ij ch'a.... hoo ch'akapolo xpe wi c'o quik'alibal....quitem quich'acat*[87] *c'o quimuj ruc'..ubak cham*[88] *e worom e c'akom are c'u ri worbal quech k'echa tumumcha tzocotz lakam*[89] *nima kaj tzijom....c'ucumam*[90] *c'aam are c'u xpe re....ri mixkabij quibi ronojel ....ikabij chic quibi wae tat........*

Page 19. *rech chituy que....na tata quech wi joob a....rajawal chituy quejnay....bij chupam wae titulo poder....mixco....lotajic rajawal chituy..ejnaiyib xa....wi pu queje juwinak cai..pop c'aam*[91] *....paq'uiche c'o upop c'o uc'aamj..jujun chi....ajawab xawi c'u queje jujun uk'alel rajpo.... c'o naipu utzam uchinimital rajtz'*[92] *....tatama ri c'o te ix ruc'ajol ix....chiwila chitaa*[93] *usuc'u.... c'ojeic ajauarem rech ..mam ika....nima k'ak'al tepewal*[94] *x..n paq'uiche chi....chwach kachum kasajcab chila pu xqui.... wi xpok' wi ronojel wae k'ula xelaju*[95] *.... chaj ruc' ronojel sija pamalaj pa....jil xawi pu queje ajnakaj ajtaa.... xiquin ajuwila ajam.. ajxoya........teaj/ ch'ulimal/ ....c'aba ....quin/ saki....wej/..../ruc' a....*

Page 20. *....najpu/ ri aja....yabaj/ ajraxacha*[96] *....c' jun uchuch ukajaw ri....marcaj chi ismachi*[97] *panq'uib panpacay chi..ic ruc' mukuis ilocab..huchaxic..n chic roxq'uiche chun sajcab nima k'ak'al tepewal xbanic cumal aj.. e kamam e kajaw ta xwimar q'uiche are c'ut xchikatiq'uiba chic....xic utz'ibaxic*[98] *wae k'al utepewal q'ui ....nimal ajawa e n..woric c'akic tax....p..cob chanal ta xbinaaj tojil auwilis....k'awitz*[99] *chuchaxic mayijabal*[100] *xban pa....che taxban ..utinem possesion bij .. un nima c'utbal ilbal*[101] *xbanic taxban....cuj pachojib*[102] *xban choloj tziquin k'ij*[103] *lak'ajaw zenteut*[104] *woric c'akic ta xoc puch .. ix xuchucat alicat aca wi..chu ch..nenepu tunapulul*[105] *ruc'..ch'ob k'a....u q'uexel rech........rio....n xawi quej........ tun..jail....*

Page 21. *ixajil tun ruc' tzala tun*[106] *ch'aw....xecha chirech queje ri ox..o bixa....subakibal*[107] *quech ajawab ta que..quec'astajic*[108] *cajib mul oxib*[109] *.... bul chitaltic*[110] *are c'ut caja..n aja....ri xpe relebal k'ij xbequic'amari/ be....jeb k'ij/ ajwaliom*[111] *xeberewal k'ij....nam quibe ruc' rech cawe.... ijai....ka choo ch'aka* *polo* c'o quimuj c'o qui.... *k'alibal coj k'alibal balam tzic wil coj....wil balam cot chiom aztapulul.... matacus quel samajal*[112] *ta.... uis cal camul belej cal*[113] *oxlaj....chi k'echa chi tumumcha ujalc'at....rem retal woric c'akic' xpe rel.... ch'aka cho ch'aka polo c'axaja*[114] *....k'ic chisiq'uinic oxlaju winak....wuklaju winak mwaji*[115] *....c'a te c'ut nima aj........homchaj........ ajawarem....*

Page 22. *....al chik'echa tumumcha chic'ow....c'ajol ta chulok sak amak*[116] *eka....ak'e kaley siwan tinamit....c'ut ichitaje chic ronojel....wachin....q'uiawic utzatzaric uquiri ajic wi....pokic winak paq'uiche chi....an....npacay chuchaxic ri tina........ acamic c'ut xchik'alajinic ronojel qui.... quichabem e kamam e kakajaw re....w..oic rutz..nic unojixic labal ta xeel....ronojel ajcha ajc'aam ajtzolaj ....che ajch'ab ajpocob*[117] *oyew achij*[118] *....amak'tinamit uk'alechij rajopa....ajtz'alam achij ruc' ronojel julajuj....oj k'alel ajaw k'ale sakic' ruc' rono....cawek q'uiche winak nijaib....ruc' ronojel wach belej ch'ol.... k'alechij chituy cajnay......jit Aj wuk'm ....cuc' cono....*

Page 23. *wi c'ajol xebe chupam labal....wi c'ajol ajawab xbecatzixel cha....ma na xata jalun ma na xata....xbec oxlajuj k'ulaja ajxelaju....lajuj tzijbachaj ruc' xw....c'oxtun sija*[119] *xbec are c'ut....ulok xwubax*[120] *quic'u ..x xc....wach cumal ajawab are....alak alak koyowal kachajilal*[121] *....chibe alak alak c'ulelaay*[122] *rech....tecpan yoc k'anchebex tzicol ba....nima amak' chibe yec'oj alak to.... mesquel alak*[123] *xeuchaxic kamam ...... waeic*[124] *uk'alechij c'o........*

Page 24. *....tecpan q'uiche petinak wi quit....acat ri e uxequi uxeoj sakcor....uchaxic catbec at watz....matok'ic matbisonic mawu....wicatalic xawi catpetic....wi ixc'ulelaay rech wuk*[125] *....cpan ajpoxajil*[126] *coon bu*[127] *....tzuja/ ruc' bamak'/ nima....k' anchebex/ tzitzol/ chele ....chaxic/ chun ruc' acalotema....balam colob queuchaxic atoloc'a....quel*[128] *chayec'uj xeuchix ulok ja.... nam kakajaw ta xeel ulok paq'uiche....panq'uib panpacay nima cu........*

Page 25. *kasay rech amak' tinamit e nimak ajlabal e kamam e kakajaw oj chit.. y quejnay ta xcokotaj mam e sakiulewa*[129] *.... nak chwach quijuyubal qui..jal....chila quijuyubal quitak'ajal ..uwila*[130] *a.. re ronojel quijuyubal quitak'ajal....quijebal quitz' akibal wakle ajawarem rumal don q'uikab c'awisimaj*[131] *ruc'..jaw* *baca ruc' 9 aj c'oyoi xeeleşan ubic..bal ta xeminic ri mam sakiule-wab..nak xawi e oyew achij xeel c'ut cwin..kamam kakajaw chwach quijuyubal paiqutyu ruc' iquilaja[132] xeokotax chwach chich'ab chipocob ta xeel chiri chwach tena/ ruc' lotz/ tzakibalja[133] ruc' xoch'o ruc' chukuljuyub palin quej[134] paquemeyo patziquiche patzala.. choo patuloa xec'ul chuwi quilaja ruc' xelaju chichaj/ chichaj/ ruc' sunil k'anteel ruc' pabaca/ xequi....paxtoca/ ruc' pac'uc'um....*

Page 26. *jel c'ut quijuyubal quitak'ajal e sakiulew winak ruc' ak'aab balam colob[135] ....yik'oxic[136] xeel c'ut chwach quijuyubal.... e kamam kakajaw nabe capitan ..kamam kakajaw oj c'oyoi sakcorwach uxequi uxeoj cojuchaxic rey q'uiche chapowinak[137] kamam kakajaw tecpan q'uiche chapowinak chi tzocotz lakam xul uyik'oj ulew junam quichiquiwach chi nima conojel ruc' cawek nijaib ajaw q'uiche ruc' tamub cuc' ajawab ilocab rokche cajib Aj wukmi.... sic'a juanija[138] xkaj c'ut quitinamit amak' cumal xoquibek c'ut quijuyubal quitak'ajal xsach c'ut quichiquiwach xk'up c'ut quik'inomal quitiq'uilem xturutix c'ut qui tz'ak quijaibal xc'am c'ut c'wal yamanic tatil k'ana abaj xkup[139] c'ut....tzij pwak quik'okol xteco[140].*

Page 27. *sochoj yamanic[141] xkupic xmajic rumal cawekib q'uiche winak ruc' chituy quejnay kamam kakajaw ruc' cakoj ikomak' ruc' rokche cajib aj wukmil sic'a ta xeel chiri chuo....ijuyubal quitak'ajal queje c'....xban chupam q'uiche juyub tak'aj ta xeul conojel oyew achij paq'uiche xepe chupam labal e yik'oy ulew e ch'a cot ulew[142] e kasay rech siwan tinamit ta xquijojij c'ut quitzij ajawab ta xeulic ta xquicuch quib conojel nima quicotem xban pa q'uiche[143] chwach kachun kasajcab ta xeoc apanok ajchaa ahc' aam oyew achij ta xtzucux c'ut ta xwae c'ut umam ajaw uc'ajol ajaw kitzij uchak' ajaw uc'ajol ajaw atzixel chak'ixel xbec ma na xata jalum ma pu xata al c'ajol[144] xbe..oxlajuj k'ulaja ajxelaju cablajuj tzijbachaj wajxakib tzalam c'oxtun sija Are c'ut ta xepixabax[145] ulok rumal nima ajaw don q'uikab xawi Alak catze..*

Page 28. *jic alak oyew achij alak kasay rech tinamit alak yik'oy ulew chibe alak alak lak'abey rech ulew chwach wukamak' tecpan rech mawi queul chic chiri ch....ik' alak ch'acom alak alak ajtz..l aj....unche xawi jutzu[146] chibam nimak xojuc'ulbatil ulew alak chujutak tzobajil siwan tinamit xeuchixic utz queje lal ajaw xecha conojel ruc' al alak c'ajol alak chibe alak alak koyowal kachajilal chibe ta alak c'ulelaay rech wukamak' tecpan chibeyec'*

*oj alak toloc' alak mesquel alak chwi ch'ab pocob xeuchaxic kamam
kakajaw queje c'u wi ix ajawab ix kamam kac'ajol chita usuc'
uliquil kelic ulok chupam q'uiche juyub tak'aj ta xojul waral chupam kajuyubal xelaju*[147] *xawi mawi kitzij ta waral xela xojul
wi c'o chi na usuc'uliquil xchikabij e nimak ajtzolaj tz'ununche e
rij siwan tinamit*

Page 29. *kamam kajaw mana xataki quirai. . . .k'alelal cajpopol
e nimak capitan rumal tecpan q'uiche petinak wi quitem quich'acat
catbec at watz at nu chak'. . . .tok'i. .matbisonic mawuchaj ac'ux*[148]
x. . . .tulic xa wi cojol awila[149] *chic oj ich. . . . kajaw xecha ajawab
xok'ojawab*[150] *quichuch quikajaw e kamam kakajaw oj chituy cajnaib junam quelic junam quipixabaxic ulok e oxch'ob chiuwa
q'uiche xeel ulok e. . . .lak'abei rech ulew chiquiwach winak e
sakiulewab e yoc k'anchebex tz'itzol bamak' nima amak' atoloc'
amesquel cha yec'uj at banol labal chibana iwoyowal iwachijilal*[151]
xeuchaxic janic' chiok'ej chibis xquibano xquimes quiwi[152] *xquiu. .
baj quic'ux xcok'en quichiquiwach ja. . . . la chiok'ej chibixab
xquibano kitzij catz kitzij quichak' ajawab ri xeel ulok lak'abeya
chulew xek'alun canaquib xemeso ucana quiwi queje c'ut xquiban
ri ix*

Page 30. *kac'ajol chi ta usuc'uliquil quelic ulok quipetic puch
kamam kakajaw oj ajxelaju cuc' ajmik'ina c'u cajsija cuc' ajxtoca
ajxoch'o ajxec'ut ah xo. . . .huwa tz'ak*[153] *ruc' ronojel amak' ruc'
rono. . . .malaj winak tz'utujil winak junam quelic ulok pa q'uiche
ta xejel ulok kamam kakajaw/ xec'ulun chiri tzam chicojaj xeak'an
ulok chocol capapec*[154] *xeel chi c'u chiri xeak'an chic chipatzam/
xeel chi chiri xec'ulun chic chi cak q'uix chay bamat cakiquil
cuchaxic c'a chiri c'ute xejachow wi quib ruc' k'ulaja ajxelaju/
are c'u ri tzijbach xkaj chwa joyam k'anak*[155] *xawi c'u c'a chiri
xechaw wi chi k'alelal chi ajpopol ri cablajuj chi tzijbachaj are
chi c'u ri wajxakib chi tzalam c'oxtun sija cabajojout raxq'uim*[157]
sebache[156] *yacalic*[158] *xekaj pa rax tum pec chiri nabe xetique wi
chisubic c'oje cana quicimiento chiri Are c'o ri ka*

Page 31. *mam kakajaw oj ajxelaju yacalic xekaj ula chirij c'oxtun
chiri xecanaj wi ajxtoca xec'oxtun are c'u kamam kakajaw yacal
chic xekaj ulok pac'uc'umabal xeq'uiak*[159] *chiri xeca. . . .ajsajcab
ajnima tz'ak q'uiche are. . . .ajaw k'ale ch'o cakoj*[160] *yacalic xoc
ubi chuwi quilaja are c'u ri kamam kakajaw oj chituy quejnay
ri ajaw uk'alechij c'oyoi belejeb aj cuchaxic ruc' nima ajpop achij*

*c'oyoi yacalic xeoc ubic pa baca ruc' junam quiwach ruc'ajaw
k'ali c'amja looquin*[161] *cuchaxic chiri xak'an wi quijebal quitz'ak
e kamam kakajaw oj chituy quejnay oj uxequi uxeoj oj c'oyoi sakcorowach cuchax kak'ajaric nima labal xuban . . kamam kajaw chwach
ronojel amak' wukamak' tecpan coon buxija/ tzuja/ ruc' bama/
nima amak'/ ruc' yoc k'anchebe tzizol chele. .n queuchaxic ruc'
ajalo xemache balam colob xrokotaj . .*

Page 32. *mam kajaw oj chituy quejnay junam quiwach chic oxch'obi
chauwa q'uiche queje c'u ucanajic ri chupam kacimiento pa baca
ri kakamam kakajaw oj c'oyoi s . . . . rowach uk'alechij belejeb aj c'oyoi
cuchaxic ruc' rajpop achij c'oyoi ruc' nima c'aamja looquin queje
c'u ri xkaj ajaw cortes k'ale rokche saknoi isuy sakpoklaj*[162] *yacal
c'u ajaw xak'an chuwi lajun quej runum c'abwil k'alel ajaw xoc
c'u ubi ajaw quemaxitapul chic'wa*[163] *junam quibe ruc' belejeb
aj uxecha uxeabaj mejia cuchaxic chiri c'o wi quicimiento xetuj*[164]
*ruc' yacal ajaw xic'owic ajcot ajbalam mama ajpop rax chiri
xepach*[165] *xc'oje wi cuc' conojel chic rajop achij ch'uti rajop achij
cuc' cal quic'ajol cachbilam ta xetequeic chiqui jutak tzobajil chil
amak' tinamit que. . . . c'ut ulaca. .xic aretak ulew rij chwach
wukamak'*

Page 33. *tecpan ix kamam kac'ajol chic'ama inaoj chupam wae
ititulo*[166] *proban. . . .ipoder uyaom tecpan q'uiche xec'ujeke lok
chiquijujunal*[167] *ta xquiban chic quitzij ajawab waral . . . .u chi
nima conojel ta x. .n. .ij ubanic retc'amaxic ronojel uchi. . . .chiri
xbeticara wi ulok retaxic retal paraxq'uim chupam tz'ak quiculbat
ajsija cape c'u chiri c. .chuchija xawi. .a. .raxq'uim cape chi c'u
chiri caculun chac'ulbat ajaw xcamparij ajxtoca*[168] *cape chi c'u
chiri xawi capakmaij ula chwa juyub xawi paraxq'uim quel ula
chwa juyub. .xule chi c'u ulok xawi chwa ri juyub ca. .lun chwa
tz'ibam pec*[169] *cape chi c'u chiri. . . . chuwi juyub q'uiak c'o jun
nima tz'ak pauwi ri q'uiak quitz'akibal e sakiulewab winak*[170]
cape chi c'u chiri chuwi q'uiak cakaj ula pa rakan tak'aj[171]
quic'ow. . . . chilemob[172] *xa chiwi catzal c'o. . . .*

Page 34. *quiculbat ajxtoca chwa c'abawil chaj*[173] *catzolk'omij chi
c'u ulok c'ulbat uchi siwan capetic quic'ow la chiri sajc'aja*[174]
quicow la chwa nima caja[175] *xaki uchi siwan cape. .ul c'u tij ulok
chwa xak cuk'at nim. .a pu. .ula*[176] *quicow la chwi pa ba. .quel
c'u chiri c'a copon pachun quel c'u chiri copon tzam abaj*[177] *copon
tzam ixim ulew quic'ow pa. .almet copon chi c' . .chila chijaya*

xbe chwa tz'olojche[178] *copon chi c'u wuk xiquincan quel c'u chiri quel c'u chiri cakal pa ucus quel c'u chiri juyub cabec palajunoj c'a chila chiquic'ulbat aj tak'ajal..ak xbe quitanaba wi kamam kaka....oj ajxelaju xbanatajinak achi c'u ri ronojel ri mixkacho xnojitajinakok cumal ajawab junam quichiquiwach xquicojo retal culew are c'ut usuc'uliquil wae ix ajawab ix nuc'ajol chinbij canajok usuc'uliquil chwech ma.... mich'u ma ta pu chisa.. ic'ux ix....nu c'ajol*

Page 35. *oxib roxc'al*[179] *tzij wae rulic nima aja....Adelantado capitan don p° albarado conquistador utakom ulok kanima ajawal dios Rey castilla yaol re..utzij dios pakawi oj q'uiche winak chi nabe....wi xetulul*[180] *jun batz ta..quibex.... xetulul/ caib e*[181].. *ta xoquibex ....ajxepach ajcot ajbalam xexim....tulul aj-xepach*[182] *e k'alel e ajpop ta....nima tz'alam abaj ronojel tzalam c'ostum k'atibal*[183] *rech winak sak utiojil e soltad..rech don p° albarado nima capitan ru c'aam lanza Albarado ruc' c'am al-cabuz c'o upocob c'o respada ....tz'akat ronojel murion jolom.... ch'ic xak pota ch'ich'*[184] *c'o chirij ma...cabinta chirakan relem rumal quej cabinic ju k'ataj xkaj ronojel tzalam costun rumal xwilijic....kaj ..onojel abaj cumal k'ek....*

Page 36. *yaqui winak*[185] *rachbilam nima rajop achij don p° de albarado conquistador cape españa ruc' kanima ajawal dios rey c'ate c'ut uyiquiyobic conojel k'alel ajpop rajop achij.... lechij.... jpop achij chiwaral xelaju....etakan ruc' nima ajaw don q'ui ....ila tecpan q'uiche pa nima tz'ak c'o.... chupam pu nima chun sajcaj tz'u..un quisamajel xbe pa q'uiche*[186] *xawi are k'ij xc'ulunic bi ta xiquin*[187] *chiri c'ute chuwi mik'ina pa tzijbachaj xel wi nima rajop achij adelantado tecum umam rey q'uiche don q'uik'ab*[188] *wukub k'ij xtelex*[189] *chiri pa q'uiche xol tak ja telem pa k'uk' chupam puch c'wal yamanic tatil k'ana abaj ta xul uk'ijil upetic telem rumal ronojel tinamit ri nima ajaw tecum adelantado capitan rech q'uiche nima bi..xajoj cham cham*[190] *catajin ruc' ta ....*

Page 37. *xpetic xawi queje caquiban conojel k'a....pop uk'alechij rajop achi ruc' rajpop a....chiri xelaju janic' lalo chi cham cham ....bix chi xajoj catajin pa nima tz'ak c'oxtun xelaju ta xoc apano tecum ..m capitan rachbilam laju k'ob ju..ju k'o b....nak juwinak belej lajuj ka..ak wi lakam*[191] *chiquixol ruc' su uk'o.. m*[192] *xawi queje tzatz chi ajawab e rachbi..rachijpop rachij c'aamja achi q'ui nima.... pop ta xic'aja pa bamlimaja*[193] *xel wi....*

nol labal waral pa q'uiche c'a chwa tuj tok'ol wi banol labal[194]
q'uiche winak cachuwi[195] *cab..yoc*[196] *tok'ol wi ronojel c'ut k'alel*
ajpop roxɪche..wuch q'uiche tamub ilocab ruc' ronojel ajxelaju
cawekib nijaib ajaw q'uic....hituy cajnai ruc' ronojel ajnakaj
ajta....ajxiquin waral q'uiche/ aj uwila[197] *aj ch'ulimal/ ruc'abala*
tziquin/ sakiya/ xojbaquiej ruc' ajwajxaklajuj/ ajtinamit/ aj-
pachiqui/ ruc' la....bola/ ajc'akolquej/ ruc' aj i....

Page 38. *ajcabrakan ajtzapik'ak'/ ruc' ajchi..ajpu/ ruc' ajraxacha/*
tucurub c'oyoi sakcorowach uxequi uxeoj ruc' ajamak' tam aj-
sakmolob/ ruc' ajtabij/ ruc' a..quiya ruc' ajcak'alaj/ aj..xit/
..c'aj amak' mes ajpokoba/..aj k'ojomeb[98]*/ ruc' ajchich'alib/*
ronojel..cawek q'uiche winak nijaib ajaw q'uiche ..tuy cajnai
ruc' ajawab ajpop tam k'aletam k'ale cakoj atzij winak[199] *cakoj*
xawi ruc' ajpop/ ajpop c'aamja alel atzij winak uk'alechij rajpop
achij rajpop achij chituy cajnayib ruc' atzij winak rokche k'alel
cajib Aj utzampop rokche ilocab ri c'ute ajawab e ujolom tzij
uwi ajawarem xebe pa labal ruc' ronojel cal quic'ajol xeel chiri
xelaju xec'ulan rech don pedro de albarado capitan conquistador
espanol chiri xban wi labal chwaraal nic'aj chaj[200] *mawi ajilam*
chiwinak chuwi calab uk'u[201] *u..a juyub tak'aj xeche xec'aam ta*
xban ....waral xelaju tzanabaj chiri xeju..xel wi ujolom uquej
nima ajaw[202]

Page 39. *adelantado capitan don p° albarado conquistador xel*
ujolom uquej rumal capitan tecum ajaw chi ch'ami chaal[203] *camul*
c'ut upetic c'uc'umam ajaw tecum chicaj cape wi ta xul uyaa rib[204]
..i capitan ca..chiquixol castilan winak....tecum raj xti[205] *cumal*
nima ....ulew x.. ri q'ui chirij ch..que i sac'a[206] *españo.. chi-*
wilari cap..jim oxib corona[207] *i..lemo chwa chuq'u..c'.. m ruc'*
k'uk' rismal[208] *elenak ulok chupam utiojil queje ri xkaj ulok*
jun k'ij ch.. caj kitzij nima k'ak'tepe[209] *chi ri c'ute xuta wi..*
xutz'onoj ubi ri juyub chiquech yaqu..winak nakipa ubi wae
juyub xeuchax..tenanco c'uchax usiq'uixic señor xech..conojel yaqui
winak chire don p° albar..utzbala queje Quetzaltenanco bach......
rumal mixcam jun nima capi....tzai ajaw chupam ruc'chupam....
as espiritu san[210] *mixnuch'aco....xawi are chubinaa..are ic'..*

Page 40. *u..chuchajij xcha ajaw chitaco quibe....c'ut ajcha ajac'*
am ajlabal oyew....rachbil tecum mawi ajilam chi wi..nak xcamic
rachbil tecum xcakar uwa k'ij chi caj rumal quic'[211] *xawi queje*
ja quiq'uel....rumal quic' are ru....aaj quiq'uel queje c'u xban

. . . .*mam kac'ajol queje pu ka ch'a* . . . .*ri queje c'u* . .*ko quia ri chi xptia*[212] . . . .*chupam uch'a* . .*dios* . .*mal nima capitan don p° Alvarado jun kakajaw oj c'oyoi sakcorowach xcam pa labal nima rajop achij c'o chirij rach camic tecum*[213] *pa labal are c'u ri 9 Ah uk'alechij c'oyoi jun chi kamam kajaw ri wae in c'olic in uc'ajol in ch'uti c'ajol ala ta xkaj* . .*hapan wi chiri xinalax wi pa ujebal utz'akibal*[214] *numam nukajaw chiri pa baca are quilak'abem canok kamam k* . .*jaw ri nima tz'ak c'ostun waral xela* . . . .*pum junam quiwach elem* . . . . . .*taj* . .*atinak chuwi ja nima tz'a* . . . .*xeoquibex rumal* . . . .

Page 41. . .*capitan conquistador jutzuc xquik'aluj* . . *quik'oj quic'*[215] *xquiluc quib chwach ri ajaw xquicubachu jun nima tem ch'acat petinak pa relebal k'ij raj c'ut xeximic ma c'u jabi xcaj p^e xeximic*[216] *ruma* . .*caqu* . .*quemelaj quib nakila c'u upa* . . . .*wex* . .*ta xesiq'uix c'ut conojel* . . . . *don p° Albarado* . . . . . .*onojel winak e* . . . .*lic xcha chi* . . . . *c'ajol conojel e baka* . . . .*wi e c'o waral chupam* . . . .*tz'akibal wae ja c'olic e* . . . .*xecha conojel al c'ajol* . . . .*chwach don p° Alb* . . . .*xeuchax* . . . .

Page 42. . .*xiban ri labal ma ta xojilabalij xa* . .*ta xcam ri capitan tecum xeuchaxic que* . .*c'u ri ix kamam kac'ajol chi ta usuc'uliquil nabe xkaj pa pauwi ajaw k'alel ajaw ruc' umial uc'ajol don Andres de chavez xubinaaj ucab ajaw 9 Ah don min mejia* . . . .*rox ajaw k'ale xc'ub don Ju°* . . . .*aj ucaj ajaw k'ale rokche don*[217] . . . .*nu kajaw uk'ale* . . . .*c'oyoi xkaj ja pakawi* . . . .*c'oyoi xinbina* . . . .*ri' ralc'wal xkaj ja* . . . .*castilan winak soldado* . . . .*unic chiquiwach p^e aj* . . . .*bilam ajaw don p° Alba* . . . .*wa ja tzij pwak/* . . . .*ajaw rumal* . . . .*don p°* . . . .

Page 43. . . . .*Lopez witorio xubin* . . . .*oi Andres basqu*[218] . . . . *xkaj wi ja pakawi xelaju* . . . .*wab xkaj ja paquiwi ruc' qui* . . . . *don di° quemaxitapul ruc' don* . . . .*k'ale cho e uwi ajaware* . . *ar* . . . . *ajpop k'alel ajxepach k'a* . . . .*paquiwi chiri xkaj wi ja pa* . . . .*bal c* . .*wi pach* . . . .*mam e kakajaw* . . . .*c'amol cristianoil* . . . .*quimial quica* . .*mi* . . . .*jujunal xbanataj* . . . .*ok jun nima solda* . . . .*chuchaxic teniente ca* . . . .*al xelaju ruc' toton*[219] . . . .*eul chi c'u* . . . .*re xak'an chic* . . . . *ri xeul chi ch* . . . .*chiwi xchwiban* . . . .*nic mawi ca* . . . .*ak'ajal mawi* . .

Page 44. . . . .*retal rulew tinamit*[220] . . . .*chi c'u chiri cac'ulun chuqu* . . . .*mparij ajxtoca xawi are jun* . . . .*inakil retaxic ulew capakmaij* . . . .*yub xawi paraxq'uim quel ula chwi* . . . .*le chi c'u*

ula chwa juyub takal....ac cape chi c'u chiri cul chuwi....lun
wi matz'ak pauwi ri q'uiak....c'u chiri chuwi....tak'aj cac'ulu
....c'u ucok chiquic'ul....bawil chaj ca....c'ulbat xaki uchi
siwan....chwa xak cuk'at....ac'ulun chuchibe nim....ina xawi
cabe pa puju....ro wi c'ulbat chi rech ca........xiquin[221] ta
........camic ta....bil quisachic....xquitao utz....mam e ka
....cachbilam....

Page 45. ..quinjij........uwakle ajawarem ta xa....aj uk'alechij c'oyoi ta....hanal upok'oj siwan tinamit....uejnayib ta xel
ubic oyew....siwan tinamit tzucunel....nakaj xopon wi........
ta xecha........ri pa q'ui[222] ....ka....alaj....kulew ...xawi
...jij....xawi ....chiri xepaca....paka....abaj ch....wi....
baj........al c'u ....ubi chipi........ don c........p°
gomez........p° s........

Page 46. ....ix kamam ix kac'ajol....c'uliquil tzij ri cakabij
ca ....ech ix kamam kac'ajol....chikatiquiba chic uk'alaj....
nok chiwach kulic pa q'uiche........q'uib panpacay oj nabe[223]
....tala culew chiquiwach........xak'an........ siwan........
paca....anta cruz....cat saku....lbarado.... wex........

Page 47. ..ubic copon pa pajaca caxul....c'ulbat chuchi wi c'ul-
ba........ajmik'....xulan....tianoi....ajxequi.... quin....
....xequiq'uel....quiq'uel ....are ta xya....bat cuc'....ele....
copon tza....wi tinamit..wila....copon....ik'ijax........
xquin........ajawa....nukulo........em..xtza....oyoi ta....
....c'ajol aj....xawi........axic siwa........binaa....belej
........San....ubij per....ixim....tinam........

Page 48. ....lbat mixquikasaj conoj....chi c'u chiri copon wuk....
chi c'u chiri xkaj pau....ek....tzamba....tin........chuchi....
capetic....yik' tz'i....ajaw pa....e winak....cabe chi....xax
....chwach....ula chu....wi....quic'ulb....quista....sic'a....
ca c'u....xejacho....xecha....mak' chi q'u.... iche ta xe
........ruc' ....tzam........c'u e c'o chu.... etal ....tinak
e....canok q'ui....ox wi....santa crux.... p° alba

Page 49. ....sion....lo oje.... albarado....e mamaxel e....
tz'ak pa costun pa q'ui....tao ajaw ca....ta xeusiq'u....jaw
....kaban........inak e.... icar laba....oyotaj....ej chiban
laba.... bala cojcamic xecha....ajaw xaki..aj cam....quib chi
coxichal cuc'

Page 50. ....*ajaw....Albarado conquistador....ajaw xe..*
..sochoj yama....k'ab chincuy tzi....xquiyao....ecoc c'ut....
lucas de....cahij c'o........ok'ibaj co....uc'uliquil....lal xa
....xcokotaj chi q'u....macutura....naj....xemolomanic xech'ij
....ochoch quijuyabal qu

Page 51. ....*na ta....quitzij....in Ju^o....ticar ucoj....*
chiri........tz'aki....ri ya....chiri....canay........

Page 52. ....*con....aja capetic....il chupam....español..*
......c'u e ka....xawi....tok'o........umal....alak aja....ri
ulew....chi........

Page 53. ......*akaw cumal......españoles......an fran^co p^e e*
ra........ ado tonatiu xca....quikul kamam .... nuyao usa..
español adelantado capitan ....quistador e are c'u ri kamam
ka ....k'ijilonic xquik'ijilabej....nic tatil k'ana abaj k'al....
ma pwak k'ana puakim ....quik'ijil abaj c'wal yamanic ....
xuk'ijila....ukajaw fran^o[224] ....ruc' rajpop.... sakimox......
..

Page 54 ....*queje ulo....rib chupam wae utitulo ....de putan-*
za[225] c'oyoi uk....don fran^co ....cak........pala....quic'ulbat
....felipe re....espiritu san....uchax usi........och cochoch
....xatulic....ta xquiyao in ....rado xax e ajawab....wi-
mul rumal don ....e wi ajawab xpe k'ij xpe ....ajolaxel rumal
rey c'opa.... che xecha chic/ xere ic'ux....ri espanol ta xeuc'am
....ij ri conojel ajawab kamam kaka....tuba chupam silla ma
na xa ta....as iwuc' xeuchaxic are....mawi ..

Page 55. ....*jawib........c'ut....xawi na........santa*
cruz mixb............xpe k'ij........

Page 56. ....*iqui....parij........k'ale s....wi....a Cruz*
.... xequic'........xion....wej....ban........k'aya....
....retal........rumal....don ju^o....saknoy[226] ....don mi....
mik'e....tapul....rakan....ju^o bautista ajpop/ don....xia don
fran^co gomze ju^o ca....don....perez xchaob utzamachij utzam....
don....de roja k'ale par..in....don jor....santa cruz mix....
(in different handwriting)....titulo....los antig....c'oyoi....

ENGLISH TRANSLATION OF THE TÍTULO C'OYOI

Page 1. Today at....in the year[1]....(we) begin here the first account[2] of the existence....(of the fathers) and the grandfathers, we the Q'uiche ....below the woods and stones; and we....(the C'oyoi Sak) corowach[3] they speak of our whitened stone structures[4]....(the Chi)tuy Quejnay,[5] the 19.... lordships here; our grandfathers, in....(the mountains) and plains;[6] we the grandfathers and sons....(Balam Quitze, Balam) Ak'ab, Maj(ucotaj, Iq'ui Balam)[7]....(our) grandfathers........

Page 2. ....Sakcorowach....here today....afterwards, you, my grandfathers, you (my fathers)....of the entire account of the sons....our lordship, we the lords....(Chit)uy Quejnay arrived at....the lords.... they truly were joined together[8].... the existence of the great lordship[9] of our (grandfathers and) fathers; one people and two lordships....the whole account....and (their) coming........

Page 3. in the Q'uiche world; then (they) came from the East[10].... (from the other side of) the water, the other side of the sea, from the canyons of Tulan....the seven caves and seven canyons ....they are (our grandfathers and fathers); the first people were Balam Q'uitze (Balam) Ak'ab; Majucotaj; Iq'ui (Balam) .... our grandfathers and fathers.... then Cawek,[11] Nijaib, Ajaw Q'uiche....we, the grandchildren and sons of the Lord Iq'ui (Balam)....so also the second Q'uiche (branch), the Tamub.... (Aj)chojlan, Majquinalo, Ajk'anail....Ilocab (branch) also came together....Yalchitun....Chiyatziquin....together....

Page 4. ....they came from the East; and there they counseled among themselves....on the mountain; then their account was spoken there.... its name is Chipixab;[12] they were thirteen.... the names of all.... the Q'uiche; Tamub; Ilocab....(C)akchiqueleb;[13] Tzutujileb....Mayuc Ajtzun(unija) ....Ajch'umilala; La(mak'ib) ....(Cu)matz; Cakajib;....all of the thirteen groups....our hamlets and fortified centers,[14] when they....

then our grandfathers (and fathers)....Balam Q'uitze....all the settlements....

Page 5. "Tamub[15] is your name," they say; "so likewise yours.... (Ilo)cab, this is your name," they say; "so likewise, Rabinaleb, this is your name," they say; "so likewise yours, Cakchiqueleb, this is your name," (they say) ...."so likewise yours, Tzutu-jil(eb)....(you) come to be; likewise here....the Tujal people you come to be; you the Cubulcaal come to be....yours, you the Zakajib Cakajib....so likewise you, the Balimja, this is (your)....name," they say; "likewise here is your, the Ch'umilaja, this is your name," they say; "likewise here is yours, the Lamak'ib (C)umat, this is your name," (they) ....say; thus our grand-fathers and fathers said to all the groups when they were glori-fied (and dignified with names), when they counseled them on the mountain called Chi(pixab) ....the groups....

Page 6. ....then there at Amak'tan,[16] the name of the mountain, the red place, (was) Amak'tan, as they say today; this....when it dawned they were kneeling, they were occupied....shouting, when the great star came out....the dawning it was said to them, "they....Mixtan Pom,"[17] they say to them, when.... three festive days[18] there....mountain it dawned there, you our grandfathers (and fathers)....when they began to travel .... left the dawning....memorial was given when they came; (and when) they arrived there, they were hungry; the Tamub and Ilocab were established, the two of them when they met with our grandfathers and fathers, (the first)....Q'uiche; so it was far away there that they made....they established the two of them on top of the ....far away they did it there, the three established the two of them on top of the....far away they did it there, the three companion groups.... when they came there, (when) they arrived....

Page 7. they did it there; just the young of wasps and bees[19].... they covered themselves with bark clothing;[20] then they left and arrived there at Ticaj Ch'alib;[21] they went up and....there they took out the stone that was brought from the East, (along) with the Pisom C'ac'al;[22] there was no fire.... one time they ate at Tic'oj, far away....every day; in truth they were belov-ed people, they....lords, Balam Q'uitze, Balam A(k'ab, Ma-juco)taj, Iq'ui Balam, they the first people.... lords; then

they abandoned (that place), and later....arrived at Jo Balam
K'ana Uleu....then they arrived there, at Waam....K'uk'
they stayed there awhile; there they did (things), there they
passed the time[23]....then they left and arrived at Xch'ayab
Xinbuxuc'; likewise they took out (the) stone that came from
the East, with the Pisom C'ac'al, (the sign) of the lordship; then
they abandoned (that place).... behind Tzutuja, and there
(they went), and then....above....Tuja Sak ....the (Sakco)-
rowach....

Page 8. ....then they left there, and arrived at....in Tzekeb
Chiyaqui, as the mountain was called, when....the place where
they calmly settled in the canyons and roads, in the mountains
and forests; (they) are our grandfathers and fathers, Don Balam
Quitze, Don Balam Ak'ab, (Don Majucot)aj, Don Iq'ui Balam;
then they left.... (they became) sick there at K'alena....,
(Cucu)rabaj;[24] so they went up to their houses....the young
of wasps and bees they.... their sickness; they became yellow,
they weakened (softened up), they....our grandfathers and
fathers truly were magical beings;[25] then they (began to) search,
and they made known our mountains and plains....their grandchildren and sons; they abandoned then (that place) and arrived
at Pache Chik'ojom, as the mountain was called; it was far
away where they did (all this), our grandfathers and fathers,
the Aj Q'uix and Aj Cajb;[26] then they abandoned that place,
and arrived at Chiq'uix[27].......

Page 9. the lords, and our grandmothers, their women, (were)
Xur,.... Xpuch, Xtax[28] as they were called; then....by our
grandfathers and fathers, likewise....the pink-colored clouds,[29]
and then the mud, the placid water....the clouds and mist,
the lightning[30] ....wasps and bees came to them....at the
corner of the settlement, when they became lost.... thus, you,
our grandfathers, you (our fathers)....at Chiq'uix, Chic'at by
our (grandfathers and fathers); in truth, oh,[31]....they were
called Tibil Xc'alakam K'uy[32] at the corner (of the settlement);
so, it is said, they disappear, they died at Chiq'uix, Chich'at,
when they came there; then they left, (and arrived) at Jumetaja
Culba Cawinal,[33] far away, just above Jumet they made their
houses, they made them there; likewise they met the lord of
the Ak'aab of Cawinal,[34] as they say, but they talked with hu-

Page 10 of the *Título C'oyoi*. Photograph from the original document at Princeton University Library.

mility in their hearts in those times, when he spoke at Cawinal; certainly....the gilded fabrics,[35] the gilded....they say to him;

Page 11 of the *Título C'oyoi*. See plate 7.

they payed tribute[36] (before him); when they came to Jumetaja;
then they arrived here at Ismachi........the stone structures
of mortar and whitewash[37]........by the lords....

Page 10. (The inscription in the middle of the pictorial states): Castle[38] of the second Q'uiche king of Utatlán.[39]

Page 11. (The inscription above the pictorial states): Castle[40] of the calpul of Juan Penonias de Putanza,[41] the Third.[42]

Page 12. Executive proof........the first people, our grand-fathers and fathers arrived....here in Ismachi;[43] then they made .... this (título) before the buildings....in the título; there are today many....in Q'uiche, one for Ca(wek, one) for Nijaib, one for Ajaw (Q'uiche) with Chituy Quejnay; when the small power (or majesty) was created; then the Pokob Chanal[44] was celebrated, and (they danced) the one Ajpu C'oy, and the seven Cakix[45]....grouped together (in) Liquinca,[46] they say; Cakix ....was celebrated in the plaza, with parakeets[47]....then the feathers, when it was done, when marriage was consummated[48] .... the small power there, when they became drunk, when they.... in the great time of joy, the Pokob Chanal dance; then they gave their daughters as gifts....the place of punish-ment,[49] the place of oration and announcements;[50] they say the Quiche lords ate (large tamales);[51] they say....their daughters at the same place of presentation[52] where....our handwhipping ....anciently. This....(Bala)m Quitze

Page 13. Balam Ak'ab, Ma(jucotaj,[53] Iq'ui Balam), (their grand-fathers) and fathers, the lords....Chituy Quejnay, likewise.... (Aj)chojlan, Majquinalo, those of ....with the Ilocab lords, Yal-chitun, Chira(mak')....Chiyatziquin, the seven.... (Tzunu)nija Rokche;[54] the four (lords of) Ta....here in Ismachi; three.... Nima Q'uiche, the second Q'uiche, the third (Q'uiche); they divid-ed up among themselves when the Nima Q'uiche....so that our grandfathers and fathers (stayed) at Ismachi; thus, it hap-pened there....at Panq'uib, Panpacay;[55] it is said that they ....our grandfathers and fathers; the Ilocab then entered there at Mukuis[56] Ilocab, so they say........

Page 14. ....was spied upon....the completion of their.... with the Nima Q'uiche, with the Malcatz[57]....their existence, with their appreciation one for another[58]....(the older brothers) the younger brothers; until in the fourth (succession)....when the great lordships were begun....our grandfathers, all the grandfathers (or grandsons) of the lord(s)....the older brother, the younger brother; then the....began....the fortified center;

the great....were made; (one section), two floors, three floors[59] ....houses crowded....arm's length measurement[60] on this side, an arm's length measurement....great extension at the.... already, from within the people began to be afraid and to feel lost;[61] then was begun the taking (seizing) and measuring of.... the three of them grow, the powerful lordships[62] of the Nima Q'uiche; likewise those of the Tamub and Ilocab grow; (it was after) five or six successions[63] that the.... began.... the battle squadron[64] of the fortified structures........

Page 15. in truth it was done anciently in Q'uiche, you, our grandchildren and sons; anciently there were many powerful ones, warriors;[65] our grandfathers and fathers (were) magicians;[66] they knew the east,[67] they knew the west, also they knew the middle of the sky, the middle of the earth; this was done in the past, it is said (in the) tradition left (for us by) our grandfathers and fathers; we asked that they tell us, we the lords; we saw the coming of the work of God with Don Pedro de Alvarado[68] the great Captain, Adelantado, Conquistador, (who) came from Castilla from the great Lord God and king;[69] thus, we will establish the order (of occurence) of that great war which they made against the settlements and fortified centers[70] of the subject peoples; they pushed aside all the settlements and fortified centers; the Rabinal center was brought down; the (Cak)chiquel,[71] the Tzutujil, the Tujaleb, the Cubulcaal, Cunen Cakquilaj, Booj, the Choxa..naj Xjil people, the structures of the Tzitzol; then the center of the....was brought down........

Page 16. they came into existence, with all the lords, the great Rajpop Achij, the small Rajpop Achij[72] in Xicaja, in Balimaja;[73] the warriors left then; they went (away); now we will give the names of the lords, under the rule of the Quiche; we are one of the Q'uiche.... Chituy Quejnay; these are the first lords, the first groups;[74] the great Ajpop Sakimox with the lord K'ali Camja.... with the lord Uk'ale....(C'o)yoi Nine Aj[75] the....the lord Rajpop Achij C'oyoi, the second.... with the lord Utzam Achij Sitai Sitalan[76]....the lords, the spokesmen, the heads of speech; these then are the first multitudes, the second and third older and younger brothers; likewise we will relate and put forward the....the appearance of all the nine lords of Chituy Quejnay, with the spokesmen, the two groups, the earliest groups, indeed their existence....there is no word........

Page 17. the lordship; these are the first groups of Don Martín Mejía, Nine Aj,[77] as they say; likewise it is true that those of the Cawekib are here, the eagle and jaguar warriors,[78] the first group of the great[79] Ajpop; and likewise the Ajaw Q'uiche (are here); this is the ancient people of the great masculine idol,[80] the K'alel Ajaw; so the two (or three) chief spokesmen are here; in truth they....near and far; likewise then the second Q'uiche group, the Tamub (are here): the K'ale Cakoj,[81] the Atzij Winak Cakoj, the K'ale Tam, the Ajpop Tam; they (too are) lords and chief spokesmen of the first grouping; likewise then, the lords of the Ilocab (are here); they are of the first grouping: Cortés K'alel Rokche, with the Atzij Winak Rokche, with....Four Aj, the Utzam Pop Rokche[82]....the Q'uiche lords arrived....
....together they........

Page 18. the great Rajpop Achij; then, in truth, this is Cortés, the K'alel Rokche Saknoy; in truth these are the lancers and slingers[83] that we will tell about; these are the lords, annointed with black and yellow,[84] who propelled the spears and stones, and (who) encircle and sacrifice[85] (their captives) against a tree;[86] the jaguar bone, the black and yellow magical colors....the hooves of the deer, the claws of the lion and jaguar....the mantle .... the feathers of the macaw, the (feathers of) the heron; (these things) came from the East, from the other side of the water and the sea; they came here; they had their throne.... their little benches and stools;[87] they had their parasols, with bone flutes and little flutes (or drums);[88] they are the lancers and slingers; these then are the piercing instruments of the military invaders, the lancers, the flag bearers,[89] the great spikesmen....C'ucumam[90] C'aam; they came (from the East) all of whose names we have given....we will give their names again; these are the....

Page 19. of the Chituy Que(jnay)....the father of the five.... the lord Chituy Quejnay....in this Q'uiche título of power.... the lord Chituy Quejnayib; so only the twenty-two (Aj)pop C'aam(ja),[91] and the Pop and C'aamja....several of the lords in Q'uiche; so likewise several K'alel, Ajpop; also there are the Tzam Chinimital, Ajtz'(alam)[92].... the fathers, (and) afterwards, you the sons, you....in Chiwila, Chitaa;[93] truly the lordship of the grandfathers and fathers (came into) existence; at the great, powerful and majestic[94] walls in Q'uiche, before our structures of mortar and whitewash; also here those of the K'ula Xelajuj[95] multiplied and spread forth, with all those of Sija in Malaj....likewise the Ajnakaj, the Ajtaa....Xiquin, those of Uwila, Ajam...., those of Xoyabaj....Ch'ulimal, Aba(la, Tzi)quin, Zak(iya....Xajbaq)uej........

Page 20. ....(J)unajpu; the A(mak'tam)....the Raxachax[96] ....one mother and one father that....(K'u)marcaj in Ismachi,[97] at Panq'uib, Panpacay....with the Ilocab at Mukuis, so it is said of the third Q'uiche (center) of mortar and whitewash; great power and glory was created by the lords, our grandfathers and fathers, when the Q'uiche expanded; this then we will put (here in).... this writing;[98] the....power and glory of the Q'uiche, the great lordship of the lancers and bowmen; when the....the Pokob Chanal dance....when Tojil, Awilix, and Jak'awitz[99] were named; it is said that wonders[100] were done in Q'uiche when they made the demonstration of possession there....a great demonstration and display[101] was made, when they did....at Chojib;[102] when the month Tziquin K'ij[103] was counted; when the sacred lords of the military squadron,[104] the lancers and slingers (came); and ....*chucat alicat aca wi*.... *nenepu tunapulul*,[105] with the (three) groups....the punishment of the....so likewise....the dance of....

Page 21. the drum dance, with the war dance[106]....they said to them ; so the three....songs accompanied by the flute[107] of the lords, when they originated[108] the four parasols, the three parasols[109] ....above the earth;[110] this then is the....lords that come from the East, who started (it all); (the) nine days; the Waliom[111] people came from the East, together they came with the Cawek, Nijaib (from) across the water and the sea; they had their parasols, their lion throne, their jaguar throne, the claws of the lion, jaguar, and eagle, the feathers of the macaw, the feathers of the heron, the mantles; then the messengers[112] leave, when the twenty (day) period ends, the 360 (day period)[113] ....the thirteen invaders, the lancers; (so) was the changing (of the lordship) by the symbols of the spearing and slinging which came from the east, from the other side of the sea; the foaming ones,[114] so they call the thirteen valiant ones....the seventeen valiant ones of Mwaji[115]....then the great lords.... (Ch)om chaj, the military invaders....the lordship....

Page 22. ....the invaders, the lancers that celebrate....when the people of the open places[116] were esteemed; our (fathers), our lineages of the canyons and fortified centers....then their appearance was to be put in order, at (the time of) the multiplying, the increasing, adding....the spreading forth of the people in Q'uiche, in Panq'uib Panpacay, as they call the fortified center.

Today we will declare all (about) the....the sayings of our grandfathers and fathers....the completion and fulfillment of the war, when all of the flag bearers, ensigns, warriors, lancers, bowmen, shield bearers,[117] the valiant warriors[118] left....the K'alel Ajaw, the K'ale Sakic', with all....Cawek Q'uiche people, the Nijaib....with all the nine Ch'ol....K'alechij Chituy Quejnay....those of the subject towns, settlements....with all....

Page 23. the sons went to battle....the sons of the lords; their older brothers went....this testimony is not false, the thirteen K'ulaja from Xelajuj went....the Twelve Tzijbachaj, with .... (the eight Tz'alam) C'oxtun Sija;[119] these then....their thorns were blown out (?);[120] they.... by the lords; these.... "you, you our valiant watchmen[121] ....go, do battle with[122] ....the fortified center of the Yoc K'anchebex, Tzicol (Bamak'), the great settlements; go and take (them)....by the arm pits (and sacrifice them);"[123] so it was said to our grandfathers.... these (are)[124] the K'alechij........

Page 24. ....the fortified Q'uiche center; they came there.... those of Xequi and Xeoj, the Sakcorowach....so they say: "Go, you our older brothers....do not cry, do not be sad.... just arrive there, just go (there) ....do battle with the settlements of the enemy peoples[125]....the fortified center of the Ajpoxajil,[126] the Coon Bu(xija)[127]....tzuja, with the Bamak', the Nima Amak' ....the Yoc K'anchebex, the Tzitzol, the Chele....as they say, the Chun, with the Acalotem....the Balam Colob;" they were told to take them by the armpits and sacrifice them;[128] "Take them," it was said to our grandfathers and fathers, when they left there in Q'uiche, Panq'uib, Panpacay, the great........

Page 25. our conquerors of the hamlets and fortified centers, they are the great warriors, our grandfathers and fathers, we the Chituy Quejnay; then the Mam of Zakiulew[129] were driven out ....before their mountains and plains, there the mountains and plains were taken;[130] these were all their mountains and plains, their beautiful places, their structures; this was the 6th succession of the lordship by Don Q'uikab, C'awisimaj,[131] with Ajaw Baca, with Nine Aj C'oyoi; our grandfathers and fathers cast them out, when they inserted themselves (among) the Mam of Zakiulew....indeed they were fierce warriors; then our grandfathers and fathers left....(they arrived) in front of the mountains at Iquiya and Iquilaja;[132] (these places) were abandoned from before the arrow and shield; then they left there in front of Tena, Lotz, and Tzakibalja;[133] at Xoch'o, Chukuljuyub, Palin Quej,[134] Quemeyo, Tziquiche, Tzoloj, Choo, Tuloa; they arrived at the top of Iquilaja; (later they went to) Xelaju and Chicaj, Sunil, K'antel, Baca; they arrived at Paxtoca, and C'ucum(am)....

Page 26. all their mountains and plains; the Sakiulew people, with the Ak'aab Balam Colob[135] were beaten down;[136] our grandfathers and fathers left then from before the mountains; the first captain of our grandfathers and fathers, we the C'oyoi Sakcorowach, from Xequi, Xeoj ; it was spoken to us by the Q'uiche king when our grandfathers and fathers were made chiefs[137] (there) in the fortified center of Q'uiche; (and) the flag bearer received his office; they left to trample the lands; the speech and appearance of all the great ones was the same: the Cawek, Nijaib, Ajaw Q'uiche, with the Tamub, and the Ilocab Rokche lords, the Four Aj, the Wukmil Sic'a Juanija;[138] the fortified centers and settlements were brought down by them when they entered into the mountains and plains; their....were lost, their riches and wealth were fragmented, their structures and residences were torn into pieces,[139] their precious stones and jewels, and black and golden stones were carried off, their.... precious metal and stones[140] were forcefully torn up....

Page 27. the precious rattle[141] was taken away by force from them by the Cawek Q'uiche people, with the Chituy Quejnay, our grandfathers and fathers, along with the Cakoj and Ikomak', and the Rokche, the Four Aj, Wukmil Sic'a; when they left the place in front of the plains and mountains, there in the mountains and plains of Q'uiche; then all of the valiant warriors arrived at Q'uiche, they came (from) warring, the treaders of the lands, the eagle warriors who take the lands with bow and arrow,[142] the conquerors of the canyons and fortified centers; the lords gave a full report when they arrived; when they all gathered together, a great celebration was held in Q'uiche[143] in front of the whitened stone structures, when the flag bearers, the valiant warriors entered from outside; than the grandsons and sons of the lords were sought; in truth, the younger brothers and sons of the lords, the beloved older and younger brothers went; it is true that they were not vassals;[144] the thirteen K'ulaja from Xelaju, the twelve Tzijbachaj, the eight Tz'alam C'oxtun Sija went; this is when they were given instructions[145] by the great lord, Don Q'uikab: "You must return,

Page 28. you valiant warriors, you conquerors of the fortified centers, you treaders of the lands; go and be inhabitants of the lands, at the fortified centers of the subject peoples, so that they do not arrive there again....conquer, you warriors, lancers; likewise go back and forth[146] continually, make many land boundaries for us at each milpa in the canyons of the fortified center," it was said to them; "Good," they said to the lord; "Go with your sons, you, our valiant warriors, our watchmen, be fighters of the subject peoples of the fortified center; with bow and arrow and shield, go and trample them, grab them by the armpits and sacrifice them," it was said to them, our grandfathers and fathers, and our sons; then indeed we left the Q'uiche mountains and plains and arrived here in the mountains of Xelaju;[147] in truth we arrived not far from Xela(ju); truly we will tell about (them), the great warriors and lancers, the old ones of the canyons of the fortified center,

Page 29. our grandfathers and fathers; they were not few in number, the....K'alel, Ajpop; many captains (were made) at the fortified center of Q'uiche, (from where) their thrones and stools came: "Go, you our older and younger brothers....do not be sad, do not be worried[148]....now get yourselves in order;[149] we are your....your fathers," said the lords and the ladies,[150] their mothers and fathers, our grandfathers and fathers, we the Chituy Cajnaib; together they left, together they were counseled there (by) the three groups, above Q'uiche; the inhabitants of

the lands left (and went) before the Sakiulew people, the Yoc
K'anchebex, Tz'itzol, Bamak', Nima Amak'; "Grab them by the
armpits and sacrifice them, trample them, make yourselves valiant warriors, and watchful guardians,"[151] so it was said to them
when they cried, and were sad; they endearingly put hands on
their heads[152]....their hearts, they cried before them; in truth
(they were) the older and younger brothers of the lords, (those)
who left there, the inhabitants of the lands; they embraced each
other, they put hands on their heads; this then they did, you
Page 30. our sons, when indeed they left there, and our grandfathers and fathers came; we the people of Xelaju, with those
of Mik'ina, Sija, Paxtoca, Xoch'o, Xec'ut, Xo....Chuwa Tz'ak,[153]
with all the settlements, with all the people of Malaj, the Tz'utujil people; together they left Q'uiche, when our grandfathers
and fathers left there; they came to Tzam Chicojaj, and climbed
up to beautiful Cakapec;[154] then they left there and went up
to Patzam; they left and came again to Cak Q'uix, Chay Bamat
Cakiquil, as they say; later they separated from the K'ulaja
of Xelaju; these then are the Tzijbach who went down to Joyam
K'anak';[155] likewise then, the K'alel and Ajpop spoke there, the
twelve Tzijbachaj: these are the eight Tz'alam C'oxtun Sija,
the two Jojout, Raxq'uim[156] Sebache[157] placed up high;[158] they
went down to Raxtumpec, where earlier the Subic were established, and their stone foundations still existed there; these then are
Page 31. the grandfathers and fathers of the Xelaju people;
from on high, they dropped down behind the fortress, (and)
there they left the people of (Pa)xtoca; below the fortress are
our grandfathers and fathers; from up there they went down
to C'uc'umabal, below Q'uiak,[159] where they left the Q'uiche
people at the whitened stone structures and great walls....
(with) the lord K'ale Ch'o Cakoj[160] they went up to the top of
Iquilaja; these are our grandfathers and fathers, we the Chituy
Quejnay; the lord K'alechij C'oyoi, Nine Aj, as they say, with
the great Ajpop Achij C'oyoi; they went up and entered Baca,
with the lord of equal (rank), K'ali C'(a)amja Looquin,[161] as
they say, where our grandfathers and fathers climbed their
beautiful residences and stone structures; we the Chituy Quejnay
of Xequi and Xeoj, we the C'oyoi Sakcorowach, as they say;
the great and famous warriors, our grandfathers and fathers did

this in the presence of all the settlements of the palace of the captive peoples, the Coon Buxija, the Tzuja, with the Bama, Nima Amak', and the Yoc K'anchebex, the Tzizol, Chele.... as they say, with those of Alotemache, Balam Colob; (then) our grandfathers and fathers left;

Page 32. we the Chituy Quejnay; the rank of the three groups at Q'uiche were equal; then our grandfathers and fathers, we the C'oyoi Sakorowach, remained at our center of stone structures at Baca; we the K'alechij C'oyoi, Nine Aj, as they say, and the Rajpop Achij C'oyoi, and the great C'aamja Looquin; then the lord Cortés, the K'ale Rokche Saknoi Isuy of Sakpoklaj[162] came down, (and) climbed to the top of Lajum Quej, (the place) of the great masculine idol; then the K'alel Ajaw, named lord Quemaxitapul Chic'wa,[163] came, together with Nine Aj Mejía, as he is called; there below the stones and woods they have their structures, below the hot springs;[164] and with the lord they pass over to the (place of the) eagle and jaguar warriors of the old Ajpop Rax, there at Xepach[165] they exist with all the other Rajop Achij, the small Rajop Achij, with the vassals and companions; then they began to establish each milpa in the hamlets of the fortified center, when each one began to inhabit the ancient lands in front of the fortress and rural area of the captive peoples;

Page 33. you our grandsons and sons, receive wisdom in this our título,[166] (which is) your power, and proof, given at the fortified center of Q'uiche; they established the foundations and order of each group[167] when the lords again spoke there.... all the great ones then....a knowledge of all their (lands) there; they began setting the boundary signs at Paraxq'uim, at the boundary-marking structure of the people of Sija; then it comes alongside the river, likewise at Paraxq'uim; then it comes to where it meets the boundary of the Lord Xcamparij of (Pa)xtoca;[186] it comes there, and goes up over the same Paraxq' uim mountains; they leave then, (and go) up to Mount.. xule; then likewise on top of the mountain it comes to....above Tz'ibampec;[196] then it comes to the top of Mount Q'uiak; a fortress, a large structure is located on top of Q'uiak, the structures of the Sakiulew people;[170] then it comes above Q'uiak, and goes down to the plains shaped like a leg,[171] (and) passes over.... at the rose tree;[172] then it returns....

Page 34. the boundary of the Paxtoca people is above C'aba-wil Chaj;[173] then it turns around at the canyon boundary and passes over at Sajc'aja;[174] it passes above the large rock on the hillside,[175] just along the edge of the canyon; then it comes.... wide, there above the earth formation; it passes over a great (river), Pujula;[176] it passes above Pa....; then it leaves there, and later arrives at the limestone; it leaves there and arrives at Tzamabaj,[177] and Tzam Ixim Ulew; it passes by ..almet, and arrives there at Chijaya.... above Tz'olojche;[178] then it arrives at Vuk Xiquincan; it leaves there, and goes to Cakal in Ocus; it leaves the mountains there and goes to Palajunoj, and later to the boundary of the people of Tak'ajal.... there our grandfathers and fathers, we the people of Xelaju finished it; it was done by everyone, together it was completed by lords of the same rank; they placed the markers of the land, which in truth, (are yours), you the lords, you my sons; I must leave these words, in truth, they are yours; do not let....do not for get, you.... my sons.

Page 35. (Here we will put) a few words[179] (about) the coming of the great lord, Adelantado Capitán Don Pedro de Alvarado, conquistador, sent here by our great Lord and God, the king of Castilla, he who gives us the word of God, we the Q'uiche people; first (they arrived) at Xetulul;[180] on 1 Batz they entered there at Xetulul; on Two E[181] they entered....the people of Xepach,[182] the eagle and jaguar warriors; they tied up the people of Xetulul and Xepach, the K'alel and Ajpop; then the great stone walls, all the civil buildings[183] were....by the people with white skin, the soldiers of Don Pedro de Alvarado, the great captain; they carried lances, battle axes, rifles, shields, and swords; all the chiefs were finished, killed by the metal[184] weapons they used against them; they do not travel on foot, they come on horseback; they came and quickly brought down all of the stone buildings; they took them, knocking down all the stones by the K'ek....

Page 36. Yaqui people,[185] the great military lords (who) accompanied Don Pedro de Alvarado, the conquistador who came from España, from our great God and king; later they routed

all the K'alel, Ajpop, Rajop Achij ....K'alechij, Rajop Achij
from here at Xelaju.... they had been sent by the great lord
Don Q'(uik'ab), from the fortress of Q'uiche, at the great walls
and stone structures, among the mortar and limestone buildings....their messenger went to Q'uiche,[186] (and) on that same
day he met (them) there and (they) listened to him;[187] afterwards above Mik'ina, at Tzijbachaj the great Rajop Achij, Adelantado Tecum, the grandson of the Q'uiche king, Don Q'uik'ab,[188]
departed; for seven days he was carried on their shoulders[189]
at Q'uiche among the (great) houses; (he was) carried in feathers
and precious stones, with black and yellow annointing, when
he got his glory and was carried throughout all of the fortified
center; the great Lord Tecum, the Adelantado and Captain of
the Q'uiche, for whom they performed a great song and dance
with flutes (or drums)[190] when

Page 37. he came; so likewise, all the K'al(el, Aj)pop, the K'alechij, Rajop Achi, with the Rajpop here in Xelajuj performed
the song and dance with the flutes at the walls and stone buildings of Xelaju; then the great Captain Tecum entered from
outside with 8,400 people, and 39 flagbearers[191] among them,
and drum instruments;[192] thus there were many lords who accompanied him; the Rachij Pop, Rachij C'aamja Achi, many
great....Pop; then they carried him on their shoulders at
Bamlimaja(?);[193] the warriors left Q'uiche (and went) to (a place)
above the mineral springs, and bled themselves by piercing;[194]
there were 8,000[195] warriors of the Q'uiche people who showed
reverence,[196] and pierced themselves; all the K'alel and Ajpop
of the three groups of Q'uiche; the Tamub, Ilocab, with all the
people of Xelaju, the Cawek, Nijaib, Ajaw Q'uiche, Chituy
Cajnai, with all those of Nakaj, Ta... Xiquin, here in Q'uiche;
those of Uwila,[197] Ch'ulimal, with the Abala Tziquin, the Zakiya,
Xojbaquej, the Wajxaklajuj, the Tinamit, Pachiqui, the La..
bolo, C'akolquej....

Page 38. those of Cabrakan, Tzapik'ak', with the Ajpu, the
Raxacha, Tucurub, the C'oyoi Sakcorowach from Xequi and
Xeoj, with the Amak' Tam, Sakmolob, the Tabiij, Iquiya, Cak'
alaj, Na(jxit), those of Amak' Mes, Pokoba, K'ojomeb,[198] and
those of the Chich'alib; all the Cawek Q'uiche people, the Nijaib,
Ajaw Q'uiche, Chituy Cajnai, with the lords Ajpop Tam, K'ale

Tam, K'ale Cakoj, Atzij Winak[199] Cakoj; and likewise the Ajpop, Ajpop C'aamja, the (K')alel Atzij Winak, K'alechij, Rajop Achij, Rajpop Achij of the Chltuy Cajnaiyib; and the Atzij Winak Rokche, K'alel Four Aj Utzampop, Rokche of the Ilocab; and also the lords, the spokesmen and heads of the lordship; they went to war with all their vassals; they left there at Xelaju, and encountered Don Pedro de Alvarado, the Spanish captain and conquistador; they did battle at Chwaraal in the middle of the pines;[200] the people (were so numerous) that the units of 8,000, 20, and 400 could not be counted,[201] there in the mountains and plains, below the trees and woods; then....was made here at Xelaju, at Tzamabaj, there below (the mountains)....the head of the horse of the great lord[202]

Page 39. Adelantado, Captain Don Pedro Alvarado the conquistador was taken off; the head of his horse was taken off by captain Tecum, the lord of the banners and staffs;[203] two times feathered grandfather, the Lord Tecum came from the sky, when this captain gave himself (to the fray)[204] among the Spaniards....Tecum was pierced[205] by the great....earth....then against....the trotting horses[206] of the Spaniards in the plains.... three crowns[207]....the rose tree at the edge of....with quetzal feathers on his head;[208] he was deprived (of life) in his body; thus he went down that day before heaven and the great fire-mountain;[209] afterwards he (Alvarado) asked the Mexican people the name of the mountain: "What is the name of this mountain?" it was said to them; "(Quetzal)tenanco is what it is called, Señor," all the Mexican people said to Don Pedro Alvarado; "Good, then *Quetzaltenanco....* because a great captain died....lord in (it), and on....Espiritu San(to)[210] I fought ....likewise this will be called....

Page 40. in order to guard (them)," the lord said; when the flag bearers and valiant warriors, the companions of Tecum forced their way (into the battle); one cannot count the number of companion people of Tecum who died, (but) the sun in the sky turned red because of the blood,[211] likewise (a) river of blood ....because of the blood; this (is) the.... the blood; thus was done....our grandsons and sons; so is our (tradition?) .... when the Christians[212] ....under the word of God, by the great captain Don Pedro de Alvarado; one of our fathers, from the

C'oyoi Sakcorowach, died in war; he was the great Rajpop
Achij, who in the war accompanied from behind the deceased
Tecum;[213] he is Nine Aj, the K'alechij C'oyoi; he was one of
our grandfathers and fathers; I was a child, a little child when
it came down over me here; I was born there in the beautiful
stone buildings[214] of my grandfathers and fathers....the great
walls and stone structures, here at Xelaju....together (they)
had left....above the houses, the great walls....they forced
their way in on behalf of Don (Pedro de Alvarado)....

Page 41. captain and conquistador; repeatedly they embraced
(them), they played the drum,[215] and bowed down before the
lord; they sat down at the great throne and stool which had
come from the East; then they wanted to tie (them) up,[216] (but)
the padres still did not want to tie them up so they would humble
themselves; who....when all the....were called ....Don Pedro
Alvarado....all the people....said....sons, all the.... they
were here in....the stone buildings of this house were.... they
say all the vassals....before Don Pedro de Alvarado....so
they are told, ...

Page 42. "You made war, did you not make war against us
....when Captain Tecum died?" they were told; (so now we
tell) you, our grandsons and sons, when indeed long ago the house
of the Lord K'alel Ajaw fell down on him and his daughter and
son; he was named Don Andrés de Chávez; the second lord,
(was) Nine Aj, Don Martín Mejía....the third lord, K'ale
Xc'ub, Don Juan....the fourth lord (was the) K'ale Rokche;
Don[217] ....my father, the K'ale....C'oyoi; the houses fell down
on us.... the C'oyoi, I was named ....old one, his family;
the house fell down....the soldiers of the Spanish people....
before the padres, the people of....the companions of the
lord Don Pedro de Alvarado....jewels and riches....the lord
by.... Don Pedro........

Page 43. ....López, *escribano*, made....(C'o)yoi, Andrés Vásquez[218] ....our houses fell in on us at Xelaju....lords the
houses fell in on them with the ....Don Domingo Quemaxitapul,
and Don....K'ale Cho; they are the heads of the lordship,
they are....Ajpop, K'alel from Xepach....over them here;
the houses fell in on....our grandfathers and fathers.... the
coming of Christianity....our daughters and sons....(to) each

one it was done....a great soldier....they say *Teniente*, Captain
.... Xelaju and Totoni(capán)[219].......

Page 44. ....the boundaries of the territory of the fortified
center[220] ....then here they encounter....(Xcam)parij from (Pa)-
xtoca; likewise there is one....putting the boundaries of the
lands; it goes up....mountains, and also Paraxq'uim; they leave
there on top of....then above the mountains and plains....
it comes here then, and arrives above....the large stone structure on top of Q'uiak....here above....plains it encounters
....they will encounter....(C'a)bawil Chaj....the boundary
marker just at the border of the canyon....above the earth
formation it passes over....encounters alongside the road of
the big....likewise it goes to Puju(la)....the boundary marker
of the[221].......

Page 45. ....the seventh succession of the lordship, when....
Nine Aj, the K'alechij C'oyoi, when....the dispersion into the
canyons of the fortified centers....the Quejnayib; then the
valiant (warriors) left there ....the canyons of the fortified
center the searchers....nearby they arrived....when they said
....at Q'uiche[222].......

Page 46. ....you are our grandsons and sons....in truth the
words that we speak....you, our grandsons and sons....we
will begin the clarification....before you (when) we arrived
in Q'uiche....(Pan)q'uib, Panpacay, we the first[223]....their land
before them....he went up....the canyons.......

Pages 47-56. (These pages are so badly torn that I am unable
to establish their order, or to translate a coherent narration,
nor am I certain that there were no other pages which are now
missing. The numbering of the text from page 47 on is arbitrary,
except for the pairing together of matching pages of fragments.
In the comments which follow, I attempt to give a synopsis
of what seems to be the subject of the various fragments, including translations of phrases in the text where they are com-
prehensible and seem to add to our understanding of the document.)

Two matching pages of fragments (pp. 47-48) contain what
appears to be a continuation of the postconquest recognition
of the boundaries of the lords of Quezaltenango. Some native
peoples and places listed here are mentioned in an earlier part

of the document: Baca, Mik'ina, Xequi, Xequiq'uel, C'oyoi, Wuk Xi(quincan), (Wukum)il Sic'a J(uanija). Alvarado and the Spaniards are again mentioned as knocking down native residences at some places.

Two other matching pages of fragments (pp. 49-50) appear to contain a continuing account of the conquest. One fragment (p. 49) has the statement, "we will die, they said," apparently referring to the native reaction to the onslaught of the Spaniards. The precious rattles (*sochoch yamanic*) of the Quiche lords are again mentioned (p. 50), possibly in the context of having to give them to the Spaniards as spoils (they were adorned with precious stones and, perhaps, gold).

Another page with a large fragment (p. 53) contains a list of the political symbols and riches possessed by the Quiche lords: *tatil k'anabaj, k'ana pwak*. There is a brief description of the honor paid to the lords and their symbols, perhaps as part of the ritual carried out at the time this título was produced. One of the Quiche lords mentioned here is the Ajpop Sakimox, and a certain Don Francisco.[224] The author also appears to refer again to his father, ...(n)u kajaw, "my father," but alas, the account is torn away at this place.

Another fragment (p. 54) contains a statement that, "this is the título....de Putanza[225] C'oyoi the K'(ale)...."

Finally, there are two almost completely illegible pages which appear to have become stuck to the leather binding which covered the document (pp. 55-56). One of the two pages is certainly the last page of the document, for it contains the names and titles of the Quiché lords who witnessed its writing. At the bottom of this final page, there is a statement in Spanish which can be partially translated as follows: "(this is) the título....of the ancient.... C'oyoi." The legible names listed on this page are as follows: Don Juan Cortés Saknoy,[226] Don Domingo Pérez (Quemaxi)tapul, ...Rakancoj, Don Juan Bautista Ajpop, Don (Martín) Mejía, Don Francisco Gómez, don.... Pérez Utzam Achij, Don (Juan) Rojas K'ale from Tecpán (Q'uiche) Don Jorge from Santa Cruz.

NOTES ON THE TRANSLATION OF THE TÍTULO C'OYOI

Page 1.

1. *ruc' junab.* Apparently, the date of the document was given here, but unfortunately it is torn away. From the general contents, a date of composition roughly contemporaneous with that of the *Popol Vuh* and Totonicapán document (1550-1560) can be estimated. Some persons mentioned at the end are found in other Quiche sources, especially the Nijaib títulos (see note 218).

2. *nabe tzij.* "The first memorial" (Vico n.d.a), or "history" is the idea intended here; it is an expression found in the preamble of the *Popol Vuh.* (Recinos 1953:81). A more literal translation, "talk" or "speak," suggests that the author is basing his account on oral tradition, handed down from ancient times. I have argued (Carmack n.d.c) that the traditions were often used as aids to the interpretation of prehispanic codices, and this is probably the case here (for a similar use by the Mexicans of combining written and oral traditions, see León-Portilla 1961:63-70).

3. *(sak)corowach.* Later, we learn the word refers to the main kin-based political unit mentioned in this document. Before fragmenting the full name was given as *c'oyoi* (from monkey, *coy*) and sakcorowach (quail, from "white is its face") (Ximenez n.d.). According to the *Annals of the Cakchiquels*, the sakcorowach came under control of the Quiché at an early time; later some fell under Cakchiquel rule (Villacorta 1934:202-204).

4. *chun sajcab.* Literally, "whitened limestone," it refers to the political-religious stone structures of the fortified Quiche centers. The expression is used in the *Popol Vuh* (Villacorta 1962a:325).

5. *(Chi)tuy Quejnay.* As revealed in other places in the document, the complete title is Chituy (place of the small

animal?), *Quejnay* (increased or understanding deer). From other sources we learn that Chituy was an office in the Quiche political organization (Villacorta 1962a:336), and Quejnay was a lineage branch of the Cawek kin group (Recinos 1953:249-250).

6. *tak'aj*. This is the second half of a pair of words which invariably go together: juyub (mountain) and *tak'aj* (plain). Ethnographic studies in modern Quiché communities make it clear that the reference is to the sacred earth, a divinity with multiple forms, powers and manifestations (Bunzel 1952; Mendelson 1958b; Carmack n.d.b).

7. *Ak'ab, Maj....* This is a reference to the founding ancestors of the Quiché: Balam Quitze, Balam Ak'ab, Majucotaj, and Iq'ui Balam.

Page 2.

8. *quitunisaj*. From the verb root *tun*, (to unite or join together) which gives the meaning, "they cause to unite or come together."

9. *rajawarem*. The term derives from the title ajaw, (lord, chief). These terms are widely employed in the Quiche sources, and an extensive analysis beyond the scope of the present translation would be required fully to explain their meanings. Therefore, I propose to use the noncommittal terms, "lordship," and "lord."

Page 3.

10. *rele(bal k'ij)*. The reference here is to the Tulan of the East mentioned in most of the other Quiche sources (Carmack 1968). The same language is used in the other accounts and was the standard way of showing a connection between the founding forefathers and the Toltecs.

11. *Cawek.* This page contains a list of the three divisions of the Quiché—the Nima Quiche, Tamub Quiche, Ilocab Quiche. It conforms with a similar list found in the Totonicapán document (Recinos 1950:215-216). Only two of the five Ilocab forefathers listed in the *Título Totonicapán* remain in this badly fragmented page, but all the Nima and Tamub Quiche names are accounted for.

A Case Study: *Título C'oyoi*

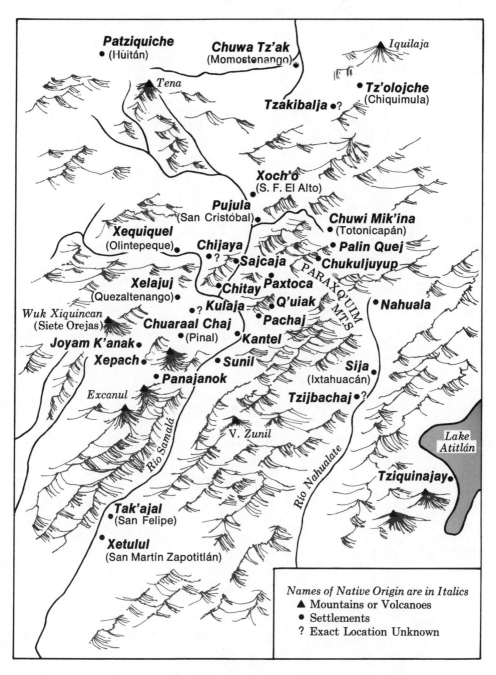

Patziquiche
• (Húitán)

Chuwa Tz'ak
(Momostenango)•

▲ Iquilaja

▲ Tena

• Tz'olojche
(Chiquimula)

Tzakibalja •?

Xoch'o
(S. F. El Alto)

Pujula
(San Cristóbal)•

Xequiquel
(Olintepeque)•

Chijaya

Chuwi Mik'ina
• (Totonicapán)

•? •Sajcaja

• Palin Quej

Chukuljuyup

Xelajuj
(Quezaltenango)•

•Chitay

Paxtoca

•? Kulaja

• Q'uiak

• Nahuala

Wuk Xiquincan
(Siete Orejas)▲

•Pachaj

Chuaraal Chaj
• (Pinal)

Joyam K'anak •

Kantel

Xepach •

• Sunil

Sija
(Ixtahuacán)•

•Panajanok

Tzijbachaj •?

Excanul

V. Zunil

Lake
Atitlán

Río Samalá

Río Nahualate

Tziquinajay•

Tak'ajal
• (San Felipe)

• Xetulul
(San Martín Zapotitlán)

PARAXQ'UIM MTS

Names of Native Origin are in Italics
▲ Mountains or Volcanoes
• Settlements
? Exact Location Unknown

3. Geographic locations mentioned in the *Título C'oyoi*.

Page 4.

12. Chi pixab. This is a mountain mentioned in the *Popol Vuh* and other sources where the forefathers of the Quiche gathered upon entering the highlands after their journey from the East (Villacorta 1962a:253). It is located north of present-day Santa Cruz del Quiché.

13. *(C)akchiqueleb.* The list of kin-based political groups given here corresponds closely to the one given in the *Popol Vuh*, where they are also said to be thirteen in number (Villacorta 1962a:230-231). The only group not listed in the *Popol Vuh* is the mayuc ajtzunu(nija).

14. *amak' tecpan.* The two terms have social referents of complex meanings; I can only give a brief exposition here. *Amak'*, (hamlet, lineage, or settlement) refers to permanent but dispersed settlements located outside the fortified centers. *Tecpan*, "palace," is of Nahua derivation, and when used by the Quiché refers to their fortified centers. The two words form a pair (a typical case of Quiche dualism), referring to the rural and semiurban settlements of the prehispanic Quiché.

Page 5.

15. *Tamub.* The main political divisions of the highlands in prehispanic times are listed here. Probably listed first was the Nima Quiche group from Utatlán, while the other groups, and the approximate locations of their political centers are as follows: Tamub (between Santa Cruz del Quiché and Patzité), Ilocab (San Antonio Ilotenango), *Rabinaleb* (between Joyabaj and Rabinal), *Cakchiquelab* (Iximché), *Tzutujileb* (Chuitinamit, Atitlán), *Tujal* (Sacapulas), *Cubulcaal* (Cubulco), *Zakajib Cakajib* (?), *Ak'aab* (Santa Lucía La Reforma), *Balimaja* (Aguacatán), *Ch'uimilaja* (?), *Lamak'ib* (Xolchún, just east of Sacapulas). In the *Popol Vuh* account of this same event at *chi pixab*, ony the first six divisions are mentioned (Villacorta 1962a: 253-254).

Page 6.

16. *Amak'tan.* The same place is mentioned in the *Popol Vuh* as Amak'Tam, (place of the Tamub), (Villacorta 1962a:259-260). The "dawning" described here is also given in greater detail in that source.

17. *mixtam pon*. This should be mixtan pom, which is mentioned in the *Popol Vuh* as one of three incenses brought from the East (Villacorta 1962a:265). Jiménez Moreno suggests (1942:136) its association with a settlement in the southern Veracruz area by the name of Mixtan, which was conquered by the people of Tehuacán in A.D. 1351. Recinos (1953:197, note 306) further etymologizes the word from the Nahua *mictlan*, (place of the dead), and suggests it was an incense burned in honor of Mictan Ajaw, the Quiche god of the underworld.

18. *nimak k'ij*. Literally, "great days," but also "ceremonial or festive days." The term is still used in Quiche-speaking communities to refer to the festive days of the Christo-pagan ritual cycle.

Page 7.

19. *wal wonen, wal sitan*. The young (pupae?) of bees and wasps was the food they had to survive on. The *Popol Vuh* describes the same conditions of hardship (Villacorta 1962a:278).

20. *ratz'iak che*. "Clothing of wood," presumably a reference to bark cloth, which was known to the peoples of highland Guatemala.

21. *Ticaj Ch'alib*. Both the Tamub and Totonicapán títulos list this as one of the places where the Quiche forefathers stopped during their early migrations in the highlands (Recinos 1957:41; 1950:227). The exact site is unknown, but it probably was in the western part of present-day Baja Verapaz.

22. *pisom c'ac'al*. pisom k'ak'al, the sacred bundle brought from the East. It is mentioned in the *Popol Vuh* (Villacorta 1962a:211) and Totonicapán document (Recinos 1950: 216). Its significance is discussed by Recinos (1953:217, note 341), and myself (Carmack 1968), while Mendelson (1958a) has recorded a modern survival of it at Santiago Atitlán.

23. *xemay*. "Pass time," or "remain" in some place (Vico n.d.a). Literally, "to pass twenty-year periods," for it derives from *may*, a unit denoting periods of twenty years (400-day years).

24. *K'alena....rabaj.* Apparently the reference here is to the site mentioned in the Totonicapan título as *K'ale Mial Cucurabaj* (Recinos 1950:228). In both documents the next place mentioned is *Pache Chik'ojom.*

25. *c'axc'ol.* I am unable to find this word in the dictionaries, though it obviously has as its basic root, *c'ax*, pain or hurt. It suggests two other Quiche forms, *c'axtoc'* and *c'axol*, both of which contain the idea of magical beings or demons (Edmonson 1965).

26. *ajq'uix, ajca(j)b.* Recinos (1953:1823) translates the two words as "priests" and "sacrificers" and notes their association with the Yaqui or Mexicans. In Vico (n.d.a) the roots of these two words are given as "thorn" or "spine" and "cut to pieces," and he gives their meanings as "idolators" and "sacrificers." *ajq'uix*, (he of the spine), would appear to refer to the autosacrificer, and *ajcajb*, (he who cuts in pieces), to the sacrificer of animals and humans.

27. *Chiq'uix.* This place is also mentioned in the *Popol Vuh* (Recinos 1953:224) as one of the places near Cawinal where the Quiché passed on their way from Jakawitz to the Utatlán area.

28. *Xur....Xpuch, Xtax.* These are the maidens sent by the Wuk amak' to tempt the Quiche forefathers, according to the *Popol Vuh* (Recinos 1953:209). The names of only two maidens are given in the *Popol Vuh* (Ixtaj, Ixpuch); three in the Totonicapán document (Puch, Taz, Q'uibatzunaj) (Recinos 1950:221); and four in the Torres Macario document cited by Fuentes y Guzmán (Xur, Xbit, Xpuch, Xtas) (1932-1933:7:387). Obviously, the C'oyoi document is closest to the Torres account (from Santa Catarina Ixtahuacán) on this point.

29. *cak sutz'.* "Pink-colored clouds seen at sundown."

30. *cakulja.* Literally, "reddish water," it refers to flashes of lightning. As with the natural phenomena listed just before this (*sutz', mayul*, cloud, mist), the Quiche associated their deities with nature (Recinos 1953:86).

31. *aroka.* I do not find this word in the dictionaries. It probably has an exclamatory function, like *acaroc* (hail, oh), a word which appears frequently in the *Popol Vuh.*

32. *Tibil Xc'alakam K'uy.* These are settlements inhabited by enemies of the Quiché, according to the *Título Totonicapán* (Recinos 1950:228).

33. *Jumetaja Culba Cawinal.* These settlements are also listed in the *Popol Vuh* as places where the Quiche stopped during their migrations (Recinos 1953:224; see also *Título Totonicapán*, Recinos 1950:228). This is the area around present-day Cubulco. Apparently the ruins at *Pueblo Viejo*, just north of the present location of Cubulco, were called Cawinal (Brasseur 1861:cclxic; Shaw and Neuenswander 1966:28; Recinos 1957:111, note 30).

34. *Ak'aab Cawinal.* The *Ak'aab* (the night people) were a powerful Quiche-speaking group extending from the Cubulco area in the East to below Sacapulas in the West. They are mentioned in connection with this area in several other native sources (Recinos 1950:229; 1957:111).

35. *(k'a) na pwakin boj.* K'ana pwak refers to the metal gold, and *boj* is cotton worked into fabric. The idea of this phrase seems to be "gilded fabric." Just how these obviously luxurious cotton materials were gilded is difficult to say. Perhaps the reference to gold had a metaphorical meaning of "luxurious" or "fine."

36. *xqui(pa)t(a)nij.* This contains a verb widely used in the native sources, *patan.* Its root meaning appears to have been "to give service," but it was extended to refer to tribute paying as well.

37. *(Is)machi....chun sajcab.* Chun sajcab is a reference to the lime mortar and whitewash used to construct the religious-political centers of the Quiche. As in the *Popol Vuh*, it is only after Ismachi is founded that this form of construction is mentioned (Recinos 1953:225, note 353).

Page 10.

38. *castillo.* The structure pertaining to the second Quiche king is similar to the one in the other pictorial. except that a portaled wall has been added. The representation of the sun and moon showing through two arches

A Case Study: *Título C'oyoi*

of the wall might mean that astronomical observations were made by lining up astral bodies in openings of stone buildings. The true arches here undoubtedly are the result of Spanish influence, and were probably horizontal in the original structures. None of the structures at Utatlán were ever used as Christian churches, and this is perhaps indicated by the absence of crosses on the three roof structures at the bottom of this pictorial.

39. *segundo rey Q'uiche utlatlecat.* "The second Q'uiche king of Utatlan." Presumably, this refers to the Nijaib Quiche. The "second king" is mentioned so as to be able to refer to the "third king," that is, the C'oyoi ruler. The fact that this second ruler is specifically placed at Utatlán appears to be an indication that the palace of the ruler in the other pictorial was not situated at Utatlán.

40. *castillo.* The building portrayed in this pictorial apparently represents the prehispanic structure which the C'oyoi Quejnay had in the Quezaltenango area. As in the other pictorial, there are three spires or roof structures. The style portrayed appears to be an interesting mixture of Spanish and native motifs.

41. *Putanza* is a Christian name, apparently taken from "Pedro de Pontasa," one of the first friars to begin the work of conversion at Quezaltenango (Gall 1963:25). As Gall has pointed out the Franciscan friars did not accompany the conquistadores, as the Indian tradition would have us believe, but came several years later.

Page 11.

42. *calpul de Juan Penonias de Putanza, tercero.* Further on in the document, we learn that the Quiche name of Penonias de Putanza was C'oyoi, and that he is the instigator of this título. He apparently also bore the title, Chituy Quejnay, which lineage, perhaps along with the Ajaw Quiche was considered to be third in rank in the Quiche political system. The "tercero" written below Putanza's name presumably refers to this ranking.

Page 12.

43. *Ismachi.* "In the whiskers." This was the political center of the Quiche prior to founding K'umarcaaj (Utatlán),

and it is mentioned in the *Popol Vuh* (Recinos 1953:224) and other sources. It was located on a wedge of land on the Quiche plateau, just across from Utatlán. Archaeological remains still exist there.

44. *pokob chanal.* "Pillar and whistle." *Pokob* is given in the dictionaries as "pillar," apparently the kind which supports a roof. *Chanal* is a kind of whistle. The Pokob Chanal was a dance, according to the dictionaries (Basseta n.d.; Ximenez n.d.), which apparently involved playing of whistles and dancing in their pillared plazas.

45. *x(quixaj)oj jun Ajpu C'oy, wukub Cakix.* "They danced the One *Ajpu* Monkey and the Seven *Cakix* (Macaw)." Seven *Cakix* and One *Ajpu* are demigods mentioned in the *Popol Vuh* (Recinos 1953:98ff, 133ff). Apparently, the stories about their exploits were recounted in drama and dance in prehispanic times (Recinos 1953:136), and this refers to such a presentation.

46. *liquinza (liquinca).* The third and fourth months in the Quiche calendar (Berendt n.d.). Apparently, this refers to the time of the year when these dances were performed.

47. *quel cuyuch.* Both words apparently refer to two different varieties of parakeets (Guzmán n.d.). The first word should be *q'uel.*

48. *xtijto.* The context helps suggest the meaning here of "consummated marriage" (Sáenz 1940), for below we are told that the lords were giving their daughters as gifts.

49. hubabal or (c)h'ubabal. The root word seems to be *chub,* "spit at, abuse," and may refer to the public punishment which was meted out by the native rulers. According to this interpretation, *chubabal* would mean, "place of abuse," and would be close to the *ch'ubic'abal* given in Varela (Sáenz 1940), as "place where the condemned are whipped."

50. *sic* or *sic'* . In this case, the meaning seems to be "announcement," rather than "tobacco" (Sáenz 1940).

51. *sub....ak', tibaac'.* Possibly suban nimak, "tamal grande," which the Quiche eat on festive occasions. *Tibaac'* must mean, "you chew" or "masticate," though I do not understand the grammatical function of the postfix -*c'* in this case.

52. *k'ebal*. In this case I believe the meaning to be, "place of presentation," (from *k'e*, "to introduce" (Varela)). The narration continues to focus on the public square where the ceremony took place. As the author states later, it is the same place where people were punished.

Page 13.

53. *Ma(jucotaj)*. Again, the founding fathers of the Tamub and Ilocab Quiche are given. The only names which can be reconstructed that do not appear in the fragment of page 3, are the Ilocab lords, Chira(mak') and (Tzunu)-nija (Recinos 1950:216).

54. *rokche*. This is the oak tree, though the literal meaning is "yellow tree," from *rokoroj*, "very yellow," and *che* "tree" (Sáenz 1940). This is the highest title of the Ilocab rulers, and is listed in the other sources. It is sometimes given as *roxche*, "third tree," which might be a reference to the ranking of the Ilocab below the Quiche and Tamub.

55. *Panq'uib, Panpacay*. Both place names have the locative *pan* "in" or "at." This may be an archaic form which is not otherwise used in the documents, though the dictionaries state that the *-n* is added to *pa-* when a vowel follows. *Q'uib* may mean "farm" or "place where people live;" whereas *pacay* is a palm tree with an edible flower (Varela) (see also Recinos 1950:232, note 25). The two sites, in the vicinity of Ismachi, are mentioned in the Torres Macario document cited by Fuentes y Guzmán (1932-33:7:387), but not in the other sources.

56. *Mukuis*. This place is mentioned in the Tamub document as Mukuitz. I would suggest an etymology of *muku*, "to bury" or "hide," and *itz*, "magic" or "witchcraft." The meaning might be "magical burial place."

Page 14.

57. *malcatz*. Though I cannot find the word in the form it is given here, it is probably closely related to *malcan*, "wide river." Here the reference seems to be to a specific political unit.

58. *quilok'quib*. The probable meaning is "their appreciation or love, one for another."

59. *catak wikab, oxtak wikab*. This is a numerical phrase,

the units of which in this case may be levels or sections of buildings (from *wik*, an addition, floor, adornment). Hence the translation, "two floors, three floors."

60. *tanata....mej ulok, mej*. The basic idea here is one of size and measurement. *Tanata* is related to *tanataj*, "to crowd" (Edmonson 1965), while *mej* is a measurement of approximately an arm's length (Sáenz 1940).

61. *chixibin chic chisach....(wi)nakil upam*. I believe the meaning of this phrase is related to the greatness of the growing kingdom, which is described here: "Already, inside themselves the people began to be afraid and to feel lost" (i.e., filled with doubt because of the growing power of the Quiche).

62. *cakan ajawa(rem)*. "The red lordship." The metaphorical meaning of *cak*, "red," is one of emotion. I suggest that when applied adjectively, as in the present case, it attributes to the object qualities of power (which cause others to be angry or at least emotionally distraught).

63. *role, wakle*. *le* has usually been translated as "generation", though I have elsewhere noted (Carmack n.d.c) that it more accurately suggests points or nodes along a line or string. The meaning of this phrase would be, "5 successions, 6 successions" (i.e., of rule, or generation).

64. *zinteut*. This word appears on page 20 as *zenteut*. It may be related to the Quiché word, *sin*, "centipede" or "millipede" (Edmonson 1965), though more likely it is of Nahua derivation. In Nahuatl, *cen-* is a root with a quantitative meaning (*centetl* is one, *cenca* means much or many), and *-teut* or *teotl* is "a god" or "god-like conqueror" (*teuhtil* is prince) (Garibay 1961). *Centeotl* or *centeuhtil* would mean, "many princes" or "military lords." A closely related Nahua term is *centecutli*, "battle squadron" (Molina 1944).

Page 15.

65. *achijilal*. Derived from *achi*, "male" or "man," this substantive form is associated with warriors or soldiers. Vico (n.d.a) says it is the name for fortress, and other sources refer to the warriors who defend and fight from such fortified centers. It is used in this sense in the *Ra-*

A Case Study: *Título C'oyoi*

binal Achi, where Brasseur translates it as "valiance" (1862:38-39).

66. *e nawal winak*. "They were magical people." Nawal is a term widely used in the Quiche sources to refer to powerful ancestors and rulers. It derives from the nahua term, *nahualli*, a "generic term for magician" (Nicholson n.d.b). In Central Mexico these religious practitioners were closely connected with the idea of transformations from human to animal form. This seems to be one of the basic meanings attached to the term as used in highland Guatemala (e.g., Recinos 1957:89; Saler 1964).

67. *relebal k'ij....ukajibal k'ij....unic'ajal caj unic'ajal ulew.* Literally, "the coming of the sun, the falling of the sun, the middle of the sky, the middle of the earth." These are the four sacred directions of the Quiche, corresponding to the east, west, above and below. As in Yucatán, each direction was associated with a deity, and the cross formed by lines linking the four directions was also a sacred symbol.

68. *Don Pedro de Alvarado*. He was the conquistador of Guatemala sent there from Mexico by Cortés in 1523. He later became the first *Capitán General and Gobernador* of the province.

69. *kanim(a kaja)wal dios rey*. As in other native sources, the king of Spain is represented in deified terms. This is indicative of the "divine kingship" principle which was operative in Quichean culture.

70. *wuk amak'*. "Seven settlements or hamlets." Vico (n.d.a) defines amak' as "hamlet" or "town subject to another (group)." According to Brasseur (1861), the wuk amak' against whom the Quiche fought in the early part of their history were Pokomán-speaking peoples (Recinos 1953:206 passim). That was probably a correct interpretation, but the context must be studied carefully in each case to determine the correct referents for these general terms.

71. *Rabinal, (Cak)chiquel....* These peoples, who came under attack from the Quiche, were located in the central part of the highlands of Guatemala. Specifically, the areas mentioned are Lake Atitlán (the Cakchiquel, X(a)jil Cakchiquel, and Tzutujil), Sacapulas (Tujaleb, Cunen, Bali-

maja, Booj), Huehuetenango (Yoc K'anchebex, Tzitzol, Chele?), and Baja Verapaz (Rabinal, Cubulcaal).

Page 16.

72. *rajpop achij.* "Warrior of the mat." The *Popol Vuh* (Recinos 1953:237) confirms that this was a military office, and indicates that late in Quiche history these officials were elevated in rank and privilege.

73. *xicaja, balimaja.* I cannot identify Xicaja with any known geographical place, but Balimaja or Balamija is the aboriginal name of the people in the Aguacatán area.

74. *culel.* Should be *cubulel*, as seen in the text below. The meaning in the present context is "group" or "collection." (Sáenz 1940).

75. *Uk'ale Chi(tuy C'o)yoi Nine ·Aj.* In this important phrase we are given the titles and calendric name of an important C'oyoi lord. In the page that follows he is referred to by his Christian name, Martín Mejía. The calendric name comes from the 260-day sacred calendar: the 9th number, 7th day (*Aj*, or "reed"). According to an 18th century Quiche calendar from Quezaltenango (Berendt n.d.; see Secondary Sources), this was a day of good luck, "a day of the lords." Hence, it was an appropriate name for one of the great ones of the Quiche ruling class.

76. *Ajpop Sakimox....Utzam Achij Sitai Sitalan.* These and the other officials listed here apparently specify the clans or lineages which they represent. We have here the Ajpop of the Sakimox (some kind of insect or fruit?) lineage, and the Utzam of the Sitalan (wasp) lineage. A member of the Sakimox lineage witnessed the writing of the Huitzitzil Tzunun document (Gall 1963:28).

Page 17.

77. *Don Martín Mejía, Nine Aj.* Martín Mejía is listed as a signer of both the Nijaib I and II títulos (Recinos 1957: 93:116). In the latter case his origin is given as Quezaltenango. The calendric name of Nine Aj identifies him with the C'oyoi lord mentioned in the preceding page. In a 1588 list of calpules at Quezaltenango (AGC, A3: 2800-40485; see Judicial Records), the name C'oyoi appears in the Pérez rather than the Mejía calpul. The lists

are not complete however, and there may have been C'oyoi people in both groups.

78. *ajcot ajbalam.* "The eagle and jaguar warriors." They are mentioned in several other sources, though most clearly in the *Rabinal Achí* (1862). In that document they are designated as warriors, but they also participate in the ritual sacrifice of a captured Quiche lord. In the *Relación Atitlán* it is stated (Betancor and Arboleda 1964: 100) that native warriors wore eagle feathers and "tiger" skins into battle, a practice well known for Central Mexico. I have suggested (Carmack 1968) the possibility of eagle and jaguar "orders" in prehispanic highland Guatemala, similar to those in Mexico.

79. *raxaj.* This is an attributive form deriving from *rax*, "green" or "blue." Metaphorically this word meant "beautiful" or "great," due no doubt to its association with the feathers of the Quetzal and other tropical birds.

80. *runum c'abawil.* I have been unable to find this name in other sources, though separately both words are found in most of the early dictionaries. Runum is the male genital organ, and by extension, male sexuality, tear drops, and stick-shaped objects (Varela). C'abawil is the Quiche word for the idols of wood, stone, and clay which represented their deities (Vico n.d.a; Coto n.d.). In the present context, I would suggest a meaning of the "great masculine idol (or god)."

81. *Tamub....cakoj.* From the Tamub document (Recinos 1957:24-67) we learn that Cakoj was one of the moieties into which that descent-based group was divided. The other moiety was the Ekoamak'.

82. *Cajib Aj, Utzam Pop Rokch(e).* Cajib Aj, "four reed," appears to be another calendric name, though one cannot be certain because the preceding word is missing. According to the Quiche calendar from Quezaltenango (Berendt n.d.), this was "a bad or unlucky day." It does not mean that it was so interpreted by the Ilocab, however, for the divinatory meaning of the different days apparently varied from one settlement to another (to judge from the situation in modern times). Or, this might have meant that the

Ilocab lord referred to here was magically "dangerous," at the same time that he was powerful (i.e., another case of Quiche dualism).

Page 18.

83. *e worom e c'a(ko)m.* "They are the lancers and slingers." From *wor-*, "to pierce or perforate," hence "to spear;" and *c'ak*, "to throw rocks," hence, "the slingers."

84. *xeworic, xec'akic chi tatil, chi k'ana abaj.* Tatil and K'ana abaj are listed in the *Popol Vuh*, along with other symbolic objects brought by the Quiche from the East (Recinos 1953: 221). Recinos has translated them as "yellow (magical) pieces," and finds cognate words in Yucatecan Maya. To this may be added the suggestion that tatil is the Nahua form of *tlatlil-* "black" or "dyed black" (Molina 1944), so that tatil k'ana abaj becomes, "black and yellow magical stones pieces." Vico (n.d.a), explains their symbolic significance as follows: "*tatil, k'ana abaj, cak, cakuleuj*, colors that were put on those who were lords, like an annointment." This undoubtedly is a custom deriving ultimately from the famous Toltecs of central Mexico (Brasseur 1857: I:374).

85. *lotzqui....* Its verbal form means "to bleed," in the sense of sacrifice (Varela; Chinchilla A. 1963:9). Its precise meaning here is unclear because the next word is obliterated, though it apparently refers to the sacrifice of enemies, carried out by the warriors.

86. *(c)ak che ri xtz'akcot.* This difficult phrase follows the root *lotz-*, which, as noted in footnote 85, is connected with the idea of sacrifice. If, as it appears, *cak*, "red," is the next word, then *cak che ri xtz'akcot* might be translated as, "the red tree which is encircled by the construction." This may be a reference to the "tree sacrifice," in which the enemy is tied to a tree and sacrificed by a circle of warriors who shoot arrows into his body (Villacorta 1934:210).

87. *quitem, quich'acat.* "Their benches and their stools." These were the seats of authority for the Quiche. Vico (n.d.a) states that *tem* was "a little bench that they gave, and (they) sat on it as a sign that they were heads of the calpul,

(and) of great authority; and (they were) careful to incense it." For *ch'acat* he gives the following gloss: "the wooden seat or little bench or chair, smoked with incense, which the Indians used when they establish a chief of the town."

88. *balam bak, tatil, k'ana abaj....pich quij, tzic uwil coj, tzic uwil balam....matacuz, (chi)yom, aztapulul....k'alibal ....qui muj....(s)ubak cham.* This is a list of symbolic objects brought back from the East. Their meanings have been interpreted by Recinos (1953:221, note 346) and myself (Carmack 1968:73), and I will not repeat the analysis here.

89. *k'echa, tumumcha, tzocotz lakam.* Except for *lakam*, "flag" or "ensign," these seem to be archaic forms, for they do not appear in the early dictionaries. K'echa apparently derives from k'e, "to penetrate," and may mean the "penetrators" or better, "military invaders." Tumumcha is probably to be equated with *tzununche* of the other sources, "lancer." *Tzocotz lakam* is possibly, "flag bearer," from *tzocon* "to discharge an obligation," and lakam, "flag" (Edmonson 1965). In the military organization of the Quiche, the flag bearer was an important position restricted to persons of noble rank (Recinos 1957:86).

90. *c'ucumam.* This is an interesting form similar to the name of the famous Quiche ruler, *K'uk'umatz* (feathered serpent) (Carmack 1966a). In the form given here, the serpent part of the word has been replaced by *mam*, "grandfather." The word would mean, therefore, "feathered grandfather," and metaphorically, "majestic" or "powerful grandfather." The reference here is to an office, and not a person.

Page 19.

91. *(aj)pop c'aam(ja).* A high official second in command below the ajpop. While it has long been known that ajpop means, "he of the mat," the meaning of c'aamja has not been adequately clarified. Because *c'aam* means, "part" or "piece" (Sáenz 1940), and because it was an office of a lineage (*ja*) offshoot from the ajpop lineage, I suggest that the meaning of *c'aamja* was "branch" or "part of the Ajpop lineage." The Ajpop C'aamja was a kind of assistant or auxiliary official and lineage.

92. *aj tz'(alam)*. I have given the etymologies of these various political titles elsewhere (Carmack 1967; 1968), though not satisfactorily in the case of Aj tz'alam. According to Coto (n.d.), this official was the head of a clan or lineage (*chinamital*), and as such had the right to name policemen or guardians in early posthispanic times.

93. *Chiwila, Chitaa*. Chiwila is Chichicastenango (Recinos 1953: 236), but I have not been able to find Chitaa in the other sources. In listing the settlements over which the Quiché exercised dominion, Chiwila or Uwila is usually given first.

94. *k'ak'al, tepewal*. "Powerful and majestic." K'ak'al derives from *k'ak'*, " fire," which metaphorically expressed the power and authority of the ruling class. *Tepewal* is of *Nahua* derivation, and, as pointed out by Thompson (1943b:23), connotes "greatness, glory."

95. *kula xelajuj*. This reference to the people of Quezaltenango begins a list of settlements similar to lists in several other sources (Recinos 1953:234-236; 1957: 71-73, 105). (*Ru)c'aba(la) Tziquin, Ch'ulimal, Uwila, Zaki(ya), (Xajba)-quej, Xoya(baj)* were all located close to Ismachi, while Sija and the closely associated Pamalaj were near present-day Santa Catarina Ixtahuacán. I cannot identify *Aj Nakaj*, and *Aj Taa....*

Page 20.

96. (*J)unajpu, Aj(Amak'tam)....Aj Raxacha*. A continuation of the list of settlements surrounding the Quiche capital (Recinos 1953:236; 1957:72-73).

97. (*K'u)marcaj chismachi*. These two names are often combined in the sources referring to the Quiche capital late in their history. K'umarcaj became known as Utatlán after the conquest, and is still clearly visible as an archaeological site just west of present-day Santa Cruz del Quiche. As noted in No. 43, Ismachi was located on a small mesa just across the canyon to the south of Utatlán.
The etymology of K'umarcaj has never been adequately explained. Ximénez (1929-1931:1) translated the word as "rotten huts," and Recinos (1953:228, note 362) noted the similarity between this meaning and that of Utatlán, "among the reeds," the Nahuatl translation which the

Mexican warriors gave to it. *K'umar* means "rotten," but also "old" or "ancient" (Carmack n.d.b). *Caj* means "the reeds" or "canes," and apparently by extension, "reed huts." The etymology of the word might be, "the old reed huts," perhaps a reference to simple structures standing there at the time the Quiche first began to build their capital.

98. *utz'ibaxic.* "The painting or writing." The reference seems to be to the writing of the document under discussion here, and not to any prehispanic codex.

99. *Tojil, Auwilis, (Ja)k'awitz.* Three of the four gods brought back from the east, according to the *Popol Vuh* (the other god was *Nic'ajtak'aj*) (Recinos 1953:184-185). These gods became the patron deities of the three most important ruling descent groups of the Quiche. Recinos (1953:185, note 271) has provided an etymology for Tojil, and I have suggested one for Jakawitz (1968:68). Auwilis or *Awilix* still has no satisfactory explanation, though Edmonson has suggested (1965) a possible derivation from *C'abawil Ix,* "the goddess *Ix.*" This etymology would agree well with the argument (especially, Recinos 1953; Carmack 1968; Nicholson n.d.a) that the Quiche rulers came from the Tabasco-Verapaz region—an area where the goddess *Ix Chel* was of paramount importance.

100. *mayijabal.* A word with several meanings, all suggesting "wonder," "awe," or "greatness," and by extension, "the universe" (Sáenz 1940; Edmonson 1965). In the present context it should be translated as, "great thing" or "wonder."

101. *nima c'utbal, ilbal.* "The great demonstration and display." The reference is to a council held by the Quiche lords at Ismachi, where their power and lordship were demonstrated in dress, dance, and word.

102. *Chojib.* *Choj* means "hole in the ground," as for an oven, so that *pa chojib* would be, "at the ovens." There is such a place within the bounds of present-day Chichicastenango (Edmonson 1965).

103. *xban choloj Tziquin K'ij.* "The month *Tziquin K'ij* was counted." Here we have recorded the month of the 365-day calendar on which the celebration took place. An 18th century calendar from Quezaltenango begins with

the words: *"wae chol powal k'ij, macewal k'ij,"* "this is
the count of the cycle of days, the ordinary days" (Berendt
n.d.; Edmonson 1965). The Quiche apparently conceived
of the days as a series of units arranged in circular form.
The 8th 20-day unit (month) of the series was Tziquin K'ij.

104. *lak'ajaw zenteut.* I have already suggested a meaning for
zenteut (see Note 64). Though I do not completely understand the grammatical form of *lak'ajaw*, it apparently is
related to *lak'aj*, "sacred, consecrated" (Sáenz 1940). Perhaps the meaning here is, "the consecrated group of military lords (i.e., squadron)."

105. *xuchucat alicat aca....nenepu tunapulul.* None of these
appear to be Quiche words, but rather of Nahua derivation.
The Nahua forms are apparently archaic, and probably
corrupted. The following glosses must be considered as
tentative, and I am sure a Nahua specialist could improve
them.

The *-cat* suffix of *chucat* and *alicat* is a personalizer used
with place nouns or verbs. The closest possible equivalents to *chuc-* and *ali-* in Nahuatl are "to cry" or "roar"
(*choca*), and "to sacrifice before idols" (*altia*) (Molina 1944;
Simeon 1963). A speculative translation of these two
terms would be, "those who howl and sacrifice before
the idols."

aca is a Nahua relative pronoun, meaning "all those that"
(Garibay 1961). It appears to be followed by the Quiché
locative, *wi* ("there" or "here").

nenepu(l). Perhaps derives from the Nahua noun, *nenetl*,
"female nature, or idol," and *-pol*, "excessiveness" (Molina 1944; Bright n.d.). Hence, a powerful fertility goddess,
with accompanying idol is suggested. *nene-* however, also
appears in Quiche dictionaries from the Rabinal area (Edmonson 1965), where it means "to resound, roar." This
suggests another Nahua word, *nenepilli*, "tongue." An
alternate meaning here, then, would be, "the great roaring,"
and would be related to *chucat* ("those who roar") already
discussed.

tunapulul suggests the Nahua word *tonalpohualli*, the sacred
divinatory calendar of Central Mexico. It would be equi-

valent to the Quiche *choloj k'ij*. The reference here might be to the diviners who interpreted the calendar, rather than to the count itself.

In summary, the authors have apparently left us an esoteric Nahua phrase which was recited at the time of important ritual occasions. It seems to be an expression of the roaring sounds made by the warriors dressed in their animal skins, as they go before the idol and consult the sacred calendars.

Page 21.

106. *ixajil tun ruc' tzala tun.* "The drum dancing and the war dance." This is a continuation of a list of dances beginning at the bottom of the preceding page. The *tun* was a hollow log drum, sometimes referred to in the Quiche sources by its Nahua equivalent, *teponaztli.* Apparently, it was the basic musical instrument employed during the dance drama of the Quiche, and generically came to express such dances. We find it in the name of several prehispanic dances mentioned in the sources, such as *Xajoj tun* (Brasseur 1961), *Loj tum* (Chinchilla 1963:9), and *Ox tun* (Edmonson 1965).

Xajil is the name of an important Cakchiquel descent group, but etymologically means "the dancing." xajil tun, therefore, would be "the drum dancing."

107. *ox....bixa....subakibal.* Too much of this phrase is missing to be able to reconstruct it completely, but the general idea is clear. *Ox....* is part of a numerical classifier meaning "third;" *bixa-* is derived from the verbroot "to sing;" *subakibal* is a little bone flute which the Quiche played during their dances (Coto n.d.). The reference here is to a number of songs or chants, accompanied by the flute.

108. *c'astajic.* This is the word used by the Quiche today to refer to the Christian concept of "resurrection," but one of its original meanings was "to give birth" (Varela).

109. *cajib mul, oxib m(ul).* "The four parasols, the three parasols." This is a reference to the elaborate tiers of parasols (probably of feathers), placed above the throne of the Quiche rulers (Recinos 1950:224; Las Casas 1958).

The highest Quiche ruler had the right to four tiers, the second highest three, and so on down.

110. *chitaltic*. This appears to be another Nahua word, cognate with the Aztec term, *tlalticpac*, "the world above the earth." The meaning here would be, "above the earth," referring to the tiered parasols. *Chi* is the Quiche locative, "at," "on," or "in."

111. *(aj)waliom*. I cannot find this form in the early dictionaries. Perhaps it is a reference to the people of Walil, who are mentioned in the *Annals of the Cakchiquel* (Recinos 1950:67). Miles (1957) identifies them as the inhabitants of Acasaguastlán, a place in eastern Guatemala where both Pokomán and Pipil speakers resided.

112. *samajal* or *samajel*. "Messenger." This is a general term widely used in the sources. It can refer to emissaries sent by political officials, or to the mythological owl messengers sent by death gods from the underworld (Villacorta 1962a:94).

113. *camul belej c'al*. Assuming that *cal* in the text is an erroneous rendering of *c'al*, the translation of this phrase would be, "two times nine times twenty." The product of this is 360, the number of days in the solar calendar minus the five closing days. Apparently this numerical unit was conceived of in calendrical terms, 18 (2 times 9) representing the "months" of the calendar, and 20 the days of each "month."

It is surprising to find a 360-day unit used by the Quiché, as a count of elapsed time.

The 360-day *tun* was the fundamental unit of the Yucatec long-count system (Thompson 1950:141-156), while the 400-day *may* was apparently its equivalent among the Quiche peoples (see Native Sources). Obviously, there is still much about Quichean chronology that we do not understand.

114. *c'axaja(i)*. The text is broken at the end of this word, so one cannot be certain of its form. It is apparently derived from *c'axaj*, "to salivate, foam." Perhaps the meaning here is, "the foaming ones," a reference to the animal-like fierceness of the warriors. Dressed in their jaguar and lion skins they also howl and scream.

A Case Study: *Título C'oyoi*

115. *Mwaji....* Perhaps the text here is a continuation of the description of the Pokomán people of Acasaguastlán. Among the four leaders mentioned for the Pokomán in the *Annals* (Recinos 1950:67) is Mewac, possibly related to the Mwaji....given in the text.

Page 22.

116. *sak amak'.* Literally, "the white hamlet." In Totonicapán I was told by informants that *sak* is used to refer to plains or open places in the rural areas. I suggest the reference here is to "the hamlet or people of the open places (plains)."

117. *ajcha(a), ajc'aam, ajtzolaj, (tzunu)nche, ajch'ab, ajpocob.* This is a listing of the components of a Quiche military squadron. The same warrior types are given in the other native sources (Recinos 1957:104-10), and may be roughly translated as follows: "the flag bearers," "the bearers (ensigns)," "the warriors," "the lancers," "the bowmen," "the shield bearers."

118. *oyew achij.* "The valiant warriors." The meaning of *oyew* is given in the dictionaries as "anger, ire, rage," and when applied to the warriors is a reference to their fierceness and violence. I suspect that it originally derives from a Nahua word, though similar forms in Molina's dictionary (1944) have a meaning almost the reverse of that in Quiché: *Oyeiujco,* "smiling."

Page 23.

119. *oxlajuj k'ulaja ajxelaj(uj)....lajuj tzijbachaj ruc'....c'oxtun sija.* These contingents of warriors were all from the valley of Quezaltenango. The K'ulaja were located just west of present-day Quezaltenango, according to a document, from the national archives in Guatemala (AGC, A1:5946-52050; see Judicial Records). The Tzijbachaj were apparently located south of present-day Totonicapán (Carmack 1966b), near Sija, the aboriginal name of Santa Catarina Iutahuacán. This list is almost identical with one given in the *Título Totonicapán*, where it is associated with conquests made in this same region during the reign of Quik'ab (ca. 1444-1484 A.D.) (Recinos 1950:237).

120. *xwubax.* I do not find the verb form of this word in the early dictionaries. Perhaps it is related to *wubi-,* "to blow

out" (Edmonson 1965), though it makes the phrase of which it is a part incomprehensible—"their thorns were blown out."

121. *chajilal.* From *chajij*, "to guard or watch," hence, "guards or watchment." Also, the word is often given as *chajal*, "guard," a term still used in Quiche-speaking communities to refer to cofradía or municipal officials with minor police duties.

122. *alak c'ulelaay.* A proper translation of this phrase would be, "be fighters," from *c'ulelway*, "to fight with another" (Sáenz 1940).

123. *mesquel alak. Mesquel*, "armpits, odor," is used here in the sense of grabbing the victim by the armpits (to sacrifice him). In the *Popol Vuh*, the gods of the Quiche are said to have commanded the priest-rulers to take the enemy peoples by the armpits (mesquel) and sacrifice them (Villacorta 1962a:247-248).

124. *xeuchaxic...xwaeic.* This appears to be an intentional case of antiphony. Thompson long ago pointed to this technique in Yucatán Mayan poetry (1950:61), and Edmonson believes the *Popol Vuh* to be entirely composed in such couplets (n.d.).

Page 24.

125. *c'ulelaay rech wuk(amak').* This same phrase appeared on the previous page, without the wuk amak'. It can be translated as, "make war with the enemy peoples."

126. *Ajpoxajil.* The leading ruler of the Xajil line of the Cakchiquel. He apparently resided at Iximché, though after the conquest that line was transferred to Sololá, from where the *Annals of the Cakchiquels* was written (Recinos 1950).

127. *Coon Bu(xija).* Probably a Tsutujil settlement along the shores of Lake Atitlán, near modern Panajachel (Recinos 1957:149). The peoples listed here are the traditional enemies of the Quiche—the Cakchiquel, Tzutujil, and Mam. Most of the same Mam names appear in the Nijaib I document (Recinos 1957:75).

128. *atoloc'a (mes)quel.* The second person singular command form is given here: "Take (them) by the armpits and

sacrifice (them)." This is the same phrase that was used in the preceding page, though part of it is missing there (see Note 123).

Page 25.

129. *Mam e Sakiulew.* "Mam people of the white land." This is a reference to the Mam speakers in the area of present day Huehuetenango. The ruins of the fortified center there have been excavated and restored (Woodbury and Trik 1953), and are still called Zakuleu. This same conquest is described in one of the Xpantzay documents (Recinos 1957:145), and the Sakulew Mam are listed in the título from Santa Clara (Recinos 1957:179).

130. ....*wila.* Perhaps this should be *xquiwila,* "they obtained" or "took," a reference to the subjugation of the mountains and plains of Sakulew.

131. *Don Q'uikab, C'awisimaj.* The two highest rulers of the Quiche political system at the climax of Quiche history, according to the *Popol Vuh.* Q'uikab (or Quik'ab) became the most famous of all the rulers. As in the reference here, the authors of the *Popol Vuh* place him in the 6th succession of rulers (Villacorta 1962a:342). Other sources indicate, however, that he was ninth in the line of succession, beginning his rule in about A.D. 1444 (Carmack 1966a).

132. *Iquilaja.* There is a sacred mountain by this name situated just north of the *cabecera* of modern Santa María Chiquimula. Quiche priest-shamans still visit the site to practice *costumbre* (Carmack n.d.b). From this reference it is clear that the conquest had shifted toward the south, away from Huehuetenango.

133. *Tena, ruc' Lotz, Tzakibalja.* These are names of places in the territory of present-day Momostenango (Carmack 1967). Tena is a sacred mountain which juts upward to the north of aldea San Vicente Buenabaj (Carmack 1967).

134. *Chukuljuyup, Palin Quej....* This is a list of settlements in the Quezaltenango valley (see Recinos 1950:128; Appendix II in this study; Carmack 1966b). Chukuljuyub, Palin Quej, and Paxtoca are all hamlets of present-day Totonicapán. Other recognizable places are San Francisco

el Alto (Xoch'o), Huitan (Patziquiche), Cantel (K'antel), Chiquimula (Patzoloj), and Zunil.

Page 26.

135. *Ak'aab Balam Colob.* Here we learn that Balam Colob is a settlement or group of people of the Ak'aab branch of the Quiche. The Ak'aab, located just south of Sacapulas are mentioned in most sources (Carmack 1967; Recinos 1957:111; *Título Lamaquib*, Appendix X). Balam Colob is listed by Vico in 1553 (Remesal 1932:5:334) as a settlement near Sacapulas.

136. *(xe)yik'oxic.* I am not certain of the meaning of the verb root here, though Vico (n.d.a) gives the meaning of the word *yik'* as, "to tread (beat down)." A possible translation here would be, "they were beaten down (i.e., conquered)."

137. *chapowinak.* "Were made chiefs." The general meaning of the verb root *chap-* is "to take" or "grasp." It apparently denotes the act of receiving a political office, when symbols of some kind are seized at the time of accession. This expression is still used in Quiche-speaking communities to refer to the taking of the alcalde or regidor staffs at the beginning of each year (Schultze-Jena 1933:148-154).

138. *Wukmil Sic'a Juanija.* This is one of the Quiche political descent groups not mentioned often in the sources. I find it listed in the *Título Nijaib I* (Recinos 1957:77), and the *Título Chacatz-Tojin* (see Appendix IX). Apparently, this group was located in the general vicinity of Utatlán.

139. *xkup.* "To tear up by force." The authors have used very expessive verb forms to describe the destruction by the Quiche warriors of the prestige possessions of their enemies. They "fragmented" (*xk'up*) their riches, "tore into pieces" (*xturatix*) their structures, "carried off" (*xc'am*) their gold and jewels, and "forcefully tore up" (*xkup*) their precious metal and stones.

140. *c'wal, yamanic, tatil, k'anabaj....(wa)tzij pwak, xtecoc....* This is a list of most of the precious stones worked by the Quiché and other peoples of the highlands. Missing is *xit*, "green stone," apparently the general term used to refer to jade and amazon stone by the Quiche (and hence,

corresponding in meaning to the Nahua term, *chalchihuitl*) (Foshag 1957; Ximénez 1929-1931:1). I have already suggested that tatil k'anabaj refers to black and yellow obsidian, of which there are ancient deposits around San Marcos, Chimaltenango, and just northeast of Guatemala City (McBryde 1947). C'wal yamanic is given in the dictionaries as "emeralds, precious stones;" watzij pwak as "jewels, riches;" and xtecoc as "precious stones" (Guzmán n.d.; Sáenz 1940; Coto n.d.). Obviously, it is not possible to make specific identifications of the stones referred to in such general terms. However, based on minerological and archaeological studies made in the highlands, one can assume that among the precious stones referred to were jade (Foshag's type III), albite, jasper, microline (Amazonstone), serpentine, steatite (Soapstone), and obsidian (Foshag 1957; Woodbury 1965).

Page 27.

141. *sochoj yamanic.* "The precious rattle." Precious, probably, because of its use in the sacred dance ceremonies, as well as its adornment with "jewels."

142. *e ch'a cot ulew.* The meaning here would seem to be, "the eagle warriors who conquer the lands with bow and arrow."

143. *nima quicotem xban pa Q'uiche.* This is a reference to the great victory celebrations held at the capital after successful military expeditions. There is a fairly detailed account of such a celebration in the Nijaib documents (Recinos 1957:83-84, 107-109).

144. *al, c'ajol.* "Vassals." The authors are careful to distinguish this form, which literally means, "children of man and woman," from the children and brothers of the lords (*uc' ajol ajaw, atzixel, chak'ixel*), who were not vassals.

145. *xepixabax.* "They were taught the law." That is, Don Quik'ab gave the warriors instructions and advice. When the leaders of lineages in modern Quiche-speaking communities give counsel and advice to the whole group, this is still referred to by the verb root, *pix-* (Carmack n.d.b). Quik'ab's advice to them continues on the next page.

Page 28.

146. *jutzu.* The meaning of the root *jutziu-* is, "to go back and forth," apparently a reference to the vigilance the warriors were to keep at their new outposts.

147. *ta xojul waral chupam kajuyubal Xelaju.* "When we arrived here in the mountains of Quezaltenango." Here the authors explain how their fathers were sent to the Quezaltenango area to serve as watchmen against the encroach ment of the Mam enemies who had formerly controlled it.

Page 29.

148. *mawuchaj ac'ux.* "Do not guard your heart." I do not find this expression in the dictionaries, but the context suggests a meaning similar to the English expression, "let not your heart be troubled" (do not worry).

149. *cojol awila.* This phrase is difficult to translate. Cojol can mean "belief," or "placement, arrangement," or "intermediate distance" (not far), while awila is the command form of *wil*, "to get" or "obtain" (Sáenz 1940; Edmonson 1965). The most likely meaning is, "you must put yourself in order" (i.e., arrange yourselves).

150. *xok'ojawab.* "The ladies (i.e., wives of lords)." This derives from *ixok*, "woman, wife," and *ajaw*, "lord."

151. *iwachijilal.* The meaning here is "watchful guardians," from *wachij*, "to watch, look with the eyes." The reference is to the military colonists who were sent from Q'uiche to guard the area of Quezaltenango.

152. *xquimes quiwi.* This is another puzzling expression. *mes* is a verb root meaning, "to sweep, clean, forget" (Varela; Edmonson 1965). Vico (n.d.a) gives another meaning which apparently applies here: "put hands on the head" (endearingly, as when holding a child). The expression probably means, "they endearingly put hands on their heads" (as sign of endearment and sadness at parting).

Page 30.

153. *Aj Mik'ina....(Ch)uwa Tz'ak.* A list of the political centers receiving military guards is given here. Most were situated in the Quezaltenango valley (e.g., Mik'ina, Totonicapán), or nearby (Chuwa Tz'ak, Momostenango).

154. *Tzam Chicojaj....ch'ocol Cakapec.* "Point of the lions," "beautiful red cave." These are sites apparently located south of Quezaltenango, in the direction of the passageway leading to the coastal lowlands. *Tz'ibampec,* "the painted cave," is mentioned in the *Título Nijaib I* as being one of the places near Excanul (Volcán de Santa María) which Quik'ab conquered (Recinos 1957:77).

155. *Cak Q'uix, Chay Bamat, Cakiquil....Joyam K'anak'.* "The red thorn," "obsidian stone *bamat,*" "red thorns," "yellow cavity." These same places are listed in the *Título Totonicapán* (Recinos 1950:237), where it is intimated that they are all close together. The area indicated is apparently the strip of land extending below Volcán de Santa María and Cerro Quemado called, Panajunok' (Gall 1963:26; Anonymous 1963). This name has been retained for a barrio of Quezaltenango, called San Antonio Palajunoj (Bode 1961:241).

156. *Raxq'uim.* "The green bunch grass." Paraxq'uim is the name of a mountain chain which runs from southwest to northeast, between Lake Atitlán and the valley of Quezaltenango. It is still known by that name (Gall 1963: 30, note 44).

157. *cab AjOjout....Sebache....* The same peoples ("the two *Ojout*"? and the "*Sebache*") are mentioned in the *Título Totonicapán* (Recinos 1950: 237-238). I am unable to specify their location, though it must have been in the same passage leading to the coast. There is a place of worship near Santa Catarina Ixtahuacán called, Tzibache which may be the Sebache mentioned here (Hernández Spina 1932).

158. *yacalic.* "Placed." The root of this word, *yac-* has as one of its meanings, "the return of animals to their lair," and so denotes something placed up high (as a lion's lair) (Edmonson 1965).

Page 31.

159. *xeQ'uiak.* "Below Mount Q'uiak." Q'uiak provides us with a positive identification of the specific location of the C'oyoi group. Q'uiak is a large hill in the northeastern part of the modern municipality of Cantel. In this same

vicinity, the modern maps (1:50,000) show a number of places which can be identified with those given in this document: Chitay (Chituy), a *caserío* of Quezaltenango, about four kilometers west of Q'uiak; Paxtoca, a canton of Totonicapán, about four kilometers north of Q'uiak; Pachaj, an aldea of Cantel, about two kilometers southwest of Q'uiak; Parraxquim, a caserío of Ixtahuacán, some nine to ten kilometers from Mount Q'uiak. Xequi and Xeq'uiakuleu are *parajes* of Quezaltenango, probably situated close to Mount Q'uiak (DGC, 1961).

160. *k'ale ch'o cakoj.* This appears to be a reference to the ruler at (Xo)ch'o (San Francisco el Alto). Cakoj is one of the Tamub moiety names.

161. *k'ali c'(a)amja looquin.* I do not remember seeing this title in the other native sources.

Page 32.

162. *ajaw Cortés K'ale Rokche Saknoi Isuy Sakpoklaj.* The same lord appears as a signer of other Indian títulos from this area (e.g., Recinos 1957:93, 115; *Títulos Paxtoca, Retalulew*). The ruler of *Sakpoklaj* (modern San Pedro Almolonga) is specifically mentioned in the *Título Nijaib I* as having received a message from the rulers at Quezaltenango, advising him of the arrival of the Spanish conquistadores (Recinos 1957:86).

163. *ajaw Quemaxitapul Chic'wa.* This lord also appears as a signer of several native documents (Recinos 1957:93, 103; *Título Retalulew* Appendix VII), where his Spanish name is given as Don Alonso Pérez). Chic'wa, "at the well," is mentioned in the Totonicapán document, along with Chuwiztoca (Paxtoca), as places where four of the sons of Quik'ab built their residences (Recinos 1950:238-39). One of the sons was named Xitapul, from which (Quema)-xitapul apparently derives.
    Quemaxitapul is a Nahua-derived word, possibly combining *quema-*, "fixed, firm," *xiutla*, "place of bushes or herbs," and *-pol*, attribute of excessiveness (Molina 1944: Bright n.d.). Hence, the meaning of the name might be translated as, "fixed place of many bushes."

A Case Study: *Título C'oyoi*

164. *Xetuj.* "Below the hotsprings." There are several natural hot springs in the vicinity of Quezaltenango: just south of the modern city, at the crossroads between San Cristóbal and San Miguel Totonicapán, just south of Almolonga, and others.

165. *Xepach.* This place may still be identified by a caserío of that name in the southern part of municipio Quezaltenango (DGC 1960). According to the *Título Nijaib I,* Xepach was located in the Palajunaj zone near Chwabaj, and provided 3,000 warriors for the battle against the Spaniards (Recinos 1957:87).

Page 33.

166. *chic'ama inaoj chupam wae ititulo.* "Receive your wisdom in this, your título." The elders of the C'oyoi prepared this land title for their sons and grandchildren. The boundaries are then listed below.

167. *xec'ujeke lok chiquijujunal.* "They established the foundation and order of each group." This is a reference to the procedure by which the boundary markers of each political descent group were publicly outlined.

168. *c'ulbat ajaw Xcamparij Ajxtoca.* "The boundary marker of the lord Excamparij of Paxtoca." The territory of the Xcamparij, corresponding to the modern hamlet of Totonicapán still called Paxtoca, is given in detail in the Paxtoca document (see Appendix VI).

169. *tz'ibampec.* "Painted cave." This same place is mentioned in the *Título Nijaib I* in the vicinity of Volcán de Santa María (Excanul) (Recinos 1957:77). Since it is listed after Paxtoca and before Q'uiak, perhaps it was situated somewhere near modern Salcajá.

170. *quitz'akibal e Sakiulewab winak.* "The stone structures of the Sakiulew people." We are informed that there were fortified structures at the top of Mount Q'uiak, and that they had been constructed by the Mam. It would be interesting to examine any ruins, which might still exist there, and compare them with artifacts at typical Quiche sites.

171. *rakan tak'aj.* "The foot plains." Apparently a reference to the fertile plains which extend east of Mount Q'uiak

to the beginning of the Paraxq'uim mountain chain. It is a narrow plain, which the Quiche apparently conceptualized in the shape of a foot. Hernández Spina's account from Ixtahuacán (see Secondary Sources) lists this place, and indicates that there were three Maya priest-shamans residing there, two of whom were named Tay, perhaps a name derived from (Chi)tuy.

172. *chi lemob.* "At the Alizo tree." This is a tree of the rose family, with white or rose-colored flowers (La Rousse 1963).

Page 34.

173. *C'abawil Chaj.* "Pine tree idol." This boundary marker is described in the Paxtoca document as follows (see Appendix VI): "And they followed the boundaries to where there is a pine tree called, *cabaguil abaj*, among the pine trees, at the road coming from Quezaltenango."

174. *Sajc'aja.* "White water." This is the aboriginal name of modern Salcajá, located along the Samalá river between Quezaltenango and San Cristóbal. It is called Zakcaha, and Zahcaha by Vazques (1937-1944:14:19, 187).

175. *nima caja.* "Lone piece of rocky hillside" (Edmonson 1965). This is apparently a reference to a topographical feature located near Salcajá. Another land formation in the next phrase is called, *xak*, "earth rock" (Maynard and Xec n.d.).

176. *Pu(j)ula.* The name of this large river is repeated at the end of the document. It is probably the Samalá river as it flows on its southward course just west of San Cristóbal. One of the aboriginal names of San Cristóbal was Papula or Pujila (Appendix VI; AGC, A1:5968-52387), which is apparently equivalent to the Pujula.

177. *Tzamabaj....* "point of stone." This is a mountain situated between modern Olintepeque and San José Chiquilajá (an aldea of Quezaltenango) (Gall 1963:30, note 37). Enough of the boundaries listed here can be identified to roughly plot the direction of the territory being outlined. Chijaya may be the aboriginal name for Chiquilajá (San José). Vuk Xiquincan, "seven ears," is a volcano about six kilometers southwest of Quezaltenango, and now called Siete Orejas.

Cakal pa Ucuz apparently refers to a site along the Ocós River, a branch of which has its beginning at Volcán Siete Orejas. Palajunoj, as noted above, is the strip of land extending down the passageway to the coast, created by the Samalá river. Tak'ajal is San Felipe, as indicated in the text, though it was crossed out in favor of its Quiche form. This territory appears to be the same as the one outlined in the *Título Huitzitzil Tzunun* (Gall 1963:29-30), but some what different from the one given in the *Título Nijaib IV* (Appendix IV).

178. *Tz'olojche.* "Alder tree." This is the name generally used to designate Santa María Chiquimula in the native sources (e.g., Recinos 1957:74). In this case, however, it appears to refer to some other place located between Olintepeque and Volcán Siete Orejas. A caserío in Quezaltenango by that name probably identifies the place listed here.

Page 35.

179. *oxib roxc'al.* "Three and sixty." This number is recorded in the vigesimal system of counting used by the Quiche and other peoples of highland Guatemala. *c'al* is a unit of twenty; *rox-* "three" as a multiplying factor; and *oxib*, "three," gives the number of units. Hence, we have three plus three times twenty, for a total of sixty-three. Used with *tzij*, "word" or "discourse," the metaphorical meaning is apparently, "many words."

180. *Xetulul.* "Below the Zapotes." This is the Quiche name for the prehispanic settlement which was located near present-day San Martín Zapotitlán. It was the first Quiche center attacked by the Spaniards, and is described briefly by Alvarado in his report to Cortés (Alvarado 1946:457).

181. *jun Batz....caib E.* "One monkey, two tooth." *Batz* and *E* are the fifth and sixth of the twenty day names in the Quiche calendar. The associated numerical coefficients (1, 2) indicate that successive days of the calendar are indicated here. The *Título Nijaib I* also records the arrival of the Spaniards at Xetulul on the day 1 Batz, but states that they stayed there three months (*vs.* the implication here that they were at Xetulul only one day) (Recinos 1957:85). In the *Título Huitzitzil Tzunun* there

is no arrival date, but is it stated that Alvarado stayed in the zone extending between the coast and the highlands (Panajunoj) for one month (Gall 1963:26). Alvarado himself indicates that the Spaniards spent about five days in the Xetulul area, and another two days in traveling to the highlands (1946:457).

According to the *Annals of the Cakchiquels* (Recinos 1950: 124-125), the Spaniards subdued Xetulul on the day 1 *K'anel*, and seventeen days later (4 *C'at*) burned the Quiche rulers at Utatlán. The date 1 *K'anel* is about six months removed from 1 *Batz*, so there is a wide discrepancy between the Quiche and Cakchiquel dating of the entry of the Spaniards into the coast of Guatemala. This could not be due to differences between their 260-day calendar systems, for they have been shown to be correlated even in modern times (Miles 1952:281). The date given in the *Annals* should be accepted over the Quiche sources in view of the extensive chronology in that document, and the close correspondence with dates given by Alvarado in his letters (e.g., Alvarado wrote from Utatlán on April 11th, which would be a reasonable month after the date given in the *Annals* for the execution of the Quiche lords). I am still unable to explain why the Cakchiquel have left us a detailed illustration of their long-count chronological system while the Quiche have not. The isolated and problematic calendric citation in the C'oyoi document only further reveals the lack of a chronological character in the Quiche writings.

182. *Aj Xepach.* Other native accounts of the conquest mention Xepach as one of the first places in the Valley of Quezaltenango to offer resistance to the Spaniards (Recinos 1957:87; Gal 1963:26). The 3,000 warriors which Alvarado says attacked the Spaniards when they reached the highands (1948:457) were apparently from Xepach.

183. *tzalam costum or c'oxtum k'atibal.* "The sculptured stone buildings where judgment was pronounced." The reference here is to the civil function of structures which existed at the fortified centers. Modern municipal buildings in the Quiché area are called *K'atbal tzij* by the Indians.

A Case Study: *Título C'oyoi*

184. *ch'ich'*. "Iron, bronze metal." The term is applied to any metal object, and apparenty in this case the reference is to the metal rifles and cannons used by the Spaniards.

Page 36.

185. *Yaqui winak.* This is a reference to the Mexicans (Texcocans, Tlaxcalans, Mexican, Cholultecans) who aided the conquistadores in the conquest of Guatemala. The term Yaqui is widely used in the native documents of Guatemala to refer to peoples of Mexican or Toltec origin, who came in contact with the Quiche (in some areas, long before the conquest) (Recinos 1953:183; 200). By extension the term also designated certan weapons, presumably introduced by the Mexicans: "the lance, club, sword, and hatchet" (Brasseur 1862:28; Sáenz 1940). I have commented elsewhere on the possibe introduction of Mexican weapons into Guatemala (Carmack 1968:78-80). The word *Yaqui* itself is of Nahua origin, and means, "departed, or gone to some place" (Molina 1944).

186. *quisamajel xbe pa Q'uiche.* "The messenger went to Q'uiche." This same event is mentioned in the *Título Nijaib I*, where his title is given as *Ukalechij* (Recinos 1957:86).

187. *ta xiquin.* "Then (he was) attended to." *Xiquin* in its substantive form means, "ear" or "corner," but the verb form is apparently used here: "to listen, attend."

188. *Tecum Umam Rey Q'uiche Don Q'uik'ab.* Tecum is the national hero of Guatemala who was killed by the Spaniards in the battle over Quezaltenango (Anonymous 1963). Here we learn that he was the grandson (umam) of the Quiche ruler, and that his own title was *Rajpop Achij.* Apparently, at that time he was residing at Tzijbachaj, in the mountains near present-day Ixtahuacán.

189. *wukub k'ij xtelex.* "Seven days he was carried on their shoulders." Tecum was ceremonially carried about on a litter at Quiche for seven days, decorated with the most sacred symbols of the state. The *Título Huitzitzil Tzunun* also refers to the seven days during which he was *festejado* by the captains (Gall 1963:26).

190. *nima bi(x), xajaj cham cham.* "The great song and dance with flute (or drum)." This is again a reference to the

ceremony at Quiche in honor of Tecum, presented before he left to lead the Quiche warriors to war against the Spaniards.

Page 37.

191. *laju k'ob, julaju k'ob chi winak, juwinak belej lajuj....wi lakam*. This is a count of those accompanying Tecum: 10 × 400 (4,000), 11 × 400 (4,400), making 8,400 people, in addition to 20 + 19 (39) flagbearers (Brasseur 1961). This is the contingent which Tecum brought with him from Quiche. It perhaps corresponds to the army of 10,000, which the *Título Nijaib I* says Tecum organized from "many towns" (Recinos 1957:86).

192. *su' uk'o(jo)m*. "The drum instrument." *Su'* is said to mean, "clarinet," and *aj su'ab*, "musician" (Edmonson 1965). Some specific instrument may be implied here, but in the absence of further information, I will assume it to be a generic adjective applying to *k'ojom*, the hollow-log drum.

193. *ta xic'aja pa Bamlimaja(?)*. *Bamlimaja* (the writing is not clear) is apparently a toponym for a place near Quezaltenango. Perhaps *xic'aja* should be *xicaja*, "they carried (him) on their shoulders," and hence, a reference to this honor given to the great military lords.

194. *tok'ol wi banol labal*. "The warriors who are bled by piercing." This appears to be a continuation of the ritual by which the warriors prepared themselves for the imminent battle with the Spaniards.

195. *cachuwi*. *Chuwi* is a bag with 8,000 cacao beans in it, and is equivalent to the number 8,000 (the Aztec *Xiquipilli*); cachuwi would be 2 × 8,000, (16,000).

196. *cab(an)?yoc*. The meaning of *yoc* is given in the Sáenz dictionary as, "to lower the head as a sign of reverence" (1940). The warriors show signs of reverence before the lords by bleeding themselves.

197. *Ajuwila....* This is part of the same list of peoples situated around Utatlán given earlier in this document (Recinos 1953:236; 1957:55-61, 71-73).

Page 38.

198. *AjNajxit, AjAmak'Mes, AjPokoba AjK'ojomeb*. A contination of the list of peoples participating in the war

against the Spaniards. Najxit is a hamlet just north of Utatlán, where an impressive temple mound still stands. Amak' Mes was an Ilocab settlement which was probably located just northwest of Utatlán, and may now be identified by a hamlet of that name (Pamak'mes) within the territory of San Antonio Ilotenango. Pokoba, "shield," is the aboriginal name of Chimaltenango (Recinos 1957:73). *K'ojomeb* was apparently a settlement near modern Patzité (Edmonson 1965).

199. *Atzij Winak....* This is one of a list of the political offices of the Quiche state, which were also lineage positions. The offices of the major lineage components are listed here (cf. Recinos 1953:231; 1957:489)—Cawek, Nijaib, Ajaw Quiche, Quejnay, Cakoj Tamub, and Ilocab.

200. *Chwaraal nic'aj chaj.* "*Chwaraal*, in the middle of the pines." This same site is given in other native documents as the place where the decisive battle between the Quiche and Spaniards was fought (Gall 1963:26; Recinos 1957: 88-89). Situated about five kilometers east of present-day Quezaltenango, it is now known as Llanos de Pinal, "the plains of pine" (DGC, 1959; Gall 1963).

201. *chuwi, c'alab, uk'u.* "8,000, units of 20, units of 400." The authors explain that there were so many Quiche warriors that they could not be counted, either in units of 8,000, 20, or 400.

202. *xel wi ujolom uquej nima ajaw.* "The head of the horse of the great lord was taken off." This same incident, when Tecum cut off the head of Alvarado's horse, is repeated in the other native accounts of the conquest (Recinos 1957:90; Gall 1963:26). Alvarado does not mention this, though he states that the fighting was so tight that the Indians had crowded up to the very tails of their horses (1946:458).

Page 39.

203. *ch'ami chaal.* "The staffs and banners." Tecum was the leader of the army, including the banner-bearers.

204. *uyaa rib.* "Giving himself." Tecum enters into the fray, personally fighting as well as directing the Quiche army.

205. *raj xti.* "Wanted (caused?) to bite (like a mosquito)."

The meaning here must be that Tecum was pierced or stuck by Alvarado, though this is stretching quite far the grammatical meaning of raj.

206. *que i sac'a.* I am unsure of the meaning here because of the fragmentary nature of the document. The phrase might be, *quej sac'a,* "the trotting horses" (of the Spaniards).

207. *oxib corona.* "Three crowns." The authors of the *Título Nijaib I* state that Tecum wore "three crowns of gold, silver, diamonds, emeralds, and pearls" (Recinos 1957:90).

208. *k'uk' rismal.* "Quetzal feathered hair." The authors of the *Título Nijaib I* also comment on this, stating that Tecum was beautifully adorned with feathers (on his head), and that Alvarado was so impressed, he had the other Spaniards come and look at him after he had fallen (Recinos 1957:90). They then named the place "Quezaltenango," in memory of the quetzal feathers which adorned Tecum.

209. *nima k'ak' tepe.* "The great fire-mountain." This is apparently a reference to Volcán de Santa María (Excauul). Interestingly, the last part of the word is of Nahua derivation: *tepetl,* "mountain."

210. *Espiritu Santo.* "Holy Ghost (The Day of Pentecost)." The text places the death of Tecum on the Day of Pentecost, which is said to be the day when the first Indians of Quezaltenango were baptized, according to the *Título Nijaib I* (Recinos 1957:92). Gall (1963:9-13) has clarified the fact that the Day of Pentecost celebrated in 1529, not 1524, was the source of these traditions, for on that day the town of Quezaltenango was formally established under the vocation of the Holy Ghost.

Page 40.

211. *xcakar uwa k'ij chi caj rumal quic'.* "The sun became red because of the blood." The text goes on to state that so much blood was spilled that it turned the waters of the river red. The same tradition is contained in other native accounts, where we also learn that the river flowing southward from Olintepeque received its name, Quiq'uel, "the blood," at that time (Recinos 1957:91).

212. *xptia.* This is an abbreviated form of *Christianos.*

213. *c'o chirij rach camic Tecum.* "He accompanied from behind the dead Tecum." The C'oyoi lord, Nine Aj, died in battle with Tecum. The author of this account was related to that lord.

214. *xinalax wi pa ujebal, utz'akibal.* "I was born there in the beautiful place of stone buildings." We have a clear statement here that the lords resided within the walls of the fortified center. The author was a child when the Spaniards arrived, probably some 30 to 40 years earlier.

Page 41.

215. *(x)quik'oj quic'.* "They played the drum with rubber-tipped sticks." The drum was played when the Spaniards came to Baca. In some Quiché communities the drum (though not usually of the hollow log variety) is still used to signal festive occasions or important announcements.

216. *ma c'u jabi xcaj P^e xeximic.* I am uncertain about the meaning of the abbreviation, *P^e*. It connot be Pedro (de Alvarado), for he is always referred to as Don *P^o*. It later occurs following the words "(S)an Francisco" (page 51), suggesting that it might be an abbreviation for the "Padres" of the Franciscan order. The phrase would then read, "the Fathers did not want to tie them up." Apparently, there was a question of whether or not to tie up the Quiché lords in order to make them humble themselves before the Spaniards.

Page 42.

217. *Don Andrés de Chávez....Don Martín Mejía....K'ale Xc' ub, Don Juan....K'ale Rokche, Don....* The first three persons listed here are also given at the end of the *Título Nijaib I* (Recinos 1957:93); and in the *Título Huitzitzil Tzunun* it is claimed that they were among the first Indians baptized by the friars (Gall 1963:28). The K'ale Rokche would be a lord of the Ilocab branch of the Quiche, perhaps the Don Juan Gómez mentioned in the *Títulos Nijaib III* and *IV* (Appendices III, IV). In the *Título Nijaib I* the K'ale Xc'ub has the Christian name Don Domingo (Recinos 1957:90), whereas here the bearer of that title is Don Juan. The name and titles of the author's father were recorded here, but tears in the document deprive

us of all but the first and last part of his names and titles, Uk'ale ....C'oyoi. Since the title of the most prominent figure in document was Nine Aj, Uk'alechij, Martín Mejía, it seems likely that Don Martín was either the author's father or a very close relative. The author seems to have inherited these same titles (See Note 225).

Page 43.

218. *López (esc)ritorio....Andrés Vásquez.* The scribe appears to be the same Bartolomé López who transcribed the *Título Huitzitzil Tzunun* (Gall 1963). I find no Andrés Vásquez listed among the rulers at Quezaltenango in that document.

Inasmuch as the *Título Huitzitzil Tzunun* account was written in 1567 (Gall 1963:21), and many of the same persons listed in the C'oyoi document (including the scribe) are mentioned in it, we can be sure of the approximate time period in which it was composed—ca. 1550-1567.

219. *Toton(icapán).* From this point on, the narration is unintelligible.

Page 44.

220. *retal rulew tinamit.* "The boundaries of the territory of the fortified center." This part of the text appears to be a posthispanic recognition of the same boundary signs which are listed for the prehispanic period on pages 33 and 34.

221. *xiquin.* From this word on the fragment yields no coherent translation.

Page 45.

222. *pa Q'ui(che).* "At Q'uiche." This refers to the historical events which occurred at Utatlán, and gave rise to the C'oyoi ruling rights in the Quezaltenango area.

In the fragments below the piece of text which I have translated, parts of three Christian names can be detected: Don C...., Pedro Gómez, and Pedro La....

Page 46.

223. *oj nabe.* "We are the first." As with the preceding page of fragments, the text here may refer to the prehispanic period. However, we find evidence of postconquest references in the small fragments at the bottom of the page.

One of them contains the names (S)anta Cruz, and Alvarado. I have not included in the text several additional parts of words from other fragments of this page for they are unintelligible.

Page 47-56.

224. *Don Francisco.* Unfortunately, the rest of the titles and the name of this lord have been torn away, so that it is not possible to identify him with certainty. Speculatively, he might be identified with one of the two Franciscos, K'ale Xcona, and Utsamachij Xchapo, who were among the first baptized Indians from Quezaltenango (Gall1963:28).

225. *de Putanza.* From these fragments we learn that the instigator of the document was Juan Penonias de Putanza. In one place this was apparently stated outright, but the page is torn, and all that remains is, "I am Juan...." His title appears to have been Uk'alechij (page 54), so his full aboriginal names and title were Uk'alechij C'oyoi Zacorowach Quejnay.

226. *Don Juan (Cortés) Saknoy.* This lord from Quezaltenango, and most of the other witnesses are listed in the *Títulos Nijaib I*, and *Huitzitzil Tzunun* (Recinos 1957:93; Gall 1963:22). Racan(coj) must be Don Gerónimo K'ale Rakancoj (from the Buenabaj version of the *Nijaib I* document). Juan de Rojas was the grandson of the supreme ruler of the Quiche state at the time of the conquest, the Ajpop, Three Quej (Recinos 1950:241; 253; 244). Don Jorge is possibly the Jorge Nijaib, listed in the *Título Totonicapán* (Recinos 1950:241). The other lords, Juan Bautista, Don....Pérez, Francisco Gómez, may be identified with the "Batista," "Pérez," and "Gómez" calpules known to have existed at Quezaltenango shortly after the conquest (Appendix XX).

Appendices

APPENDIX I : Native Picture Writing as Described by Fuentes y Guzmán.

The following pictorial and its interpretation is from the second volume of Fuentes y Guzman's famous, *Recordación Florida* (1932-33:7:112; see Secondary Sources, Colonial Histories). The pictorial was placed immediately after his discussion of Pipil writing, and was introduced with these words: "....*porque para describir la vida del rey* Sinacam, *que era el que dominaba á* Cacchique, *á el tiempo de la conquista, usaron de la figura empresa que se propone*: [the pictorial]."

The following interpretation was then given by Fuentes y Guzmán: "*Con que para representar a* Sinacam, *pintaban un murciélago, que era el nombre ó la divisa, y armas, de semejante personaje, y para decir que era el Rey, puntaban una corona sobre la figura del murciélago, y los años de su reynado los representaban con aquellos guarismos, o caracteres, que parecen ceros en esta forma* ⊙*; y los que imperó aquel gran cacique parece que fueron nueve, las batallas en que venció, demuestran haber sido cinco, con este género de demostración, y parece que estas fueron cinco, luego en otra grada de aquella empresa, que es la segunda en orden, miradas del pavimento arriba, los partidos que sujetó y agregó á su dominio. Pero en la primera grada pintando un sombrero de que ellos no usaban en el tiempo de la gentilidad, dieron a conocer que fué dominado de la española bizarría; por donde podrá verse, y conocerse, si carecían de entendimiento....*"

APPENDIX II: Passages from *Título Nijaib II*.

The following is a translation of passages from the Nijaib II document based on the Quiche text (Recinos 1957:96ff), Recinos' trans-

---

Illustration: Native picture writing as described by Fuentes y Guzmán. Adapted from a drawing by Fuentes y Guzmán (1932-33:7:112).

lation of that text, and a translation of it now in possession of the
aldea San Vicente, municipio Santiago Momostenango (Carmack,
n.d. c.). I have altered the orthographic signs of the Quiche text
to make them correspond to usage explained in the introduction
to Primary Native Documents.

Quiché Text

Recinos 1957:98 ...*rumal kitzij utzuculiquil chic uc'ajol ajawab
xquekaya c'u chupam quik'alibal, zqueka c'u caj chupa c'u quim
roxo nim xilla, chupa c'u nima k'ij santa cecilia, xchikayao maquit-
zal bak, ubakil coj, ubakil balam, quich'amiy ruc' yachwachchim
puak xch'oc chiquiwach; are c'u rumal xquech'ap chwi quik'alelal
cajpopol xchiban c'ut quiposesion rumal e c'u chul amak' tinamit,
xqueoc wi tzam tak juyup, pa tak ciwan, xquebequic'ama wi xch'ey
pu c'u chwi waklajuj chi tz'ak xquibano cochoch cal, quic'ajol rumal
queje utzij ajaw don pedro alvarado donadiu chiwech e c'u chul amak'
tinamit....*

Recinos 1957:106 ....*xquiya puch ucuenta capitan oyew achij, xuyao
ucuenta chu k'ucumatz, chwa tepe; e ajilom chirech patan xquimolo-
ba c'ut xch'acom quixic chwach oxib chi corona, e c'o chupa tz'ak, chupa c'oxtum, cajaw xol ciwan, e aj ismachi' chi K'umarcaj, xk'at c'u
ubi tzij pa wi cajawal aj rabinaleb xtz'elej ubic chupa u juyubal xa
c'u utz'ak upatan, uc'ajol ruc' chij xk'at ubi chirij cajawalaj aj rabinaleb....*

Recinos 1957:110-112 ....*xeel chi c'u chiri, xeopon c'u xtemmaij wi
quiwach achijab ronojel xok'i pu xiwal siq'uibal quech jutzic'....xel
chi c'u chiri, xopon chi k'uki juyup uc'ulel tena chiri c'ute chi c'ace
wi wal nu c'ajol chuxic, jomaji' chi c'ut, xila bica culaja aj xelaju'
chu aj e pu aj xelajun quej, rumal xa junam coyewal cachajilal; xel
chi c'u chiri rilic cul k'ana puak; chwi ri juyup tzijbalchaj, tzijabalak
c'u xa juyub; ju wuk xc'oje chwi, xel chi c'u chiri xopon chupa quijuyubal, juyubal ak, chupan pa quijuyubal tis, chuwach aponak tziquiche
....xopon chi c'ut chupa quic'ulbat yoc canchebes chupa pu quic'-
ulbat, xq'ueje china c'u uk'ijil, ta xemin yoc canchebex; xpe c'u ajaw,
xeyajuj c'u aj tz'ol, aj tzununche' chu paxchun q'ueje wach k'imos
k'ab ajaw, chu tzam nima juyub, juyub c'ula juyub....*

Spanish Translation.

Recinos 1957:98 ...*porque de verdad son hijos de principales y los
ponemos en sus palacios, arriba en pajón en sillas de plumas adorna-
das, y el día de Santa Cecilia les damos lo que llaman el hueso ma-
quitzal, hueso de león, y hueso de tigre que les sirve de bastón, y las
coronas de plata que se les ponen en su frente, y los nombran por grandes
principales y caciques, que se llaman, K'alel, Ajpop. Y se les hace
la profesión porque son fundadores de las aldeas ordinarias y los pueblos, y que entraron por las laderas y cerros y quebradas, trayendo
vigas para hacer las 16 estructuras y casas de sus hijos y vasallos,*

porque así les mandó don Pedro de Alvarado a los de las aldeas y de los pueblos....

Recinos 1957:106 *....dando su cuenta el capitán que llaman valiente guerrero, ante al que llaman* K'ucumatz *y* Tepe, *que son los contadores de los tributos. Y juntaron lo que habían ganado, las plumas, ante los 3 coronados que están en el dorsal y palacio dentro del castillo, los señores de las barrancas, los de* Ismachi *en* K'umarcaaj. *Y les mandaron a los señores de* Rabinal *que habían de llevar entre las montañas y pagar su tributo y estar sujeto a pagar sus tributos en algodón, él y sus hijos y plebeyos de aquel pueblo de •*Rabinal....

Recinos 1957:110-112 *....y de allí se fueron y llegaron en un cerro que llaman* Tena; *y allí se juntaron todos los soldados y allí tocaron una bocina (concha) para llamarlos y juntarse en aquel lugar, que le pusieron el nombre de* Tena, *por haberse juntado a toda la gente y los soldados en aquel paraje.... Y se fue de allí y llegó a* K'uk'-ijuyup *que confronta con el cerro* Tena, *que allí buscarán la vida mis hijos y vasallos; en adelante que no sean perjudicados por los que llaman* K'ulaja, *que son los de Quezaltenango, porque el señor de ellos es tan valiente y digno de respeto como nosotros. Se fue y llegó en un cerro llamado* Tzijbalchaj, *y allí topó con el oro, y estuvo 7 días sobre el cerro; y paraje de las dantas, a un paraje que llaman* Tz'ic'ache....*Llegó entonces al mojón y lugar de los que llaman* Yoc K'anchebex. *Se tardaron mucho en esta ocasión; y después entraron a conquistar y echar a los* Yoc K'anchebex. *Llegó el señor, y les regañó a los guerreros y lanceros en* Paxchun, *ante* K'imox K'ab, *el cacique y señor del cerro grande, cerro* C'ulajuyub....

APPENDIX III: *Título Nijaib III*

The Quiche text of the document comes from the Archivo General de Centroamérica (Al:6074-54879). The Spanish translation is the result of my additions and modifications of a Spanish version located in the alcaldía indígena (Auxiliatura) of municipio Santiago Momostenango (see Carmack 1967). I have modified the orthography of the Quiche text.

Quiché Text.

Wacamic cakatiquiba retal wae ulew rech ajaw don franco Itzquin Nejaib yic' u yic' ayaw Itzquin; queje cubij impormacion kitzij rech ri ulew quech'a conojel ajawab kitzij re uyic' uch'acom ajaw Itzquin rumal queje cubij titulo probanza are c'u rumal; achikaban quitor chirech ajaw Itzquin ri ulew yic 'chikawach konojel oj ajawab rajawal Quiche quewek, Nejaib, Ilocab, Roxche, in ajaw Don Pedro Chi Ilocab, in aj Santa Antun Ilocab, in ajaw Allso Gomez Uz, aj Chiquimula, aj Tzolojche, in ajaw Don Oxorio Cortes, Saknoy Isuy, aj Xelaju, ruc' chiquiwach aj palotz aj sakibalja.

Katzij rech ri ulew ri yic' ri xcuch wi ri tinamit aj utzakibala aj pa-
lotz, are xcuchu utinamit ri Don Franco Itzquin Nejaib cuchul tina-
mit, ruc' ajaw Don Juo Basquez Roxche Ilocab cuchul tinamit, are
c'u rumal xchikachiquiba retaxic wae ulew rech ajaw Don Franco
Itzquin; xchiticaric retaxic chu pachalib, requen quitinamit aj Chi-
quimula, aj Tz'oloche; xel c'u etabal chiri xopon chuchi' nima' Xiquin
Chila; xel chi c'u etabal chiri xopon pa Ak'a; xel xchi c'u etabal chiri
xopon ibayal pa tapal pa chanim, chi c'u utz'ak Tuja ajaw aj Tz'iquin-
aja' achi, chuchi' ya nima ja', tz'ukubal car; xopon wi ri yic' tz'uku-
bal car ajaw Don Francisco Itzquin e quieb chi ajawab Don Juan
Gomez e aj utzakibala; xpakmayij c'u ulok' chuchi' nima' tujala,
xul c'u etabal chiri xul chuchi' quiyik' yoc k'anchebex tz'icol chu pa-
chalu uxalcatja', cuc'ul wi rib chi nimak' ja'; uchi' ya c'ut xpe culok'
xul chirij c'usmak', chiri c'ute xbe nu waram chupam juwinak' jun
k'ij xawi etabal chiri.

Xcha' c'u ajaw Don Juan Gomez Rok'che aj utzakibala chirech ajaw
Don Francisco Izquin Nejayib, xatachibeticar ulok' retaxic ulew chila'
chuchila utzakibalja', c'ut pakmayij c'u ulok'; xchiquitzij e c'u e oj
je' ajawab utzbala lal aj ...xaja c'ut ajaw Tziquin; ma pa mixetata
otuk chi mil ruc' ox c'al chi etabal ri yik' lal ajaw Izquin; uj aj tzo-
laj tz'ununche xech'a c'ut xopon c'u chu chi ri ja' palotz utzakibala
xeq'uik'ab juyub; xpakmayij c'u la retaxic ulew, xul wi caj juyub
...chuchi' nima ciwan; xpe chi c'u a...capa aj xech'o cha uchi chun
xul uk'...xetzolk'omij....ulok' etabal chu K...ri xo...on chi c'ut
pa tz'icache; xel chi c'u eta...xopon chi c'ut waliic ixok' abaj ri
c'u etabal chiri xoponic chuch....

Wae cubij titulo probanza jecutorio fiel jecutorio rumal are ri qui
tzij e kanan amak; queje inpormazion mixquiyao chirij titulo pro-
banza e yoc k'anchebex chiquiwach nejaibab, chiquiwach i(l)ocab rok'-
che, chiquiwach puch ajawab q'uiche winak'; mixuya u tzij yoc k'an-
chebex q'uizol; mixquicajo xalcatja' chiri c'u temiska wi ju etabal
xalcaj ja rech ulew ix uyik' ajaw Don Franco Izquin aj utzabala
aj palotz qui c'ulbat; cumari ulew xebal....mi c'u xpe ulok' etabal
...patzalic mixpetic quebetabala xol queban....ruc' ri cabaxolacul
quicoxon xe cabe chi quetabal chiri cul c'u chiri sakcolaj cabawilal
chiri c'ute mixul wi etabal quitexena wi ajawab; chi nimajel c'ache
winak' ruc' mam tz'icol xban c'u jun nima conbitar.

C'ate cajawal xe am...mal ajaw Don...quin xchiquetabal chiri....
yik' yoc k'anchebex; xtzolk'omaj chi in ulok' xul chi quetabal chiri
chwi wa k'iribal cakixa; xpe chi quetabal chiri xul chirij paxchun
juyub; xchiquetabal chiri, xul chirij tena; xpe chiquetabal chiri, xul
chwi juyub q'uixal k'ak'i juyub, relebal....wa puak.

Wacamic c'ut xchikabano wi ronojel chirij wa ulew yik' u yik' ajaw
Don Franco Itzquin ruc' ajaw Don Juan Gomez Rok'che Ilocab, ru-
mal mixkil chikawach chi nima ronojel oj ajawab, rumal queje cubij

titulo probanza, uj jujun chi nima kajawab xchijun chi tinamit, ka juicio c'u retal wae...lo probanza; taza chok' chupam olajuj...rajilabal ic' junio ruc' junab 1542 años. Wacamic Xchikal...kapirma chi nima konojel ajuwab. Don Juo Oxorio Cortés Saknoy, aj xelaju'; Don Pedro Gomez....k chi ilocab rok'che, aj Sant Antun; Allso Gomez Utz ajaw Chiquimula, aj tz'olojche; Don Juo Gomez Rok'che, ajpalotz, ajtzukibala; ruc' ch'ajcar chic ajawab aj Mumustenango; ....mo don Franco Itzquin yikoy ulew ajpalotz ajutzakibala, yic' a rech ulew, yik' rij lotz utzakibalab. Bartolome Lopez, unum quiescribano.

Spanish Translation:

Hoy comenzamos a señalar esta tierra del señor Don Francisco Izquin Nijaib, poderoso señor Izquin; ciertamente así dice el informe de tierra, dicen todos los señores de la conquista, gananza del señor Izquin, porque así dice el Título y probanza por él; haremos auditor por el señor Izquin, conquistador de tierras, delante de nosotros, todos los señores, señores de los Quiché; Cawek, Nijaib, Ilocab; yo el señor Rok'che, Don Pedro Chilocab de San Antonio Ilocab; yo el señor Alonso Gómez Utz de Chiquimula Tz'olojche'; yo el señor Don Osorio Cortés Saknoy Iswi de Xelajú; con la presencia de los señores de Palotz y Tzakibalja.

De verdad, es conquistador de la tierra, que juntó por aquí al pueblo de Palotz-Utzakibala, Don Francisco Izquin Nijaib juntó al pueblo, pone en orden (?) al pueblo; con el señor Don Juan Vásquez Rok'che Ilocab pone en orden (?) al pueblo. Por él fijaremos un tiempo para medir esta tierra del señor Don Francisco Izquin. Empezamos a medir en un paraje que llaman Pachalib, abajo del pueblo de los de Chiquimula, que llaman Tz'olojche'. Y de allí corrió la medida y llegó junto al río que llaman Xiquin Chila. Y de allí corrió la medida y llegó en un paraje que llaman Ak'a, y de allí corrió la medida y llegó a Pabojal, Patapal, Pachalim, junto a los edificios Tuja del señor Tz'iquinaja' Achi, junto a un río grande donde pescaban y sacaban pescado para el cacique Don Francisco Izquin; hasta allí llegó lo que conquistó, los dos con Don Juan Gómez que se llamaban de Tzakibala. Y vino subiendo junto al río Tujala', y llegó a la medida junto a los de Balamja', otra banda del río. Y de allí vino la medida, y llegó al señorío de los Yoc K'anchebex Tz'icol en Pachalum, donde se juntan los ríos grandes. Y de allí vino por el río y llegó detrás del C'uxmak, y allí se durmieron, al cabo de 21 días llegó la medida allí.

Y dijo el principal, Don Juan Gómez Rok'che de Utzakibala al cacique y señor, Don Francisco Izquin que llaman Nijaib, que se fueran a empezar a medir las tierras allá en Chilotz Utzakibalja', y subieron por aquí. Así nos dicen los señores Utzbala, vosotros de.... xaja y el señor Izquin. Y, acaso no se han medido 2.060 cuerdas

que Vosotros, señor Izquin, que habéis conquistado? Nosotros somos
Tz'oloj Tz'unumche' *dijeron unos a los otros. Y llegaron junto al*
río Palotz Utzakibala' *bajo el cerro* Q'uik'ab. *Y de allí vino subien-*
do y llegó a la medida del cerro....a la orilla de una barranca grande;
y de allí vino la medida arriba del pueblo de los de Totonicapán y
los de Xoch'o *al paraje que llaman* Chuchichun. *Y dieron vuelta la*
dicha medida por donde pone el sol, y vino detrás del C'uxmak, *y de allí*
corrió la medida y llegó en Tz'icache. *Y de allí corrió la medida*
y llegó en un paraje que llaman Walic Ixok Abaj; *allí llegó....*

Esto dice el título, probanza, y ejecutoria fiel, porque son las palabras
de nuestros padres de los cantones; así, es la información que dieron
sobre el título y probanza de los Yoc K'anchebex *delante de los* Nijaib,
los Ilocab Rok'che, *y los señores* Q'uiche Winak. *Entonces habló*
el Yoc K'anchebex Q'uizol. *Bajaron a la unión de los ríos, aquí*
en el temascal, el mojón, la unión de tierras del conquistador señor
Don Francisco Izquin, de Utzabala Palotz, (son) sus mojones. Fué
a recibir el terreno bajo...entonces vino la medida...por un lado,
viene su medida entre...con el Cabaxolacul, *su caja (?); va su me-*
dida aquí, llega junto a Sakcolaj Cabawilal; *después llegó la medida*
todavía con los principales. Con los principales Q'uiche Winak *y*
los Mam Tz'icol *fue hecha una gran celebración.*

Después, los señores....el señor Don Izquin *siguen con la medida*
aquí....junto a las tierras de los Yoc K'anchebex. *Allí dió vuelta*
y llegó la medida al principio del río Cakixa; *y de allí vino la medida*
y llegó aquí en el cerro Paxchun; *y aquí llegó la medida detrás de*
Tena; *y vino la medida aquí, llegó sobre el cerro* Q'uixal, K'akijuyub.

Y ahora escribimos este auto sobre estas tierras conquistadas por el
cacique Don Francisco Izquin *y el señor Don Juan* Gómez, Rok'che
Ilocab, *porque lo hemos visto entre todos nosotros los principales,*
porque así dice el título y probanza. Hoy 15 de junio de 1542 años,
y lo firmamos entre nosotros todos los principales. Don Juan Osorio
Cortés Saknoy, *de Quezaltenango. Don Pedro Gómez* Ilocab Rok'che,
de San Antonio. Alonzo Gómez Utz, *señor de Chiquimula* Tz'olojche'.
Don Juan Gómez Rok'che, *de Palotz Utzakibala, con los demás se-*
ñores de Momostenango. Firma Don Francisco Izquin, *conquista-*
dor de las tierras de Palotz Utzakibala. Bartolmé López, Unum,
su escribano.

APPENDIX IV: *Título Nijaib IV*

The Spanish translation comes from the Archivo General de Centroamérica (Al:18:6074-54884). Except for minor grammatical changes,
the original version is retained.

"Aquí comienzan los títulos y probanzas de los caciques y prin-
cipales de los pueblos que abajo se van citando, compuestos én el idio-

ma Achí y rubricado por su escribano público en el año de 1505; y al presente sacados en el original que queda en romance y en el idioma Achí.

Romance. Nombres de sitios, purujes y lugares señalados de nuestros antepasados, bisabuelos y abuelos nuestros. Primeramente Quebek y Nejaib antiguo Izquin, principales y antiguos caciques. Estos dos principales fueron los que mandaron que se recogieran todos para venir a pelear a estas tierras que eran de indios Mames, nombrados los calpules Yoc K'anchibixes, Bamak', Nimabamak', e Tzixoles. Estos sabían de una y otra lengua a lo cual mandamos referir a los de Santa Cruz Utatlán y a los de Momostenango por las hazañas de Don Francisco Izquin. Yo Don Quebek y Don Nejaib por tener experimentado la hazaña y valentía de dicho Don Francisco Izquin; por el tanto suplicamos nosotros los del paraje de Otzoya a estos tres reyes se nos libran títulos... Por la presente volvemos a referir la posesión de dicho Don Francisco y de su hermano Don Juan Izquin y de los dichos Don Quebek y Don Nejaib, y los damos por nuestros nombres las cabezas de los dichos lugares y pueblos. Y juntamente dada por nuestro monarca los títulos que se van refiriendo de una y otra parte a dichos capitanes y dada por nosotros, Don Juan Cortés. Y para que certifique ser verdad así van los nombres de cada lugar y paraje; en primer lugar Satzol tzununche, Ajwila, Ajchuimal, Aj Rok'obala tziquin, Aj tzaquibalja, Ajxok'bakiej, Ajtemaj y los 18 pueblos nombrados Ajpatiqui, Ajchobolo, Ajk'ak' olkiej, Culchip, Cabrakam, Tzak'ijk'ak', Nimajpu, Raxaja, Tucurub, Coyoy, Sak'corowuach, Uxek'i, Uxeoj, Amak' Ajsakmolob, Ajtabil, Ajkiyak'ak abaj, Najxit, Makmet, Pok'oba, K'ojomeb, Ajchichalib, Tzutubaja, Ajsack'inom. Estos son los parajes, lugares y pueblos que ganó el referido Don Francisco, con más otros Ajtucurub, Kajbon, Yitzal... Aquí fue donde quitaron estos capitanes el oro, la plata y demás tesoros y joyas que tenían; en donde se experimentaron sus esforzados valores; y se pasaron a otro paraje llamado K'alchak' donde entraron destrozando, en este paraje. Allí también mostraron sus esforzados valores con sus soldados, en donde también quitaron cuanto tenían. Dieron parte al paraje que se sigue Quiché por todo lo que habían gandado; y de allí se pasaron al paraje de Rabinal y con los de Cubulco, donde hallaron las minas de plata; en el paraje de Rabinal, allí fue donde quitaron (el) tesoro (que) habían cogido. Y después vinieron a dar al Quiché a dar parte de lo que traían a los reyes cabezas del lugar, en donde se les devolvió cuanto habían ganado en recompensa de las hazañas ante los principales y cabezas, que son Don Iki Balam, Don Majocotaj, Don Balam Ak'ab y Don Balam Quiché. Aquí fue(ron) todas (las) cuentas y la cuenta que dió el capitán valeroso, en donde dijo el referido que pagasen tributos ante los tres coronados que gobiernan esos parajes nombrados por la barranca, en donde les amonestaron que en breve tiempo les mandasen lo amonestado. Se volvieron a sus lugares y esto sucedió *ante Don* Iki Balam *coronado, Don* Majocotaj *y Don* Balam Ak'ab. *Estos eran los tres reyes....Y al tiempo de despedirse estos capitanes de los tres coronados les respondieron que no tan luego dispusieron tal viaje, que entre 3 ó 4 días se habían a sus lugares que nos obedecieran. Respondieron que sí, obedecían al mandato que nuestros superiores y los demás cabezas de todas las parcialidades obedientes a todo cuanto nos mandaren. Aquí fue donde les hicieron una gran función y una gran veneración a los dichos capitanes por sus honores y famas, que se tardaron 8 días en la función que hicieron estos 3 coronados al dicho* Izquin *y sus capitanes y a los dichos de* Otzoya Mam *y a sus capitanes de arcos y flechas. Aquí fue el esmero y agradecimiento de estos coronados por el registro de plantas y tierras y por montañas y barrancas, pues les costó a todos ellos su trabajo, por el tanto, les dieron sus parabienes y les fueron señalando sus parajes, lugares y sitios de una y otra parte como estos de* Otzoya, *y a los dichos Don Francisco* Izquin *y sus hermanos y a todos sus capitanes....*

Auto. En el nombre de nuestra Real Corona, yo el primero Don Iki Balam, *Don* Majocotaj, *Don* Balam Ak'ab, *los tres reyes que gobiernan el paraje de Santa Cruz Quiché, damos en nuestros nombres a Don* Quebek *y a Don* Nejaib *y a los calpules nombrados* Yoc, K'anchibix, Tzisol, Bamak', Nima Bamak', *el cual capitán Don* Quebek, *quien gobierna todos estos sitios, lugares y parajes de la Mamería. Hoy 20 días del més de Marzo en el año de 1501 dámosle a Don* Quebek *títulos, egidos de sus tierras para todos sus parajes que las gocen mientras Dios fuere Dios, y la licencia adquerida de nuestro monarca* Montesuma, *que por sus mandatos reales mojoneamos dichas tierras de Don* Quebek, *sus sitios y lugares, juntamente con las de Don* Francisco Izquin, *capitán y cabeza de los parajes de Momostenango. Y porque en adelante conste, firmamos y lo rubricamos ante los caballeros testigos, que son Don Juan Cortés cabeza del paraje de Santa Cruz Quiché, y Don Martín del mismo Quiché; Don Juan Perez* Chilocab *cabeza de San Antonio; Don Juan Osorio* Saknoy *y Don Martín Megía, cabezas de Quezaltenango; y de todos los mas principales de Santa Cruz Quiché, y lo firmo por todos. Escribano público, Francisco Hernández.*

Egidos. Por cuanto nosotros los 3 reyes coronados que gobiernan los lugares de Santa Cruz Quiché dámosle a los dichos capitanes a quienes por sus hazañas y valentías, que son Don Quebek *y Don* Nejaib, *nombrados del paraje de* Otzoya, *a quienes damos título y posesión de sus egidos. Y por medida y vista de ojos empiezan desde el paraje de* Sak'ol ajcabawil abaj, *aquí fue donde llegaron a ver alto con Don Francisco* Izquin *y Don Juan su hermano, y (el) paraje donde les hizo un gran convite el dicho Don Francisco a los capitanes de* Otzoya; *de aquí partieron y fueron a dar al paraje de San Sija; y de aquí fueron caminando para el sur, y llegaron a un volcán que le llaman, el* Excanul, *y en* Twipach; *y de aquí caminamos para abajo, pasando por el paraje de San Luís como cosa de 2 leguas, hay "*

piedrones con 2 cruces en cada una de ellas; y de aquí se partieron
hasta el mar, siempre siguiendo el río de Nagualate; *allí donde hace*
una comba hicieron alto para después siempre del mar caminando
para el poniente hasta llegar a los parajes nombrados Mazatan; *y*
de allí salieron y entraron en los parajes de Naguadecat; *de aquí*
salieron caminando para hacia el norte arriba en los parajes Ayude-
cat, *donde llegan los parajes y poblaciones de los dichos capitanes*
nombrados de Otzoya, *para que él a cada poblado o paraje de estos*
de su jurisdicción les vaya señalando y amojonando de cada lugar o
paraje y reconociendo cada uno lo que es suyo. Por en cuanto le supli-
camos cumpla lo referido en toda su parcialidad, proceda y cumpla
por mandado de nuestro monarca, para que los gocen él y sus here-
deros y los hijos de estas 3 reales Coronas, que cumplan los dichos
capitanes con su obligación, y que los gocen por igualmente, hijos
y herederos mientras Dios fuere Dios. Dámosle los títulos reales,
firmados por nuestros nombres y dados por nuestros capitanes y por
las cabezas de cada parcialidad de Santa Cruz del Quiché, San Antonio,
Tzolojche, *nombrado* Chiquimula. *Y damos firmados por nosotros*
3 coronados y por el dicho Don Francisco Izquin, *y Don Juan Iz-*
quin, *y por Don Juan Gómez* Rok'che, *por Don Juan Osorio Cortés*
Saknoy, *y por Don Pedro Gómes* Aj Chilocab *de San Antonio, y Don*
Alonso Gómez Rok'che Aj Polotz Ajaw Tzquibala, *y por todos los*
calpules de esta nuestra provincia, y cabezas de los lugares, y en el
nombre de nuestro monarca, y de los 3 reyes coronados. Y porque
consta, lo firmo por todos, yo el escribano público, Don Bartolomé
López."

APPENDIX V: Map and Postscript to the *Título Sacapulas*.

The map and small document appear to have originally been attached to the *Título Sacapulas*, and are now part of the collection
of the Archivo General de Centroamérica. I have altered the orthographic signs of the Quiche text to make them conform to standard
usage. The translations into Spanish are mine.

Sacapulas Map (AGC, A1:337-7091).

The map consists of three concentric rings, the outermost of which
is partitioned into 28 sections. Each section has an inscription,
and so have the two inner rings. There is a small explanation in
the upper left section of the map.

Quiche Text.

(Inscription at the upper left section) *Nawal winak wae waral*
nabe xojul wi ulok chumul k'ak' e kakajaw xawi are xel chi wi ta xel
ubic ta xetzalejic nabe wae uxerulic upetic xutiquiba wi uyuk'uxic
juyub tak'aj.

(Inscription in the innermost ring) *Esta posesión se llama re-
cumbalación tiro a tiro donde empieza ahí se acaba número uno; número 28 perteneciente a esta medida destas tierras que costó a este
título viejo de 1151 (1551?) año en el idioma lengua Quiche.*

(Inscription in the thin middle ring) *Xa wi c'u ri xuc'....apa-
nok chumul ubi ri xoc wi ulok ri muul chumul k'ak' kakajaw chuch
..ic....*

(Inscription in each of the 28 sections of the outermost ring,
beginning with the first section which also has above it, *nabe etamabal*, "first information".)

1. *nuul ubi juyub nabe xitiquiba wi uyuk'uxic—xkaj c'u ulo xe-
   juyub xwinakir ja xec'oje wi.*
2. *ucam ubi juyub chic xico uwi ulok chiri.*
3. *rox xkaj ulok chuxe chicotz c'o chun chiri wacamic c'o muxul
   chiri chuchi ja.*
4. *ucaj etamabal xol pujil c'o muxul chiri caib c'o wi c'o ukajibal
   abaj.*
5. *roo etamabal choy juyub c'u xol sak coral ubi c'o chun chiri ruc'
   muxul.*
6. *waka k'ak' etamabal xoc ulok pa kolok'om luego chun chiri quej
   e komal winak.*
7. *wuk etamabal xoc ulok chwi muxyac lajab c'o muxul chiri jun
   quej e kom winak jun quej toltecat.*
8. *wajxak etamabal chwi cotz juyub c'o mux chiri quech toltecat.*
9. *ubelej etamabal setesic xak xakan wi ulok c'o chiri.*
10. *ulajuj etamabal xicoy chwi juyub muchulic abaj ubi cakmway
    ubi.*
11. *ujulajuj etamabal jun chic juyub sesecon quej chuchaxic ajaw
    sakil ubi.*
12. *ucab lajuj etamabal chwi pok balam c'o chiri.*
13. *urox laj etamabal chwi nima che mixule ulok xulan upetic.*
14. *ucajlaj etamabal chitepero mixculun wi.*
15. *rolajuj etamabal xpapal chwach cruz.*
16. *uwaklaj etamabal chi juyub abaj patz'ak.*
17. *wuklaj etamabal chwi wisilabaj.*
18. *wajxaklaj etamabal chi k'apoj.*
19. *ubelejlaj etamabal chwi pacruz.*
20. *ujuwinak etamabal chwi atzam amak'aleb.*
21. *ujuwinak jun etamabal chwi ul chwa cruz.*
22. *wae chi c'ut pa tz'ak xetocoy ipan i....*
23. *tzam chila c'am c'ux ubi juyub 23 etamabal.*
24. *chwi c'ut k'ana abaj 24 etamabal.*
25. *chwi c'ut lawibal seb juyub.*
26. *chwi s..maj c'ajol.*
27. *chwi (c)ajbab ch'ulel cunen.*
28. *ta xel aponok xopon c'ut pa xichal xopon sak c'ujel.*

Spanish Translation.

(Inscription at the upper left section) *"Estos son los hombres mágicos; llegamos aquí antiguamente, el* Chumul K'ak *(Conejo de Fuego), (y) nuestros padres; así, salió de allí, salió y regresó antiguamente; esta es la llegada, la venida, (cuando) se comenzó a sujetar a las montañas y los planos."*

(Inscription in the middle ring) *"Entonces, solo la cabeza que ....afuera llamado* Chumul *(el Conejo) que entró allí en el montón, el* Chumul K'ak *(Conejo de Fuego), nuestro padre, (así) se dice....*

(Inscription in the 28 sections of the outermost ring)

1. *Nuul (mi venida) es el nombre del cerro donde antiguamente se comenzó la sujeción—bajó entonces debajo del cerro allí a* Xwinakir Ja *(se brotaba el agua).*
2. *Segundo (es) otro cerro allí que se llama* Xico *(gavilán?).*
3. *El tercero, se bajó debajo de* Chi Cotz *(en las flores), donde hoy hay cal, hay un baño (?) allí al lado del río.*
4. *El cuarto informe,* Xol Pujil *(entre lo podrido), donde hay baño, y segundo hay una piedra pendiente.*
5. *Quinto informe, entonces (es) el cerro de agua llamado* Xol Sak Coral *(entre el corral blanco), hay cal allí, y un baño.*
6. *Sexto informe de fuego, entró allí por* Ko Lok'om *(loro? comprado), hay cal allí, el venado de los* Komal *(los de caña).*
7. *Séptimo informe, entró arriba de* Mux Yac Lajab *(trampa del tigre que nada), hay baño allí, un venado de ·los* Kom(al), *un venado de los* Toltecat.
8. *Octavo informe, arriba de* Cotz Juyub *(cerro de flor), hay un baño allí de los* Toltecat.
9. *Noveno informe, está* Setesic Xak *(peñasco redondo), subió allí.*
10. *Décimo informe,* Xicoy *(?) arriba del cerro llamado* Muchulic Abaj *(piedra desconsolada), llamado* Cak Meway *(ayuno fuerte).*
11. *Undécimo informe de otro cerro* Xesecon Quej *(bajo el olfato del venado), se dice por nombre* Ajaw Sakil *(señor blanco).*
12. *Duodécimo informe, está arriba de* Pok Balam *(arena de jaguar).*
13. *Décimo tercio informe, arriba del* Nima Che *(árbol grande), donde tocó la flauta (cuando) llegó, (cuando) vino.*
14. *Décimo cuarto informe de* Chi Tepe(ro) *(en el monte?), donde lo encontraron.*
15. *Décimo quinto informe donde se paró delante de la* Cruz.
16. *Décimo sexto informe,* Chi Juyub Abaj *(en el cerro de piedra) en la estructura.*
17. *Décimo séptimo informe arriba de* Wisil Abaj *(piedra del mensajero).*
18. *Décimo octavo informe,* Chi K'apoj *(en la señorita).*
19. *Décimo noveno informe, arriba de* Pa Cruz *(en la Cruz).*
20. *Vigésimo informe, arriba de* Atzam Amak'aleb *(sal de los pueblitos).*
21. *Vigésimo primer informe, arriba de* Ul *(llegar), arriba de la* Cruz.

22. *Este está en la estructura,* Xetocoy Ipan (*bajo la avispa,   ?*).
23. *Vigésimo tercer informe, allá en el punto del cerro llamado* C'am C'ux (*recibir dolor?*).
24. *Vigésimo cuarto, arriba de* K'ana Abaj (*piedra amarilla*).
25. *Arriba del cerro,* Lawibal Seb (*dobladura cerrada*).
26. *Arriba de* S..maj C'ajol (? *el hijo*).
27. *Arriba de* Cajbab Ch'ulel (*sacrificio de suciedad*) *de* Cunen.
28. *Entonces salió afuera y llegó a* Pa Xichal (*en lo sucio*), *llegó a* Sak C'ujel (*troje? blanca*).

Postscript. (AGC, Al:337-7091).

Quiche Text.

"*Waral mixkatz'ibaj wi quic'olem kamam kakajaw ojer winak, nawal winak chi k'ekumal chi ak'abil; ajaw chumul k'ak' ajaw xkanil ajaw toltecat ajaw can zakitzol ubi, chuchaxic; xecha e kawixal kacutamil; upetic puch kacolom chi k'ij, oj tultecat, oj c'o wacamic; uyaic juyub tak'aj uyuk'uxic c'ut cumal caib nawal winak queuchaxic, ta xquetaj ronojel juyub tak'aj ta xquicoj pu retal; mawi xalok xebinic juluc xc'oje mumus tz'ak cumal e nabe winak; ri biba xkatz'ibaj mixkaban peresasion chi ruj juyub ta kaj xebin wi ta xquiyuk'uj juyub tak'aj mixac titulo mibaxkatz'ibaj nabe xoc ulok muul ulew xutiquiba wi uyuk'uxic i.. kaj wi ulok chuwi chicotz xecruz jusuc xwinakir atzam om.... xbe wi chakaja aponok ta xkaj c'u ulok xawibakalaj xak'an ulok ta xkaj wi ulok; xawi mixkatz'ibaj wi juyub xak'an wi; ta ukajic c'ut chila ajsic pa k'eka ulew ta xkajic ta xopon chila pa tz'ak inop xelab xetocoy chuchaxic; ta xak'an c'ut chuwach juyub lakam abaj; ta xel ulic c'ut xbe urikari xoc wi ulok muul tz'ak; ta utzalejic xya k'umaja chic juyub tak'aj cumal xchomachic retal ronojel; ta xtzalejic ta xequic'ama xcachbilaj pu ulok quiquial winakil; ta culic quipetic puch ronojel ri winak chak'acho palow; queje c'ut cach petic conojel winak xawi cul quicabawil, ta xepetic ruc' jun can saketzal ajaw ubi chuchaxic; cachbilam ta xepetic; mana c'o ta xquitzucuj waral; ma jabi c'a chila omuch inop omuch cakja ubi juyub ta xepetic c'a chila; c'ut xepe wi chak'acho chak'apalo xa xecojena chiri oomuch inop oomuch cakja; xecojena chiri ta xepetic chumul k'ak' e kakajaw; queje usuc'uliquil mixtz'ibax wi, ruc' puch xawi queje baxal c'ulbat xawi bakalaj; usuc'uliquil ronojel ta c'o alachinak chi banoy chaoj chuxapanok waral; c'ut chil wi chetamax wi usuc' uliquil chajix lax c'ut chiquiwach e uc'ulel ajchaoj cumal k'ana winak; nabe c'ut chuc'ut retal ulew ri ajchaoj we alachinak chibanoy chaoj cojcha oj ajawab; are uc'ojeic kamam kakajaw ojer puch quik'ij e kawinakil e mama e tata ti e wixal e ucutamil toltecat c'o wacamic.*"

Spanish Translation

"*Aquí hemos escrito sobre la existencia de nuestros abuelos y padres, la gente antigua, la gente* nawal, *en la oscuridad y la noche; el señor*

Chumul K'ak (*Conejo de Fuego*) *el señor* Xkanil (*Cabrito*), *el señor* Toltecat, *y el señor* Can Sakitzol (*Serpiente de Plumas Alumbrantes*), *se llaman, así se decía, son nuestros progenitores; (escribimos de) la venida de nuestro tronco y la salvación, la gloria de nosotros, los Tolteca, nosotros que hoy existimos; se dieron cuando las montañas y los planos fueron conquistados por los 2 hombres* nawales, *se les dice; cuando organizaron todo el mundo, cuando fijaron los mojones; no viajaron en vano, porque establecieron estos primeros hombres las murallas y los edificios; la razón porque hemos escrito esto es que hemos posesionado estas montañas y planos, al tiempo en que viajaron aquí, cuando conquistaron las montañas y los planos; el título lo escribimos antes (cuando) vino aquí el montón de tierra, cuando se comenzó la conquista; se bajó por aquí sobre* Chicotz (*en las flores*), *bajo la cruz, directamente donde se brinda la salina. . . . se fué al otro lado del río; luego se bajó por un corto tiempo, y se subió, y luego se bajó; así hemos pintado la montaña donde se subió; entonces se bajó allí arriba de la tierra lodosa y llegó allí en la estructura de ceiba, en* Xelab (*debajo del oráculo*) *y* Xetocoy (*debajo de la avispa*) *se dice; entonces se bajó ante el monte* Lakam Abaj (*piedra de bandera*); *entonces se salió, y va a la estructura amontonada; entonces regresa y da con* K'umaja (*casa podrida*), *ya en las montañas y los planos donde está el mojón que se puso por todos ellos; entonces regresaron, los acompañaron amistosamente; llegaron y vinieron también toda la gente del otro lado del mar; así juntos vinieron todos; también sus dioses llegaron cuando vinieron con un señor llamado* Can Saketzal *se dice que juntos vinieron; no buscaban este lugar; no había aquí las 400 ceibas, y las 400 casas rojas, que así se llamaban los montes cuando vinieron aquí; vinieron del otro lado del mar, del otro lado del agua; vivieron allí en las 400 ceibas, las 400 casas rojas; vivieron allí cuando vinieron* Chumul K'ak', *los poderosos señores; así, ciertamente se pintó también todos los mojones de cal y relleno; entonces estaban los que hacen disputas fuera de aquí; se verá, se conocerá, ciertamente se guardará por los testigos ante los enemigos, los que hacen disputas; primero entonces al lado del mojón de tierras de los de las disputas, los que hacen disputas, decimos, nosotros los señores; esta es la existencia de nuestros abuelos y padres, en los días antiguos; es nuestra gente, nuestros abuelos y padres, los progenitores, el tronco de los Toltecas que existen hoy en día.*"

APPENDIX VI: *Título Paxtoca.*

The document begins with the words, "*Memoria de la Conquista y Títulos de mojones, Paxtoca*" (AGC, Al:6074-53386). It has never been published, though I included an extract of it in my doctoral dissertation (Carmack n.d.c.), and Crespo recorded the entire Spanish text in his thesis (Crespo n.d.). The following extracts were taken from the text in the Guatemalan Archives. A few grammatical changes have been made for clarity.

"*Don Alonzo Pérez de Torres, que llaman por sobrenombre* Excamparitz, *que vivió en el lugar de la tierra que se llama* Paxtoca.... *Estos fueron los principales y caciques que fueron ante el Capitán Don Pedro de Alvarado,* Tonatiuh....*que fuesen asentados sus nombres en el título y puesto....y (en) verdad que son dones que fueron de nuestros caciques que poseen la tierra de* Paxtoca.

Por Don Carlos V fue testigo, y por el Emperador fue elevado Don Juan Cortés, principal de Santa Cruz Quiché....Don Francisco, que fuese cacique en San Cristobal Papula, *y se dio información por Don Pedro de Alvarado de como era este cacique sobre todos los naturales de dicho pueblo de* Papula.

Yo, cacique (del) Quiché, que ante mi están sujetos los de Paxtoca, *por ser yo el cacique menor del cacique mayor, y así me ha venido de derecho el gobierno de esta gente. Yo, Alonzo Pérez de Torres* Excamparitz, *nieto del cacique mayor que poseyó en* Paxtoca....

....*empezamos a medir las tierras nosotros, los de San Sebastián y de* Paxtoca, *con los principales de Quezaltenango y los de Totonicapán y los de Santa Catarina* Sija, *que son testigos de esto, y los de nuestra parte de* Paxtoca, *y los principales de San Cristobal* Papula. *En 13 días del mes de Julio de 1557 años empezamos a medir las tierras....y fueron siguiéndose los mojones donde está un pino, llamádose,* Cabawil Abaj, *entre los pinos; y se llega al camino que viene de Quezaltenango, y va subiendo donde está hecho un castillo sobre el cerro, que es de Alonzo Pérez de Torres* Excamparitz.

....*y aquí se juntaron los mojones de las tierras de un calpul de Alonzo de Torres* Excamparitz *y otro llamádose, Juan Gomez* Calel Ajaw ....*y que nadie los malquiste en sus tierras porque son de sus antepasados, como verdad.*

Alonzo Pérez Excamparitz, *Juan López* Calel
Y *Francisco López* Calel Ajaw Excamparitz.
Don Domingo Cortéz de Quezaltenango,
Don Juan Cortés Sacnoy,
Don Pedro Alvarado Ramírez,
    y 4 regidores de cabildo y otros principales,
Don Baltasar, cacique de Totonicapán,
Don Pedro Alvarado, alcalde,
Don Juan López Calel, *alcalde*
    y 4 regidores de cabildo con otros tres,
Don Francisco Mexía Cortés de San Christóbal,
Francisco Gómez Cux, *alcalde,*
Juan Gómez, alcalde
    y 4 regidores del pueblo,
Don Christóbal, alcalde de Santa Catarina
    y 4 regidores y principales.

....*y con voto de todos los principales doy por escrito con fe y testimonio las dichas tierras de* Paxtoca, San Sebastián, *una parcialidad de calpul de San Sebastián* Paxtoca *del dicho Alonzo Pérez* Excamparitz."

APPENDIX VII: *Título Retalulew*

Following is a copy of a document found in the Archivo de la Escribanía, Guatemala, Sección de Tierras, in the packets from Departamento Suchitepéquez, No 2. A few minor grammatical changes have been made in order to clarify the account. Also included, at the end of the Spanish text, is a copy of two coats of arms which were attached to the Título. They were painted in black and white.

"*En el pueblo de San Antonio* Retaluleuj, *en 15 días del mes de Marzo de 1537 (1557?) años, le damos a Don Francisco* Tatzuy *su título y probanza, por haberse apropiado de estas tierras para poblar en ellas. Siendo los dueños de estas tierras los de la generación* Ideota, *queriendo ellos que fuera a poblar a la orilla del río de* Samalá. *No siendo esto permitido, se le tomó información al susodicho para que se le confiriese facultad grave, y fuese respetado con sus hijos. Y todo lo....de su ascendencia, y no fuesen quitados por ninguna de las maneras. Y dádoles el estado y puestos que merecen.*

Este auto se ha expedido en el pueblo de San Antonio Retaluleuj *entre nosotros los justicias de Santa Cruz Quiché y los demás antiguos y superiores de los demás pueblos, con testigos de asistencia, los que irán al fin de este auto. Y por ser nominados, y por haberlo trabajado, le concedemos este título y probanza, Don Francisco Cortés, rey, Don Francisco de Rojas, y Don Francisco de Rosales, y por haber quedado dichas tierras con buena disposición. Y en tan buen paraje bien arreglado vinieron los demás pueblos a acabar de formalizar y a echar los pocos que habían quedado. En dicho lugar que fueron a vivir al Pueblo Viejo, donde el dicho Don Francisco* Tatzuy *había vivido, en la otra banda del Río de* Samalá. *De ellos nació el decir; era de la generación y ascendencia que arriba dijimos, que eran águilas, que eran tigres, que eran* Guisisiles, *que eran* Alcabuseros. *Tan parecidos a nuestra calidad y ....son jactancia. Mas, parecía a Don Pedro Alvarado, y Don Francisco* Tatzuy *en cara, en habla, y finalmente, en todas sus facciones.*

Y como se había dicho que el nominado Guegueg *Baptista era hijo de susodicho, se volvió pasar al lugar que llaman, Palma Verde, que linda con las tierras de Cuyotenango, al oriente. Y volviéndose a convocar los pueblos se acabó de fundar y formulizar de esta suerte. Salieron de allí, de Palma Verde, y se fueron con Don Domingo de San Felipe, y el dicho* K'alel, *buscando el mismo lindero para arriba, buscando la margen del Río de* Samalá *al oriente. Y de allí se fueron buscando al norte el lindero que llaman,* Joc'alin, *a rematar*

*a la Piedra Bubosa, que es el tercer mojón. De allí volvieron a salir
para abajo, buscando el poniente derecho, buscando el paraje que llaman, Oc'us, hasta la orilla del río de Tilapa, que linda con las tierras
de los Provincianos, al margen de la mar. Suben hasta la Barra San
Luís, buscando el sur en la misma línea, hasta llegar al primer mojón, que es Palma Verde, en donde se quedaron las 4 esquinas y mojón
este.*

*Y por eso le han conferido muchos méritos para uno de las may-
ores facultades a Don Francisco* Tatzuy, *Don Pedro Alvarado, con
un capitán español y 100 Españoles. Y por eso todos los pueblos
le rinden obediencia, por tenerlo ya granjeado, y bien merecido. Y
son los siguientes: Totonicapán, Santa Catharina, Pasija, Quezaltenango, Santo Tomás Samayaque, San Francisco Zapotitlán, San
Luís, todos estos pueblos. Como hemos dicho, están a la obediencia
de dicho Señor Don Francisco* Tatzuy, *y se colman sus asenos, que
con 2 méritos le hacen acreedor de mayores empleos.*

*Aquí da fin la historia y explicación, según la información de
dicho Señor Don Francisco Cortés, Reyes* K'ak'noy, *y Don Osorio,
para instrucción: de dicho poder, auto, títulos, y probanza de Don
Francisco* Tatzuy, *para que le libre* tequios *y demás molestias, por
haberlo trabajo mas que los demás habitantes y estantes. Y habiendo
visto el Rey y nuestro Señor este auto, Don Carlos Quinto, certifica
como los dichos* Ideotas *eran los dueños de estas dichas tierras, como
y de que manera las quitó el dicho Señor Don Francisco* Tatzuy, *por
cuyo motivo decimos que ni el Señor Presidente, ni la Real Audiencia,
ni S.V.Y. el Señor Arzobispo, ni otro algún señor juez, así eclesiático
como secular, no nos puede obscurecer y deshelar de esto; por habernos
concedido su Magestad nuestro deseo. Y porque dichos pueblos dieron palabra seria de concederle a dicho Señor Don Francisco* Tatzuy
esta merced en este dicho pueblo de San Antonio Retaluleuj, *como
son Don Francisco Cortés y Osorio, caballero del pueblo de San Felipe; Don Francisco de Rosales, caballero y superior del pueblo de
Quiché; Don Francisco de Rojas, caballero del pueblo de San Luis.
Y para que en todo tiempo conste, lo firmaron todos los testigos como
van nominados en la vuelta. En dicho día, mes, y año, marzo, 15
de 1537 años.* Ut supra coronas opus.

*Don Francisco Cortés, Don Martín Mexía, Don Francisco Cor-
tés Reyes* K'ak'noy, *Don Pedro Alvarado, Don Christobal* Pasija, *Don
Francisco Izq'uin atzuicaj, Don Domingo de San Phelipe, Don Alonso
Básquez, gobernador de Mazatenango, Don Francisco de Rosales, Don
Joseph Cortés, Don Pedro Alvarado de Totonicapán, Don Pedro Pérez*
Quemagitasul, *Don Francisco* Tilam, *Don Francisco Ixk'an de San
Martín Zapotitlán, Don Francisco Aj Yabacoj, Don Pedro López,
Don Pedro Básquez de San Francisco, Don Joseph Aj Ric'las, Don
Francisco Básquez* Xolochic'ax, *Don Francisco Xac'tocja, Don Pedro
Básquez Aj Wiasej. Escribano, Bartolomé López* Inum."

Coat-of-arms of the Ideata lineage. From a pictorial attached to the *Título Retalulew*.

APPENDIX VIII: *Título Chuachituj.*

The título located in the Archivo de la Escribanía, Guatemala, Sección de Tierras, is filed with other documents from Departamento Totonicapán, packet No. 1. It was accompanied by a crude map, a free hand copy of which follows the transcription below.

"*Escrituras, testamentos, y títulos de un pedazo de tierra sacado en el original, año de 1592. Nosotros los naturales y principales de Santa Cruz del Quiché, y el rey Montesuma, y el rey Quiché, conquistador que vino en la Nueva España; el rey Cortés y Don Pedro, y los muy reverendos padres, y los soldados. Don Juan Rojas, gobernador, que estuvo en Santa Cruz del Quiché. Martín Pérez* Quicab.
Título de un pedazo de tierras, lo hago yo, monarca Montesuma. Y me estuve en el reino de Santa Cruz del Quiché, y llamado mi casa de Patzak, y Quextun. Y delante el rey Quiché, y los vasallos Cobok'ak, y todas las jurisdicciones mías. Vieron hice señal de todas las tierras donde yo me estuve, uno de los de Santa Cruz del Quiché cogen atrás de la Iglesia, a llegar en el sitio llamado Xexal, *a lindar con los de Zacualpa. Y las tierras que dejo, yo, en orden de unos vasallos míos, llamados Juan Bautista* Soc *y Cristóbal Bautista* Soc, *dos hermanos naturales del pueblo de Santa María Chiquimula de las Mercedes; el sitio y llamado de las tierras del paraje de* Chuachituj. *Y que en adelante ninguno los inquieten en sobre las tierras; son para sus hijos en adelante. Delante los testigos dejo estos renglones, e instrumentos de papeles, porque me vinieron a traer el conquistador, el rey Cortés, y el señor Don Pedro Alvarado, y los reverendos padres, Fray Bartolomé de Olmedo y Fray Martín de Balencias. Son de España, vinieron con un gran ejército de soldados. Y todos mis bienes y mi palacio me embargaron. En uno del mes de junio de 1592 años, yo, Martín Pérez, natural y criollo del pueblo de Quezaltenango, me hicieron llamar los naturales de este pueblo de Santa Cruz del Quiché, en sobre de un pedazo de tierras llamado el sitio de* Chuchituj. *Como caballería de tierras que ha dejado el rey Montesuma en poder de Juan Bautista* Soc *y Cristóbal Bautista* Soc. *Y eran 2 hermanos legítimos. Las tierras son realengas no se han puesto en el título real de Santa Cruz Quiché porque los dichos Juan Bautista y Cristóbal Bautista* Soc *han servido muchísimo tiempo en poder de sus antepasados, los naturales de Santa Cruz Quiché. Por eso le dieron el pedazo de tierras e estos Juan y Cristóbal Bautista* Soc. *Ni ellos tienen tierras en su mismo pueblo de Santa María de las Mercedes Chiquimula. Y yo soy testigo de Montesuma, Martín Pérez, natural del pueblo de Quezaltenango, en 5 días del mes de Junio de 1592 años.*
Yo el rey Quiché soy nacido y más antiguamente de Santa Cruz de Quiché; hermano menor de Montesuma. Delante nosotros hicieron este instrumento. Que quedó el pedazo de tierras en poder de los dichos Juan Bautista Soc *y Cristóbal Bautista* Soc. *Han servido muchísimo tiempo en casa de Montesuma; eran barberos del señor; se han acomodado mucho en la casa, y no tienen tierras Juan Bautista* Soc *y Cristóbal Bautista* Soc *en el pueblo de Santa María de*

las Mercedes Chiquimula. Que en adelante no se inquieten estos dichos en sobre de las tierras. Y para que conste verdad, lo firmo, rey Quiché, Junio, 8 días del mes próximo año de 1592 años, en el valle de Santa Elena y Santa Cruz de Quiché. Yo, el conquistador que vino de la Nueva España, juntamente con mi señor Don Pedro Alvarado, y mis muy reverendos Padres fray Bartolomé de Olmedo, Fray Martín de Valencia, dos personas apostólicas. En nuestra presencia dejó el Montesuma un pedazo de tierras en poder de unos pobres naturales de Chiquimula, que son Juan y Cristóbal Bautista Soc. *Que en adelante no les embarguen dichas tierras que les dejamos, los citados nombrados.*

Y (damos) cada mojón y esquina con nombre. Su primera esquina y mojón se llama, Questun Paismachiy, *en un lado de la casa de Montesuma. Que la casa de Montesuma....señal de todo que está, como iglesias que no se pierda en todo la vida. Y el otro mojón en medio llano de* Panajxit. *Y viene a dar vuelta en el agua tibia, donde se encuentra un río que le llaman Río Colorado,* K'akaa, *con riachuelo* Joj. *Y coje el camino para arriba, pasa en* Pacawib, *en el llano. Y coje el camino real que va a Totonicapán, loma por loma, pasa en* Xexak. *Pasa en* Cotoluk. *Llega en* Ticachamiy, *y coje la montaña. Pasa en* Tzam Jibache, *hasta dar esquina en* Pacan Abaj. *Y da vuelta atrás, y coje el otro camino real que viene de Quiché y Santo Tomás Chichicastenango. Pasa en* Pachoc, *a llegar en el cerro* Quikiquil, *a llegar en el sitio,* Macsul, *a lindar con las tierras de Santo Tomás Chichicastenango. Y sale de allí, coje por abajo a llegar en el sitio,* Patzak Paismachi. *Y allí, dió fin donde empezó. Que por otro nombre le llaman de* Chuachituj. *Estos renglones e instrumentos que dejamos en poder de Juan Bautista* Soc *y Cristobal Bautista* Soc. *No tiene más que hacer....posesiones a los señores y jueces en adelante, porque ya están apuntados los mojones. Y firmamos por ser verdad.*

Y el conquistador Cortés, y Don Pedro Alvarado, y los predicadores Padres, Fray Bartolomé de Olmedo, Fray Martín de Balencias, y el reverendo Padre Fray Díaz, en 8 dias del mes de junio de 1592. Montesuma, rey Quiché, Martín Pérez, escribano. En el cabildo de Santa Cruz de Quiché, nosotros los alcaldes, justicias, y principales, y gobernador, todo el común del pueblo. Ya hemos registrado este título y testamento de tierras que hicieron nuestros antepasados, que quedó en poder de Juan Bautista Soc *y Cristóbal Bautista* Soc. *Ya han apuntado los mojones y esquinas. Ni pasa ni menos de dichos mojones, y nombrados de* Chuachituj. *Y que en adelante no les inquieten los hijos ni nietos de Don Juan Bautista* Soc *y Cristóbal Bautista* Soc. *Eran naturales de Santa María Chiquimula por nombre de Montesuma, y el señor conquistador, y el señor Don Pedro Alvarado, y los muy reverendos, Padres predicadores fray Bartolomé de Olmedo y Fray Martín de Balencias. Y firmamos nosotros de Quiché, yo, el gobernador y alcalde, Don Juan Rojas Qui-*

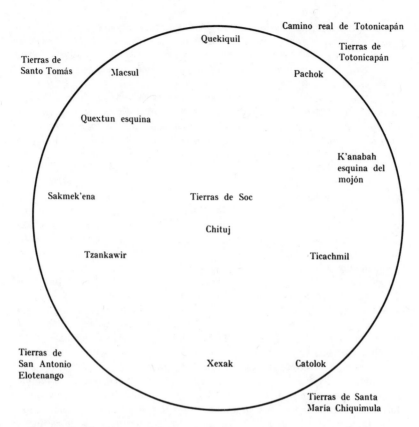

Camino real de Totonicapán

Quekiquil

Tierras de
Totonicapán

Tierras de
Santo Tomás

Macsul

Pachok

Quextun esquina

K'anabah
esquina del
mojón

Sakmek'ena

Tierras de Soc

Chituj

Tzankawir

Ticachmil

Tierras de
San Antonio
Elotenango

Xexak

Catolok

Tierras de Santa
María Chiquimula

cab, *nombrado por su Magestad, mi título real de España. En 25 días del més de agosto de 1594 años. Fecho.*"

APPENDIX IX: *Título Chacatz-Tojin.*

The document is a copy of a *protocolo* in the Archivo General de Centroamérica (Al:1497-9974). It was registered in the Departamento de Totonicapán, though it pertains to Indians from Santa Cruz del Quiché. The orthography has been slightly modified for clarity.

"*En 7 días del mes de agosto de 1783 años, nosotros (somos) los barrios y calpules llamados Juan* Chacatz, *Joseph* Chacatz, *Gabriel* Chacatz, *Lucas* Chacatz, *Pablo* Tojin, *Miguel* Tojin, *Gaspar* Tojin, *y Pedro* Tojin, *Diego* Tojin, *Nicolás* Tojin. *Y un barrio grande,* todos nosotros hicimos trasladar nuestra copia documentada, y pusimos en lengua castellana ni mas ni menos, porque nos llama Dios, y no hay quien explica delante él....y para que consta virtud, firma el escribano del cabildo, Miguel Lamistoy.

Con 9 días del mes septiembre de 1688 años, somos 4 hermanos, son.... Yo Pedro Chacatz, Juan Chacatz, Nicolás Tojin, Diego Tojin, y Manuel Tojin, Juan Chacatz, y Gaspar Tojin. Ya hicimos trasladar nuestro documento, libro y título que nos han dejado nuestros antepasados. Ni bajamos, ni subimos de las palabras que están aquí aportadas, que todo lo que reza el título original, porque está creciendo nuestro barrio, porque nos llama Diós mañana. Y lo trasladó Pedro de Vico por ser virtud. Y soy de Santa Cruz de Quiché, y aquí se acabó.

Copia sacada de su original, esta escritura, año de 1607. Jesús, María y Joseph.

Ahora en 14 días del més de febrero de 1607 años, hacemos y quedamos nuestra escritura y título, se sirve en adelante.

Primeramente se llaman los antiguos, unos se llaman Bail c'atz, segundo Bail os, tercero Bail bel, quarto Bail tum, los nombres de los antepasados. Y otros se llaman Estayul, Came, y otro se llama Taom, y otro, yo Sannik; y otro Cheraquik; y los otros se llaman, los quartos, se llaman Sande Balan, y otro Cotziwa, y otro Atzawal ekom, y otro Tecum; quinto se llama Quizi, y otro Iqui Balam, otro Maic', y otro Estayul.

Seis siglos primero cuando vino Donati. Le nombraron Francisco, Pascual, y otro Juan Uluch, otro Francisco Tojin, y otro Miguel Chacatz. Y ahora hacemos estas palabras para que se sirvan en delante para nuestros hijos. Uno se llama Miguel de Chawik, segundo Francisco Gómez Tojin, los viejos. Y nuestros hijos se llaman Juan Pérez, y otro se llama Martín Gómez Tojin, otro Pedro Chacatz, y otro Gerónimo Tojin, y otro Baltasar Lorenzo. Ya dimos parte.

Ahora dejamos estas palabras para que se sirvan en adelante, y damos noticia de una suerte de tierra, porque somos bisabuelos del Señor Don Juan de Rojas, gobernador del Pueblo de Santa Cruz Quiché, entre los calpules y barrios de San Marcos. Era muy antiguo, se llama Ra poj se está con los barrios San Marcos. Primero se entró en el Tzununja, y se llegó bajo el cerro llamado, Iquilija, entre los calpules Ajcotepet, Ajcutun, Ajcame, ya los sitios.

Primeras tierras dónde entran, ahora empezamos a puntar los nombres y esquinas: Primero, se llama Chichirik, y se sube en Pabal mizquinaa, en sobre él, se linda con Rokcha. Y coje la loma, se va a lindar en sobre el sitio llamado Chuchub, y se baja en el riachuelo llamado, Exkayil, se linda con Antún Chituy. Y coje el río por arriba, y coje otra loma, llegan en el sitio llamado, calcat Chinaj. Llega también en el sitio Mumutzim ulew, y se linda con Tucutzi, y se llega en el sitio Chuwijolom. Y se va a salir en el mojón Quikec;

y se baja en el Coxom, *linda con* Rokchub; *se linda con* Juanitzaib
*en la punta de una piedra. Y coje una loma por arriba, y se pasa
en* Pajom, *y topa el camino grande por arriba, y se llega donde se
bebe agua. Y se llega sobre de un cerro, donde está un pocito, y coje
él sobre el cerro. Y viene a dar con el sitio* Kabelon, *en una piedra
donde da golpe en riachuelo llamado* Uwal caam. *Y se sube en
la loma, llega en* Chicakatux, *y topa en una punta de un cerro.
Y viene bajando las tierras* Chinub, *y se va subiendo, y se va a lindar
con los* Cakojib, *se dice,* Wajxakib Chinamit. *Y se viene a acabar
en el río, y coje el río por arriba, y se llega en* Xalcatz Tziris. *Y allí
di fín.*

Y otro pedazo de tierras, llamado Saktol, *donde está (el) local
del señor* Quicab, *y se llama* Chisatzam jebal, *atrás de los* Estayul
Came, *junto* Wukij. *Son dos (que) están aguardando el agua caliente.
Y sale allí, y se llega en el cerro llamado* Iquilija, *y se linda con* Ka-
lito. *Y linda y se viene y se llega en* Chikaxul. *Sale de allí, y llega
en* Chwi Camja, *y va bajando* Chiracan atz, *y pasa* Chuwacutum,
y se llega en sobre del cerro, y coje la loma. Llega en Chwi Sakchojox.
Y se va cojiendo una loma, llega en Chwi tasabal quej. *Y se bajan
(a) un riachuelo, se llama* Pakichina. *Y de allí, coje* Racan Chinaj,
y llega en Paxok'ol. *De allí llega en* Panawal, *y se va colindante,
llega* Saklecaam; *de allí llega en el lago, y se pasa y va a lindar
donde (es) espeso, en* Chwi Ikilija.

*Di fín, y pusimos en lo cierto, y que en delante no hay esturbio
ni pleito. Y si alguno levanta pleito, se llevará esta escritura con
el señor Alcalde Mayor, o con regidores. En 14 días del més de febrero
de 1607 años, firmamos por ser virtud,* Miguel de Chawi Pacal, *Francisco Gómez* Tojin, *los hijos,* Juan Pérez Pacal, *y Martín Gómez* Tojin, *Pedro Gómez* Chacatz.

*Ahora llegamos en las tierras, yo Don Joseph Cortés del pueblo
de Santa Cruz Quiché. Doy parte a cada uno para que en adelante
no busca pleito. Hicimos (esto) delante los calpules llamados* Jua-
nitzayib, *y los viejos. Y ya hizo justicia con averiguación; hicimos
poseción. Primero, se nombra* culbat *las tierras* Chinib, *se linda
con* Cak. *En el agua coje el hijo de cerro, y se baja en el río, y allí
se acaba. Y para que consta virtud, firmamos con su poseción, en
13 días del més de enero de 162 años.* Don Joseph Cortés, Don Francisco de León."

APPENDIX X: *Título Lamaquib*

The small document was written in 1595 by the elders of Sacapulas.
It was attached to the litigation papers of a 1739 land dispute between
Sacapulas and Aguacatán, and is now in the Archivo General de
Centroamérica (A1:5978-52518). I am indebted to that institution
for providing me with a Xerox copy of the document. The version

given here was taken from the copy, with punctuation changes added for clarification.

"*En el pueblo de Santo Domingo Sacapulas de la jurisdicción de Huehuetenango, en cuatro días del mes de enero del año de 1595 se hizo reconocimiento de los mojones pertenecientes al dicho pueblo de Santo Domingo de Sacapulas, y particularmente las que pertenecen al calpul del glorioso apóstol Santo Thomás y demás parcialidades que es como se sigue. Se reconoció el primer mojón que le llaman* ce cale k'apoj; *este mojón linda con los de San Pedro Jocopilas. Luego prosigue al otro mojón que le llaman* chuwi cajbab, *vecino de los de* Ak'aab. *Luego prosigue al otro mojón que le llaman* chichim; *luego prosigue el mismo lindero teniendo a la vista* Ak'aab. *Luego llega al otro que le llaman* chi macute, *vecino con el pueblo de Chalchitán y Aguacatán. De allí prosigue al otro lindero de chi juchom, en frente de los de Aguacatán, siguiendo la línea llega a* Suluquej; *prosigue el mojón hasta* ajtzibab. *Sale de allí y llega a* chi pak balcaco, *nombrado así, vecino con los de* Motomal Winak. *Y de allí llega al otro lindero de* cok'ojaw. *Prosigue hasta* Uchubaja. *Prosigue al otro lindero llamado* Tzam cak'abtze, *vecino con los de* Cumatz, *en donde tuvieron su sitación los del calpul de Santo Thomás. Sigue al otro lindero de* Achulaja, *tierra de los de* Cumatz. *Sigue y llega al paraje de* Tzam bakinay, *en donde está la señal de los de* Cumatz; *y de allí prosigue al otro lindero que le llaman* Chuwi k'um, *perteneciente a los de* Cumatz. *Prosigue al otro lindero que le llaman* Sol chi ic, *vecino con los de* Cumatz. *Y de allí prosigue al otro lindero que le llaman* Cheybal, *hasta llegar al paraje llamado,* Chi sulu, *cerca de los de* Cumatz. *Y aquí estuvo también en la situación antigua llamada* Tinamicot sacaribal solya. *También estuvo otra situación....llamada* Ical Atzam wae, *donde estuvo el pueblo de Santa María Magdalena, llamado el paraje por los antiguos,* Aj lemo.

Decimos nosotros (los) principales Lamaquib *ser verdad lo que llevamos dicho del reconocimiento de nuestras tierras, y para que conste en qualquier tiempo lo firmamos: Don Francisco de Velasco, alcalde ordinario; Gabriel de Zepeda, alcalde segundo; regidores Andrés Pérez, Diego López, Gaspar Barroz; principales Bartolomé Sánchez, Gaspar López, Juan* Bobtixti, *Marcos Díaz, Bartolomé Gómez, Francisco López, Juan de Velasco, Matheo Sánchez, Andrés Joseph, Nicolás Pérez, Diego Pérez, Pedro Velasco, Pedro* Tzalam, *Pedro Hernández, Diego López, Diego Aj, Diego Vásquez. Yo, escribano Francisco* Cenenaz."

APPENDIX XI: *Título Uchabaja.*

The small land title was attached to litigation papers from Sacapulas, now preserved in the Archivo General de Centroamérica (AI:

5936-51914). I have modernized the orthographic symbols of the Quiche text, and provided a Spanish translation.

Quiché Text.

"Chupam 28 de agosto, 1600 años. Catz'ibax wi nu tzij, in, Don "Chucisco Azeituno, Uchabaja, chiquiwach k'ana winak; ta canubij rumal are ri ulew Chok'olaj ubi quech Tolthecatl ri ulew; chupam mawi ajilam chijunab xquic'amo xeoc chuwach ri ulew xabix quimam quikajaw quech nabek ri ulew quech puch kamam kajaw Uchabaja are c'ut, ta xul quiche winak ajlabal xoc c'ut labal chiquij kamam kakajaw, ta xc'am c'ut ri ulew Chok'olaj ta roquic c'ut ri Tolthecatl chuwach ri ulew chupam tziquin che abaj, ta xquic'amo mawi ajilam chijunab ta xquic'amo; are c'ut xnataj chikac'uxwaj canakaj rumal quech ri ulew quech puch kamam kakajaw, queje c'ut we ta pu roquic chikac'amo; we ta pu chi quech aj jumul chic xojcha macu xbanataj kumal, ma pu xutzinic xalok xkabano xapulok xkatzijoj rumal xax rech in ri winak Tolthecatl wacamic quincha, in Don Francisco, majabi jumul chic chikatzijoj ma pu jumul ta chic chikachao rumal quech ri Tolthecatl ronojel ri ulew xax quech wi chupam quiya junab mawi ajilam chi junab, ta xquic'amo queje c'ut jumul chic canubij carelesaj nu k'ab chirij majabi jun ta wal nu c'ajol chopon chila chabix ta pu chila chuwach ri ulew Chok'olaj queje c'ut canipowaj wi ronojel tzij xkabano mawi lo mawi chuwach chic chinchao quic'ama Tolthecatl ulew ruc' xax ojer wi quic'amom; mawi xopon ta kak'ab chirij ulew quech Tolthecatl xawi xcoje cuc' quincha, in Don Francisco Azeituno, xere wi nutzij canubij, mawi jalan ta chic tzij chinbij petinak ruc' wanima; ta canubij chuwach Dios ruc' chuwach k'anawinak, ta canubij cattz'ibax. 18 de agosto 1600 años. In Don Francisco Azeituno."

Spanish Translation.

"El 28 de agosto de 1600 años. Aquí se escriben mis palabras, yo Don Francisco Aceituno Uchabaja, delante de los testigos; entonces lo digo porque esta es la tierra Chok'olaj de los Toltecas; en un año que ya no se puede contar la recibieron, y entraron en la tierra de milpa los abuelos y padres, los primeros dueños, y la tierra también de nuestros abuelos y padres, los Uchabaja; entonces llegaron los guerreros de los Quichés, y vino la guerra contra nuestros abuelos y padres, cuando fue recibida la tierra de Chok'olaj, cuando entraron los Toltecas delante de la tierra en Tziquin che abaj; la recibieron en un año que no se puede contar; esto descubrimos cerca, porque es tierra de ellos y de nuestros abuelos y padres; así si entraron ellos, tenemos que recibirla también si era de ellos una vez; hemos dicho que no fue hecho por nosotros; no en vano se completa lo que hicimos; no en vano hablamos, porque de verdad es mía, de la gente Tolteca de hoy, digo yo, Don Francisco; no lo diremos otra vez, no hablaremos otra vez de ello, porque es de los Toltecas toda la tierra; de verdad era de ellos

*blli en el año que ni se puede contar, cuando la recibieron; así tam-
aién otra vez lo digo, y se saca mi poder sobre ello; no tuve hijos cuando había de llegar y hacer milpa allí en la tierra de* Chok'olaj; *así
también aquí echo todas las palabras que hicimos; tal vez no lo diré
otra vez de la recepción de la tierra* Tolteca, *que de verdad recibieron
antes; no llegó entonces nuestro poder sobre la tierra de los* Toltecas,
*solo existió con ellos; así digo, yo, Don Francisco Aceituno; así de
la palabra que doy; no cambian las palabras que digo, (son) venidas
de mi corazón; esto entonces digo delante de Diós, delante de los testigos, cuando doy mi escritura. 18 de agosto de 1600 años. Yo, Don
Francisco Aceituno.*"

APPENDIX XII: Buenabaj Pictorials.

The photograph is a page of certain ancient papers in possession
of the elders of aldea San Vicente Buenabaj, municipio Santiago
Momostenango. Following the photograph is a transcription and
translation of the Quiche inscriptions accompanying each pictorial.

Inscription: The names inscribed on each church, from left to right,
are "Santa Cruz" (below the belltower), "Sta Antún Chijlocab,"
and "Stiago Chwa Tz'ak" (below base of center and right hand
church). The three names correspond to the present-day communities of Santa Cruz del Quiché, San Antonio Ilotenango, and Santiago Momostenango.

Quiche Inscription: "Emperador chupa mexico rajawal quiche cu-
luna ojer ruc' e caib u mial malintzin qui bi, e umial ajaw mendect-
zum....emperador ajawal quiche ri xoc patan chwach ojer iboy-
ooca chwach cumal ajauab chupa tinamit quiche utladecat oj."

Spanish Translation: "El emperador en Mexico y el señor Quiché,
a quien antes casó a dos de sus hijas, nombradas Malintzin, hijas
del señor Montezuma....El señor Quiché, ante quien entraron los
tributos antiguamente, por los señores en nuestro centro Quiché
de Utatlán."

APPENDIX XIII: Testament Catalina *Nijay*

The document is in the Archivo General de Centroamérica under
the title, "*Título de tierras de San Antonio Suchitepéquez*" (1586)
(Al:5930-51849). Both the Nahuatl and the Spanish versions have
been preserved. Following is a modification of the Spanish translation, corrected by comparison with the Nahuatl text.

"*Este es un testamento trasjuntado de lengua Mexicana en Castellano por mandado del Juez, Señor Francisco de Perea, Teniente
General desta provincia, en 14 días del més de agosto de 1586 años,
que es como se sigue:*

En el nombre de diós Padre, Hijo y Espíritu Santo, yo, Catalina
Nijay, *natural deste pueblo de San Antonio, estando enferma del*
cuerpo y sana de mi ánima y voluntad delante de mi señor, hago yo
mi testamento ante el escribano y testigos, si diós fuere servido de lle-
varme esta vida haya misericordia de mi ánima. Y ruego a la Virgen
María ruegue a su Hijo haya misericordia de mi ánima, y en mi cuer-
po entierre el padre en esta iglesia de santa autoridad, y se dirán por
mi dos misas. Darán la limosna Andrés, Francisco, y Francisco.
    Yo, Catalina Nijay, *mi marido se llama Alonzo* Aj K'ucumatz.
Tengo aquí tres hijos (piluan), Andrés, Francisco, y Francisco Ajquiyb Yaqui Winak. *Tengo un nieto que se llama Francisco.*
    Declaro una milpa de cacao (cacauamilli) de mi marido, Miguel
Ajquiyb Yaqui Winak. *Y agira esta tierra de* Ixch'al junajpu
pula Yeocatu *a la orilla de la tierra (en) la· expediente de Andrés,*
Francisco, Francisco; que tiene estos linderos junto a Juan Ichal,
y Pedro K'epux, *Juan* Yuj, *Antonio* Lenamak, *Juan* Ichal, *que*
parece erdre los mojones (que han) de tomar mis hijos Andrés, Fran-
cisco, y Francisco. Porque así les dijo su padre. La tierra y la mil-
pa de cacao eran de su padre. Hanla de tomar Andrés, Francisco,
y Francisco. La justicia lo ha de hacer y dar a cada uno de mis hijos
su parte que se ha de hacer tres partes. Así lo digo.
    Hay unas milpas de maíz y de cacao (cacauatoctli, cacauamilli)
que compré junto con Domingo Quewek, *Miguel* Tzwitzin, *Francisco*
K'iboy, *Alonzo* Ajk'ucumatz, *mi marido. Es mi compra, porqué*
bien los trabaja Alonzo mi marido.
    Un pedazo de tierra pequeña (tlalli) que es de Miguel Yaqui
Winak, *padre de Andrés, Francisco, Francisco. Ya la sembró Alon-*
zo. *Ahora y hay árboles de cacao hasta la orilla del río* Chewes. *Así*
mismo, la ha de tomar Andrés, y Francisco, porque Alonzo es mi
marido. Tengo, una piedra de moler. Y no digo más, yo Catalina,
en presencia de los caciques (tlatoque), digo mis palabras todas. Trés
son mis hijos, Andrés, Francisco, y Francisco que han de tomar sus
milpas de cacao porque eran tierras de su padre, que se decía, Miguel
Yaqui Winak. *La justicia lo ha de repartir entre Andrés, Francisco,*
y Francisco, porque es del padre de mis hijos. Y no digo mas, yo,
Catalina Nijay, *en presencia de mis testigos.*
    Don Francisco de la Cueva....regidor; Francisco Bacaj, *Diego*
C'ux; *Francisco Baciles, alguacil mayor; Miguel* Chimal; *Domingo*
Xutut; *Pedro* Tabal; *Francisco* Raxawach; *Francisco* Chimal: *Fran-*
cisco Chial....*Francisco* Ahzic; *y otros ante mí, Gonzalo Rodríguez.*
Fecho a 28 diciembre de 1596 años. Gonzalo Rodríguez, escribano."

APPENDIX XIV: Testament *Ajpopolajay.*

The document is in the Archivo General de Centroamérica, Guatemala (Al:5942-51997). I obtained a xerox copy, from which the
following transcription was taken. I have altered spelling and gram-

mar in some places to make the account conform, more closely, to modern usage.

"*En el nombre de Diós Padre, Diós Hijo, Diós Espíritu Santo, trés personas (y) un solo Diós verdadero en quien creemos fiel y verdaderamente, de la siempre Virgen Madre de Nuestro Señor y Salvador, Jesucristo, a quien pongo por intercesora ante la Divina Majestad. Amén, Jesús.*

Yo, don Jerónimo de Mendoza ahora estoy muy enfermo en la justicia de Diós, y mi ánima y entendimiento están sanos, si mi Diós fuere servido de sacarme de esta vida; pido que el maestro de capilla y los demás cantores vengan por mi cuerpo, y me digan trés responsos en el camino cuando me llevaren en el camino; y también me digan la vigilia; digo que cada año me digan una misa cantada de requi? mi mujer e hijos tendrán cuenta; y esta casa y solar se los dejo a mi mujer y a mi hijo don Faliano; y cuando mi mujer fenesca se los dejará a mi hijo don Faliano; y otra casa se la dejo a mi hijo don Bernardino; también no tengan....porque así lo mando; y también digo que una milpa de cacao que yo tengo en San Bartolomé, y donde está esta milpa de cacao, buluba, *se la dejo a mi hijo don Bernardino y a mi hijo don Gaspar; y en muriendo mi mujer entonces les partirá esta milpa de cacao, la mitad por Bernardino, la mitad a mi hijo don Gaspar; mas otra milpa de cacao que también está más arriba de* buluba *se la dejo a mi hijo don Juliano y mi hijo don Francisco, si Diós los deja vivir; se ha de partir la mitad por Francisco y otra mitad por don Juliano; y también otra tierra de cacao que me la dió dada mi cuñado Pedro de Castillo, se la dejo a mi hijo Serafín, está este en el pueblo de San Bartolomé; y también un pedazo de tierra que está medida an....llamada niek', en San Bartolomé, milpa que fue de Francisco* Tzuul, *que Diós sea en gloria, se la dejo a don Faliano mi hijo; y también otras tierras donde sembraba* quatzin, *llamadas,* xebojob, *se las dejo a mi mujer; y también otras tierras que están hurto del pueblo de San Andrés de la Costilla, el cual me las dió dadas Martín* Coquixolj *se las dejo dadas a mi hijo don Esteban; y también otras tierras de sembrar juntas al pueblo llamado,* ajawl, *y* nima chiy cakj *se las dejo a mi hijo Juan de León, y Francisco López su hermano; y también otras tierras llamadas* quisacaribal ujpani, *y también otro nombre* xequecaabak, *se las dejo a mis hijos Juan Xabino y a su hermano Gaspar y Serafín; y esta tierra me la dió Gaspar Loma* ajpan *y Andrés Rom* ajtojj *y también otra tierra llamada* tzam queca ciwan, *que fue de mi abuelo y abuela, la cual está amojonada* cawisicaj quiutis tzam juyubj *se la dejo a mi hijo Bernardino para él solo; no la venda, si la vendiere la justicia se la quite, y la entrasen a sus hermanos; y también otra tierra llamada,* pacacas, *donde están las tierras llamadas* itz ak'bal, *a que las dejo a don de Léon y Francisco López, se las dejo a los dichos mis hijos; y también otra tierra llamada* xeajponil sempucuuj quixa sotzal chupan, *se la dejo a mi hijo don Juan Juliano, así lo mando; y otra tierra llamada* saquiribal uleuj tzamulujay *y el mojón llamado* mumus, *y otro nombre* saquipoj, *ante de las tierras así llamadas* mumus tzan c'uj, *donde sembró antiguamente el cacique* Chial, *junto a la laguna; y mando que ningún....no la venda, no otra persona o cacique; y también otra tierra llamada* saquiribal uleuj c'umuj quixac che tzan cakquic'uy cacachea ru nic'ajol uleuj; *es tierra mía, yo, el cacique* ajpopolajay, *don Jerónimo Mendoza; el principal mojón llamado* tzan chicok *y otro mojón* raxaj conop *y* pac'utijom tzam xulquej; *y va bajando así otro nombre* payatza, *y va* cak'baltzala *hasta llegar por* nawala; *y de allí hasta* xebojob; *allí acaba donde sembramos por* chaquij panan; *y se va siguiendo hasta* chwach abaj, *y otro nombre* racan tzi, *hasta encima de un cerro hasta otro cerro, pasa de una barranca llamada* chicapoj, *y otro nombre llamado* jololila abaj, *y otro* caca abaj, *hasta otro mojón llamado* quiwiacha.

Y estos son los años donde están señalados estas tierras; son de mi parcialidad, don Jerónimo de Mendoza, ajpopolajay; *dejo para mis hijos y nietos y para los de mi parcialidad; y esto dejo mandado, y también una casa que es mía, donde está Pedro de Castillo, que fue de mi padre y abuelo, que dejo para mis hijos Juan de León y Francisco López, don Bernardino, don Juliano; y todos los principales hagan voto en cabildo; y este testamento mío lo hice por mi voluntad ante todos los principales, don Francisco de Rivera, gobernador, y don Joseph de Santa María, alcalde, y Bartolomé Villa Vicencio, alcalde, y los regidores, Juan de Benivides y don Diego de Mendoza; y todos en presencia de los demás principales, Gaspar Lora* Tepan, *Francisco de Castro, y Andrés de Velásquez, y Antonio* Nepan, *y Francisco* Quiej Ajuc'an, *Juan de Capriel, y Francisco Alvares, Martín Guerra, y delante de mis hijos. Hoy en 27 de noviembre de 1569 años."*

APPENDIX XV: Fragment of the *Crónica Franciscana* (?).

The document is part of a collection of Guatemalan manuscripts in the library of the Peabody Museum, Harvard University. I have argued in the section on Primary Native Documents that it is part of the *Crónica Franciscana*, written near the turn of the sixteenth century.

"Lo siguiente es tomado de un historiador anónimo de San Francisco, cuyo manuscript existe en el archivo del mismo Convento.

Capitulo 4º. De las grandes ciudades y poblazones del Reyno de Guatemala, su aumento y extensión, su gobierno y policía y magestad de sus reyes y personas.

Que había recios pueblos o de mucha gente en la provincia de Guatemala y ricas minas, ahora que las casas en que moran los in-

dios no son suntuosas sino bién humildes y que no se benefician minas, nos parece que fue esto algún rinconsillo habitado de gente montañosa. Y yo, aunque no con pleno acertimiento estaba en ese engaño, hasta que he tratado con todo concerto los libros de historia, y papeles mas fidedignos de los naturales; oía yo decir que en Santa Cruz del Quiché están hasta hoy los vestigios de los palacios de los reyes y reynos que manifiestan lo suntuoso de los edificios que allí hubo, la casa y los corredores de juego de la pelota tan grande y de tanta fábrica que hasta hoy admira; y casi lo mismo en el pueblo de Tecpán Guatemala, el antiguo que llaman Ojer Tinamit, *lo del* Tunabaj, *que es una piedra hueca que trasmina muchas leguas, y que en el pueblo de San Miguel Pochutla hay relequías de un cañon fortísimo de tan rara arquitectura que siendo argamasa y cal y canto parece de una piesa, y que viene por bajo tierra hasta donde era la corte de Tecpán Guatemala (que ay más de 10 leguas de andadura) por donde dicen que venían los mensages secretos y la sangre de los sacrificios que llegaba caliente; y que en el paraje llamado, Parrasquin, bajando de Totonicapa hacia la costa, están patentes las ruinas de una soberbia fortaleza de notable simetría; es extraña sólidas donde asistían 80,000 guerreros (que es cosa notable y que indica mucha grandeza), y que es tan eminente el lugar que desde él se descubren mas de 60 leguas en contorno; es cogido por esta razón para que los atalayas y vigías divisasen las naciones contrarias, cuando venían a darles guerra.*

Estas y otras noticias semejantes me persuadían lo grande y populoso que fue este reino de Guatemala, mas con el decurso de cerca de 200 años que ha que esto entró en poder de Españoles, y con no estar en caminos reales los referidos vestigios y ruinas, me hallaba en alguna perplejidad para el asenso, hasta que leer en el Padre Torquemada, refiriendo las muchas y grandes poblazones que había en este nuevo mundo cuando se descubrió; estas fórmulas palabras, aquí unas palabras de Torquemada en el t. 1, L.3, Cap. 29; y luego continúa: bien se conoce por lo dicho y se verá por lo de adelante lo numeroso grande y opulento que fue el reino de Guatemala, y que si.... no lo parece es porque ya todo el oro que los indios tenían recogido en muchos siglos, salió en cantidades grandes a los principios y sale cada día en plata su remesa, descaeciendo al mismo por ser? el valor de sus veneras, por haberlos trasplantado en otras partes.

Pobláronse pues las tierras de este hemisferio y refió de cuatro hermanos Tultecas, el uno pobló y propagó la nación de los Tzoziles, Tzoblenes y Quelenes que tuvieron muchas y grandes poblaciones, y es en la provincia de Chiapa, con que confinan estas naciones por el nordeste con Guatemala, por el mediodía, y alcansa hasta oriente tierras y despoblados del Lacandón, y por el poniente, confina con Soconusco.

El otro hermano pobló hacia la parte de la Verapaz, Cajabon, y Pochutla, y otros recios pueblos en distancia de casi 50 leguas, hasta el Golfo Dulce en cuyo distrito aun hay algunos por reducir, que un tiempo fueron conquistados, que apostataron de la fe, huyendo de la sujeción y vasallage a S.M., como son los del Chol y *la provincia del Próspero, a que se han agregado otras naciones y parcialidades de indias.*

El otro hermano fue progenitor de los Mames y Pocomanes, *que habiendo habitado en su gentilidad muchas de las tierras que hoy son de las naciones que abajo diré en el riñon de esta provincia; las guerras que se dieron consumieron muchos, y los que quedaron de los* Mames *los retiraron los* Quichés *hasta las sierras altas del norte, donde hay hoy muchos pueblos; los* Pocomanes *tambien fueron arrinconados de los* Cacchiqueles *hacia al oriente, y hay hoy de ellos muy buenos pueblos.*

Del otro hermano, que era el mayor de todos, se pobló todo lo que son hoy Quiches, Kacchiqueles *y* Subtujiles; *estas tres naciones se enseñorearon a fuerza de armas de lo que es riñon del reino de Guatemala; tierras mucho mejores y de más regalo convenientes y buenos temperamentos que las otras, porque creciendo y aumentándose, olvidados de sus humildes principios, les entró la ambición, y sin otro motivo o con leves causas les conspiraban los unos contra los otros; y unidos al principio los* Quichés, Kacchiqueles, *y* Subtujiles *fueron formidables a las demás naciones; y divididos en tres reinos como luego veremos fueron terror de todos y enemigos unos de otros entre sí, sin respetar los parentescos de su origen....*

Volviendo a la población de este reino Guatemalteco, el mayor de los hermanos Tultecas *se quedó a esta parte que llaman* Utatlán, *el cual que se llamaba* Axopal *tuvo dos hijos en su muger que se llamaba* Oceloxoj; *el primero de ellos se llamo* Xijutemal *y el segundo* Acxocuaj, *entre los cuales, viendo el aumento en que iba su desendencia distribuyó; pasados muchos años de su llegada sus grandes provincias, porque si bien al principio eran como solo un reino gobernados todas por el dicho* Acxopal, *llegando a edad de mas de 200 años hizo dos señoríos uno dió al hijo mayor llamado* Xiutemal *(que dira? a su reino de Subtujiles), y él se quedó en la parte de* Utatlán *(de donde todo el reino se llamó así); dispuso estos tres estados con este orden que por muerte suya entrase en el gobierno de* Utatlán *como rey soberano su hijo mayor y el segundo pasase al estado que tenía el primero, y si este tuviese hijo entrase al del segundo o el pariente mas allegado al tronco, y si hubiese hijos de todos se graduasen por su edad y cercanía y hubiese orden, no solo en la entrada de los oficios mayores y* ajauarem *(que así llamaban el senorío) sino el dos asientos; por manera que siempre venía el reyno a personas ancianas....*

Hizo su asiento y corte el hijo mayor Xiutemala *ocho leguas de esta ciudad de Guatemala en un paraje que llamó,* Chiximche, *que quiere decir, "en el árbol de maiz," por uno que hallaron; llamose también* Patinamit *como si dijéramos, "la ciudad antonomástica," u origen de las ciudades; estos nombres tuvo en el gobierno de* Xiutemala; *y después asendiendo este a* Utatlán *por muerte de su padre como ya diremos, y entrando en su lugar su hermano* Acxocuajuj, *se llamó* Quautemal, *y corrompido el nombre* Guatemala; *y después de la conquista* Tecpán Guatemala, *que quiere decir "palacio real de Guatemala."*

Creció este estado como los otros dos en populosísimo número, y se llegó a hacer reyno aparte del de Utatlán; *extendiose en muchos pueblos, hasta el lugar en donde hicieron los Españoles la primera fundación de esta ciudad; eran 38 ó 40 pueblos los que vivían bajo el dominio del rey* Kacchiquel, *cuyos nombres son los siguientes*: Uocabul, Atexo, Ualic, Uitanin, Lajub Belecuyac, Xubabac, K'ak'-lix, Nultucus, Zamael TuK'um, Chik'otuk', Chicak'ik'?, Coja, Ajcusuia, Zutum, K'ixjal, Molobak Toxlomane?, Zualay, Uchabajay, Acumilajay, Lamak', Cumatz, Rapak, Chicak, Uxa, Ajalquik', Molonucabaj, Nim posam, Nacuxcuix, Bulbuxyal, Panaj, Chiojom, K'akinan, K'uk'uyu, K'axcan, Uuxuciwan, Xerapit. *El parage pues que hoy se llama* Almolonga *era un pueblo pequeño que servía de guarda a muchas milpas, y se llamaba* Bulbuxyal, *que traducido por los Mexicanos le dijeron*, Atlomloni, *que quiere decir, "agua que brota."*

El segundo hijo llamado Axoquauj *hizo su corte en* Atitlán, *que en lengua* Subtujil *llaman* Axiquinijay, *que quiere decir, "casa de águilas"; creció también, y fue reino aparte de los otros dos, y se llamó* Subtujiles; *extendiéronse por la costa del sur, en donde tenían haciendas muy cuantiosas de cacao, que eran sus minas ricas.*

Solo Axopal, *que hizo su asiento en* Utatlán,....

APPENDIX XVI: *Título Tzutujil* Used by Brasseur

The account was taken from the second volume of Brasseur's, *Histoire des Nationes Civilisées du Mexique et de l'Amerique Centrale* (1857:II:83-84). As Brasseur's footnotes show, his summary came from the famous *Crónica Franciscana*, now lost (see Secondary Documents).

In translating the brief passage from the French, I gratefully acknowledge the help of Rochelle Silva of San Diego, California. She provided an initial translation as a basis for my translation.

I have altered Brasseur's punctuation in order to clarify the meaning of several phrases.

"The traditions of the various nations conquered by the Spaniards in the state of Guatemala are all equally in accord in giving themselves the same origin. According to these traditions [2], they were part of a powerful people established on the other side of the seas. After having grown considerably, they wanted to invade the neighboring states; they found themselves involved in a series of wars and battles which ended with their humiliation. Persecuted

[2] Ms. Zutujil, en la Chron. de San Francisco de Goattemala.

and pursued, they decided to abandon the fatherland to seek a refuge against the vengence of their enemies beyond the ocean.

A squadron, composed of a large number of boats, brought the exiled with their families; they are supposed to have embarked at the places called "Wucub Pek, Wucub Ciwan," the Seven Caves and the Seven Ravines [3]. From there they directed their vagrant trip as far as the region which they designated under the name of Xenimain [4], where after another extremely arduous trip, they settled in deserted localities, which for that reason received the name Tolan [5]—that is to say, "the solitude."

It is there that, tired of their nomadic life, the tribes prospered considerably, spread themselves far, and must have founded various states, of which the most flourishing was that of Tula[6]. But as a result of new dissensions, war broke out, and they were chased out of this other land. Finally, after another very long peregrination, they arrived in the mountains of Quiché.

Such is the quick sketch of the Tzutujil traditions preserved by the Guatemalan chronicle."

APPENDIX XVII: *Relación Cerrato*

The account was contained in a letter sent by Licenciado Alonso López Cerrato, Governor of Guatemala, to the emperor on the 25th of May, 1552. An extract of it may be found in the Muños collection (T. 68:1390), Real Academia de la Historia, and it was published in a collection of 16th century documents in Spain (CDI 1875).

"*Mandóme V.M. informarte de lo que se había antiguamente. Lo que yo he podido averiguar es que en esta tierra había 4 señores.... Sinaca que era señor de los Utlatecas.... Sacachul de los Guatemaltecas, otro de Comalapa, y otro de Jilotepeque; aunque estos dos postreros reconocían a los otros dos. A estos servían muchas personas, pero no les daban pecho ni servicio ordinario, sino lo que habían menester. Con estos había 24 diputados que entendían en las cosas de gobernación y justicia; y eran tantas partes que si el señor mas principal hacía alguna cosa indebida, le cortaban la cabeza. Estos señores principales ponían caciques en todas las provincias allí sujetas, los quales los indios tambien servían en hacerles sus sementeras, y traerles leña y agua, y en hacerles sus casas, y darles lo que habían menester.*

---

[3] Ms. Zutujil, *ibid.*

[4] Xe-nim-ain, that is to say, literally, "below the great Caiman."

[5] Tolan effectively means, "solitude," "a desert" in the language of the Quiché, Cakchiquel, Tzutujil, etc.

[6] There is a question as to whether this settlement of Tula, also called Tollan, the capital of the royal Toltecs, is the place whose founding the Tzutujil attribute to their ancestors. The answer to this is hard to decide."

Cuando los Españoles entraron en esta tierra, a unos caciques mataron, a otros quitaron los cacicazgos; por manera que en toda esta provincia casi no hay cacique natural ni legítimo. Y si estos han de llevar un tributo como antes, y otro los encomenderos, implica muy gran contradición a lo que V.M. tiene mandado....que los indios paguen menos tributo a los encomenderos que solían pagar a sus caciques; y si hubieron de pagar a unos y otros no se podría sufrir. En esto hay confusión, y en que vengan la justicia y gobernación hay otro daño grande, porque la justicia que ellos hacían era por su voluntad sin proceso ni causa alguna, y por muy livianas causas ahorcaban al que querían, y le tomaban sus hijos y mugeres por esclavos, y hacían otros insultos. Sería inconveniente consentirlo ahora. Se ha entendido en volver a algunos señores o sus hijos los cacicazgos; y muchos aun usan sus tiranías, mandando dar 20 al que se reparten 10 de tributo. Quéjanse que no les tienen el acatamiento que solían....porque antiguamente los reverenciaban como a dioses, y si esto durara podrían los señores levantar la tierra facilmente. Ahora preciánse de vasallos del Emperador y no tienen aquella obediencia."

APPENDIX XVIII: *Relación Garcés.*

The relación consists of two letters written by the alcalde mayor of Zapotitlán, Diego de Garcés. The first letter was sent to the audiencia in Guatemala in 1570, the second was sent to the Crown in 1572. The copies of both letters were taken from the Archivo General de Indias (Guatemala 968, and 55).

1570 Letter.

"Muy Ilustrísimos Señores. Porque de cada día se ofrecen cuentas y repartimientos de tributos en los pueblos desta provincia y su jurisdicción, y porque podría ser que las personas que vienen a hacer las dichas cuentas diesen diferentes pareceres de lo que conviene al servicio de Su Magestad, y por de los naturales en las posibilidades y frutos y riqueza o pobreza de los dichos pueblos, o por ser mal informados dello, o por otras causas que muchas veces acontece entre los hombres, he acordado enviar a Vuestra Señoría la relación que con ésta va como criado de Su Magestad, y que desea servirle y acertar en lo que se me encargare y mandare como persona que he visto y visitado los pueblos desta dicha jurisdicción, y sé lo que es y puede cada uno dellos, así los de la costa como los de la sierra; todo aunque son muchos y el distrito largo y muy trabajoso de caminar, por la cual se entenderá con mucha facilidad en que y como y cuanto puede tributar cada un pueblo y vecinos dél, poco más o menos conforme al mejor parecer de Vuestra Señoría, cuya muy Ilustrísima Persona Nuestro Señor guarde, prospere, y ensalce por tiempos muy largos, como por sus servidores, es deseado.

Los pueblos de la sierra no pueden ni deben tributar en cacao por ninguna vía, porque ni lo hay ni se cría en ella, y de ir los indios a buscarlo fuera de sus tierras enferman y mueren unos, y otros se quedan amancebados en los pueblos de cacao, y aun se casan segunda vez, teniendo viva la primera mujer, y hay pueblos que tributan en cacao estando como están en la sierra donde no se da.

Y también aunque en los dichos pueblos de la sierra tributan en mantas, generalmente en todos ellos se ha de tener atención que no se cría ni coje algodón en toda la serranía, y se lleva desta costa, aunque es cosa necesaria que tributen en mantas, así por el pro de la tierra como porqué es gente desocupada y no tienen en que entender, y pueden tejer y hacer las dichas mantas; tienen mucho maíz y gallinas todos ellos que poder tributar así mismo.

Y también se ha de tener atención que las mantas que tributan los naturales son como la lenzería, que hay delgadas y bastas y unas chicas y otras grandes, porqué hay mantas que valen a 8 tostones, y hay otras de a 4, y en otras partes de a 5, y así van de diferentes maneras y precios.

Y también partes de la sierra donde las gallinas valen a real y partes que a medio real, y el maíz así mismo hay partes donde vale a dos reales la fanega y partes que a 4 y otras a 8, y por ser muchos los pueblos de la sierra no va especificado aquí en cuales dellos vale a un precio y en cuales a otro y en cuales se hacen mantas de a 8 tostones y en cuales de a 5 y en cuales de a 4; espacificarlos cada que va se me lo mande porque he visto y visitado toda mi juridicción, aunque es muy larga y la más trabajosa de caminos que hay en las indias, y lo he visto todo por vista de ojos.

Los pueblos de cacao son desde las estancias de Atitlán de la real corona hasta Santa Catalina de la encomienda de don Francisco de la Cueva por el camino real que va por esta costa a Mexico, según aquí irá declarado.

Y la Magdalena, que por otro nombre se llama el Patulul, *y San Miguel, estancias de Tecpán Atitlán de la real corona, y de Tecpán Guatemala de la encomienda de Marroquín , aunque son pueblos que están en la costa no son pueblos de cacao, no lo hay en ellos; estos deben tributar conforme a sus cabeceras.*

San Francisco y Santa Barbara y San Andrés y San Bartolomé, estancias de Atitlán de la real corona son pueblos ricos de cacao, y lo mismo los vecinos de Atitlán, que tienen milpas de cacao en los dichos 4 pueblos, y en estos se cría y coje algodón y cualesquier otras semillas y legumbres de la tierra; muy bien pueden tributar unos con otros a diez y ocho contles *de cacao sin otra cosa, y no más porque en los pueblos de cacao ocúpanse los indios en el beneficio dél, y no pueden entender en otras labranzas, si no es maíz para su sustento de los pasajeros.*

San Juan de Nagualapa, de la encomienda de Gaspar Arias de Ávila, que es en los Suchitepéquez es el mas rico pueblo desta cos-

ta, y en toda la tierra no hay indios que más gasten y compren que los deste pueblo, porque tienen mucho cacao y bueno, y pueden pagar a 20 contles de cacao unos con otros, porque en los pueblos ricos de cacao no se dan ni pueden sembrar algodón ni otras cosas, aunque lo lleva la tierra, por la ocupación de sus milpas.

San Antonio de la encomienda de Juan Méndez de Sotomayor y Francisco de Ayllón así mismo es en los Suchitepéquez, es pueblo rico de cacao y podrán tributar como los de las estancias de Atitlán, porque no son los indios en general tan ricos como los de Nagualapa.

Xicalapa de la encomienda de Juan Rodríguez Cabrillo está desviado de todos los demás pueblos desta costa, distancia de 12 leguas, y está junto a la mar del sur; es el pueblo mas rico de cacao en su tanto de toda la tierra, y pueden tributar a 30 contles de cacao, que es media carga unos con otros, y no otra cosa; es tierra muy cálida y enferma, mas que ninguna otra deste distrito.

Santo Tomás en el cual hay indios de la real corona y Gaspar Arias de Avila y de Alonso Gutiérrez de Monzón, está 2 leguas de los Suchitepéquez a la parte de la sierra de Totonicapán; es tierra templada, y no es muy fértil de cacao por ser mas fría que las dichas; pueden tributar en cacao y maíz y gallinas, como no pase todo de a 7 tostones por tributario unos con otros.

San Gregorio es pueblo muy chiquito que tendrá hasta vecinos, y son de las mismas encomiendas que Santo Tomás; está otra legua más arriba, llegado a la dicha sierra; es tierra fría; son pobres y tributan en cacao a mucha costa y trabajo suyo; debían tributar en dinero como Totonicapa y Quezaltenango de la real corona o mandarlos pasar a Santo Tomás donde serían mas bien doctrinados y visitados de su vicario de lo que son.

Zamayaque de la encomienda de Alonso Gutiérrez de Monzón, está a una legua del pueblo de San Antonio Suchitepéquez en el mismo camino real; es pueblo de cacao aunque no tan rico como los Suchitepéquez, porqué aquí empieza a adelgazar la tierra y no es tan fértil de cacao como los Suchitepéquez; pueden tributar en cacao y maíz y gallinas con que no pase de a 6 tostones y medio, hasta 7 por tributario unos con otros, contando las gallinas a real y el maíz a 6 reales.

San Pablo de la encomienda de Lorenzo de Godoy y de Juan de Morales y de Zavallos y de Juan Rodríguez Cabrillo; está 3 tiros de arcabuz de Zamayaque; es de la misma arte, y puede tributar lo mismo que Zamayaque.

San Bernardino estancia de Totonicapán de la real corona está a una legua de Zamayaque, abajo hacia la mar del sur; es buena tierra de cacao, salvo que no tienen tierras, y las de Santo Antonio Suchitepéquez llegan hasta las mismas casas de San Bernardino, y alquilan tierras en que sembrar su maíz; pueden tributar en cacao y no en otra cosa por no tener tierras; y pueden pagar a 14 contles de cacao, unos con otros y no más.

Zambo de la encomineda del secretario Diego de Robledo y de Gaspar Arias de Ávila y del menor Diego de la Barrerra está en el camino real a 2 leguas de Zamayaque; es pueblo templado; tienen cacao y pataste y algodón y maíz y gallinas; y en todo ello pueden tributar aunque las milpas de cacao deste pueblo y sus comarcanos son muy menores y de menos llevar que ningunas de todas las otras declaradas, y la tierra más delgada y flaca que todas las dichas; no pueden tributar los deste pueblo más de hasta valor de 7 tostones, unos con otros en todo lo que tributaren, teniendo atención que las gallinas valen a real y el maíz a 6 reales fanega.

San Pedro, estancia de Totonicapa de la real corona, está cerca de Zambo; son pobres y aunque tienen cacao es poco, y tienen ruines tierras; pueden tributar en cacao y no otra cosa, y pagar a 12 contles unos con otros; este pueblo es de muy pocas o casi ninguna granjería.

Zapotitlán de la encomineda de Juan Maldonado de Guzmán y Doña Juana de Sayavedra está en el camino real quarto de legua de Zambo; las milpas de cacao deste pueblo son ruines y de poco llevar, aunque tienen muchas tierras y buenas, son pobres por no ser trabajadores; tienen cacao y pataste aunque poco; tienen algodón harto; pueden tributar en mantas y cacao y pataste, maíz y gallinas, como lo tienen de uso, con que no pase de a 6 tostones cada tributario uno con otros; las mantas de aquí aunque son bastas son grandes y sirven de costales para el cacao, y para este efecto son los mejores de toda la tierra; valen a 7 tostones y el maíz a 6 reales y las gallinas a real, y a veces vale el maíz a 4 reales.

Mazatenango y Cuyotenango, sujetos del dicho pueblo de Zapotitlán y de la misma encomienda, tienen cacao y pataste y mejores milpas de cacao que Zapotitlán, porque caen a legua de Zapotitlán mas abajo a la mar; y es tierra más caliente y dase mejor el cacao, y los indios son mejores trabajadores; pueden tributar en lo mismo que la cabecera, y hasta valor de 7 tostones cada uno unos con otros, que en cacao vienen a ser 14 contles, a razón de a 30 tostones (la) carga, que es el precio mas ordinario, aunque el cacao de Zapotitlán siempre vale más.

San Martín de la misma encomienda y sujeto así mismo de Zapotitlán está en el camino real a 2 leguas dél; puede tributar como Zapotitlán.

San Felipe estancia de Quezaltenango de la real corona está al lado de San Martín, obra de media legua hacia la sierra; las milpas de cacao deste pueblo son como las demás de Zapotitlán y Zambo, porque es tierra mas fría; tienen algodón, maíz, gallinas, cacao y pataste, tributan en cacao aunque con trabajo, empero pagan su tributo mejor que sus comarcanos; pueden dar hasta 12 contles cada uno de tributo unos con otros, no dando otra cosa si no fuese una gallina.

San Luís así mismo estancia de Quezaltenango de la real corona es de la misma arte y puede tributar lo mismo.

Santa Ursula, barrio de San Luís y sujeto a Totonicapa de la real corona, son pocos indios y pobres y no pueden jamás pagar tributo, ni la pagan a derechas, ni cosa que deban; y no pueden tributar en cacao; deberían tributar en dineros como la cabecera.

Santa Catalina estancia de Oztuncalco de la encomienda de don Francisco de la Cueva está a 2 leguas de San Luís; y es tierra mas cálida y muy mejor de cacao; aquí torna a engrosar la tierra, y corresponde con la de la provincia de Soconusco con quien confina, porque deste pueblo al de Tilpa, que es el primero de la provincia de Soconusco, hay 9 leguas de despoblado, y al medio se parten los terminos; tiene buenas milpas de cacao aunque son nuevas; tributan en mantas y cacao, y las mantas de aquí valen a 8 tostones.

A la parte de arriba deste pueblo hay muchos pueblos de la misma encomienda de don Francisco de la Cueva que confina con la provincia de Soconusco, y tienen buen cacao conforme al de la dicha provincia, que son la Magdalena Coatepeque, San Pablo, Santa Lucía Malacatlán, Zazitepeque, Tecpantepeque.

Y todos los cuales son estancias y sujetos de Zacatepeque y Oztuncalco sus cabeceras, y de la dicha encomienda; su posibilidad se especificará más por entero al tiempo de contarlos; y hase de advertir en una cosa en que va mucho, y es que los dichos pueblos de Zacatepeque y Oztuncalco que son las cabeceras no tienen cacao ni se cría en ellos, porque es tierra muy fría, y está en la sierra; y así los vecinos dél no deben tributar en cacao, salvo algunos dellos que tienen milpas de cacao en las dichas estancias; las mantas de estos pueblos y sus estancias son de una suerte y las mejores de toda la tierra.

Y ha se de advertir más que Santa Catalina está 15 leguas de Oztuncalco y acude a ella son su tributo, lo cual no es justo ni se debe permitir.

Hay otras estancias sujetas de los dichos 2 pueblos de Oztuncalco y Zacatepeque, como son Chiquirrichapa y San Martín y Texutla y Comitlán, los cuales están en la sierra y tierra muy fría; y no se cría ni coje cacao en ella y así no deben tributar en cacao porque de irlo a buscar a la provincia de Soconusco, y a otras partes cálidas con la mudanza del temple de la tierra enferman y mueren muchos.

En toda esta jurisdicción no hay más pueblos de cacao porque es todo serranía, y la provincia de Cuilco que se incluye en ésta no lo tiene, si no es Motozintla la Baja, que confina con la provincia de Soconusco por la parte del poniente; y por la otra parte hacia el norte, confina esta provincia con la de Chiapa, y en toda ella ni en la sierra de Jacaltenango, ni en la de Huehuetenango no hay cacao niguno, porque toda ella es tierra fría, y no se da cacao ni algodón ni frutas de la tierra no otras legumbres apenas, y es tierra pobre y estéril, salvo de maíz y gallinas que hay en abundancia. Diego Garcés."

1572 Letter.

"Los gobernadores indios son muy perjudiciales en los pueblos, y de ningún fruto; porque, como son gobernadores y principales, temen los pobres indios; y por muy grandes fuerzas y robos y cohechos y prisiones que les hagan, no se osan quejar; y si alguno se queja, le buscan luego por donde destruirlo; y le dicen que el Alcalde Mayor se ha de ir, y que ellos han de quedarse allí siempre; y que se lo han de pagar de que Vuestros vasallos reciben grandes vejaciones y trabajos perdidos.

Que por ninguna vía ni modo se consienta tesquilar a india ninguna por graves y enormes delitos que cometa, porque esta orden y manera de hacer justicia creo sin duda la introdujo el demonio para su contento; y ha sido y es cosa muy usada y guardada por frayles y clérigos y por Vuestras justicias; y es que como las indias andan destocadas y en cabello, en viendo a una india tresquilada, todos cuantos ocurren al pueblo ponen los ojos en ella y la persiguen porque entienden que es mujer errada, y que por tal la tresquilaron; y es como el ramo de la taverna y tablilla en el mesón, y es causa que se vengan a hacer las indias públicamente malas y pierdan la vergüenza.

Y también conviene así mismo que en los sermones que se les hicieren a los naturales nunca se trate de los adulterios que hubo en los tiempos antiguos, como fue el de David con Bersabe, ni otros porque los indios son grandemente y demasiados de viciosos en este pecado; y a sus propias deudas no perdonan, y como oyen cosas semejantes y son livianos e incapaces paréceles que pues a aquellos bien aventurados y santos hicieron aquello, que no es mucho que ellos lo hagan; y aun les parece que no es mal hecho ni pecado, y así los que gobiernan entre ellos, así en lo espiritual como en lo temporal se deben mucho abstener y guadar deste vicio....

Que en los pueblos donde se coje y cría cacao no tributen en cacao, porque el cacao se cría en tierra caliente, y cuanto más mejor y yendo los indios de tierra fría a buscar cacao a la caliente para pagar sus tributos enferman y mueren; y muchos se casan segunda vez en ellos, teniendo viva su primera mujer, y yo he castigado a hartos por ello....

Y también de casarse los indios de poca edad, se les siguen muchos e infinitos daños; y es que en siendo casados hácenlos tributarios, y no tienen cuenta con la edad; y como son niños ellos y ellas ni tienen fuerzas ni abilidad para proveer sus personas y casas de lo necesario y pagar sus tributos; andan rotos y pobres y desnudos y buscan entre sus parientes quien les pague su tributo, y pónense a servir en casa de otros; y el marido va para una parte y la mujer por otra, y es gran lástima a verlos; y en esto hay tan mala orden que niños y niñas de 8 y 10 años y menos estan casados; sobre lo cual yo proveí un auto....

Y también de casárselos indios de unos pueblos en otros se recrecen grandes ofensas contra Diós Nuestro Señor, y de servicios deba muy grandes daños y pérdidas y pleitos a los naturales....y es que como son gente incapaz y no entienden lo que es el matrimonio, por cualquier enojitos que entre ellos haya, se vuelve la mujer a su tierra, y a casa de sus padres, y acontece estar mucho tiempo que no se vuelven a juntar; y a muchas he hecho yo volver de sus pueblos a poder de sus

*maridos dos y tres veces; y acontece no tener remedio este daño; y así
mismo, hay otro muy grande, y es que si el marido hubo con su mujer
alguna milpa de cacao, tributa por si en su pueblo, y tributa en el
pueblo de la mujer por razón de la milpa que con ella hubo; y es tanta
carga esta que de cada día hacen dejación de las milpas, y las quieren
perder antes que pagar tanto tributo; y otras veces les ponen pleitos
los del pueblo de donde tienen la tal milpa, y prenden por cualquier
inconveniente que haya...."*

APPENDIX XIX: Judicial Records of Claims to Servitude Rights by Descendants of Quiche Rulers

The extracts were taken from documents located in the Archivo
General de Centroamérica and Archivo General de Indias. I have
arranged them in chronological order and have included the citation at the beginning of each extract. Spelling and punctuation
have been slightly changed from the originals in order to facilitate
their study.

Cédula Real, 1557. (Carrasco 1967a:253-254)

"Presidente e Oidores de la nuestra Audiencia Real de los Confines.
*Don Juan Cortés cacique de Utlatlán y de todos sus pueblos y
sujetos, hijo legítimo que dizque es de Don Juan Chicueyquiagut y
nieto de Yeymazatl, me ha hecho relación que siendo los dichos sus
padre y abuelo señores de la dicha provincia de Utlatlán y teniéndola
y poseyéndola entró en ella Don Pedro de Alvarado y sus capitanes
y la conquistaron juntamente con la provincia de Guatimala, y que
el dicho Don Pedro de Alvarado había quemado a su abuelo porque
no le daba oro, y muerto que fue el dicho Don Pedro y sus lugarte-
nientes despojaron al dicho Don Juan Chicueyquiagut casi de toda
la dicha provincia, y que había hecho muchos repartimientos de ella
en los Españoles que con él iban, y dividió los pueblos, y que así cada
uno de los encomenderos hicieron y nombraron cacique a los indios
que les parecían y de quien mejor se podían aprovechar; y que como
murió el dicho su padre y él había quedado muchacho no le habían
querido obedecer ni tener por señor y cacique de la dicha tierra como
lo habían sido todos sus pasados, y que aunque él lo ha pedido los
encomenderos de los dichos pueblos lo defendían que no había de ser
señor de tantos pueblos, ni le habían de obedecer, y que ha requerido
muchas veces a las justicias de esa dicha provincia para que lo pro-
vean, las cuales no lo han querido proveer, en lo cual recibía mucho
agravio y notorio daño, y que por esta causa vivía muy alcanzado y
necesitado, y me suplicó que pues no nos éramos servidos que ningún
fuese despojado ni quitado de su cacicazgo, Vos mandase que le me-
tiésedes en la posesión de la dicha provincia de Utlatlán, y le resti-
tuyésedes el señorío y cacicazgo de ella y de todos sus pueblos y sujetos según y de la manera que lo habían tenido y poseído el dicho su*

*padre y abuelo, o como la mi merced fuese. Lo cual visto por los del
nuestro Consejo de las Indias fue acordado que debía mandar esta
mi cédula para Vos, y yo lo tuve por bien porque Vos mandó que veáis
lo susodicho y llamadas todas las partes a quien tocarse hagáis e ad-
ministréis sobre ello entero y breve cumplimiento de justicia, de manera que las partes le hayan y alcancen y por defecto de ella no tengan
causa ni razón de se nos venir ni enviar a quejar sobre ello. Fecha
en Valladolid a 30 de noviembre de 1557 años. La princesa. Re-
gistrada de Ledesma, señalada de Vriviesca, Don Juan Villagómez."*

Autos, 1596. (AGC, Al:1587-10231)

*"En la ciudad de Santiago de las provincias de Guatemala a 28 dias
del mes de julio de 1561 (sic) años ante el Ilustrísimo Señor, licenciado Francisco Briceño, gobernador por Su Magestad de la dicha
provincia parecieron Don Juan Cortés, cacique del pueblo de Utlatán,
y Cristóbal Lucas, alguacil, y Diego de Mendoza y Pedro Gómez, y
Juan Pérez y los demás vecinos que dijeron ser del pueblo de Santa
Cruz Utlatán ante el dicho señor gobernador; se averiguó la diferencia
que hay entre el dicho Don Juan Cortés y los dichos indios cerca de
que el dicho Don Juan dice que no complen con el contenido en el auto
y mandamiento del dicho señor gobernador; y los dichos indios dicen
que el dicho Don Juan Cortés excede del suso dicho y en pedirles y
llevarles más del contenido en el dicho mandamiento... en que les
manda a los dichos indios hacer otra semetera demás de media fanega, demás la sementera que por el dicho auto y mandamiento son obligados hacer y no les da por lo suso dicho paga suficiente; y los dichos
indios no la quieren hacer de su voluntad; y también exceden en que
envía recojedores del dicho pueblo para que recojan el tributo de los
pueblos y estancias de la costa; y los dichos recojedores cuando van
al dicho llevan cargados de los indios de dicho pueblo de su ropa que
reciben agravio en dos cosas, la una en llevarlos cargados y sin paga,
y la otra en el servicio que habían de hacer los dichos recojedores la
semana que les cabe ayudar hacer la milpa demás; y en las otras cosas
que todos deben hacer no las hacen y carga el trabajo y servicio sobre
los demás vecinos del dicho pueblo... excede en que tiene 2 indios
casados en su estancia de lleguas y guarda dellas, que está en el dicho
pueblo, los cuales no sirven en cosa alguna más dello en lo dicho; también pareció el dicho Juan Cortés lleva el tributo aparte de 8 indios
vecinos del dicho pueblo que llaman los Mac achis ... lo cual se les
dió a entender por lengua de Gaspar Martínez, intérprete, que le cum-
plirían; y el dicho señor gobernador lo firmó a su nombre, el licenciado Briceño... en la ciudad de Santiago de Guatemala, a 29 días
del mes julio de 1569 años."*

Memoria, 1574. (AGC, Al:1587-10231)

*"...de la dicha memoria de los indios nimac achies y de un man-
damiento del licenciado Briceño, que así presentaron la parte de dichos*

indios es éste que se sigue. En nombre de los indios que se llaman nimac achies, *que fueron esclavos de los antecesores de Don Juan Cortés y Don Juan de Rosales que han pagado tributos son los siguientes: Diego* Sunun, *tributario, Isabel* Nun *su mujer, y un hijo llamado Diego; Juan Gómez y Catarina Gómez su mujer, tributario; Juan* Conum (?) *y Catarina Gómez su mujer, tributario; Juan Godoy y María Godoy su mujer; Catarina, vieja viuda, reservada de tributo, es suegra del dicho Juan* Canil; *Pedro Gómez y Juana Gómez su mujer; Juan Gómez y Catarina Gómez su mujer; Cristóbal López y Magdalena López su mujer; este tiene en su casa a Isabel, viuda vieja su madre reservada; Diego* Chacchal *y Magdalena* Chacchal *su mujer; Juan* Chacchal Teupatlaca, *Catarina* Chacchal *su mujer; Luis* Quiawit, *viejo reservado, Catarina* Quiawit *su mujer; Juan* Quiawit *y Magdalena* Quiawit *su mujer; Diego* Quiawit *y Magdalena* Quiawit *su mujer; Baltasar Alonso, Catarina Alonso su mujer; Diego* Tun *y...? Tun su mujer; Diego Eli e Isabel Eli su mujer; Tomás* Coloc, *Mercía* Colol *su mujer; Diego de Mendoza y Catarina de Mendoza su mujer; Miguel de León y Catarina de León su mujer; Pedro de Angulo y Ana de Angulo su mujer. Don Juan Cortés, Don Juan de Rojas.*"

Petición, 1575. (AGC A1:1587-10231)

"parece que por petición que en ella presentó Francisco Sánchez en nombre de los dichos caciques...del año pasado de 1574 años nos hizo relación diciendo que los dichos sus partes como sucesores de los señores del dicho pueblo y de toda la provincia de Utlatán, conforme a nuestras leyes y ordenanzas habían sido amparados aunque no tanto como les pertenecía, como en los privilegios y excepciones y provechamientos que eran suyas, y particularmente de muchos años a esta parte habían tenido por tributarios ciertos indios nimac achies *que eran esclavos propios suyos y de sus padres, y aquellos que los cautivaron en la guerra, a los cuales los tenían por sus esclavos; y cuando estas provincias se conquistaron y después acá les habían tributado en reconocimiento de su señorío y así se había mandado por los gobernadores pasados, particularmente en las ordenanzas que hizo el Licenciado Zorita, oidor, y Licenciado Briceño, gobernador que fue de la dicha provincia de Guatemala, como dijo que constaba y parecía por los autos que presentaba; y con el tiempo, aunque solían ser muchos más, llegaron los del pueblo de Utlatán a hacer 8, y ahora eran 20..."*

Padrón, 1574. (AGC, A1:1587-10231)

"...en el dicho pueblo de Santa Cruz Utlatlán, a 19 de octubre de 1574 años, el dicho señor oidor mandó que los indios que parecía que tenían los dichos Don Juan Cortés y Don Juan de Rojas caciques por sus tributarios que llaman Nimac achies, por decir que antiguamente eran esclavos de sus pasados, que son los de la nunciación; que contra los dichos caciques hizo Alonso Telles en nombre de la Ha-

cienda Real, por no los haber declarado al tiempo que se empadronasen juntamente con los demás; los cuales declararon los dichos caciques y pareciendo algunos de ellos en precencia del dicho señor oidor, los que estaban en el dicho pueblo, y declarando así...? mujeres e hijos en la manera siguiente (the list of tributaries by family is given)... según que lo suso dicho consta y parece por el dicho padrón cuenta que al fin de ella parece están firmados del dicho Doctor Arévalo Sedeño, y Pedro de Grizalua, escribano, y Francisco de Abalos, intérprete...Alonso Telles, y Juan de Alsa...a mandamineto de los dichos señores, presidente y oidores de la dicha Real Audiencia...mes de diciembre de 1574."

Petición, 1593. (AGC, Al:205-4985)

"Muy poderoso señor don Juan Cortés, cacique de la mitad de la parcialidad de indios Nimac achies, *y a don Juan de Rojas, cacique de la otra mitad; en la provincia de Utlatán, visita de Sacapulas. Decimos que el doctor Pedro de Aguero vuestro oidor y visitador de la dicha provincia nos reservó de tributo por ser como somos tales caciques decendientes de los antiguos caciques nuestros....enpadronó a nuestros hijos, así los primogénitos como los menores casados; a lo cual Vuestra Alteza no debe dar lugar, pues la dicha exempción les viene por derecho de sangre y costumbre inmemorial, y por otros antiguos justos y derechos títulos de que consta notoriamente; y de la dicha costumre a Vuestra Alteza pedimos y suplicamos que sin embargo del dicho enpadronamiento declare por reservados del dicho tributo y otros servicios a los dichos nuestros hijos....(se dan los nombres de sus hijos) debían ser reservados no solamente los primogénitos sino también los demás, siendo como son hijos legítimos....que viniendo como viene el cacicazco y señorío que hoy tienen por vía de linaje y sangre; militaba la misma....en los demás hijos que en los primogénitos; y porque los hijos y nietos de nobles son nobles, aunque no sean primogénitos, ni hayan de ser caciques; y porque entre todas las gentes del mundo hay diferencia entre los nobles y los que no le son, así en tributos como en otras cosas...."*

Carta, 1595. (Carrasco 1967a:262)

"Los caciques del pueblo de Santa Cruz Utatlán y sus sujetos en su gentilidad tuvieron muchas guerras con sus vecinos. A los que de ellos cautivaban hacían esclavos y por esta razón los llamaban nimac achies, *y hoy les dura este nombre a los descendientes de estos cautivos, pero luego se concertaban los caciques con estos vencidos y les daban la libertad, con que se quedasen en sus tierras y les pagasen cierto tributo ellos y los que de ellos procediesen. Este tributo y pecho han cobrado y cobran hasta hoy los caciques de los dichos indios* nimac achies, *y los oidores que han visitado aquellas provincias han conservado los dichos caciques en la posesión de este tributo y en ella también han sido emparados por esta Audiencia. Yo he vuelto sobre este*

pleito pareciéndome que con este tributo duran entre estos naturales vestigios de las servidumbres bárbaras reprobadas por Vuestra Majestad, y que implica contradicción que del tributo formal que a Vuestra Majestad como a su rey universal deben los indios lleven los caciques parte, mayormente que a estos caciques les acuden todos los indios con los servicios que como a tales caciques se les deben, que son repararles las casas, hacerles una milpa de maíz, proveerles la casa de agua y leña y darles indios que les sirvan. Conclúyose la causa y la Audiencia la remitió a Vuestra Majestad.

APPENDIX XX: Judicial Record of Rezago Tributes from Tecpán Guatemala and Quezaltenango.

The following are pertinent extracts from a large expediente in the Archivo General de Centroamérica (A3:2800-40485). Parts of these I have used in an appendix to my dissertation (Carmack n.d.a). The extracts are identified by the names and positions of the persons making the statements.

Statement by the legal defender of the two towns, Licenciado **Tomás Espinosa.**

"el común y maceguales de los dichos, pues pagaron enteramente los tributos de dichos 3 años a los tlatoques y cabezas de calpules, y estos se entendió por los jueces se hacía la reservación porque delinquieron los dichos tlatoques y calpules gravemente gastar en sus borracherías y quedarse con el tributo que los maceguales pagaron; y los dichos maceguales pagaron bién, y así no es justo paguen dos veces; porque de costumbre inmemorial a esta parte los dichos tlatoques y cabezas de calpules cobran los tributes y son cogedores dellos con poder y consentimiento que de los oficiales reales; y este consentimiento atenta la larga costumbre se presume expreso; a los menos es tanto así y permisión evidente, por tan largo tiempo aprobada por los dichos oficiales, los cuales siempre llaman destos principales y a estos escriben sobre las cobranzas; e estos dan las rentas de pago, y por ellas dan por libres al pueblo; y por esta verdad los maceguales acuden con el tributo a los dichos tlatoques y calpules y a ellos reconocen por cobradores, comisarios, y se han tenido y tiene hasta hoy por libres del tributo con la paga que hacen a los dichos principales."

Testimony of Diego de Paz Quinones, the official who had collected tribute in Tecpán Guatemala and Quetzaltenango and many other towns.

"que sabe este testigo que el gobernador, alcaldes, y regidores de los pueblos tienen cuidado de cobrar los tributos y tienen calpules que son indios principales de cada parcialidad, y estos calpuleros cobran el tributo de los vecinos de sus barrios, y andan con todo lo que cobran

al gobernador y alcaldes y regidores; y se haga un montón para pagar
su tributo; y esto ha visto hacerse este testigo en muchos pueblos de
esta provincia....que ha visto este testigo como los alcaldes y regi-
dores de los pueblos cobran los tributos y tienen sus memoriales en
su lengua escritos, donde asientan lo que van cobrando de los vecinos
por estar ellos obligados a la paga de los tributos."

Name list of deceased and other nontributaries from Que-
zaltenango according to calpul affiliation, prepared by Fray
Alonso de la Cruz, from Quezaltenango (1578-1580).

"Calpul don Juan de Chávez: *Mach, Quej, C'urun, Xibit, Xatom,*
Zij, Xok'chite, Cucmaotzay, Xquetey, Pobol, Cabjacutz, Atzcabatzuu,
C'um, Ajtun, Con, Cazcal, Zakik', Cax, Tzalam, Ajcabatz....Coo,
Xc'...., K'al.., Puj (?), C'ac'...., Cotoc (all deceased); Pobol
(deserted).

Calpul Alonzo García: *Zkcun, Bolotuj, Tz'iquina, Zij, Coroc, C'ubal,*
Corox, Zoknow, C'in, Reinoso C'amum, Xk'uh, Iz, Velasco, Gómez,
Mibaboj, Gómez (deceased). (There is also a Francisco, probably de-
serted.)

Calpul Francisco Hernández: *Tz'alic, Chajcan, Chajcan, Ch'amicoj,*
Tunzic', Chowik', Tzoc', Macario, Xub, K'alel, Chojlam, C'ujc'at,
Xujumatzin, Tebalan (deceased). (Two names partially destroyed, prob-
ably deserted).

Calpul don Francisco Mejía: *Tojin, Xc'om, Zajcab, Tzajaq'uit, Juk'*
ab, Yas, Boy, Tazor, Mutic, Cleo Chávez, Jucub, Xiyab, Chin, Nuu
Mutic, Hernández, Uztun, Chapalric', Joron, Xcam....Tac'....Juan
....(deceased). Xuwatic, Uztun....(deserted).

Calpul Juan Macario: *Xic, Ch'aol, Lucas Zatic', Tzamquej, Ralom-*
cot, Zabic', Chacaj, de Sosas Catzol Tz'iqui, Tzamquej, K'ak'awitz,
K'ak'awitz, Yac, Taom, Cabtzutzuj, Tzalanic, Tzamquej, Zic'ol (de-
ceased). Coroc (deserted).

Calpul don Juan Gómez: *Fraco Nijaib, Xic, Xc'ab, Ch'ubat, Jur,*
Tecpan, C'obatil, Tiez, Xic, Tecpan, Paratum, Xeltepa, Cantunaj,
Chochom, Zacayom, Ayaz, Mos, Mich', Xer, Xc'ubchac....Mich',
Lus, Cajt....Xc'a....Racha....Tzin, Toxc'om, Xic, Tucur, Xtz-
iaren Ztamay, Agustín, Rachabuc', Chay, Xtus, Tzarab (deceased);
Yob, Xic, Tuk'ur, Xec (deserted).

Calpul don Juan Pérez: *Xuchi, Xtan, Zat, Uyak'balquej, Yabacoj-*
quej, Q'uis, C'oyoy, C'otuja, Jut, Zop, Luys, Yab, Poz, Zop, C'oyoy,
Xc'ot, Ch'ulim, Ch'ay, López Yac....Tiuj, Cham....Xhin, Poz (de-
ceased); Zicoy, K'ok', Pz (deserted).

Calpul don Juan Batista: *López Pac, Pac, Penec, Penec, Pérez Penec,*
Joron, Car, Zamauz, Juk'ab, Coxujij, Car, Joron, ?enes, Car, Tay,

Gaves, Jocol, Xmay, Tay (deceased); Jocol, Ban...(apparently deserted).

The following name list consists of 3 groups of women:

Catarina viuda tributaria, Isabel v. triba, Catalina Cot viuda, Mag^{na} Yas triba, Magna viuda tributaria.

Isabel mujer Juo Zatic', $Cata^{na}$ mujer, Nua Taon viuda muerta, Ana viuda, Magna viuda triba; María Zajcab triba, Ana Iciwa Juo Rasacatche, Mag^{na} v. triba, Cat^{na} v. triba, $Cata^{na}$ Boy v. triba, Juana v. triba, Mag^{na} v. triba, Jua Ch'nay viuda; $Cata^{na}$ v. C'obakil, $Catan^a$ Xic v., Jua Zc'aran v., Isabel Chochon v., Catana tributaria; Isabel v. triba Ana v. triba, Franca Tutis, viuda.

Mag^{na} v., Isabel v., Isabel Juyub v. triba, Mª Mibaboj v. triba, M^a muerta tributaria."

Name list of deceased and other nontributaries from Tecpán Atitlán, according to calpul affiliation. Probably prepared by a priest.

"Calpul de Don Pedro de Soliz Ajpopo: Po de Soliz viejo, Pérez, Noc, Zit, López viejo, Quec, Bautista viejo, Biuto (viudo), Cantil, Canel viudo viejo, Yu viejo, Canel, Méndez, Tz'iquin viejo, Iquec viejo (Quec), Quec, Robio, Ziquin, Batz'in, Quec viejo, Pérez?, Razam, Izinral, Zaclan, Pepech, Canuz, Pepech viejo, Tesalamanca viejo, Noc Viejo, Bazin viejo, Xuc, Acbal viejo, Tojin, Hernández, de Tapiz viejo, Iquec viejo, Bernabé.... Vásquez Chial, Iyu, Acbal, Pérez, Hernández, López Tlcopantacatl, Balam, Camey viejo, Afin, Hernández, Pérez, mozo soltero, Quin, Baras, Quec viejo, Gómez viejo, Moxin viejo, Bazin viejo, Acbal viejo, Gudiniz, Chanacha, Tazen, Chicop, Ajmac, Pacal, Tepepul, Pacal, Hernández (all deceased); Chenol, Yac, Puzul (all absent); Bernabé, Ziquin (recently married).

Calpul don Gaspar Manrique; Pérez, Quec, de León, Sánchez, Iyu, Blanco, Batzin, López viejo, Hernández, Pérez viejo, Ic, de Paz, Min García, Min Pérez, Gómez viejo, Acbal?, Francisco.

Calpul de Matheo García: Pérez, Canel, Tiax, Bernabé, Moro, Zalte, Noc, de Vera, Chávez, An'a Vinak, Rubio, Zacuj, Acmac, Noc, Rodríquez viejo, Zian viejo, Acmac viejo, Pérez viejo, Iyu (deceased).

Calpul de Diego Sánchez Chiroy: Can Zuluwi, Zuluwi, López Zacquiy, Catu, Chiroy, Rodríguez, Pérez, Acmac viejo, Canel, Iyu viejo, Hernández viejo, Méndez viejo, Batzin....(deceased). Can Zacquiy, Sebastián, Chiroy (deserted); Junacpu (absent).

Calpul de don Pedro K'ekac'uch: Ambrosio, Leonardo, Hernández Nimapam, Xtuluc, López, C'atym Ajmak, Batz'in, Tijax, Cokti, León, López, Min Zibaquijay, Luís Zibakijay, Ajmak, K'anel (deceased).

Calpul de Alonso Pérez Nimak achi: *García Tum viejo, Batz'in, López Tum, Junajpu, Matan, Can viejo, K'anel, Gómez viejo, Ye, Díaz, Batz'in, Méndez, López, López, Tij....(deceased); Cate, Ziquin (absent); Pérez, Junajpu viejo (deserted).*

Calpul de Pablo Ximénez: *Can, Pocob viejo, Ordóñez, Vásquez, Min viejo, Arana, Rafael, López, murió durante la cuenta, Min de Arana, Bueno, Ocoma viejo, López viudo viejo, Alinam, P....viejo, Alva ....Iyu, Franc....López, de Paz, Hernández, Catu, de Buenaventura, Mueun viejo, Noc (deceased); Vásquez, Álvarez, Min (deserted); López recién casado. Mozo soltero.*

Calpul de Juan Martín Ajzic'ajauj: *Can viejo, Camey, Díaz (deceased); Tz'iquin (absent).*

Calpul de Domingo Hernández Xayi: *Do Hernández viejo, Zian viejo, López viejo Tiax, Ajin, López, Banatzij viejo, Junacpu, Gómez viejo, Noc viejo, Tojin viejo, Curuy, Canuy viejo, Moxin, Junajpu, Juo....Noueyo?, Popan, Noc, Pérez (deceased); Rodríguez recién casado (deserted).*

Calpul de Juan de Vera Xitayul: *Pérez, Méndez, Pérez, Cauti viejo, Catu, López, Zian, Ziquin, Ajin viudo, Ziquin, Sánchez viejo, López viejo, Cauti viejo (deceased); Estamel (deserted).*

Calpul de don Diego Maldonado Xulwi: *Gómez, Amac, de Figueroa viejo, Ajmac, Balam viejo, Junajpu, López viejo, Méndez viejo, Méndez viejo, López, Tiax, Junajpu, Iyu, Ajin, Can viejo (deceased).*

Calpul....Tz'quin Baran: *....Pérez viejo, Cauti, hijo Juan Cati (deceased); Pérez Tullido (deserted). ....ran (absent).*

Calpul de Francisco Hernández Arana: *Camey, Quec, Can viejo, Catu viejo, Méndez, Hernández viejo, López viejo, Iquec, Moxin viejo, Gómez viejo, Ajin, López, Junacpu viejo, Acbal, Acmac, Comuyuc viejo, Catu, ...casado, ...viejo, ...tzin viejo, Pérez, Ziquin, Ramírez, Moxin viejo, Moxin, Tiax, Gómez, Vásquez, Noc, Aguilar, Ziquin viejo, Can, Escobar viejo, Lacam (deceased); Acbal, Zico, Camey, Acbal, Zac (deserted); Mozo soltero."*

APPENDIX XXI: Judicial Record Listing Tributaries from Sacapulas (ca. 1572).

The list is of tributaries from two parcialidades at Santo Domingo Sacapulas (AGC, Al:5942-51995). It was prepared in conjunction with a dispute over land between the two parcialidades in 1572. I have included only extracts of the account which precedes and follows the tributary record.

"En este dicho día, mes, y año suso dicho, yo, Francisco del Puegare, hice la dicha cuenta del número de los vecinos de la parcialidad

*de Sacapula y Coatlán, y Sacualpa, y Citalá, y de Iztapanecas en
precencia de todos los caciques, señores, alcaldes y regidores, y los
demás principales; que ellos mismos me fueron nombrando los nombres
de cada maceguat; los cuales hice de ellos una memoria de cada parcialidad de la manera siguiente:*

Parcialidad de Sacapula (*la encomienda de Diego de Salvatierra*).
*Don Francisco Marroquín, Francisco López, alcalde, Pedro Her-
nández, Juan López, Juan Ramos, Simón, Domingo López, Juan
Chaol, Juan Sánchez, Martín Pérez, Francisco Chay, Juan Sebastián,
Juan Sánchez, Pedro López, Juan Chacab, Juan Mejía, Diego Her-
nández, Francisco Tziquin, Francisco Ramírez, Juan Mendoza, Juan
Zontec, Alonso Iztaul, Pedro Cuxun de Pacheco, Francisco Yac,
Diego Reynoso, Pedro Xiuj, Diego Quichiy, Francisco de Castro,
Juan Sante, Diego Quix, Francisco de Paz, Andrés Marroquín, Juan
Chocon, Andrés Méndez, Pedro Zitzum, Juan de Vico, Cristobal López,
Pedro de Velasco, Pedro Pen, Francisco Capal, Pedro Tay, Juan
Contreras, Juan de Vico, Juan López, Juan Olicuan.*

    (*La encomienda de Alonso Paez*): *Don Martín Pérez, Francisco
Nil, Martín de Guzmán, Diego Hernández, Juan Calinto, Pedro Ca-
mey, Juan Quez, Diego Tatzin, Pedro Ajquic, Martín Coch, Miguel
Tul, Juan Zopoca, Diego Quej, Juan de Mendoza, Cristóbal Girón,
Pedro Cimaj, Diego, Pedro Caj, Juan Gómez, Juan Ramos, Martín
Gómez, Francisco Ixtacachi, Mateo, Juan Calel, Andrés Noj, Diego
Muñoz, Francisco Calindo, Juan Iscup, Francisco Nuj, Diego Ca-
caj, Juan Tzut, Pedro Cun, Pedro Quey, Francisco Mani, Cristóbal
López, Juan Martín, Alonso Jamac, Diego Vásquez, Juan Xixilio,
Juan Camey, Francisco Zuac, Pedro Tol, Diego Pu, Diego Méndez,
Diego Pérez, Juan Noj, Juan Solís, Francisco Cordero, Diego Áviles,
Andrés Méndez, Pedro Osorio, Francisco Porcelo, Diego de la Cruz,
Juan Pérez, Martín Liajeza, Francisco Mox, Domingo Bonoco, Juan
de Aguilar, Diego Hernández, Mateo, Francisco Cuxan, Gonzalo Cha-
caj, Juan Lax, Pedro Noj, Juan Calo, Lucas, Domingo Ramos, Diego
Pérez, Juan López, Francisco Baz, Juan Solís, Francisco, Miguel,
Miguel de Vera, Jiram Cac.*

Los Iztapanecas (*encomienda de Juan Griego*).
*Don Francisco Acetuno, Don Francisco Mendo, Andrés Calel, Diego
Ajpopachi, Juan Ajtzalan, Martín Gómez, Juan Martín Tuj, Martín
Ajitza, Andrés Pu, Pedro Tuwiz, Pedro Pu, Diego Biz, Diego Pérez,
Martín Quic, Pedro Tuj, Francisco Sastre, Diego Chizirin, Diego
Lol, Diego Ajanel, Miguel Tu, Juan Méndez.*

Parcialidades Citaltecas, Coatecas, Sacualpanecas (*encomienda de Cristóbal López*).
    Citaltecas: *Don Diego Jaj, Domingo Lajpop, Antonio Pérez,
Juan Pérez, Francisco Pérez, Pedro Choj, Martín Cuch, Felipe, Domingo Girón, Diego Pérez, Sebastián, Juan Baz, Andrés Pac, Diego*

Alquej, Andrés Ajmac, Francisco, Juan Pochol, Juan Polanco, Diego Tel, Diego Pucaj, Domingo Tec, Francisco Tziquin, Pedro Tajwi, Juan Oslaj, Pedro Quez, Martín Xiwit, Juan Calan, Francisco Catin, Pedro Alarcón, Alonso Cican, Juan Malca.

Sacualpanecas: *Don Juan Calel, Cristóbal Toyon, Juan Zac, Antonio Coz, Francisco Pacheco, Diego Méndez, Pedro de Velasco, Juan López, Pedro López, Pedro Martín, Pedro Aczalan, Diego Ajjuleuj, Francisco Bac, Diego Cuj, Juan Zuc, Diego Tun, Andrés Jajmay, Diego Ojer, Alonso Chimay.*

Coatecas: *Antonio Pérez, Pedro de Velasco, Alonso Lajpop, Diego Méndez, Diego Ajanel, Antonio Zac, Pedro Hernández.*

Todos estos indios suman y montan los unos y los otros 200 indios juntos; y según la cantidad y número de la parcialidad de Sacapula, los Iztapanecas, para en comparación de las otras 3 parcialidades, les cabe la cuarta parte de la división y partición...."

APPENDIX XXII: Judicial Record of a Dispute between Alotenango and Escuintla.

The extracts were taken from a document belonging to a private party in Guatemala City. They consist of a series of testimonials given before the audiencia in 1565.

Witness 1, cacique from Tziquinala, ca. 80 years old.

"....*en tiempo de los señores de los Guatemaltecos, que eran* Sinaca *y* Sacachul *y* Potocope, *tenían guerras con los de Esquintepeque y otros pueblos de aquella comarca; los dichos indios Guatemaltecos llegaban a poner su gente de guarnición hasta la tierra que llaman* Xeococo *o* Silosuchil....*y en la dicha tierra tenían dos sacrificaderos de piedra, donde los dichos indios Guatemaltecos sacrificaban a sus ídolos; y que la gente de los dichos Guatemaltecos tenían muchas casas pobladas en aquel tiempo de la guerra que llegaban con ellas, hasta la dicha tierra que tenían por sus términos; y por allí hicieron una cerca alrededor donde llaman los* Chiaguitze, *sembraban maíz, frijoles, y ají, y tenían su poblazón; que después que tuvieron paces y vinieron los Españoles, los dichos indios Guatemaltecos se recogieron y se retiraron más hacia Guatemala, y poblaron el dicho pueblo de Alotenango; y estando así poblados venían e iban a las dichas tierras a hacer sus sementeras....*"

Witness No. 2, elder from Tziquinala.

"....*sabe que cuando* Canaca *y* Sacachal, *sus señores de los indios Guatemaltecos tenían guerras con los indios de Esquintepeque y su comarca tenían como por alborada y señal a donde llegaba a poner la gente de guerra contra los dichos indios de Esquintepeque, la dicha tierra llamada* Xeococo *o* Silosuchit; *y allí ponían su gente de guar-*

nición, porque hasta allí tenían los de Guatemala su término; y allí por señal dello tenían dos sacrificaderos de piedra, y que sabe que los dichos indios Guatemaltecos hacían por allí cercas donde tenían su guarnición, sementeras de maíz, y ají, y frijoles, y tenían muchas casas y poblazón donde llaman los Chiaguites; llegaban hasta el paraje de la dicha tierra que después que la dicha gente indios Guatemaltecos tuvieron paces con los de Esquintepeque y vinieron los Españoles, retiraron hasta Guatemala y poblaron el dicho pueblo de Alotenango, y todavía tenían las tierras a donde con tiempo de guerra hacían sementeras; y hasta ahora van y vienen a hacer y sembrar en ellas milpas....”

Witness No. 3, elder from Almolonga.

“....que sabe que habiendo guerra entre los indios Guatemaltecos y los de Esquintepeque yendo este testigo con la gente de guerra que enviaban los señores principales de Guatemala, llegaban a ponerse en las tierras que llaman Xeococo o Silosxil, porqué hasta allí tenían por término los indios Guatemaltecos de sus tierras; y por señal dello tenían en dicha tierra dos sacrificaderos de piedra, y cuando estaban de guerra y va a las dichas tierras ponían en los dichos sacrificaderos algunas flechas con puntas de pedernal en sangre, untadas para que dichos indios de Esquintepeque llegados a aquel término supiesen que estaban de guerra; y si estaban de paz las ponían con unas pelotillas de cera; que estas señales se acostumbraban poner en los términos de entre unos pueblos y otros que....de la dicha tierra llamada Xeococo hacia Alotenango, no pasaba los de Esquintepeque a cultivar ni labrar las tierras ni hacer sementeras, porque los de Alotenango estaban por allí poblados en tiempo de guerras; porque eran y son Guatemaltecos y hacían sus milpas y sementeras por allí alrededor en las tierras que llaman los Chiaguites, que están en el paraje de la dicha tierra Xeococo; que hasta ahora van y vienen a las dichas tierras y siembran en ellas los dichos de Alotenango maíz y lo demás. . .”

Witness No. 4, cacique from Masagua, ca. 80 years old.

“....que desde que este testigo se acuerda antes que los Españoles vinieron a estas tierras y después, ha visto que en el dicho pueblo de Esquintepeque han tenido por términos hasta el río llamado Xoxuycapa, y que este río partía los términos de las tierras entre los indios Guatemaltecos y los del pueblo de Esquintepeque; yendo por el camino real de este el dicho pueblo hacia Guatemala, y que hasta el dicho río de Xexuycapa ha visto tener y poseer y gozar a los del pueblo de Esquintepeque por tierras suyas; y que ha oído decir que los dichos indios de Esquintepeque tienen algunas milpas de cacao por aquellas tierras, que llegan hasta el paraje del dicho río, aunque este testigo no las ha visto; y que así mismo sabe que en tiempo de guerras los señores principales de los Guatemaltecos llegaban con su gente de guerra más adelante del dicho río, y la ponían en guarnición contra los de Esquinte-

peque en las tierras llamadas Siloxuchil *y los* Chiaguitles; *que allí los dichos Guatemaltecos hacían, estando en la guerra, sus milpas de maíz, frijoles, y ají, para su mantenimiento; y después que tuvieron paces los dichos Guatemaltecos y los de Esquintepeque se recojieron los dichos indios Guatemaltecos y poblaron el dicho pueblo de Alotenango; y cuando vinieron los Españoles a esta tierra, teniendo guerra con los dichos Guatemaltecos, se fueron huyendo a las faldas del volcán; y estando escondidos en los montes hacían sus milpas para mantenerse, a donde las habían hecho en tiempo que habían tenido guerras con los de Esquintepeque; que hasta estas tierras donde se hacían las milpas, que llaman los* Chiaguites, *es donde los de Alotenango dicen que llegan sus términos....*"

APPENDIX XXIII: Contents of the 1722 Quiche Calendar Book.

This is a summary of the contents of the Quiche calendars copied by Berendt in Guatemala, in 1877 (n.d.). His handwritten copy is now in the University of Pennsylvania Museum Library.

Chol Powal K'ij, Macewal K'ij (the count of the cycle or round of days, the common days).

The twenty day names: (1) *Quej,* (2) *K'anil,* (3) *Toj,* (4) *Tz'i,* (5) *Batz',* (6) *Ee,* (7) *Aj,* (8) *Ix,* (9) *Tz'iquin,* (10) *Ajmak,* (11) *Noj,* (12) *Tijax,* (13) *Caok,* (14) *Junajpu,* (15) *Imox,* (16) *Ik',* (17) *Ak'bal,* (18) *C'at,* (19) *Can,* (20) *Queme.*

The eighteen months: *Nabe Mam, Ucab Mam, Nabe Liquinca, Ucab Liquinca, Nabe Pach, Ucab Pach, Tz'izi Lakam, Tz'iquin K'ij, Cakam, Botam, Nabe Zij, Ucab Zij, Rox Zij, Che, Tequexepual, Q'uibapop, Zac, Ch'ab.* The five remaining days, *Tz'api K'ij.*

The four year-bearers: *Noj, Ik', Quej, Ee.*

Ajilabal K'ij (the count of the days).

The following 4 sets of five days each are listed here by the beginning dayname, with the associated fates in parentheses (taken from the first of the two divinatory calendars): (1) *Imox (good fate),* (2) *Ik'* (bad fate), (3) *Ak'bal* (bad), (4) *C'at* (bad), (5) *Can* (bad), (6) *Queme* (bad), (7) *Quej* (bad), (8) *K'anil* (good), (9) *Toj* (good), (10) *Tz'i* (bad), (11) *Batz'* (bad), (12) *Ee* (good), (13) *Aj* (mixed — "angry day;" this may be associated with difficulties, but also with the power of rulers); (1) *Ix* (mixed), (2) *Tz'iquin* (good), (3) *Ajmak* (bad), (4) *Noj* (bad), (5) *Tijax* (mixed), (6) *Caok* (good), (7) *Junajpu* (bad), (8) *Imox* (good), (9) *Ik'* (good), (10) *Ak'bal* (?), (11) *C'at* (bad), (12) *Can* (good), (13) *Queme* (bad); (1) *Quej* (good), (2) *K'anil* (good), (3) *Toj* (good), (4) *Tz'i* (bad), (5) *Batz'* (mixed), (6) *Ee* (bad), (7) *Aj* (bad), (8) *Ix* (bad), (9) *Tz'iquin* (mixed), (10) *Ajmak* (good), (11) *Noj* (bad), (12) *Tijax* (good), (13) *Caok* (bad); (1) *Junajpu* (good),

(2) *Imox* (good), (3) *Ik'* (good), (4) *Ak'bal* (bad), (5) *C'at* (good), (6) *Can* (*good*), (7) *Queme* (bad), (8) *Quej* (good), (9) *K'anil* (good), (10) *Toj* (*good*), (11) *Tz'i* (bad), (12) *Batz'* (good), (13) *Ee* (bad).

APPENDIX XXIV: Record of Two Land Sales from Paxtoca, San Cristóbal Totonicapán.

The texts were taken from the Archivo General de Centroamérica (Al:6047-53386). The translations are mine. I have changed spelling and grammar to conform to modern usage.

First Quiche Text.

"Wacamic chupam 4 Junio año de 1715 años, uj c'o wi camic uj justicias, c'o wi alcalde, regidores, escribano chupam tinamit San Cristobal Totonicapa; xchikaya wi jun cedula escritura crusimiento puch chirech jutzabaj uleuj; mixulok' wae ajaw Francisco Gomez Xc'amparij, chirech jun achi Chwi Mik'ina, Baltasar Tzil; mixuc'aili chirech alcalde Xc'amparij; 9 tostones mixuyao alcalde Xc'amparij; waral c'ut caticar wi mojon chirech wae uleuj chwach abaj, chuxe esquina, uc'ulbat Juan Tzil; pakal c'ut mixbec c'o abaj; parakan mixbec, copan c'ut chila chwi chwach abaj, esquina uc'ulabat Tzil; jiquil c'ut mixoc ubic chwi c'o abaj; parakan mixbec, copan c'ut chila chwach Chabaj, chwi esquina; xulon c'ut, mixpetic c'o abaj; parakan mixbetic, copan c'ut chwa Chabaj chuxe esquina; jiquil c'ut mixoc ula chuxe c'o abaj; parakan mixbec copan c'ut chiri mixc'amar nima....chirech chi(ri) mixsuteic wae....rech alcalde sc'am pa rij chwi ronojel; usuc'uliquil kapatan xchikabano uj justicias, gobernador, alcalde, xawi chiquiwach testigos xchikayao ka firma chupam 4 Junio año del 1715. Señor Andrés Vásquez, gobernador; Don Juan Mejía, alcalde ordinario; Pedro Gómez Petz, alcalde mtto; 4 regidores; Diego Pérez Simaj, testigo; Lucas Vásquez Tzil, testigo xawi ajc'ail uleuj Francisco Gómez Xc'amparij mixulok' uleuj; 9 tostones mixuyao Baltasar Tzil ruc' Lucas Vásquez Tzil; mixquic' ayij uleuj 9 tostones; mixquic'amo.... Cristóbal Vásquez Son, escribano."

Spanish Translation.

"Hoy, el 4 de junio del año 1715, nosotros estamos aquí hoy, nosotros los justicias; están aquí el alcalde, los regidores, y el escribano; (aquí) en el pueblo de San Cristóbal Totonicapán. Daremos una cédula, escritura, y "crucimiento" de una parcela de tierra que compró el señor Francisco Gómez Xcamparij a un hombre de San Miguel Totonicapán, Baltasar Tzil. La vendió al alcalde Xcamparij; le dió 9 tostones por esta tierra en Paxtoca, dice el alcalde Xcamparij. Allí entonces empiezan los mojones de esta tierra; sobre la piedra (Chwach Abaj) bajo la esquina por el límite de Juan Tzil; subió donde está una piedra (C'o Abaj); a pie fue y llegó allí sobre Chwach Abaj, en

la esquina del límite de Tzil. Recto entonces entró sobre C'o Abaj;
derecho entonces entró allí bajo C'o Abaj; *fue a pie y llegó allí, y comenzó por allí*....*dió vuelta esta*....*para el alcalde; lo tomó el viejo
delante todos. En verdad (es) nuestro oficio, lo haremos, nosotros
los justicias; el gobernador, el alcalde, delante los testigos daremos
nuestra firma, en 4 de junio del año 1715. Señor Andrés Vásquez,
gobernador; Don Juan Mejía, alcalde ordinario; Pedro Gómez* Petz,
alcalde mtto; 4 regidores; Diego Pérez Simaj, *testigo; Lucas Vásquez*
Tzil, *testigo y vendedor de la tierra; Francisco Gómez* Xcamparij,
que compró la tierra. Nueve tostones dió a Baltasar Tzil *y Lucas
Vásquez* Tzil; *vendieron la tierra en 9 tostones. Lo tomaron....
Cristóbal Vásquez Son, escribano."*

Second Quiché Text.

*"Wacamic chupam 16 k'ij rajilabal ic' marzo, año del 1715 años,
uj c'o wi camic, uj justicia, gobernador, alcalde orinario, regidores,
escribano cabildo; xawi chiquiwach e testigos; xchikaya wi jun cédula
escritura crusimiento puch chirech jutzabaj uleuj mixulok' wae ajaw
Francisco Gomez Xc'amparij ruc' uchak' Alonso Ujich'u; mixquilok'o
quicabichal chila c'o wi uleuj Paxtoca; chuchaxic 30 tostones mix-
qui(y)ao chirech wae Nicolas Velasco ruc' uchak' Baltasar Velasco,
e uc'ajol k'etzam Pedro Velasco Chwi Mik'ina; chi ronojel quic'ux
mixulquic'aij kaja(w) waral maja alaajinak chich'ojina chikech; rumal kech uyaom canaka kajow quecha chikawach, uj, justicia; nabe
c'ulbat caticar wi waral chwi Chubaj, chuxe uc'ulbat Simaj; jiquil
c'ut cabec c'o uc'ulbat c'o cabec copan c'u chuwa Tzolojche, esquina
Chwiwa mixchap rib wach ruc' uleuj rech Xc'amparij....c'ut mixpetic mixoc ulok'cul c'ut chuwa Chinimabaj, esquina; xulan c'ut
mixpetic e nima C'uxbiq'uel; parakan cul c'ut chiri chwach nima
Popaabaj ri mixc'amar wi mojon chirech; chi mixsuteic wae uleuj
rech alcalde Xc'amparij ruc' uchak' Alonso Ujich'u....suc'uliquil
kapatan xchikabano, uj justicia, gobernador, alcalde ordinario; xchikayao ka firma chupam 16 k'ij marzo, año del 1715 años. Andrés
Vásquez del Osorio, gobernador; Don Juan Mejía, alcalde ordinario;
Pedro Gómez Petz, alcalde mtto; 4 regidores; Juan García (?) Simaj,
testigo; Pedro Gómez Simaj, fiscal testigo; Francisco Gómez Xc'amparij, ruc' uchak' Alonso mixquilok' uleuj 30 tostones, mixqui(y)ao;
Nicolas Velasco ruc' uchak' Baltasar Velasco mixquic'ayij uleuj 30
tostones; mixquic'amo Cristóbal Vásquez Son, escribano cabildo."*

Spanish Translation.

*"Hoy, el dia 16 del mes de marzo, año de 1715, nosotros estamos aquí,
nosotros los justicias, el gobernador, el alcalde ordinario, los regidores,
el escribano de cabildo; así, delante de los testigos. Daremos una
cédula escritura de "cruzimiento" de una parcela de tierra que compró el señor Francisco Gómez* Xcamparij *y su hermano menor, Alonso*
Ujich'u. *Los dos compraron la tierra que está allí en* Paxtoca. *Se*

dice que a Nicolás Velasco y su hermano menor Baltasar Velasco, hijos del difunto Pedro Velasco de San Miguel Totonicapán les dieron 30 tostones. Llegaron todos unidos de parecer para vender a nuestro padre aquí. No puede ser sacado el arreglo sin nosotros; por nosotros fue dado a nuestro padre, delante de nosotros los justicias. El primer mojón comienza aquí sobre Chubaj, *debajo el límite de* Simaj; *va recto el límite de Velasco, hasta llegar sobre* Tzolojche, *en la esquina de* Chwiwa; *se cogió delante de la tierra de* Xcamparij....*entonce vino y entró ante* Chinimabaj, *en la esquina; llegó entonces al gran* C'uxbiquel; *a pie llega entonces allí delante el gran* Popaabaj, *donde comenzó su mojón. Entonces dio vuelta esta tierra del alcalde* Xcamparij *con su hermano menor,* Alonso Ajich'u....*de verdad haremos nuestro oficio, nosotros los justicias, el gobernador, el alcalde ordinario. Daremos nuestra firma en el 16 de marzo de 1715. Andrés Vázquez del Osorio, gobernador; Don Juan Mejía, alcalde ordinario; Pedro Gómez* Petz, *alcalde mtto; 4 regidores; Juan García(?)* Simaj, *testigo; Pedro Gómez* Simaj, *fiscal testigo; Francisco Gómez* Xcamparij *con su hermano menor,* Alonso, *compraron la tierra; dieron 30 tostones.* Nicolás Velasco *y su hermano menor,* Baltasar Velasco, *vendieron la tierra en 30 tostones. Lo recibió Cristóbal Vásquez* Son, *escribano de cabildo."*

APPENDIX XXV: Record of Two Land Titles from Sacapulas.

The Quiche texts are part of the papers of land disputes between several ethnic factions at Santo Domingo Sacapulas during the 17th and 18th centuries (see Secondary Documents, Records). The first document was composed in 1613, in connection with a dispute over lands between Sacapulas and Sacualpa (AGC, Al:5942-51995). I have translated it into Spanish. The second document was originally prepared in the Quiche language in 1734, apparently under peaceful conditions, but translated in 1778 in connection with an internal dispute over lands between two factions of Sacapulas (AGC, Al:6025-53126). I have slightly altered its Spanish translation to make it conform to modern grammatical usage.

First Quiche Title.

"Chupam julajuj k'ij diciembre ruc' junab 1613 años, chikawach oj, ajawab; Juan Boraja, alcalde; Tomas Osorio; y Gaspar Delgado, regidor; justicias cabildo Francisco Cordero Ucalechij; Diego Mendez, Ajaw Kanil; Nicolas Lopez, Uchabaja; ruc' Cristobal Acuto, Andres Marroquin; chiquiwach e justicias; ruc' Juan Boraja Uchabaja, fiscal de Santa Iglesia; mixojul wi chupam ulew K'ebala; mixojbin wi chupam uleuj, mixkaban wi posesion chupam retal uleuj quech ac'-alab; e c'ajolaxel cumal, e cajib caminak, c'aslic calc'ual; e Lamak'ib quichinamital; e ajawal Pedro Lopez, Diego Perez Lamak'ib; chiquiwach c'ut e Lamak'uib Diego Lopez ajulew, ruc' Rafael Ramirez,

*Bartolome Bernardo Lamak'ib, chwach Matias Ajbejay; mixutzin wi
posesion cumal justicias Poponel cabildos; mixutzin wi xbana wi
retal uleuj quech jujun chi ac'alab, calc'wal e cajib caminak; justicia
xbano usuc'uliquil ronojel c'ulbat; queje c'ut xquitzij quik'ab k'anawinak; mixkacan retal uleuj chicanaj, oj justicias; caquiya quifirmas
chirij wae posesion retal uleuj; wacamic julajuj k'ij de diciembre
ruc' junab 1613 años; cac'oje c'ut jun auto cumal oj justicias, chwi
wae Diego Perez, rumal mani xunimaj utzij justicias; mawi mixbe
chupam uleuj quech ac'alab; queje c'ut canab wi jun auto chirij majabi jumul chic jun chao; chiri c'ut mixutzin wi wae posesion. Juan
Boraja; Tomas Osorio; Gaspar Delgado, regidor; Juan Boraja, fiscal.*"

Spanish Translation.

*"El dia 11 de diciembre del año 1613, ante nosotros los señores Juan
Boraja, alcalde, Tomás Osorio, y Gaspar Delgado, regidor; justicias
de cabildo Francisco Cordero* Ucalechij, *Diego Méndez,* Ajaw Kanil,
Nicolas López, Uchabaja, *con Cristóbal Agusto, Andrés Marroquín;
delante los justicias con Juan Boraja* Uchabaja, *el fiscal de la Santa
Iglesia. Llegamos a la tierra de* K'ebala; *caminamos a la tierra e
hicimos posesión entre los mojones de la tierra. Es de los hijos, los
varones hijos de los cuatro muertos, los de su familia que viven. Son
del* chinamital *de los* Lamak'ib; *los señores Pedro López, Diego Pérez*
Lamak'ib, *delante los* Lamak'ib; *Diego López dueño de la tierra,
con Rafael Ramírez, Bartolomé Bernardo* Lamak'ib, *delante de Matías*
Ajbejay. *Llevó a cabo la posesión por los justicias de cabildo, los*
Poponel. *Se llevó a cabo haciendo los mojones de tierra de algunos
hijos, la familia de los cuatro difuntos. En verdad, la justicia puso
todos los límites; y así testificaron los testigos. Dejamos puestos los
mojones de la tierra, nosotros los justicias. Dieron sus firmas sobre
esta posesión de mojones de tierra. Hoy, el 11 de diciembre del año
1613. Es un auto (hecho) por nosotros los justicias para este Diego
Pérez, porque no obedece la palabra de los justicias; que no fuere a
la tierra de los hijos. Así, se hace auto para que no haya pleito otra
vez. Aquí se terminó esta posesión. Juan Boraja, Tomás Osorio,
Gaspar Delgado, regidor, Juan Boraja, fiscal.*"

Second Quiche Title.

*"Wacamic chupam 24 rajilabal ic', diciembre ruc' junab de 1734 años;
cakaya quiescritura chirech kalok' chuch kajaw, Domingo Uliwan;
jurabaj abixabal ulew xechun rech k'etzam Sebastian Acetuno c'u
xbekabana posesion chupam ulew; are c'u nabe etabal Raxabaj, chwa
juyub c'o wi chi rakabal k'ij; ma c'u xojxule chi ya ucab etabal, xaki
suc'ulic mixic'owkaji chupam petak c'a chi ya retal, xe retal wi ya
chi wa k'anibal k'ij macuxojpake chic chuchu k'ajibal k'ij, wox etabal
sakabaj, chi c'ulel Juan Francisco Acetuno; ma cuxojpake chic
xe juyub, mixojic'ow chwi jun etabal, c'o chiri jal ulew k'anabaj;
xax chiquil wi ba wa chak' alaj ciwan; ma cuxojxule chic iquem xaki*

xe juyub mixbe karika uwach nabe etabal; chiri mixquis wi kapatan;
are c'ut rajil ulew, 16 tostones; are la cojya wi kafirmas, oj, alcalde,
Juan Lucas Aguilar, alcalde don Juan Ciprian cuc' 3 regidores Josepa
Acetuno, Jacinto Bernardo Josep, Juan Pérez, e regidores cuc' testi-
gos Francisco Pérez Pascual Aquino, Pedro Zaries, Juan Francisco
Acetuno, e testigos; mixnuya retal, in Nicolás Chocoj, escribano rech
cabildo."

Spanish Translation.

"*Ahora en el día 24 del més de diciembre del año de 1734 años, hace-*
mos estas escrituras de nuestro chuch kajaw, *Domingo* Ulwan, *y las*
hacemos sobre un pedacito de tierras de sembrar en el paraje llamá-
dose Xechun, *que era de un difunto llamádose Sebastián Acetuno;*
a lo cual fuimos a darle conocimiento y posesión a las dichas tierras
llamadas Xechun, *y comenzamos a mojonarlas. Y el primer mojón*
es una piedra negra, llamada Raxabaj, *delante el cerro, por donde*
sale el sol; de allí bajamos hasta la orilla del río, que es el segundo
mojón; de allí anduvimos por la orilla del río dentro de unos tunales,
hasta llegar al tercer mojón que es una piedra blanca por donde cae
el sol, vecinos de Juan Francisco Acetuno; de allí fuimos subiendo
al cerro por arriba, y pasamos sobre de un mojón que está en media
tierra, k'anabaj; *y proseguimos hasta llegar al cuarto mojón que está*
en una barranquita; de allá anduvimos debajo del cerro hasta llegar
a la piedra negra donde empezamos. Allá acabamos nuestro oficio.
Y el valor de la tierra son 26 tostones; estos son los mojones. Damos
nuestras firmas, nosotros, el alcalde Juan Lucas Aguilar; alcalde
Don Juan Ciprián con los 3 regidores: Josepa Aceituno; Jacinto
Bernardo Josep, Juan Pérez, los tres regidores; con los testigos Fran-
cisco Pérez, Pascual Aquino, Pedro Zaríes, Juan Francisco Aceituno,
los testigos. Dí los mojones, yo, Nicolás Chocoj, *escribano de cabildo.*"

References

Acosta, J. R.
1956- Interpretación de algunos de los datos obtenidos en Tula
1957 relativos a la época tolteca. Revista Mexicana de Estudios
Antropológicos, Vol. 14, pp. 75-110. México.

Acuña, R.
1966 El Hunab Cakchiquel. La Palabra y el Hombre, Vol. 39,
pp. 427-439. Revista de la Universidad Veracruzana.
1968 Título de los Señores de Sacapulas. Folklore Américas, Vol.
28. Los Angeles.

Adams, R. McC.
1966 The Evolution of Urban Society: Early Mesopotamia and
Prehispanic Mexico. Aldine Publishing Co., Chicago.

Adams, R. N.
1956 Sobrevivencia en la Casa de Solteros en Mesoamérica. Antropología e Historia de Guatemala, Vol. 8, No. 2, pp. 53-
57. Guatemala.
1964 Encuesta sobre la cultura de los Ladinos en Guatemala. Seminario de Integración Social Guatemalteca, Pub. 2. Guatemala.
1968 Changes in Power Relationships in the Guatemalan National
Social Structure, 1944-1966. Thirty-seventh International Congress of Americanists. Actas y Memoriales, Vol. 1. Buenos
Aires.

AGC Archivo General de Centroamérica. Formerly, Archivo Nacional de Guatemala. Guatemala. The letter A refers to
colonial, the letter B, to postindependence documents. The
numbers after the colon refer to *legajo*, after the dash to
expediente.

AGI Archivo General de Indias. Sevilla, Spain.

Aguilar, S.
1933 Prólogo, *In*, Recordación Florida, F. A. de Fuentes y Guzmán.
Biblioteca "Goathemala," Vol. 8. Guatemala.

Alvarado, P. de
1946 Relación hecha por Pedro de Alvarado a Hernando Cortés
(1524). Biblioteca de Autores Españoles, Vol. 22. Madrid.

Andrade, M. J.
1946a Materials on the Quiche, Cakchiquel, and Tzutuhil Languages. Microfilm Collection of Manuscripts on Middle American Cultural Anthropology, No. 11. University of Chicago Library, Chicago.
1946b Material on the Kekchí and Pokomán Languages. Microfilm Collection of Manuscripts on Middle American Cultural Anthropology, No. 12. University of Chicago Library, Chicago.
1946c Materials on the Mam, Jacaltec, Chuj, Bachahom, Palencano and Lacandon Languages. Microfilm Collection of Manuscripts on Middle American Cultural Anthropology, No. 10. University of Chicago Library, Chicago.

Anonymous
1924- Catalogue des manuscrits Américains de la Bibliothèque Na-
1925 tionale. Revue des Bibliothèques, Vols. 31-32. Paris.
1934 Libro Viejo de la fundación de Guatemala, y papeles relativos a Don Pedro de Alvarado. Biblioteca "Goathemala," Vol. 12. Guatemala.
1935a Colección de Documentos antiguos del ayuntamiento de Guatemala. Archivo Municipal de Guatemala. Guatemala.
1935b Isagoge Histórica Apologética de las Indias Occidentales. Biblioteca "Goathemala," Vol. 8. Guatemala.
1935c Boletín del Archivo General del Gobierno, Vol. 1, No. 1. Guatemala.
1950 Alfabeto para los cuatro idiomas indígenas mayoritarios de Guatemala: Quiché, Cakchiquel, Mam, y Kekchí. Publicaciones Especiales del Instituto Indigenista Nacional, No. 10. Guatemala.
1952 Relación de los caciques y principales del pueblo de Atitlán (1571). Anales de la Sociedad de Geografía e Historia de Guatemala, Vol. 26, pp. 435-438. Guatemala.
1961- Diccionario Geográfico, 2 Vols. Dirección General de Car-
1962 tografía. Guatemala.
1962 Alfabetos Oficializados de Trece Principales Idiomas de Guatemala. Dirección General de Cartografía. Guatemala.
1963 La Muerte de Tecún Umán, Estudio Crítico de la Conquista del Altiplano Occidental de la República. Editorial del Ejército. Guatemala.
1966 Censo 1964, Población. Departamento de Censos y Encuestas. Dirección General de Estadística. Guatemala.

Armas Lara, M.
1964 El renacimiento de la Danza Guatemalteca, y el Origen de la Marimba. Ministerio de Educación Pública. Guatemala.

Arriola, J. L.
1956 Integración Social en Guatemala. Seminario de Integración Social Guatemalteca, Pub. 3. Guatemala.

BAILY, J.
1850   Central America: Describing Each of the States. London.

BANCROFT, H. H.
1883   The Native Races of the Pacific States of North America. 5 Vols. San Francisco.
1886   History of Central America. History of the Pacific States of North America, Vol. 1, 1501-1530. San Francisco.

BATRES JÂUREGUI, A.
1894   Los Indios: su historia y su civilización. Guatemala.

BEALS, R. L.
1951   History of Acculturation in Mexico. In, Homenaje a Don Alfonso Caso, pp. 73-82. Mexico.
1952   Notes on Acculturation. In, Heritage of Conquest, S. Tax (ed.). The Free Press. Glencoe.

BECQUELIN, P.
1966   Informe preliminar sobre las excavaciones realizadas en Acul, departamento de El Quiché, 1964-1965. Instituto de Antropología e Historia, Guatemala.

BERENDT, C. H.
1872   Report on Explorations in Central America. Annual Report of the Smithsonian Institute for 1867, pp. 420-426. Washington.
1877   Collection of Historical Documents in Guatemala. Annual Report of the Smithsonian Institute for 1876. Washington.
1878   Geographic Distribution of the Ancient Central American Civilization. Journal of the American Geographical Society of New York, Vols. 7-8.
n.d.   Calendario de los Indios de Guatemala Kiché (1722). Copy of the original manuscript in the University of Pennsylvania Museum Library. Philadelphia.

BERLIN, H.
1950   La Historia de los Xpantzay. Antropología e Historia de Guatemala, Vol. 2, No. 2. Guatemala.

BERNAL, I.
1962   Bibliografía de arqueología y etnografía: Mesoamérica y norte de México, 1514-1960. Instituto Nacional de Antropología e Historia, Mem. 7. Mexico.

BERNOUILLI, G.
1868- Briefe aus Guatemala. Mittheilungen aus Justus Perthes Geo-
1870   graphischer Anstalt. Pettermann's Geographische Mitteilungen. Gotha.

BETANCOR, A. P., and ARBOLEDA, P. DE
1964   Relación de Santiago Atitlán (1585). Anales de Geografía e Historia de Guatemala, Vol. 37, pp. 87-106. Guatemala.

1965 Descripción de San Bartolomé del Partido de Atitlán (1585). Anales de Geografía e Historia de Guatemala, Vol. 38, pp. 262-276. Guatemala.

BLOM, F., and LaFARGE, O.
1926- Tribes and Temples, 2 Vols. Middle American Research In-
1927 stitute, Tulane University, Pub. 1. New Orleans.

BODE, B. O.
1961 The Dance of the Conquest of Guatemala. Middle American Research Institute, Tulane University, Pub. 27, pp. 205-292. New Orleans.

BORAH, W. W., and COOK, S. F.
1963 The Aboriginal Population of Central Mexico on the Eve of the Spanish Conquest. Ibero-Americana, No. 45. Berkeley.

BORHEGYI, S. F.
1950 Estudio arqueológico en la falda norte del Volcán de Agua. Antropología e Historia de Guatemala, Vol. 2, No. 1, pp. 3-22. Guatemala.
1956a Settlement Patterns in the Guatemalan Highlands: Past and Present. *In*, Prehistoric Settlement Patterns in the New World. G. Willey (ed.), Viking Fund Publications in Anthropology, No. 23, pp. 101-106. New York.
1956b The Development of Folk and Complex Cultures in the Southern Maya Area. American Antiquity, Vol. 21, pp. 343-356. Menasha.
1965 Archaeological Synthesis of the Guatemalan Highlands. *In*, Handbook of Middle American Indians, Vol. 2, pp. 3-58. University of Texas Press, Austin.

BOWDITCH, C. P. (Supervisor of translation)
1939 Mexican and Central American Antiquities, Calendar Systems, and History. Translation of Several German Articles. Bureau of American Ethnology, Bulletin 28. Smithsonian Institute, 1904. Washington.

BRASSEUR DE BOURBOURG, C. E.
1857 Histoire des Nations Civilisées du Mexique et de l'Amérique Centrale, 4 Vols. Paris.
1861 Popol Vuh. Le Livre Sacré et les mythes de l'antiquité américaine (avec les livres héroiques et historiques des Quichés). Paris.
1862 Grammaire de la Langue Quichée et Rabinal-Achi. Paris.
1945- Antigüedades Guatemaltecas. Anales de la Sociedad de Geo-
1949 grafía e Historia de Guatemala, Vols. 20-25, *passim*. Guatemala.
1961 Gramática de la lengua Quiché. Editorial del Ministerio de Educación Pública. Guatemala.

Bremme de Santos, I.
1963 Aspectos hispánicos e indígenas de la cultura Cakchiquel. Anales de la Sociedad de Geografía e Historia de Guatemala, Vol. 36, pp. 517-563. Guatemala.

Brigham, W. T.
1887 The Land of the Quetzal. New York.

Bright, W.
n.d. Notes on Aztec. Manuscript used in a course taught at U.C.L.A., 1963.

Brinton, D. G.
1881 The Names of the Gods in the Kiche Myths, Central America. Philadelphia.
1884 A Grammar of the Cakchiquel Language of Guatemala. Philadelphia.
1885 The Annals of the Cakchiquels. Brinton's Library of Aboriginal American Literature. Philadelphia.
1893 The Native Calendar of Central America and Mexico. Philadelphia.
1896 The Myths of the New World. Philadelphia.
1900 Catalogue of the Berendt Linguistic Collection. Bulletin of the Free Museum of Science and Art, University of Pennsylvania, Vol. 2, No. 4. Philadelphia.

Brown, R.
1963 Explanation in Social Science. Aldine Publishing Co., Chicago.

Bucaro, M., J. I.
n.d.a San Andrés Xecul. Manuscript on file with the Instituto Indigenista Nacional, 1962. Guatemala.
n.d.b Momostenango: Algunos apuntes para la monografía de la comunidad. Manuscript, ibid., 1965.

Bunzel, R.
1952 Chichicastenango. American Ethnological Society, Pub. 22. J. J. Augustin Publisher, New York.

Burgess, D. M. de, and Xec, P.
1955 Popol Wuj. Texto de R. P. F. Ximénez. Quezaltenango.

Burkitt, R.
1902 Notes on the Kekchi Language. American Anthropologist, Vol. 4, pp. 441-463. New York.
1905 A Kekchí Will of the Sixteenth Century. American Anthropologist, Vol. 7, pp. 271-294. Lancaster.
1920 The Hills and the Corn—A Legend of the Kekchí Indians of Guatemala. University of Pennsylvania, University Museum. Anthropological Publications, No. 9, pp. 183-227. Philadelphia.

References 407

1930 Excavations at Chocolá. Explorations in the Highlands of
Western Guatemala. The Museum Journal, Museum of the
University of Pennsylvania, Vol. 21, No. 1, pp. 5-21, 41-72.
Philadelphia.
1930- The Calendar of Solomá and of Other Indian Towns. Man,
1931 Vols. 30-31, Nos. 80, 160. London.

BUTLER, M.
1940 A Pottery Sequence from the Alta Verapaz. *In*, The Maya
and Their Neighbors, pp. 250-267. New York.
1959 Spanish Contact at Chipal. Festband Franz Termer. Mitteilungen aus dem Museum für Völkerkunde in Hamburg,
No. 25, pp. 28-35.

BUTLER, R. L.
1937 A Check List of Manuscripts in the Edward E. Ayer Collection. The Newberry Library. Chicago.

CAMARA BARBACHANO, F.
1964 El Mestizaje en Mexico. Revista de Indias, Vol. 24, pp.
25-83. Madrid.

CAMPBELL, L.
n.d. On Quichean Languages. Manuscript, 1969.

CARMACK, R. M.
1966a El Ajpop Quiche, K'uk'umatz: un problema de la sociolo-
gía histórica. Antropología e Historia de Guatemala, Vol.
18, No. 1, pp. 43-47. Guatemala.
1966b La perpetuación del clan patrilineal en Totonicapán. Antropología e Historia de Guatemala, Vol. 18, No. 2, pp. 43-
60. Guatemala.
1967 Análisis histórico-sociológico de un antiguo título Quiché. Antropología e Historia de Guatemala, Vol. 19, No. 1, pp. 3-13.
Guatemala.
1968 Toltec Influence on the Post-Classic Culture History of Highland Guatemala. Middle American Research Institute, Tulane University, Pub. 26, pp. 49-92. New Orleans.
1970 Ethnography and Ethnohistory: Their Application in Middle
American Studies. Ethnohistory, Vol. 17, No. 3.
n.d.a The Documentary Sources, Ecology, and Culture History of
the Prehispanic Quiche Maya. Doctoral Dissertation, University of California, Los Angeles, 1965.
n.d.b Field Notes from ethnographic research in Santiago Momostenango. 1966-1967.
n.d.c Prehispanic Quiche-Maya Historiography. Manuscript to be
published by Revista Mexicana de Estudios Antropológicos.
Mexico.

CARRANZA, J. E.
1897   Un Pueblo de los Altos: Totonicapán, Apuntamientos para
        su Historia. Quezaltenango.

CARRASCO, P.
1950   Los Otomíes, cultura e historia prehispánicas de los pueblos
        mesoamericanos de habla otomiana. Instituto Histórico, Pub.
        15. Mexico.
1961a   The Civil-Religious-Hierarchy in Mesoamerican Communi-
        ties: Pre-Spanish Background and Colonial Development.
        American Anthropologist, Vol. 63, pp. 483-497. Menasha.
1961b   El Barrio y la Regulación del Matrimonio en un Pueblo del
        Valle de México en el Siglo XVI. Revista Mexicana de Es-
        tudios Antropológicos, Vol. 18. Mexico.
1963   La Exogamia según un documento Cakchiquel. Tlatocan,
        Vol. 6, No. 3. Mexico.
1964   Los Nombres de Persona en la Guatemala Antigua. Estudios
        de Cultura Maya, Vol. 6. México.
1967a   Don Juan Cortés, Cacique de Santa Cruz Quiché. Estudios
        de Cultura Maya, Vol. 6, pp. 251-266. Mexico.
1967b   El Señorío Tz'utuhil de Atitlán en el Siglo XVI. Revista
        Mexicana de Estudios Antropológicos, Vol. 21, pp. 317-331.
        Mexico.

CASO, A.
1963   Land Tenure Among the Ancient Mexicans. American An-
        thropologist, Vol. 65, pp. 863-878. Menasha.
1966   Prólogo, Los Imperios Prehispánicos en Mesoamérica. Re-
        vista Mexicana de Estudios Antropológicos, Vol. 20. Mexico.

CASTEÑEDA, C. E., and DABBS, J. A.
1939   Guide to the Latin American Manuscripts in the University
        of Texas Library. Harvard University Press. Cambridge.
CDI
1875   Colección de documentos inéditos relativos al descubrimiento,
        conquista, y organización de las antiguas posesiones espa-
        ñolas de América y Oceania. Vol. 24. Madrid.
1925   Documentos del Consejo de Indias. Colección de documen-
        tos inéditos relativa al descubrimiento, conquista, y organi-
        zación de las antiguas posesiones españolas de ultramar,
        2d Series, Vol. 17. Madrid.

CERWIN, H.
1963   Bernal Díaz, Historian of the Conquest. Universtiy of Okla-
        homa Press, Norman.

CESAR DE LA ROCA, J.
1966   Biografía de un Pueblo: Síntesis Monográfico de Quezalte-
        nango. Editorial "José de Pineda Ibarra". Guatemala.

CHARENCEY, H. DE

1883 Sur le pronom personnel dans les idiomes de la famille Maya-Quiché, *and* Sur le système de numération chez le peuple de la famille Maya-Quiche. *In*, Mélanges de Philologie et de Paléographie Américaines, pp. 123-139, 151-157. Paris.

1885 Título de los Señores de Totonicapán. Actes de la Societé Philologique, Paris.

1891 Des suffixes en langue Quichée. Mémoires de l'Académie Nationale des Sciences, Arts et Belles-Lettres de Caen, pp. 205-278.

1896 Mélanges sur quelques dialects de la famille Maya-Quiché. Journal de la Société des Américanistes, Paris, Vol. 1, Pt. 1.

CHAVERO, A. (ed.)

1892 Lienzo de Tlaxcala. *In*, Antigüedades Mexicanas, 2 Vols. Mexico.

CHINCHILLA AGUILAR, E.

1957 El mundo mágico en un catecismo Quiché-Español del Siglo XVII. Humanidades, Vol. 2, pp. 1-8. Universidad de San Carlos, Guatemala.

1961 Historia y Tradiciones de la Ciudad de Amatitlán. Biblioteca Guatemalteca de Cultura Popular. Ministerio de Educación Pública, Guatemala.

1963 La danza del sacrificio y otros estudios. Ministerio de Educación Pública, Guatemala.

CLINE, H. F.

n.d.a Gates Collection in the Brigham Young University. Handbook of Middle American Indians, Working Papers. Washington.

n.d.b A General Survey: The Relaciones Geográficas of the Spanish Indies, 1577-1586. Handbook of Middle American Indians, Working Papers. Washington.

COE, M. D.

1959 Una investigación arqueológica en la costa del Pacífico de Guatemala. Antropología e Historia de Guatemala, Vol. II, No. 1, pp. 5-15. Guatemala.

1961 La Victoria, an early site on the Pacific Coast of Guatemala. Papers of the Peabody Museum, Harvard University, Vol. 53. Cambridge.

1963 Cultural Development in Southeastern Mesoamerica. Smithsonian Institution, Miscellaneous Collection, Pub. 146, pp. 27-44. Washington.

COLBY, B. N., and VAN DEN BERGHE, P. L.

1969 Ixil Country: A Plural Society in Highland Guatemala. University of California Press, Berkeley and Los Angeles.

CONTRERAS R., J. D.
1951 Una rebelión indígena en el partido de Totonicapán en 1820:
el Indio y la Independencia. Guatemala.
1963 Temas y motivos Bíblicos en las crónicas indígenas de Guatemala. Antropología e Historia de Guatemala, Vol. 15, No.
2, pp. 46-58. Guatemala.
1965 El último cacique de la casa de Cavec. Cuadernos de Antropología, Vol. 5, pp. 37-48. Guatemala.
n.d. Breve historia de Guatemala. Editorial del Ministerio de
Educación Pública, Vol. 15. Guatemala.

CORREA, G.
1958 La Loa en Guatemala. Texto de un Baile del Diablo. Middle
American Research Institute, Tulane University, Pub. 27,
pp. 1-96, 97-104. New Orleans.

CORTES, H.
1961 Cartas de relación de la conquista de Mexico. Espasa-Calpe
Mexicana, Mexico.

CORTES y LARRAZ, P.
1958 Descripción Geográfico-Moral de la Diócesis de Goathemala,
2 Vols. Biblioteca "Goathemala," Vol. 22. Guatemala.

COTO, T.
n.d. Vocabulario de la lengua Cakchiquel u Guatemalteca. (c. 1690).
Manuscript at the American Philosophical Society Library,
Philadelphia.

CRESPO, M. M.
1956 Títulos indígenas de tierras. Antropología e Historia de
Guatemala, Vol. 8, No. 2. Guatemala.
n.d. Títulos Indígenas de Guatemala. Tesis inedita. Facultad
de Humanidades, Universidad de San Carlos, 1967. Guatemala.

DGC
1959- Dirección General de Cartografía, Guatemala. Cartographic
1960 Maps of The Republic of Guatemala. Individual maps, published at different times, are cited by year of publication.

DIAZ, B. DEL CASTILLO
1933 Historia Verdadera de la Conquista de la Nueva España.
Espasa-Calpe, S. A. Madrid.

DIEBOLD, A. R.
1960 Determining the Centers of Dispersal of Language Groups.
International Journal of American Linguistics, Vol. 26, pp.
1-10. Baltimore.

DIESELDORFF, E P.
1904 Extracto del libro antiguo que conserva la cofradía de Carchá. Fourteenth International Congress of Americanists, Proceedings, pp. 399-402. Stuttgart.

1925- Los Dioses prominentes de la religión Maya. Anales de la
1926 Sociedad de Geografía e Historia de Guatemala, Vol. 2, pp. 378-386. Guatemala.
1928- Religión y Arte de los Maya. (Translation from the German.)
1929 Anales de la Sociedad de Geografía e Historia de Guatemala, Vol. 5, pp. 66-86, 184-203, 317-335, 432-453. Guatemala.

DOLLFUS, A., and MONT-SERRAT, E. DE
1868 Voyage Géologique dans les Républiques de Guatemala et de Salvador. Paris.

DUNLOP, R. G.
1847 Travels in Central America: being a journal of nearly 3 years residence in the country. London.

DUNN, H.
1828 Guatimala, or the United Provinces of Central America. Sketches and Memorandums made during a Twelve months' Residence in that Republic (1827-1828). New York.

DURAN, C. M.
1963 El Obispo Marroquín y la Fundación del Hospital de Santiago. Anales de la Sociedad de Geografía e Historia de Guatemala, Vol. 36, pp. 79-84. Guatemala.

DUTTON, B. P. and HOBBS, H. R.
1943 Excavations at Tajumulco, Guatemala. School of American Research, Monograph 9. Santa Fe, New Mexico.

EDMONSON, M. S.
1964 Historia de las tierras altas Mayas según los documentos indígenas. Desarrollo Cultural de los Maya, Universidad Autónoma de Mexico, Mexico.
1965 Quiché-English Dictionary. Middle American Research Institute, Tulane University, Pub. 30. New Orleans.
1967 Classical Quiche. In, Handbook of Middle American Indians, Vol. 5, pp. 249-267. University of Texas Press, Austin.
n.d. Literary Style in the Dresden Codex. Paper delivered at the American Anthropological Association Meetings in Denver, 1965.

EGGAN, F.
1954 Social Anthropology and the Method of Controlled Comparison. American Anthropologist, Vol. 56, pp. 743-763. Menasha.

ESCOBAR, A. DE
1841 Account of the Province of Verapaz in Guatemala. Journal of the Royal Geographical Society of London, Vol. 11, pp. 89-97.

ESTEVE BARBA, F.
1964 Historiografía Indiana. Editorial Gredos, Madrid.

ESTRADA, J. DE
1955 Descripción de la Provincia de Zapotitlán y Suchitepéquez. Anales de la Sociedad de Geografía e Historia de Guatemala, Vol. 28, pp. 68-84. Guatemala.
1966 Mapa de la costa de Suchitepéquez y Zapotitlán (1579). Anales de la Sociedad de Geografía e Historia de Guatemala, Vol. 39, pp. 96-99. Guatemala.

EVANS-PRITCHARD, E. E.
1962 Anthropology and History. In, Essays in Social Anthropology. The Free Press, New York.

EWALD, R. H.
1956 Bibliografía Comentada Sobre Antropología Social, 1900-1955. Seminario de Integración Social Guatemalteca. Guatemala.

FOSHAG, W. F.
1957 Minerological Studies on Guatemalan Jade. Smithsonian Miscellaneous Collections, Vol. 135, No. 5. Washington.

FOSTER, G. M.
1967 Tzintzuntzán: Mexican Peasants in a Changing World. The Little, Brown Series in Anthropology. Boston.

FOX, D. G.
1965 Lecciones Elementales en Quiché. Ministerio de Educación Pública, Guatemala.
1966 Gramática (Quiché). In, Lenguas de Guatemala, pp. 87-124. Seminario de Integración Social Guatemalteca, Pub. 20. Original title, Languages of Guatemala, 1966.
1968 Quiche-English Dictionary, by Edmonson, M., A review. Language, Vol. 44, pp. 191-197. Baltimore.

FREEMAN, J. F.
1962 Manuscript Sources on Latin American Indians in the Library of the American Philosophical Society. Proceedings of the American Philosophical Society, Vol. 106, pp. 530-540. Philadelphia.

FUENTES y GUZMAN, F. A. DE
1932- Recordación florida. Guatemala. Discurso historical y de-
1933 mostración natural, material, militar y política del Reyno de Guatemala. Biblioteca "Goathemala," Vols. 6-8. Guatemala.

GAGE, T.
1958 Thomas Gage's Travels in the New World. Introduction by J. E. S. Thompson. University of Oklahoma Press, Norman.

GALL, F.
1962 Quezaltenango Quiché. Anales de la Sociedad de Geografía e Historia de Guatemala, Vol. 34. Guatemala.

1963   Título del Ajpop Huitzitzil Tzunún. Probanza de Méritos de los de León y Cardona. Ministerio de Educación Pública, Guatemala.

GAMIO, M.
1926- Cultural Evolution in Guatemala and its Geographic and
1927   Historic Handicaps. Art and Archaeology, Vols. 22-23. Baltimore.

GARCIA DE PALACIO, D.
1866   Relación hecha por el Licenciado Palacio al Rey D. Felipe II, en la que describe la Provincia de Guatemala, las costumbres de los indios y otras cosas notables. Colección de Documentos Inéditos del Archivo de Indias, Vol. 6. Madrid.

GARCIA ELGUETA, M.
1932   Ahavarem quauhtimalan. Maya Society, Vol. 1, pp. 147-149. Baltimore.
1939   Etimología de los nombres de Totonicapán y Momostenango. Etimología del nombre de Guatemala. Etimología de Quezaltenango. Anales de la Sociedad de Geografía e Historia de Guatemala, Vol. 15, pp. 245-258, 336-358, 504-508. Guatemala.
1962   Descripción Geográfica del Departamento de Totonicapán. Guatemala Indígena, Pub. 8, pp. 115-192. Guatemala.

GARCIA ICAZBALCETA, J.
1886- Nueva colección de documentos para la historia de México,
1892   5 Vols. México.

GARCIA PELAEZ, F. de P.
1943   Memorias para la Historia del Antiguo Reino de Guetemala, Tipografía Nacional. Guatemala.

GARIBAY, K., A. M.
1961   Llave del Nahuatl. Editorial Porrúa, S. A. Mexico.

GATES, W. E.
1937   The Maya Society and Its Work. The Maya Society, Pub. 19, Baltimore.
n.d.   Mayance and other Manuscripts in the Gates Collection. Manuscript in the Princeton University Library. Princeton.

GAVARRETE, F.
1868   Geografía de Guatemala. Guatemala.

GAVARRETTE, J.
1929   Antigüedades de Cotzumalguapa, 1866. Anales de la Sociedad de Geografía e Historia de Guatemala, Vol. 5, pp. 308-311. Guatemala.
1932   Advertencia sobre el autor de esta obra y su tercera parte (1875). In, Recordación Florida, A. de Fuentes y Guzmán. Biblioteca "Goathemala," Vol. 6, pp. xix-xx. Guatemala.

GIBSON, C.
1952   Tlaxcala in the Sixteenth Century. Yale University Press, New Haven.
1964   The Aztecs Under Spanish Rule: A History of the Indians of the Valley of Mexico, 1519-1810. Stanford University Press, Stanford.
1966   Spain in America. Harper Torchbooks, Harper and Row, New York.

GILLIN, J.
1951   The Culture of Security in San Carlos: A Study of a Guatemalan Community of Indians and Ladinos. Middle American Research Institute, Tulane University, Pub. 16. New Orleans.

GIRARD, R.
1948   El Calendario Maya-México: Origen, función, desarrollo, y lugar de procedencia. Colección Cultura Pre-Colombina. México.
1949   Los Chortís ante el Problema Maya, 5 Vols. Antigua Librería Robredo, Mexico.
1966   Los Mayas, su civilización, su historia, sus vinculaciones continentales. Libro México, Editories. México.

GLASS, J. B.
n.d.   The Robert Garrett Collection of Middle American Manuscripts, 1968. Manuscript.

GLEASON, H. A.
1961   An Introduction to Descriptive Linguistics. Holt, Rinehart, and Winston, New York.

GOETZ, D.
1953   Title of the Lords of Totonicapán. Translation from the Spanish version of A. Recinos. University of Oklahoma Press, Norman.

GOETZ, D. and MORLEY, S. G.
1950   Popol Vuh, the Sacred Book of the Ancient Quiché Maya. Translation from the Spanish version of A. Recinos. University of Oklahoma Press, Norman.

GOMEZ CANEDO, L.
1961   Los archivos de la historia de América, 2 Vols. Mexico.

GOUBAUD CARRERA, A.
1935   El "Guajxaquip Bats"-ceremonia calendárica indígena. Anales de la Sociedad de Geografía e Historia de Guatemala, Vol. 12, pp. 39-52. Guatemala.
1946   Distribución de las lenguas indígenas actuales de Guatemala. Boletín del Instituto Indigenista Nacional, Vol. 1, Nos. 2, 3. Guatemala.

1964   Indigenismo en Guatemala. Seminario de Integración Social Guatemalteca, Pub. 14. Guatemala.

n.d.   Notas etnográficas sobre Rabinal. Manuscript on file in the Instituto Indigenista Nacional, Guatemala, 1944.

GOUBAUD CARRERA, A., ROSALES, J. DE D., and TAX, S.

1944   Reconnaissance of Northern Guatemala. Microfilm Collection of Manuscripts in Middle American Cultural Anthropology, No. 17. University of Chicago Library, Chicago.

GRIMES, J. L.

1968   The Linguistic Unity of Cakchiquel-Tzutujil. International Journal of American Linguistics, Vol. 34, pp. 104-114. Baltimore.

1969   The Palatalized Velar Stop in Proto-Quichean. International Journal of American Linguistics, Vol. 35, pp. 20-24. Baltimore.

n.d.   The Phonological History of the Quichean Languages. Doctoral Dissertation, University of Texas, 1969.

GUILLEMIN, J. F.

1958   La Pirámide B6 de Mixco Viejo, y el Sacrificatorio de Utatlán. Antropología e Historia de Guatemala, Vol. 10, No. 1, pp. 21-27. Guatemala.

1959   Iximché. Antropología e Historia de Guatemala, Vol. 11, No. 2, pp. 22-64. Guatemala.

1961   Un Entierro Señorial en Iximché. Anales de la Sociedad de Geografía e Historia de Guatemala, Vol. 34, pp. 89-105. Guatemala.

1965   Iximché, Capital del Antiguo Reino Cakchiquel. Instituto de Antropología e Historia. Guatemala.

1967   The Ancient Cakchiquel Capital of Iximche. Expedition, Vol. 9, No. 2. University Museum, University of Pennsylvania.

1969   Exploration de Groupe C d'Iximche (Guatemala). Societé Suisse des Americanistes, Bulletin No. 33, pp. 23-33. Geneva.

GUZMAN, P. DE

n.d.   Compendio de nombres en lengua Cakchiquel y significado de verbos por imperativos y acusativos recíprocos. 1704. Photocopy from the Bibliothèque Nationale, Paris, in the Newberry Library, Chicago.

HALPERN, A. M.

1942   The Theory of Maya ts-sounds. Carnegie Institution of Washington, Notes on Middle American Archaeology and Ethnology, No. 13. Washington.

HANKE, L.

1949   Bartolomé de Las Casas, pensador político, historiador, antropólogo. Spanish version by A. Hernández Travieso. Habana.

HARRIS, M.
1964 Patterns of Race in the Americas. Walker and Co., New York.

HERBRUGER, A., and DIAZ B., E.
1956 Método para aprender a hablar, leer, y escribir la lengua Cakchiquel, Vol. 1. Guatemala.

HERNANDEZ SPINA, V.
1932 Ixtlauacan Quiche Calendar (1854). Translation by E. J. W. Bunting. Maya Society Quarterly, Vol. 1, Baltimore.

HERRERA y TORDESILLAS, A. DE
1934- Historia general de los hechos de los castellanos en las islas
1957 y tierra firme del mar océano, Vols. 1-17. Tipografía de Archivos, Madrid.

HERSKOVITZ, M. J.
1965 A Genealogy of Ethnological Theory. In, Context and Meaning in Cultural Anthropology, Melford E. Spiro (ed.). The Free Press, New York.

HIGBEE, E. C.
1947 The Agricultural Regions of Guatemala. Geographical Review, Vol. 37, pp. 177-201. New York.

IBARRA, J. A.
1959 Apuntes de Historia Natural y Mamíferos de Guatemala. Colección Popular, No. 21. Ministerio de Educación Pública, Guatemala.

IXTLILXOCHITL, F. DE ALVA
1952 Obras históricas, 2 Vols. A. Chavero (ed.). Editora Naciona, S. A., Mexico.

JIMENEZ MORENO, W.
1942 El enigma de las Olmecas. Cuadernos Americanos, Vol. 5, pp. 113-145. Mexico.

JUARROS, D.
1823 A Statistical and Commercial History of the Kingdom of Guatemala in Spanish America. Translation by J. Baily. London.
1937 Compendio de la historia de la cuidad de Guatemala. Tipografía Nacional, Guatemala.

KAUFMAN, T. S.
1964 Materiales lingüísticos para el estudio de las relaciones internas y externas de la familia de idiomas mayanos. Desarrollo Cultural de los Mayas, Universidad Nacional Autónoma de Mexico. Mexico.

KIDDER, A. V., JENNINGS, J. D., and SHOOK, E. M.
1946 Excavations at Kaminaljuyu, Guatemala. Carnegie Institution of Washington, Pub. 561. Washington.

KINZHALOV, R. V.
n.d.   Indian Sources on the History and Ethnography of Mountain Indians of Guatemala in the X-XVI Centuries. Manuscript, English translation of an article in Ot Aliaski do Ognennoi Zemli Moskva, 1967, pp. 222-233, in possession of Howard F. Cline.

KIRCHHOFF, P.
1952   Mesoamerica. In, Heritage of Conquest, S. Tax (ed.). The Free Press, Glencoe.

KONETZKE, R.
1953- Colección de documentos para la historia de la formación
1962   social de hispanoamérica (1493-1810), 3 Vols. Madrid.

KURATH, G. P.
1967   Drama, Dance, and Music. Handbook of Middle American Indians, Vol. 6, pp. 158-190. University of Texas Press, Austin.

KURATH, G. P., and MARTI, S.
1964   Dances of Anahuac. Viking Fund Publications in Anthropology, No. 38. New York.

LA FARGE, O.
1947   Santa Eulalia: The Religion of a Cuchumatán Indian Town. University of Chicago Press, Chicago.
1962   Maya Ethnology: The Sequence of Cultures. In, The Maya and Their Neighbors, pp. 281-291. New York.

LA FARGE, O., and BYERS, D.
1931   The Year Bearer's People. Middle American Research Institute, Tulane University, Pub. 3. New Orleans.

LAMADRID, L.
1937   Prólogo, In, Crónica de la provincia del santísimo nombre de Jesús de Guatemala, F. Vázquez. Biblioteca "Goathemala," Vol. 14, pp. ii-xx. Guatemala.

LANDAR, H.
1967   Bibliographic Note: Quiché. International Journal of American Linguistics, Vol. 33, No. 1. Baltimore.

LARDE, J.
1926   El Popol Vuh: El monumento literario de los pueblos Maya-Quiché. Taken from a version by F. Ximénez. In, El Salvadoreño, San Salvador.

LA RENAUDIERE, P. F. DE
1843   Mexique et Guatemala. Paris.

LA ROUSSE
1963   Nuevo Pequeño La Rousse Illustrado. Diccionario Enciclopédico. Paris.

LAS CASAS, B. DE
1909 Apologética historia de las Indias. M. Serrano y Sanz. Nueva Biblioteca de Autores Españoles, Vol. 13. Madrid.
1951 Historia de las Indias, 3 Vols. A. Millares C. and L. Hanke (eds.). Mexico.
1958 Apologética historia de las Indias, 2 Vols. Biblioteca de Autores Españoles, Nos. 105, 106. (Unless specified with "I", references are to No. 106). Madrid.

LEACOCK, E.
1961 Symposium on the Concept of Ethnohistory (Comment). Ethnohistory, Vol. 8, pp. 256-261.

LEHMANN, H.
1968a Mixco Viejo, guía de las ruinas de la plaza fuerte Pocomám. Guatemala.
1968b Arts Mayas du Guatemala: Mixco Viejo. Réunion des Musées Nationaux, Ministère d'État. Paris.

LEHMANN, W.
1911 Der Kalender der Quiche Indianer Guatemalas. Anthropos, Vol. 6, pp. 403-410. St. Gabriel-Mödling bei Wien.
1920 Zentral-Amerika. Teil I. Die Sprachen Zentral Amerikas in ihren Beziehungen zueinander sowie zu Süd-Amerika und Mexico. Berlin.

LEON-PORTILLA, M.
1961 Los Antiguos Mexicanos a trevés de sus crónicas y cantares. Fondo de Cultura Económica, Mexico.

LEWIS, O.
1963 Life in a Mexican Village: Tepoztlan Restudied. University of Illinois Press, Urbana.

LINCOLN, J. S.
1942 The Maya Calendar of the Ixil of Guatemala. Carnegie Institution of Washington, Pub. 528, Contribution 38. Washington.
1946 An Ethnological Study of the Ixil Indians of the Guatemalan Highlands. Microfilm Collection of Manuscripts in Middle America Cultural Anthropology, No. 1. University of Chicago Press, Chicago.

LOPEZ DE VELASCO, J.
1952 Geografía y descripción universal de las Indias y demarcación de los reyes de Castilla (1571-1574). Anales del Museo Nacional "David J. Guzmán" San Salvador, Vol. 3, pp. 33-62. San Salvador.

LÓPEZ DE GÓMARA, F.
1946 Historia general de las Indias. Biblioteca de Autores Españoles, Vol. 22. Madrid.

LOTHROP, S. K.

1926 A Quiché Altar. Man, Vol. 26, No. 55. London.

1928 Santiago Atitlán, Guatemala. Museum of the American Indian,
Heye Foundation, Indian Notes, Vol. 5, pp. 370-395. New
York.

1929 Further Notes on Indian Ceremonies in Guatemala. Canoes
of Lake Atitlán, Guatemala. Museum of the American Indian,
Heye Foundation, Indian Notes, Vol. 6, pp. 1-25, 216-221.
New York.

1930 A Modern Survival of the Ancient Maya Calendar. Proceedings of the Twenty-third International Congress of Americanists, pp. 652-655. New York.

1933 Atitlán: An Archaeological Study of Ancient Remains on
the Borders of Lake Atitlán, Guatemala. Carnegie Institution of Washington, Pub. 444. Washington.

1936 Zacualpa: A Study of Ancient Quiché Artifacts. Carnegie
Institution of Washington, Pub. 472. Washington.

1952 Zutugil Dugout Canoes. Notes on Middle American Archaeology and Ethnology, Carnegie Institute of Washington, Pub.
4, Contribution 3, pp. 203-210. Washington.

LOWIE, R. H.

1937 The History of Ethnological Theory. Holt, Rinehart and
Winston, New York.

LUNA, J. J. R.

1958- La fauna Guatemalteca. Anales de la Sociedad de Geografía
1959 e Historia de Guatemala, Vols. 31-32, pp. 152-158. Guatemala.

MACE, C. E.

1961 The Patzcá Dance of Rabinal. El Palacio, Vol. 68, pp. 151-
167. Santa Fe.

1967 Dance Dramas of Rabinal. Xavier University Studies, Vol.
6, pp. 1-19. New Orleans.

n.d. Brasseur de Bourbourg. Article to be published in an up-
coming volume of the Handbook of Middle American Indians
(1968).

MADSEN, W.

1967 Religious Syncretism. Handbook of Middle American Indians, Vol. 6, pp. 369-391. University of Texas Press, Austin.

MARTINEZ, M.

n.d. Arte de la lengua Utlateca o kiché, vulgarmente llamado el
Arte de Totonicapán. Photocopy of a Manuscript in the Bibliothèque Nationale, Paris, in the Newberry Library, Chicago.

MARTIR, P. A.

1912 De Orbe Novo. The Eight Decades of Peter Martyr D'An-
ghera. Translation from the Latin, F. A. MacNutt. G. P.
Putnam's Sons, New York, London.

MAUDSLAY, A. P.
1899 A Glimpse at Guatemala and Some Notes on the Ancient Monuments of Central America. London.

MAYERS, M.
1966 Languages of Guatemala. Juna linguarum, series practica, 23. The Hague.

MAYNARD, G., and XEC, P.
n.d. Diccionario preliminar del idioma Quiché. Manuscript.

MC BRYDE, F. W.
1933 Sololá: A Guatemalan Town and Cakchiquel Market-Center. Middle American Research Institute, Tulane University, Pub. 5, pp. 45-152. New Orleans.
1942 Studies in Guatemalan Meteorology. American Meteorological Society, Bulletin, Vol. 23, pp. 754-763, 400-406. Caston, Pa.
1947 Cultural and Historical Geography of Southwest Guatemala. Smithsonian Institution, Institute of Social Anthropology, Pub. 4. Washington.
1955 Census Atlas Maps of Latin America. U. S. Bureau of the Census, Department of Commerce. Washington.

MC QUOWN, N. A.
1955 The Indigenous Languages of Latin America. American Anthropologist, Vol. 57, pp. 501-570. Menasha.
1956 The Classification of the Mayan Languages. International Journal of American Linguistics, Vol. 22, pp. 191-195. Baltimore.
1964 Los orígenes y la diferenciación de los mayas según se infiere del estudio comparativo de las lenguas mayanas. Desarrollo Cultural de Los Mayas. Universidad Nacional Autónoma de México, México.

MENDELSON, E. M.
1958a A Guatemalan Sacred Bundle. Man, Vol. 58, pp. 121-126. London.
1958b The King, the Traitor and the Cross: An Interpretation of a Highland Maya Religious Conflict. Diogenes, Vol. 21, pp. 1-10. The University of Chicago Press for UNESCO, Chicago.
1959 Maximón: an iconographical introduction. Man, Vol. 59, pp. 57-60. London.
1962 Religion and World-View in Santiago Atitlán. Microfilm Collection of Manuscripts in Middle American Cultural Anthropology, No. 52. University of Chicago Library. Chicago.
1965 Los Escándalos de Maximón. Seminario de Integración Social Guatemalteca, Pub. 19. Guatemala.
1967 Ritual and Mythology. Handbook of Middle American Indians, Vol. 7, pp. 392-415. University of Texas Press, Austin.

MENDEZ DOMINGUEZ, A.
1967 Zaragoza, la estratificación social de una comunidad Ladina Guatemalteca. Seminario de Integración Social Guatemalteca, Pub. 21. Guatemala.

MILES, S. W.
1952 An Analysis of Modern Middle American Calendars: A Study in Conservation. In, Acculturation in the Americas, S. Tax (ed.). Proceedings and Selected Paper of the Twenty-ninth International Congress of Americanists. University of Chicago Press, Chicago.
1957 The Sixteenth-Century Pokom-Maya: A Documentary Analysis of Social Structure and Archaeological Setting. Transactions of the American Philosophical Society, Vol. 47, pp. 731-781. Philadelphia.
1965 Sculpture of the Guatemala-Chiapas Highlands and Pacific Slopes, and Associated Hieroglyphs. In, Handbook of Middle American Indians, Vol. 2, pp. 237-275. University of Texas Press, Austin.

MILLA, J. (SALOME JIL)
1963 Historia de la América Central, Vol. 1. Ministerio de Educación Pública. Guatemala.

MIRANDA, F. M. DE
1954 Descripción de la Provincia de la Verapaz. Anales de la Sociedad de Geografía e Historia de Guatemala, Vol. 27, pp. 342-358. Guatemala.

MOLINA, A. DE
1943 Antigua Guatemala: Memorias del M. R. P. Maestro Fray Antonio de Molina, continuadas y marginadas por Fray Agustín Cano y Fray Francisco Ximénez de la Orden de Santo Domingo. Prologue and notes by J. del Valle Matheu. Guatemala.

MOLINA, FRAY ALONZO DE
1944 Vocabulario en lengua castellana y mexicana. Colección de Incunables Americanos, Vol. 4. Madrid.

MONTEFORTE TOLEDO, M.
1965 Guatemala, monografía sociológica. Universidad Nacional Autónoma de Mexico, Mexico.

MONTERDE, F.
1955 Teatro indígena prehispánico: Rabinal Achi. Mexico.

MORELET, A. M.
1871 Travels in Central America. Translation of Voyage dans L'Amérique Centrale, by Mrs. M. F. Squier, 2 Vols., New York.

MUÑOS, B.
n.d. Colección de Don Juan Bautista Muños. Manuscript. Real Academia de la Historia, Madrid.

NAGEL, E.
1952 Some Issues in the Logic of Historical Analysis. Scientific Monthly, Vol. 54, pp. 162-169. Washington.

NASH, M.
1957 Cultural Persistence and Social Structure: The Mesoamerican Calendar Survivals. Southwestern Journal of Anthropology, Vol. 13, pp. 149-155. Albuquerque.
1958 Political Relations in Guatemala. Social and Economic Studies, Vol. 7, pp. 65-75. Mona, Jamaica.
1967a Machine Age Maya: The Industrialization of a Guatemalan Community. Phoenix Books, University of Chicago Press, Chicago.
1967b Introduction to Volume on Social Anthropology. Handbook of Middle American Indians, Vol. 6. University of Texas Press, Austin.
1969 Guatemalan Highlands. In, Handbook of Middle American Indians, Vol. 7. pp. 30-45. University of Texas Press, Austin.

NAVARRETE, C.
1962 La Cerámica de Mixco Viejo. Cuadernos de Antropología, Vol. 1. Universidad de San Carlos de Guatemala, Guatemala.

NICHOLSON, H. B.
1955 Native Historical Traditions of Nuclear America and the Problem of Their Archaeological Correlation. American Anthropologist, Vol. 57, pp. 594-613. Menasha.
1960 Ethnohistory: Introduction. Handbook of Latin American Studies, Vol. 23. Gainesville.
1968 Middle American Ethnohistory: An Overview. Working paper No. 72. To be published in the Handbook of Middle American Indians.
n.d.a Topiltzin Quetzalcoatl of Tollan: A Problem in Mesoamerican Ethnohistory. Doctoral Dissertation, Harvard University, 1957.
n.d.b Prehispanic Central Mexico: Religion. To be published in Handbook of Middle American Indians.

NOVAL, J.
1964 Materiales Etnográficos de San Miguel. Cuadernos Antropológicos, No. 3. Universidad de San Carlos de Guatemala, Guatemala.

OAKES, M.
1951 The Two Crosses of Todos Santos. Bollingen Series, No. 27. Princeton University Press, Princeton.

O'NEALE, L. M.
1945 Textiles of Highland Guatemala. Carnegie Institute of Washington, Pub. 567. Washington.

Ordoñez Ch., M. J.
1957 Prácticas Eleccionarias de los Indígenas del Municipio de
Sololá. Boletín del Instituto Indigenista Nacional, Vol. 1,
pp. 57-59. Guatemala.

Osborne, L. de J.
1931- Ensayo sobre temas indígenas: Historia y simbolismo en la
1932 indumentaria. Anales de la Sociedad de Geografía e Historia de Guatemala, Vol. 8, pp. 295-304. Guatemala.
1935 Guatemala Textiles. Middle American Research Institute,
Tulane University, Pub. 6. New Orleans.
1960 Así es Guatemala. Ministerio de Educación Pública. Guatemala.

Parsons, L. A., Borhegyi, S. F., Jenson, P., and Ritzenthaler, R.
1963 Excavaciones en Bilboa, Santa Lucía Cotzumalhuapa: informe preliminar. Antropología e Historia de Guatemala,
Vol. 15, No. 1, pp. 3-14. Guatemala.

Parsons, L. A., and Jenson, P. S.
1965 Boulder Sculpture on the Pacific Coast of Guatemala. Archaeology, Vol. 18, pp. 132-144. Cambridge, Mass.

Paso y Troncoso, F. del
1939- Epistolario de Nueva España, 16 Vols. Mexico.
1942

Paul, B. D.
1959 La Vida de un Pueblo Indígena de Guatemala. Original English title, Life in a Guatemalan Indian Village. Cuadernos
del Seminario de Integración Social Guatemalteca (Número Extraordinario). Guatemala.

Paul, B. D., and Paul, L.
1962 Ethnographic Materials on San Pedro La Laguna, Sololá,
Guatemala. Microfilm Collection of Manuscripts on Middle
American Cultural Anthropology, No. 54, University of Chicago Library. Chicago.

Pineda, J. de
1925 Descripción de la Provincia de Guatemala. Anales de la
Sociedad de Geografía e Historia de Guatemala, Vol. 1, pp.
327-363. Guatemala.

Pollock, H. E. D., Roys, R. L., Proskouriakoff, T., and Smith,
A. L.
1962 Mayapán, Yucatán, Mexico. Carnegie Institute of Washington, Pub. 619. Washington.

Pomar, J. B.
1941 Relación de Tezcoco. Editorial Salvador Chávez Hayhoe.
Mexico.

PONCE, A.
1873   Relación breve y verdadera de algunas cosas de las muchas
       que sucedieron al Padre Fray Alonso Ponce en las Provincias
       de la Nueva España, 2 Vols. Madrid.

RAMIREZ, J. F.
1930- Proceso de residencia contra Pedro de Albarado....Notas y
1931   noticias biográficas, críticas arqueológicas. Anales de la So-
       ciedad de Geografía e Historia de Guatemala, Vols. 7-8. Gua-
       temala.

RANDS, R. L., and SMITH, R. E.
1965   Pottery of the Guatemalan Highlands. In, Handbook of
       Middle American Indians, Vol. 2, pp. 95-145. University
       of Texas Press, Austin.

RECINOS, A.
1913   Monografía del Departamento de Huehuetenango. Ministerio
       de Educación Pública, Guatemala.
1950   Memorial de Sololá: Anales de los Cakchiqueles. Título de
       los Señores de Totonicapán. Fondo de Cultura Económica,
       Mexico.
1952   Pedro de Alvarado, conquistador de México y Guatemala.
       Fondo de Cultura Económica, Mexico.
1953   Popol Vuh: Las antiguas historias del Quiché. Fondo de
       Cultura Económica, Mexico.
1957   Crónicas Indígenas de Guatemala. Editorial Universitaria,
       Guatemala.
1959   Algunas ideas sobre el origen de las razas indígenas de Guate-
       mala. Mitteillungen aus dem Museum für Völkerkunde in
       Hamburg, Vol. 25, pp. 114-117. Hamburg.

REDFIELD, R.
1939   Primitive Merchants of Guatemala. Quarterly of Inter-
       American Relations, Vol. 1, pp. 42-56.
1946   Notes on San Antonio Palopó. Microfilm Collection of Manu-
       scripts on Middle American Cultural Anthropology, No. 4.
       University of Chicago Library. Chicago.

REDFIELD, R., LINTON, R., and HERSKOVITZ, M. J.
1936   Memorandum on the Study of Acculturation. American An-
       thropologist, Vol. 38, pp. 149-152. Menasha.

REDFIELD, R., and VILLA ROJAS, A.
1934   Chan Kom, a Maya Village. Carnegie Institute of Washing-
       ton, Pub. 448. Washington.

REINA, R. E.
1959   Continuidad de la Cultura Indígena en una Comunidad Guate-
       malteca. Cuadernos del Seminario de Integración Social Gua-
       temalteca, No. 4. Guatemala.

1960   Chinautla, A Guatemalan Indian Community. Middle American Research Institute, Tulane University, Pub. 24, pp. 55-130. New Orleans.
1966   The Law of the Saints. The Bobbs-Merrill, Indianapolis and New York.
1969   Eastern Guatemalan Highlands: The Pokomames and Chortí. *In*, Handbook of Middle American Indians, Vol. 7, pp. 101-132. University of Texas Press, Austin.

REMESAL, A. DE
1932   Historia general de las indias occidentales, y particular de la gobernación de Chiapa y Guatemala. Biblioteca "Goathemala," Vols. 4-5. Guatemala.
1964   Historia general de las indias occidentales y particular de la gobernación de Chiapa y Guatemala. Biblioteca de Autores Españoles, Vol. 175. Madrid.

RODAS N., F.
1925-   Creencias religiosas de los antiguos quichés. Anales de la
1926   Sociedad de Geografía e Historia de Guatemala, Vol. 2, pp. 60-71.

RODAS N., F., and RODAS CORZO, O.
1938   Simbolismos (maya-quichés) de Guatemala. Guatemala.

RODRIGUEZ, M.
1965   Central America. Prentice-Hall, Englewood Cliffs, New Jersey.

RODRIGUEZ, R., and CRESPO, M.
1957   Calendario Cakchiquel de los indios de Guatemala (1685). Antropología e Historia de Guatemala, Vol. 9, No. 2, pp. 17-27. Guatemala.

ROJAS, G. DE
1927   Descripción de Cholula. Revista Mexicana de Estudios Históricos, Vol. 1, pp. 158-170. Mexico.

ROSALES, J. DE D.
1949   Notes on Aguacatán, and Notes on San Pedro La Laguna. Microfilm Collection of Manuscripts on Middle American Cultural Anthropology, Nos. 24-25. University of Chicago Library. Chicago.

ROWE, J. H.
1965   The Renaissance Foundations of Anthropology. American Anthropologist, Vol. 67, pp. 1-20. Menasha.

ROYS, R. L.
1943   The Indian Background of Colonial Yucatan. Carnegie Institute of Washington, Pub. 548. Washington.
1957   The Political Geography of the Yucatan Maya. Carnegie Institute of Washington, Pub. 613. Washington.

SAENZ, C. DE SANTA MARIA

1940 Diccionario Cakchiquel-Español. Tipografía Nacional, Guatemala.

1959 Una ojeada a la bibliografía lingüística Guatemalteca. Revista de Indias, Vol. 19, pp. 255-271. Madrid.

1963 Vida y escritos de Don Francisco Marroquín, primer Obispo de Guatemala (1499-1563). Anales de la Sociedad de Geografía e Historia de Guatemala, Vol. 36, pp. 85-314. Guatemala.

1964 Estudio preliminar, Fray Antonio de Remesal, O. P. y su obra. Biblioteca de Autores Españoles, Vol. 175, pp. 7-68. Madrid.

1966 Remesal, la Verapaz, y Fray Bartolomé de Las Casas. Estudios Lascasasianos. Escuela de Estudios Hispano-Americanos de Sevilla, 175, pp. 329-349.

SAHLINS, M. D.

1958 Social Stratification in Polynesia. The American Ethnological Society, University of Washington Press. Seattle.

SALER, B.

1962 Migration and Ceremonial Ties Among the Maya. Southwestern Journal of Anthropology, Vol. 18, pp. 336-340. Albuquerque.

1964 Nagual, Witch, and Sorcerer in a Quiché Village. Ethnology, Vol. 3, pp. 305-328. Pittsburgh.

n.d. The Road from El Palmar: Change, Continuity, and Conservatism in a Quiché Community. Ph. D. Dissertation, University of Pennsylvania, 1960.

SANDERS, W. T., and PRICE, B.

1968 Mesoamerica: The Evolution of a Civilization. Random House, New York.

SAPPER, D. E.

1925 Costumbres y Creencias religiosas de los indios Quekchí. Anales de la Sociedad de Geografía e Historia de Guatemala, Vol. 2, pp. 189-197. Guatemala.

SAPPER, K. T.

1890 Die soziale Stellung der Indianer in der Alta Verapaz. Pettermann's Geographische Mitteilungen, Helt 4. Gotha.

1894 Grundzüge der physikalischen Geographie von Guatemala. Pettermann's Geographische Mitteilungen, No. 113. Gotha.

1897a Ein altindianischer Landstreit in Guatemala. Globus, Vol. 72, pp. 94-97. Braunschweig.

1897b Das nördliche Mittelamerika, Ausflug nach dem Hochland von Anahuac. Reisen und Studien aus den Jahren 1885-1895. Braunschweig.

1898   Die Ruinen von Mixco. Internationales Archiv für Ethnographie, Vol. 11, pp. 1-6. Leiden.

1899   Uber Gebirgsbau und Boden des nördlichen Mittelamerika. Aus Justus Perthes Geographischer Anstalt, Vol. 27, Hefte 125-130.

1901   Speise und Trank der Kekchi-Indianer. Globus, Vol. 18, pp. 259-263. Braunschweig.

1902   Mittelamerikanische Reisen und Studien, aus den Jahren 1888-1900. Braunschweig.

1904a   Religiöse Gebräuche und Auschauungen der Kekchi-Indianer. Archiv Religionswiss, Vol. 7, pp. 453-470.

1904b   Sitten und Gebräuche der Poconchi Indianer. Fourteenth International Congress of Americanists, Vol. 14, pp. 403-417. Stuttgart.

1905   Der gegenwärtige Stand der ethnographischen Kenntnis von Mittelamerika. Archiv für Anthropologie, Vol. 3, pp. 1-39.

1906   Chols und Chortis. Fifteenth International Congress of Americanists, Proceedings. Pt. 2, pp. 423-465. Quebec.

1924   Die Zahl und Volksdichte der Indianischen Bevölkerung in der Gegenwart. Twenty-first International Congress of Americanists, Proceedings, pp. 95-104. Göteborg.

1925   Über Brujeria in Guatemala. Twenty-first International Congress of Americanists, pp. 391-405. Göteborg.

1936   Die Verapaz im 16. und 17. Jahrhundert. Ein Beitrag zur historischen Geographie und Ethnographie des nordöstlichen Guatemala. Abhandlungen der Bayerischen Akademie der Wissenschaften. Neue Folge, Heft 37. Munich.

SAQUIC C., R.

n.d.   Santa Catarina Ixtahuacán. Manuscript on file with the Instituto Indigenista Nacional, Guatemala.

SCHERZER, K.

1855   Sprache der Indianer von Ixtalavacan (Quiche) von Quezaltenango, Guatemala. Klasse der Kaiserlichen Akademie der Wissenschaften, Vol. 18, pp. 227-241. Berlin.

1856   Die Indianer von Santa Catalina Istlavacan. Vienna.

1857   Las Historias del Origen de los Indios de esta Provincia de Guatemala. Copy of the Ximénez version of the Popol Vuh. Vienna.

1864   Aus dem Natur- und Völkerleben im tropischen Amerika. Leipcig.

SCHULTZE JENA, L.

1933   Leben, Glaube und Sprache der Quiche von Guatemala. Indiana I. Gustav Fischer, Jena.

1944   Popol Vuh: Das heilige Buch der Quiche Indianer von Guatemala. Stuttgart, Berlin.

1947   Indígenas Quichés de Guatemala. Biblioteca de Cultura Popular, Guatemala, Vol. 49, 1947. Editorial del Ministerio de Educación Pública, Guatemala.

SELER, E.
1901   Die alten Ansiedelungen von Chacula. Berlin.
1960   Gesammelte Abhandlungen zur amerikanischen Sprach- und Alterumskunde, Vols. 1-5. Graz, Austria.

SERVICE, E. R.
1955   Indian-European Relations in Colonial Latin America. American Anthropologist, Vol. 57, pp. 411-425. Menasha.
1964   Primitive Social Organization: An evolutionary perspective. Random House, New York.

SHAW, M. and NEUENSWANDER, H.
1966   Achi. In, Lenguas de Guatemala, pp. 27-71. Original English title, Languages of Guatemala, 1966. Seminario de Integración Social Guatemalteca, Pub. 20. Guatemala.

SHOOK, E.
1949   Historia arqueológica de Puerto de San José, Guatemala. Antropología e Historia de Guatemala, Vol. 1, pp. 3-22. Guatemala.
1952   Lugares arquelógicos del altiplano meridional central de Guatemala. Antropología e Historia de Guatemala, Vol. 4, No. 2, pp. 3-40. Guatemala.
1965   Archaeological Survey of the Pacific Coast of Guatemala. In, Handbook of Middle American Indians, Vol. 2, pp. 180-194. University of Texas Press, Austin.
n.d.   Field Notes, 1942-48, for the Carnegie Institution of Washington. Peabody Museum, Harvard, Cambridge, Mass.

SHOOK, E., and KIDDER, A. V.
1952   Mound E-III-3, Kaminaljuyú, Guatemala. Carnegie Institution of Washington, Pub. 596, Contribution 53. Washington.

SIEGEL, M.
1941   Religion in Western Guatemala: a product of acculturation. American Anthropologist, Vol. 43, pp. 62-76. Menasha.
1943   The Creation Myth and Acculturation in Acatán Guatemala. Journal of American Folklore, Vol. 56, pp. 120-126. Philadelphia.

SILVIA L., F.
n.d.   La conquista de Utatlán: drama histórica, escrito bajo el plan de un antiguo manuscrito de cuyo original se conservan los nombres y locuciones indígenes, y se refiere al año de 1524. (1887?). Guatemala.

SIMEON, R.
1963   Dictionnaire de la langue Nahuatl ou Mexicains. Graz, Austria.

SMITH, A. L.
1955 Archaeological Reconnaissance in Central Guatemala. Carnegie Institution of Washington, Pub. 608. Washington.
1965 Architecture of the Guatemalan Highlands. *In*, Handbook of Middle American Indians, Vol. 2, pp. 26-94. University of Texas Press, Austin.

SMITH, A. L. and KIDDER, A. V.
1943 Explorations in the Motagua Valley, Guatemala. Carnegie Institution of Washington, Pub. 546, Contribution 41. Washington.
1951 Excavations at Nebaj, Guatemala. Carnegie Institution of Washington, Pub. 594. Washington.

SMITH, R. E.
1952 Pottery from Chipoc, Alta Verapaz, Guatemala. Carnegie Institution of Washington, Pub. 596, Contribution 56. Washington.
1955 Pottery Specimens from Guatemala: II. Carnegie Institution of Washington, notes on Middle American Archaeology and Ethnology, No 124. Washington.

SOLANO PEREZ LILA, F. de P.
1963 Los Mayas del Siglo XVII. Antropología e Historia de Guatemala, Vol. 15, No. 2, pp. 3-34. Guatemala.

SQUIER, E. G.
1858 The States of Central America: their Geography, Topography, Climate, Population, Resources, Productions, Commerce, Political Organization, Aborigines, etc. Harper and Bros., New York.

STADLEMAN, R.
1940 Maize Cultivation in Northwestern Guatemala. Carnegie Institute of Washington, Contributions in American Anthropology and History, Vol. 6, No. 33, pp. 83-266. Washington.

STARR, B.
1951 The Chortís and the Problem of the Survival of the Maya Cultures. American Anthropologist, Vol. 53, pp. 355-369. Menasha.

STEPHENS, J. L.
1853 Incidents of Travel in Central America, Chiapas, and Yucatan. Harper and Bros., Publishers, New York.

STEWARD, J. H.
1963 Theory of Culture Change: the methodology of multilinear evolution. University of Illinois Press, Urbana.

STOLL, O.
1884 Zur Ethnographie der Republik Guatemala. Zurich.

1886   Guatemala: Reisen und Schilderungen aus den Jahren 1878-1883. Leipcig.
1887   Die Sprache der Ixil-Indianer. Leipcig.
1888   Die Maya-Sprachen der Pokom-Gruppe, 1. Teil. (*Also*, Die Sprache der Pokonchi-Indianer). Vienna.
1889   Die Ethnologie der Indianerstämme von Guatemala. E. Steiger and Co., New York.
1896   Die Maya-Sprachen der Pokom-Gruppe, 2. Tiel. (*Also*, Die Sprache der K'kechi Indianer, Die Uspanteca). Leipcig.
1901   Die ethnische Stellung der Tz'utujil-Indianer von Guatemala. Festschrift der Geographisch-Ethnographischen Gesellschaft, pp. 27-59. Zurich.
1904   Título del barrio de Santa Ana, agosto 14, de 1565. International Congress of Americanists, Proceedings, Vol. 14, pp. 383-397. Stuttgart.
1912   Zur Psychologie der indianischen Hochlands-Sprachen von Guatemala. Jahresbericht der Geographisch-Ethnographischen Gesellschaft, Zurich.
1928   Das Vokabular der Sprache von Aguacatan, No. 2. Mittheilungen der Geographisch-Ethnographischen Gesellschaft, Supplement 1, Zurich.
1958   Etnografía de Guatemala. Seminario de Integración Social Guatemalteca, Pub. 8. Guatemala.
1960   Los Indios Ixiles. Primeros trabajos etnológicos en Guatemala. Boletín del Instituto Indigenista Nacional, Vol. 2, pp. 59-64. Guatemala.

STURTEVANT, W. C.
1968   Anthropology, History, and Ethnohistory. *In*, Introduction to Cultural Anthropology, Clifton, James A. (ed.). Houghton Mifflin Co., Boston.

SWADESH, M.
1960   Interrelaciones de las lenguas Mayas. Anales, Instituto Nacional de Antropología e Historia, Vol. 11, pp. 231-267. México.

SWARTZ, M. J.
1958   History and Science in Anthropology. Philosophy of Science, Vol. 25 (1), pp. 59-70. Baltimore.

TAX, S.
1937   The Municipios of the Midwestern Highlands of Guatemala. American Anthropologist, Vol. 39, pp. 423-444. Menasha.
1946   The Towns of Lake Atitlán. Microfilm Collection of Manuscripts on Middle American Cultural Anthropology, No. 13. University of Chicago Library. Chicago.
1947a   Notes on Santo Tomás Chichicastenango. Microfilm Collection of Manuscripts in Middle American Cultural Anthropology, No. 16. University of Chicago Library. Chicago.

1947b Miscellaneous Notes on Guatemala. Microfilm Collection of Manuscripts in Middle American Cultural Anthropology, No. 18. University of Chicago Library. Chicago.
1953 Penny Capitalism in a Guatemalan Indian Economy. Smithsonian Institution, Institute of Social Anthropology, Pub. 16. Washington.
1964 El Capitalismo del Centavo. Spanish translation, *Ibid.*, Seminario de Integración Social Guatemalteca, Pubs. 12, 15. Guatemala.

TAX, S. (ed.).
1952 Heritage of Conquest: The Ethnology of Middle America. Viking Fund Seminar on Middle American Ethnology. Glencoe.

TAX, S., and HINSHAW, R.
1969 The Maya of the Midwestern Highlands. *In*, Handbook of Middle American Indians, Vol. 7, pp. 69-100. University of Texas Press, Austin.

TEJEDA, A.
1947 Drawings of Tajumulco Sculpture. Carnegie Institution of Washington, Notes on Middle American Archaeology and Ethnology, No. 77. Washington.

TELETOR, C. N.
1946 Memorial de Tecpán Atitlán (última parte). Guatemala.
1951 Epítome Quiché. Guatemala.
1955 Apuntes para una Monografía de Rabinal (B. V.), y algo de nuestro Folklore. Ministerio de Educación Pública, Guatemala.
1959 Diccionario Castellano-Quiché y Voces Castellano-Pocomám. Guatemala.

TEMPSKY, G. F. VON
1858 Narrative of Incidents and Personal Adventures on a Journey in Mexico, Guatemala, and Modes of Life in Those Countries. London.

TERMER, F.
1930a Archäologische Studien und Beobachtungen in Guatemala in den Jahren 1925-1929. Tagungsberichte der Gesellschaft für Völkerkunde, pp. 85-102. Leipcig.
1930b Zur Ethnologie und Ethnographie des nördlichen Mittelamerika, Ibero-Amerikanisches Archiv, Vol. 4, no. 3. Berlin and Bonn.
1930c Los bailes de culebra entre los indios quichés en Guatemala. Twenty-third International Congress of Americanists, Proceedings, pp. 661-667. New York.
1931 Zur Archäologie von Guatemala. Baessler-Archiv, Vol. 14, pp. 167-191. Berlin.

1936a Die Bedeutung der Pipiles für die Kulturgestaltung in Guatemala. Baessler Archiv, Vol. 19, Heft 1-2, pp. 108-113. Berlin.
1936b Zur Geographie der Republik Guatemala. Beiträge zur physischen Geographie von Mittel- und Südguatemala. Mitteilunge der Geographischen Gesellschaft in Hamburg, Band 44.
1939- Apuntes sobre Geografía y Etnografía de la Costa Sur de
1940   Guatemala. Anales de la Sociedad de Geografía e Historia de Guatemala, Vol. 16, pp. 25-41. Guatemala.
1946- Nuevas investigaciones sobre los Mayas altenses del Norte
1949   de Guatemala. Anthropos, Vol. 40/44, pp. 561-576. St. Gabriel - Mödling bei Wien.
1957   Etnología y Etnografía de Guatemala. Seminario de Integración Social Guatemalteca, Pub. 5. Guatemala.
1958   Apuntes Geográficos y Etnográficos acerca de la Zona de Nebaj. Anales de la Sociedad de Geografía e Historia de Guatemala, Vol. 31, pp. 150-165. Guatemala.

THOMPSON, G. A.
1829   Narrative of an Official Visit to Guatemala from Mexico. London.

THOMPSON, J. E. S.
1938   Sixteenth and Seventeenth Century Reports on the Chol Mayas. American Anthropologist, Vol. 40, pp. 584-604. Menasha.
1943a A Trial Survey of the Southern Maya Area. American Antiquity, Vol. 9, pp. 106-134. Menasha.
1943b Pitfalls and Stimuli in the Interpretation of History Through Loan Words. Middle American Research Institute, Tulane University, Pub. 11. New Orleans.
1948   An Archaeological Reconnaissance in the Cotzumalhuapa Region, Escuintla, Guatemala. Carnegie Institution of Washington, Pub. 574, Contribution 44. Washington.
1950   Maya Hieroglyphic Writing: Introduction. Carnegie Institute of Washington, Pub. 589. Washington.

TORQUEMADA, J. DE
1943   Monarquía Indiana, 3 Vols. Mexico.

TOVILLA, M. A.
1960   Relación histórica descriptiva de las provincias de la Verapaz y de la del Manché (1635). Editorial Universitaria, Guatemala.

TOWNSEND, W. C.
1960   Cakchiquel Grammar. Mayan Studies I. Publication of the Summer Institute of Linguistics, University of Oklahoma, Norman.

TOZZER, A. M.
1941   Landa's Relación de las Cosas de Yucatán: a translation, edited with notes by A. M. Tozzer. Papers of the Peabody

Museum of American Archaeology and Ethnology, Harvard University. Cambridge, Mass.

Tumin, M. M.
1952 Caste in a Peasant Society. Princeton University Press.

Ubieto, A., Regla, J., Jover, J. M., and Seco, C.
1967 Introducción a la Historia de España. Editorial Teide, S. A. Barcelona.

Valois, A. de
1861 Méxique, Havana et Guatemala, notes de voyage par Alfred de Valois. Paris.

Vazquez, F.
1937- Crónica de la provincia del Santísimo Nombre de Jesús de
1944 Guatemala de la Orden de Nuestra Seráfico Padre San Francisco (1714-1717). Biblioteca "Goathemala," Vols. 14-17. Guatemala.

Vazquez de Espinosa, A.
1968 Description of the Indies (c. 1620). Translation by C. U. Clark. Smithsonian Miscellaneous Collections, Vol. 102. Washington.

Vela, D.
1935 Geneonimia maya-quiché. Guatemala.
1944 Instituciones y normas jurídicas entre los pueblos maya quichés. Revista de la Facultad de Ciencias Jurídicas y Sociales de Guatemala, Epoca II. Vol. 6, No. 1. Guatemala.

Viana, F. de, Gallego, L., and Cadena, G.
1955 Relación de la Provincia de la Verapaz, hecha por los religiosos de Santo Domingo de Cobán (1574). Anales de la Sociedad de Geografía e Historia de Guatemala, Vol. 28, pp. 18-31. Guatemala.

Vico, D. de
n.d.a Vocabulario de la lengua Cakchiquel y Kiché (no date). Photocopy from a manuscript in the Bibliothèque Nationale, Paris, in the Newberry Library, Chicago.
n.d.b Arte de la lengua Quiché o Utlateca. Photocopy of a manuscript in the Bibliothèque Nationale, Paris, in the Newberry Library, Chicago.

Villa Rojas, A.
1967 Los Lacandones: su origen, costumbres y problemas vitales. América Indígena, Vol. 28, pp. 25-53. Mexico.

Villacorta C., A. J.
1934 Memorial de Tecpán-Atitlán (Anales de los Cakchiqueles). Tipografía Nacional, Guatemala.
1938 Prehistoria e historia antigua de Guatemala. Sociedad de Geografía e Historia de Guatemala. Guatemala.

1962a Popol-Vuh. Crestomatía Quiché. Tomo I. Ministerio de Educación Pública. Guatemala.
1962b Popol-Vuh: Exégesis crestomática del manuscrito Quiché. Tomo II. Ministerio de Educación Pública. Guatemala.

VILLACORTA C., J. A., and RODAS N., F.
1927 Manuscrito de Chichicastenango. El Popol Buj. Guatemala.

VILLAGUTIERRE SOTO-MAYOR, J. DE
1933 Historia de la conquista de la provincia de El Itza. Biblioteca "Goathemala," Vol. 9. Guatemala.

WAGLEY, C.
1941 Economics of a Guatemalan Village. American Anthropological Association, Memoir 58. Menasha.
1949 The Social and Religious Life of a Guatemalan Village. American Anthropological Association, Memoir 71. Menasha.
1957 Santiago Chimaltenango: estudio antropológica-social de una comunidad indígena de Huehuetenango. Seminario de Integración Social Guatemalteca, Pub. 4. Guatemala.
1969 The Maya of Northwestern Guatemala. In, Handbook of Middle American Indians, Vol. 7, pp. 46-68. University of Texas Press, Austin.

WARREN, J. B.
n.d. An Introductory Survey of European Writings on Colonial Middle America, 1503-1818 (1968). Handbook of Middle American Indians, Working papers.

WAUCHOPE, R.
1948a Excavations at Zacualpa, Guatemala. Middle American Research Institute, Tulane University, Pub. 14. New Orleans.
1948b Surface Collection at Chiche, Guatemala. Middle American Research Records, Vol. 1, pp. 211-250. Tulane University, New Orleans.
1949 Las Edades de Utatlán e Iximché. Antropología e Historia de Guatemala, Vol. 1, No. 1, pp. 10-22. Guatemala.
1964 Southern Mesoamerica. In, Prehistoric Man in the New World, pp. 331-386. University of Chicago Press, Chicago.
1965 They Found the Buried Cities. University of Chicago Press, Chicago.

WHETTEN, N. L.
1965 Guatemala: The Land and the People. Yale University Press, New Haven.

WHORF, B. L.
1943 Loan Words in Ancient Mexico. Middle American Research Institute, Pub. 11. Tulane University. New Orleans.

WICK, S. A.
1966 Spoken Quiché (Maya). Book 1. (Wick was assisted by R. Co-chojil-Gonzáles.) Dept. of Anthropology, University of Chicago.

WISDOM, C.
1940 The Chortí Indians of Guatemala. University of Chicago Press, Chicago.
1961 Los Chortís de Guatemala. Seminario de Integración Social Guatemalteca, Pub. 10. Guatemala.

WOLF, E. R.
1953 La formación de la nación: un ensayo de formulación. Ciencias Sociales, Vol. 4, pp. 50-62, 98-111, 146-171. Puerto Rico.
1955a The Mexican Bajío in the Eighteenth Century: an analysis of cultural integration. Tulane University, Middle American Research Institute, Pub. 17, No. 3. New Orleans.
1955b Types of Latin American Peasantry: a preliminary discussion. American Anthropologist, Vol. 57, pp. 452-471. Menasha.
1962 Sons of the Shaking Earth. Phoenix Books, University of Chicago Press, Chicago.

WOODBURY, R. B.
1965 Artifacts of the Guatemalan Highlands. In, Handbook of Middle American Indians, Vol. 2, pp. 163-179. University of Texas Press, Austin.

WOODBURY, R. B., and TRIK, A. S.
1953 The Ruins of Zacaleu Guatemala, 2 Vols. The William Byrd Press Richmond, Va.

XIMENEZ, F.
1929- Historia de la provincia de San Vicente de Chiapa y Guate-
1931 mala. Biblioteca "Goathemala," Vols. 1-3. Guatemala.
1967 Historia Natural del Reino de Guatemala (1722). Editorial "José de Pineda Ibarra ", Guatemala.

ZAVALA, S.
1967 Contribución a la historia de las instituciones coloniales en Guatemala. Editorial Universitaria, Guatemala.

ZORITA, A. DE
1909 Historia de la Nueva España, Vol. I. M. Serrano y Sanz (ed.). Colección de Libros y Documentos Referentes a la Historia de America, Vol. 9. Librería General de Victoriano Suárez, Madrid.
1941 Breve y sumaria relación de los señores....en la Nueva España. Editorial Salvador Chávez Hayhoe, Mexico.
1963a Breve y sumaria relación de los señores de la Nueva España. México.
1963b Life and Labor in Ancient Mexico: The Brief and Summary Relation of the Lords of New Spain by Alonso de Zorita. Translated by B. Keem. New Brunswick, New Jersey.

Index

in dictionaries, 115, 117; recorded after conquest, 164-168; used for naming, 175; in *Crónica Franciscana*, 194; modern studies of, 228, 234, 236, 238, 239, 240, 241, 253, 256; in *Título C'oyoi*, 271, 315, 324ff., 327, 338f.

Canil. *See* Sacapulas Quiche

Cantel, 254, 331, 334

Carchá, San Pedro, 70

Cauque, Santa María, 115

Cawek, 28, 30, 35, 43, 44, 45, 85, 309f., 342. *See also* Ruling lines

Cawinal, 312, 313

Censuses (modern), 262f.

Cerrato, Alonso, 84, 123-124, 138, 143, 145f.

Chajoma. *See* Cakchiquel

Chajul, 183, 257

Chicaj, 255

Chamá, Santa Ana, 69

Chamelco, San Juan, 69, 70, 255

Chicacao, San Bartolomé (*Aguacatepec*), 67, 133-135

Chiche, 204, 255

Chichicastenango, 24-25, 145, 150, 162, 174, 175, 183, 189f., 236f., 239, 248, 251-252, 323, 324

Chimaltenango, 97, 140, 144, 151f., 199, 332, 342

Chimaltenango, Santiago, 256

Chinautla, 257

Chiquilajá, San José, 337

Chiquimula, de la Sierra, 128n., 198, 199

Chiquimula, Santa María, 35, 58, 115, 204, 255, 330, 331, 338

Chiquirichiapa, Concepción, 68

Chol, 69, 179, 182, 192, 235. *See also* Languages of highland Guatemala

Chorti, 85, 241, 256

Christianity: in posthispanic documents, 21; in P.V., 28; in *Título Tamub*, 32; in Nijaib documents, 36; in *Título Sacapulas*, 39; in *Título C'oyoi*, 40, 56, 271; in *Título Huitzitzil Tzunun*, 42; in

lineage disputes, 52, 72; in dictionaries, 112, 115, 118; teaching aids for, 160ff., 171-173

Chuachituj, 59, 204

Coast, Pacific, 126-128, 132ff., 146, 150f., 153, 199, 206, 235, 236, 248f., 334, 338

Coatán, 149, 207

Cobán, 69, 102n., 103n., 120f., 128, 129, 141, 153, 205, 226

Codices (codex): prehispanic forms, 11ff., 13ff., 105, 107; scribes of, 16, 17; uses of, 18; basis of P. V., 27; of Tamub, 32; of Nijaib, 36; of Zapotitlán, 43; basis for *Annals*, 49f.; of *Xpantzay*, 51f.; Tzutujil forms, 54f., 153; of Pokoman, 56; Pipil scrolls, 74; claims by Fuentes y Guzmán, 77f.; of Tlaxcala, 95f.; from Cobán area, 127; basis for calendar, 166f.; basis for *Título C'oyoi*, 307, 324

Comalapa, 115, 140, 205

Conquest, Spanish, 33, 47, 54, 58, 68, 72, 73f., 75, 89-90, 144, 145, 146, 152, 156, 168ff., 179, 185f., 188, 190, 192, 206, 232, 270f., 339ff.

Conquistadores, 59n., 87, 89-99, 169n., 183, 189

Conservatives, 217, 220f.

Cortés, Hernán, 59n., 67, 89, 91, 92, 94, 171, 179

Cortés, Juan de, 124f.

Cortés y Larraz, Bishop, 89, 165, 166f., 195, 196, 199-201, 211

Costilla, Santa Lucía de la, 206

Cotzal, 256

Cotzumalhuapa, 206, 232, 249

C'oyoi, 39-41; 265-346. *See also* *Quejnay* Quiche

Creoles, 148n., 157, 159f., 186, 187, 202, 212, 214

Crónica Franciscana, 73n., 76, 77, 84, 85, 88, 100, 165, 193, 230

Dances: in the P. V., 18; *Rabinal Achí*, 44-46, 168; Colonial, 168-

37; their role in Quiche state, 36; at Momostenango, 213; in *Título C'oyoi*, 314, 342, 346

Office titles, Quichean, 17, 20, 148, 154; in *Título C'oyoi*, 309, 319, 322, 323, 328, 340, 342, 344f., 346
Officials. *See* Spanish officials
Olintepeque (*Xequiquel*), 75f., 97, 337, 338, 343
Oral tradition: as basis for títulos, 28, 30, 40, 52, 53; in using Sacapulas map, 38-39; case of *Rabinal Achí*, 45-46; as basis for *Relación Pacal*, 65; used by Felipe Vásquez, 66; to pass on calendar, 166f.; modern texts of, 228, 236f., 239f., 251, 254; in *Título C'oyoi*, 307
Ostuncalco, San Juan, 68

Pacal. See Cakchiquel
Paché, Santa María de Jesús, 161
Palapó, San Antonio, 253f.
Pamaca. See Sacualpa
Panajachel, 253, 329
Panpacay, 316
Panq'uib, 316
Parra symbols, 22n., 40, 61, 115, 116, 117, 161, 162, 269
Párramos, 152
Patulul, 117, 154
Patzicía, 205
Patzité, 31n., 73, 203f., 255, 310, 342
Paxtocá, San Sebastián, 57, 176, 330, 335, 336
Petapa, 140, 181
Pictorials: list of early ones, 13-16; possible use in *Título Totonicapán*, 30; map from Sacapulas, 37, 62; in *Título C'oyoi*, 39, 40, 271, 314; with *Título Zapotitlán*, 42; Tzutujil paintings, 54; from Buenabaj, 62-63; by Kekchi, 70; for título Ixtahuacán, 72f.; Lienzo de Tlaxcala, 95; Atitlán map, 133f.
Pinula, 181

Pipil. *See* Mexican
Pokoman: *Título Cajcoj*, 55f.; dictionaries, 120-121; studied by Miles, 121, 140, 151ff.; described by Gage, 181; at Yampuc, 190; modern studies of, 235, 257; archaeological sites of, 246; in *Título C'oyoi*, 327f.
Popoloca, 175, 198
Popol Vuh: prehispanic uses, 17ff.; general evaluation, 24-28; translated by Ximénez, 162ff.; modern studies of, 217, 237, 258, 260; compared with *Título C'oyoi*, 266f., 272, 307ff.
Post classic, 244, 247, 249, 250
Priest-shaman (*Aj k'ij, Chuchkajaw*): record calendar, 168; prayers of, 228; modern studies of, 235, 236, 251, 337; prehispanic antecedents, 312; visit mountains, 330

Quauhtemallan. See Guatemala
Quejnay Quiche, 39, 42-43, 308f., 342-346
Quezaltenango (*Xelaju'*), 16, 33, 36, 39n., 40, 41, 59, 68, 73, 76, 93, 115, 123, 148, 150, 166f., 169, 170, 174, 177, 197, 198, 199, 210, 235, 241, 267, 271f., 314, 319, 320, 323, 325, 328, 330, 333ff.
Quik'ab, 23n., 29n., 30, 33, 40, 44, 51, 52n., 58, 169, 229, 328, 330, 332, 334, 335

Rabinal, 175, 176, 179, 183, 189f., 227, 230; early area of Quiche conquest, 42, 169; place of *Rabinal Achí*, 44-46; relations with Joyabaj, 53, 204; visited by Las Casas, 101ff.; Tequicistlán, 102f., 103f.; land disputes of, 150, 153, 205; dictionaries from, 162; modern studies of, 241, 254, 255; in *Título C'oyoi*, 310, 319, 325
Rabinal Achí, 18, 44-46, 171, 229, 271, 317f., 320
Records, Spanish, 158, 174f., 195f.,